ONLINE CONTRACT FORMATION

N. Stephan Kinsella
Andrew F. Simpson
General Editors

First Edition

Oceana Publications, Inc., Dobbs Ferry, New York

You may order this or any Oceana publication by visiting Oceana's website at <http://www.oceanalaw.com>.

Library of Congress Control Number: 2004105815

ISBN 0-379-21519-5

Manufactured in the United States of America on acid-free paper.

TABLE OF CONTENTS

PART 2
SAMPLE FORMS AND AGREEMENTS

PART 3
GENERAL COMMENTARIES

PART 4
PRIMARY SOURCE MATERIAL

INDEX

INTRODUCTION

Whether "electronic commerce law" is a distinct body of legal knowledge is a question that has generated some controversy.[1] According to one view, online business merely throws up new manifestations of familiar problems that existing law can readily resolve. Certainly the tremendous growth in the volume of transactions initiated or completed by electronic means has tested the law's claims to adaptability. Regardless of whether online business is regarded as generating new problems or merely new manifestations of old problems, the editors consider that lawyers and businesspeople can benefit from a knowledge of how contract law applies to agreements reached online.[2]

The legal maxim *pacta sunt servanda*—agreements must be honored—expresses one of the most fundamental of all legal principles.[3] This principle lies at the heart of all jurisdictions' contract laws, from ancient to modern. As individuals and businesses increasingly are forming their contracts online, the same principle has come to apply in respect of written and electronic agreements alike. Online business has presented considerable challenges to the world's legal systems, which have had rapidly to develop ways of dealing with circumstances unforeseen only a decade ago. Though contemporary modes of agreement could not have been foreseen, courts have aspired to a far-sighted application of the foundation principles of contract doctrine. As our US contributor Chip Rainey notes, a New Hampshire court commented as early as 1869, in finding that a telegraphed contract was a sufficient writing under the statute of frauds, that:

> It makes no difference whether that operator writes the offer or the acceptance . . . with a steel pen an inch long attached to an ordinary penholder, or whether his pen be a copper wire a thousand miles long. In either case the thought is communicated to the paper by use of the finger resting upon the pen; not does it make any

1 See, e.g. Sommer, J.H. "Against Cyberlaw" (2000) 15 Berkeley Tech. L.J. 1145 and works cited therein.

2 This belief also underlies Simpson and Kinsella (eds.) *World Online Business Law* (Oceana).

3 See Josef L. Kunz, *The Meaning and the Range of the Norm Pacta Sunt Servanda*, 39 AJIL 180-197 (1945); Hans Wehberg, *Pacta Sunt Servanda* <http://tldb.uni-koeln.de/php/pub_show_document.php?pubdocid=129500 >.

> difference that in one case common record ink is used, while in the other case a more subtle fluid, known as electricity, performs the same office.[4]

Business has been conducted "online," in a broad sense, since the invention of electronic communications. From telegraph and telex to electronic document interchange (EDI), facsimile, and the World Wide Web, businesspeople have always been quick to apply new developments in communications to the transaction of business. The advent of the Internet, followed shortly by the Web, has provided a tremendous spur to a wide range of businesses. In turn, business exploitation of the Internet is influencing people's use of the Internet. In *Online Contract Formation* the editors have aimed to bring together the knowledge and insights of legal professionals from Europe, Asia and the Americas, to provide practical guidance for those forming contracts by electronic means and for their advisors.

It is instructive to consider how legal systems have responded to the various challenges posed by online commerce. As the examples in the following pages show, the development of sound new laws—or the correct application of existing laws—will require that legislators, judges and lawyers have a deep understanding of the electronic media used in such transactions and of the transactions themselves.

In order to assist the practitioner in navigating the issues that arise in relation to online agreements, *Online Contract Formation* contains:

- country-specific chapters summarizing the online contract law of key jurisdictions around the world;
- sample agreements and checklists related to online business, from key jurisdictions;
- topical commentary on contract-related issues; and
- key sources and documents.

The country-specific chapters include concise summaries by local experts of the law as it pertains to online contract formation for several representative, and commercially significant, countries. These country-specific chapters, prepared by local experts, cover each jurisdiction's law of online contract formation in a consistent format, so far as that is possible. These synopses include discussion of the sources of law, the general scheme of online business regulation, general principles of contract formation, the status of digital signatures, jurisdiction issues and a review of key statutes affecting online contract formation. Key jurisdictions from Asia, Europe, and the Americas are covered, as are developing and developed economies, and both civil-law and common-law states. Complementing the country-specific chapters are a selection of sample agreements and checklists related to online business, again prepared by local experts from vari-

4 *Howley v. Whipple*, 48 N.H. 487 (1869).

ous jurisdictions. These include checklists for online agreements; guidelines for click-through agreements; sample arbitration clauses; sample terms and conditions for a website; and a website development checklist.

In addition, several topical commentaries are provided, some covering similar topics from different perspectives. This section includes articles on jurisdiction in international online commerce from both common law and civil law perspectives; as well as general commentary on contract formation, and basic contractual issues that will be relevant to practitioners from many jurisdictions. Finally, several key sources and documents are reprinted, including key digital signature laws and guidelines and electronic commerce model laws.

It is our hope that this volume will serve as a useful guide to practitioners representing clients conducting online business in this increasingly borderless and online world.

N. Stephan Kinsella
Houston, Texas

Andrew F. Simpson
Hong Kong

CONTRIBUTORS

GENERAL EDITORS

N. Stephan Kinsella
Applied Optoelectronics, Inc
13111 Jess Pirtle Blvd.
Sugar Land, TX 77478
United States
Tel: 713-416-0006; Fax: 281-966-6988
Stephan@KinsellaLaw.com
www.KinsellaLaw.com.

N. Stephan Kinsella is General Counsel and Vice President-Intellectual Property with Applied Optoelectronics, Inc., in Sugar Land, Texas. Before joining AOI, he was a partner in the Intellectual Property Department of Duane Morris LLP. He has taught Computer Law at South Texas College of Law, and is author of numerous articles about intellectual property law, international law and other topics, including economics, and political and legal theory. Mr. Kinsella is co-author of *Protecting Foreign Investment Under International Law: Legal Aspects of Political Risk* (Oceana 1997), co-editor of *Digest of Commercial Laws of the World* (Oceana 2003-present), co-editor of *World Online Business Law* (Oceana 2003-present) and editor *Trademark Practice & Forms* (Oceana 1998-present). He received an LL.M. (international business law) from King's College London—University of London, his J.D. from the Louisiana State University Law Center, and an M.S.E.E. and B.S.E.E. from Louisiana State University. Registered to practice before the United States Patent and Trademark Office, he is also licensed to practice law in Texas, Louisiana, and Pennsylvania.

Andrew F. Simpson
Arculli and Associates
2012 Hutchison House
Central, Hong Kong
Tel: +852 2882 0880; Fax: +852 2882 0888
andrew@e-chidna.com

Andrew Simpson is an Associate with Arculli and Associates, Hong Kong. Previously he practised in Sydney with Gilbert + Tobin. He has contributed articles on online commerce, telecommunications regulation, securities regulation and competition law to a range of books and periodicals. Dr. Simpson is co-editor, with Mr. Kinsella, of *World Online Business Law* (Oceana 2003-present). Dr. Simpson received B.A., LLB.(Hons.) and LL.M.(Hons.) degrees from the University of Canterbury, New Zealand. Subsequently, he completed LL.M. and Ph.D. degrees at the University of Sydney, Australia. He is admitted to practise in New Zealand, New South Wales, England and Wales, and Hong Kong.

COUNTRY COMMENTARIES

AUSTRALIA

Peter Leonard
Gilbert + Tobin
2 Park Street
Sydney, NSW 2000
Australia
Tel: +61 2 9263 4000
Fax: +61 2 9263 4111
pleonard@gtlaw.com.au

Peter Leonard's focus is on commercial and corporate transactions and structuring for corporations active in the technology, media, communications and e-commerce industries. He has had a long career with Gilbert + Tobin, joining as the third partner in 1989.

His commercial and corporate experience includes e-business implementations, systems integration, outsourcing, development and hosting arrangements in Australia and the Asia Pacific region. He also has extensive experience in communications regulation in Australia and South East Asia and is a co-editor of *Communications Law and Policy in Australia.*

Peter writes and lectures extensively in his areas of practice. He is a member of the Technology Law Committee of the International Bar Association. Peter was a member of the Australian Attorney-General's Expert Group on Electronic Commerce, which issued the report leading to the Australian *Electronic Transactions Act.*

Peter holds a Bachelor of Economics and a Masters of Laws from the University of Sydney.

BRAZIL

Momsen, Leonardos & Cia
Rua Teófilo Ottoni, 63/10º andar
Centro
20090-080 Rio de Janeiro—RJ
Brazil
Tel: +55-21-2518-2264; Fax: +55-21-2518-3152
momsen@leonardos.com.br
www.leonardos.com.br

Momsen, Leonardos has 85 years of experience protecting and enforcing intellectual property's assets. Among its clients are some of the largest companies in the world. Today the Firm has 27 Partners and over 50 lawyers, as well as engineers and scientists, who find support in a staff of more than 240 employees. Its main office is located in Rio de Janeiro and it also has a branch in São Paulo. Momsen, Leonardos is committed to provide the highest quality of technical and legal services in all areas of intellectual property law such as patents, trademarks, copyrights, industrial designs, unfair competition, anti piracy, trade secrets, technology transfer, computer law, internet law, e-commerce and software protection. Its practice includes IP portfolio management, litigation and licensing.

CANADA

Gary N. Bouchard
Fogler, Rubinoff LLP
77 King Street West
T-D Centre, Royal Trust Tower
Toronto, Ontario M5K 1G8
Canada
Tel: 416-941-8845; Fax: 416-941-8852
gbouchard@foglerubinoff.com
www.foglerubinoff.com

Gary N. Bouchard is a partner of Toronto-based firm Foglers LLP. Gary heads up the firm's technology law practice group.

Gary's key practice areas are in information technology and business law, with a focus on technology law, mergers and acquisitions, international distribution law, contract negotiations and litigation strategy. He represents clients that extend from small, start-up ventures to Fortune 500 companies. He is a member and panelist of the World Intellectual Property Organization Arbitration and Mediation Centre Panel of Neutrals where he's presided over domain name disputes. Gary attended McGill University in Montreal, Canada, and graduated with an LL.B. from Queen's University in Kingston, Canada. He is a member of The Law Society of Upper Canada, the Canadian Bar Association, the American Bar Association and the Licensing Executives Society.

Prior to joining Foglers, Gary established the technology business solutions group at a large Toronto firm which he joined after operating his own technology law practice. Gary's legal career began as a contract specialist at one of the largest automated light rail transit manufacturers in Canada for their logistics and procurement subsidiary, handling technology and EPC related matters. He was also a litigator for the largest poverty law clinic in Ottawa, Ontario, where he appeared before various courts, boards, and tribunals. Gary has also held a number of senior legal counsel positions in some of Canada's largest corporations. He was Corporate Counsel and Secretary to Kellogg Canada Inc., Legal Counsel and Assistant Secretary to ISM Information Management Systems and Legal Counsel to International Semi-Tech Microelectronics Inc., one of Canada's largest consumer products companies and parent company to several multinational corporations, including The Singer Company.

Fogler, Rubinoff LLP is a full service law firm located in Toronto, Canada, and is recognized as one of Canada's premier business law firms. The firm's lawyers work in all areas of the law, including corporate/commercial, securities, technology, tax, bankruptcy, insolvency and restructuring, litigation and alternative dispute resolution, employment and labour, governmental and regulatory affairs, commercial real estate and leasing, banking, institutional lending and asset securitization, and estates and trusts.

CROATIA

Mladen Vukmir, mr.sc., partner
Olena Manuilenko, associate
VUKMIR & ASSOCIATES
Pantovcak 35
10000 Zagreb

Croatia
Tel: +3851 376 0511; Fax: +3851 376 0555
vukmir@vukmir.net
www.vukmir.net

Mladen Vukmir, the founding partner of Vukmir & Associates, obtained his law degree from the University of Zagreb in 1985. In 1989, he obtained his Masters degree in Intellectual Property from Franklin Pierce Law Center in the U.S. After that he worked separately for the California-based law firm Fenwick & West, for the Italian law firm Pavia e Ansaldo and for the United Nations Industrial Development Organization. In 1992, Mladen was retained as an expert advisor by the Croatian IP Office during its founding. Today his work includes specialization in intellectual property, licensing, commercial law, litigation and arbitration. Mladen Vukmir is the Honorary Royal Danish Consul General in Zagreb. He is an arbitrator for domestic disputes under the Permanent Arbitration Court of the Croatian Chamber of Commerce and a panelist on the WIPO Domain Name Administrative Panel.

Olena Manuilenko obtained her law degree at the University of Split in Croatia. She is currently taking postgraduate studies in corporate and commercial law at the University of Zagreb while working as an associate for Vukmir & Associates. Olena's practice areas are in copyright and computer law.

Vukmir & Associates is a partnership specializing in intellectual property. Within this field, the firm acts as a patent and trademark agent and works on developing IP strategies and marketing identities for local clients. Moreover, this partnership litigates IP infringement cases and advises on copyright issues in the entertainment and software industries. In the field of computers and software, the partnership is particularly experienced in registering domain names for foreign companies, drafting/concluding computer contracts and overseeing counterfeiting and anti-piracy issues. Work in the commercial law field includes the drafting and reviewing of licensing and distribution contracts. Corporate law matters include the incorporation of limited liability and joint stock companies and due diligence procedure.

ECUADOR

Amani Harrison
Bustamante & Bustamante
Patrias and Amazonas Avenues
COFIEC Building, 5th Floor
P.O. Box 17–01–02455
Quito
Ecuador
Tel: +5932 2562 680; Fax +5932 2564628
aharrison@bustamante.com.ec
www.bustamante.com.ec

Ms. Harrison received a bachelor of science from the Massachusetts Institute of Technology, a juris doctor degree from the Georgetown University Law Center and is a member of the Bar of the State of New York. While at Georgetown, Ms. Harrison served as a staff member and editor of the American Criminal Law Review. Her publications include "Securities Fraud." *American Criminal Law Review.* 36(3) Summer: 1095-1155, which she co-authored while serving as a member of the American Criminal Law Review. Prior to joining Bustamante & Bustamante Intellectual Property, Ms. Harrison worked as a project finance associate in the Washington, D.C. office of Freshfields Bruckhaus Deringer.

Bustamante & Bustamante has provided intellectual property legal services since the firm's foundation in 1956 and has one of the largest intellectual property practices in Ecuador. The intellectual property practice encompasses a broad array of legal services including registrability, validity, infringement, unfair competition, patent and trademark prosecution and administration, copyright, trademark licensing, trademark searches, health registrations and technology transfer. The patent practice includes prosecuting and administrating patents, counseling, conducting due diligence investigations, U.S. and international patent, trade secret matters, negotiation of licenses and other patent-related agreements and handling the prosecution or defense of infringement claims. Intellectual property practitioners also assist clients with the registration and maintenance of plant varieties and with obtaining health registrations which are necessary for importing perishable items, cosmetics and pharmaceutical goods into the Republic of Ecuador.

FRANCE

Professor Michel Vivant
Home & Private Office:
Les Chênes-verts
868, route de Ganges
F– 34090 Montpellier
University: Faculty of Law
36, rue de l'Université
F–34060 Montpellier Cedex
Office in Paris:
Denton Wilde Sapte
43, rue du Faubourg Saint-Honoré
F–75008 Paris
France
Tel: + 33 6 03 51 19 44; Fax: + 33 4 67 54 03 40
m.vivant@wanadoo.fr
http://arbiter.wipo.int/domains/panel/profiles/vivant.pdf

Michel Vivant is a professor at the University of Montpellier and he was the Dean for three years. He is also an honorary doctor ("*honoris causa*") of the University of Heidelberg, associate professor of several Universities (Beirut, Mexico, Quebec, Rio).

Appointed as, member of the French "High Council of Industrial Property", member of the Legal Advisory Board of DG "Information Society" of the European Commission, he is also an expert for several international organisations (in particular he was "scientific expert" for the Council of Europe: Committee of Experts on Crime in Cyberspace) and French public authorities (Prime Minister, Minister of Industry, Minister of Research).

Director of the Research Team "*Créations immatérielles et Droit*" (Immaterial Creations and Law) (ERCIM), he is a specialist in intellectual property rights in general and the new technologies in particular, recognised within and outside Europe. He has published extensively on the following themes: patents, trade marks, copyright, computer law, communication, networks (internet), in six languages in more than ten countries (from Argentina to Vietnam).

He is called upon to be a national and international arbitrator (in particular he is a member of the WIPO Arbitration Center) and is a regular consultant for lawyers and companies. He is acting as a consultant "of counsel" within the law firm Denton Wilde Sapte (Paris).

HONG KONG

Andrew Simpson
Arculli and Associates
2012 Hutchison House
Central, Hong Kong
Tel: +852 2882 0880; Fax: +852 2882 0888
andrew@e-chidna.com

Andrew Simpson is an Associate with Arculli and Associates, Hong Kong. Previously he practised in Sydney with Gilbert + Tobin. He has contributed articles on online commerce, telecommunications regulation, securities regulation and competition law to a range of books and periodicals. Dr. Simpson received B.A., LLB.(Hons.) and LL.M.(Hons.) degrees from the University of Canterbury, New Zealand. Subsequently, he completed LL.M. and Ph.D. degrees at the University of Sydney, Australia. He is admitted to practise in New Zealand, New South Wales, England and Wales, and Hong Kong.

Arculli and Associates provides innovative, specialist legal services in the technology, communications and content industries. Arculli and Associates is affiliated with Gilbert + Tobin, one of Asia Pacific's leading corporate, communications and technology practices. Working effectively in Asia is about trust, local knowledge and local relationships. But in a globalising economy, leading edge knowledge and skills are also crucial. Arculli and Associates and Gilbert + Tobin create a trusted Asian legal services provider with world class expertise in the technology and communications industries. Our two firms act for industry leaders in diverse sectors throughout Asia Pacific. Our base is the Asia Pacific region and our people, resources and skills are located here. Our core value is to create a law firm which integrates Asian and Western lawyers, perspectives and cultures. We have Chinese, Australian and Malaysian lawyers. We speak Cantonese, Mandarin/Putonghua, Japanese and English. We work in Hong Kong, the mainland of China and throughout the Asia Pacific region.

HUNGARY

Dr. Katalin Grósz, Esq., Szabolcs Gall, Esq., Daniel F. Visoiu, Esq., and Dr. András László
Szecskay–Attorneys at law
Kossuth tér 16–17
H–1055 Budapest
Hungary
Tel: +36 (1) 472–3000; Fax: +36 (1) 472–3001
info@szecskay.hu
www.szecskay.hu

Dr. Katalin Grósz, Esq., a Senior Associate with the Firm, is a Hungarian attorney admitted to the Budapest Bar. Dr. Grósz received her JD, cum laude, from the Pécs Faculty of State and Legal Science in 1989. She worked at the Hungarian Ministry of Justice, where, as member of the EU Harmonization Department, she was involved in the preparation of draft laws (company and civil law) from October 1991 until May 1993, at which time she joined the Firm. In 1992, Dr. Grósz participated in a six–month training program at the legal department of the EU Commission in Brussels. She has co-authored a treatise on commercial law. Dr. Grósz is fluent in English, French and German.

Szabolcs Gáll, Esq., an Associate with the Firm, is a UK and Canadian qualified solicitor of Hungarian background and is a member of the Law Societies of England and Wales and Upper Canada. Mr. Gáll received his law degree from the University of Western Ontario in 1998, and also has a Bachelor of Arts degree from the same university. Mr. Gáll worked at the firm of Blake, Cassels and Graydon LLP while in Canada, and in 2001 Mr. Gáll joined Clifford Chance LLP in London, UK, where he was an associate in the Banking and Finance group until joining the Firm in February of 2004. Mr. Gáll specializes in finance, including bank lending, capital markets and securitization and is a guest lecturer at Pázmány Péter University—Faculty of Law. He is fluent in English and Hungarian.

Daniel F. Visoiu, Esq., an Associate with the Firm, is a Romanian–born American attorney admitted to the Florida (USA) Bar. Mr. Visoiu joined Moquet Borde & Associés in May 1997. He graduated from the University of Florida (College of Law, JD 1996, and the College of Journalism, BS 1993). Mr. Visoiu was the Executive Articles Editor of the Florida Journal of International Law and a member of the National Moot Court Board. He is co–author of the booklet Doing Business in Romania (1996), as well as the author of numerous articles on Hungarian and Romanian legal topics, in such publications as the International Lawyer, the International Law News, the World Securities Law Report, BNA's Eastern European Reporter, and the Eastern European Forum Newsletter. Mr. Visoiu is also currently co–chair of the American Bar Association's Central European Law Committee (CELC). Mr. Visoiu is fluent in English and Romanian.

Dr. András László, a Junior Associate with the Firm, is a Hungarian attorney. Dr. László received his JD, cum laude, from Eötvös Loránd Faculty of State and Legal Sciences in 2002. In 2001 he studied in France at the University of Paris– X. (Nanterre) on an Erasmus Scholarship. Dr. László joined the Firm in 2002. Dr. László is fluent in English and French.

Szecskay–Attorneys at law is one of the premier Hungarian firms providing a full range of legal advice and assistance to the business community. The Firm specializes primarily in international business, corporate and commercial law, and has a vast amount of experience with all aspects of intellectual property, securities transactions, mergers and acquisitions, corporate financing, banking, antitrust (competition), tax, labor law, commercial transactions, litigation and arbitration.

The Firm's attorneys provide efficient legal consultancy services to local and international clients in Hungarian, English, German and French. Each of the Firm's attorneys is equally at home in counseling and with litigation. The approach of the Firm is practical and client-oriented, and our Firm is committed to providing efficient, effective, and top-quality legal services.

The Firm's clients are typically large and medium-sized businesses from Hungary and abroad that represent the full spectrum of industry, trade and services. The Firm endeavours to establish long-lasting relationships with its clients and every assignment is preceded by a careful assessment of the work, costs and realistic results. The Firm carries out assignments in close consultation with its clients which explains in part why it is justifiably proud of its many long-standing and close client relationships.

The attorneys of the Firm regularly publish in Hungarian (e.g., Magyar Jog, Védjegyvilág, Céghírnök, etc.) and foreign (International Financial Law Review, Eastern European Forum News Letter, BNA's East European Reporter, International Law Office Newsletter/ Hungarian IP, Banking, E-Commerce Chapters of the IBC Newsletter) legal publications addressing topical legal issues arising from their day-to-day practice.

ISRAEL

Neil J. Wilkof, Karen L. Elburg, Nicholas Cannon and Lee-Anne Berns
Herzog Fox & Neeman
Asia House
4 Weizmann Street
Tel-Aviv 64239
Israel
Tel: (972)-(3)-692-2020; Fax: (972)-(3)-696-6464
hfn@hfn.co.il
www.hfn.co.il

Herzog, Fox & Neeman (HFN) is one of Israel's foremost corporate and commercial law offices representing leading companies worldwide. The firm was founded in 1972 by three prominent lawyers: the late Chaim Herzog, later to become the sixth President of the State of Israel, Israeli Ambassador to the United Nations, and member of the Israeli Parliament; Michael Fox, formerly a solicitor, known for his corporate work and his legal contributions to the development of the infrastructure, energy and natural resources of Israel; and Yaakov Neeman, author of numerous books and articles on tax law and respected tax advisor to the government and major local and foreign corporations.

As a full service international law firm with a diversified corporate practice and the largest tax department of any general commercial law office in Israel, HFN is especially equipped to handle multinational transactions of all types. This includes legal advice with respect to complex Mergers and Acquisitions, Investments, Joint Ventures, Securities Offerings, Corporate Reorganizations and Tax, as well as Venture Capital and Private Equity Funding; Banking & Finance; Infrastructure Development and Project Finance; Intellectual Property and Information Technology; Internet and E-Commerce; Telecommunications; Commercial Litigation; Property & Construction; Energy and Natural Resources; Employment; and Anti Trust and Competition. Involved from the beginning in the privatization and liberalization of the Israeli market, the firm has also been active in the drafting process of the regulations and legislation that shape that market. The firm's internationally educated and multilingual team of lawyers, as well as administrative staff is proficient in English and Hebrew, with French and German capabilities.

Also assisting with the preparation of this chapter: Eldar Ben-Ruby, James Franks, Ayelet Berman, Shai Kagan, Yaron Kupfer, Saar Pauker, Eliot Sacks, Gil White and Moran Yemini.

JAPAN

Haig Oghigian; Toru Yamada
Jones Day Reavis & Pogue
Shiroyama MT Bldg., 6th Fr.
4-1-17, Toranomon, Minato-ku
Tokyo 105-0001
Japan
Tel: +81-3-6800 1819 (Direct line); Fax: +81-3-5401 2725
hoghigian@jonesday.com
tyamada@jonesday.com
www.jonesday.com/

Haig Oghigian is a graduate of McGill University (B.A. Hons 1976) and its Law School (LL.B. 1979) in Montreal, Canada and has also researched Japanese law at Harvard University's East Asian Legal Studies Program (1984-86). Mr. Oghigian specializes in cross-border transactions such as joint-ventures, licensing & distribution agreements and mergers & acquisitions. He also practices in the field of international commercial arbitration. He has acted as counsel, arbitrator and mediator in a variety of proceedings, as well as assisted clients with significant ADR related issues. Mr. Oghigian obtained a Diploma in International Commercial Arbitration by completing a program at Keble College, Oxford University (1998) and was made a Fellow of the Chartered Institute of Arbitrators. He is a contributing author and editor of The Law of Commerce in Japan: A Collection of Introductory Essays published by Simon & Schuster. Mr. Oghigian served as a diplomat in the Canadian Department of External Affairs with a four year assignment at the Canadian Embassy in Japan. He speaks English, French and Japanese.

Toru Yamada, with over ten years of experience in structured finance and corporate law, is a graduate of the Law Faculty of the University of Tokyo (1990) and Harvard University (Fulbright Scholar, LL.M. 1997). He is admitted in Japan after completion of the Legal Training and Research Institute (1992) and New York (1998). He has a varied Japanese commercial capability and has considerable e-commerce transactional experience, including co-authorship of a Japanese publication on the subject with Arthur Andersen. He is fluent in English, Japanese, and Russian.

MALAYSIA

Michael Raj
Shahrizat Rashid & Lee
Level 12 & 13, Menara Milenium,
8 Jalan Damanlela, Damansara Heights
50490 Kuala Lumpur
Malaysia
Tel: +603 2710 5555; Fax: +603 2710 3106
michael.raj@srl-law.com.my

Michael Raj currently heads the communications and intellectual property practice of Rashid Lee. He joined the Intellectual Property Department of Rashid & Lee in 1994. Michael has done considerable work in all aspects of intellectual property, telecommunications and information technology law and is currently the principal legal advisor to a large telecommunications group in Malaysia. Michael has been advising both local and international clients on e-commerce and Internet related issues, the new cyberlaws regime in Malaysia and the current competition regulatory framework in the telecoms industry. Michael is an executive committee member of the Malaysian Intellectual Property Association.

Rashid & Lee was established in 1965 and currently has a large domestic and regional intellectual property practice. Michael and a number of Rashid & Lee partners and lawyers are registered patent, industrial designs and/or trademark agents. Rashid & Lee is licensed to directly initiate and prosecute applications for registration in respect of trade marks, designs and patents in Malaysia. Rashid & Lee have participated actively in Intellectual Property Association meetings and conferences both in Malaysia and abroad, and has presented country reports on intellectual property rights matters at these conferences. In support of Rashid & Lee's practice in the intellectual property rights area, Rashid & Lee has a team of advocates experienced in intellectual property rights laws.

NEW ZEALAND

Mary-Anne Borrowdale
Chapman Tripp
1-13 Grey St
PO Box 993, Wellington
New Zealand
Tel: +64 4 499 5999; Fax: +64 4 472 7111
mary-anne.borrowdale@chapmantripp.com
www.chapmantripp.com

Mary-Anne Borrowdale BA LLB LLM (Hons) joined the litigation department of Chapman Tripp in mid 2001. Before joining Chapman Tripp, Mary-Anne was a senior associate with a national Australian law firm, practising in the fields of insurance, banking, corporate law and commercial litigation. Mary-Anne undertakes general commercial litigation, with an emphasis on company and contract law. She has a strong interest in professional negligence law and defamation. Mary-Anne has published numerous articles in the areas of negligence and the liability of company directors, and has lectured corporations law at the University of Canterbury. Mary-Anne trained as a mediator with the LEADR organisation in Sydney, and is a member of the New Zealand provisional panel of mediators.

Nicholas S. Wood LLB (Hons) BA (Hons) has practised in the litigation department of Chapman Tripp since joining the firm at the start of 2001. Nicholas works primarily in the area of commercial litigation, including intellectual property law. Nicholas has a strong interest in the law of civil obligations and intellectual property, and has published articles in the areas of copyright law, privacy law and the doctrine of precedent.

Chapman Tripp, is one of New Zealand's largest commercial law firms. Our 500 staff are committed to excellence in both legal advice and client service. We practise in all areas of commercial, corporate, securities, property, environmental and public law. Chapman Tripp lawyers play key roles in mergers, acquisitions, dispositions, takeovers, financing, banking and capital restructurings in New Zealand and overseas. Our specialist areas of expertise include privatisation, taxation, superannuation, litigation, dispute resolution, legislative drafting and advice to statutory and government bodies. We are one of very few truly national New Zealand firms, with offices in Auckland, Wellington and Christchurch and clients located throughout New Zealand, and across the world.

REPUBLIC OF THE PHILIPPINES

Vicente B. Amador
SyCip Salazar Hernandez & Gatmaitan
105 Paseo de Roxas, Makati City 1226
Philippines
Tel: (632) 817-9811; Fax: (632) 817-3896
vbamador@syciplaw.com
www.syciplaw.com

Vicente B. Amador: Born Candelaria, Quezon, Philippines, December 18, 1948; admitted to Bar, 1976; Preparatory education, University of Sto. Tomas (Ph. B. magna cum laude); legal education, University of the Philippines (LL.B.); Registered Trademark and Patent Attorney; Former President, Licensing Executives Society-Philippines; Named as one of Asia's leading intellectual property lawyers in Asia Law Profiles (1997); Cited as recognized authority on IP law in The Asia Pacific Legal 500 (2002-2001); Member: Philippine Bar Association; Professorial Lecturer in intellectual property law, College of Law, University of the Philippines (1999 to present); Author: Copyright, Trademarks and Patents Under the Intellectual Property Code (3 volumes; 2000); E-Commerce Act and Other Laws of Cyberspace (2002); The Law on Strikes (2000); Labor Standards Administration (2000).

SyCip Salazar Hernandez & Gatmaitan, founded in 1945, is the largest commercial law firm in the Philippines with a diverse practice reflecting the nature and quality of the national and international industries and corporations for whom it acts. Four of the partners are admitted to the New York bar, giving an indication of the firm's international connections and capabilities. The firm is active in construction, energy, manufacturing, mining, banking and financial services, intellectual property and all other aspects of commercial law practice and litigation.

ROMANIA

Catalin Baiculescu, Partner
Horatiu Dumitru, Ph.D., Senior Associate
Musat & Asociatii
43 Aviatorilor Blvd., 1st District, Code 011853,
Bucharest
Romania
Tel: (40-21) 223 3717; Fax: (40-21) 223 3957; 223 0495
general@musat.ro
www.musat.ro

Catalin Baiculescu, Law Degree (RO), is a partner at Musat & Asociatii. Former Parliamentary advisor and legal consultant to the World Bank. He has participated on a number of high profile Romanian privatisations having a wide and considerable experience of the due diligence process and on the pre and post legal aspects and issues in the privatisation field. He has acted on major cross border mergers and acquisitions and in the emerging corporate and telecommunications field. Being involved in major transactions in Romania, he has gained extensive experience in aviation, banking, communications & information technology, and insurance. He has published frequent articles on foreign investment and corporate matters, privatisations and communications. He teaches general theory of law at the Bucharest University. He speaks Romanian, English and French and is a Member of the Bucharest and Romanian Bar Associations as well as a number of international legal organisations.

Horatiu Dumitru, Law Degree (RO), Ph.D., is a senior associate at Musat & Asociatii. He acted previously as legal advisor at the Legal Department of the Romanian Government and subsequently as chief-assistant to the Secretary General of the Chamber of Deputies in the Romanian Parliament. He has much expertise in drafting laws, commercial law, securities and e-commerce. He has published numerous articles in Romanian law journals regarding securities law and cyberspace law. He speaks Romanian, German and English and is a Member of the Bucharest and Romanian Bar Association.

SINGAPORE

Anne Choo
CitiLegal LLC
Advocates & Solicitors
7 Temasek Boulevard
#21-02 Suntec Tower One
Singapore 038987
Tel: 65-63331611; Fax: 65-63386277
mail@citi-legal.com
www.citi-legal.com

Anne Choo is the Chief Executive Officer of CitiLegal LLC. A senior member of the Singapore Bar, Anne obtained her LL.B.(Hons) from Queen Mary College, University of London. She was called to the UK Bar (Lincoln's Inn) in 1980 and the Singapore Bar in 1981 and commenced practice in Allen & Gledhill. In 1988, she co-founded Koh & Choo, which subsequently underwent corporatisation on 1 July 2001 to form CitiLegal LLC. Anne heads CitiLegal's corporate & commercial, technology and intellectual property departments. With the rapid advances in technology, liberalisation of Singapore's telecommunications' market and the government's push towards the life sciences sector in the Singapore economy, her practice now is increasingly focused within the technology and intellectual property arena. Anne handles matters pertaining to e-commerce and related activities, telecommunications and the full spectrum of IT-related agreements including software development, licensing and distribution, system integration, network management and consultancy services, reseller arrangements, co-branding and outsourcing arrangements. Anne also acts as trusted lead counsel for the Asia Pacific region for many multi-national corporations.

Anne is a Commissioner for Oaths and Notary Public. Since 1987, Anne has served and continues to serve as the Chairperson to the late Justice Tan Ah Tah-SAWL Education Fund for disabled children. She has also conducted classes for law graduates attending the Practical Law Course organized by the Board of Legal Education. Anne was awarded the Asian Legal Business, Legal Who's Who Singapore 2003 award for the Information Technology category.

CitiLegal LLC is a boutique-size full service law corporation. Areas of practice include corporate, corporate finance, commercial, info-communications and technology, intellectual property, labour and tax laws, litigation, arbitration and dispute resolution. website; www.citi-legal.com.

SPAIN

Enrique Jimenez Batalla; Ana Martinez Gomez-Tejedor; Nuria Gonzalez Mejia
Batalla Abogados
C/ Goya 67, 6º Dcha
28001 Madrid
Spain
Tel: + 34 91 781 1626; Fax: +34 91 575 1494
enrique.batalla@lawoffice-batalla.com

Enrique Jimenez Batalla, born Málaga, Spain. Education: University of Granada; Studies in Washington, D.C.; International Juridical Practices in Washington D.C. (1972). Member: Madrid Bar Association (1973); International Associations: LES, IPBA, AIPPI, ECTA, IBA (officer of the Committee R), COMPUTER LAW ASSOCIATION (advisor of the Board of Directors); Hispano-Chinese, Hispano-Japanese and Hispano-Taiwandese Bilateral Committees Spain Chambers of Commerce High Council. Languages: Spanish and English. Practice areas: Information Technology Law, Mercantile and Administrative.

Ana Martinez Gomez-Tejedor, born Madrid, Spain. Education: Universities of Madrid and Utrecht. Member: Madrid Bar Association (2000). Languages: Spanish and English. Practice areas: Intellectual Property, New Technologies, Unfair Competition, Software and Telecoms Law, Transfer of Technology Contracts, Patent, Trademark and Copyright Litigation.

Nuria Gonzalez Mejia, born Madrid. Education: University of Madrid. Master on Telecommunication Law, Audio Visual Services Law and Information Technology Law. Member: Madrid Bar Association (2002). Languages: Spanish and English. Practice areas: Information Technology Law, International Business Law, Software and Telecoms Law, Transfer of Technology Contracts.

Batalla Abogados was formed with the main objective of giving the client absolutely professional and complete service, as well as personalized treatment. The firm has expertise in the following areas of practice: Intellectual Property: IP & e-Commerce Law, Patent, Trademark and Copyright Litigation, Anticounterfeiting Activities, Information Technology, Unfair Competition, Software and Telecoms Law, Transfer of Technology Contracts, Licensing, Technology Due Diligences, Technology Appraisals, Intellectual Property Arbitration; and Corporate Law and Legal Assistance: General Commercial Practice, Commercial Litigation, Tax Law, Real Estate Law, Labour Law, International Trade, Chapter XI, Bankruptcy, Administrative Law, Acquisitions, Minority Shareholders. The Firm also acts as an Industrial & Intellectual Property Agency.

SWITZERLAND

Dr. Mark A. Reutter; Dr. Markus R. Frick
Walder Wyss & Partners
Attorneys at Law
Münstergasse 2
CH–8022 Zürich
Switzerland
Tel: +41–44–265 75 11; Fax: +41–44–265 75 50
reception@wwp.ch
mreutter@wwp.ch, mfrick@wwp.ch
www.wwp.ch

Dr. Mark A. Reutter is a partner in the information technology and intellectual property practice of the law firm Walder Wyss & Partners in Zurich, Switzerland. Mr. Reutter's practise focuses both on a comprehensive legal advising of clients who are active in the information technology and e–commerce field and on the advising of corporate and private clients in relation to technology, e–commerce and intellectual property matters. Mr. Reutter is counsel to clients in computer, software and other technology related industries as well as to major listed and non–listed Swiss and foreign companies for information technology related purposes and projects. He has frequently written and spoken on topics related to his practice. Mr. Reutter received his Doctorate in Law from the University of Zurich School of Law in 1992 and his LL.M. from Harvard Law School in 1998.

Dr. Markus R. Frick is an associate in the information technology and intellectual property practice of Walder Wyss & Partners. He specializes in all aspects concerning the acquisition and enforcement of intellectual property rights. His litigation experience includes numerous trademark, patent and unfair competition trials and appeals. He frequently advises clients in the information technology and e–commerce field. Mr. Frick received his Doctorate in Law from the University of Zurich School of Law in 2000 and his LL.M. from New York University School of Law in 2001. He is also admitted to the New York Bar.

Walder Wyss & Partners is one of Switzerland's leading law firms, specializing in corporate and commercial law, banking and finance law, intellectual property and competition law, dispute resolution, and tax law. It has been named Leading IT Firm in Switzerland by The Legal European 500. The IT practice of Walder Wyss & Partners–one of the largest in Switzerland–has a broad experience in dealing with IT and IP issues, including in particular the comprehensive structuring and implementation of major IT–projects and the creation of IT and IP structures.

UNITED KINGDOM

Nick Lockett
D L Legal
Cornhill, London
United Kingdom
Tel: +44 845 456 9800; Fax: +44 870 831 4798
nick.lockett@dllegal.com
www.DLLEGAL.com

Nick Lockett is a founding partner of London-based firm DL Legal. Nick originally qualified as a biologist and then trained in the finance industry where he specialised in investment through bio-tech, environmental and computer/IT issues. Nick's Internet site "the netlaw files" (now at www.netlaw.co.uk) were first published in December 1993 when he began specialising in the then emerging field of Internet law and computer security. Later Nick re-qualified as a barrister to specialise in the legal side of these issues and practised in England and Wales until 1998, at which time he commenced practise as a solicitor to provide a more direct service to his e-commerce and e-communications clients. He is a member of the English and Flemish Bars. He is the co-founder of the CANEU project in relation to the .eu domain name and part of the EU industry taskforce drafting registry concepts for the .eu domain name. Nick advises many e-commerce companies and venture capitalists concerning all aspects of e-commerce, cyber-insurance, on-line intellectual property protection and infringement, Internet electronic payment mechanisms and related matters. He has sat on various UK government Internet advisory panels and is currently advisor to various governments internationally on e-commerce, e-communication and e-crime, mediation and arbitration. Nick sits as an arbitrator for numerous bodies involved in providing Hi-Tech mediation and arbitration, including the UK domain provider Nominet and as a project arbitrator for the European Commission. He travels extensively around Europe, the Balkans and the former Soviet Union.

DL Legal (.DLL) is a specialist European and UK technology practice, based in London. DL Legal (www.dllegal.com) is engaged in providing advice in all areas of high-tech law including Internet and e-communications, Intellectual Property, Bio-technology and related commercial and non-contentious issues. A small specialist contentious unit also handles mediation, arbitration and litigation. DL Legal lawyers work in all areas of non-contentious hi-tech practice and recent work has involved computer-based forensic issues, data protection, computer security, analysis of technological contract performance, outsourcing and software disputes, brand protection and anti-piracy (including online anti-piracy and closure of pirate websites), domain disputes, anti-competitive behaviour in technology fields, mediation and arbitration and emergency court and non-court injunctive, seizure and conservation remedies.

UNITED STATES

John S. "Chip" Rainey
Locke Liddell & Sapp LLP
100 Congress, Suite 300
Austin, Texas 78701-4042
United States
Tel: (512) 305-4787; Fax: (512) 391-4787
crainey@lockeliddell.com

Mr. Rainey is a partner with **Locke Liddell & Sapp LLP** practicing in the area of technology and commercial transactions. Extensive transaction experience in all areas of commercial law with emphasis on copyright, trademark, software licensing and telecommunication issues. His practice specializes in computer law, E-commerce, and other commercial transactions, particularly those involving the transfer or licensing of technology and intellectual property rights, including computer related issues. Much of his practice involves the international aspects of e-commerce, including international joint ventures, cross-border data flows, international issues on privacy and transnational technology transfer agreements. His practice also includes the regulation of financial institutions with respect to e-banking activities and the use of technology.

Locke Liddell & Sapp LLP is a United States law firm with attorneys practicing in virtually every area of the law, representing and protecting the interests of not only Fortune 500 corporations, but newly formed entrepreneurial companies and individuals, as well. Locke Liddell has a large intellectual property practice that assists clients in the prosecution and registration of all forms of intellectual property rights, as well as litigating disputes regarding such rights. Separately, its Technology and Commercial Transactions section has a practice devoted just to the development, use and licensing of technology, including associated intellectual property rights, by both online and traditional clients, including issues involved in website development and operations, outsourcing, and e-commerce. Established in 1891, Locke Liddell & Sapp LLP is recognized as one of the leading law firms in Texas and throughout the nation. A full service law firm with offices in Austin, Dallas, Houston, and New Orleans, Locke Liddell & Sapp has approximately 400 lawyers who represent a broad range of businesses and individual clients having extensive domestic and foreign business interest. For additional information on the firm, please visit www.lockeliddell.com.

Joseph F. Ruh, Jr.
Eastman Kodak Company
3457 S LaCienega Blvd
Los Angeles, CA 90016
United States
Tel: 310-204-7160; Fax: 310-204-7177
jruh@kodak.com

June M. Besek
Executive Director and Director of Studies
Kernochan Center for Law, Media, and the Arts
Columbia University
435 West 116th St.
New York, NY 10027-7297
www.law.columbia.edu/center_program/kernochan

June M. Besek joined the Kernochan Center in 1999, where she oversees studies on national and international intellectual property issues. She was formerly Director of Intellectual Property at Reuters America Inc. and, before that, a partner at Schwab Goldberg Price & Dannay in New York. She is an active member of the ABA Intellectual Property Section and the Copyright Society of the U.S.A., and serves on the Editorial Board of the Journal of the Copyright Society of the U.S.A. She received her B.A. from Yale and J.D. from New York University.

Susan E. Colman
Attorney at Law
International Square, PMB 400
1825 I St., N.W., Suite 400
Washington, DC 20006
United States
Tel: (202) 775-4937; Fax: (301) 469-7862
colman@colmantechlaw.com
www.colmantechlaw.com

Ms. Colman is currently a sole practitioner with more than 23 years of experience as an attorney in Washington, DC. She concentrates her practice in the areas of computer law, IT-law, trademarks and copyrights, including extensive experience in hardware, software and database protection and licensing, as well as trademark and copyright prosecution and litigation. She also has an extensive background in information technology and was a computer scientist for 10 years in systems and applications, including aerospace engineering and human genetics graphics programming before entering the legal profession. Her client base is international, and she has substantial involvement with the European computer law community, particularly in Scandinavia, and in Africa.

In addition to her legal practice, Ms. Colman frequently lectures and writes on legal topics relating to technology, both in the United States and internationally. She is fluent in

Swedish and has reading fluency in Norwegian and Danish, offering translation services in all three languages.

Joost J. Linnemann
Kennedy Van Der Laan
Haarlemmerweg 333
1051 LH Amsterdam
The Netherlands
Tel: +31 20 5506666; Fax: 020-5506 777
Joost.Linnemann@kvdl.nl
www.kvdl.nl

Joost Linnemann worked in the ICT industry as a software programmer for several years before completing his law degree and joining the ICT department at Kennedy Van der Laan in 1992. His practice focuses on complex international contracts and ICT projects and on the legal aspects of Internet developments, subjects on which he frequently writes and speaks. He is a member of a number of associations of lawyers in the ICT area, including the Association for Information Technology and Law and the Association for Copyright Law.

Oliver R. Smoot, Jr.
Executive Vice President
Information Technology Industry Council
1250 Eye Street NW, Suite 200
Washington, DC 20005
United States
Tel: 202-737-8888; Fax: 202-638-4922
osmoot@itic.org
www.itic.org

VIETNAM

Ngo Ngoc Thu
Of Counsel
Russin & Vecchi, LLC
8 Nguyen Hue Blvd, District 1
Ho Chi Minh City
Vietnam
Tel: (84-8) 824-3026; Fax: (84-8) 824-3113
NNThu@russinvecchi.com.vn

Ms Thu is Of Counsel to **Russin & Vecchi, LLC**. She was born in Saigon, Vietnam in 1948. She received her LLB from the University of Saigon in 1972, and was admitted to the bar in Ho Chi Minh City in 1996. Ms Thu's principal practice areas are banking, foreign investment; commercial relations, and litigation.

GENERAL COMMENTARIES

EFFECTIVE FORMATION OF CONTRACTS BY ELECTRONIC MEANS AND DISPUTE RESOLUTION IN THE NEW E-CONOMY: STILL MORE QUESTIONS THAN ANSWERS

Karen Mills
Chartered Arbitrator
J.D., F. C.I.Arb., F. S.I.Arb., F. H.K.I. Arb.
KarimSyah Law Firm
Level 11; Sudirman Square Office Tower B
Jl. Sudirman Kav. 45-46
Jakarta 12930, Republic of Indonesia
Tel: (+6221) 577-1177; Fax: (+6221) 577-1947
kmills@cbn.net.id
www.karimsyah.com

Karen Mills has practiced in Indonesia for over 20 years and is one of the founders of the KarimSyah (formerly Karim Sani) law firm in Jakarta. Ms. Mills is a Chartered Arbitrator and Fellow of the Chartered Institute of Arbitrators and of the Singapore and Hong Kong Institutes, serves as special advisor to the Board of Indonesia's arbitral institution, BANI, for which she drafted their new procedural rules, and is on the panel of arbitrators of a number of other regional and international institutions.

A graduate of New York University School of Law and member of the New York bar, Ms. Mills commenced her legal career with Haight, Gardner Poor and Havens, specialising in financing. Today she often sits as arbitrator or mediator and also specialises in financing transactions and restructurings, Oil & Gas and Energy matters, information technology and general investment and other cross-border transactions. She teaches and writes extensively on arbitration and other Indonesian legal matters and has published over 60 papers in various books and international professional journals.

KarimSyah Law Firm

Formerly known as Karim Sani, KarimSyah is recognised as one of the most trusted and respected law firms in Indonesia. The firm's practice consists of almost all aspects of commercial legal matters, both contentious and transactional. KarimSyah is one of very few firms in Indonesia with both litigation and transactional divisions, and the two work hand-in-hand so as to provide a full spectrum of experience, advice and assistance to clients of all nationalities.

KarimSyah is internationally recognised as Indonesia's market leader in dispute resolution. International Arbitration as well as Alternative Dispute Resolution (ADR) and is a strong advocate of amicable, party-driven resolution, such as mediation and other forms of ADR.

The major substantive strengths of the firm include all aspects of banking and financial transactions, including capital market, mergers & acquisitions, project finance, debt restructuring and bankruptcy. KarimSyah is also active in oil, gas, energy and mining matters, with a large number of clients in these fields, as well as in all nature of general trade, industry, Telecommunications and Information Technology.

INTERNATIONAL JURISDICTION IN EUROPEAN UNION E-COMMERCE CONTRACTS

Norel Rosner
Faculty of Law
University of Groningen
P.O. Box 716, 9700 AS Groningen,
The Netherlands

Tel: 31-50 363 7046
Fax: 31-50 363 8934
N.Rosner@rechten.rug.nl
http://www.rug.nl/rechten

Norel Rosner is an assistant professor of law at the University of Groningen, the Netherlands. His fields of expertise include conflict of laws and international civil procedure. He is currently involved in extensive research covering the area of recognition and enforcement of foreign money judgments, as well as the current development of European private international law. The legal aspects of international commercial transactions online, in particular with regard to courts' jurisdiction and the applicable law, forms yet an additional field of expertise. Mr. Rosner has an LL.B. from Iasi, Romania, LL.M. from Central European University in Budapest and a postgraduate degree in European and International Relations from the University of Amsterdam. He was a visiting scholar at various academic institutions, among other New York University School of Law, Max Planck Institute in Hamburg and Brigham Young University.

The section of Private International Law within the Department of Private and Notary Law at the University of Groningen is one of the largest research groups in the field within Netherlands. The research conducted stretches from private international law aspects of securities law and successions, to maritime law and conflict of laws in commercial matters. Likewise, it places a strong emphasis on the field of international civil procedure, in particular the regime for recognition and enforcement of foreign judgments in various countries, stretching from the U.S. to Europe and South-East Asia. Private international law aspects of e-commerce transactions is yet an additional area of focus for this group. The research targets not only the academics, but has also strong practical aspects. Most staff members are also affiliated with prestigious law firms in the Netherlands.

BASIC CONTRACTUAL ISSUES; PERSONAL JURISDICTION IN INTERNET-RELATED LITIGATION

George W. Thompson
Neville Peterson LLP
1900 M Street, NW Suite 850
Washington, DC 20036
Tel: 202-861-2959; Fax: 202-861-2924
www.npwtradelaw.com

George W. Thompson is an attorney in the Washington, D.C. office of Neville Peterson LLP, where he specializes in import and export regulation, administrative practice, trade policy, and litigation. From 1987 to 1993, Mr. Thompson served in the Office of General Counsel of the U.S. International Trade Commission. While there, he participated in numerous investigations, represented the Commission in judicial proceedings throughout the United States, and served as Special Assistant to the Commission's Vice Chairman. While in the government, he was selected to provide legal assistance to the United States Trade Representative, and represented the United States before the General Agreement on

Tariffs and Trade. He also has extensive expertise in Customs, export control, import regulation, antidumping and countervailing duty cases, and international business matters.

Mr. Thompson co-authored the books, *Exporting: Regulations, Documentation, Procedures* and *International Ocean and Air Transportation*, and has written many published articles and lectured widely on international trade topics. He is an Adjunct Professor at the graduate School of Public Policy of George Mason University, where he teaches courses on International Contract Negotiation and ABCs of Importing and Exporting. Mr. Thompson is a 1981 graduate of Cornell Law School and a 1978 graduate of the State University of New York.

The law firm of **Neville Peterson LLP** concentrates its practice in international and domestic trade regulation. The firm provides legal counsel and representation to foreign and domestic corporations, trade associations, governments, Customhouse brokers, freight forwarders, carriers and individuals with respect to international trade, Customs, antitrust, shipping, product safety, export controls, domestic and foreign product standards, and Federal and State legislation and regulations.

The firm represents clients before a wide array of Government agencies, including the United States Customs Service, the United States Departments of Commerce, Treasury and State, the United States International Trade Commission, the Office of the United States Trade Representative, the Federal Trade Commission, the Consumer Product Safety Commission, Congressional Committees, and Federal and State Courts—including, particularly, the United States Court of International Trade and the United States Court of Appeals for the Federal Circuit. Members of the firm write, lecture and teach extensively concerning their respective areas of expertise.

The firm also supports its clients with extensive and timely information resources. The firm's monthly Global Trade Report newsletters highlight selected developments of importance to clients in international and domestic trade regulation. The firm's Website (www.npwtradelaw.com) connects to international trade and legal databases worldwide. The firm also sponsors seminars on topics of interest for various industry groups throughout the year, including the firm's innovative and respected Corporate Counsel Institute.

HOW TO USE ONLINE CONTRACT FORMATION

Online Contract Formation consists of four parts. Part 1 contains twenty country chapters that discuss the laws and regulation of online contract formation in each jurisdiction. The commentary for each country chapter is organized into three major subject areas. They are: Sources of Law, Online Business Regulation, and Electronic Transactions & Contract Formation. Each major subject area contains discussions of topics including, but not limited to: jurisdiction, evidentiary issues, digital signatures, online offer and acceptance, regulatory bodies, and e-commerce legislation.

Part 2 contains sample agreements and checklists relevant to contracting online. These are illustrative of documents that are currently in use. A list of the sample agreements and checklists can be found in the table of contents on page iv.

Part 3 contains four general commentaries that deal with dispute resolution, basic contractual issues, jurisdiction in the European Union, and personal jurisdiction in the United States.

Finally Part 4 contains primary source material.

A detailed subject index is located at the end of the book.

PART 1
COUNTRY COMMENTARIES

AUSTRALIA[1]

by
Peter Leonard and Lucas Sork
Gilbert + Tobin

A. SOURCES OF LAW

1. Australian Law

Australia is a Federation of six States (New South Wales, Victoria, Queensland, South Australia, Western Australia and Tasmania) which by the Australian Constitution ceded certain powers to the Federal Parliament (also referred to as the "Commonwealth" or "Australian" Parliament) and its executive branch, the Commonwealth Government. There are also two internal Territories—the Northern Territory and the Australian Capital Territory—which today have systems of self-government and enact laws on a similar basis to the six States.

The *Australian Constitution* (the Constitution) implements the doctrine of separation of powers, providing for a Commonwealth (or Federal) Parliament, the Executive and Federal Judicature. The Executive consists of the Prime Minister, Ministers of State and Departments of the Federal Government administered by those Ministers. The Federal Government consists of the Prime Minister, Ministers of State and other Members of the Federal Parliament in the political party or parties in majority in the Lower House of the legislature, the House of Representatives.

While the separation of the judicial from the legislative and executive powers is strict, the separation between legislative and executive powers is somewhat blurred. Firstly, the Prime Minister and other Ministers are members of the legislature. Second, the practice of the Federal Parliament in enacting legislation is to confer on the Federal (Commonwealth) Executive power to make delegated legislation such as regulations, rules and by-laws under particular Acts of the Commonwealth Parliament. As a result, subordinate and delegated legislation in

1 Section A was edited by Peter Leonard of Gilbert + Tobin. Section B was edited by Madura Wijewardena and Nick Alston, Gilbert + Tobin, and revised by Peter Leonard and Lucas Sork, Gilbert + Tobin. Section D was edited by Brendan Scott of IT Law, and revised by Peter Leonard and Lucas Sork, Gilbert + Tobin

various forms as permitted by express provisions in relevant statutes are important sources of law in Australia. This subordinate and delegated legislation takes a variety of forms—Regulations or Statutory Rules or By-laws made under an Act, Ministerial Determinations or Directions, or Determinations or Statutory Rules made by statutory bodies such as the Australian Communications Authority or the Australian Broadcasting Authority.

Similarly, at the State and Territory level of government, delegated legislation is an important source of law. However, State statutory bodies generally have a more limited role and authority than statutory bodies established under Commonwealth law.

The judicial power of the Commonwealth is vested in the High Court of Australia and other Federal Courts, which include the Federal Court and the Federal Magistrates Court. The High Court has the responsibilities of interpreting and applying the laws of Australia, hearing and determining appeals by special leave from Federal, State and Territory Courts, and deciding cases of special Federal significance, including challenges to the constitutional validity of laws.[2]

2. Division of Law Making Between the Commonwealth and the States

The Parliament of the Commonwealth is authorised under the Constitution to make laws on or in respect of particular matters, including interstate and international trade, taxation, defence, external affairs, corporations, marriage and divorce, immigration, bankruptcy and interstate industrial arbitration.[3]

The States enjoy significantly wider powers to legislate for their "peace, order and good government" and accordingly regulate important matters such as education, crimes and roads. The Constitution confines the powers of the States in respect of specific matters, including levying customs and excise duties, maintaining armed forces, issuing money and taxing Commonwealth properties.[4]

With particular relevance to online business, the Commonwealth Parliament has the power under section 51 of the Constitution to make laws for:

- "trade and commerce with other countries, and among the States";[5]
- "postal, telegraphic, telephonic, and other like services";[6]
- "currency, coinage and legal tender";[7]

2 Commonwealth Constitution, Chapter III.

3 Commonwealth Constitution, ss 51 and 52.

4 Commonwealth Constitution, ss 112, 113, 114 and 115.

5 Commonwealth Constitution, s 51(i).

6 Commonwealth Constitution, s 51(v).

7 Commonwealth Constitution, s 51(xii).

- "banking, other than State banking; also State banking extending beyond the limits of the State concerned, the incorporation of banks, and the issue of paper money";[8]
- "copyrights, patents of inventions and designs, and trade marks";[9]
- "foreign corporations, and trading and financial corporations formed within the limits of the Commonwealth";[10] and
- "external affairs."[11]

Because the Commonwealth imposes income tax and customs and excise duties exclusively, the States depend on grants of financial assistance from the Commonwealth. The Commonwealth is able to influence the States by attaching conditions to certain of these financial grants.[12]

3. Application to Online Business

In practice, online business in Australia is affected by a matrix of Commonwealth, State and Territory laws which exhibit considerable divergence in their handling of key matters.

Network infrastructure and operators are regulated primarily by the *Telecommunications Act 1997 (Cth)* and associated legislation and by Parts XIB and XIC of the *Trade Practices Act 1974 (Cth)* which pertain specifically to telecommunications. Privacy of communications in the course of online business is affected by the provisions of Part 13 of the *Telecommunications Act 1997 (Cth)* and the *Privacy Act 1988 (Cth)*. Matters such as privacy, fair trading, non-discrimination and electronic signatures are also subject to State legislation.

Through the exercise of the Commonwealth's constitutional powers over interstate commerce, telecommunications and corporations, Commonwealth law exerts the primary influence on online business in Australia. State laws remain important in some fields, such as regulation of online gaming, consumer credit, fair trading, computer crime and censorship. Particularly over the last decade there has been a significant move towards substantive harmonisation of State laws, including laws affecting online business. However, State based differences remain significant in areas such as employee entitlements and stamp duty on documents.

The Commonwealth Government's approach to the regulation of online business is generally light-handed and facilitating, rather than interventionist or prescriptive. Legislative measures generally reflect principles of technology

8 Commonwealth Constitution, s 51(xiii).

9 Commonwealth Constitution, s 51(xviii).

10 Commonwealth Constitution, s 51(xx).

11 Commonwealth Constitution, s 51(xxix).

12 Commonwealth Constitution s 96.

neutrality (not favouring one electronic mechanism over another) and functional equivalence of electronic and physical world transactions. Commonwealth policy is that the government should only intervene to create and safeguard a business environment which:

- inspires consumer confidence, through transparency and consistency;
- minimises non-tariff barriers to trade and commerce; and
- treats online and paper based transactions in a non-discriminatory manner in terms of taxation and regulation.

A number of government agencies perform significant roles in relation to regulation of online commerce. The Australian Competition and Consumer Commission (ACCC) and its State equivalents, generally named Departments of Fair Trading, administer consumer protection laws relevant to online business. The Australian Broadcasting Authority (ABA) administers Internet content rules. The Australian Securities and Investments Commission (ASIC) administers corporations law and securities and investment offers. Internet access services are generally under the authority of the ACCC in relation to antitrust, access and consumer pricing issues, and the Australian Communications Authority (ACA) in relation to technical and telecommunications interception matters.

The Telecommunications Industry Ombudsman (TIO) is an independent and alternative dispute resolution scheme for small business and residential consumers in Australia who have a complaint about their telephone or Internet service. The role and powers of the TIO are provided in the *Telecommunications (Consumer Protection and Service Standards) Act 1999.* The TIO plays an important role by

- identifying Internet Services industry issues;
- alerting the relevant government and industry organisations to the issues, including systemic problems; and
- providing information and assistance to those organisations when law requires it, or where it will help the industry and consumers.

On 8 April 2004, the existing Australian Government Information Management Office (AGIMO) replaced the National Office of the Information Economy (NOIE). AGIMO's role is to promote excellence in the way that information and communication technology is used to develop and deliver Government policies, information, programs and services. AGIMO has assumed control of IT and Internet projects across multiple government agencies and it co-ordinates the use of IT within the government. It also provides strategic IT advice for government programs and services, and manages online initiatives. The old NOIE functions relating to broader policy, research and programs have been transferred to the Department of Communications, Information Technology and the Arts (DCITA).

The only Federal statute specifically directed solely at online transactions is the *Electronic Transactions Act 1999 (Cth)* which is largely replicated in State and Territory electronic transaction legislation [and which is further described in the Electronic Transactions chapter of this commentary]. Many Commonwealth and State statutes that have an impact on online business at large will affect online transactions. Some of the more important Acts having a broad commercial application are the *Trade Practices Act 1974 (Cth)*, the *Corporations Act 2001 (Cth)*, and State and Territory *Fair Trading Acts*, the *Copyright Act 1968 (Cth)*, the *Telecommunications Act 1997 (Cth)*, the *Income Tax Assessment Act 1942 (Cth)*, the *A New Tax System (Goods and Services Tax) Act 1999 (Cth)* and from the perspective of importers and exporters, the *Customs Act 1901 (Cth)* and subordinate and delegated legislation stemming from those Acts. The *Broadcasting Services Act* now includes specific provisions creating an internet censorship regime. This regime includes substantial fines for publishing illegal content over the Internet.

References

Legislation

Commonwealth

Commonwealth Constitution—given formal legal status by the Commonwealth of Australia Constitution Act 1900 (UK)

Acts Interpretation Act 1901 (Cth)

Australia Act 1986 (Cth)

Judiciary Act 1903 (Cth)

Jurisdiction of Courts (Cross-vesting) Act 1987 (Cth)

State Grants Acts

Australian Capital Territory

Australian Capital Territory (Self-Government) Act 1988 (Cth)

Interpretation Act 1967 (ACT)

New South Wales

Constitution Act 1902 (NSW)

Interpretation Act 1987 (NSW)

Queensland

Constitution Act 1867 (Qld)

Acts Interpretation Act 1954 (Qld)

Northern Territory

Northern Territory (Self-Government) Act 1978 (Cth)

Interpretation Act 1978 (NT)

South Australia

Constitution Act 1934 (SA)

Acts Interpretation Act 1984 (SA)

Tasmania

Constitution Act 1934 (Tas)

Acts Interpretation Act 1983 (Tas)

Victoria

Constitution Act 1975 (Vic)

Interpretation of Legislation Act 1984 (Vic)

Western Australia

Constitution Act 1889 (WA)

Constitution Acts Amendment Act 1899 (WA)

Interpretation Act 1984 (WA)

Secondary Material

Carvan J, Understanding of the Australian Legal System (3rd ed, LBC Information Services, Sydney 1999)

Chisholm R & Nettheim G, Understanding Law (6th ed, Butterworths, Sydney 2002)

Waller P L, An Introduction to Law (8th ed, LBC Information Services, Sydney 2000)

Websites

Australasian Legal Information Institute (AustLII)—www.austlii.edu.au

ScalePlus—scaleplus.law.gov.au

National Office of the Information Economy—www.noie.gov.au.

B. SCHEME OF ONLINE BUSINESS REGULATION

1. Introduction

In Australia, the regulation of online business is largely the same as the regulation of traditional business transactions. The general laws of contract that apply to traditional business transactions apply to online business transactions and on that basis, statutory instruments and regulatory agencies that regulate traditional business transactions also apply to the regulation of online business transactions. However, over recent years there has been a movement away from this approach with Australian Parliaments, regulatory agencies and Courts examining the unique features of online business and approaching regulation on a case-by-case basis.

2. Regulatory Bodies and Functions

The main regulatory bodies for online business are the Australian Competition and Consumer Commission (ACCC) and its state equivalents, the Australian Broadcasting Authority (ABA), the Australian Communications Authority (ACA), and the Australian Securities and Investment Commission (ASIC). The Australian Government Information Management Office (AGIMO) is an executive agency of the Commonwealth Department of Communications, Information Technology and the Arts (DCITA) and is Australia's central policy making agency in respect of online business.

As an independent statutory authority, the ACCC administers the *Trade Practices Act 1974 (Cth)* (TPA) and the *Prices Surveillance Act 1983 (Cth)* and has additional responsibilities under other legislation. In broad terms, the TPA covers anti-competitive and unfair market practices, mergers or acquisitions of companies, product safety/liability and third party access to facilities of national significance. The ACCC is the largest national agency dealing with competition matters and the only agency with responsibility for enforcement of the TPA and associated State/Territory legislation.

The ACCC enforces the TPA and other statutes in respect of online businesses in a manner similar to their application to traditional businesses. Despite this general approach, the ACCC has acknowledged the unique features of online business. The ACCC's approach is particularly relevant in relation to the enforcement of consumer rights where the ACCC has taken an active role in regulation. In 2002-2003, the ACCC received and investigated 2926 complaints regarding online trading and e-commerce.[13]

The ABA was established by the *Broadcasting Services Act 1992 (Cth)* (BSA), and began operations on 5 October 1992. The BSA defines the role of the regulatory authority, gives the ABA a range of powers and functions, and sets out explicit policy objectives which include:

- promoting program diversity,
- limiting the concentration of ownership and foreign control of the mass media; and

13 p36, ACCC Annual Report 2002-2003.

- fostering an Australian cultural identity;
- encouraging fair news reporting; and
- advocating the respect for community standards.

The ABA plans the availability of segments of the broadcasting services bands (the radiofrequency spectrum used by AM and FM radio and VHF and UHF television) for analogue and digital broadcasting. It is authorised to renew, suspend and cancel broadcasting licences and collect any fees payable for those licences. It also allocates pay TV licences and administers the class licence regime for subscription radio broadcasting and open and subscription narrowcasting services.

In terms of content regulation, the ABA assists the different sectors of the television, radio and Internet industries to develop codes of practice relating to content and complaints handling and investigates complaints about inappropriate content on broadcasting services and the Internet. It also develops and administers program standards about Australian content and children's programs on commercial television and conducts research into community attitudes on programming matters.

In relation to online business, the ABA regulates the nature of Internet content under Schedule 5 of the BSA. The broad aim is to restrict access to Internet content that is likely to offend adults and to protect children from content that is unsuitable. Under this scheme the ABA has the authority to issue "take down" notices in respect of Internet content hosted in Australia that it determines to be in violation of these rules. In respect of content hosted outside of Australia, the ABA enforces prohibitions by notifying the suppliers of filter software. All ISPs are required to provide filters on a cost recovery basis to all its customers.

The ACA was established under the *Australian Communications Authority Act 1997* and exercises powers under the *Telecommunications Act 1997*, the *Radiocommunications Act 1992* and other related legislation as a regulator of radiocommunications and telecommunications. The ACA's roles include management of the radiofrequency spectrum, promotion of industry self-regulation and other significant consumer responsibilities. The ACA's functions are designed to encourage and assist industry and consumers to take advantage of the opportunities presented by current and future technologies, while providing safeguards for consumers. The ACA is involved in internet regulation through its regulatory authority over the terms and conditions that telecommunications service providers, including internet service providers, offer carriage services, enforcement of privacy protection afforded to telecommunications users by telecommunications legislation, and regulation of unsolicited e-mail communications pursuant to the *SPAM Act 2003*. ASIC is an independent Commonwealth government body established by the *Australian Securities and Investments Commission Act 1989 (Cth)*. In July 1998 ASIC received new consumer protection responsibilities. ASIC enforces company and financial service laws to protect consumers, investors and creditors. It regulates and informs the public about Australian companies, financial markets, financial service organisations and professionals who deal and advise in investments, superannuation, insurance, deposit taking and credit.

3. Governing Legislation

The principal pieces of legislation governing online business in Australia are the TPA and the state and territory Fair Trading Acts, the *Copyright Act 1968 (Cth)*, the *Corporations Act 2001 (Cth)*, the *Electronic Transactions Act 1999 (Cth)*, the *Telecommunications Act 1997(Cth)*, the BSA and the *New Tax System (Goods and Services Tax) Act 1999(Cth)* and, from the perspective of importers and exporters the *Customs Act 1901 (Cth)*.

The TPA governs all consumer protection and competition issues and, as outlined above, is administered by the ACCC. Section 52 of the TPA deals with misleading and deceptive conduct, which can be of particular relevance to online business advertising their services via the Internet. Other general consumer protection provisions (relevant to merchantability of goods and unconscionability relating to business transactions) also have a role in the regulation of online businesses.

The *Electronic Transactions Act* was introduced to facilitate the use of online transactions and promote confidence in the use of electronic business transactions. The *Electronic Transactions Act* establishes a technology neutral regime whereby a transaction is not held to be invalid merely because it took place by means of electronic communication.

The *Corporations Act* is the principle piece of corporate legislation in Australia dealing with establishing and maintaining public and private companies in Australia. The *Copyright Act* is one of the many Acts establishing Australia's intellectual property regime.

4. Contracting on the Internet

Australian law generally places no restrictions on the manner in which commercial contracts can be executed or evidenced (with exceptions in relation to conveyance of land, consumer credit and certain other transactions deemed to require particular formality). Subject to the intention of the parties being clear and unambiguous, the parties may agree to use any means to conclude an agreement. On this basis, the parties may agree to enter into agreements by using:

- 'click-through' options
- e-mail exchanges; and
- digital signatures.

The *Electronic Transactions Act* and state and territory counterpart statutes have largely removed impediments for execution of documents through electronic means. There is a general presumption of equality between electronic and paper based agreements. These statutes in general do not apply to private transactions and only apply to transactions with governments or transactions mandated by statute. That is, in respect of private transactions, the common law rules will apply.

5. Jurisdiction on the Internet

Australian courts have generally applied ordinary principles of private international law where possible (consistent with conflict of laws principles), when attempting to regulate online businesses. In this respect Australian law is very similar to English common law. However, in recent years Australian courts have made some significant decisions in relation to the determination of jurisdiction on the Internet. In particular, Australian courts have taken an activist role is in relation to defamation which occurs via the Internet, including by means of e-mail. [Please refer to the *Defamation and Online Content* section of this commentary for further discussion of this topic].

C. ELECTRONIC TRANSACTIONS AND CONTRACT FORMATION

There is a common belief that the method of entering into a contract can affect its legal validity. Under Australian common law, there are no formal requirements which need to be met in order for a contract to be valid and binding. The basic elements of common law simply require that there has been a "meeting of minds" which is sufficiently certain to allow the court to enforce the agreement, and consideration must flow from each party. The common law position has been modified in a number of instances by legislation at both State and Federal level.

The modifying legislation has its roots in the *Statute of Frauds 1677 (Imp)* which required that, for certain categories of transactions, a contract will not be enforceable unless specific evidence is available supporting that transaction. This is particularly relevant in relation to transactions which relate to real property. These transactions, while not void, won't be enforceable unless they are evidenced in writing signed by the parties.

A number of Australian jurisdictions have similar requirements for the sale of goods above a certain value. In one instance it is arguable that a sale of goods at a price above a nominal value (about AUD30) will be unenforceable without this evidence. This strange requirement is the result of inheriting a GBP10 limit from the *Statute of Frauds* in the former British colonies, without any adjustment for 300 years of inflation.

Examples of contracts which need to be in writing include contracts for the sale of land under, for example, section 54A(1) of the *Conveyancing Act 1919* (NSW) and the sale of goods above a nominal value. Additional issues arise from the meanings given by interpretation Acts to terms such as "document," "sign" and "writing."

1. Postal Acceptance Rule

At the time a contract is formed electronically there can be questions regarding where and when the contract was formed. The familiar "Postal Acceptance Rule" provides that an offer can be accepted at the time a properly pre-paid and addressed letter is posted (as opposed to the time that that letter is received). While the common law is not settled, it seems that if communication is instantaneous (such as by telephone), acceptance will occur and a contract will form, when the offeror receives the acceptance.[14] It is not clear that e-mail is instantaneous in this sense. It is certainly "more instantaneous" than the post, but not necessarily as instantaneous as a telephone or facsimile. The Electronic Transactions Acts in the various Australian jurisdictions include provisions that determine the time and place at which sending and receipt of an electronic message occurs when the message is communicated electronically. These provisions are based on the UNCITRAL Model Law and include rules which revolve around the time and place a message enters or leaves the relevant party's e-mail system.[15]

Electronic transactions are often multi-jurisdictional and transnational. The legally defined moment and place of a contract's execution may vary depending on the laws of the competing jurisdictions. It is important for parties to an electronic transaction to consider the potential jurisdictions and to contemplate the effectiveness of the postal acceptance rule in those jurisdictions.

2. Click-wrap, E-mail and Electronic Data Interchange (EDI) Contracts

Contracts can be formed using information systems. Information systems are defined as systems for generating, sending, receiving, storing or otherwise processing electronic communications[16], and which are comprised of hardware and software. Most electronic contracts created via information systems are executed using a click-wrap, e-mail or EDI.

Click-wrap contracts

Click-wrap contracts are usually formed when an internet user purchases goods or services via the internet. The purchaser pays the vendor online, often using a credit card. Once the payment details are entered, the purchaser is presented with either

- the content of the purchase terms and conditions; or

14 *Entores Ltd v Miles Far East Corp* [1955] 2 QB 327.

15 See, for example, section 13 of the Electronic Transactions Act 2000 (NSW).

16 Section 5 of the Electronic Transactions Act 1999 (Cth).

- a link to the purchase terms and conditions, which the purchaser must click in order to continue with the transaction.

After the purchaser has been presented with the terms and conditions, they will then need to click another link—usually titled, for example, 'I Agree', 'Buy Now', 'I Accept' or 'Submit'—to complete the transaction. This affirmative consent distinguishes such transactions from the 'ticket' cases referred to below, although questions arise as to the extent to which consumers read or can reasonably be expected to read 'click-through' terms. These questions are becoming increasingly important as States in Australia revise Fair Trading Acts to include provisions enabling Courts to declare void provisions in consumer contracts, and in particular terms in contracts that consumers do not have a reasonable opportunity of negotiating (so-called 'adhesion' contracts), that are unfair—see, for example, Part 2B introduced in 2003 in the Fair Trading Act 1999 (Victoria).

While there is currently no Australian case law that directly upholds the enforceability of a click-wrap contract, a US District Court held that a defendant breached an ISP's terms and conditions which had been accepted via a click-wrap agreement.[17] It is generally accepted by legal practitioners that 'click-wrap' agreements which require a form of affirmative consent by consumers will be upheld, subject however to the general strictures on consumer contracts and in particular limitations on unfair contract terms.

E-mail

E-mail contracts are simply contracts executed via e-mail. As opposed to contracts executed via EDI, an e-mail contract is read by each party to the contract, rather than processed automatically by an information system. An e-mail contract can assume any form the parties are willing to accept, however, it will need to contain all the elements required for a normal written contract for it to be enforceable.

EDI

EDI allows contracting parties to execute a contract via a specific and identical application installed on each party's information system. The contracting parties' information systems are discreetly linked and they use an EDI message which is only decipherable by each other's information systems.

'Ticket' case law precedents have a potentially important influence when courts are determining if a click-wrap, e-mail or EDI contract has been formed. These cases usually involved the provision of services by vendors such as car park or public transport operators. The terms and conditions for the use of those services were often inaccessible, or at least not prominently displayed and subject to an affirmative consent by the customer, at the time the services were acquired. In

17 Hotmail Corp v Van$ Money Pie Inc 47 USPQ 2d 1020 (1998) (ND Cal).

ticket cases, the courts have attempted reconcile the requirements of contract law with situations where purchasers deal with a vendor displaying a sign or proffering a ticket. Courts will normally consider:

- whether or not the terms and conditions were sufficiently brought to the attention of the other party;
- whether a reasonable person ought to have been aware of the terms and conditions;
- whether the terms and conditions gave unusually generous rights to or imposed unusually onerous obligations on one of the parties;
- whether the other party had a reasonable opportunity to review the terms and conditions; and
- whether that party was able to negotiate any of the terms and conditions of that agreement.[18]

The prospects of a click-wrap being upheld can be enhanced by:

- making the terms and conditions sufficiently prominent;
- bringing the terms and conditions to the attention of the end user or customer at every reasonable opportunity;
- requiring the end user or customer to click a button marked with, for example, 'I accept' 'I agree' before proceeding with a transaction; and
- refraining from incorporating onerous or unreasonable terms and conditions into the contract, keeping in mind that an end user or customer will normally be unable to negotiate the terms and conditions.

3. Evidentiary Issues

The discussion above is strictly related to the theoretical requirements for a contract to be enforceable at law. However, in order to sue on a contract it will first be necessary to prove to a court that the contract exists.

At the Federal level, and in some of the State and Territory jurisdictions, revised Evidence Acts[19] provide that electronic documents are admissible in court in the same or equivalent fashion as hard copy documents. The main common law barrier to the admission of electronic documents is the "best evidence" rule. This rule states that the best evidence of a fact should be tendered as proof of that fact. Where the best evidence is not available an explanation of why it is not available should be given to the court. For electronic documents, the best evi-

18 See generally, *Parker v South Eastern Railway Co* (1877) 2 CPD 416, *Causer v Browne* [1952] VLR 1, *Thornton v Shoe Lane Parking Ltd* [1971] 2 QB 163 and *Interfoto Picture Library Ltd v Stiletto Visual Programmes Ltd* [1989] QB 433.

19 In particular, see the *Evidence Act 1995 (Cth)* (expressed to apply to the Territories) and the *Evidence Act 1995 (NSW)*.

dence is the original or first copy of a document which is an arrangement of magnetism on a hard disc or physical peaks and valleys on a CD ROM, as opposed to the display on a computer screen or a print out of the document in a hard copy form.

The Evidence Acts, which have been amended more recently, provide the courts with a broad discretion to admit electronic documents into evidence. This discretion is augmented by the enumeration of specific methods that can be used to prove the contents of an electronic document, including by printing that document out and tendering that print out in evidence.[20]

Another issue is the weight that should be accorded to an electronic document, given that electronic documents do not have the same forensic evidence associated with them to readily permit the identification of tampering. For example, word processing systems are specifically designed to allow changes to be made to documents easily and quickly. In most cases no audit trail is available to determine the changes made, when the changes were made, or the order in which changes were made. The lack of physical evidence associated with electronic documents can be contrasted with tangible documents for which impressions on a page, the type of ink used, the pattern of pressure applied while writing a signature, or the humidity of the air at the time that pen is put to paper can signify when specific changes were made to a document and whether or not the document is authentic.

The Evidence Acts allow courts to presume the validity of electronic documents, and that presumption cannot be rebutted simply on the basis that they are electronic.

Those courts in jurisdictions that don't have a new generation Evidence Act are taking a pragmatic approach to the admissibility of electronic documents. Indeed, in some instances courts appear to have adopted substantial contortions of the ordinary English meanings of some existing legislative provisions in order to preserve the admissibility of electronic documents. For example, section 59B of the *Evidence Act 1929* (South Australia) appears to impose a very strict prescriptive regime for the admissibility of electronic documents. These provisions potentially prevent the admission of many electronic documents. However, South Australian courts have interpreted section 59B as providing permissive rather than prescriptive requirements, thus preserving the admissibility of electronic documents.[21]

---

20 See, for example, section 10 of the Electronic Transactions Act 2000 (NSW).

21 See, for example, *Mehesz v. Redman (No. 2) (1980)* 26 S.A.S.R. 244, *R v. Weatherall* (1981) 27 S.A.S.R. 238). However, the more recent case of *Steiner v Modbury Towing Services & Ors* SCGRG-96-1993 Judgement No. S6774 [1998]; SASC 6774 (5 August 1998) refers to the *Weatherall* case and states *". . . in inserting 'Part VIA—Computer Evidence' in the* Evidence Act, *Parliament in effect codified the law relating to the admissibility of computer output."*

4. Administrative Requirements Regarding Electronic Contracts

There are many circumstances when persons or companies are required to keep records. For example, insurance legislation and regulations sometimes require the storage of hard copies of claims, even if the claims have been lodged electronically. Failure to comply with these regulations can result in monetary penalties or, potentially, the loss of a licence to operate. It is these types of requirements that the Electronic Transactions Acts[22] intend to address. The Electronic Transactions Acts are all modeled on the Federal legislation, however, not all jurisdictions within Australia have an Electronic Transactions Act. These Electronic Transactions Acts provide that where a piece of legislation requires a document to be stored, or provided to a Government authority, that document may be kept or presented in an electronic form. The various Electronic Transactions Acts achieve this through two key principles: technology neutrality and format independence. For example, individual legislation cannot require that a document be written using a pencil, because that would be a specific technology requirement which attempts to restrict the methods by which a document can be stored and presented under the various Electronic Transactions Acts.

A summary of the requirements of the Electronic Transactions Acts is set out below.

Where an Act Requires Material To Be in Writing:

(a) the information must be readily accessible for subsequent reference;

(b) if given to a government entity, any particular technology requirements or receipt verification requirements specified by that entity must be complied with; and

(c) if given to a non-government entity, the recipient must consent to that information being provided electronically.

Where an Act Has Requirements for the Production of Documents:

(a) the method chosen must provide a reliable means of assuring the integrity of the information contained in the document, that is, the document must remain complete and unaltered apart from 'endorsements' and 'immaterial changes';

The Court goes on to make other comments which indicate that there may nevertheless be other avenues available for the admissibility of computer output.

22 See the *Electronic Transactions Act 1999 (Cth), the Electronic Transactions Act 2000 (NSW), the Electronic Transactions (Victoria) Act 2000, the Electronic Transactions Act 2000 (SA), the Electronic Transactions Act 2000 (Tas)and the Electronic Transactions (Queensland) Act 2001.*

(b) the information contained in the document must be readily accessible for subsequent reference;

(c) to a government entity, that entity may specify the use of a particular technology or method of verifying the receipt of the document; and

(d) to a non-government entity, the recipient must consent to the production of the document in electronic form.

Where an Act Has a Requirement for a Document to Be Signed:

(a) having regard to the circumstances at the time, a reliable and appropriate method must be used to identify the person and to indicate the person's acknowledgement and approval of the information communicated;

(b) if a government entity is a party to the agreement, that entity's particular information system requirements must be met; and

(c) if a non-government entity is a party to the agreement, that entity must consent to using an electronic signature.

5. Tax Law Requirements

Australian tax payers may be required to store electronic documents, including contracts, used for income taxation purposes. Those documents may be stored in an electronic format provided:

- they are in writing in the English language or so as to enable the records to be readily accessible and convertible into writing in the English language; and
- the records are kept so as to enable the person's tax liability to be readily ascertained.[23]

Companies may also keep financial records, including contracts, in an electronic form, but they must be convertible into a hard copy that must be made available within a reasonable time to a person who is entitled to inspect the records.[24]

6. Public Key Cryptography (PKI)

There has been a large increase in the use of PKI, corresponding with the growth in the use of electronic transactions. PKI is a useful tool which parties to an electronic contract can utilise to protect the integrity of a transaction.

PKI is a means of encrypting messages which are received and decrypted by a receiving party. PKI achieves this through the use of two encryption keys (very large prime numbers), one of which encrypts while the other decrypts a mes-

23 See, for example, section 262A(3) of the Income Tax Assessment Act 1936 (Cth).

24 See section 288 of the Corporations Act 2001 (Cth).

sage. Neither key can be used to decrypt a message which it has encrypted. PKI can be used as a means of:

- identifying: a party who sends a message;
- keeping the message confidential;
- identifying any changes that have occurred to the message during transit; and
- ensuring only the intended party receives the message.

The use of PKI raises difficult ancillary issues. First, the security of any information system is only as secure as its weakest link. The value of the strongest encryption system in the world will be greatly diminished if someone leaves their computer unattended and their e-mail application open. Indeed, strengthened electronic security may actually reduce the security on the human or social side of the equation. Second, the use of encryption on a broad scale has potentially negative consequences for record keeping and archiving. If an encryption key is lost there may be no way to decrypt the respective electronic document. For example, if the Australian Tax Commissioner's officers are unable to access relevant documents because they cannot be decrypted, an organisation may be in breach of tax laws.

The implementation of a PKI regime can be expensive and complicated; therefore, it would be wise for a person or organisation to weigh the benefits against the costs before using PKI on all electronic communications.

Within Australia, the distributed authentication framework for PKI has organically evolved. Commonwealth Government agencies wishing to use digital certificates to identify their clients and trading partners are required to use Gatekeeper[25] accredited services and service providers. Gatekeeper is a government-administered scheme to encourage trust and reliability in online transactions. Under the Gatekeeper system, the government conducts audits of potential participants against a number of criteria such as the processes that that participant has in relation to maintaining the privacy and security of information, the type of contracts that they propose to have with their customers and some aspects of their internal processes and procedures. In this way the Government attempts to encourage trust by providing procedurally based assurances. That is, the Government does not say that an entity is trustworthy, but rather that entity has processes in place which meet certain minimum standards. Although the Government disclaims liability in relation to its Gatekeeper project, it remains to be seen whether they can be successful in excluding that liability.

Another issue which has the potential to undermine the implementation of PKI within Australia is, ironically, also its source of strength. Creating information systems in which all trust is reposed within a single object or facility means that a compromise of that facility results in a much broader compromise of trust than

25 < http://www.agimo.gov.au/infrastructure/gatekeeper >.

would otherwise occur. That is, a failure can be catastrophic because the same facility is used for identification in a number of different circumstances. While this means that the barriers to fraud are improved, the adverse consequences of a fraud also increase.

The occurrence of identity theft is increasing in Australia and the creation of regimes that allow identity to be conveniently packaged into, for example, an encryption key means that the abduction of that key is equivalent to the abduction of a person's or organisation's identity with all of the adverse consequences which flow from that.

BRAZIL

by
Momsen, Leonardos & Cia[1]

A. SOURCES OF LAW

1. Introduction

The Brazilian legal system follows the Roman-Germanic tradition and its principles are inspired in Roman law and based on ethical principles of Christianity. The law is codified and created by the Legislative Branch of government. Differently from Common Law systems, judicial precedents do not necessarily have to be followed by judges, as they are not considered to be law.

When the courts do not find any law applicable to a particular situation, they may refer to the alternative sources listed in Article 4 of the Brazilian Civil Code Introduction Law (Decree-Law no. 4657/42) which are: (i) analogy; (ii) usages; and (iii) the general principles of law.

2. The Brazilian Constitution

The current Brazilian Federal Constitution was promulgated in 1988 and is Brazil's first democratic constitution, following twenty-five years of military government and almost twelve years of gradual re-democratization. Its promulgation was a landmark in Brazilian history and represents a great conquest for Brazilian citizens, since it provides an extensive list of civil and political rights.

The structure of the Brazilian State is based on the doctrine of the separation of powers, as established by Article 2 of the Constitution. Each branch has a specific function and the duties of each are defined by the Constitution:

- The Legislative Power is responsible for the lawmaking process, performed nationally by the National Congress (which comprises the Senate and the House of Representatives), members of which are elected by the citizens.

---

1 This text was written under the coordination of Gabriel F. Leonardos and Clarisse Escorel by and with the assistance of the following members and associates of Momsen, Leonardos & Cia (in alphabetical order): Clarisse Escorel, Christiana Lamazière, Daniele M. Teixeira Coelho, Elisa Bastos Mutschaewski, Gabriel F. Leonardos, Gabriela Acciaris Pinto Vieira and Gabriela Muniz Pinto. This article takes into consideration the changes in the applicable laws through 2003.

- The Executive Power is incumbent with the public administration and is represented nationally by the President and by the ministries of the government.
- The Judiciary Power's function is to apply the law to concrete cases in order to resolve conflicts between individuals.

Brazil is organized as a federation and is divided into twenty-four states, each of which has its own local constitution as well as the same three spheres of power, that is, the Legislative, performed by the members of the State House of Representatives; the Executive, represented by the Governor; and the Judiciary.

One interesting feature of the Brazilian federation is the fact that the municipalities have considerable autonomy in relation to the states and to the federal government, each having its own Executive Power, represented by the Mayor, and Legislative Power, represented by the City Council (there is no municipal Judiciary Power) as well as its own taxation system.

There are clauses in Brazil's Constitution that may not be abolished by amendment, that is, those that establish: (i) the federative form of government; (ii) the direct, confidential and universal form of the vote; (iii) the Separation of Powers; and (iv) civil rights. The only way to modify these provisions would be through the promulgation of a new Constitution.

3. The Legislative Process

The Constitution defines the Brazilian State as a democratic state of law, meaning that no one shall be obliged to do or refrain from doing something unless expressly required by law.

The creation of laws is the function of the Legislative Power. Nonetheless, the Executive Power also takes part in the lawmaking process by vetoing or sanctioning proposed legislation being discussed by the legislators.

The Constitution allows the following entities to take legislative initiative, i.e, to submit a bill for analysis by the Legislative Power: (i) members of the House of Representatives; (ii) members of the Federal Senate; (iii) the President; (iv) the Supreme Federal Court; (v) the Superior Courts; (vi) the General Attorney of the Republic; and (vii) the citizens.

A proposed legislation (a bill) is submitted to the House of Representatives and Senate members and then remitted to the President, who will either veto or sanction it. If sanctioned, the bill becomes law and is published in the Brazilian Official Gazette. If the President vetoes the bill, it returns to the Congress, where its members will vote either for maintaining the veto, in which case the bill will be dismissed, or for overruling the veto, in which case it will become law.

It should be noted that the above-mentioned lawmaking process may be carried out by the Legislative and Executive Powers of the states or of the municipalities, depending on the subject matter of the law to be created and on its range of application. For example, a law created by the National Congress and signed by the President, namely a federal law, has national applicability, while a law created by the City Council and signed by the Mayor of a certain municipality is only applicable locally.

4. Normative Acts of the Executive Power

One of the Executive Power's functions set forth by the Constitution is to issue normative acts in order to explain, define or clarify the text of a law. An executive normative act, therefore, always derives from a specific law and shall not exceed its scope by creating obligations different from those established by the legislators.

Exceptionally, normative acts may be issued by the Executive Power in order to rule on a subject not yet regulated, supplementing an omission. However, it is not possible to enact these supplementary normative acts in order to regulate subjects that, according to the Constitution, may only be regulated by law, such as tributary matters.

In this essay we mention some normative acts enacted by the Executive Power, such as decrees and normative rulings.

5. The Brazilian Judicial System

The function of the Judiciary Power is to apply the law to concrete cases in order to resolve disputes between individuals. It should be stressed that in the Brazilian legal system the courts do not have a law-making function as in Common Law systems. Thus, as mentioned, precedents are not binding and do not have the force of law, serving only as a reference for Brazilian judges.

The Judiciary Power reposes in the following courts:

- The Supreme Federal Court;
- The Superior Court of Justice;
- Federal Courts of Appeals and Federal Judges;
- Federal Courts and Judges;
- State Courts and Judges;
- Labor Courts and Judges;
- Electoral Courts and Judges; and
- Military Courts and Judges.

The Supreme Federal Court, located in Brasilia, the capital of Brazil, is the highest court of the Brazilian judicial system, and is mainly responsible for dealing with Constitutional matters, i.e., ruling on the constitutionality of a law. It comprises eleven justices nominated by the President and approved by the Senate, chosen from Brazilian citizens who are between thirty-five and sixty-five years of age and who have a flawless reputation as well as outstanding juridical knowledge.

The Superior Court of Justice is the highest court of appeals concerning federal law and comprises, at minimum, thirty-three justices. It is mainly responsible for cases involving a federal law.

The Federal Courts of Appeals and the Federal Judges form what we call the federal justice system. The cases under the jurisdiction of the regular federal justice system are ones in which the federal government, federal autarchies or state-owned companies are involved either as plaintiff, defendant, assistant or intervener, and are decided in the first stage by the federal judges.

The Federal Courts of Appeals reexamine the decisions of the regular federal judges and the decisions of the state judges. They are formed by, at minimum, seven justices recruited in the respective district and nominated by the President.

The Labor Justice system is part of the Special Justice system and is formed by the following bodies:

- Labor Courts;
- Regional Labor Courts; and
- the Superior Labor Court—the highest stage of appeal of the Labor Justice system, located in Brasilia, the national capital.

The Electoral Justice system is also a part of the Special Justice system, and comprises:

- Electoral Boards;
- Electoral Judges;
- Regional Electoral Courts; and
- the Superior Electoral Court, which is the highest stage of appeals of the Electoral Justice system, located in the Brazilian capital.

The Military Justice system is entitled to prosecute and judge military crimes, which are defined by law, and comprises the Courts and Military Judges and the Superior Military Court.

Each state of the federation also has its own judicial system to judge those cases in which the government and its agencies are neither the defendant nor the plaintiff. The State Judge and the Courts of Justice, which are courts of appeals, form what we call the State Justice system.

B. THE SCHEME OF ONLINE REGULATION

1. Introduction

The National Congress is the legislative body entitled to create and analyze bills relating to the Internet, since according to the Constitution the enactment of any law regulating water, energy, informatics, telecommunication and broadcasting subjects shall be made by the federal Legislative Power, so that it may be applied nationwide.

Nevertheless, despite the evident juridical relevance of such themes, the Brazilian legal system still does not have any specific law regulating the use of the Internet in Brazil. A series of Internet-related bills is currently before the National Congress for analysis, and the subsidiary application of existing legislation in order to try to resolve conflicts originating from the use of the Internet.

In spite of the lack of specific Internet legislation, since 1995 the Federal Government has started to define the policy for Internet regulation by enacting administrative rulings and creating committees to manage some aspects of the Internet in Brazil.

Apart from these committees, some federal autarchies with regulatory power, i.e., power to issue normative acts, such as the Brazilian Securities and Exchange Commission and the Brazilian Central Bank (discussed later in this commentary), have already enacted rulings related to the Internet which are within their scope.

The structure of Brazil's online legislation is still being developed. Up to now Brazil has merely an attempt to diminish the harm caused by the absence of Internet-specific laws.

2. The Internet Management Committee

Administrative Ruling no. 147, enacted jointly by the Ministry of Communication and the Ministry of Science and Technology, on May 31, 1995, created the Internet Management Committee (IMC).

This ruling has been highly criticized. It was considered to be unconstitutional, given that the Constitution did not confer to government ministries the power to create administrative bodies, such as the IMC, through the enactment of rulings.

The IMC was created to meet the need to coordinate and integrate Internet services throughout the country. Its aim is to guarantee: (i) the quality and efficiency of Internet services; (ii) free competition between Internet service providers; and (iii) the maintenance of a standard of behavior for users and service providers.

The main duties of the IMC are to:

- stimulate the development of Internet services in Brazil;
- recommend patterns of operational and technical procedures for the Internet;
- coordinate the attribution of Internet addresses, the registration of domain names and the interconnection of backbones; and
- collect, organize and publish information about Internet services.

It should be noted that the IMC has delegated the registration of domain names to another governmental institution, "Fundação de Amparo à Pesquisa do Estado de São Paulo" (FAPESP), but is still entitled to regulate this matter.

The IMC is constituted of representatives of the Ministries of Communication and of Science and Technology, as well as of representatives from different sectors of society, such as one representative each from academia and Internet service providers.

3. The E-Commerce Executive Committee

In order to reduce problems caused by the delay in the enactment of a special law regulating online commerce in Brazil, the Ministry of Development, Industry and Foreign Commerce; the Ministry of Science and Technology; and the Ministry of Economy, Treasury and Planning jointly enacted Administrative Ruling no. 47, on August 3, 2000 in order to promote the development of online commerce, along with its corresponding technologies and associated infrastructures, as well as to encourage the integration and coordination of projects in this field.

The Administrative Ruling also created the Executive Committee of Electronic Commerce, with the following duties:

- acting as an intermediary in the relationship between the Government and the economic sectors;
- monitoring the growth of online commerce in Brazil, as well as the corresponding technologies and products developed in the country, and to present an annual report on online commerce development, particularly regarding the services offered to the public, to small and medium size companies and to the exporting sector;
- enacting recommendations related to: (i) the development of methods, technologies and products that provide comparative advantage to the country; (ii) education and training of small and medium size companies in order to increase their use of online commerce, and (iii) actions that facilitate and stimulate the use of online commerce;
- promoting research and publicize information about the development of online commerce, its technologies, its potential for improving the quality and the cost reduction of services offered to the public, aiming thus to enhance access to it by the public and by service providers, especially for small and medium size companies;
- recommending a pattern of use, and technical and operational procedures, as well as to create a code of ethics for the use of online commerce services in Brazil;
- promoting events on this subject aiming to attract society's interest;
- technically reviewing proposals and projects about the employment of technology in online commerce;
- submitting proposals, including projects involving partnerships between the private and the public sectors of the economy; and

- debating and proposing concrete actions to improve the use of online commerce by small and medium size companies as well as to improve exportation.

4. The Brazilian Securities and Exchange Commission

The Brazilian Securities Exchange Commission (SEC) is a federal autarchy created by Law no. 6.385, of December 7, 1976, and is empowered to discipline, rule and supervise the activities of the securities market as well as the subjects related to it.

The law that instituted the SEC established the following goals to be achieved by said body:

- assuring the proper functioning of the exchange and over-the-counter markets;
- protecting all securities owners against fraudulent practices and illegal actions performed by company managers, controlling shareholders, or mutual fund managers;
- preventing or inhibiting any kind of fraud or manipulation which may give cause to artificial price formation in the securities market;
- ensuring public access to all relevant information about available securities and the companies which have issued them;
- ensuring that all market participants adopt fair trading practices;
- stimulating the formation of savings and investment in securities; and
- promoting expansion and efficiency in the securities market, as well as the capitalization of publicly held Brazilian companies.

As already mentioned, the SEC has regulatory power concerning matters related to the Brazilian securities market, such as: the registration of public offerings; securities trading and intermediation; and organization of the stock exchange. Therefore, although the SEC is not an agency specifically created to discipline the use of the Internet, it has the power to enact rulings regulating the use of the Internet in securities market operations in order to pursue the achievement of the above listed goals.

5. The Brazilian Central Bank

The Brazilian Central Bank (BCB) is a federal autarchy created by Federal Law no. 4.595, of December 31, 1964, whose main attributions are:

- controlling foreign capital;
- authorizing, supervising and disciplining the activities of the Financial Institutions;
- dealing, on behalf of the Brazilian Government, with foreign and international financial institutions;
- acting in order to maintain the regular functioning of the exchange market, the relative stability of exchange rates, and the balance of the clearance system;

- authorizing and monitoring the activities of exchange brokers; and
- regulating clearance services.

The BCB has the power to enact rulings related to its own attributions, which may be, for example, related to the use of the Internet in banking activities.

C. ONLINE TRANSACTIONS AND CONTRACT FORMATION

Despite the lack in Brazil of enforced legislation on online contracts, it is a common position in Brazilian standing doctrine that already existing laws, namely the Brazilian Civil Code, can be applied to contracts derived from online transactions.

1. The Brazilian Concept of Contract

According to the Brazilian Civil Code, every contract comprises an agreement between the contracting parties over a determined subject matter, fulfilling the legal requirements of the contract form (if existing) or not violating the express legal prohibitions concerning such formalities.

In addition, the contracting parties must have the legal capacity to perform civil obligations (i.e., being over eighteen years of age). The subject matter dealt with in the contract must not be illicit and must be of viable execution (feasible).

Brazilian Civil Legislation has no express prohibition concerning an agreement to be entered into or performed by digital means. Therefore, whenever a legal formality is not required for the formation and validity of a contract, it can be executed in an online transaction.

It is worth emphasizing that the vast majority of the contracts executed through a computer in Brazil are consumption contracts (i.e., "B to C" or "Business to Consumers" contracts) and, therefore, are controlled by the Brazilian Consumer Protection Code (see discussion under the heading "Consumer Protection in the Online Business" in this commentary).

Application of the Brazilian Consumer Protection Code does not obviate the subjective and objective requisites of contract formation ruled by civil law.

2. The First Step in Executing a Contract: The Proposal

According to Brazilian doctrine, the proposal, after reaching the proposed party, is mandatory for the party that proposed (i.e., the latter cannot modify the terms of the proposal without the agreement of the proposed party) under penalty of having to pay an indemnification for losses and damages. It should also be noted that a valid proposal must contain the necessary information about the subject covered (such as: price, quantity, date of delivery—if applicable) since, after the proposed party's acceptance, this proposal will turn into the contract itself.

Thus, whenever an individual accesses a site and a certain product is offered to him or her, this offer is considered to be a proposal and (the site) binds the proposer to it, if indeed it contains all the necessary information about the goods or services (to be) purchased. The Brazilian Consumer Protection Code (especially Article 30—which rules advertising about services and products binding the advertiser) applies to such a contract.

On the other hand, should this contract not be settled between a supplier and a consumer but between two companies which will resell the purchased goods (and, therefore, are not considered final consumers) the applicable law is the Brazilian Civil Code.

3. The Parties' Agreement

Regardless of whether the Brazilian Consumer Protection Code or the Brazilian Civil Code applies, the analysis of contracts engaged in through online transactions must focus on the subtle question: is the agreement between the parties an agreement *inter praesentes* or *inter absentes* (i.e., between two persons physically in front of each other, or not)?

If the offer is presented through, for example, the Internet Relay Chat or through a Web camera and microphone, the parties are considered to be present (since the proposed party can respond to the offer almost simultaneously) and should the proposal not be accepted, the proposer is no longer bound to the proposal.

On the other hand, if the offer is presented through, for example, an electronic mail message, the parties are considered to be absent (since the proposed party cannot respond to the offer almost simultaneously) and the proposer is bound to the proposal for a reasonable period while awaiting the proposed party's response.

4. The Contract Formation

After the proposal, the contract shall be reputed to be executed when the proposed party expresses its acceptance of the proposed terms and conditions. When taking into consideration online transactions, the same criterion established in the previous item shall be once again considered valid: (i) if the parties are considered to be present to the negotiation, the contract is concluded at the time the proposer receives and understands the agreement of the proposed party (as per Article 1086 of the Former Brazilian Civil Code); (ii) if the parties are considered to be absent, the contract shall be reputed to be concluded at the time the proposed party sends its agreement by, for example, electronic e-mail or by clicking on a site "accept" button.

There is as yet no law regulating the matter in question, only bills (like PLS 672/99, PLS 1483/99 and 1589/99, for example). The President of Brazil has issued, with force of law, "Provisional Measure nº. 2.200"—PM nº. 2.200, which established the "Infra-structure of Brazilian Public Keys" (IBPK). The purpose of the IBPK is to guarantee the authenticity, the integrity and legal validity of electronic documents, as well as applications using digital certificates, and to protect electronic transactions. It should be noted that all kinds of electronic documents are regulated by PM nº. 2.200. The problem PM nº. 2.200 attempts to solve is not so much the legal validity of electronic commerce but the fact that electronic documents can constitute valuable proof in court cases.

5. Law Applicable to Contracts Executed in Online Transactions

Whenever these contracts are executed between Brazilian parties, the applicable law is the Brazilian Civil Code or the Brazilian Consumer Defense Code, depending on whether the legal relationship between the parties is a direct consumer relation ("B to C") or not.

Controversy arises when the contract is executed between a Brazilian consumer and a foreign supplier as to whether: (i) the Brazilian Consumer Defense Code should be applicable, binding the foreign supplier; or (ii) Article 9, paragraph 2, of the Brazilian Conflict of Law applies.

This is a highly controversial subject among Brazilian legal scholars and, at present, no settled opinion has been reached on the subject.

6. Bills of Law Covering Contracts Executed in Online Transactions

Even though there is no enforced legislation in Brazil as of yet, the Brazilian Congress is analyzing several bills covering this theme. We present below a brief analysis of the two most important of these.

a. Bill no. 1589/1999

In Articles 6, 7 and 8, it is provided that goods and services purchase proposals must be made in a safe environment and that unsolicited e-mail ("spam") must be identified as such, even if the computer user does not open the message.

The provision of Article 13 determines that all the rules of the Brazilian Consumer Defense Code are equally applicable to electronic commerce.

b. Bill no. 4906-A/2001

Bill 4906-A/2001 is focused on contractual issues in electronic commerce. In Article 11, it is stated that when executing a contract, the proposal and its acceptance can both be expressed by electronic messages. By Article 12, every willful manifestation expressed by the parties by electronic mail is valid and can incur legal effects.

CANADA

by
Gary N. Bouchard
Fogler, Rubinoff LLP

A. SOURCES OF LAW

1. Introduction

Canada is an independent federal parliamentary state comprised of ten Provinces and three Territories. Technically, Canada is a constitutional monarchy, the monarch of the United Kingdom playing a largely ceremonial role in its governance. Canada began as part of the British Empire established by the *British North America Act* of 1867 (now the *Constitution Act, 1867*), an Act of the British Parliament. Canada gained independence through a gradual legislative and political process that culminated in the *Constitution Act, 1982*, which repatriated the *Constitution Act, 1867*, formally ended all British control and made Canada responsible for all changes to its own constitution.

There are two levels of government in Canada, federal and provincial/territorial. Located in Ottawa, Ontario, the federal government has three branches: legislative, executive, and judicial. The federal government's legislative authority vests in the Parliament of Canada, which consists of the Queen and two legislative houses.[1] The Parliament is bicameral, meaning that it is composed of two legislative houses. As of April 22, 2003, the lower house, the House of Commons, has 301 members[2] who are popularly elected for maximum terms of five years. The leader of the political party that wins the most seats in the House of Commons becomes Prime Minister. The leader of the political party winning the second highest number of seats becomes the Leader of the Official Opposition,

---

1 The *Constitution Act, 1867*, 30 and 30 Victoria, c.3, section 17.

2 Parliament of Canada website "Senators and Members" (viewed on April 26, 2003) at <http://www.parl.gc.ca/information/about/people/house/mpscur.asp?lang=E>. The *Constitution Act, 1867*, 30 and 30 Victoria, c.3, section 37 provides that the House of Commons shall consist of 295 members, unless otherwise provided for in the Act. Section 52 provides that Parliament can increase the number from time to time, provided the proportionate representation of the Provinces prescribed by the Act is not disturbed.

which is responsible for providing intelligent and constructive criticism to the government.

There are 105 seats in the upper house,[3] the Senate, which is based on the House of Lords in the United Kingdom. In contrast to members of the House of Commons, the Prime Minister appoints Senators for life terms subject to mandatory retirement at the age of 75. The Sovereign is also part of Parliament. The Governor General represents in the Sovereign in Canada and exercises the Sovereign's authority in relation to the federal government.

The Prime Minister is responsible for forming the Cabinet, the executive arm of the federal government. The Cabinet is responsible to the House of Commons, and Cabinet members—referred to as Ministers—may hold office only so long as they retain the confidence of the House. Each Minister has a portfolio of governmental responsibility and heads the relevant department or ministry.

The provincial governments resemble the federal government. The only significant structural difference is that the provincial legislatures are unicameral. The leader of the provincial government is referred to as the provincial Premier. The Sovereign's representative is appointed by the Governor General and is referred to as the Lieutenant Governor. Provinces have the authority to establish local governments. Accordingly, there are systems of municipal government unique to each Province.

The federal government administers the territories, so they are structured differently from the Provinces. Nunavut is the only territory with a formal legislature. Yukon and the Northwest Territories have Councils of elected persons who advise their Commissioner in Council, the Sovereign's representative, on legislative matters. Each of the Territories is entitled to one member in the House of Commons.[4]

The judicial branches of the federal and provincial/territorial governments are discussed later in this section.

Canada is referred to as a "bijural" country, meaning that it has two legal systems—the civil law in the Province of Québec and the common law in the remaining provinces and territories. The civil law and common law are equally authoritative and recognized sources of the law on property and civil rights in Canada.[5] In the Province of Québec, as a general rule, the civil law system applies to private law matters within the provincial government's jurisdiction while the common law system applies to public law matters. The common law

---

3 The *Constitution Act, 1867*, 30 and 30 Victoria, c.3, section 21. As of February 7, 2003, there were 98 members of the Senate: Parliament of Canada website "Senators and Members" (viewed on April 26, 2003) at <http://www.parl.gc.ca/information/about/people/Senate/SenIdx.asp?lang=E&Hist=N>.

4 The *Constitution Act, 1867*, 30 and 30 Victoria, c.3, subsection 51(2).

5 *Interpretation Act*, R.S. I-21, sections 8.1 and 8.2.

system is based on the common law tradition of the United Kingdom. Accordingly, principles in areas such as tort, contract and property are similar to those of the United Kingdom and the United States of America. The civil law system is based on the civil law and *Napoleonic Code* of France.

2. Constitution

The Constitution of Canada (the "Constitution"), as defined in the *Constitution Act, 1982*,[6] is the supreme law of Canada.[7] Any law that is inconsistent with its provisions is of no force or effect. The Constitution applies to all acts of the federal and provincial governments within the jurisdiction of their respective legislatures.[8] Accordingly, any court in Canada can review an act of government if there are grounds to believe that the act violates the Constitution. If a violation is found, the court can declare the act, or any part thereof, of no legal effect. The Constitution also applies to the common law insofar as it provides the basis for some governmental action.[9] It does not apply to relations between private persons.

In addition to the written Constitution, Canada has an "unwritten constitution" composed of constitutional conventions and judicial interpretations developed and adopted over time. For example, the laws of Parliamentary privilege (the implied powers needed to operate Parliament) and the laws of Crown prerogative were developed by judicial decisions.

a. Division of Powers

The Constitution sets out the division of powers between the federal and provincial governments. The legislative powers of the Territories are set out in their respective founding statutes.[10]

The federal government has authority over issues concerning the "peace, order and good government of Canada,"[11] generally meaning issues of national importance that transcend provincial boundaries. Certain matters are specifically mentioned as falling within federal jurisdiction. These include responsibility for the armed forces, regulation of trade and commerce, banking, credit, currency and bankruptcy, criminal law and procedure, postal services, fisheries, intellectual property, immigration, foreign affairs, the census and national statistics, taxation, navigation, shipping, railways, canals and telegraphs. In addition, the federal government enjoys a residual authority over matters that are not specifically assigned to the Provinces.

---

6 The schedule to the *Constitution Act, 1982*, R.S.C. 1985, c.11, refers to the written documents that make up the Constitution and includes the *Constitution Act, 1867*.

7 *Constitution Act, 1982*, R.S.C. 1985, c.11, section 52.

8 *Constitution Act, 1982*, R.S.C. 1985, c.11, section 32.

9 *Retail, Wholesale, and Dept Store Union v. Dolphin Delivery Ltd.*, [1986] 2 S.C.R. 573.

10 The *Nunavut Land Claims Agreement Act*, 1999, c.29, and the *Nunavut Act*, 1993, c.28 established Nunavut. The Yukon Act, R.S. c.Y-2, The *Northwest Territories Act*, R.S. c. N-22.

11 The *Constitution Act, 1867*, 30 and 30 Victoria, c.3, sections 91, 94-94A.

The provincial governments have jurisdiction over issues regional in nature, such as direct taxation within the province, education, social programs, property rights and commerce.[12] They are also responsible for the administration of justice within provincial boundaries. While territorial governments are subject to federal jurisdiction, they have authority over local government programs and initiatives. They also have limited legislative powers, which are set out in their respective constituting documents.[13]

b. Charter of Rights and Freedoms

The Constitution also contains the *Charter of Rights and Freedoms*[14] (the "*Charter*"), the Canadian equivalent to the American Bill of Rights. The rights guaranteed by the *Charter*, however, are not absolute and are subject to "such reasonable limits prescribed by law as can be demonstrably justifiable in a free and democratic society." Specifically, *Charter* rights may be limited under section 1 of the *Charter* if: (1) the infringing act has a pressing and substantial legislative objective; and (2) the means chosen by government is reasonably and demonstrably justified, meaning that (a) they are rationally connected to the legislative objective, (b) they are the least restrictive means possible on the rights and freedoms being infringed, and (c) their limiting effect on the right or freedom is proportionate to the legislative objective of sufficient importance.[15]

In addition, section 33 of the *Charter* permits governments to exclude their Acts, or provisions contained therein, from the application of sections 2 and 7-15 of the *Charter of Rights and Freedoms*[16] simply by way of an express declaration within the Act to the effect that the Act (or a specified provision therein) will operate notwithstanding the *Charter*. The exclusion may extend over a maximum period of five years from the date the Act comes into effect, which is renewable by re-enacting a declaration.

The Province of Québec's *Charter of Human Rights and Freedoms* applies in the Province of Québec, not only to the Parliament but also to persons, corporations, partnerships and trusts.

---

12 The *Constitution Act, 1867*, 30 and 30 Victoria, c.3, sections 92-93A, 95.

13 The *Nunavut Land Claims Agreement Act*, 1999, c.29, and the *Nunavut Act*, 1993, c.28 established Nunavut. The Yukon Act, R.S. c.Y-2, The *Northwest Territories Act*, R.S. c. N-22.

14 *Constitution Act, 1982*, R.S.C. 1985, Part 1.

15 This test is commonly referred to as the *Oakes* test, which was established by the Supreme Court of Canada in *R v. Oakes*, [1986] 1S.C.R. 103. An interesting discussion of the evolution of the *Oakes* test can be found in Leon E. Trakman, William Cole-Hamilton, and Sean Gatien, "R. v. Oakes 1986-1997: Back to the Drawing Board" in *Osgoode Hall Law Journal*, Vol.36, No.1, Spring 1998, pp.83-149.

16 *Constitution Act, 1982*, R.S.C. 1985, c.11, section 33.

3. Legislation

a. Federal

The federal and provincial legislative processes are similar. In Parliament, either the Senate or the House can originate a Bill proposing a change to the existing law or the introduction of a new law, but only the latter can introduce Bills regarding the expenditure of public funds or imposition of taxes.[17] A Bill goes through three "readings" in each of the Senate and the House during which members debate the Bill. Before the final reading, the Bill is sent to a committee where it is reviewed in detail and revised. Both the Senate and the House must pass a Bill before it receives royal assent from the Governor General and becomes law. Practically, the Governor General only exercises the power to proclaim Bills as law in consultation with and on the advice of the two legislative houses.

b. Provinces

The provincial law-making process mirrors the federal one, but the provincial legislatures are unicameral. A provincial Bill comes into effect either upon royal assent or upon a date specified within the Bill. In the latter case, the date must typically be approved by the Lieutenant Governor and fixed by royal proclamation.

While the Province of Québec is unique as the only civil law jurisdiction in Canada, its legislative processes resemble those of the rest of the provinces. The current *Civil Code of Québec* (the "*Civil Code*") came into effect on January 1, 1994 after undergoing a massive overhaul in the 1980s. The *Civil Code* is essentially a statute that is divided into ten books: (1) Persons, (2) Family, (3) Successions, (4) Property, (5) Obligations, (6) Hypothecs (mortgages and the sale of land), (7) Evidence, (8) Prescription (statute of limitations), (9) Publication of Rights (property registration), and (10) Private International Law. The Province of Québec also has statutes and regulations of general application within the Province, which typically contain more detailed provisions than those found in the *Civil Code*. Amendments to the *Civil Code* are introduced through the same process as the introduction of any new law.

c. Territories

The Governor General's representatives in the Territories are referred to as Commissioners. In Yukon and the Northwest Territories, law-making authority rests with the Commissioners who are able to legislate by way of Ordinance on the advice and with the consent of their Councils. The Ordinances, or any part thereof, are subject to veto by the Governor General.[18] Nunavut is the only

17 The *Constitution Act, 1867*, 30 and 30 Victoria, c.3, section 53.

18 *Yukon Act*, section 22; *Northwest Territories Act*, section 21.

Territory has a formal legislature that has direct law-making authority.[19] Its laws are also subject to veto by the Governor General.[20]

Most statutes empower their overseeing authority to make legally-binding regulations, which are enacted simply by publication in the federal or provincial Gazette. Regulations are sometimes considered a backdoor method of lawmaking because government officials are able to introduce them bypassing the lengthier legislative process that statutes undergo.

4. Common Law

All the Provinces and Territories, excluding the Province of Québec, are common law jurisdictions, based on the common law tradition of the United Kingdom. This means that, in addition to legislation they enact, they follow laws based on the decisions of judges over time using the doctrine of precedent. While the Province of Québec is a civil law jurisdiction, the common law is still applicable. Generally, the civil law system applies to private law matters that fall within the Québec government's legislative jurisdiction while the common law system applies to public law matters.

Laws are applied and interpreted by the federal or provincial bureaucracy responsible for regulating their application as well as the court system and legal practitioners.

Pursuant to the Constitution, authority for the judicial system is divided between federal and provincial governments.

5. Federal Courts

The federal government has the authority to create "a General Court of Appeal for Canada and any additional Courts for the better Administration of the Laws of Canada."[21] Based on this authority, the federal government established the Supreme Court of Canada in 1875, the Federal Court (trial and appellate levels) in 1971, and the Tax Court in 1983.[22]

The Supreme Court is the last court of appeal for the federal and provincial court systems in contrast to its American counterpart, which only hears appeals from its federal court system. In addition, it has a special "reference" jurisdiction unique to Canada among the common law countries. This special jurisdiction permits the Supreme Court to opine on important questions or law or fact referred to it by the Governor-in-Council. The Governor-in-Council is responsible for appointing nine judges to the Supreme Court pursuant to the *Supreme Court*

---

19 *Nunavut Act*, sections 14, 23 and 25-27.

20 *Nunavut Act*, section 28.

21 The *Constitution Act, 1867*, 30 and 30 Victoria, c.3, section 101.

22 See the *Supreme Court Act*, R.S.C. 1985, c. S-26, the *Federal Court Act*, R.S.C. 1985, c. F-7 and the *Tax Court of Canada Act*, R.S.C. 1985, c. T-2.

Act, one of whom is designated as the Chief Justice and at least three of whom must be from the Barreau du Québec.

The Federal Court of Canada (Trial and Appeal Divisions) replaced and expanded the jurisdiction of the old Exchequer Court. In addition to the traditional powers over revenue, the Crown in Right of Litigant, industrial and intellectual property, the admiralty, and certain other matters regulated by federal legislation, the Federal Court was given jurisdiction over other federal matters like inter-provincial transportation and bills of exchange and the power to judicially review decisions of federal administrative tribunals. The Tax Court primarily hears appeals in the area of income tax.

6. Provincial Courts

Provinces are responsible for the administration of justice within their borders, which includes the "constitution, organization and maintenance" of civil and criminal courts as well as civil procedure. The federal government appoints and removes judges to and from the provincial superior court benches (trial and appellate levels).[23] It is also responsible for their remuneration.[24] The provincial government appoints, removes and remunerates judges on the benches of the lowest level of provincial courts (e.g. Traffic Court, Small Claims Court, Family Court), known simply as "provincial courts." Two provincial courts act as courts of appeal for the three territories.[25]

In the Provinces, there are provincial superior courts and provincial courts. The jurisdiction of provincial superior courts is not limited to matters within the legislative jurisdiction of provincial governments. If federal legislation requires the exercise of judicial authority, but does not specify which court is to exercise that authority, it is assumed that reference is to provincial superior courts. As mentioned earlier, provincial courts are the lowest level of court. As such, they handle the bulk of the cases that enter the court system.

7. Administrative Tribunals

Administrative tribunals are not a formal component of the judicial system, but are an integral part of the dispute resolution process. Disputes arising in areas such as human rights, labour relations, employment are brought before administrative tribunals, and the decisions of those tribunals are legally binding and, in some cases, may only be reviewed by the courts in very limited circumstances, for example, where a tribunal has exceeded its jurisdiction as defined in its founding statute. Generally, tribunals have the final say on questions of law that

23 The *Constitution Act, 1867*, 30 and 30 Victoria, c.3, sections 96 and 99.

24 The *Constitution Act, 1867*, 30 and 30 Victoria, c.3, section 100.

25 The judges of the British Columbia Court of Appeal also sit on the bench of the Yukon Court of Appeal. The judges of the Alberta Court of Appeal are also judges of appellate courts for the Northwest Territories and Nunavut.

arise within their jurisdiction, which are reviewable by a court in select situations. It should be noted that courts have demonstrated considerable deference to tribunal judgments on law.

8. Judiciary

The Constitution guarantees the independence of the judiciary in Canada. In Canada, all judges are appointed from a provincial or territorial bar. Where the federal government is responsible for appointing judges, federal statute requires candidates to have been a member of a provincial or territorial bar for at least ten years.[26] Applications are vetted by local committees and ultimately decided upon by the federal Cabinet. The appointment process is similar for provincial courts within the respective provinces.

Superior Court judges appointed by the federal government must retire at the age of 75.[27] All other judges must retire at either 75 or 70, depending on the court and the applicable statute.

9. Lawyers

In Canada, the regulation of the legal profession and the practice of law falls within provincial/territorial jurisdiction. Lawyers are accredited and governed by Provincial and Territorial law societies (or their equivalent), which are statutorily charged to govern in the public interest lawyers practicing within their jurisdiction pursuant to their relevant provincial and territorial legislation. Each law society works to ensure the independence, integrity and honour of its members by establishing standards for professional conduct and competence.

B. SCHEME OF ONLINE BUSINESS REGULATION

1. Introduction

There is no comprehensive regulatory regime exclusively devoted to the governance of online commerce. For our purposes, online commerce refers to commercial transactions using Transmission Control Protocol/Internet Protocol. Generally, all existing laws applicable to traditional commerce apply to the conduct of commercial transactions online. This includes laws concerning incorporation, business name registration, taxation, import/export, consumer protection, and product safety and standards. Some federal statutes more specifically applicable to online commerce issues include the *Competition Act*, the *Copyright Act*, the *Investment Canada Act*, the *Telecommunications Act*, the *Trademarks Act*,

26 *Judges Act*, R.S., c.J-1, section 3.

27 The *Constitution Act, 1867*, 30 and 30 Victoria, c.3, subsection 99(2).

the *Personal Information Protection and Electronic Documents Act*[28] and the computer misuse provisions of the *Criminal Code*. Businesses must comply with the laws of whatever jurisdiction(s) where they are deemed to be "carrying on business." The type and level of activity that constitutes "carrying on business" may vary between jurisdictions. This is discussed later on in this commentary.

On September 22, 1998, the Prime Minister announced *Canada's Electronic Commerce Strategy*, which outlined the following four objectives in making Canada a world leader in adoption and use of online commerce:

- Building trust in the digital economy by addressing security, privacy and consumer protection concerns;
- Clarifying marketplace rules, creating a technology-neutral regulatory environment with transparent rules on how the law treats electronic transactions;
- Strengthening the information infrastructure through the standardization of technology; and

Increasing economic growth and making the government a model user of e-commerce technology.[29] Generally, the Federal government, through Industry Canada, leads the development and implementation of online commerce and Internet policy and law in Canada. Its policies are reflected in those of the Canadian Intellectual Property Office, the Communications Research Centre, Spectrum Management, and Telecommunications, Copyright Board of Canada, the Canadian Radio-Television and Telecommunications Commission, and Technology and Innovation Research policies. Different aspects of online commerce fall within the jurisdiction of the federal and provincial government depending on the kind of issue. Both levels of government, in consultation and collaboration with the private sector, have taken initiatives to develop a legal and regulatory infrastructure governing electronic transactions that is consistent with the principles articulated in *Canada's Electronic Commerce Strategy*. They are discussed below.

2. Security, Privacy, and Consumer Protection

In October 1998, the federal government adopted an online commerce cryptography policy to protect the security of electronic transmissions and prove their origin, receipt and integrity. The federal government's Public Key Infrastructure (PKI) Initiative is a system enabling Federal departments and agencies to participate in secure transactions within government, with external clients and the general public. Users register with a central authority (the Certificate Authority), which issues to each user special encryption software and a unique pair of

---

28 *Personal Information Protection and Electronic Documents Act*, S.C. 2000, c.5.

29 A copy of *Canada's E-Commerce Strategy* can be found at <http://e-com.ic.gc.ca/english/strat/doc/ecom_eng.pdf> (viewed April 27, 2003).

keys (a "public key" and a "private key"). The user's public key is listed in a publicly available electronic directory. Another registered user can access the first user's public key to encrypt messages to be sent to that user. The recipient then uses his or her private key to decrypt the message. The PKI policy was completed in May 1999 under the auspices of the Treasury Board of Canada Secretariat.

On April 13, 2000, the Federal government passed the *Personal Information Protection and Electronic Documents Act*[30] ("PIPEDA"), the first national legislation to protect the privacy of personal information in the private sector. PIPEDA came into force on January 1, 2001. As will be discussed later on in this commentary, PIPEDA currently applies to the inter-provincial and international exchange of personal information (including exchanges within an organization), provided the personal information itself is the subject of the transaction and consideration is given for the information. It also applies to the intra-provincial personal information activities of "federal works, undertakings and businesses," meaning any work, undertaking or business within the legislative authority of Parliament. As of January 1, 2004, PIPEDA will apply intra-provincially unless the provincial government enacts privacy protections that are substantially similar. As of April 27, 2003, Québec is the only Province with privacy legislation applicable to the private sector.

General consumer protection laws applicable in that jurisdiction apply to online commerce transactions. Alberta introduced the Internet Sales Contract Regulation under the *Fair Trading Act*,[31] which applies to consumer contracts formed by text-based Internet communications for goods or services exceeding CAD50. This regulation came into effect on October 15, 2001. Ontario's *Consumer Protection Act*[32] was amended in 2002 to address Internet agreements. These instruments are discussed later in this commentary.

In August 1999, the Working Group on Electronic Commerce and Consumers released a set of consumer protection principles specifically tailored to the online shopping experience. The Working Group on Electronic Commerce and Consumers is a consortium of federal and government offices, industry associations, and consumer groups. The Principles of Consumer Protection for Electronic Commerce complement the Guidelines for Consumer Protection in the Context of Electronic Commerce issued by the OECD.[33] This is discussed in detail later in this commentary. While the adoption of these consumer protection

30 *Personal Information Protection and Electronic Documents Act*, S.C. 2000, c.5.

31 *Fair Trading Act*, R.S.A. 2000, c. F-2. This Act came into effect on September 1, 1999 and essentially replaced and expanded the scope of *Unfair Trade Practices Act, Collection Practices Act, Consumer Credit Transactions Act, Direct Sales Cancellation Act, Licensing Trades and Businesses Act, Public Auctions Act*, and the *Wage Assignments Act*.

32 *Consumer Protection Act*, S.O. 2002, c.30.

33 Both are available on the Industry Canada website at <http://strategis.ic.gc.ca/SSG/ca01180e.html> (viewed on April 27, 2003).

principles and their supporting documentation is not legally required, they contribute to the normative environment of online commerce and act as important guidance documents for online business and consumers.

3. Electronic Documents and Signatures

The Uniform Law Conference of Canada (the "Conference") is a conference of commissioners representing the Federal government, the Provinces and the Territories whose primary object is to harmonize legislation where it is considered to be advantageous. At the request of its constituent jurisdictions, the Conference develops Uniform Acts, Model Acts, Statements of Legal Principles and other documents deemed appropriate. On September 30, 1999, the Conference adopted the *Uniform Electronic Commerce Act* ("UECA"), a model Act based on the 1996 UNCITRAL *Model Law on Electronic Commerce* and broadly similar to the *Uniform Electronic Transactions Act* adopted by the American National Conference of Commissions on Uniform State Laws.

The UECA is divided into three parts. Part 1 sets out basic functional equivalence rules applicable where parties have expressly or impliedly agreed to use electronic documents. Part 1 also permits governments to set their own rules for incoming electronic documents while requiring outgoing documents to conform to UECA standards unless otherwise provided for by some other legislation. Part 2 addresses contract formation and sets rules for particular kinds of communication. For example, section 23 provides that a person is presumed to have received an electronic document under certain circumstances. Part 3 deals with the carriage of goods.

Except for Québec, all of the Provinces, the Federal government, and the Yukon Territory have passed laws based on the UECA. The federal government enacted PIPEDA, Part 2 of which addresses the use of electronic signatures and electronic documents where federal laws contemplate the use of paper records. Part 3 amends the *Canada Evidence Act* to make electronic signatures and documents admissible as evidence.

The Provincial online commerce statutes vary slightly in their provisions and should be consulted individually.[34] For example, unlike other provincial online

34 *Electronic Transactions Act* (British Columbia), S.B.C. 2001, c.10; *Electronic Transactions Act* (Alberta), S.A. 2001, c. E-6.5; *Electronic Commerce and Information Act* (Manitoba), S.M. 2000, c.E55; *Electronic Transactions Act* (New Brunswick), S.N.B. 2001, c.E-5.5; *Electronic Commerce Act* (Nova Scotia), S.N.S. 2000, c.26; *Electronic Commerce Act, 2000* (Ontario), S.O. 2000, c.17; Electronic Commerce Act (Prince Edward Island), S.P.E.I. 2001, c.31; *Electronic Information and Documents Act, 2000* (Saskatchewan), S.S. 2000, c.E-7,222; and *Electronic Commerce Act* (Yukon), S.Y. 2000, c.10.

commerce legislation, Ontario's *Electronic Commerce Act*[35] expressly excludes from its application the use of biometric information or other personal identifiers, unless another Act expressly provides for the use of such information or unless all parties to the transaction consent to its use.

In 2001, Québec enacted *An Act to establish a legal framework for information technology*.[36] Substantively, it is not vastly different from UECA and the remaining provincial online commerce statutes. It is broader in its objectives—for example, it promotes the harmonization of technical systems, norms and standards—but still achieves many of the same objectives of the UECA and the UNCITRAL *Model Law on Electronic Commerce*.

4. Technology-neutral Regulatory Framework

In September 1998, the Prime Minister stated that Canada was committed to a technology-neutral approach to online commerce taxation, meaning no new tax for online commerce.[37] On May 17,1999 the Canadian Radio-Television Telecommunications Commission (CRTC) issued a report wherein the CRTC stated its intention to exempt Internet-based services from certain licensing and regulation requirements.

5. Standardization

In March 1999, the Telecommunications Standards Advisory Council of Canada approved the *Standards Framework for Electronic Commerce*,[38] which is intended as a practical guide for private and public sector players engaged in developing online commerce standards. Industry-led initiatives to promote online commerce standardization includes the establishment of the Electronic Commerce Council of Canada (ECCC), which is a not-for-profit industry association whose mandate is to promote and maintain global standards relating to supply chain management, for example, the identification of goods, services, locations and related online commerce communication such as bar code issuance and maintenance. The ECCC disseminates information on best practices and industry standards to its constituents.

---

35 *Electronic Commerce Act, 2000*, S.O. 2000, c.17. "Biometric information" is defined in subsection 29(2) as "information derived from an individual's unique personal characteristics, other than a representation of his or her photograph or signature."

36 *An Act to establish a legal framework for information technology*, S.Q. 2001, c.32.

37 Industry Canada, E-Commerce website at <http://e-com.ic.gc.ca/english/strat/index.html> (viewed on April 27, 2003).

38 *Standards Framework for Electronic Commerce* is available at <http://e-com.ic.gc.ca/english/strat/doc/standards.pdf> (viewed on April 27, 2003).

C. ELECTRONIC TRANSACTIONS AND CONTRACT FORMATION

1. Introduction

The same rules of contract law that apply to traditional transactions apply, generally, to electronic transactions, they are subject to certain modifications introduced by legislation intended to clarify their application in the electronic context. They are also subject to legislative provisions reflective of the different policy issues surrounding business-to-business and business-to-consumer contracts, including provisions protecting consumers and the privacy of personal information

2. Contract Law: General Principles

The bulk of contract law is judge-made law, the application of which has been modified and clarified by legislation for various circumstances. The fundamental principles of contract formation, however, remain the same. A contract is a promise that the law will enforce.[39] To establish a legally binding contract, one party must extend an offer to another party, the latter must have communicated to the former unconditional acceptance of the offer, and value must have been exchanged to seal the bargain. These acts should all reflect the determinative element of a legal contract, that being the intention of the parties to be legally bound to one another at the time of entering into the agreement.

An "offer" has been described as a manifestation of willingness by one party to enter into a legally binding contract with another party upon such party's acceptance of the offer.[40] To constitute an offer at law, the manifestation must induce a reasonable expectation that acceptance of the offer will result in a valid contract. The offer is effected at the time it is communicated to the offeree. An offer to contract is distinguished from an "invitation to do business," also referred to as an "invitation to treat." Courts have held that advertisements made in press or trade catalogues or goods displayed in a store are "invitations to do business" and not contractual offers.[41]

"Acceptance" has been described as the outward expression, by words or conduct, of assent to the terms of an offer in the manner prescribed or indicated by the offeror. The acceptance must be unequivocal and without qualification to the terms of the offer. Merely acknowledging receipt of the offer is insufficient, and an acceptance that attempts to modify the terms of the original offer will be con-

39 S.M. Waddams, *The Law of Contracts* (4th ed.), (Toronto: Canada Law Book, 1991), p.11.

40 S.M. Waddams, *The Law of Contracts* (4th ed.), (Toronto: Canada Law Book, 1991), pp.20-21.

41 *Grainger & Son v. Gough*, [1896] A.C. 325 (H.L); *Pharmaceutical Society of Great Britain v. Boots Cash Chemists (Southern) Ltd.*, [1953] 1 Q.B. 401 (C.A.).

sidered a counter-offer at law.[42] Also, to create a legally binding contract, the acceptance must be communicated to the offeror or someone authorized by the offeror to receive it.[43] The offeror can specify how his or her offer should be accepted and whether that is the exclusive method of acceptance. An offer cannot be accepted after it has been revoked or rejected. Only the offeree may accept the offeror.

If there are circumstances where an offeror did not get the acceptance due to his or her own fault, the offeror may be estopped from saying that he or she did not receive the communication. There is no contract, however, where technical failures are to blame, which are not attributable to the fault of either party.[44]

There are cases where acceptance does not have to be communicated to the offeror to effect a legally binding agreement. The resultant agreement is sometimes referred to as a "unilateral contract."[45] In such instances, where a promise is made in return for the performance of an act, the offeree needs only to perform the act in reasonable reliance on the promise to make that promise binding. Cases in which unilateral contracts have been found include promises to give prizes, a listing in a railway timetable, and an implied promise by a newspaper to exercise care in giving financial advice to readers.[46]

Generally, acceptance is effected at the time the offeror receives communication of the offeree's acceptance and at the place of such receipt.[47] An exception to this is the "mailbox rule," which deems an acceptance delivered by conventional mail to have been communicated upon entering the postal system, provided that it was within the parties' contemplation that an offer may be accepted by post. This exception has been extended to telegrams and couriers. (Note that the "mailbox rule" does not exist in the Province of Québec where contracts are made when acceptance is received by the offeror, regardless of the method of communication used, and even though the parties have agreed to reserve agreement as to secondary terms.[48]) The time and location of a contract is objectively determined by examining facts and circumstances of each case, including the

---

42 S.M. Waddams, *The Law of Contracts* (4th ed.), (Toronto: Canada Law Book, 1991), p.46.

43 S.M. Waddams, *The Law of Contracts* (4th ed.), (Toronto: Canada Law Book, 1991), p.67.

44 *Entores Ltd. V. Miles Far East Corp.*, [1955] 2 Q.B. 327 (C.A.).

45 *Carlill v. Carbolic Smoke Ball Co.*, [1893] 1 Q.B. 256 (C.A.). In this case, an advertisement offered money to anyone who contracted influenza after using the advertised product according to its printed instructions and indicated that a sum had been deposited to show the sincerity of the company's offer. The plaintiff became ill despite using the product according to its instructions and claimed the sum of money. The court awarded the plaintiff the money.

46 S.M. Waddams, *The Law of Contracts* (4th ed.), (Toronto: Canada Law Book Inc., 1999), p.124.

47 *Re Viscount Supply Co.* (1963), 40 D.L.R. (2d) 501 (Ont.S.C.).

48 *Civil Code of Québec*, S.Q. 1991, c.64, Book V, Article 1387.

place of contracting, the place of performance, the places of residence or business of the parties, and the nature and subject matter of the contract.[49]

In addition to the offer and communication of unconditional acceptance, consideration must be given to bind the parties to the agreement, meaning that something of value must be given or promised in exchange for the promise that is sought to be enforced. The exchanged things do not have to be equal in value. Parties are free to make good or bad bargains. However, courts may set aside an exchange as unconscionable where a contracting party used or abused its superior bargaining power to reach an agreement.

Generally, there is no formal requirement that an agreement be in writing to be legally binding. Contracts can be made by any means of communication, and the common law has evolved to confirm this. However, there may be statutory requirements that a contract be written to be enforceable, so local laws should be consulted. The essential terms of the contract must be certain, and the language used must be comprehensible.[50] Also, the contracting parties must be legally capable of entering into the transaction. What constitutes "legally capable" may vary from jurisdiction to jurisdiction. The case law on which law governs capacity to contract in an international context is inconclusive, but some courts have held that the proper law of the contract will govern.[51]

3. Electronic Commerce Legislation

Recent legislative initiatives across Canada have clarified and codified how general contract law principles and related statutory requirements apply to electronic transactions. They established what is referred to as "functional equivalency" for electronic communications, meaning the rules that set out the conditions that must be met if an electronic communication is to be used to satisfy a legal requirement for a "written" communication. In common law Provinces, there are essentially two types of legislation that specifically address electronic contract formation: legislation based on the *Uniform Electronic Commerce Act* ("UECA") and legislation based on the Internet Sales Contract Harmonization Template (the "E-Contract Template"). The Province of Québec has enacted *An Act to establish a legal framework for information technology* (the "Québec E-Commerce Act"),[52] a piece of legislation developed independent of the UECA.

The UN Commission on International Trade Law ("UNCITRAL") developed a Model Law on Electronic Commerce and a Model Law on Electronic Signatures as guides to which UN member states, including Canada, could reference when

---

49 *Re Viscount Supply Co.* (1963), 40 D.LR. (2d) 501 (Ont.S.C.).

50 Barry Sookman, *Sookman: Computer, Internet and Electronic Commerce Law* (Release 3), (Scarborough: Thomson Canada Ltd., 2002), p.10-12.

51 *Charron v. Montréal Trust Co.*, [1958] O.R. 597 (C.A.); *Bodley Head Ltd. v. Flegen*, [1972] 1 W.L.R. 680 (Ch.D.).

52 *An Act to establish a legal framework for information technology*, S.Q. 2001, c.32.

drafting their own online commerce legislation. In 1999, the Uniform Law Conference of Canada adopted the UECA, which builds upon the UN Model Law on Electronic Commerce and expands the application of its principles beyond just "commerce" to nearly every legal relationship that may require documentation. The UECA was intended as a template on which the provinces and territories could draft their own provincial legislation. The goal was to harmonize local online commerce laws so as to increase legal certainty for businesses that operate in a medium that does not really recognize geopolitical boundaries.

Part 1 of the UECA establishes basic functional equivalency rules which apply when people involved in a transaction have agreed, expressly or by implication, to use electronic documents. Note that the UECA does not make the use or acceptance of information in electronic format mandatory.[53] Part 1 also establishes special rules applicable to governments, permitting them to set their own rules for incoming electronic documents. Part 2 sets out rules for particular kinds of communications including the formation and operation of contracts, the effect of using automated transactions, the correction of errors when dealing with a computer, and the deemed time of delivery and receipt of messages. Part 3 deals with the carriage of goods.

All of the provinces (excluding the Province of Québec) and the Yukon Territory have drafted and enacted online commerce legislation based on the UECA.[54] Accordingly, the provincial Acts establish *prima facie* functional equivalency for electronic documents, electronic contracting, electronic agents, electronic signatures, and official filings. They follow the UECA closely. They typically apply where a contract was formed within their jurisdiction or governed by the laws of their jurisdiction. They apply to all legal relationships and documents, except wills and codicils, and powers of attorney concerning personal health or financial matters, documents transferring land, negotiable instruments, and other prescribed documents. All the provincial Acts, excluding New Brunswick's Act and the Québec E-Commerce Act, state that they do not limit the operation of any provision of law that expressly authorizes, prohibits or regulates

53 *Uniform Electronic Commerce Act*, section 6. A person's consent to use or accept information in an electronic format may be inferred from his or her conduct. This does not apply to government actions, however. Government's consent to the use or acceptance of information in an electronic format must be expressed by a "communication accessible to the public or to those likely to communicate with it for particular purposes."

54 *Electronic Transactions Act* (British Columbia), S.B.C. 2001, c.10; *Electronic Transactions Act* (Alberta), S.A. 2001, c.E-5.5; *Personal Information Protection and Electronic Documents* (Canada), S.C. 2000, c. 5; *Electronic Commerce and Information Act* (Manitoba), S.M. 2000, c. E55; *Electronic Transactions Act* (New Brunswick), S. N.B. 2001, c. E-5.5; *Electronic Commerce Act* (Newfoundland and Labrador), S.N. L. 2000, c. E-5.2; *Electronic Commerce Act* (Nova Scotia), S.N.S. 2000, c. 26; *Electronic Commerce Act* (Ontario), S.O. 2000, c. 17; *Electronic Commerce Act* (Prince Edward Island), S.P.E.I. 2001, c. 31; *Electronic Information and Documents Act* (Saskatchewan), S.S. 2000, c.E-7.22; and *Electronic Commerce Act* (Yukon), S.Y. 2000, c. 10.

the use of electronic documents or the operation of a legal requirement for legal information to be posted, displayed, or transmitted in a specified manner.

Substantively, the Québec E-Commerce Act[55] is not vastly different from the UECA and the derivative provincial Acts. It is broader in its objectives—for example, it promotes the harmonization of technical systems, norms and standards—and is perhaps more detailed in its provisions, but the Québec E-Commerce Act is substantially consistent with many of the UECA's objectives.

Federally enacted legislation that was drafted according to the UECA's principles is the *Personal Information Protection and Electronic Documents Act* ("PIPEDA"). PIPEDA makes electronic transactions or documents functionally equivalent to paper documents for the purposes of provisions in federal statutes and regulations that require or contemplate paper documents, unless expressly stated otherwise. PIPEDA also addresses secure electronic signatures, authorises federal agencies to use electronic means to manage information, receive certain filings and publish certain official documents, and introduces legal provisions meant to protect the privacy of personal information.

On May 25, 2001, federal, provincial and territorial ministers responsible for consumer affairs approved the E-Contract Template which provinces and territories will rely on to draft their legislation regarding consumer protection in electronic transactions. The E-Contract Template introduces mandatory terms into electronic agreements. Such terms provide that copies of contracts must be sent to consumers, credit charges be reversed after a contract has been properly cancelled and no refund has been received within 15 days after such time. The E-Contract Template imposes other obligations on sellers and creditors. Manitoba and Alberta both passed electronic commerce consumer protection laws before May 25, 2001. They are addressed in detail later in this commentary.

In addition to legislation that specifically targets electronic activities, there are laws and regulations of general application that affect the rules of electronic contract formation. For example, statutory requirements for "writing" or signatures will apply to all contracts before the court in which proceedings are brought. Consumer protection legislation and some other legislation require parties to deliver or retain copies of their agreement in order for it to be valid. Canada has ratified and enacted the United Nations Convention on Contracts for the International Sale of Goods (the "UN Convention") which applies to contracts for the sale of goods between parties whose places of business are in different countries where the countries are signatories to the UN Convention, or when the rules of private international law lead to the application of the law of a signatory

55 *An Act to establish a legal framework for information technology*, S.Q. 2001, c.32.

country.[56] Privacy statutes and industry-specific legislation (e.g. health care and banking) may require firms to retain and destroy on a specified schedule certain types of information they collect in the course engaging in their commercial activities.

4. Effectively Forming Electronic Contracts

It is now established in Canadian law that information shall not be denied legal effect or enforceability solely because it is in electronic form and that contracts shall not be denied their legal effect, validity or enforceability solely because an electronic document was used in their formation.[57]

As already mentioned, the rules of electronic contract formation do not differ dramatically from those applicable to contracts, generally. There are aspects to contracting that are unique to online commerce. For example, the contracting parties do not have to come into personal contact to reach an agreement. Websites are easier and cheaper to create than conventional retail stores, making it possible for almost anyone to set up an online business and, accordingly, raising greater consumer protection concerns. By and large, however, an analysis of the elements of electronic contracts proceeds in substantially the same fashion as conventional contracts.

a. When and how is an offer made to create an e-contract?

The UECA and its derivative legislation (the "UECA laws"), excluding New Brunswick's Act, provide that offers can extended by means of: (a) an electronic document, (b) an action in electronic form, including touching or clicking on an appropriately designated icon or place on a computer screen, or (c) otherwise communicating electronically in a manner intended to express the requisite willingness to contract.[58]

---

56 *International Sale of Goods Contracts Convention Act*, S.C. 1991, c.13, Article 1(1) of the Schedule. The UN Convention and its enacting legislation prevail in the event of inconsistencies with other laws: section 6.

57 *Uniform Electronic Commerce Act*, section 5 and subsection 20(2). Note that the New Brunswick Act does not contain a provision relating directly to the general formation and operation of electronic contracts. Courts in Canada have also established in common law that, generally, online agreements are binding and must be "afforded the sanctity that must be given to any agreement in writing." See *Rudder et al. v. Microsoft Corp.* (1999), 2 C.P.R. (4th) 474 (Ont.S.C.J.), para 17. See also *Kanitz et al. v. Rogers Cable Inc.* (2002), 58 O.R. (3d) 299 (S.C.J.) wherein Nordheimer J. upheld the unilateral amendment of an Internet subscription contract which was made by posting a notice of new contract terms online. In that case, the original agreement provided that the defendant could amend the agreement by posting notice of changes on the website.

58 *Uniform Electronic Commerce Act*, section 20. The New Brunswick government did not include this provision in its legislation on the grounds that the principle was already law: Barry Sookman, *Sookman: Computer, Internet and Electronic Commerce Law* (Release 3), (Scarborough: Thomson Canada Ltd., 2002), p.10-18.1.

An offer communicated electronically is effected at the time of communication. The UECA laws provide that, unless the parties agree otherwise, an electronic communication is sent when it enters an information system outside the control of the originator or, if they are in the same information system, when it becomes capable of being retrieved and processed by the addressee.[59]

Unless agreed otherwise, the UECA laws (excluding New Brunswick's Act) deem an electronic communication to have been sent from the originator's place of business or, where there is none, habitual residence. Where there is more than one place of business, delivery is deemed to have occurred at the place that has the closest relationship to the underlying transaction to which the electronic communication relates or, if there is no underlying transaction, the principal place of business.[60]

The offeror should unequivocally express (and document) his or her intention to contract to avoid confusing his or her offer with a mere invitation to do business. Note that in respect of the international sale of goods, the UN Convention provides that a proposal will be considered an invitation to make offers and not an offer itself, unless it is addressed to one or more specific persons or unless the contrary is clearly indicated by the offeror.[61] In the international context, this reduces the risk that offers communicated through the Internet become offers to the world capable of being accepted by anyone and governed by the laws of a variety of different jurisdictions. To further reduce the risk, the offeror can tailor the terms of the offer to narrow the pool of offerees and specify the governing law of the contract.

The UECA laws provide that a contract may be formed by the interaction between an electronic agent and natural person or another electronic agent.[62] An "electronic agent" is defined as a computer program or any electronic means used to initiate an action or respond to an electronic document or action in whole or in part without review by a natural person at the time of the response or action.[63] An electronic agent can be used to extend an offer to contract, provided the agent can effectively convey the offeror's intention to contract in a manner that would lead a reasonable person to believe that the offeror had intended to effect legal relations with the offeree. For example, if a computer is pro-

59 *Uniform Electronic Commerce Act*, section 23.

60 *Uniform Electronic Commerce Act*, section 23.

61 *International Sale of Goods Contracts Convention Act*, S.C. 1991, c.13, Article 14(2) of Schedule.

62 *Uniform Electronic Commerce Act*, section 21.

63 *Uniform Electronic Commerce Act*, section 19.

grammed to make or accept offers in predetermined circumstances, the intention of the programmer or user to create legal relations may be reasonably inferred.[64]

Also, to constitute a valid offer, all of the material terms of the offer must be communicated with reasonable specificity. In online commerce, like in traditional retail businesses, standard forms dominate business-to-consumer contracts.[65] There are special common law rules in relation to standard form contracts, to which businesses will have to be sensitive.[66] Generally, businesses must sufficiently draw consumers' attention to the terms of the agreement and take other reasonable measures to give fair notice to consumers of any onerous or unusual terms at the time of entering into the agreement. These rules may vary between the jurisdictions, so local laws should be consulted.

In Québec, the Charter of the French Language, commonly referred to as Bill 101, imposes French language requirements on product advertising and distribution within Québec. These requirements may apply to a supplier's website, even if it is situated outside of Québec, in the event that the supplier's products are available in Québec and the supplier has any type of physical presence in Québec, whether involving distribution, maintenance or a sales branch or subsidiary office.[67]

b. How are such offers accepted?

The UECA laws (excluding New Brunswick's Act) provide that offers can be accepted by means of: (a) an electronic document, (b) an action in electronic form, including touching or clicking on an appropriately designated icon or place on a computer screen, or (c) otherwise communicating electronically in a

64 Barry Sookman, *Sookman: Computer, Internet and Electronic Commerce Law* (Release 3), (Scarborough: Thomson Canada Ltd., 2002), p.10-18.6.

65 Robert A. Hillman and Jeffrey J. Rachlinski, "Standard-Form Contracting in the Electronic Age"(2002) 77 N.Y.U.L. Rev. 429, p.446 citing Robert W. Gomulkiewicz, "The License Is the Product: Comments on the Promise of Article 2B for Software and Information Licensing," 13 Berkeley Tech. L.J. 891 at 897-99.

66 *Tilden Rent-A-Car Co. v. Clendenning* (1978), 17 O.R. (2d) 601 (Ont.C.A.); *Craven v. Strand Holidays (Canada) Ltd.* (1982), 40 O.R. (2d) 186 (Ont.C.A.)

67 Article 52 of the *Charter of the French Language*, R.S.Q. c. C-11, requires catalogues, brochures, leaflets, commercial directories and other publications of a similar nature to be in the French language. The *Office de la langue française* (OLF) takes the position that this includes content on websites or sent by fax or e-mail. In a notice dated June 21, 1997, the OLF stated that all companies with a place of business or an address in Québec must provide Québec consumers with a French language version of any commercial publication appearing on their websites: *Alan Gahatan, Martin P.J. Kratz, J. Fraser Mann, Internet Law: A Practical Guide for Legal and Business Professionals* (Scarborough: Carswell Thomson Professional Publishing, 1998), p.221.

manner intended to express acceptance.[68] Prior to the enactment of the UECA laws, an Ontario court held that an online membership agreement became an enforceable contract upon the would-be subscriber clicking the "I Agree" button.[69]

If an offer is made electronically, it may be implied that the offeror consents to the electronic communication of acceptance of the offer. If it is not specified that acceptance must be communicated electronically, the offeror risks the possibility of entering into a unilateral contract. Common law principles in relation to unilateral contracts are echoed in the UN Convention, which provides that an offeree may indicate assent to the offer by performing an act without notice to the offeror, in which case acceptance is effective the moment the act is performed, depending on the terms of the offer, established practice between the parties, or usage.[70]

c. When and where is an electronic contract formed?

As noted above, generally, a contract is formed when acceptance is communicated to the offeror and where acceptance is received by the offeror, but this may vary from jurisdiction to jurisdiction. The UECA laws presume receipt of an electronic communication:

- when it enters an information system designated or used by the addressee for the purpose of receiving that type of document and the addressee is capable of retrieving and processing it, or
- if the addressee has not designated or does not use an information system for the purpose of receiving documents of the type sent, when the addressee becomes aware of the document in his or her information system and is capable of retrieving and processing it.[71]

Under the UECA laws, this is a rebuttable presumption in contrast to the equivalent provision found in the UN Model Law on Electronic Commerce. In the context of international agreements for the sale of goods, the UN Convention provides that acceptance is effective the moment the indication of assent reaches the offeror within a reasonable time, taking into account the circumstances of the transaction, or within the time frame fixed by the offeror.[72]

---

68 *Uniform Electronic Commerce Act*, section 20. As mentioned, the New Brunswick government did not include this provision in its legislation on the grounds that the principle was already law.

69 *Rudder et al. v. Microsoft Corp.* (1999), 2 C.P.R. (4th) 474 (Ont.S.C.J.).

70 *International Sale of Goods Contracts Convention Act*, S.C. 1991, c.13, Article 18 of the Schedule. Acceptance, oral or otherwise, will not be effective if the indication does not reach the offeror within the time frame fixed by the offeror or, if no time is fixed, within a reasonable time, given the circumstances of the transaction.

71 *Uniform Electronic Commerce Act*, section 23.

72 *International Sale of Goods Contracts Convention Act*, S.C. 1991, c.13, Article 18 of the Schedule.

The UECA laws (excluding New Brunswick's Act) also provide that, unless otherwise agreed, the acceptance is deemed to have been sent from and received at the originator's and addressee's respective places of business or, where there are none, their respective habitual residences. Where there is more than one place of business, delivery or receipt (as the case may be) is deemed to have occurred at the place that has the closest relationship to the underlying transaction to which the communication relates or, if there is no underlying transaction, the principal place of business.

Consumers typically enter into two types of contracts online: "click-wrap" agreements and "browse-wrap" agreements. Click-wrap agreements are formed when people click at electronic standard forms on websites while installing software.[73] They typically require consumers to click through one or more steps to conclude an agreement. Browse-wrap agreements are agreements for the visitation and use of a website.[74] Generally, the website terms provide that using the website to purchase the goods or services offered (or even just visiting the site) constitutes acceptance of the conditions contained therein.

The UECA laws[75] and the common law[76] have established that clicking through terms of use may sufficiently communicate acceptance to conclude a contract. The issue of acceptance is more problematic in relation to browse-wrap contracts because users typically have to voluntarily follow a hyperlink to the terms of use, bringing into question the adequacy of the presentation of those terms. This has led some to argue that browse-wrap agreements are likely unenforceable in Canada unless the user takes positive action that manifests assent to the terms or the operator made reasonable attempts to bring the user's attention to the terms and the user had a reasonable opportunity to read them.[77]

In April 2003, the Québec Superior Court granted an injunction against a real estate agency's practice of modifying and reposting on its own website real estate listings found through The Canadian Real Estate Association's (CREA) website, which operated as a gateway to various real estate listing services.[78] The homepage of the CREA website referred to and contained a hyperlink to

---

73 Robert A. Hillman and Jeffrey J. Rachlinski, "Standard-Form Contracting in the Electronic Age"(2002) 77 N.Y.U.L. Rev. 429, pp.431 and 464.

74 Robert A. Hillman and Jeffrey J. Rachlinski, "Standard-Form Contracting in the Electronic Age"(2002) 77 N.Y.U.L. Rev. 429, pp.431 and 464.

75 *Uniform Electronic Commerce Act*, section 20. As mentioned, the New Brunswick government did not include this provision in its legislation on the grounds that the principle was already law.

76 *Rudder et al. v. Microsoft Corp.* (1999), 2 C.P.R. (4th) 474 (Ont.S.C.J.).; *Kanitz et al. v. Rogers Cable Inc.* (2002), 58 O.R. (3d) 299 (S.C.J.).

77 Barry Sookman, *Sookman: Computer, Internet and Electronic Commerce Law* (Release 3), (Scarborough: Thomson Canada Ltd., 2002), p.10-18.1.

78 *The Canadian Real Estate Association v. Sutton (Québec) Real Estate Services Inc.*, (April 10, 2003), Montréal 500-05-074815-026 (Que.S.C.).

terms of use which clearly prohibited licensed real estate agents from modifying, reposting, and making unauthorized use of listings found through that website. The CREA website did not, however, require the user to take any positive action communicating acceptance of the terms of use.

The issue of acceptance in browse-wrap agreements was addressed in the widely-cited American decision *Specht v. Netscape Communications Corp.*[79] In this decision, the court held that the website in question did not give users sufficient notice of the existence and terms of a software license agreement and that, as a result, the act of downloading the software did not sufficiently evidence a user's assent to be bound by the agreement. In that case, the website was designed so that there was no requirement for a user to affirmatively accept, agree or even read the terms of the agreement before downloading the software. The only reference to the agreement was an invitation to view it and a hyperlink located at the bottom of the webpage. Also, users could download the software simply by clicking a "download" button and could download it from a third party shareware site wherein there was no reference to the license agreement at all. Netscape's failure to require users to indicate assent to the license terms as a condition to downloading and using the software was fatal to its argument that a contract had formed.

The CREA decision may be an early indication of how Canadian courts will treat browse-wrap agreements in the future, particularly with respect to agreements between businesses, but it is by no means definitive.[80] Canadian courts will often refer to and be guided by legal developments in the United States and other Commonwealth countries. The *Netscape* decision is persuasive authority which suggests that browse-wrap agreements will be enforceable if the website: (i) requires users to view the terms of the agreement; (ii) indicates that downloading the software will evidence the user's assent to be bound by such terms; and (iii) requires that the user positively indicate his or her acceptance before he or she is able to download and use the software. An Ontario court upheld an electronic agreement structured in this manner.[81]

79 *Specht v. Netscape Communications Corp.*, 150 F. Supp. 2d 585, US Dist. LEXIS 9073, 45 U.C.C. Rep. Serv. 2d (C.B.C.) 1 (S.D.N.Y.2001).

80 In its decision, the Quebec Superior Court notes that the terms of use found on the defendant's website were very similar to the terms of use found on the CREA's website. The court stated that the defendant should have been aware of the CREA's terms of use and their significance given the defendant's own practices: *The Canadian Real Estate Association v. Sutton (Québec) Real Estate Services Inc.*, (April 10, 2003), Montréal 500-05-074815-026 (Que.S.C.).

81 In *Rudder et al. v. Microsoft Corp.* (1999), 2 C.P.R. (4th) 474 (Ont.S.C.J.), a "Member Agreement" for the use of the defendant's Internet access and other online services was provided to potential users in a computer readable form on a computer disk or on the defendant's website. The sign-up process presented the terms of membership to the potential user twice, requiring the potential user to positively indicate acceptance each time. Declining the terms terminated the process. The second time terms were presented to the potential user, the website advised that clicking "I Agree" would communicate his/her agreement to be bound by those terms

d. Does an electronic contract have to be in writing?

The common law does not require agreements to be in writing to be legally valid. Legislation, on the other hand, may sometimes impose "writing" requirements. Examples include: sale of goods legislation in several common law provinces;[82] the *Copyright Act* which requires assignments of copyrights to be in writing;[83] the *Patent Act*, which requires assignments of patents to be in writing;[84] and the *Statute of Frauds* (Ontario) which requires contracts of guarantee, contracts for the sale of land, and contracts not to be performed within a year to be in writing.[85] There are often writing requirements in respect of credit disclosure in various provincial consumer protection and federal banking statutes.

Reasons for requiring documents or communications in writing include: (a) to secure tangible evidence of the existence and nature of the parties' intent to bind themselves legally; (b) to help the parties think through their agreement and the consequences of it; (c) to provide a universally legible document; (e) to provide a permanent record of the transaction that can be copied and retained by the parties; (f) to provide a document in a form acceptable to public authorities and courts; (g) to finalize the intent of the authors and provide a record of that intent; and (h) to facilitate control and subsequent audit for accounting, tax or regulatory purposes.[86]

The federal and provincial *Interpretation Acts* define "writing" and "written" as words printed, typewritten, painted, engraved, lithographed, photographed or represented or reproduced by any mode of representing or reproducing words in visible form. There is very little case law that provides any guidance on whether electronic communications constitute "writing" or "written" communications. However, on a plain reading of the definition, an electronic document, in which words are reproduced in visible form, should fall within the meaning of "writing" or "written."

The UECA laws and PIPEDA make electronic documents functionally equivalent to paper documents for the purposes of any legislative requirement that information be provided to a party in writing,[87] provided that the electronic document is given to, accessible by and capable of being retained by that party for subsequent use.

---

irrespective of whether he/she read them. Winkler J. upheld the Member Agreement, stating that it "must be afforded the sanctity that must be given to any agreement in writing."

82 *Consumer Protection Act* (Ontario), R.S.O. 190, c.C.31, s.19.

83 *Copyright Act*, R.S.C. 1985, c.C.42, s.13.

84 *Patent Act*, R.S.C. 1985, P.4, s.50.

85 *Statute of Frauds* (Ontario), R.S.O. 1990, c.S.19.

86 UNCITRAL Model Law on Electronic Commerce with Guide to Enactment (1996), paragraph 48 (slightly modified).

87 Note that the Manitoba Act limits the application of the functional equivalence provisions to any laws designated in the regulations by the Lieutenant Governor in Council: see *Electronic Commerce and Information Act*, S.M. 2000, c.E.55, sections 7-11.

e. Does an electronic contract have to be signed?

The function of a signature is to affix in some way "...whether by writing with a pen or pencil or by otherwise impressing upon the document, one's name or "signature" so as to personally authenticate the document."[88] Signatures are also evidence that the signatories agreed to be bound by the document. They can identify the signatory by name or identify another particular characteristic of the signatory such as status. A signature does not have to be the entire name fully written out; any mark or notation is acceptable if it identifies the party and authenticates the document and it is the customary way of identification of the person.[89] Generally, in the absence of fraud or misrepresentation or *non est factum*,[90] a signed contract is binding.

Contracts do not have to be signed to be legally enforceable, but there are situations in which the law will require signatures. As mentioned, the *Statute of Frauds* (Ontario)[91] requires different documents (like declarations and assignments of trust) to be signed as well as in writing, otherwise they are void and of no legal effect. The *Sale of Goods Act* (Ontario) provides that if documents are required to be in writing, they must be signed as well.[92]

The UECA laws makes an electronic signature valid for all purposes where the law requires a signature, provided it is reasonably reliable for that purpose.[93] The definition of "electronic signature" varies between the UECA laws. The UECA defines it as information in electronic form that a person has created or adopted in order to sign a document and that is in, attached to or associated with the document.[94]

---

88 *Goodman v. J. Eban Ltd.*, [1954] 1 All E.R. 763 (C.A.), the leading Commonwealth case on what constitutes a signature, has been followed in Canada. See *Botiuk v. Collison* (1979), 26 O.R. (2d) 580 (C.A.) and *Atkinson et al. v. Municipality of Metropolitan Toronto* (1976), 12 O.R. (2d) 401 (C.A.), reversed on other grounds (1977), [1978] 1 S.C.R. 918.

89 *Milliken & Co. v. Interface Flooring Systems (Canada) Inc.*, [1998] 3 F.C. 103 (T.D.), aff'd (2000), 5 C.P.R. (4th) 209 (Fed.C.A.), para 42.

90 *Non est factum* is a phrase used to refer to circumstances that made the signing of the contract not the signator's act.

91 *Statute of Frauds* (Ontario), R.S.O. 1990, c.S.19.

92 *Sale of Goods Act* (Ontario), R.S.O. 1990, c.S.1.

93 *Uniform Electronic Commerce Act*, section 10. Again, the Manitoba Act limits the application of the functional equivalence provisions to any laws designated in the regulations by the Lieutenant Governor in Council: see *Electronic Commerce and Information Act*, S.M. 2000, c.E.55, sections 7-11.

94 *Uniform Electronic Commerce Act*, subsection 1(b). "Electronic signature" is a technology-neutral term that refers to all the methods by which one can sign an electronic record, including a typed name, unique codes, algorithms, letters, devices, biometric information, and digital signatures based on public key cryptography: Barry Sookman, *Sookman: Computer, Internet and Electronic Commerce Law* (Release 3), (Scarborough: Thomson Canada Ltd., 2002), p.10-68 quoting from Thomas J. Smedinghoff, "Moving with Change: Electronic Signature Legislation as a Vehicle for Advancing E-Commerce," *John Marshall Journal of*

Certain federal laws require signatures on certain documents to be witnessed. PIPEDA provides that such requirement can be met electronically if each signature and witness signs the electronic document with their "secure electronic signature," the federal law or provision is listed in schedule 2 or 3 to PIPEDA, and the related regulations have been complied with.[95] PIPEDA establishes functional equivalency for electronic signatures and secure electronic signatures in relation to other federal requirements, for example, sworn statements of truth. The Governor in Council can make regulations under the *Canada Evidence Act*,[96] establishing evidentiary presumptions in relation to electronic documents signed with electronic signatures.[97]

PIPEDA defines a "secure electronic signature" as a signature resulting from a person's use of a technology or process that is unique to him or her where: (a) the use of such technology or process is under his or her sole control; (b) the technology or process can be used to identify such person; and (c) the electronic signature can be linked with an electronic document so as to determine whether it has been changed since it was electronically signed.[98] Secure electronic signatures are thought to ensure confidentiality of information, authenticity of the sender's intention to be associated with the communication and the ability to hold the sender accountable for the communication, and integrity (accuracy and completeness) of the communication. Electronic signatures can be secured using encryption technology and certification authorities.

f. Can electronic contracts be "original" contracts?

The law sometimes requires documents to be "original" documents. For example, there are legal provisions requiring original documents for weight certificates, agricultural certificates, inspection reports, insurance certificates, birth and death certificates and documents of title and negotiable instruments. Electronic documents are easy to copy, so technically making one "original" is difficult. The UECA laws set out the functional equivalency rules to make electronic documents "original" for the purposes of law.

The UECA laws provide that a legal requirement that requires the original form of a document is satisfied if:

- there exists a reliable assurance as to the integrity of the information contained in the document from the time it was first made in its final form, whether as a paper or electronic document;

Computer and Information Law, vol.XVII, no.3, Spring 1999, at 723. Internationally, legislation has taken different approaches as to what type of electronic signature should be legally equivalent to a hand-written signature, so the relevant definitions should be consulted when doing business in a particular jurisdiction.

95 *Personal Information Protection and Electronic Documents Act*, S.C.2000, c.5, section 46.

96 *Canada Evidence Act*, R.S.C. 1985, c.C.5.

97 *Personal Information Protection and Electronic Documents Act*, S.C.2000, c.5, section 31.4.

98 *Personal Information Protection and Electronic Documents Act*, S.C.2000, c.5, section 31.

- where the document in original form is to be provided to a person, the electronic document is accessible by the person and capable of being retained by the person so as to be usable for subsequent reference; and
- where the original document is to be given to government, government has consented to accept electronic documents in satisfaction of the requirement and the electronic document meets the information technology standards and acknowledgement rules, if any, established by the government.[99]

The Québec E-Commerce Act sets out different functional equivalency rules for the different reasons for needing to establish originality.[100] In every case, the integrity of the document must be ensured.[101] If the need is to assure that the document is the first from which copies are made, the components of the source document must be retained for subsequent use as a reference. If the need is to ensure that the document is unique, the electronic document's components or its medium must be structured by a process, based on approved technical norms and standards, that makes it possible to verify that the document is unique through the inclusion of an exclusive or distinctive component or the exclusion of any form of reproduction. If the need is to ensure that the document is the first form of a document associated with a person, the process must make it possible to verify the document is unique, to identify the associated person and to maintain the link throughout the life cycle of the document.

PIPEDA provides that a requirement under federal law for an original document is satisfied by an electronic document if:

- the law is listed in Schedules 2 or 3 to PIPEDA;
- the document contains a secure electronic signature that was added when the document was first generated in its final form and can be used to verify that there have been no changes since; and
- the relevant regulations have been complied with.[102]

There are common law and statutory rules of evidence that require original documents for the purposes of authentication and producing the "best evidence." For example, the best evidence rule stipulates that, where the terms of a docu-

99 *Uniform Electronic Commerce Act*, section 11. Note that Nova Scotia's Act limits the functional equivalence between electronic documents and "original" document requirements under the *Personal Property Security Act* (Nova Scotia), establishing that control of an electronic document does not constitute "possession" of an original document for the purposes of that piece of legislation: see *Electronic Commerce Act*, S.N.S. 2000, c.26, section 12.

100 *An Act to establish a legal framework for information technology*, S.Q.2001, c.32, section 12.

101 See *An Act to establish a legal framework for information technology*, S.Q.2001, c.32, section 6.

102 *Personal Information Protection and Electronic Documents Act*, S.C.2000, c.5, section 42.

ment are material, the original document must be submitted as evidence.[103] In addition to the general functional equivalence provisions in the UECA laws, various provincial Evidence Acts establish rules with respect to authentication and best evidence as they apply to electronic documents.[104] Generally, these rules are similar to those set out in the *Canada Evidence Act*.

Under the *Canada Evidence Act*, an electronic document can satisfy the best evidence rule if:[105]

(i) the integrity of the electronic documents system by or in which the document was recorded or stored is proven;

(ii) if a printout has been manifestly or consistently acted on, relied on or used as a record of the information recorded in the printout;

(iii) at all material times the computer system or similar device used by the electronic documents system was operating properly or, if not, did not affect the integrity of the electronic document and there are no other reasonable grounds to doubt the system;

(iv) it was recorded stored by a party who is adverse in interest to the party seeking to introduce it; or

(v) it was recorded or stored in the usual and ordinary course of business by a person who is not a party and who did not record or store it under the control of the party seeking to submit it.

The person seeking to admit an electronic document must prove its authenticity by evidence capable of supporting a finding that the electronic document is that which it is purported to be.

g. Are electronic contracts made in error enforceable?

Generally, contracts made by mistake are not enforceable because they lack the requisite intention to enter into a legally binding arrangement.[106] The UECA laws address errors made in dealings between natural persons and electronic agents. They provide that an agreement will have no legal effect and will not be enforceable if:

- the natural person made a material error in the document;

---

103 *R. Betterest Vinyl Manufacturing Ltd.* (1989), 52 C.C.C. (3d) 441 (B.C.C.A.); *R. v. Donald* (1958), 121 C.C.C. 304 (N.B.C.A.).

104 These Acts include *Saskatchewan Evidence Act*, R.S.S. 1978, c.S-16, sections 29.1 to 29.6; *Evidence Act* (New Brunswick), S.N.B.C., c.E-11, sections 47.1 to 47.2; *Evidence Act* (Nova Scotia), R.S.N.S. 1989, c.154, sections 23A to 23H; *Evidence Act* (Ontario), R.S.O. 1990, c.E-23, section 34.1. *Manitoba Evidence Act*, C.C.S.M., c.E150, sections 51.1 to 51.8; and *Electronic Evidence Act* (Yukon), S.Y.2000, c.11.

105 *Canada Evidence Act*, R.S.1985, C-5, sections 31.1 to 31.8.

106 *Steller Properties Ltd. v. Botham Holdings Ltd.*, [1994] B.C.J. No.639 (B.C.C.A.); *Denham v. Denham*, [1993] O.J. No.4317 (Ont.Gen.Div.).

- the agent did not provide an opportunity to prevent or correct the error;
- the natural person notifies the other person of the error as soon as practicable when the former learns of it and indicates that he or she made an error in the electronic document;
- the natural person takes reasonable steps, including steps that conform to the other person's instructions to return or destroy the consideration received, if any, as a result of the error; and
- the natural person has not used or received any material benefit or value from the consideration, if any, received from the other person.[107]

All the above conditions must be met before a transaction will be considered void. The Québec E-Commerce Act contains a provision that is similar in principle, but is not as detailed.[108] Businesses would be well-advised to allow parties to review and reconfirm contract terms and correct errors at the time of contracting online.

The anonymity of the Internet raises concerns about the identity of the parties who contract through it. Internet users can lie about their identities, ages, and even geographic location. Identification protocols tend to identify a particular computer instead of a particular user.[109] Different technologies have been introduced to reduce the level of uncertainty such as third party certification and digital certificates.

h. What laws govern an electronic contract?

Generally, the validity and effect of a contract are governed by the proper law of the contract, meaning the law that the parties intended to apply. Where the parties have expressly selected which laws should govern their agreement, their choice will generally be respected unless there is a strong reason not to, but a court is not bound to give effect to an exclusive jurisdiction clause.[110] The party seeking to set aside the choice of law bears the burden of proving a strong cause. Canadian courts will only recognize an express choice of law clause if the choice:[111]

(i) is not illegal;

(ii) not contrary to public policy;

---

107 *Uniform Electronic Commerce Act*, section 22.

108 *An Act to establish a legal framework for information technology*, S.Q.2001, c.32, section 35.

109 Robert A. Hillman and Jeffrey J. Rachlinski, "Standard-Form Contracting in the Electronic Age"(2002) 77 N.Y.U.L. Rev. 429, p.472.

110 *Texserv Inc. v. Incon Container U.S.A. Ltd.* (2000), 48 O.R. (3d) 427 (S.C.J.); *Rosenthal v. Kingsway General Insurance Co.*, [2002] O.J. No. 1785 (S.C.J.); *Barber v. Height of Excellence Financial Planning Group Inc.*, [2001] S.J. No.294 (Q.B.).

111 Richard T. Pfohl, "Jurisdiction and Procedural Issues," in Alan Gahtan, Martin Kratz and J. Fraser Mann (eds.), *Electronic Commerce: A Practitioner's Guide* (Toronto: Thomson Canada Ltd., 2003), p.22-11.

(iii) is made *bona fide*; and

(iv) is not chosen to specifically evade a mandatory legal provision of the jurisdiction with which the transaction is otherwise most closely connected.[112]

In the absence of express selection by the parties, in Canada, a contract is governed by the system of law with which the transaction has the most "real and substantial connection."[113] This determination is made in consideration of a variety of factors, including the currency in which payments are made, use of a particular language, the nature and location of the subject of the contract, the residence of the parties, head of a corporate party to the contract, legal terminology used, implied choice of law, and any choice of forum clause. The case law is unclear as to whether an express choice of law clause will be upheld where the choice is different from the law with which the contract is most substantially connected.[114]

Canadian case law is not very developed on the subject of jurisdiction over disputes involving the Internet. Courts will likely look to legal developments in the United States, the United Kingdom and other Commonwealth jurisdictions for guidance. The British Columbia Court of Appeal held that the Internet alone did not constitute a real and substantial connection between British Columbia and Texas. In that case, the court refused to enforce a default judgment issued by a Texas court in a defamation lawsuit brought against a Vancouver resident who had posted criticism of the company on the Internet.[115] Leave to appeal was refused by the Supreme Court of Canada.

Other laws may apply in addition to the proper law of the contract. As mentioned, statutes like the *Statute of Frauds* (Ontario) are procedural in nature and apply regardless of the proper law of the contract. Statutory requirements for "writing" or signatures will apply to all contracts before the court in which proceedings are brought regardless of the proper law.

---

112 Greenshields Inc. v. Johnston (1981), 119 D.L.R. (3d) 714, affirmed (1981), 131 D.L.R. (3d) 234 (C.A.).

113 *Imperial Life Assurance Co. v. Colmenares*, [1967] S.C.R. 443.

114 Barry Sookman, *Sookman: Computer, Internet and Electronic Commerce Law* (Release 3), (Scarborough: Thomson Canada Ltd., 2002), p.10-36.

115 *Braintech, Inc. v. Kostiuk*, [1998] B.C.J. No.3201 (B.C.S.C.), reversed [1999] 9 W.W.R. 133 (C.A.), leave to S.C.C. refused (2000) 253 N.R. 395. The Court of Appeal appears to rely on an American decision, *Zippo Manufacturing Company v. Zippo DotCom, Inc.* 952 F.Supp. 1119 (W.D.Pa. 1997) at 1122, which held that the exercise of a court's jurisdiction over a non-resident entity's Internet activities should depend on the nature and quality of commercial activity that the entity conducts over the Internet. Where the entity clearly does business over the Internet and knowingly enters into contracts with non-residents, personal jurisdiction is proper. However: "[a] passive website that does little more than make information available to those who are interested in it is not rounds for the exercise of personal jurisdiction. The middle ground is occupied by interactive websites where a user can exchange information with the host computer. In these cases, the exercise of jurisdiction is determined by examining the level of interactivity and commercial nature of the exchange of information that occurs on the website."

A court will usually exercise or assert jurisdiction over a defendant located outside of Canada if the parties specified in the contract or relevant document that such court would have jurisdiction or if any of the following occurred within the boundaries of the court's jurisdiction:

- the business was conducted;
- damages were sustained;
- contract obligations were to be performed;
- the wrong was allegedly committed; or
- the dispute involves real property within the boundaries.

i. What provisions should be included in an electronic contract?

When forming an electronic contract, parties should identify the products and services to be delivered and include provisions dealing with the method of payment and delivery, the governing law, the risk of loss, warranties and product liability, limitations of liability, and acceptance and returns. In addition, parties should consider the following:

- the scope of transactions to be covered (as electronic contracts are not suitable for all transactions);
- each party's electronic signature;
- the parties' acknowledgement that they intend to be bound by the messages received and will not challenge them alter in court on the grounds that they are sent electronically;
- the need to keep transaction logs and enforce security procedures;
- agreement as to when an offer is deemed accepted;
- who bears the risk of error in messages and any remedial procedures in the event of error;
- a dispute resolution procedure; and
- risk allocation and liability.[116]

116 Michael Erdle and Heather Watts, "Electronic Contracting" in Alan Gahtan, Martin Kratz and J. Fraser Mann (eds.), *Electronic Commerce: A Practitioner's Guide* (Toronto: Thomson Canada Ltd., 2003), p.13-3.

CROATIA

by
Mladen Vukmir, mr.sc.
Vukmir & Associates

A. SOURCES OF LAW

1. Introduction

In 1991 Croatia declared its independence from the former Yugoslavia,[1] proclaiming the Republic of Croatia as an autonomous and sovereign state. In December 1990 the new Constitution[2] was adopted according to which Croatia is a unitary and indivisible democratic and social state. Croatia is a parliamentary republic guaranteeing, promoting and protecting equality, human rights and liberties, as well as economic, cultural and social progress and welfare.

In accordance with the *Act on Territories of Counties, Cities and Municipalities in the Republic of Croatia,*[3] the state territory is divided into 20 counties (*zupanija*) and the City of Zagreb, the capital of Croatia. There are around 420 municipalities (*opcina*) and over 70 cities in Croatia.

The Croatian government is organized on the principle of separation of powers into the legislative, executive and judicial branches, based on mutual cooperation and reciprocal checks and balances provided by the Constitution and law. The Croatian supreme legislative authority is vested with the Croatian *Sabor*—the Parliament of the Republic of Croatia, as a representative body of Croatian citizens. The Parliament is unicameral since the amendments to the Constitution adopted in 2001. The President of the Republic of Croatia is the formal head of and represents the state in domestic and international relations;

---

1 *The Constitutional Decree on Sovereignty and Independence of the Republic of Croatia* (*Ustavna odluka o suverenosti i samostalnosti Republike Hrvatske*), NN 31/91. *Declaration Proclaiming the Sovereign and Independent Republic of Croatia* (*Deklaracija o proglasenju suverene i samostalne Republike Hrvatske*), NN 31/91.

2 *The Constitution of the Republic of Croatia*, consolidated text (*Ustav Republike Hrvatske*, prociscení tekst), NN 41/01.

3 *The Act on Territories of Counties, Cities and Municipalities in the Republic of Croatia* (*Zakon o podrucjima zupanija, gradova i opcina u Republici Hrvatskoj*), NN10/97, 124/97, 117/99, 128/99, 44/00, 129/00, 92/01.

provides for regular and coordinated performance and stability of the government; and ensures the protection of independence and territorial integrity of the Republic of Croatia. The Government of the Republic of Croatia performs the executive authority in compliance with the Constitution and law. The head of the Government is the Prime Minister. The Government is responsible to the *Sabor*.

The judicial power is executed by the courts autonomously and independently. Croatia belongs to the countries that adopted continental law system. The courts adjudicate in conformity with the Constitution and law, as well as international agreements and treaties. Namely, subject to Article 140 of the Croatian Constitution, the international agreements and treaties duly executed, ratified, published and in force in Croatia constitute the integral part of the Croatian legal system and prevail over the statutory law provisions.

The justice is administered by misdemeanor courts, municipal courts, county courts, commercial courts, the High Misdemeanor Court of the Republic of Croatia, the High Commercial Court of the Republic of Croatia, the Administrative Court of the Republic of Croatia and the Supreme Court of the Republic of Croatia. Other, specialized courts may be established in compliance with a statute regulating specific legal areas. The Croatian Constitution, the *Act on Courts*[4] and the *Act on Territorial Jurisdiction and Seats of the Courts*[5] comprise the majority of provisions regulating Croatian judicature. Generally, Croatian judicial process is administered within two-instance system. The Supreme Court of the Republic of Croatia, as the highest regular court, ensures the uniform interpretation and application of the law and equal justice to all. The jurisdiction of the Constitutional Court of the Republic of Croatia is prescribed by the Constitution and the *Constitutional Act on the Constitutional Court of the Republic of Croatia.*[6]

2. Sources of Croatian Law

Upon proclaiming its independence, Croatia started building its legal system on the legislature inherited form the former Yugoslavia by gradually adapting, amending and renewing it in accordance with new political, social, economic and legal regime. Croatia has succeeded the former Yugoslavia as the party to numerous international agreements and treaties by virtue of notification on

4 *The Act on Courts* (*Zakon o sudovima*), NN 3/94, 100/96, 115/97, 131/97, 129/00, 67/01.

5 *The Act on Territorial Jurisdiction and Seats of the Courts* (*Zakon o podrucjima i sjedistima sudova*), NN 3/94, 104/97, 59/01.

6 *The Constitutional Act on the Constitutional Court of the Republic of Croatia*—organic statute (*Ustavni zakon o Ustavnom sudu Republike Hrvatske*), NN 99/99.

succession or accession. For instance, such fundamental statutes as the *Obligations Act*,[7] *Civil Procedure Act*[8] and the *Conflict of Law Act*[9] adopted from the federal law of the former Yugoslavia still apply in Croatia as amended. On the other hand, for example, the new *Commercial Companies Act*,[10] a number of statutes regulating intellectual property issues,[11] new criminal legislature,[12] and recently the *Electronic Signature Act*[13] were enacted by the Parliament in consideration of the modern legal science and practice, international law standards and experiences of the developed countries.

The hierarchy of Croatian sources of law is as follows in descending order: the Constitution of the Republic of Croatia, organic statutes, duly executed, ratified published international agreements and treaties in force in Croatia, statutes and regulations other than statutes (decrees, orders, rules and the like). Court practice can be considered as a secondary source of law, since it has more of a reasoning effect, rather than the role of a binding precedent. Needless to say, the important role in interpreting, developing and improving legislature belongs to legal science.

All Croatian legislation published after 1991 is available online at the website of the Official Gazette of the Republic of Croatia—*Narodne Novine* (NN), at www.nn.hr. Online search of the Official Gazette's contents is available to the general public free of charge. There also are numerous commercial databases of legislature, most of them in the Croatian language.

---

7 *The Obligations Act* (*Zakon o obveznim odnosima*), SL SFRJ 29/78, 39/85, 46/85, 45/89, 57/89; NN 53/91, 73/91, 111/93, 3/94, 107/95, 7/96, 91,96, 112/99, 88/01.

8 *The Civil Procedure Act* (*Zakon o parnicnom postupku*), SL SFRJ 4/77, 36/77, 6/80, 36/80, 43/82, 69/82, 58/84, 74/87, 57/89, 20/90, 27/90, 35/91; NN 53/91, 91/92, 112/99, 88/01.

9 *The Conflict of Law Act* (*Zakon o rjesavanju sukoba zakona s propisima drugih zemalja u odredenim odnosima*), SL SFRJ 43/82, 72/82; NN 53/91, 88/01.

10 The *Commercial Companies Act* (*Zakon o trgovackim drustvima*), NN 111/93, 34/99, 52/00.

11 *The Patent Act* (*Zakon o patentima*), NN 78/99, 127/99. *The Trademark Act* (*Zakon o zigu*), NN 78/99. *The Industrial Design Act* (*Zakon o industrijskom oblicju*), NN 78/99, 127/99. *The Geographic Indications of Goods and Services Act* (*Zakon o oznakama zemljopisnog podrijetla proizvoda i usluga*), NN 78/99, 127/99. *Semiconductor Integrated Circuit Layouts Protection Act* (*Zakon o zastiti planova rasporeda integriranih sklopova*), NN 78/99, 127/99.

12 *The Criminal Act* (*Kazneni zakon*), NN 110/97, 27/98, 50,00 129/00, 51/01. *The Criminal Procedure Act* (*Zakon o kaznenom postupku*), NN 110/97, 27/98, 58/99, 112/99. *The Juvenile Courts Act* (*Zakon o sudovima za mladez*), NN 111/97, 27/98. *The Amnesty Act*, consolidated text (*Zakon o pomilovanju*, procisceni tekst), NN29/93, 38/93. *The General Pardon Act* (*Zakon o opcem oprostu*), NN 80/96. *The Act on Execution of the Imprisonment Sanctions* (*Zakon o izvrsavanju kazne zatvora*), NN 128/99, 55/00, 59/00, 129/00, 59/01, 67/01.

13 *The Electronic Signature Act* (*Zakon o elektronickom potpisu*), NN10/02.

3. The Legal Profession

The legal profession is represented by the Croatian Bar Association headquartered in Zagreb. The Croatian attorneys practice law in compliance with the Constitution, the *Advocacy Act,*[14] the By-Laws and other regulations of the Croatian Bar Association and the Attorneys' Code of Ethics. Lawyers may professionally practice law as attorneys upon passing the Bar examination, taking the attorneys' oath and joining the Croatian Bar Association. Attorneys may practice as sole practitioners, they may open joint offices and law firms, having more bureaus, providing there is at least one full-time employed attorney working in each bureau. Consequently, sole practitioners may have only one office. All attorneys' offices, joint law offices and law firms practicing in Croatia are registered with the Croatian Bar Association. Associations of domestic and/or foreign law offices for the purposes of carrying out activities of common interest and providing mutual services may be founded. Attorneys and law firms may request that the Croatian Bar Association recognize their specialization in a particular legal area, such as commercial law, international commercial law, intellectual property law and so on.

As a general rule, according to the law in force, foreign attorneys are not permitted to represent clients in Croatian courts, nor may foreign law firms open their branch offices in Croatia. However this issue has recently been widely discussed in legal circles in pursuit of liberalization of the present situation. Currently, foreign attorneys, who are members of any foreign bar association, may represent their clients in proceedings before the Permanent Arbitration Court of the Croatian Chamber of Economy[15] in legal matters with a foreign element.

B. SCHEME OF ONLINE BUSINESS REGULATION

1. Constitutional Provisions

The Constitutional provisions on economic rights and liberties embody the following foremost constitutional guarantees applicable to conducting business in Croatia: protection of private property, entrepreneurial and market freedom, freedom of scientific, cultural and artistic expression, and other provisions. The Croatian Constitution provides certain protection to foreign investors, specifically guaranteeing the right to acquire ownership and to freely transfer and repatriate their profit and invested capital. On the other hand, the Constitution prescribes that in certain instances the statutory law may impose restrictions on

14 *The Advocacy Act* (*Zakon o odvjetnistvu*), NN9/94.

15 More information about the Croatian arbitration law is available on the official website of the Croatian Chamber of Economy at www.hgk.hr/komora/eng/eng.htm (the Permanent Arbitration Court at the CCE link), where one can particularly find an English translation of the *Arbitration Act* (*Zakon o arbitrazi*), NN 88/01.

ownership and entrepreneurial freedom for the purposes of protecting the interests and security of the state, environment and health.[16]

2. International Agreements and Treaties

Subject to the *Constitutional Decree on Sovereignty and Independence of the Republic of Croatia*, the international agreements and treaties concluded by the former Yugoslavia shall apply in Croatia, unless contrary to the Croatian Constitution and the public order, in compliance with the international law on succession. This provision is elaborated in the *Act on Conclusion and Execution of International Agreements and Treaties.*[17]

Croatia is at present the party to the majority of the foremost international treaties in the field of the international trade and intellectual property law, including the United Nations Convention on Contracts for International Sale of Goods,[18] *Agreement Establishing the World Trade Organization*[19] along with the

---

16 Article 48: The right of ownership is guaranteed./ Ownership implies obligations. The owners shall contribute to the general good./ A foreign person may acquire ownership rights under the conditions prescribed by the statutory law./ The right of inheritance shall be guaranteed.

Article 49: Entrepreneurial and market freedom shall be the basis of the economic system of the Republic of Croatia./ The state shall ensure that all entrepreneurs have equal status on the market./ Monopolies shall be prohibited./ The Republic of Croatia shall stimulate the economic progress and social welfare and support the economic development of the regions./ Neither the statutory law nor any other legal act shall not reduce the rights acquired through investment of capital./ Foreign investors shall be guaranteed free transfer and repatriation of profit and the invested capital.

Article 50: In the interest of the Republic of Croatia, ownership rights may be restricted or property may be appropriated against market value indemnity subject to the special provisions of the statutory law./ The statutory law may exceptionally prescribe restrictions of entrepreneurial freedom and property rights for the purposes of protecting the interests and security of the Republic of Croatia, the nature, the human environment and health.

Article 68: The scientific, cultural and artistic freedom is guaranteed./ The state promotes and facilitates the development of science, culture and art./ The state protects scientific, cultural and artistic goods as the spiritual national values./ The protection of moral and economic rights on scientific, cultural, artistic, intellectual and other creations is guaranteed./ The state promotes and facilitates physical education and sports care.

17 The *Act on Conclusion and Execution of International Agreements and Treaties* (*Zakon o sklapanju i izvrsavanju medunarodnih ugovora*), NN 28/96.

18 *The United Nations Convention on Contracts for International Sale of Goods of 1980* (*Becka konvencija o ugovorima o medunarodnoj prodaji robe od 11. travnja 1980.*), SL SFRJ MU 10/1/84; NN MU 15/98. Croatia became a party to the Convention as of October 8, 1991, subject to the Notification on succession. The adopted text of the Convention is available on the UNCITRAL official website at www.uncitral.org/en-index.htm.

19 *The Protocol on Accession of the Republic of Croatia to the Marrakesh Agreement Establishing the World Trade Organization, signed in Geneva on July 17, 2000* (*Protokol o pristupanju Republike Hrvatske Marakeskom ugovoru o osnivanju Svjetske trgovinske organizacije, potpisan u Zenevi 17. srpnja 2000.*), NN MU 13/00, 14/00. The adopted text of the Agreement is available on the WTO official website at www.wto.org/english/docs_e/legal_e/04-wto_e.htm. Croatia has been the Member of the WTO since November 30, 2000; www.wto.org/english/thewto_e/countries_e/croatia_e.htm.

Agreement on Trade-Related Aspects of Intellectual Property Rights,[20] *Convention Establishing the World Intellectual Property Organization,*[21] *Paris Convention for the Protection of Industrial Property,*[22] *Patent Cooperation Treaty,*[23] *Strasbourg Agreement Concerning the International Patent Classification,*[24] *Madrid Agreement Concerning the International Registration of Marks,*[25] *Nice Agreement Concerning the International Classification of Goods and Services for the Purposes of the Registration of Marks,*[26] *Locarno Agreement Establishing an International Classification for Industrial Designs,*[27] *Berne Convention for the Protection of Literary and Artistic Works,*[28] *Universal Copyright*

20 The TRIPS is Annex 1C *Marrakesh Agreement Establishing the World Trade Organization.* The adopted text of the TRIPS is available on the WTO official website at www.wto.org/english/docs_e/legal_e/27-trips_01_e.htm.

21 The *Convention Establishing the World Intellectual Property Organization*, signed in Stockholm on July 14, 1967 as amended on September 28, 1979 (*Konvencija o osnivanju Svjetske organizacije za intelektualno vlasnistvo*, Stockholm, 14. srpnja 1967. i izmijenjena 2. listopada 1979.), SL SFRJ MU 31/72, 4/86; NN MU 12/93, 3/99. The adopted text of the Convention is available on the WIPO official website at www.wipo.int/treaties/convention/index.html.

22 *The Paris Convention for the Protection of Industrial Property* (*Pariska konvencija za zastitu industrijskog vlasnistva*), SL SFRJ MU 5/74, 7/86; NN MU 12/93, 3/99. The adopted text of the Convention is available on the WIPO official website at www.wipo.int/treaties/ip/paris/index.html. Croatia became a party to the Convention as revised at Stockholm on July 14, 1967 (Stockholm Act) as of October 8, 1991.

23 *The Patent Cooperation Treaty* (*Ugovor o suradnji na podrucju patenata*—PCT), NN MU 3/98, 10/98. The adopted text of the Treaty is available on the WIPO official website at www.wipo.int/treaties/registration/pct/index.html.

24 *The Strasbourg Agreement Concerning the International Patent Classification* (*Strasbourski sporazum o medunarodnoj klasifikaciji patenata*), NN MU 11/99,4/00. The adopted text of the Agreement is available on the WIPO official website at www.wipo.int/treaties/classification/strasbourg/index.html. Croatia became a party to the Agreement as of November 25, 2000.

25 *The Madrid Agreement Concerning the International Registration of Marks* (*Madridski sporazum o medunarodnoj registraciji zigova*), SL SFRJ MU 2/74; NN MU 12/93, 3/99. The adopted text of the Agreement is available on the WIPO official website at www.wipo.int/treaties/registration/madrid/index.html. Croatia became a party to the Agreement as of October 8, 1991.

26 *The Nice Agreement Concerning the International Classification of Goods and Services for the Purposes of the Registration of Marks* (*Nicanski sporazum o medunarodnoj klasifikaciji proizvoda i usluga radi registracije zigova*), SL SFRJ MU 51/74; NN MU 12/93, 3/99. The adopted text of the Agreement is available on the WIPO official website at www.wipo.int/treaties/registration/madrid/index.html. Croatia became a party to the Agreement as of October 8, 1991.

27 *The Locarno Agreement Establishing an International Classification for Industrial Designs* (*Lokarnski sporazum o ustanovljenju medunarodne klasifikaije za industrijske uzorke i modele*), SL SFRJ MU 51/74; NN MU 12/93, 3/99. The adopted text of the Agreement is available on the WIPO official website at www.wipo.int/treaties/classification/locarno/index.html. Croatia became a party to the Agreement as of October 8, 1991.

28 *The Berne Convention for the Protection of Literary and Artistic Works* (*Bernska konvencija za zastitu knjizevnih i umjetnickih djela*), SL SFRJ MU 14/75, 4/86; NN MU 12/93, 3/99. The adopted text of the Convention is available on the WIPO official website at www.wipo.int/treaties/ip/berne/index.html. Croatia became a party to the Convention as of October 8, 1991.

Convention,[29] *WIPO Copyright Treaty,*[30] *WIPO Performances and Phonograms Treaty,*[31] *Rome Convention for the Protection of Performers, Producers of Phonograms and Broadcasting Organizations,*[32] *Convention for the Protection of Producers of Phonograms Against Unauthorized Duplication of their Phonograms,*[33] and other multilateral as well as bilateral international agreements and treaties.

It is also important to mention Croatia's aspiration to join the European Union, manifesting itself in concluding the *Stabilization and Association Agreement*[34] stipulating the framework for Croatia's accession process. In compliance with the obligations undertaken under the *Stabilization and Association Agreement*, Croatia has been implementing a number of measures, including adjusting its legislation to meet European standards. It is foreseeable that Croatia shall continue adopting the European guidelines and legislation in the field of electronic commerce and intellectual property. Thus, the recent Croatian *Electronic Signature Act* was drafted in consideration of the guidelines laid down in the *Directive on a Community Framework for Electronic Signatures,*[35] as well as the *UNCITRAL Model Law on Electronic Signatures.*[36]

---

29 *The Universal Copyright Convention* as revised at Paris on July 24, 1971 (*Svjetska (Univerzalna) konvencija o autorskom pravu*, s prilozima izmijenjena u Parizu, 24. srpnja 1971.) SL SFRJ MU 54/73; NN MU 3/99. The adopted text of the Convention is available on the UNESCO official web site at www.unesco.org/culture/laws/copyright/html_eng/page1.shtml.

30 *The WIPO Copyright Treaty* (*Ugovor o autorskom pravu Svjetske organizacije za intelektualno vlasnistvo*), NN MU 6/00, 11/02. The adopted text of the Treaty is available on the WIPO official web site at www.wipo.int/treaties/ip/wct/index.html.

31 *The WIPO Performances and Phonograms Treaty* (*Ugovor o izvedbama i fonogramima Svjetske organizacije za intelektualno vlasnistvo*), NN MU 6/00, 11/02. The adopted text of the Treaty is available on the WIPO official web site at www.wipo.int/treaties/ip/wppt/index.html.

32 *The Rome Convention for the Protection of Performers, Producers of Phonograms and Broadcasting Organizations* (*Medunarodna konvencija za zastitu umjetnika izvodaca, proizvodaca fonograma i organizacija za radiodifuziju*, sastavljena u Rimu 26. listopada 1961.), NN MU 12/99, 4/00. The adopted text of the Convention is available on the WIPO official web site www.wipo.int/treaties/ip/rome/index.html. Croatia became a party to the Convention as of April 20, 2000.

33 *The Convention for the Protection of Producers of Phonograms Against Unauthorized Duplication of their Phonograms* (*Konvencija za zastitu proizvodaca fonograma od neodobrenog umnozavanja njihovih fonograma*, sastavljena u Zenevi 29. listopada 1971.), NN MU 12/99,05/00. The adopted text of the Convention is available on the WIPO official web site www.wipo.int/treaties/ip/phonograms/index.html. Croatia became a party to the Convention as of April 20, 2000.

34 *The Stabilization and Association Agreement between the Republic of Croatia and the European Communities and Their Member States*, signed in Luxemburg on October 29, 2001 (*Sporazum o stabilizaciji i pridruživanju između Republike Hrvatske i Europskih zajednica i njihovih država èlanica*, potpisan u Luksemburgu 29. listopada 2001.), NN MU 14/01. More information is available on the official web site of the Ministry of the European Integration at www.mei.hr/default.asp?ru=144&gl=200107270000002&sid=&jezek=1.

35 Directive 1999/93/EC of the European Parliament and the Council of the European Union of 13 December 1999 on a Community Framework for Electronic Signatures (the Official Journal L 013, 19/01/2000 p. 0012-0020); http://europa.eu.int/eur-lex/en/lif/dat/1999/en_399L0093.html

36 www.uncitral.org/en-index.htm.

In conclusion, considering the globalization process, particularly evident in increasing and extensive presence of online business, one may expect gradual unification of the national legislations in the line with the growing body of the international law.

3. Legislation

The law governing business activity in Croatia, for instance the *Obligations Act*, *Civil Procedure Act*, *Conflict of Law Act*, *Commercial Companies Act*, and other regulations shall *mutatis mutandis* apply to online business. There is practically no specific legislation on electronic commerce, except for the recently enacted *Electronic Signature Act* and pertinent regulations.

4. Practice

Given the low percentage of online population and general cautiousness of the local entrepreneurs as well as consumers towards online transactions, online business is fairly limited in Croatia. Essentially, as minor as is the business practice, the legal practice in this field is even more negligible in Croatia. Lack of comprehensive legislation often persuades against establishing and conducting an online business. Should a dispute over any issue in the online environment arise, the parties would most likely opt for the alternative dispute resolution, rather than time-consuming, expensive and rigid court proceedings.

C. ELECTRONIC TRANSACTIONS AND CONTRACT FORMATION

1. Introduction

This section outlines the Croatian law provisions regarding contract formation, as this legislature represents a general legal frame applicable to all kinds of contracts, including any contract executed in electronic form. Generally speaking, most of the contracts are informal, i.e. there is no requirement that contract be in writing. The regular legal principles regarding contract formation and enforcement apply also to contracts made in electronic environment, unless there is specific legislature regulating electronic commerce. The challenge posed by electronic commerce is to adapt existing contract law to regulate fast evolving electronic transactions, taking into consideration its specific features.

The regulations concerning execution of contracts apply both to natural persons or legal entities as contracting parties, keeping in mind there are some specific rules in case of commercial transactions. Below is a short summary of the relevant provisions of the *Obligations Act*.

2. Fundamental Principles in the Croatian Contract Law

The main principle in the Croatian contractual law is the freedom of the parties in arranging their mutual obligations according to their wishes. The contract is the primary instrument for their respective obligations. However, although the contractual parties are in large part free in this sense, there are some mandatory provisions contained in the *Obligations Act*, as the main source of contractual law in Croatia which provides a general framework. Also, the provisions of this law apply in all cases when the parties omit to stipulate certain aspects of their relationship in the contract. Said law may be applied basically to all contracts, unless a specific law regulates a certain specific area of law (for example, the provisions contained in the *Electronic Signature Act* would prevail over the general provisions of the *Obligations Act*).

The following would be the basic principles from the *Obligations Act*, which might possibly be considered as the borders of the parties' freedom in contractual obligations. One of the basic principles, that contractual parties have to abide by, is the principle of acting in good faith (*bona fide* conduct). Said principle is one of the standards accepted in commercial transactions, and its scope and application is construed by the court in each particular case. It all comes down to a morality issue, requesting the parties to a contract to avoid abusing their rights at the expense of another party, to cooperate with the other, in particular providing notification to the other party on any aspects that it should be aware of, and in general to apply observance of reasonable commercial standards of fair dealing in a given trade or business, as well as to act in such a way that enables the other to perform its obligations without abuse of trust. This standard in Croatia does not significantly differ in its content compared to the European or American practices.

Additional general requirement from said law would be reasonable equality of the consideration given by one party to another. Namely, if the considerations of the parties are not in a reasonable mutual balance, the contract might, under certain circumstances, become vulnerable to request of the other party for its invalidation, for example in case of *laesio enormis*.

One of the basic provisions also forbids parties to undertake actions whereby damages are incurred to the other. This principle originates from the Roman law principle *neminem laedere*. Acting in this way may create an obligation of compensating damages.

All the above principles are basically confirmed by the last, but not the least, *pacta sunt servanda* principle (agreements must be kept), according to which the parties are obliged to fulfill the obligations they committed to, unless there are reasons that justify non-conformance (such as acts of God).

Besides the above general rules that apply to all contracts, the fundamental importance of the provisions of the above law are obvious concerning the main preconditions that have to be fulfilled in any kind of a purchase-sales agreements, including the ones executed in electronic format. Those essential preconditions are the ones that make the gist, the foundation of a contract, as the contract may not exist without them. The parties are free to broaden such prerequisites by stating some additional in their contract, but may not exclude the ones expressly stated in the *Obligations Act* (this is so-called *ius cogens*, disabling the parties to avoid their application). Namely, the *Obligations Act* itself covers this for each particular nominate contract, by expressly stating its essential prerequisites, whereas the business practices developed the same for the inominate contracts. For example, the *Obligations Act* stipulates that a sale-purchase contract, in order to be valid and binding, has to state the item, i.e. the object of the sale; and the price. Should those two not exist, the sale-purchase contract would be null and void.

However, even if the parties omit to state the price, but only provided those are persons involved in commercial transactions, the law offers a general clause for determining such price. According to this clause, if the parties for some reason do not state the price in their contract, the purchaser shall pay the price that was regularly charged by the seller at the time of conclusion of the contract, or if such is not available, a "reasonable price". In other words, the mandatory part of each sale-purchase contract has to be specification of the object of the sale (this may also concern rights which are not exclusively personal in their nature, i.e. copyrights and all other intellectual property rights).

However, the fact that there are detailed provisions on execution of a contract, still it is highly questionable whether those and other regulations provide a decent frame and a necessary base for the specific needs of electronic commerce, and whether all this will be at all sufficient to enable growth and development of this new form of conducting business transactions. The amendments of the *Obligations Act* are indeed a current issue, but it is very difficult to foresee whether they will cover so many specific issues that need to be dealt with in this subject matter.

3. Offer and Acceptance

General provisions on execution of a contract, as contained in the *Obligations Act*, leave very little doubt regarding the time of execution of a contract when it all concerns execution of a written instrument. According to the *Obligations Act*, a contract is deemed to be perfected at the moment when the offered party accepts the offer in its full content. Possible proposals on the change of the offer actually represent rejection of the so-made offer, and are considered as a new offer under different terms. Namely, the offer has to contain the essential prerequisites of the future contract, so that by its full acceptance there is no need to conduct further negotiations, as the contract becomes thus legally binding. For example, the offer in sale-purchase agreements necessarily has to contain the specification of the object of the sale and the price (with certain exceptions, as explained above).

If the parties are in direct negotiations (also including *via* telephone, teletype, direct radio contact), the contract is perfected when the other party, immediately upon being presented with an offer, accepts it (unless the offering party leaves a certain term for the other to accept). If we are talking about the distant acceptance of the offer (which actually relates to written correspondence, including telegram or facsimile), Croatian law accepted the theory of receipt. When the contract is executed between the distant parties, the offer is accepted once the party who offered it receives acceptance from the offered party.

4. Electronic Transactions Law

Croatian practices concerning electronic commerce are currently indeed at the beginning of the first developmental phase and it is almost impossible to talk of the electronic commerce practices in Croatia. Although we adopted the *Electronic Signature Act*, thus starting to build the legislative network necessary for future electronic commerce field, we are still rather far from having a full body of legislature in this respect. However, Croatia endeavors to follow the European practices and the development of the European law, so it may be expected that the future law on electronic transactions would also be along the lines of the *EU Model Law on Electronic Commerce*, just as the *Electronic Signature Act* is.

5. Documenting Contracts in Croatia

The basic principle is that a contract executed between the parties becomes binding for them as of the moment of execution, regardless of the form in which it was executed (written or oral) or its further recording with any authority. The law only expressly states (for some certain kinds of contracts) that they have to be executed in writing in order to have effect. Namely, due to specific features of certain contractual relations, there are some formalities that need to be satisfied in those cases. To name just a few, any contract on transfer of ownership over real estate, construction contract, handwritten will, or a license contract, has to be executed in writing.

On the other hand, certain contracts have to be executed before governmental authorities, either in a form of court minutes (donation contract without actual hand-over), or need to be executed in a form of a notarial act (such as pre-nuptial agreements, contracts relating to real estate owned by minors, contracts where any of the parties is a deaf or blind natural person etc), whereas some have to have certification of the signature before a notary public.

6. Electronic Signature Act

On April 1, 2002 the *Electronic Signature Act*, drafted in consideration of the guidelines laid down in the *Directive on a Community Framework for Electronic Signatures* and the *UNCITRAL Model Law on Electronic Signatures*, entered into force in Croatia. The *Electronic Signature Act* prescribes the right of natural and legal persons to use electronic signatures in administrative, judicial and other proceedings, commercial and other activities, as well as their rights, duties and liabilities related to certification services. The *Electronic Signature Act* comprises 45 articles arranged into seven parts: General Provisions; Electronic Signature and Advanced Electronic Signature; Certificates and Providing of Certification Services; Rights, Duties and Liabilities of Certification Service Provider; Supervision and Inspection; Penal Provisions; Transitional and Final Provisions.

The *Electronic Signature Act* recognizes two kinds of electronic signatures: the electronic signature, meaning electronic data identifying the signatory and verifying the authenticity of the data message; and the advanced electronic signature, meaning such an electronic signature which is uniquely linked to the signatory and which indubitably identifies the signatory. Further, an advanced electronic signature must be created by the means independently and solely controlled by the signatory; and must be directly linked to the data it refers to in a way that indubitably enables detecting of any change to the original data. An advanced electronic signature has the same legal effect and substitutes for handwritten signature or handwritten signature and a seal, when applicable.

As a general rule, an electronic document signed by an electronic signature has the same legal effects as a paper-based hand-signed document, providing the electronic signature is appropriately secured and signatory's identity is ascertained by the signatory or a certification services provider. Certain legal transactions cannot be executed in the electronic form, such as real estate, inheritance, (pre)nuptial, and other transactions.

The *Electronic Signature Act* recognizes a certificate and a qualified certificate, the former being an electronic authentication of a signatory's identity for the purposes of electronic correspondence, while the latter being an electronic authentication issued by a certification services provider verifying an advanced electronic signature. The *Electronic Signature Act* further prescribes the requirements for a qualified certificate, a certification services provider and a certification services provider issuing qualified certificates. A certification services provider issuing qualified certificates needs to obtain a license from the Ministry of Economy before starting his or her business. The Ministry of Economy keeps the official registries of certification services providers and certification services providers issuing qualified certificates in Croatia. The registries are public books kept in an electronic form. Only the registered providers may provide certification services in Croatia.

A signatory chooses his or her certification services provider or providers. A signatory may choose to engage the services of a foreign provider. A certification services provider issues a certificate to a signatory on a contractual basis. A signatory shall undertake all necessary organizational and technical security measures to prevent damage, which may be caused to other signatories, certification services providers or third parties. A signatory is obligated to notify his or her provider on any and all changes affecting the accuracy of his or her electronic signature within two days when the change occurs. A signatory shall immediately request a withdrawal of his or her certificate in case of losing or damaging the data related to his or her electronic signature.

A certification services provider shall keep record of all issued and withdrawn certificates for at least ten years as of their issuance. A certification services provider is obligated to provide his or her services *lege artis* and undertake all security measures necessary to protect the certification and all related documentation and equipment. Certification services providers must enable interconnection of their records of all issued and withdrawn certificates.

Certification services may be provided by certification services providers seated abroad and registered in one of the European Union member states, on condition that they meet the requirements for providing certification services of issuing qualified certificates laid down in the *Electronic Signature Act*. Qualified certificates issued by a provider seated in one of the European Union member states enjoy the same legal effects as qualified certificates issued in Croatia. Qualified certificates issued by a provider seated abroad outside the European Union enjoy the same legal effects as qualified certificates issued in Croatia on the following conditions: the provider meets the conditions for issuing qualified certificates set out in the Act and is registered in Croatia; a domestic registered certification services provider issuing qualified certificates guarantees such a qualified certificate; it is prescribed by a multi- or bi-lateral agreement between Croatia and other countries or international organizations; a qualified certificate or a certification services provider issuing qualified certificates is recognized subject to a multi- or bi-lateral agreement between the European Union and third countries or international organizations.

Penal provisions of the *Electronic Signature Act* prescribe misdemeanor liability and monetary sanctions against signatories and certification services providers for violating legal provisions and their obligations, as well as against third parties for unauthorized access and use of data and means for creating an electronic or advanced electronic signature, *et cetera*.

The *Electronic Signature Act* is the first piece of legislature enacted in this legal field in Croatia. The enactment of the *Electronic Commerce Act* and pertinent regulations would provide the essential legal framework admitting Croatia to the advantages of electronic business in the light of the globalization tendencies.

ECUADOR

by
Amani Harrison
Bustamante & Bustamante

A. SOURCES OF LAW

1. Introduction

The Political Constitution of the Republic of Ecuador, promulgated in 1998, provides the structure of the political and legal system for the Republic. The first constitution of Ecuador was instituted in 1830 after Ecuador dissolved its union with the Federation of Gran Colombia. Due to the turbulence that has characterized Ecuador's social, political and economic history, the Republic has undergone numerous changes in its system of governance as well as modifications and wholesale revisions to its constitutions. The Republic has had eighteen constitutional texts since it became an independent country in 1830.

The 1998 Political Constitution stipulates that the government of Ecuador is "republican, presidential, elective, representative, responsible, alternative, participative and decentralized." The government is divided into three principal branches: executive, legislative and judicial. There also exists an autonomous electoral agency, the Supreme Electoral Tribunal, which organizes and supervises elections for political office.

The country is divided into twenty-two provinces, each of which is further divided into cantons and parroquias. As of 1998, Ecuador has embarked upon a process of administrative decentralization in order to increase the participation of the citizenry in government as well as to augment the efficiency of public services. However, the Republic of Ecuador remains a unitary rather than a federal state, and the local political office holders act as representatives of the President of the Republic. Local administrative bodies include provincial and municipal councils as well as wards or districts for the indigenous and Afro Ecuadorian communities.

The Ecuadorian legal tradition is based upon the Spanish colonial origins of the Republic and is, therefore, a civil law tradition. However, similar to many Latin American countries, the constitutional theory and practice and structure of government has been influenced by legal developments in the United States.

2. Constitution

Historically, Ecuador was a colony of the Spanish crown and, therefore, subject to Spanish colonial governance until its liberation in 1822. Ecuador joined together with New Grenada and Venezuela under the rule of Simon Bolivar to form Gran Colombia immediately after military victory against Spanish loyalist troops. Since its secession from Gran Colombia in 1830, Ecuador has been governed under nineteen constitutions, two of which have been promulgated since 1979 when Ecuador returned to constitutional, civilian rule after a decade of military dictatorship. In spite of the numerous constitutions that have been enacted by successive governments, constitutional governance in Ecuador has been the exception rather than the rule. There have been eighty-six changes in government since Ecuador became a republic, each regime averaging 1.75 years.

The new constitution entered into force in 1998 after a constitutional assembly was convened by popular mandate in order to revise the prior Ecuadorian Constitution. The 1998 constitution seeks to strengthen the executive branch by eliminating mid-term congressional elections and restricting Congress' power to challenge and remove cabinet ministers.

The State institutions are:

- The agencies and branches of the Legislative, Executive and Judicial Offices;
- The electoral agencies;
- The control and regulation bodies;
- The entities that form the autonomous departmental system;
- The agencies and entities created by the Constitution or the law for the exercise of the state power, for the provision of public services or for the development of economic activities assumed by the State;
- The juridical persons created by departmental legislative act for the provision of public services.

3. Election of Government

The Republic of Ecuador is a representative democracy, and voting is mandatory for all literate Ecuadorians who have reached the age of eighteen, save for those citizens who are older than sixty five years of age, in which case voting is optional. Active members of the public forces, which are comprised of the Armed Forces and the National Police, may not exercise their right to vote.

The Tribuno Supremo Electoral (TSE) organizes and supervises the electoral process and also adjudges the accounts submitted by political parties, organizations and candidates. The Tribunal is an independent government agency, which enjoys administrative and financial autonomy. The public force is obliged to cooperate with the Tribunal in order to guarantee the freedom and purity of the vote.

Political parties that have been legally recognized may present or promote candidates for election; however, non-party affiliated candidates are also eligible for elective office. There are no limits on the number of times that an elected candidate may be re-elected. Citizens may select from among a list or lists of candidates in multi-candidate elections. Law concedes this principal through proportional representation of minority party candidates.

Due to the structure of its electoral process, Ecuador is remarkable in the number of its political parties. The largest political parties in terms of congressional representation are the center-right Partido Social Cristiano, the Partido Roldosista Ecuatoriano and the center-left Izquierda Democratica. Neither of these parties is an unfamiliar participant in the Ecuadorian political process as each has held power since the democratic transition in 1979. In the 2002 presidential elections Lucio Gutierrez, a former colonel in the Ecuadorian army (and responsible for the resignation and flight to Panama of former President of the Republic, Abdala Bucaram), was elected President.

Even prior to the election of Colonel Gutierrez, the military had exercised an important role within the government of Ecuador. Military juntas governed the Republic immediately after its establishment. And, in recent times, the military has acted to resolve intransigence between civilian political factions. The military historically was more often respected then civilian politicians due to the perceived lack of corruption within military ranks, the stability that characterized military governance and the provision by the military of physical infrastructure and social services in rural communities.

The system of government is unicameral, the Congreso Nacional or National Congress forms the only national legislative body. Each of the twenty-two provinces elects two *diputados* and one more representative is elected for each 200,000 provincial inhabitants. As of January 2003, there were 123 representatives in the national legislature, twenty national representatives and 103 provincial representatives. Parties or movements that form at least ten percent of the National Congress may form a legislative block or minority parties may unite to form such a block. The National Congress elects a president and two vice presidents every two years.

4. The Courts

The Constitution provides for the Ecuadorian court system as a means to carry out justice, guarantee due process and oversee compliance with the principles of mediation, speed and efficiency in the administration of justice. The judiciary is composed of the Supreme Court of Justice, appellate or provincial superior courts, other courts and tribunals as established by the Constitution and Ecuadorian Law, and the National Judicial Council. There are also military and police tribunals, which have the same status as circuit courts. The criminal, provincial and cantonal courts serve as courts of first-instance. Indigenous communities are also empowered by the Constitution to exercise judicial functions, applying their own community norms and procedures so long as such norms and procedures do not conflict with the Constitution or laws of Ecuador.

The supreme judicial power is vested in the Supreme Court of Justice, which is formed by sixteen judge ministers and one fiscal minister. There are five chambers, each containing three judge ministers. Each minister is elected for a life term. The Supreme Court of Justice, seated in Quito, has jurisdiction over all cases within the territory of the Republic of Ecuador and acts as the final court of appeal. The Supreme Court of Justice as well as other judicial bodies is governed pursuant to the Organic Law of the Judicial Function. Each province has a superior court whose duties include hearing criminal cases of first and second instance against certain elected officials, customs officials, as well as high-ranking officers of the police and Public Forces. Judges of the provincial superior courts are also charged with visiting jails and penitentiaries in order to hear the complaints of all detainees and prisoners. Each province also has criminal and civil court judges, whose numbers are determined by the Supreme Court of Justice. Civil court justices will hear cases of first instance in which the amount at issue exceeds at least one thousand sucres.[1] Political deputies hear cases in which the sum is less than one thousand sucres.

There are two types of judges: ordinary and special. Judges have both legal and conventional jurisdiction with ordinary judges superior in rank to special judges. The Ministers of the Supreme Court and Superior Courts, criminal and civil judges are ordinary judges. Special judges are those dealing in labor, rental and traffic matters who exercise coercive jurisdiction as well as those from the police and others established by special laws. Arbitrators are judges with conventional jurisdiction.

Substantiation of the processes which includes the presentation and contradiction of proofs shall be performed within an oral system in accordance with the principles of depositions, concentration and intervention. Proceedings are generally public, with express exceptions provided under the law.

5. Sources of Ecuadorian Law

Ecuador has a civil law tradition based in Spanish colonial history, and this civil law system largely controls and influences private and commercial law. However, as a result of the American Revolution, Ecuador has adopted many of the principles resulting from legal tradition in the United States for constitutional and public law. The content of civil, commercial and procedural codes, the influence of jurists and the role of the judge in the judicial process in Ecuador

1 In 2000, the Republic of Ecuador joined the small group of thirteen nations that have dollarized economies, that is, the United States dollar (abbreviated "USD") is used as their official currency. Despite this change, many fees and fines are still denominated in the previous official currency of Ecuador, the sucre.

conforms to the civil law tradition as exercised in Spain and other western European nations.

The Constitution of the Republic supercedes any and all other legal norms within the Republic. Any law, decree, statute, ordinance, regulation, resolution or public act must be in conformity with the Constitution. In the event of non-conformity with the Constitution, such legal dispositions will have no value if they contradict or alter the prescriptions within the Constitution.

Following the Constitution in authority are international treaties and conventions approved by the National Congress. After determination of the conformity of such international agreements with the Constitution, they must be approved by an absolute majority of the National Congress in a single debate. After international agreements in the legal hierarchy are laws, decrees, statutes, ordinances, regulations, resolutions and other public Acts. Laws are either organic or ordinary with organic laws being superior to ordinary laws. Organic laws are (1) those which regulate the organization and activities of the Legislative, Executive and Judicial branches, of the autonomous sectional regime and of the State organizations established in the Constitution; (2) those which are relative to political parties and to the exercise of political rights and to the electoral systems; (3) those which regulate the guarantees of fundamental rights and the procedures for their protection; and, (4) any other laws which the Constitution determines should be issued with the character of organic. All other laws are ordinary.

If there is a conflict between norms of different hierarchy, the courts and administrative authorities must resolve the conflict by applying the rule of superior rank within the hierarchy. The Constitutional Court, a nine-member body designated by the National Congress, determines the constitutionality of laws and other legal dispositions and administrative acts. The Constitutional Court also reviews resolutions denying *habeas corpus* and *habeas data*, rules objections by the President of the Republic to Bills based upon their unconstitutionality, rules upon the constitutional conformity of treaties and international conventions and settles conflicts regarding the abilities or powers assigned by the Constitution.

6. The Legal Profession

There are two types of legal practitioners in the Republic: doctors in jurisprudence (*doctores en jurisprudencia*) and attorneys (*abogados*). Each of these practitioners must have obtained degrees from an Ecuadorian university and are only authorized to practice upon registration in an Ecuadorian bar association. All of the doctors in jurisprudence and attorneys must be registered by the Supreme Court as well as in their respective superior courts of the provinces in which they have matriculated. There a such list or roll of doctors of jurisprudence and attorneys in the Republic and only documents signed by such listed professionals are admitted before tribunals and courts.

Attorneys who have obtained their degree from non-Ecuadorian universities or law schools may also practice law within the Republic of Ecuador provided they have fulfilled the requirements outlined in international treaties to which Ecuador is a party and have had their degrees revalidated in the form and under the conditions prescribed by Law. Such requirement only applies if the principal of reciprocity is observed between Ecuador and the country from which such attorneys have received their degrees.

Legal education and the structure of the legal profession in Ecuador are similar to most civil law jurisdictions. The basic training is an undergraduate degree in law. Upon graduation, students choose among several branches of the legal profession including judge, public prosecutor, private practice or notary.

B. SCHEME OF ONLINE BUSINESS REGULATION

Currently, there is no wholly integrated scheme for the regulation of online business within the Republic of Ecuador. However, the Congress has passed a law supportive of online contracting and commerce and has included within the consumer rights law protections for the rights of consumers' purchases over the Internet and protections within the intellectual property law against infringements using digital communications networks.

1. Relevant Legislation

The relevant laws in this area are:

- Law, 2002-67, Law on Electronic Commerce, Electronic Signatures and Data Messages (published April 17, 2002).
- Executive Decree No. 3496, General Regulation to the Law on Electronic Commerce, Electronic Signatures and Data Messages (published December 31, 2002).
- Law No. 2000-21, Organic Consumer Defense Law (published July 10, 2000).
- Executive Decree No. 1314, Regulation to the Organic Consumer Defense Law (published on March 19, 2001).
- Law No. 83, Law on Intellectual Property (published May 19, 1998).
- Executive Decree No. 508, Regulation to the Law on Intellectual Property (published February 1, 1999).
- Articles 202, 262, 415, 553, 563 and 606 of the Penal Code.
- Executive Decree No., Regulation of CONATEL with respect to Internet Service Providers.
- Decision 345 of the Andean Community Commission, Common Provisions on the Protection of the Rights of Breeders of New Plant Varieties Regulation to Decision 345 (published April 15, 1996).
- Decision 351 of the Andean Community Commission, Common Provisions on Copyright and Related Rights (published January 25, 1994).
- Decision 486 of the Andean Community Commission, Common Industrial Property Regime (published February 2, 2001).

2. Administrative Bodies

The following administrative bodies have functions in relation to online business:

a) The Office of the Superintendent of Telecommunications is the organization charged with control of the entities that certify accredited information. Duties of the Office of the Superintendent with regard to certification include:

- Overseeing the observance of constitutional and legal provisions regarding the promotion of competition and restrictive commercial practices, unfair competition and consumer protection by certifying entities.
- Exercising control over certifying entities within Ecuador and overseeing their efficient functioning.
- Performing technical audits on certifying entities.
- Requesting information from certifying entities.
- Imposing administrative sanctions.
- Issuing reports.
- Suspending certification services to prevent infractions.

b) The National Telecommunications Board (CONATEL) is the entity responsible for authorization, registration and regulation of the entities that certify accredited information. As the authorizing body, CONATEL may also:

- Cancel or suspend authorization of certifying entities in accordance with a previous report by the Office of the Superintendent of Telecommunications.
- Revoke or suspend certifications of electronic signatures in accordance with a prior report from the Office of the Superintendent of Telecommunications.[2]

c) The National Foreign Trade and Investment Board is responsible for the promotion and dissemination of electronic services, including electronic commerce and the use of electronic signatures in the promotion of foreign trade and investment.

d) NIC.EC is the entity authorized by the Internet Corporation for Assigned Names and Numbers (ICANN) to register domain numbers in Ecuador with the suffix ".ec" according to international directives for registering country code Top Level Domains (ccTLD's).

e) Furthermore, according to the text of the Intellectual Property Law, intellectual property authorities have jurisdiction over intellectual property violations that occur over the Internet. However, this competence or jurisdiction is disputed as the Ecuadorian Institute of Intellectual Property has decided that it lacks competence to sanction trademark infringements using domain names.

---

2 The Regulation to the Electronic Commerce Law currently contains certain provisions indicating that CONELEC, or the National Electricity Council, is the authorizing entity with regarding to certifiers. Apparently, this is a drafting error, and CONATEL continues to be the authorizing entity. See, Arts. 8, 15-18 and 23 of the Regulation to the Electronic Commerce Law.

C. ELECTRONIC TRANSACTIONS AND CONTRACT FORMATION

1. Introduction

The main principals governing all contracts, including online contracts, are contained within the Ecuadorian Civil Code and the Commercial Code. The Electronic Commerce Law attempts to adapt certain principals to the online environment and to amend others in order to protect consumers and other contracting parties.

2. Fundamental Principles in Ecuadorian Contract Law

The essence of contracts lies in the parties' mutual obligations. The Ecuadorian Civil Code defines a contract or convention as "an act whereby one party is bound towards another party to give, do or not do something."[3] Contracts may be of a civil or commercial nature, and the above-cited definition is applied, regardless of whether it is a civil or a commercial.

3. Offer

In the statement of consent for entering into a contract, the first step is an offer from one individual who is fit to enter into contracts. It must be complete and meet all of the essential requirements of the proposed contract as well as comply with the format necessary for the proposed act or contract.

An offer may be oral or written. A written offer is an indispensable requirement for formal commercial contracts, i.e., those which are necessarily executed in writing. A written proposal or offer must be accepted or rejected within twenty-four hours if the parties reside in the same area and if they reside in different areas, then by return mail within twenty-four hours after receiving the proposal. Proposals will not be valid after these deadlines have expired.

4. Acceptance

In order for an oral proposal for a business to be binding for the individual proposing it, it must be accepted immediately by the individual it is addressed to. When there is no such acceptance, then the individual making the proposal is released (Article 141 of the Commercial Code).

A bid may be valid if it contains conditions and contains special validity. The first case pertains to those bids or offers conditioned to a period of time for acceptance, with the effects offered intact and without changes in the price.

Offers with special validity are firm proposals. The individual making the proposal may desist within the period of time between the forwarding of the proposal and acceptance only if the offer states that he or she is not bound to await a response or to not release the object being offered within a determined time pe-

3 Ecuadorian Civil Code, Article 1481.

riod. As a general rule, offers are valid within the time periods agreed to by the parties or established under the law unless the individual making the offer dies or is legally incapacitated, the periods expire or the individual making the proposal retracts it. Offers for unspecified amounts commonly presented in catalogues, advertisements and any other type of printed notices are not binding for the individuals offering them.

Once pure and simple acceptance of the proposal has been given, the contract is completed with a written document and generates obligations and legal effects between the parties. However, if acceptance is conditional or changes are made in the original offer, then it will be deemed a new proposal.

The Commercial Code establishes the possibility for an individual making a proposal to change his or her mind within the period between the date when the proposal is made and the acceptance date, except if he or she has agreed to await a response or not release the object of the contract but after rejection or the expiration of a determined time period. Changing one's mind or retraction are not assumed.

Retraction without cause binds the individual making a proposal to compensate the expenses the individual receiving the proposal has incurred along with damages he or she may have suffered. However, legislation adds that the individual making a proposal may be exempt from the obligation of payment of compensation by complying with the proposed contract.

The individual receiving the offer may choose payment or compliance and the individual making the proposal must accept compliance or lose payment of expenses and damages it is bound to pay.

5. Capacity to Contract

Being legally fit is an essential requirement for the commitments between the parties to a contract or convention to go into effect and be legally valid. According to the norms of the Civil Code, legal fitness consists of the power an individual has to enter into obligations in his or her own right, to contract obligations and to acquire rights without the need for authorization from another individual. Legislation also recognizes all individuals' legal fitness except for those expressly denied such condition.

There are three types of legal unfitness: absolute; relative; and special cases.

a. Absolute Unfitness

This type of unfitness is applicable to individuals who, due to natural causes, lack will or cannot express it, as in the case of the insane, minors (males under fourteen years of age and females under twelve years of age), and the deaf-mute who cannot be understood in writing.

b. Relative Unfitness

Applies to certain individuals based on specific legal circumstances:

Underage adults defined in legislation as males between 14 and 18 years of age and females between 12 and 18 years of age;

Those prohibited from administering or disposing of property such as alcoholics, drug addicts, and spendthrifts, who require a statement from the court to determine or declare this type of prohibition.

Corporations are considered relatively unfit since in order to enter into obligations and contract obligations it is necessary for them to act through a legal representative. It is considered that these individuals' acts may be valid under certain circumstances established in laws, e.g. a minor may enter into a labor contract with his or her parents' authorization.

c. Special Cases of Unfitness

Some special cases of unfitness are based on a prohibition imposed by the law for certain individuals to execute certain acts under determined circumstances.

6. Formal Requirements of a Contract

a. General Requirements

In order for an individual to enter into an obligation with another individual through an act or declaration of will, it is necessary that:

- he or she be legally fit and compliant with assumptions listed in the section above;
- he or she consent in such act or declaration and such consent is free of flaws;
- it involves a lawful object;
- it has a lawful cause; and
- it complies with certain formalities according to the object of the contract.

Consent may be flawed due to *factual* errors in relation to the act or contract to be executed or signed. A factual error also renders consent flawed when the essential substance or quality of the object to which the act or contract pertains is different from what it is believed to be.

A *legal* error does not make a contract flawed; nor does an error regarding any other characteristic of the matter at hand; nor is consent flawed regarding the individuals entering into the contract, except when the characteristic is the main reason for one of them to enter into the contract and that reason is known to the other party.

An *error about an individual* with whom it is intended to enter into a contract does not render the contract flawed unless consideration regarding that person is the main reason for the contract.

Force duress is another flaw in consent when it can produce a strong impression on an individual who is mentally fit bearing in mind his or her age, gender or condition. Force is seen as all acts causing justified fear in an individual if he or she, his or her spouse or any of his/her forebears or descendents are exposed to irreparable and serious harm. In order for force to flaw consent it is not necessary that it be exercised by the individual benefiting from it. It is sufficient for force to be used by any individual for the purpose of obtaining consent.

Finally, *deceit* (fraud) flaws consent when it is the work of one of the parties and it is clear that without it they would not have entered into a contract. Otherwise, deceit results only in a damage action against the individual or individuals perpetrating it or that have gained from it.

Certain contracts need to be executed in writing. In these cases no other proof is admissible. If this formality is missing, then the contract will be understood as not having been executed. For example:

- Article 569 of the Commercial Code establishes that a pledge contract must be executed in writing;
- Article 5 of the Law of Internships in the Business Sector requires the execution of a written contract for student interns until they have been inducted or graduated; and
- The Intellectual Property Law requires this formality for contracts pertaining to the authorization for third parties' use or exploitation of works.

Another type of formality required in both civil as well as commercial contracts is recording or registration of the contract. Thus, for example, in order for a sales contract for property to be legally valid it must be recorded in the registry for this purpose at the Office of Property Records. Likewise, the Commercial Code requires that industrial pledge contracts be recorded with the Office of Commercial Records. Licensing agreements for trademarks, patents, utility models, industrial designs, trade names and slogans and, in general, transfer of technology contracts, must be recorded with the Ministry of Foreign Trade, Industrialization and Fishing.

b. Notarization

Among the formalities required by law for certain contracts to be legally valid is that they be executed before a notary public in such cases as purchase and sale of property, execution of mortgages, formation of corporations, among others.

Execution of a contract via public deed is a formal declaration before a public official that the parties to the contract are expressing their will to enter into a contract and obligations.

However, any type of contract may optionally be executed before a notary public in order for it to be considered a public deed.

c. Performance of Contracts

Execution of a contract carries with it the obligation between the parties to the contract to comply with the terms agreed to in accordance with laws applicable to each case.

d. Remedies for Failure to Perform

If one of the parties breaches the contract, the other party is entitled to file suit in the courts having competent jurisdiction for damages caused by such breach. Such suits may even be filed at criminal courts in some cases.

e. Distinction Between Civil and Commercial Contracts

As indicated above, contracts may be civil or commercial. Civil contracts are regulated by the Civil Code while commercial contracts are regulated by the Commercial Code. However, the latter must also conform to general norms established in the Civil Code which are also applicable based on express cross-references made by commercial norms.

Differences between civil and commercial contracts lie in certain particulars.

First, as indicated above, is that contracts must conform to the norms in the Civil Code while commercial contracts must conform mainly to the norms in the Commercial Code and secondarily to civil norms.

Intent is the main factor differentiating the two types of contracts. For example, in order for a sales contract to be a commercial contract it is indispensable that the buyer intend to resell.

The personal element in addition to intent is the defining factor for differentiating between civil and commercial contracts. The individual entering into the contract in the case of commercial contracts must be a duly registered businessperson.

It is also indispensable to bear in mind certain objective elements which because of the very nature of the contract make it a commercial contract independent of whether or not it is entered into by businesspersons. For example, cases of promissory notes and bills of exchange are necessarily commercial contracts even when they are not executed by a businessperson.

f. Special Requirements of Sales Contracts

A sales contract is a contract whereby one of the parties is bound to provide something and the other to pay for it with money. Regardless of whether it is a civil or commercial contract, a sales contract must meet the same requirements as listed above pertaining to the fitness of the parties to the contract, lawful object, and lawful reason.

Special requirements or formalities that may be applied to a sales contract are actually of a formal nature. Thus, the purchase and sale of immovable property must necessarily be executed via public deed and recorded with the respective

Office of Property Records in the respective jurisdiction where the property that is the object of the contract is located. Likewise, in sales contracts with reservation of ownership until the sale of property though installments have been paid, the seller may reserve the right to ownership until the buyer has paid the price agreed to in full.

Such contracts must be executed via public deed and recorded at the Office of Commercial Records in the respective jurisdiction.

7. Agency and Commercial Representation

a. Formation of Agency Agreements

In accordance with Law 22 promulgated on September 19, 1997, the creation of commercial agency agreements is subject to the principles of free contracts and independent will. Thus, only the parties to a contract may establish contract conditions and causes for contract termination as well as applicable compensation.

b. Rights and Duties of Principal and Agent

In accordance with the provisions of the aforementioned Law 22, agents' rights and obligations under commercial agency contracts are negotiated and established by the parties to the aforementioned contracts.

Starting with the promulgation of Law 22, termination of commercial agency contracts is done by observing the procedures established by the parties to the contracts. However, commercial agency contracts executed between December 31, 1976 and September 19, 1997 while Supreme Decree No. 1038-A containing the Law Protecting Commercial Agents, Distributors and Representatives of Foreign Companies in Ecuador was in effect, will be analyzed on a case-by-case basis to establish the scope of such Decree in each contract and thus determine the best procedure for their termination and the effect this would bring about for the party who wishes to terminate the contract.

8. Electronic Commerce Law

The Electronic Commerce Law[4] applies to electronic messages, electronic signatures, certification services, electronic contracts, protection for system users, electronic contracts, protection for system users, database use, violations and penalties.

The Law gives the same legal value to electronic messages as it does to documents on paper or other legally accepted means. By conferring the same legal value to electronic messages and written documents, the same evidentiary value is also accorded to them.

In order to provide security to electronic transmissions, the law includes a chapter on electronic signatures. To avoid disputes over the legal validity of elec-

4 Law No. 67, Official Gazette Supplement No. 557–April 17, 2002.

tronic signatures and electronic messages, the law creates Certification Entities that must be accredited by a control entity under the National Telecommunications Council. Certification entities will closely cooperate with public authorities, especially the National Telecommunications Council, to ensure the validity of documents, contracts, agreements and the like, that are made on-line.

Due to an express allowance that the law makes to other applicable laws, the law does not make any mention of the fundamental aspects necessary for the validity of contracts and electronic messages Those matters are resolved by following applicable rules of international or Ecuadorian laws, based on the standards governing written messages and contracts in general.

The law favors the execution of online agreements. The law states that it is unnecessary to make an express admission of this medium in order for online agreements to be effective.

FRANCE

by
Professor Michel Vivant
University of Montpellier

A. SOURCES OF LAW

1. Basic Principles

In France, as in other democratic countries, the separation of powers is the first and most important principle of law: separation between executive, legislative and judicial powers. Hence, sources of law (in the largest sense) are differentiated accordingly.

Like many countries of the world, France is a party to many international treaties and conventions that create additional laws within France. (The French Constitution says that a ratified treaty has a higher authority than the national Law). Moreover, in France, as in all the other Member States of the European Union, a fundamental principle is the primacy of the European Law. This means that, in the case of conflict between a national and the European Law, the latter must be applied, i.e. judges have the obligation not to apply the national rules. That relativizes the importance of the national sources of Law within the European system.

2. Executive and Legislative Powers

In the French constitutional system, there is a very specific repartition of competence between the law in the strict sense of the word ("*lo* ") which is voted by the Parliament and other kinds of rules called "*règlements*" (regulations) which are handed down from the ministers ("*décrets*"—decrees—or "*arrètés*") and other under-powers ("*arrètés*"). When fundamental principles are involved (*see* Constitution § 34), a law, in the first sense, is necessary and the "*règlements*" can only be adopted to complete the law (the Government in this case has only a residual power). In other cases, the "statutory power" ("*pouvoir règlementaire*") has sole competence. Therefore, while some questions are a matter for the law and other statutes, other questions are only a matter for statutes: "*décrets*" and "*arrètés*". The topics of law that are reserved solely for Parliament include civil rights, criminal law, taxes, election law, nationalizations, national defense, education, private property, labor unions, etc.

A law is voted by the Parliament. In the French system, Parliament is comprised of the National Assembly which has pre-eminence and whose members are directly elected by citizens, and the Senate, whose members are indirectly elected. The other texts are decided, depending on cases, by the President of the Republic, the Prime Minister, a minister or a group of ministers, or "*préfets*" or mayors. Any kind of text of an inferior level must be in accordance with the text of the upper level and the law must be in accordance with the Constitution, the Constitutional Council having the burden of this control. However, unlike the United States, a large control of constitutionality does not exist in France: this control has to be applied just after the vote of the law and not during the "life" of the text. Finally, all the texts must also be in accordance, as we have said above, with the European Law (*see below*).

3. European Law

The European Law has the primacy over the national Law (hence a European Law is also a national Law). This principle has a general impact. All the European texts and also the case law have this primacy.

There are two main kinds of texts: the "regulations" which have a direct application in the national context and the "directives" which have only an indirect but still restricting effect. The basic provision is article 249 of the European Union Treaty:

> A regulation shall have general application. It shall be binding in its entirety and directly applicable in all Member States.
>
> A directive shall be binding, as to the result to be achieved, upon each Member State to which it is addressed, but shall leave to the national authorities the choice of form and methods.

Consequently, many "national" provisions are little more than a translation of a directive and so, on software, data bases or electronic commerce, for example, the French, the UK or the German Law are the same thing, and not specifically French, British or German.

4. Judicial Power

The French legal system is basically divided into two great areas: private law (mainly civil and commercial law but also criminal law in the French tradition) and public law (mainly constitutional and administrative law), with different judges for these two fields. The judges who have competence in the private field constitute the "*ordre judiciaire*". Each sort of litigation has, in fact, its own judges and the composition of the jurisdictions is strongly different. For example, a Court of Assizes is composed of a popular jury, a civil tribunal is composed only of professional judges and a "*tribunal de commerce*" (trade tribunal) is composed with judges which are tradesmen.

The Constitutional Council apart, the two "high" jurisdictions are: the Court of Cassation for the private side and the State Council ("*Conseil d'Etat*") for the public side. For online commerce, the most important are the civil and commercial jurisdictions. On the civil side it is the "*tribunal de grande instance*" which is the tribunal that has the "ordinary" competence. In commercial: it is the "*tribunal de commerce*" which is competent if the litigants are traders. In the case where one litigant is a merchant and the other one is not, the competence depends on who is the defendant: if it is the merchant, the "*tribunal de commerce*" is competent, and in the other case it is the "Civil Tribunal".

France, as in other democratic countries, there are different levels of jurisdiction. In general, a possibility of appeal is open to the persons who are involved in a trial. The Court of Cassation, always, and the State Council, often, intervene as "judge of the Law" ("*juge du droit*"). This means that these jurisdictions do not have to re-try the entire case, but only to re-examine it and consider if the law has been correctly applied. If it has not, the Court of Cassation, would normally send the case back to another Court of Appeal or to the same Court but with a jury of another composition.

In France, as there is no force of precedent, a judge of a lower court can overrule a previous decision of a higher court. But in practice, decisions of higher courts do tend to be followed. As a consequence of the structure of the judicial system, the case law that has a specific value is, that judged, in the private area, by the Courts of Appeal and the Court of Cassation. Other decisions can be interesting but they do not have the same authority.

5. European Courts

As mentioned above, the European Courts have a specific power. There is a Tribunal and a Court of Justice, the latter being the more important of the two. The Court is entitled to interpret the European Law, which prevails over the national Law.

Article 234 of the Treaty states:

> Where such a question is raised before any court or tribunal of a Member State, that court or tribunal may, if it considers that a decision on the question is necessary to enable it to give judgment, request the Court of Justice to give a ruling thereon.
>
> Where any such question is raised in a case pending before a court or tribunal of a Member State against whose decisions there is no judicial remedy under national law, that court or tribunal shall bring the matter before the Court of Justice.

The Court of Cassation and the State Council fall within the second paragraph quoted above. The European court cannot say that the French Law is not correct or has not been correctly interpreted. Therefore, when the Court says that the correct interpretation of the European Law is "yes", it is easy to understand that it is not possible to say that the national text may be understood to say "no".

6. Customs

In relation with the Romanic tradition, France has the reputation of being a country of "written Law". It is not perfectly true because of the importance of jurisprudence. Moreover, it must be noted more that custom also has a place in the sources of Law. It is not an important place, though. A custom (in French: "*coutume*" and, in the field of commercial Law, "*usage*") is defined as a practice usually adopted, accepted as being a Law. Such a practice can be effectively recognized particularly in the commercial field, but with much more difficulty in the other branches of the Law. Having said that, it is non negligible in relation to electronic commerce.

B. SCHEME OF ONLINE BUSINESS REGULATION

In France, as in other countries, there are two kinds of online business: a complete "paperless trade" when all the operations are carried out online (offer, acceptance, delivery) and a more classical one when solely the "signing" of the contract is online, with execution in the "real" world. In both cases, the common opinion is that it is not necessary to have a specific regulation. The rules exist and can be applied in the online realm as well as in the traditional environment. The idea has been put forward in the important Report of the State Council: "Internet and the Digital Networks" (1998). Previously, this same idea had been developed in the Treaty on Computer and Networks "Lamy"[1] which is a book of reference in France.

Adaptations are welcome and, maybe, in certain cases, necessary. But the basic and usual rules can be used without problem.

This means that online business is the subject of different sorts of regulations that exist: law, jurisprudence and custom, on national, European and international levels. For instance, the regulation of contracts must be searched in the French Civil and Commercial Codes which have been influenced by European Law and the specific provisions on the protection of consumers in the French Consumer Code which has been particularly influenced by this European Law. The question of privacy is regulated by old texts, as provisions of the Civil Code, but also by original legislation such as, for example, an important Law of 1978 relating to information technology and human rights. Moreover, it must be noted that this Law has been adopted in order to regulate the phenomenon of digitalization but not specifically online business.

In fact, the regulation of online business is, very classically, a matter of a *combination* of different kinds of rules: civil, commercial, criminal, under the judges' authority and under the pressure of practice.

1 M. Vivant et al., *Lamy Droit de l'informatique et des réseaux*, annual republication.

C. ELECTRONIC TRANSACTIONS AND CONTRACT FORMATION

Online contracts are not the subject of any special attention under French law. They are covered by ordinary statutory and case law. France, like all the economically developed countries, has admitted the validity of electronic proof and signatures. The major principles of French law are applicable both in a traditional environment and in the specific environment of online commerce.

1. Content: the Fundamental Principle of Consensuality

French law, like in many other places, is dominated by the principle of consensuality. In other words, the idea that a contract must respect certain forms in order to be valid is alien to French law. It is for this reason that, when the draft Community Directive on Electronic Commerce provided that an online contract should be formed by a procedure involving the exchange of messages and counter-messages, it was seen as being against the principles of law and an unnecessarily long process. Since the Directive adopted in 2000 set aside this option, the consequence is that, whether on or off-line, a contract is formed by a simple exchange of consents.

This will, of course, pose problems with regard to evidence but, in principle, this exchange is sufficient. Furthermore, contrary to procedures existing in other legal systems, a sale is completed "solo consensu", and the transfer of property is carried out immediately—unless, of course, the parties, who control every aspect of the organization of their contract, within the extremely formal bounds of public order, decide to handle things differently.

Without going into a detailed study of international private law, the observation just made leads us to note that, for a contract that is very often international, such as those concluded online, it will be important to state which is the applicable law. As a member of the European Union, France is subject to the provisions of the Convention of Rome of 19 June 1980 pertaining to the Law applicable to Contractual Obligations. In Article I, this Convention grants the greatest possible freedom to contracting parties, subject to the laws that cover consumer protection.

On the issue of which is the duly competent jurisdiction, one should consult the Community Regulation of 22 December 2000 "relative to Jurisdictional Competence and the Recognition and Execution of Decisions in Civil and Commercial Matters". While jurisdictional competence is granted to the country of the defending party (or more precisely, to the courts of the Member State of the European Union), it is always possible, by virtue of this same text and in particular its Article 23, to appoint a judge to hear cases on contractual disputes. The judge may equally well be European or non-European.

The draft government bill for increasing "confidence in the Digital Economy" (2003), which implements European legislation, provides that the Civil Code be modified in a way that would enable guarantees to be produced to the effect that the exchange of consent was effective. It is for this reason that a new article

1369-2 is planned to be added to the Civil Code, supplemented by Article 1369-3, which is also new.

> *Art. 1369-2.*—The contract proposed by electronic means is deemed to have been concluded when the recipient of the offer, having had the opportunity to verify the details of the order and the total cost, and to correct any errors that may be apparent therein, confirms the offer in order to express his acceptance thereof.
>
> The offerer must acknowledge reception of the order that has been addressed to him, without delay, by electronic means.
>
> The order, the confirmation of the acceptance of the offer and the acknowledgement of receipt are deemed to have been received when the parties to which they have been addressed can have access to them.
>
> *Art. 1369-3.*—Exceptions are made to the obligations mentioned in parts 1° to 5° of article 1369-1 and to the first two paragraphs of article 1369-2 for contracts for the supply of goods or the provision of services that are concluded exclusively via the exchange of electronic mail. . . .

Since the principle is that parties are at liberty to transact, they may thus conclude all known forms of contract (sale, hire, services contract, etc.), without being limited to in pre-established legal frameworks (French law refers to these as "innominate contracts").

Online commerce has seen a veritable blossoming of new contractual practices and forms (for example, I. de Lamberterie and M. Vivant, "Commerce électronique: de nouvelles pratiques contractuelles?", in L'internet et le droit, Légipresse éd., 2001, p. 369.—Also: G. Decocq and A. Lepage, "Contrats conclus à distance et contrats par voie électronique", Revue Communication—Commerce électronique 2001, Comm. No. 131). In addition to the inevitable access or hosting contract signed with an ISP, we might also cite the examples of contracts for the setting up of a "virtual shop" or shopping centre, so-called "portal" contracts (which are gaining in importance), telephone helpline contracts, etc.[2]

2. Form: the Recognition of the Electronic Form

While French law as a rule is not formalistic in nature, there are nevertheless, in addition to consumer protection, a certain number of formal requirements currently developing, imposed by Community law and, in particular, by the "Electronic Commerce" Directive. It is for this reason that the draft law for increasing "confidence in the Digital Economy" would insert a new Article in the Civil Code, No. 1369-1, as follows:

> *Art. 1369-1.*—Whoever proposes, for professional purposes and by electronic means, the supply of goods or the provision of services, shall transmit the applicable contractual obligations in such as way as they may be conserved and reproduced. The offerer shall be bound by his proposal for as long as it remains accessible, due to his own action, by electronic means.

2 For all these contracts, *see* M. Vivant, Les contrats du commerce électronique, Litec, 1999.

Among other things, the offer must mention:

1. The various steps to be accomplished in order to conclude the contract by electronic means;

2. The technical means by which the user, before the contract is concluded, may identify any errors made in the keyboarding of data and correct them;

3. The languages in which the contract may be concluded;

4. If necessary, the methods used by the offerer to archive the contract and the conditions by which the archived contract may be accessed;

5. The means by which the professional and commercial rules to which the offerer intends to submit himself may be electronically consulted.

Since the publication of the Law of 13 March 2000, French law (by means of the Civil Code) fully recognizes the probative value of an "electronic writing". In reality, the courts had already accepted it, but in a country with a tradition of written law, the appearance of a law clarifies everything considerably. Among a number of important texts, Article 1316 of the Civil Code is the most central:

> Literal evidence, or written evidence, is the result of a series of letters, characters, figures or any other signs or symbols endowed with intelligible signification, regardless of the medium and method of transmission.

This leads us to make the following observations:

- writing is defined in general terms, without distinction as to the medium on which it appears;
- "paper-based" writing and "electronic" writing have equal probative value—there is no "second-rate" evidence;[3] and
- in the event of contradictions appearing between the written proofs presented to the court, it is the duty of the court to decide.[4]

When written material required as proof is involved, the draft bill on the Digital Economy goes even further and stipulates that written material demanded *ad validitatem* may henceforth be provided in electronic form. Electronic written material is now fully a part of the French legal structure.

With respect to the Law of 2000, the commentaries are abundant.[5]

As a result, electronic signatures also need to be legally recognized. Article 1316-4 of the Civil Code, after stating that the signature identifies the person who affixes it and acts as a sign of his consent, also stipulates:

---

3 Art. 1316-1 and 1316-3.

4 Art. 1316-2.

5 P.-Y. Gautier and X. Linant de Bellefonds, "De l'écrit électronique et des signatures qui s'y attachent", JCP 2000, I, 236 and éd. E, p. 1273. E. (Joly) Passant, "La loi du 13 mars 2000 portant adaptation du droit de la preuve aux technologies de l'information et relative à la signature électronique: nouvelle donne pour le droit de la preuve", Cahiers Lamy Informatique 2000, May (D), p. 7 and Rev. Lamy Dr. des Affaires 2000, June, No. 28, p. 13.

> When the signature is electronic, it consists generally of a reliable identification procedure that guarantees its link with the deed to which it is associated. This procedure is deemed reliable, until proved otherwise, when the electronic signature is created, the identity of the signatory guaranteed and the integrity of the deed ensured, under conditions to be determined by decree.

By virtue of an European Directive of 1999 relative to Electronic Signatures, the French text distinguishes between a signature that we might classify as ordinary and a signature with reinforced value (the "advanced" signature of the European texts). The first of these is deemed valid and fully effective, inasmuch as the procedure used may be held to be reliable (the assessment of this reliability falls to the judge). The second, on the other hand, is deemed reliable because it is protected by using an onerous and minutely specified system, at the heart of which we find "certifying third parties" whose role it is to guarantee that the system is reliable.

On the subject of the Decree of 30 March 2001, the text which sets up this certification system, there is a great deal of commentary.[6]

It will always be preferable to organize the production of evidence between parties. For many years now, the courts have recognized the validity of agreements relating to evidence and now Article 1316-2 of the Civil Code does so, discreetly but without ambiguity. The only limitation, and it is one of common sense, is that an agreement concerning evidence, which can amend the conditions under which evidence is produced, cannot purely and simply prevent the production of contrary evidence. The Agreement regarding evidence must not in any case be neglected either in business-to-business or consumer contracts.

---

6 I. de Lamberterie and J.-F. Blanchette, "Le décret du 30 mars 2001 relatif à la signature électronique: lecture critique, technique et juridique", JCP 2001 éd. E., p. 1269.—E. Joly-Passant, "Le décret du 30 mars 2001 pris pour l'application de l'article 1316-4 du Code civil et relatif à la signature électronique", Cahiers Lamy Informatique 2001, June (C), p. 1 and Rev. Lamy Dr. affaires 2001, July, No. 40, chr. No. 2519 p. 21.

HONG KONG

by
Andrew Simpson
Arculli and Associates

A. SOURCES OF LAW

Hong Kong is a "Special Administrative Region" of the People's Republic of China. Hong Kong's legal system has been greatly influenced by English law, as a consequence of English administration of Hong Kong as a British Colony for over 100 years. The Basic Law of the Hong Kong Special Administrative Region of the People's Republic of China is Hong Kong's foundational legal document and preserves Hong Kong's laws and "capitalist system" for fifty years after the resumption of sovereignty by the People's Republic of China.

1. Basic Law

In 1984, the governments of the People's Republic of China (PRC) and the United Kingdom (UK) signed the Sino-British Joint Declaration on the Question of Hong Kong, laying down key policies in respect of Hong Kong. The Joint Declaration required certain principles to be set out in the Basic Law of the Hong Kong Special Administrative Region of the People's Republic of China ("**Basic Law**").

The Basic Law is a fundamental constitutional document of the Hong Kong Special Administrative Region ("**HKSAR**"). It entrenches the principle of "One Country, Two Systems," meaning that the capitalist system will continue to apply in Hong Kong for 50 years after the reversion of sovereignty from the UK to the PRC in 1997.

The task of drafting the Basic Law rested with a committee made up of both Hong Kong and mainland PRC members. In addition, a consultative committee composed only of Hong Kong members was formed in 1985 to provide Hong Kong views on the drafts.

The PRC National People's Congress promulgated the Basic Law in 1990, along with the HKSAR's flag and emblem designs.

The Basic Law is divided into four parts: the main body of the documents consisting of 160 articles; Annex I lays down the method for selecting the Chief Executive of the HKSAR; Annex II sets out the method of formation of the Legislative Council and its voting procedures; and Annex III specifies the PRC national laws to be applied in the Region.

The articles in Chapter I set out the general principles of the Basic Law. The HKSAR is authorised ". . . to exercise a high degree of autonomy and enjoy executive, legislative and independent judicial power . . ."[1] despite Hong Kong being "an inalienable part" of the PRC.[2] The executive authorities and legislature will be composed of permanent residents.[3] Importantly, the "socialist system and policies" of the PRC will not be practiced in the HKSAR and the "capitalist system and way of life" will remain unchanged for 50 years.[4] The legal system, consisting of Ordinances and subordinate legislation, common law, rules of equity and customary law will remain to the extent that they do not contravene the Basic Law and are subject to amendment by the Legislative Council of the HKSAR.[5] The right of private ownership of property in accordance with law will be protected by the HKSAR.[6]

Chapter II sets out the relationship between the central PRC government and the HKSAR. In accordance with Article 11 "[n]o law enacted by the legislature of the Hong Kong Special Administrative Region shall contravene this Law." Article 12 provides that the HKSAR ". . . shall enjoy a high degree of autonomy and come directly under the Central People's Government." The central PRC government is responsible for the HKSAR's foreign affairs and authorises the HKSAR to conduct external affairs on its own.[7] The PRC will also be responsible for the defence of the HKSAR and will station military forces in the HKSAR, although responsibility for the maintenance of public order rests with the HKSAR.[8] Central PRC national laws will not apply to the HKSAR except for those listed in Annex III of the Basic Law, which are limited to laws such as those relating to defence and foreign affairs. Such laws will be enforced locally, by way of legislation by the HKSAR.[9] In the event of declaration of war by the PRC or the existence of a state of emergency or of turmoil in the HKSAR which endangers national security or unity and is beyond the control of the government

1 Basic Law of the Hong Kong Special Administrative Region of the People's Republic of China (Adopted at the Third Session of the Seventh National People's Congress on 4 April 1990) Article 2.

2 Basic Law, Article 1.

3 Basic Law, Article 3.

4 Basic Law, Article 5.

5 Basic Law, Article 8.

6 Basic Law, Article 6.

7 Basic Law, Article 13.

8 Basic Law, Article 14.

9 Basic Law, Article 18.

in the HKSAR, the central PRC government may issue an order applying the relevant national laws in the HKSAR.[10]

Chapter III deals with fundamental rights and duties of the HKSAR's residents. All residents are equal before the law,[11] and permanent residents have the right to vote and stand for election in accordance with law.[12] Residents' freedom of the person will be inviolable and no resident will be subjected to unlawful arrest, detention or imprisonment.[13]

The Basic Law also prohibits torture or unlawful deprivation of the life of any resident.[14] Residents enjoy ". . . the freedom of speech, of the press and of publication; freedom of association, of assembly of procession and of demonstration; and the right and freedom to form and join trade unions and to strike."[15] The freedom and privacy of communication shall be protected in that no department or individual may infringe upon such freedom unless the relevant authorities may make inspection in accordance with legal procedures for investigation of criminal offences or to meet public security needs.[16] Residents shall have freedom of movement within the HKSAR, to emigrate to other countries and freedom to enter and leave the HKSAR without special authorization unless restrained by law.[17] The freedom of conscience and religion is also protected.[18] The International Covenant on Civil and Political Rights, the Covenant on Economic, Social and Cultural Rights, and international labour conventions as applied to the HKSAR shall stay in force and be implemented through legislation.[19]

Chapter IV, which deals with political structure provides for the executive and legislative branches of the HKSAR's government together with an independent judiciary. In respect of executive authorities the Chief Executive must be a Chinese citizen and permanent resident of the HKSAR with no right of abode in any foreign country.[20] He or she will be selected or elected through local consultations and appointed by the central PRC government.[21] The Legislative Council shall be formed by election and in accordance with the principle of "gradual and orderly progress" with the ultimate aim of election of all members by universal

10 Basic Law, Article 18.
11 Basic Law, Article 25.
12 Basic Law, Article 26.
13 Basic Law, Article 28.
14 Basic Law, Article 28.
15 Basic Law, Article 27.
16 Basic Law, Article 30.
17 Basic Law, Article 31.
18 Basic Law, Article 32.
19 Basic Law, Article 39.
20 Basic Law, Article 44.
21 Basic Law, Article 45.

suffrage.[22] In respect of the judiciary, the power of final adjudication shall vest in the Court of Final Appeal which, if necessary, may invite judges from other common law jurisdictions to sit.[23] Courts in the HKSAR will exercise judicial power independent from interference.[24] The Basic Law maintains the practice of trial by jury[25] and upholds the right to a fair trial by judicial organs without delay,[26] as well as the presumption of innocence until conviction.[27]

Chapter V, which deals with the economy states that the HKSAR shall remain a free port[28] and the Government shall maintain an appropriate environment for the maintenance of Hong Kong's status as an international financial center.[29] It states that the HKSAR shall pursue the policy of free trade and safeguards the free movement of goods.[30]

Chapter VI deals with Education, Culture, Sports, Religion, Labour and Social Services. It allows the HKSAR to formulate its own policies on these areas.[31]

Chapter VII which deals with external affairs provides that the HKSAR may use the name "Hong Kong, China" on its own when maintaining and developing relations and may conclude agreements with foreign countries and relevant organizations including those in the economic, trade, tourism and cultural fields.

2. Structure of Government

a. HKSAR Government

Hong Kong was a British Colony between 26 January 1841 and 30 June 1997, and became a Special Administrative Region ("**SAR**") of the People's Republic of China ("PRC") from 1 July 1997. Its constitution consists of the Basic Law that came into effect upon return of sovereignty to the PRC. The Basic Law provides for a two-tier system of government headed by the Chief Executive, who is elected by an Election Committee in accordance with the Basic Law and appointed by the PRC central government.[32] Hong Kong has an independent judiciary.

The Hong Kong SAR Government consists of the Legislative Council, which legislates and enacts laws and controls and monitors budgets and government performance; and the Executive Council, which assists and advises the Chief

---

22 Basic Law, Article 68.
23 Basic Law, Article 82.
24 Basic Law, Article 85.
25 Basic Law, Article 86.
26 Basic Law, Article 87.
27 Basic Law, Article 87.
28 Basic Law, Article 114.
29 Basic Law, Article 109.
30 Basic Law, Article 115.
31 Basic Law, Article 147.
32 Basic Law, Annex A.

Executive on important policy decisions. At the local district level, there are eighteen district councils, which advise the Chief Executive on policy implementation in their respective district areas.

b. The Chief Executive

The Basic Law provides that the Chief Executive will be elected by an Elective Committee which is broadly representative and appointed by the PRC central government.[33] The Chief Executive shall have a five year term of office and cannot serve for more than two consecutive terms.[34] The Chief Executive has the authority to determine government policies and issue executive orders.

Bills passed by the Legislative Council are signed and then promulgated by the Chief Executive.[35] The Chief executive also appoints and removes judges and civil servants in public office in accordance with the law.[36]

Where provided in the Basic Law, the Chief Executive implements the central government's directives and conducts external and other affairs on behalf of Hong Kong government as authorized by central government.[37]

The Chief Executive's duties include signing budgets passed by the Legislative Council before reporting them to the PRC central government; making nominations to the PRC central government for appointment or removal of major Hong Kong officials; and approving the introduction of motions to the Legislative Council.

c. Executive Council

Executive Council members are appointed by the Chief Executive from among Legislative Council members, executive authorities officials and other public figures.[38] The Chief Executive also decides on members' removal. From July 2002 the Executive Council comprises 14 government officials and 5 non-officials.

The Basic Law requires the Chief Executive to put matters before the Executive Council which in turn advises the Chief Executive before he or she makes major policy decisions, introduces bills to the Legislative Council or makes subordinate legislation.[39] The Chief Executive is required to give specific reasons for not accepting a majority view of the Executive Council and to put those reasons on record.[40]

---

33 Basic Law, Annex A.

34 Basic Law, Annex A and Article 46.

35 Basic Law, Article 48.

36 Basic Law, Article 48.

37 Basic Law, Article 48.

38 Basic Law, Article 55.

39 Basic Law, Article 56.

40 Basic Law, Article 56.

d. Legislative Council

Members of the Legislative Council are, in accordance with the Basic Law, elected directly by geographical constituencies, elected by functional constituencies or by an election committee.[41] Under the Basic Law, the Legislative Council's functions include the enactment and repeal of laws in accordance with the Basic Law and procedures, examination and approval of taxation and budgets, raising questions on the government's work and debate of public issues.[42]

The legislative process usually starts with discussions between the government, the Legislative panels and the relevant trade organizations or district councils. In due course legislative proposals will be formed and submitted to the Executive Council for the Chief Executive to approve and introduce to the Legislative Council. The Bill will then be published in the *Gazette* and introduced for a first reading in the legislative Council, followed by a second reading in which it will be moved by a member giving a speech explaining the merits and aims of the Bill. Upon adjournment of the second reading debate, the Bill will then be transferred for consideration by the House Committee, the members of which will decide whether to form a Bills Committee or allow the Bill to be considered in some other manner. Where a Bills Committee is formed, it will consider the Bill and any necessary amendments before reporting back to the House Committee. After any discussions on the report, the House Committee will return the Bill to continue the second reading debate. If the Bill passes a second reading it will undergo a third reading and will then be signed by the Chief Executive, making it law.

e. The Judiciary

The Hong Kong judiciary is independent from both other branches of the government. The Hong Kong SAR legal system is based on the common law and its judiciary operates independently of the Executive and Legislative Councils. The courts of justice comprise the Court of Final Appeal, the High Court (which consists of the Court of Appeal and the Court of First Instance), the District Court (which includes the Family Court), the Magistrates' Court (which includes the Juvenile Court), the Lands Tribunal, the Labour Tribunal, the Small Claims Court, the Obscene Articles Tribunal and the Coroner's Court.

The Department of Justice is headed by the Secretary for Justice, who is responsible for all prosecutions in Hong Kong. It is made up of five divisions.

The Legal Policy Division and the Justices' Office provide the government with input on legal policy issues, advising the government on matters including those relating to the legal system and administration of justice. The Civil Division advises the Government on civil law and has the duties of conducting civil litigation and drafting contracts and carrying out other legal work for the Government.

41 Basic Law, Annex 2.

42 Basic Law, Article 73.

The Law Drafting Division drafts legislation and sub-legislation in both English and Chinese and helps with guiding legislation through the Executive and Legislative Councils. The Counsel of Prosecutions Division conducts the majority of criminal appeals up to the Court of Final Appeal, as well as most of the trials in the Court of First Instance and District Court. The International Law Division advises the government on public international law matters.

B. SCHEME OF ONLINE BUSINESS REGULATION

Hong Kong has been quick to adopt online services and exhibits high Internet penetration rates. According to the Hong Kong Trade Development Council, "[a]s at June 2002, Hong Kong had 2.6 million Internet users. Internet traffic volume reached 15,485 terabits via broadband networks during that month. Business receipts from selling goods, services or information through electronic means amounted to HKD7.6 billion in 2000. . . ."[43] However, "[o]nly 1.1% of Hong Kong companies have sold goods, services or information through electronic means"[44] and online transactions accounted for 0.17% of Hong Kong companies' total business receipts in 2000.[45] The Government expressly desires ". . . to drive Hong Kong's information technology development as a leading digital city in the globally connected world."[46]

Online business in Hong Kong is regulated by primary legislation (Ordinances) and subsidiary legislation (Regulations, Orders et cetera), by case law and the decisions of a number of regulatory agencies. Some primary legislation has been enacted which is tailored specifically for application in the online environment (e.g. the Electronic Transactions Ordinance (Cap. 553) and recent amendments to the Gambling Ordinance (Cap. 148), Crimes Ordinance (Cap. 200) and Copyright Ordinance (Cap. 528) have been made in an effort to ensure they are apt to apply to online conduct) but for the most part statutes that preceded the advent of the Internet apply to online transactions without having been amended.

Network operators and Internet service providers are regulated by the Telecommunications Ordinance (Cap. 106), administered by the Telecommunications Authority, and subject to licences, directions, statements and other instruments made under the Telecommunications Ordinance. The privacy of personal data is protected by the Personal Data (Privacy) Ordinance (Cap. 486), administered by the Privacy Commissioner, and online content is controlled by the Broadcasting Authority, Television and Entertainment Licensing Authority, Obscene Articles

43 See < http://www.tdctrade.com/main/si/internet.htm>.

44 See < http://www.tdctrade.com/main/si/internet.htm>.

45 See < http://www.tdctrade.com/main/si/internet.htm>.

46 Hong Kong SAR "Hong Kong: Connecting the World—Digital 21 Strategy" (May 2001), Foreword.

Tribunal and Film Censorship Authority, under their respective Ordinances.[47] A number of enactments provide protection to consumers in Hong Kong,[48] while online businesses are subject to the normal principles of companies law[49] and tax law.[50]

C. ELECTRONIC TRANSACTIONS AND CONTRACT FORMATION

Hong Kong contract law closely resembles that of England and decisions of the English courts remain of persuasive authority, though a number of local Ordinances and curial decisions modify the English common law of contract. The Hong Kong government's active stance in promoting adoption of new communications technologies is reflected in its promulgation of the Electronic Transactions Ordinance, which underpins recognition of electronic records and digital signatures.

1. Electronic records

The validity of records in electronic form and digital signatures is controlled by Parts III and IV of the Electronic Transactions Ordinance (Cap. 553). Five key sections of the Ordinance provide for the recognition of information in electronic form where, formerly, documents "written" on paper were required:

- Section 5 provides that a rule of law that requires or permits information to be in writing or given in writing, or provides for certain consequence if it is not, an electronic record will satisfy that rule ". . . if the information contained in the electronic record is accessible so as to be usable for subsequent reference."
- Section 6 provides for the validity of digital signatures (see heading (b), below).
- Section 7 provides that a rule of law requiring information to be presented or retained in its original form is satisfied by presenting or retaining that information in electronic records if there exists ". . . a reliable assurance as to the integrity of the information from the time when it was first generated in its final form . . ." and the information is capable of being presented in a legible form, where it is required to be presented. Attachment of a "digital signature" supported by a valid recognized certificate in accordance with the Ordinance would provide such "reasonable assurance".

47 Broadcasting Ordinance (Cap. 562); Broadcasting Authority Ordinance (Cap. 391); Control of Obscene and Indecent Articles Ordinance (Cap. 390); Film Censorship Ordinance (Cap. 392).

48 Including the Control of Exemption Clauses Ordinance (Cap. 71); Misrepresentation Ordinance (Cap. 284); Pyramid Selling Prohibition Ordinance (Cap. 355); Sale of Goods Ordinance (Cap. 26); Trade Descriptions Ordinance (Cap. 362); and Unconscionable Contracts Ordinance (Cap. 458).

49 Companies Ordinance (Cap.32).

50 Inland Revenue Ordinance (Cap. 112) and Stamp Duty Ordinance (Cap. 117).

- Section 8 provides that a rule of law requiring information to be retained, whether in writing or otherwise, is satisfied by retaining electronic records if the information remains accessible for subsequent reference, the electronic record "... is retained in the format in which it was originally generated, sent or received, or in a format which can be demonstrated to represent accurately the information originally generated, sent or received ..." and the information identifying the origin and destination of the electronic record and the date and time it was sent or received is also retained.
- Section 9 provides that, subject to the rules of evidence, electronic records shall not be inadmissible in evidence in any legal proceedings solely because they are electronic records.

Part IV of the Electronic Transactions Ordinance provides for certain limitations on the operation of sections 5 to 8:

- First, the Secretary for Information Technology and Broadcasting may, by order published in the Gazette exclude specified Ordinances, requirements or permissions from the operation of ss 5-8 or specify the manner and format of giving, presenting or retaining information in electronic records or verifying receipt of information or ensuring the integrity and confidentiality of information.[51]
- Secondly, ss 5-8 do not apply to information given, presented or retained or to signatures required for the purposes of legal proceedings of the kinds set out in Schedule 2 to the Electronic Transactions Ordinance, except where a rule of law relating to those proceedings (e.g. Court Rules) provides for, requires or permits the use of electronic records or electronic signatures.[52]
- Thirdly, ss 5-8 are not to be construed as affecting any express provision of an Ordinance which requires or permits use of electronic records or authentication by electronic signatures and which specifies particular requirements for that purpose or creates a discretion in a person in relation to acceptance of electronic records or electronic signatures.[53]
- Fourthly, an electronic record does not satisfy a requirement or permission for information to be in writing, or presented in its original form, if neither the person giving it nor the person to whom it is to be given are acting on behalf of a government entity, unless the person to whom it is to be given consents to it being given as an electronic record.[54]
- Fifthly, ss 5-8 do not apply to a requirement in an Ordinance for writing, or for documents to be in their original form, where satisfaction of such a requirement

51 Electronic Transactions Ordinance ss 11, 12.

52 Electronic Transactions Ordinance s 13.

53 Electronic Transactions Ordinance s 14.

54 Electronic Transactions Ordinance s 15.

by electronic records or electronic signatures would prevent compliance with any other requirement in that Ordinance or a related Ordinance.[55]

- Sixthly, ss 5-8 (and s 17, formation and validity of electronic contracts) do not apply to requirements or permissions for information to be in writing in matters set out in Schedule 1 to the Electronic Transactions Ordinance.[56]

Orders made under the Electronic Transactions Ordinance by the Secretary for Information Technology and Broadcasting have created a number of specific exclusions from the operation of ss 5-8 and have varied Schedule 2 of the Ordinance to include within its exclusion a number of additional statutory bodies which exercise quasi-judicial functions.[57] In briefing documents to the Legislative Council, the provisions excluded by Order from the operation of ss 5-8 were classified as:

> (a) provisions which have to be excluded due to the solemnity of the matter or document involved, i.e., provisions concerning the electoral process;
>
> (b) provisions which have to be excluded on operational grounds, e.g. provisions concerning the production of documents to Government authorities on the spot;
>
> (c) provisions which have to be excluded due to the involvement of voluminous submissions and complex plans which would be difficult to handle electronically, e.g. provisions concerning submission of documents and plans to the works departments;
>
> (d) provisions which have to be excluded because of international practices, e.g. provisions concerning documents to be kept by the flight crew for air navigation purposes; and
>
> (e) provisions which have to be excluded to ensure that Government would be able to meet its contractual obligations, e.g. provisions on the submission of trade-related documents which concern the franchise of the Tradelink.[58]

The ability to add or remove exclusions from ss 5-8 permits rapid tuning of the Ordinance to changes in other legislation and the use of technology.

2. Digital signatures

Digital signatures are intended to perform the functions of conventional signatures: to evince the provenance and hence the authenticity of documents, at the time they are signed. Section 6 of the Electronic Transactions Ordinance (Cap. 553) provides that a rule of law that requires a person's signature, or provides for certain consequences if a document is not signed, is satisfied by the digital

55 Electronic Transactions Ordinance s 16.

56 Electronic Transactions Ordinance s 3.

57 Electronic Transactions Ordinance ss 11, 50.

58 Legislative Council Brief—Electronic Transactions (Exclusion) Order; Electronic Transactions Ordinance (Amendment of Schedule 2) Order 2000 File Ref ITBB/IT 107/4/1 (00) XVII.

signature of the relevant person if that digital signature is supported by a recognized certificate that is valid at the time the digital signature is generated.

Section 6 is qualified by s 15(3), which provides that s 6 does not apply to render a digital signature satisfactory where neither party is a government entity or acting on behalf of a government entity, unless the person to whom the signature is to be given consents to the use of a digital signature.

An "electronic signature," by contrast, is merely ". . . any letters, characters, numbers or other symbols in digital form attached to or logically associated with an electronic record, and executed or adopted for the purpose of authenticating or approving the electronic record."[59] It is the fact of support by a "recognized certificate" that distinguishes a digital signature, which may satisfy a rule of law requiring a signature, from an electronic signature, which does not. For the purposes of the Ordinance, ". . . a digital signature is taken to be supported by a certificate if the digital signature is verifiable with reference to the public key listed in a certificate the subscriber of which is the signer."[60]

The recognition of digital signatures depends upon Parts VII, VIII, IX and X, establishing the machinery for the recognition of certification authorities and certificates.

3. Public Key Infrastructure

The certification system is premised on an asymmetric cryptography system, involving a private key that is confidential to the subscriber and a public key that is disclosed to the certification authority and may be disclosed to anyone with whom the subscriber communicates. The role of the certification regime of Hong Kong's public key infrastructure is, in essence, to provide a party who may wish to rely on another's digital signature with assurance of the identity of the person to whom a particular private key was issued and hence assurance that an action carried out by use of that key (e.g. creation of a digital signature) was performed by the same person. That assurance is provided through "recognized certificates."

A "certificate" is a record issued by a named certification authority, to an identified person, for the purpose of supporting a digital signature. A certificate must be signed by a responsible officer of the certification authority issuing it and must contain the subscriber's public key.[61]

A recognised certificate that is accepted by a "subscriber" (i.e. a person identified in a certificate as the person to whom it is issued and who holds the private

59 Electronic Transactions Ordinance s 2(1).

60 Electronic Transactions Ordinance s 2(2).

61 Electronic Transactions Ordinance s 2(1).

key corresponding to the public key listed in the certificate,[62] must be published in a repository by the recognised certification authority which issued it.[63] Information contained in a recognised certificate that is published in a repository shall be presumed correct, except for information identified as subscriber's information which has not been verified by the recognised certification authority.[64]

By publishing a recognised certificate, a recognised certification authority represents to any person who reasonably relies on information in the certificate that the authority has issued the certificate to the subscriber concerned.[65] By issuing a recognised certificate, the recognised certification authority represents to any person who reasonably relies on information in the certificate that it was issued in accordance with the applicable certification practice statement.[66] The liability of a recognised certification authority, however, is:

- excluded in respect of "... any loss cause by reliance on a false or forged digital signature of a subscriber supported by a recognised certificate issued by that certification authority, if the recognised certification authority has complied with the requirements of [the Electronic Transactions] Ordinance and the code of practice with respect to that certificate";[67] and
- is limited to the amount specified in the certificate as its "reliance limit," for a loss caused by reliance on any information that the certification authority is required to confirm and which is misrepresented on the recognised certificate or in a repository, if the recognised certification authority has complied with the Ordinance and code of practice and the misrepresentation was not intentional or due to the certification authority's negligence or recklessness.[68]

A certification authority may apply to the Director of Information Technology Services to be recognized as a "recognized certification authority."[69] The Director is empowered to revoke[70] or suspend[71] recognition of a certification authority. The principal effect of such revocation or suspension, or of the expiry of the period of validity of recognition of a certification authority, is that certificates issued by the certification authority are no longer treated as recognised certificates and digital signatures are no longer supported by any certificate previously

62 Electronic Transactions Ordinance s 2(1).
63 Electronic Transactions Ordinance s 36.
64 Electronic Transactions Ordinance s 38.
65 Electronic Transactions Ordinance s 40.
66 Electronic Transactions Ordinance s 39.
67 Electronic Transactions Ordinance s 42(1).
68 Electronic Transactions Ordinance s 42(2).
69 Electronic Transactions Ordinance s 21.
70 Electronic Transactions Ordinance s 23.
71 Electronic Transactions Ordinance s 24.

issued.[72] The revocation, suspension or expiry of the period of validity of recognition of a certification authority does not affect the valid use of a certificate issued by that authority prior to such revocation, suspension or expiry.[73]

Similarly, a recognized certification authority may apply to the Director of Information Technology Services for recognition of all certificates issued by it, of a particular class of certificates, or of particular certificates as "recognized certificates".[74] The Director is empowered to revoke[75] or suspend[76] recognition, in respect of all certificates issued by it, of a particular class of certificates, or of particular certificates. The revocation, suspension or expiry of a recognized certificate entails that digital signatures formerly supported by the certificate in question are no longer so supported. The revocation, suspension or expiry of a recognized certificate does not affect the valid use of that certificate prior to such revocation, suspension or expiry.[77]

The Postmaster General of Hong Kong is a recognised certification authority[78] and the Director of Information Technology Services has in addition recognised the following certification authorities under the Ordinance:

- Digi-Sign Certification Services Limited;
- Hi-TRUST.COM (HK) Incorporated Limited; and
- Joint Electronic Teller Services Limited.

In respect of each recognised certification authority, the Director of Information Technology Services must maintain a publicly accessible online record, containing ". . . information regarding that certification authority relevant for the purposes of this Ordinance . . ." and information required under the Ordinance.[79] The Director of Information Technology Services has issued a Code of Practice under the Ordinance ". . . specifying standards and procedures for carrying out the functions of recognized certification authorities."[80] At least annually, each recognised certification authority must submit a report to the Director of Information Technology Services, prepared by a person approved by the Director,

72 Electronic Transactions Ordinance s 26(2).

73 Electronic Transactions Ordinance s 26(4), (7).

74 Electronic Transactions Ordinance s 22(3).

75 Electronic Transactions Ordinance s 23.

76 Electronic Transactions Ordinance s 24.

77 Electronic Transactions Ordinance s 26(5), (6).

78 Electronic Transactions Ordinance s 34.

79 Electronic Transactions Ordinance s 31; see <http://www.itsd.gov.hk>.

80 Electronic Transactions Ordinance s 33; see "Code of Practice for Recognised Certification Authorities" issued by the Director of Information Technology Services <http://www.info.gov.hk/itbb/english/it/doc/cop.pdf>.

which report must include an assessment of whether it has complied with the provisions of the Ordinance and the Code of Practice.[81]

4. Online contracting

Section 17 of the Electronic Transactions Ordinance allows for contracts to be formed by the making and acceptance of offers online:

> 17. Formation and validity of contracts
>
> (1) For the avoidance of doubt, it is declared that in the context of the formation of contracts, unless otherwise agreed by the parties, an offer and the acceptance of an offer may be in whole or in part expressed by means of electronic records.
>
> (2) Where an electronic record is used in the formation of a contract, that contract shall not be denied validity or enforceability on the sole ground that an electronic record was used for that purpose.
>
> (3) For the avoidance of doubt, it is stated that this section does not affect any rule of common law to the effect that the offeror may prescribe the method of communicating acceptance.

In many cases, the time and place of formation of a contract will assume importance. Part VI of the Electronic Transactions Ordinance deals with the attribution of the sending and receipt of electronic records. Unless otherwise agreed between the originator of an electronic record and the addressee, an electronic record:

- is that of the originator if it was sent by the originator or with the originator's authority or was sent by an information system programmed by or on behalf of the originator to send the electronic record automatically;[82]
- is sent when it is accepted by an information system outside the control of the originator or of the person who sent the electronic record on behalf of the originator;[83]
- is taken to have been sent at the place of business of the originator (or, if there is more than one, that which has the closest relationship to the underlying transaction, or the originator's principal place of business, or the place the originator ordinarily resides);[84]
- is taken to have been received at the place of business of the addressee (or, if there is more than one, that which has the closest relationship to the underly-

---

81 Electronic Transactions Ordinance s 43(1).

82 Electronic Transactions Ordinance s 18.

83 Electronic Transactions Ordinance s 19(1).

84 Electronic Transactions Ordinance s 19(4)(a).

ing transaction, or the addressee's principal place of business, or the place the addressee ordinarily resides);[85]

- is received at the time it is accepted by the information system designated by the addressee for the purpose of receiving electronic records;[86] and
- is received at the time that it comes to the knowledge of the addressee, if either:
  - it is sent to an information system of the addressee that is not the designated information system;[87] or
  - the addressee has not designated an information system for the purpose of receiving electronic records.[88]

It remains to be seen whether Hong Kong courts will determine the time of receipt of an electronic record sent to an information system of the addressee that is not a designated information system on the basis of the addressee's actual knowledge, or at such time as constructive knowledge may arise in the addressee.

5. Deeds

In some circumstances, parties may wish to create binding obligations by means of deed, rather than contract. A deed is required by statute for some purposes, e.g. in order to create a power of attorney, dispose of an interest in land or make a will. The exemptions under Schedule 1 of the Electronic Transactions Ordinance will preclude the execution of deeds in electronic form for many such purposes but in other cases an electronic record might suffice.

The Electronic Transactions Ordinance contains no specific provision in respect of electronic deeds. The recognition under s 6 of electronic records as satisfying rules of law requiring information to be in writing would meet the requirement of common law that a deed be written.[89] A deed must also be executed under seal.

Section 19 of the Conveyancing and Property Ordinance applies to deeds by individuals:

> (1) A deed by an individual shall be signed by him.
>
> (2) A document shall be presumed to have been sealed by an individual if the document signed by him—
>
> (a) describes itself as a deed;
>
> (b) states that it has been sealed; or

85 Electronic Transactions Ordinance s 19(4)(b).

86 Electronic Transactions Ordinance s 19(2)(a)(i).

87 Electronic Transactions Ordinance s 19(2)(a)(ii).

88 Electronic Transactions Ordinance s 19(2)(b).

89 Electronic Transactions Ordinance s 6.

(c) bears any mark, impression or addition intended to be or to represent a seal or the position of a seal.

A deed might, therefore, be created by an electronic record where it is signed by an individual by means of a "digital signature" that is supported by, and generated within the period of validity of, a recognized certificate and can be presumed to have been sealed by virtue of describing itself as a deed, stating that it has been sealed or bearing an "addition intended to be or to represent a seal."

A company may not electronically execute a deed under seal, as the Companies Ordinance (cap. 32) requires every company to ". . . have as its common seal a metallic seal on which it shall have its name engraven in legible characters. . . ."[90] A company could, however, make a deed electronically, through an individual as its agent:

Where a person is empowered to execute a deed by a corporation, he may execute the deed as agent by signing the name of the corporation or his own name and by affixing his own seal.[91]

90 Companies Ordinance s 93(1)(b).

91 Conveyancing and Property Ordinance s 20(2).

HUNGARY

by
Szabolcs Gall, Esq., and Daniel F. Visoiu, Esq.
Szecskay—Attorneys at law

A. SOURCES OF LAW

1. Hungarian Legal System

a. General Description

Hungary, for hundreds of years part of the Austro-Hungarian Empire, has a legal system greatly influenced by Continental legal principles and traditions. Consequently, Hungary has a civil law system, with the courts interpreting and applying those provisions set forth in the relevant legislation.

At the same time, the communist period (mid-1940s to 1989) also influenced Hungary's legal system, although not as much as might be expected. For example, during this period, parts of Hungary's laws on the formation of private corporations enacted in 1875 (*Commercial Act*) and 1930 (*Act on Limited Liability Companies and Limited Partnerships*) were never abolished and remained in force—although they were very rarely used.

Negotiations between Hungary and the European Union (EU) began after the commencement of its *Association Agreement with the European Communities* on February 1, 1994. Hungary officially became an EU member on May 1, 2004. This means that Hungary's legal system now incorporates the over 80,000 page EU *Acquis Communitaire.*

b. Public, Private and International Law

Generally, Hungarian public law encompasses constitutional law and other such legislation which relates to the public order and well-being of society. On the other hand, *private law* focuses on the rights and obligations pertaining to individuals, such as contract law and the law of torts (as this concept is embodied in the Hungarian *Civil Code*). Regarding the concept of international law, numerous statutes have been adopted which have codified Hungary's membership and acceptance of several international conventions, and certain Acts, such as the

Private International Law Act apply to legal relationships between Hungarian citizens and foreign entities.

c. Administrative Procedures and Civil Procedure Code

Among others, administrative and civil procedural issues are generally subject to and regulated by *Act IV of 1957 regarding the General Rules of Administrative Procedures*, and *Act III of 1952 regarding the Civil Procedure Code*.

d. The Constitution and Constitutional Law

The Hungarian *Constitution* is the supreme law of the Republic of Hungary, fundamentally reviewed in 1989 and 1990 (see *Act XX of 1949* as amended by *Act XXXI of 1989* and *Act XL of 1990*). The Executive (the Hungarian Government) has the obligation to submit to the Legislature (the Hungarian Parliament) all draft legislation necessary for the enactment and implementation of the *Constitution* and its provisions.

The *Constitution* addresses such areas as general decrees, the Parliament, the President, the Constitutional Court, the Parliamentary Ombudsman, the National Auditing Office, the National Bank of Hungary, the national government, local governments, the court system, the Public Prosecutor, basic rights and obligations of citizens, electoral principles, etc.

e. Effect of International Law

In *Article 7* of the *Constitution*, it is stated that Hungary's legal system accepts the generally recognized principles of international law, and shall harmonize the country's domestic law with the obligations assumed under international law.

f. European Union Law—the *Acquis Communitaire*

Many of Hungary's legal rules are in conformity with the relevant *EU* legislation. Also, on May 1, 2004, Hungary became a full *EU* member, and thus the *Acquis Communitaire* became part of the Hungarian legal system.

g. Common Principles of Law

Common principles of law generally serve as instructional and interpretative sources.

h. Parliamentary Acts and Other Legislation at National and Regional Levels

The Parliament (National Assembly) is the sole legislative body with extensive law-making powers. Its structure is unicameral, consisting of 386 members elected to 4-year terms by popular vote. From the total number of 386 seats, 176 are elected in individual constituency elections, 152 are selected on the basis of 20 district lists (county and municipal), and 58 are appointed from national lists.

Parliament passes Acts by a simple majority of the MPs present; whereas a two-thirds vote is required for certain issues defined in the *Constitution*.

The Government has power to issue decrees signed by the Prime Minister. Local governments may also issue decrees, regulating local issues not disposed of in Acts or government decrees. The Government, the Ministers of the Government and the local government may also issue decrees upon authorization and within the limits set forth by the Parliament's Acts. Decrees must not be contrary to any legal provision at a higher level.

i. Other Legal Instruments

Various organs (Parliament, Government, Ministers, President of the Hungarian National Bank, etc.) may issue so-called other legal instruments (implementation or methodological norms), interpreting applicable legislation or setting forth technical details. These instruments do not have a binding effect for the public; they only bound the administrative organ in question.

j. Non-binding Administrative Opinions

Certain administrative organs, such as the Tax Authorities (APEH) or the *State Capital Markets Supervision Authority* (PSZÁF), may in fact issue letters interpreting the applicable legislation and specific provisions, upon written request but such issued letters do not have any legal effect.

2. Hungarian Court System

a. Court System

Starting in July 2003, there are four formal levels of courts: (1) local courts; (2) the county (metropolitan) courts; (3) courts of appeal; and (4) the Supreme Court.

b. Competence

Local courts generally handle law suits which are not specifically designated as falling under the jurisdiction of county courts.

County courts usually have competence over matters involving, but not limited to, property claims exceeding HUF 5 million, intellectual property, etc.

Courts of appeal in fact are not *per se* courts, meaning that with respect to cases being appealed from the local courts, the county courts shall act as the court of appeal; and for matters originating with the county courts, the *Supreme Court* is the court of appeal.

The *Supreme Court* is the highest court. However, in Hungary there is also a *Constitutional Court* which hears and decides whether Acts and legislation passed by Parliament or issued by the Government are constitutional.

c. Costs of Proceedings

For civil claims, courts fees are *six percent* of the value of the claim, to a maximum of HUF 900,000. Generally, the courts may oblige the losing party to cover the total or a part of the attorney's fees of the prevailing party.

d. Statute of Limitations

Section 324 of the *Civil Code* stipulates that the current general statute of limitation shall be five years (prior to 1993, there were different periods for different categories of persons/entities). Further, if the principal claim lapses, then all the dependent collateral claims shall also lapse. However, the running of the statute of limitation shall not prevent satisfaction from a pledge obtained as collateral (see *Section 324(3)*). The statute of limitation commences upon the so-called due date of the claim (see *Section 325*).

B. SCHEME OF ONLINE REGULATION

1. Associations, Government Agencies and Parliamentary Committees; Relevant Websites

a. Council of Hungarian Internet Providers

The *Council of Hungarian Internet Providers* ("CISP") <www.nich.hu> is the professional body of Hungarian Internet service providers, operating under a civil law association status. In addition to its professional activities, it plays an important and much debated role regarding domain name delegation under the top level domain ".hu". It operates as a public interest limited liability company founded by the CISP, responsible for the coordination and supervision of the administrative registration and maintenance tasks related to domain delegation. It publishes several model regulations widely used by the member Internet service providers, such as general contractual terms for the providing of Internet services.

b. Association of Content Providers in Hungary

The *Association of Content Providers* <www.mte.hu> is a self-regulatory body operating as the civil law association of content providers. The association was founded for the purpose of issuing opinions accepted by content providers concerning Internet content. It has issued the *Professional Code of Internet Content Provision* and an *Ethical Code* for content provision. The Association has established a conflict resolution committee, for the settlement of conflicts between content providers and users, with the issued decision to be accepted by every content provider as binding.

c. Parliamentary Commissioner for Data Protection

The legal basis for the establishment of the *Parliamentary Commissioner for Data Protection and Freedom of Information*,<http://abiweb.obh.hu/adatved/indexek/index.htm www.obh.hu/adatved/indexek/index. htm> is *Act LIX of 1993 on the Parliamentary Commissioners*, and *Act LXIII of 1992 on the Protection of Personal Data and the Freedom of Information.*

The integration of the tasks and duties of the *Data Protection Commissioner (Ombudsman)* constitutes a rather unique approach. Besides monitoring both data protection and freedom of information in general with an ombudsman's competence, the Commissioner's tasks are many-fold. They include the maintenance of the Data Protection Register, providing opinions on data protection and freedom of information-related draft legislation as well as on official secrets; and, according to the *Act LXV of 1995 on State Secrets and Official Secrets*, the Commissioner is entitled to change the classification of state and official secrets as well.

d. Ministry of Informatics and Communications (www.ihm.hu)

Pursuant to *Government Decree 141/2002 (VI.28) concerning the Scope of Authority and Powers of the Minister of IT and Communications*, the Minister is responsible for the development of a uniform and comprehensive government strategy in relation to the information society, and the co-ordination and supervision of in-country and international technical activities within its competence.

With respect to tasks related to information technology, the Minister's scope of authority extends to the planning, implementation and operation of social, public, administrative, cultural, educational and economic programs, except for the governmental IT systems, with regard to which the Minister in charge of the Prime Minister's Office is responsible for the performance of these tasks.

e. Communications Authority of Hungary

The Communications Authority of Hungary <www.hif.hu> was established pursuant to *Act XL of 2001 on Communications* and *Government Decree No. 248/2001. (XII. 18.) on the Communications Authority and the Fines by the Authority*. The Communications Authority performs its activities through: (i) the *Communications Arbitration Committee*, acting as arbitrator in disputes between market players requested by the parties involved but making decisions also on matters of principle within the framework of the given rules of law, which may have an effect on the competitive market; (ii) the *Communications Central Agency* providing the professional support necessary for the entire organization of the *Communications Authority* and for the Ministry of IT and Communications with respect to its legislative duties; and (iii) the *Communications Regional Offices* acting as a first instance authority.

f. Hungarian Patent Office

The Hungarian Patent Office <www.mszh.hu> is an administrative authority with country-wide competence in the field of intellectual property. The tasks and competence of the Office comprise the preparation of intellectual property legislation, official examinations and procedures in the field of industrial property (trademarks, industrial designs, utility models, topography of semiconductors, patents), central governmental information and documentation activities in the field of intellectual property, promotion of intellectual property activities through governmental measures.

2. Specific Legislation and Regulations

a. Law on Data Protection

Act LXIII of 1992 on the Protection of Personal Data and the Publication of Public Interest Data, as subsequently amended (the "**Data Protection Act**") generally provides that personal data may be disseminated—irrespective of the method of collection, storage, processing, utilization (including transmission and disclosure) and deletion—but only if the natural person concerned explicitly agrees thereto. Personal data is generally defined as any data relating to a specified natural person and any resulting information from such data with respect to him or her.

As a general rule, as long as the person concerned can be identified by the data, such data maintains its status having a "personal data" character. Thus, the name, address, sex, telephone and e-mail address most likely would be deemed as personal data.

Hungary's applicable legislation (the above-mentioned Act and the subsequent legislation which in part modified the Act) was modeled after *EU Directive 95/46/EC on the protection of individuals with regard to the processing of personal data and on the free movement of such data* [Official Journal L 281, 23/11/1995 p. 0031–0050].

b. E-Commerce and Information Society Services Act

In line with the European Commission's *E-commerce Directive (2000/31/EC)*, the Hungarian Parliament adopted *Act CVIII of 2001 on Electronic Commercial Services and on Certain Legal Aspects of Information Society Services*, which came into effect on January 24 2002. The Act contains rules on the following issues: (a) the exclusion of prior authorization principle; (b) information to be provided relating to information society services; (c) the conclusion of electronic contracts; (d) the liability of service providers; (e) unsolicited advertising; and (f) consumer protection.

c. Electronic Signatures Act

Act XXXV of 2001 on Electronic Signatures provides special rules in relation to electronic signatures. The Act provides that there are three types of electronic signatures, which have different legal recognition and effects: (i) electronic signatures; (ii) advanced electronic signatures; and (iii) qualified electronic signatures.

C. ELECTRONIC TRANSACTIONS AND CONTRACT FORMATION

1. Introduction—Fundamental Contract Law Principles under Hungarian Civil Code

In Hungary, the *Civil Code* addresses issues relating to contracts. The statutory provisions dealing with contracts are set forth in *sections 198–596* which encompass *Part Four* of the *Civil Code.*

a. Freedom to Contract

The principle of freedom to contract is guaranteed in section 200 of the *Civil Code*, whereby, "*. . . parties are free to define the contents of contracts, and they shall be entitled, upon mutual consent, to deviate from the provisions pertaining to contracts if such deviation is not prohibited by legal regulation*".

b. Formal Requirements of a Contract

Section 205 of the *Civil Code* stipulates that an agreement shall be deemed to have been concluded if the parties have agreed on the important or material issues relating to the legal relationship in question and the issues which any of the parties deem as important or material.

Sections 216–218 of the *Civil Code* set forth the formal requirements for concluding contracts.

Further, contracts may be concluded: (a) *verbally*; (b) *in writing*; and (c) by the *implied intent* of the parties as expressed by their conduct (see *section 216* of the *Civil Code*).

However, certain contracts, such as a pledge contract or a real property sale and purchase agreement, must be in written form (see *sections 254 (2)* and *262*) and must fulfill other formal requirements (*e.g.*, endorsement by a public notary).

c. Concept of Pre-contract

A distinctive feature of the Hungarian legal principles relating to contracts is the existence of so-called "pre-contracts" or "agreements in principle." Pursuant to *section 208* of the *Civil Code*, parties may agree to conclude a contract at a later date, which contract would be based on the parties' prior agreement on all the essential or material issues (*Civil Code section 205*).

It is important to note that the courts have the right, if so requested by a contractual party, to bring a contract into existence and to determine its content (based on the above-mentioned essential or material issues) (*section 208(3)*). However, in such a case, a party shall have the right to refuse to conclude a contract, ". . . *if it provides proof of inability to perform the contract by virtue of a circumstance that has occurred after the conclusion of the agreement in principle. . . .*" (*section 208(6)*).

2. Electronic Commercial Services and on Certain Legal Aspects of Information Society Services Act

The *Act CVIII of 2001 on Certain Issues Related to Electronic Commerce and Information Society Services* (the "**E-commerce Act**") contains rules on the following issues:

(a) the exclusion of prior authorization principle;

(b) information to be provided relating to information society services;

(c) the conclusion of electronic contracts;

(d) the liability of service providers;

(e) unsolicited advertising; and

(f) consumer protection.

a. Information Society Services

The term "information society service" covers: (i) any service provided by electronic means, at a distance, for consideration and pursuant to the individual request of a recipient of such services; and (ii) any such service provided for free, if this does not fall under the scope of the freedom of speech rights guaranteed by the *Constitution*.

b. Scope of the E-commerce Act

In compliance with the applicable EU directive, the Act is based on the "country of origin" principle—that is, an information society service will be governed by the law of the EU member state from which the service is provided. However, until Hungary joins the European Union (on May 1, 2004) this principle is not applicable with respect to services provided from EU member states.

In other words, until Hungary joins the EU on May 1, 2004, the Act's provisions will apply to all information society services provided both from and to the territory of Hungary and to all service providers and service receivers that provide or receive such services. A service is considered to be provided to the territory of Hungary if it can be inferred from the language, the currency or other relevant circumstances that the service is intended to be accessible to Hungarian recipients.

c. Exclusion of Prior Authorization

Information society services may be provided by any natural or legal person. However, such authorization shall nonetheless be subject to the application of qualifications, notifications or licensing requirements stipulated by other legal rules.

d. Information Requirements

An information society service provider must make certain information permanently accessible to service recipients and competent authorities. This information must be provided in the Hungarian language and includes the following:

- details of the service provider, including (i) its name; (ii) the geographical address at which it is established; and (iii) its contact details, including its e-mail address; and (iv) its tax identification number;
- whether provision of the service is subject to authorization and, if so, the details of the relevant supervisory authority and the relevant permit number;
- the name of the professional chamber of which the service provider is a member;
- essential information about the products or services on offer, including (i) an adequate description of these products or services; (ii) instructions for their use or maintenance, together with details of any hazards associated with such use; (iii) the quality of the products or services; and (iv) the relevant prices;
- other information that will enable the consumer to make a final decision on the product or service to be purchased; and
- basic information on the enforcement of consumer rights.

Where information society services are provided at a charge, this must be indicated clearly, unambiguously and permanently. In particular, the service provider must indicate whether they are inclusive of tax and delivery costs.

The service provider must also provide general information on the security of its systems and potential risks that might arise from their use.

e. Electronic Contracts

Before an order which forms the basis of an electronic contract can be concluded, the service provider must make the contractual terms and general conditions accessible in such a way as allows the recipient to store and reproduce them. In addition to the information listed above, it must also provide details on the following:

- all technical steps necessary to conclude the contract;
- whether the contract will have the force of a written contract;
- whether the service provider will register the contract and make it available at a later time;
- the technical means by which input errors can be identified and corrected;

– the language of the contract; and

– the rules of the code of conduct to which the respective service provider is bound.

The service provider must ensure that the recipient is able to identify and correct input errors prior to placing the order. If the technical means to do this are not available, the recipient's order will not have the legal effect of an offer.

The service provider must acknowledge receipt of the recipient's order without undue delay and by electronic means. If its acknowledgement does not arrive in the recipient's electronic mailbox within 48 hours of the recipient submitting his or her offer, the recipient will not be legally bound by the offer. The acknowledgement of receipt is deemed to have been received when the party to whom it is addressed can access it.

These rules apply to both business-to-business and business-to-consumer contractual relationships. However, in the former the parties may derogate from the provisions relating to the information requirements and the point at which the contract becomes effective. In addition, the rules will not apply to contracts concluded exclusively by exchange of e-mail or other such equivalent individual correspondence.

f. Liability of Internet Service Providers

In general, an Internet service provider (ISP) is subject to general civil law liability. However, in compliance with *Articles 12-15* of the EU directive, the new Act defines how an intermediary service provider may exclude liability with respect to its activities if these are limited merely to acting as a conduit, caching or hosting, or to the provision of search engine services.

In certain circumstances specified by the Act, there is no general obligation on ISPs to monitor the content of the material that they manage either prior to transmission or on a permanent basis. Nor are they required to investigate actively facts or circumstances which give rise to suspicions of illegal activities.

The Act introduces a so-called "notice and takedown procedure" similar to that set out in the *U.S. Digital Millennium Copyright Act*. Under this procedure, a copyright owner or owner of related rights may request that the ISP remove any illegal content or make it inaccessible within 12 hours. However, the entity which posted the disputed content has the right to challenge its removal within eight days, upon which the ISP must make the content accessible again, as long as the entity has provided its contact details. However, if the right owner initiates a court procedure within ten days, the provider must again remove the offending content. The Act expressly stipulates that the right owner and the ISP may enter into an agreement relating to the application of this procedure.

g. Unsolicited Advertising

The Act provides for opt-in registers, in which natural persons wishing to receive commercial communications can request that they be mailed the same. In other words, the receipt of unsolicited commercial communications is subject to the prior consent of the recipient.

In addition, the fact that such electronic communications are advertisements must be identifiable at the point at which they become accessible to the recipient—that is, prior to opening the message.

3. Electronic Signatures Act

Pursuant to *Act XXXV of 2001 on Electronic Signatures* (the "**E-signatures Act**"), there are three types of electronic signatures, which have different legal recognition and effects.

a. Electronic Signatures

Section 3 of the *E-signatures Act* provides that an electronic signature or electronic communication (*e.g.*, an electronic document containing an electronic signature) will be accepted as evidence and as a legal statement, and will have legal effect, although it will not be considered a "written communication". Its effects may not be disputed solely on the ground that the signature, communication or document exists only in electronic form.

b. Advanced Electronic Signatures

Section 4(1) of the *E-Signatures Act* provides that where a statute requires that a certain document be provided in written form, an electronic communication will satisfy this requirement if it contains an advanced electronic signature.

c. Qualified Electronic Signatures

Pursuant to *section 196(1)(f)* of *Act III of 1952 on Civil Procedure*, as modified by the *E-signatures Act*, an electronic communication which contains a declaration, an approval of a declaration or a commitment to abide by a declaration, and which is signed with a qualified electronic signature, shall be regarded as a public document or a private document providing full evidence, as long as the authenticity of the signature is evidenced by a qualified certificate. A qualified certificate may only be issued by a qualified certification service provider.

Following the adoption of the *E-signatures Act*, numerous Acts were amended in order to comply with its provisions. As a result, several Acts now provide for the use of electronic signatures in different kinds of transactions. For instance, *section 44* of *Act CXX of 2001 on the Capital Market* now provides that, "*. . . an offering statement made by the investor to acquire any stock shall only be valid if it is made in writing, in an electronic statement with a qualified electronic signature or through an exchange trading system approved by the authority.*" *Section 49(4)* further provides that "*an auction offer and its acceptance must be made in writing or in an electronic statement bearing a qualified electronic signature, or through an exchange trading system approved by the authority*". Similarly, *section 167(5)* of *Act C of 2000 on Accounting* provides that, "*[f]or* accounting purposes, only electronic documents which are executed by qualified electronic signature and time stamp will be accepted, and then only if they satisfy the requirements set forth in this act and if the validity of the certificate issued by the certification service provider can be guaranteed for 10 years in the case of the annual report and eight years in the case of accounting documents." In addition, *section 210(1)* of *Act CXII of 1996 on Credit Institutions and Financial Enterprises* states that, "*all contracts of financial institutions for financial services and auxiliary financial services must be made in writing or in the form of an electronic document executed with a qualified electronic signature. The financial institution must provide original copies of the written contracts to the customer.*"

In order to facilitate the practical use of electronic signatures in business transactions, supplementary regulations which implement these new provisions also had to be introduced. Consequently, rules were adopted in 2001 which govern the services provided in connection with electronic signatures, as well as the service providers themselves. Rules relating to the appointment of certification service providers were also adopted. In addition, the government recently adopted rules relating to the operation of qualified certification service providers. These decrees and rules have established a legal framework that allows for the efficient use of electronic signatures and provides for the operation of certification service providers. The standards which certification service providers must meet under these regulations are very high and thus make their operation very costly. In spite of this, the legislature intends certification service providers to be private, market-oriented entities that receive no financial support from the *Hungarian Communication Authority*.

ISRAEL

by
Neil J. Wilkof, Karen L. Elburg, Nicholas Cannon and Lee-Anne Berns
Herzog Fox & Neeman

A. SOURCES OF LAW

1. The Evolution of Israel's Legal System

The State of Israel is a parliamentary democracy. Its legal system has been influenced by a number of historical events of the 19th and 20th centuries. Until 1917, the area that is now the State of Israel was a part of the Ottoman Empire and from 1918 until 1948 was under the British Mandate. As a result, principles of Ottoman law, English common law and equity and Jewish religious law were introduced, and significantly influenced current Israeli law. In addition, judicial decisions of the United States are increasingly taken note of in the context of online business.

2. Israel's Parliament Parliamentary Supremacy

Israel's political system is based upon the principle of parliamentary supremacy. Israel's parliament, known as the Knesset, literally translated as the "meeting house", is the primary authority for both the enactment and repeal of legislation. Legislation is enacted through bills that are introduced by the Government, private members or by Knesset committees, and are then voted on by the Knesset members.

The Knesset comprises 120 members elected through the system of proportional representation. The members are selected from lists drawn up by political parties. Within the Knesset exist a number of key committees relating to major areas of national importance: Constitution, Legislation and Judicial; Foreign Affairs and Security; Finance; Labor and Welfare; Education and Culture. These consider and vote on draft legislation as well as examine and comment on government policy and issues affecting the State generally.

All citizens of Israel 18 years and older are eligible to vote for the Knesset. Since March 1992 the Prime Minister has been elected directly by the Israeli electorate.

However, in March 2001, the Knesset amended the Israeli election law,[1] and re-instated the previous system that was revoked in 1992. Under the old system, rather than being directly elected, the chairman of the party winning the most seats in the Knesset became Prime Minister, provided he could form a government that would obtain the confidence of the Knesset. This amendment will come into force at the beginning of the next Knesset period and will apply for future Israeli elections.

3. Government and President

The Government is responsible for implementing the policy of the Executive and the state authority. The doctrine of Cabinet responsibility is enshrined in the political system. The President of Israel is not part of the Executive. He is elected by a secret ballot of a majority of the Knesset members. Although he has a largely ceremonial role, he has the right to commute sentences, grant pardons, participate in the formation of the government and call general elections.

4. The Role of the Basic Laws

Since 1950, and as a consequence of the "Harrari decision",[2] the Knesset agreed that the Israeli constitution should contain separate chapters each called a "Basic Law." In some respects, the existence of the "Basic Laws", which set out specific fundamental laws, is loosely analogous to a written constitution. However, because of the principle of parliamentary supremacy, it could be argued that the Israeli constitution lies between a formal written constitution and an unwritten one.

The "Basic Laws" concern the Knesset,[3] Israel Lands,[4] the President of the State,[5] the Government,[6] the State Economy,[7] the Army,[8] Jerusalem Capital of Israel,[9] the Judiciary,[10] the State Comptroller,[11] Human Dignity and Freedom,[12] and

1 This is the third version of "Basic Law: The Government", the first one having been passed in 1968.

2 "The Harrari resolution" June 13, 1950 (named after MK Yizhar Harrari of the Progressive Party). See the vote on 5 D.K (1950), at P. 1719-1722.

3 5718-1957, 12 L.S.I. 85.

4 5720-1960, 14 L.S.I. 48.

5 5724-1964, 18 L.S.I. 111.

6 5761-2001.

7 5735-1975, 29 L.S.I. 273.

8 5736-1976, 30 L.S.I. 150.

9 5740-1980, 34 L.S.I. 209.

10 5744-1984, 38 L.S.I.101.

11 5748-1988, 42 L.S.I. 24.

12 5752-1992.

Freedom of Vocation.[13] Despite being considered fundamental laws, the Basic Laws are subject to amendment by the Knesset and interpretation by the Supreme Court.

Despite this, the Supreme Court in 1995[14] recognized that two of the Basic Laws—Human Dignity and Freedom and Freedom of Vocation—possess higher normative status and, accordingly, any amendment to these laws requires a special majority of Knesset members.

5. Judiciary

The Israeli judiciary is apolitical, and follows specific juridical principles: the power to create case law by the exercise of judicial discretion; the binding effect of decisions on lower courts; and the supremacy of the highest court, the Supreme Court which is not bound by its own decisions. The judicial system comprises Magistrates' Courts, District Courts, and the Supreme Court. Religious law as applicable to Jews, Moslems, Christians and some other minorities (for example the Druze) are subject to separate religious courts in areas concerning marriage and divorce.

As well as religious courts, special courts or tribunals exist to determine matters involving labor issues and military law. In addition, courts having quasi-judicial authority exist. These include the Restrictive Trade Practices Tribunal and the Office of Patents, Trademarks and Designs. In addition, a Family Court exists which has jurisdiction in all matters of family law except divorce, which remains under the sole jurisdiction of the religious courts. As an alternative to court proceedings, arbitration and mediation proceedings are widely used.

B. SCHEME OF ONLINE BUSINESS REGULATION

There is no single law that regulates the conduct of online business in Israel. Instead, a number of substantive laws exist which impact either directly or indirectly upon the conduct and regulation of online business.

These include at least the following statutes:

- Defamation (Prohibition) Law, 5725-1965;
- Secret Monitoring Law, 5739-1979;
- Consumer Protection Law, 5741-1981;
- Protection of Privacy Law, 5741-1981;
- Defective Products (Liability) Law, 5740-1980;

---

13 5754-1994.

14 Bank Hamizrahi Hameuchad Ltd et al v Migdal Kfar Shitufi, 49 P.D. (4) 221. See also Board of Investors Managers v. Minister of Finance et al, 51 P.D. (4) 367; Zemakh v. Minister of Defense et al., 53 P.D (5) 241. The latter two decisions were the only times that the Israeli Supreme Court declared that a regular Knesset Law is not valid because of a contradiction to the Basic Law: Freedom of Vocation or to the Basic Law: Freedom and Human Dignity.

- Standard Contracts Law, 5743-1982; Telecommunications Law, 5742-1982;
- Imported Services Charge (Temporary Provisions) (Amendment No. 2 and Extension of Validity) Law, 5746-1985;
- Prescription Law, 5718-1958;
- Computers law, 5755-1995;
- Electronic Signature Law, 5763-2001; Sale Law, 5728-1968;
- Sale (International Sale of Goods) Law, 5759-1999;
- Land Law, 5729-1969;
- Gift Law, 5728-1968; Patents Law, 5727-1968;
- Currency Control Law, 5738-1978. Sections: Commodities and Services Control Law, 5718-1957;
- Interpretation Law, 5741-1981;
- Performers' Rights Law, 5744-1984;
- Copyright Act 1911;
- Contracts (General Part) Law, 5733-1973;
- Basic Law: Human Dignity and Freedom;
- Debit Cards Law, 5746-1986;
- Value Added Tax Law, 5736-1975;
- Securities Law, 5728-1968;
- Commercial Torts Law, 5759-1999;
- Unjust Enrichment Law, 5739-1979;
- Postal Authority Law, 5746-1986;
- Torts Ordinance (New-Version);
- Customs Ordinance;
- Patents and Designs Ordinance;
- Evidence Ordinance (New Version), 5731-1971;
- Bills of Exchange Ordinance (New Version) 5717-1957;
- Income Tax Ordinance (New Version);
- Trade Marks Ordinance (New Version) 5732-1972;
- Export Control Order (Warfare Gear and Military knowledge) 5737-1977;
- Copyright Order (Bern Treaty) 5713-1953;
- Performers Rights Order (Trips Agreement) 5760-1999;
- Income Tax (Double Taxation Relief) 5724-1963;

- Telecommunications Regulations (Procedures and Conditions for Award of Satellite Broadcast Licenses) 5758-1998;
- Protection of Privacy Regulations (Conditions for Protection and Maintenance of Information Procedures for Transfer of Information Between Public bodies) 5746-1986;
- Designs Regulations;
- Customs Regulations 5727-1965;
- Civil Procedure Regulations 5744-1984;
- Merchandise Marks Ordinance 1940; Currency Control Permit 5738-1978;
- Currency Control Permit 5758-1998;
- Declaration of Control of Commodities and Services (Engagement in Encryption Items) 5735-1974;
- Telecommunications Rules (Broadcasting of a licensee) 5748-1987;
- General Import License 5738-1978; Electronic Signature Regulations (Registration and Administration of Certification Authority) 5761-2001;
- Electronic Signature Regulations (Secured Electronic Signature, Hardware and Software Systems and Requests Examination) 5761-2001.

C. JURISDICTION

The issue of jurisdiction is of prime importance in conducting online business. This section describes the main principles of Israeli law regarding jurisdiction as they apply within the context of the new online environment.

1. Submission to Jurisdiction

Under Israeli law, a court has jurisdiction over every person who can be served in Israel. Jurisdiction can arise either:

(i) as a consequence of the person being present within the Israeli jurisdiction, and in this case, it is irrelevant as to whether or not the defendant is an Israeli citizen.

(ii) by consent, subject to certain exceptions.

Under section 482 of the Civil Procedure Rules,[15] any person, corporation or entity conducting business in Israel can be served. Thus, service can be through a representative or agent whose activities are such that it may be argued that business is being conducted in Israel. Whether a person is "doing business" in Israel is a question of fact. Merely that a party has an asset in Israel, for example a bank account, will not be enough to establish that the party has submitted to the jurisdiction.

15 4685 Code of Regulations (1984) 2209, 2284 (as amended).

If a defendant is not present in the territory, jurisdiction may be extended to the foreign defendant by obtaining leave to serve outside the jurisdiction under section 500 of the Civil Procedure Rules.[16] Section 500 lays down ten different "scenarios" in which international jurisdiction may be acquired.

The application is made *ex parte* and leave is usually granted as a matter of course. When service is made pursuant to Rule 500, 60 days are generally allowed for filing a defense. In addition, service under Rule 500 must comply with the Hague Convention,[17] where applicable, and the plaintiff is usually required to translate the process documents, including the application for leave and its appendices, into the defendant's local language.

2. Jurisdiction and the Internet

An argument as to submission to Israeli jurisdiction may arise where it can be demonstrated that a foreign company's website is active in Israel. Israeli courts are yet to conclusively address the issue of jurisdiction through the Internet. To date there has only been one Israeli court decision[18] regarding this matter and this lone decision centered on the question of local jurisdiction and not international jurisdiction.

The decision in *Landau v. Chason*,[19] given in May 2002, addressed the question of whether the existence of a website by the defendant could be considered as giving rise to "residence", in the context of the territorial extent of Internet jurisdiction. Chason claimed defamation by an article published in an Israeli national newspaper and on an Israeli-based and targeted Internet site. Landau requested that the court should dismiss the claim for damages, as it did not have the jurisdiction to hear the case, basing its argument on sections 3(a)(1) and 3(a)(5) of the Civil Procedure Rules, which state that an action which is not entirely based on real estate should be brought before a court in the area of jurisdiction.

In this case, it was argued that this means either the defendants place of residence or of business,[20] or the place of the act or omission that gives rise to the cause of the action.[21] Landau's argument was that neither his place of residence nor his of business was within the jurisdiction of the magistrate's court in Kiryat Gat. Accordingly, it was argued, publication of the relevant article had not occurred within the court's jurisdiction. In response, Chason argued that since

16 4685 Code of Regulations (1984) 2209, 2286-2287 (as amended).

17 Convention on the Service Abroad of Judicial and Extra-judicial Documents in Civil and Commercial Matters, 23 *Kitvei Amana* (1972) 31.

18 CM 884/02 (CF 566/02) [Kiryat Gat] Landau v. Chason, (unpublished decision, given on 01/05/02).

19 CM 884/02 (CF 566/02) [Kiryat Gat] Landau v. Chason, (unpublished decision, given on 01/05/02).

20 Civil Procedure Rules section 3(a)(1).

21 Civil Procedure Rules section 3(a)(5).

publication on the Internet is a publication without boundaries, the civil procedure rules relating to the place of the "act" or "omission" should be ignored.

The Court did not accept Landau's argument. It reasoned that there is no difference between publication on the Internet and publication in a newspaper. Accordingly, it was held that the court in Kiryat Gat had jurisdiction to hear the case, since the act of distributing the article over the Internet was deemed to have occurred within the Court's jurisdiction.

3. Recognition and Enforcement

An issue to consider in tandem with jurisdiction is that of recognition and enforcement of judgments. Under Israeli law, a clear distinction is drawn between recognition and enforcement of a foreign judgment.

Enforcement is customary practice in cases where the judgment is in personam, such that an obligation has been imposed on a defendant to pay a sum of money.

Recognition will be relevant if it is sought in regard to proceedings taking place in Israel where the court is requested to recognize the foreign judgment. The term "foreign judgment" is defined as:

> "a judgment given by a court in a foreign state in a civil matter, and includes a judgment for the payment of compensation or damages to an injured party even though it may not have been in a civil matter".[22]

Accordingly, a foreign judgment must be shown to include:

(i) the existence of a judgment;

(ii) in respect of civil proceedings for the payment of damages or damages to an injured party, even though it may not have been in a civil matter; and

(iii) that the judgment was given by a court.

For example, a decision given by an arbitrator within the context of arbitration proceedings, would not be regarded as a judgment given by a court. A distinct procedure exists for the enforcement of an arbitration award.

An Israeli court will usually enforce a foreign judgment made by any court in any jurisdiction, subject to specific conditions being fulfilled. Accordingly, the question of the foreign jurisdiction may be relevant when the court will examine the conditions for enforcement.

Under Israeli law, a foreign judgment may only be enforced in accordance with the provisions of the Enforcement of Foreign Judgments Law 5718, 1958.[23] Enforcement is based upon reciprocity with the country in which the judgment is given. Thus, Israeli courts will only declare a judgment given in a particular

22 Enforcement of Foreign Judgments Law, 5718-1958, 244 *Sefer Hachukim* 68 s 1.

23 Enforcement of Foreign Judgments Law, 5718-1958, 244 *Sefer Hachukim* 68 s 1.

country enforceable in Israel if the courts of that country would likewise enforce a judgment given by an Israeli court. With regard to the concept of reciprocity, the Israeli courts have interpreted this condition in a wide manner. Accordingly, if the relevant foreign courts enforce Israeli judgments of the same type or nature, this will be enough for the purposes of demonstrating reciprocity.

The judgment must be final. This has been interpreted by Israeli courts as meaning that an appeal is no longer possible or that the appeal was dismissed and no further appeal is possible.

The judgment must be enforceable in its nature in accordance with Israeli law. Furthermore, the judgment must not be defective, in that its content must not be contrary to Israeli public policy. This is material within the context of the nature of the plaintiff's claim. The judgment must be capable of being executed in the county where the judgment was made. The judgment also must not have been obtained by fraud, or in a manner contrary to principles of natural justice or international law.

One of the defenses that may be raised to enforcement is that the judgment was not given in accordance with the Israeli rules of private international law. The Israeli courts have interpreted this as meaning that there must be a linkage of residence or consent in the country where the judgment was given.

A Plaintiff seeking to enforce a foreign judgment in Israel would be required to file a request with the Israeli court, attached to which should be a copy of the judgment, duly authenticated by the appropriate court officer of the court in the foreign jurisdiction. In addition, an affidavit has to be submitted confirming that the conditions for enforcement have been complied with (as referred to above).

D. ELECTRONIC TRANSACTIONS AND CONTRACT FORMATION

1. Click-wrap Agreements

There has not been any published opinion in Israel on the validity or enforceability of a click-wrap agreement. Nor is there any Israel court decision that can be applied by direct analogy to the click-wrap situation. However, it is more likely than not that a click-wrap agreement, if challenged, will be found valid and enforceable under Israel law. It is possible that one or more of the provisions of the click-wrap agreement could still be challenged as an Unduly Disadvantageous Condition under the Standard Contracts Law.[24] The Regulations of the Consumer Protection Law (Size of Letters in a Standard Contract)[25] must also be taken into account. These points are discussed further below.

---

24 See section D.3 of this Chapter.

25 The Regulations of the Consumer Protection Law (Size of Letters in a Standard Contract), 5755-1995, Regulations 5704 (1995), 1898.

2. Contract Formation

For there to be a valid contract under Israeli law, there must be offer and acceptance and each party must resolve to be bound. No consideration is necessary. Within this framework, Israeli contract law gives wide latitude to freedom of contract.

With respect to the requirement of "offer", section 2 of the Israel Contracts (General Part) Law[26] provides (in official English translation) as follows:

> A person's proposal to another person constitutes an offer if it attests to the offeror's resolve to enter into a contract with the offeree and is sufficiently definite to enable the contract to be concluded by acceptance of the offer.

While "resolve" is related to the common law concept of "meeting of the minds", it enjoys a unique status under Israeli contract law, where consideration is not an element of the offer/acceptance process.

With respect to the requirement of "acceptance", section 5 of the Israel Contracts (General Part) Law provides (in English official translation) as follows:

> Acceptance shall be by notice by the offeree delivered to the offeror and attesting to the offeree's resolve to enter into the contract with the offeror in accordance with the offer.

The effect of the offer and acceptance requirements under Israeli contract law is to place a heightened emphasis on whether the parties intended to be bound. This takes on particular importance in the click-wrap situation, where the parties are usually anonymous, one to the other.

The offeror is the master of the manner by which acceptance is to be evidenced. Under this principle, for example it would appear that a company offering a licensed product can validly fix the manner of acceptance of the terms of the license by means of the requirement that the customer must click on the "I ACCEPT" button after the agreement appears on the screen. From the vantage of the customer, clicking on "I ACCEPT" under such circumstances would appear to satisfy the notice and resolution requirements for acceptance under the law. On its face, therefore, the act of clicking on the "I ACCEPT" button in this manner would appear to constitute notice of acceptance under Israeli law.

In addition to the foregoing, several other considerations in connection with the contract formation process in a click-wrap situation are suggested. In the absence of direct Israeli law, Israeli jurisprudence recognizes foreign law in general, and U.S. law in particular, as providing guidance in appropriate

26 Contracts (general part) Law, 5733-1973, 27 L.S.I 117.

circumstances. It is noted in this context that the first three points have recently been given recognition in the U.S. case of *Specht v. Netscape*.[27]

1. *Availability of the Agreement*—The full text of the Agreement should appear in such a way that the customer cannot bypass it.

2. *Explicit Provisions of Acceptance*—It should be unequivocal that the operation of the "I ACCEPT" button by the customer constitutes his or her assent to the terms of the Agreement.

3. *Interactive Acceptance*—The operation of the "I ACCEPT" button should be the result of an active, interactive response by the customer.

4. *Size and Form of the Print*—The size and format of the license and the offer and acceptance process should satisfy the Regulation to the Israel Consumer Protection Law.[28]

3. The Standard Contracts Law

Even if the click-wrap process satisfies the requirements discussed above, the Standard Contracts Law[29] must also be complied with. Under section 2 of this Law, a "standard contract" is "the text of a contract all or part of the conditions of which have been determined in advance by one party in order to serve as conditions of many contracts between him and persons undefined as to number or identity."

Based on this definition, it would appear that a click-wrap agreement could be found to be a "standard contract." If so, pursuant to section 3 of the Standard Contracts Law, a court may "annul or vary any condition . . . which having regard to the totality of the conditions of the contract and to other circumstances—involves an undue disadvantage to customers or an unfair advantage to the supplier likely to lead to a deprivation of customers" ("Unduly Disadvantageous Condition").

Each of the following are presumed by the Standard Contracts Law to be an Unduly Disadvantageous Condition:

(1) a condition relieving the supplier, fully or partially, of a responsibility he or she would have to bear under law but for that condition, or unreasonably restricting the responsibility he or she would have to bear by virtue of that contract but for that condition;

(2) a condition conferring on the supplier an unreasonable right to rescind, or to suspend or defer the performance of, the contract, or to alter any material obligation imposed on him or her by the contract;

---

27 Specht v Netscape (US 2nd Circuit Court of Appeals October 01, 2002 Docket Nos. 01-7860(L), 01-7870(CON), 01-7872(CON) See: <http://laws.lp.findlaw.com/getcase/2nd/case/017860&exact=1>.

28 See section D.3 of this Chapter.

29 Standard Contracts Law 5743-1982, 37 L.S.I. 6.

(3) a condition conferring on the supplier the right to transfer his or her responsibility to a third party;

(4) a condition conferring on the supplier the right to alter unilaterally, after the contract has been made, a price or any other material obligation imposed on the customer, unless the alteration arises out of factors over which the supplier has no control;

(5) a condition unreasonably requiring the customer to resort to the supplier or to some other person or otherwise limiting the customer's freedom to enter or not to enter into an engagement with another person;

(6) a condition denying or limiting a right or remedy available to the customer under law or unreasonably restricting a right or remedy available to him or her by virtue of the contract or making any such right or remedy conditional on giving notice in unreasonable form or within an unreasonable time or any other unreasonable requirement;

(7) a condition imposing the onus of proof on a person who would not have to bear it but for that condition;

(8) a condition which, save as part of a customary arbitration agreement, denies or limits the customer's right to make certain pleas before judicial authorities or to take any other legal proceedings;

(9) a condition prescribing an unreasonable place of jurisdiction or conferring on the supplier the right to choose unilaterally the place of jurisdiction or arbitration where a dispute is to be settled; and

(10) a condition prescribing referral of a dispute to arbitration when the supplier has greater influence than the customer on the designation of the arbitrators or the place of arbitration.

If a condition is found to be an Unduly Disadvantageous Condition, it may be either annulled or amended, depending upon the circumstances. A supplier may seek to have the Standard Contracts Tribunal approve the terms and conditions of its standard contract in advance. If approved, the basic rule under section 14(b) of the Law is that the contract can be used and no claim can be raised for a period of five years that the contract contains an Unduly Disadvantageous Condition. If advance approval is not obtained, the validity of a condition of a standard contract may be challenged in any appropriate forum as constituting an Unduly Disadvantageous Condition.

4. Regulation of the Consumer Protection Law

The Regulation of the Consumer Protection Law (Size of Letters in a Standard Contract)[30] provides for the minimum size of the letters (2 mm), the form of the letters, the color of the letters, the spacing between lines and the proximity of

30 Regulation of the Consumer Protection (Size of Letters in a Standard Contract) 1995, Sec. 2, 3.

the letters to each other. There is no explicit legal authority that indicates the legal effect if the click-wrap agreement fails to satisfy the requirements of the Regulation. It is uncertain whether a click-wrap agreement set out in an unclear or small font might be annulled on the basis of non-compliance with the Regulation.

5. Electronic Signatures

The Israeli Electronic Signature Law, 5761-2001[31] was enacted in order to enable some types of transactions to be completed electronically. Traditionally, certain transactions under Israeli law have been required to be in writing, the actual signing of a written document being taken as evidence of the parties' intention to enter into a binding contract. The Electronic Signature Law, while allowing some of these "writings" to be electronically signed, specifically excludes certain documents, which will continue to require manual signatures, e.g. wills, affidavits and powers of attorney.[32]

a. Definitions

The definition of "Electronic Signature" in The Electronic Signature Law is a broad one, allowing for rapid advances and developments of digital technologies:

> Electronic Signature—a signature that is electronic data or an electronic sign, that is attached to or associated with an Electronic Message.[33]

Two security levels are defined under the law: secure electronic signatures and certified electronic signatures. The different levels are reflected in the effect given to each type of signature. Notably, only an electronic document or mes-

---

31 Electronic Signature Law, 2001.

32 The laws, enactments and regulations that are excluded from the Law are as follows:The Succession Law, 5725-1965, 19 L.S.I. 58, concerning wills, memorandum on an oral will, succession order and probate; The Trust Law, 5739-1979, 33 S.L.I. 154, concerning instruments of endowment; The Notaries Law, 5763-1976, 30 S.L.I. 190, and The Notaries Regulations, 5764-1977, concerning signing before a notary, and signing by a notary. Section 91 of the Chamber of Advocates Law, 5721-1961, 15 L.S.I. 196, as amended ion Chamber of Advocates (Amendment No. 15) Law, 5747-1987, 41 L.S.I. 34, concerning a power of attorney; The Land Regulations (Administration and Registration), 5770-1969, concerning requests for registration or for the cancellation of registration and transaction deeds; The Agreements for Carrying Embryos Regulations (The Authorization of an Agreement and the Status of the Infant)(Notices, Requests and Orders), 5758-1998, concerning notices and requests; The Adoption of Children Law, 5741-1981, 35 L.S.I. 360, and section 272 of the Civil Procedure Regulations, 5744-1984, concerning a parent's consent to adoption; Rules and trade guidelines for the operation of recognized fellowship society (amuta) (according to the Adoption of Children Law, 5741-1981, 35 L.S.I, 360, as amended on the Adoption of Children (Amendment No. 2) Law, 5756-1996, concerning requests and opinions; The Rules of Banking (Service to Costumer)(Proper Disclosure and Delivery of Documents), 5752-1992, concerning agreements between a banking corporation and a costumer; Any legislation, which requires a person to sign an affidavit; The Debit Cards Law, 5746-1986, 40 L.S.I. 193, concerning a debit card agreement.

33 Electronic Signature Law, 2001, Sec 1.

sage bearing a "certified" electronic signature can be considered to satisfy the writing requirement (assuming that the transaction in question is not one of those excluded from the application of this law as noted above).

b. Requirements for Secure Electronic Signature:

(1) The electronic signature is unique to the owner of the Signing Device (a Signing Device is "unique software, a unique object or unique information required for producing a secure Electronic Signature");

(2) The electronic signature allows apparent identification of the owner of the Signing Device;

(3) The electronic signature has been created using a Signing Device that is under the sole control of the owner of the Signing Device; and

(4) The electronic signature allows any change to the electronic message subsequent to signing to be detected.[34]

An Electronic Message signed with a Secure Electronic Signature is admissible in any legal proceeding as prima facie evidence that (a) the signature is that of the owner of the Signing Device, and (b) that the Electronic Message is the one that was signed by the owner of the Signing Device.

As a matter of evidence, a printout or any other output of an Electronic Message signed with a Secure Electronic Signature is granted the status of an original of the Electronic Message, rather than that of a copy, for the purpose of any legal proceeding, except for those specifically excluded in the law.

c. Requirements for a Certified Electronic Signature:

(1) It must be a Secure Electronic Signature. There is a presumption in the Law that every Certified Electronic Signature is a Secure Electronic Signature;

(2) The Signing Device used to produce the electronic signature has been verified by a Certification Authority, which is an entity, registered under the provisions of the law, which issues the electronic certification. [35]

d. Certification Authorities

The Electronic Signature Law imposes certain conditions on entities wishing to be accredited as a Certification Authority. The task of certifying an electronic signature has been entrusted to private commercial enterprises rather than any public body. The most salient conditions are:

(1) The Certification Authority must be a resident of Israel or a corporation incorporated in Israel, the purposes of which include that of acting as a

34 Electronic Signature Law, 2001, Sec 1.

35 Electronic Signature Law 2, 2001, Sec 1.

Certification Authority. A foreign Certification Authority may be registered if it fulfils similar requirements in their country of incorporation;

(2) It must utilize reliable hardware and software systems that offer sufficient protection from interruption, disruption and damage to computers and to data.;

(3) It must carry adequate third-party liability insurance;

(4) It must be registered with the Registrar of Certification Authorities. The Law has conferred upon the Registrar extensive powers of search and seizure;[36] and

(4) The Certification Authority's database of Electronic Certificates must be registered as a database in accordance with the provisions of the Protection of Privacy Law.[37]

36 See, Y. Herman "The Electronic Signature Law", URL: <http://www.interlaw.co.il/arutzim/Main.asp?id=20&page=Art&Sec=83>.

37 Section 11(4) of the Electronic Signature Law, 5761-2001.

JAPAN

by
Haig Oghigian and Toru Yamada
Jones Day Reavis & Pogue

A. SOURCES OF LAW

1. Introduction

Japan's legal system is based on civil (or Continental, code based) law. Its legislature is called the Diet. Most legislation is drafted by bureaucrats of various Ministries and other governmental agencies and is submitted by the Cabinet to the Diet, although key bills are sometimes prepared by members of the Diet. Each bill is submitted to either the House of Representatives (the Lower House) or the House of Councillors (the Upper House). Each House has various committees, and a bill is submitted to a committee that has jurisdiction over it. Members of the committee review and, if necessary, revise the bill, and if the bill is then passed by that committee, it is reported to a plenary sitting of the House. If the bill is approved with necessary affirmative votes at the plenary sitting, it is forwarded to the other House. After approvals have been obtained from both Houses, the bill is submitted through the Cabinet to the Emperor and promulgated to the people of Japan.[1]

2. The Constitution

Japan has a written Constitution, which has not been amended since its adoption in 1946. The Constitution is the supreme law of Japan, and no law or regulation contrary to the provisions of the Constitution has legal force or validity.[2]

In the Constitution, the Emperor is characterised as the symbol of the state and does not have powers related to government. Powers related to government are divided among the central government and local governments and, within the central government, further divided among the Diet, the Cabinet and the courts, to which the legislative power, the executive power and the judicial power are delegated respectively.

---

1 See: <http://www.shugiin.go.jp/itdb_main.nsf/html/index_e_guide.htm>.

2 Article 98 of the Constitution.

3. The Courts

Japan has five levels of courts: the Supreme Court, the High Court, the District Court, the Family Court, and the Summary Court. The District Court deals with general civil and criminal disputes, while the Family Court has exclusive jurisdiction over family related disputes (such as divorce and succession). The Summary Court has jurisdiction over civil claims with a disputed amount of not more than JPY 900,000 and criminal cases of certain misdemeanours. Generally, the Patent Office, under the jurisdiction of the High Court, makes decisions over patent and intellectual property disputes but in certain cases these disputes are heard in the District Court, Family Court, or Summary Court.

The Supreme Court is comprised of fifteen judges appointed by the Cabinet. The Supreme Court has three Petty Benches (each of which consists of five judges) and one Grand Bench (consisting of fifteen judges). Most of the cases appealed from the High Court are examined before one of the Petty Benches, but a matter involving an issue of the Constitution or requiring a change to a precedent of the Supreme Court is decided by the Grand Bench.

There are eight High Courts located in major cities in Japan, and several High Courts have one or two branch offices in their jurisdictions. Decisions by the High Court are made by a bench of three judges.

The other three kinds of courts (District, Family and Summary) sit in the capital city of each urban and rural prefecture, with several branch offices in their jurisdictions. Decisions by these courts are usually made by a single judge, although significant cases brought before the District and Family Courts may be heard before a bench of three judges.

All judges other than those of the Supreme Court are appointed by the Cabinet from a list of persons nominated by the Supreme Court.

The average length of a court proceeding is about 20 months, with complicated cases taking longer. Since an appeal to the Supreme Court is relatively easy to file for irreconcilable parties, one should anticipate that an appeal might take more than two years to reach final judgment.

4. Sources of Japanese Law

The Diet has the exclusive power to enact laws consistent with the Constitution. All laws enacted by the Diet are promulgated by the Emperor, and published in the Official Gazette ("*Kampou*"). The Japanese texts of current laws are available on the Japanese government website.[3] The Cabinet may conclude treaties with other states but it must obtain approval of the Diet. Treaties concluded by the Cabinet have priority over laws enacted by the Diet in the application process.

---

3 See: <http://law.e-gov.go.jp/cgi-bin/idxsearch.cgi>.

Assemblies of local governments (prefectures, cities, towns and villages) may establish local regulations to the extent permissible under the Constitution and the laws of Japan.

For the purposes of enforcing and supplementing the laws, the Cabinet and Ministries issue Cabinet Orders and Ministerial Ordinances, which are also published in the Official Gazette and are available on the Japanese government website.

In addition, in cases in which the Ministry or governmental agency that has jurisdiction over a certain law or regulation intends to provide certain guidance on how such law or regulation should be interpreted, complied with and enforced, it may issue guidelines to the public, or directives (*tsuutatsu*) to government officials. If no guidelines or directives have been issued, it is sometimes necessary for practicing lawyers to contact government officers by phone or meet them in person to seek their unofficial view and practical treatment concerning certain legal issues. Some Ministries and governmental agencies have recently adopted a system of a "no-action letter", under which parties who would be affected by how the Ministry or agency interprets and enforces a certain law or regulation may seek an official opinion of the Ministry or agency on whether and how the law or regulation should apply to a certain transaction or situation that they may encounter. Although these guidelines, directives, and unofficial or official views of the government are not laws in the literal sense, in practice they are as important as published laws and regulations.

The courts have the authority to render official and conclusive interpretations of the laws and regulations, and court precedents (judgments and decisions by the Supreme Court, in particular) are respected as such. However, not all judgments and decisions are made public. Selection and publication are at the discretion of the Supreme Court or the publishing companies.

With respect to legal issues which have no precedent, commentaries or treatises written by academics (professors of top-level Japanese universities, in particular) have some authoritative value. If there is a common view broadly shared among academics on a certain legal issue, it is highly unlikely that a court would render a different opinion.

5. The Legal Profession

The total number of lawyers (*bengoshi*) qualified to practice in Japan is about 19,000 as of 2002.[4] Due to the recent change of the national bar examination and the new legal education system to be introduced in 2004, the number of lawyers is expected to increase by three to five times in the near future. Most *bengoshi* are sole practitioners, and their services are mainly focused on litigation. Recently, however, larger-sized law firms have appeared in order to respond to an increasing demand of legal services, especially in the field of general corporate matters.

---

4 See: <http://www/nichibenren.or.jp/en/about/index.html>.

Every *bengoshi* is required to be a member of a local bar association where the law office is located as well as of the Japan Federation of Bar Associations (JFBA),[5] which consists of 52 local bar associations. Each bar association and the JFBA is managed by *bengoshi* themselves, and has the power to take disciplinary action against its members.

Lawyers qualified to practice in a foreign jurisdiction may be registered with a local bar association and the JFBA as a foreign legal adviser, or *gaikokuho-jimu-bengoshi*, if certain requirements are satisfied. As *Gaikokuho-jimu-bengoshi* may not give legal advice regarding Japanese legal issues, major U.S. or U.K. law firms have merged their offices with Japanese *bengoshi* in Japan, in order to render comprehensive legal services.

B. ONLINE BUSINESS REGULATIONS

1. Overview of IT Strategies in Japan

The current government of Japan has emphasized the importance of its policies in handling the IT revolution. In July 2000, it created the IT Strategy Council and the Strategic Headquarters of Information and Telecommunications in the Cabinet, and the IT Basic Strategy was adopted by the Council. The Basic Law on the Formation of an Advanced Information and Telecommunications Network Society (Law No. 144 of 2000) was passed in the Diet in November 2000.

The Strategic Headquarters of Information and Telecommunications was reorganised in January 2001[6] and renamed the Strategic Headquarters for the Promotion of an Advanced Information and Telecommunications Network Society (IT Strategic Headquarters). The IT Strategic Headquarters adopted the "e-Japan Strategy" and the "e-Japan Priority Policy Program," in order to make Japan the most advanced IT nation within five years. The IT Strategic Headquarters issued the e-Japan 2002 Program in June 2001 to enable each office and ministry to reflect such Strategy and Policy Program in the fiscal year 2002.[7] In June 2002, the IT Strategic Headquarters revisited the e-Japan Priority Policy Program and reissued it as a new program called the "e-Japan Priority Policy Program—2002," in order to expedite the goals described in the e-Japan Strategy.

The IT Basic Law, the "e-Japan Strategy" and "e-Japan Priority Policy Program" all focus on the following five areas:

- Formation of the World's Most Advanced Information and Telecommunications Networks;

5 See: <http://www.nichibenren.or.jp/en/index.html>.

6 The IT Strategic Headquarters consist of the members of the Cabinet, a university professor, CEOs/ presidents of financial institutions, electronic device manufacturers, telecommunications service providers, etc.

7 See: <http://www.kantei.go.jp/foreign/it/network/0626_e.html>.

- Promotion of Education/Learning and Human Resources Development;
- Facilitation of Electronic Commerce;
- Digitisation of the Administration and Utilization of IT in Other Public Areas; and
- Ensuring the Security and Reliability over Advanced Information and Telecommunications Networks.

2. IT Basic Law

The IT Basic Law provides guidelines for adopting and implementing specific policies, gives a statutory basis for the formation of the IT Strategic Headquarters, and outlines the responsibility of the IT Strategic Headquarters to issue a priority policy program.

Under the IT Basic Law, an "Advanced Information and Telecommunications Network Society" is defined as a society where creative and energetic development is enabled by obtaining, commonly possessing and transmitting various information or knowledge freely and safely on a global scale through the Internet or other advanced information and telecommunications networks.[8] The central government is obligated to take legal, financial or other measures necessary to carry out policies regarding the formation of an Advanced Information and Telecommunications Network Society.

Although the IT Basic Law does not purport to directly regulate online business, it gives express statutory grounds for the formation of a necessary legal framework to promote electronic commerce in Japan by the Cabinet and related ministries.

3. Laws Concerning Formation of the World's Most Advanced Information and Telecommunications Networks

The Ministry of Public Management, Home Affairs, Posts and Telecommunications (MPHPT), which supervises and controls the telecommunications industry, has supported this effort with the following legislation:

- Amendment to Telecommunications Business Law (Law No. 62 of 2001);
- Amendment to Provisional Measures Law for Telecommunications Infrastructure Improvement (Law No. 43 of 2001);
- Law Concerning Promotion of Development of Communication/Broadcast Fusion Technology (Law No. 44 of 2001);
- Amendment to Radio Law (Law No. 48 of 2001); and
- Broadcast Utilising Telecommunications Services Law (Law No. 85 of 2001).

---

8 The Basic Law on the Formation of an Advanced Information and Telecommunications Network Society (Law No. 144 of 2000), Article 2.

4. Laws Concerning the Digitisation of the Administration and the Use of IT in Other Public Areas

The goal of digitisation is one of convenience in handling civic matters. This would indirectly benefit business activities because certificates of registry or licenses issued by governmental agencies, such as a certified copy of residential registry, are required in various phases, e.g., when establishing a company or entering into certain bank transactions. However, because such advancement implies an increased risk of unintended leakage of personal data and improper handling or use of personal data by government officials, the need for an appropriate security system and strict handling regulations is recognised. Numerous laws have, therefore, been amended, for example:

- The Amendment to Basic Residential Registers Law (Law No. 133 of 1999) is intended to build the "Basic Residential Registers Network System," whereby all municipalities and prefectures are linked with one another and the central and local governments can share information on residents based on residential card codes.
- The Amendment to Road Traffic Law (Law No. 51 of 2001) has enabled drivers who have not violated traffic regulations for a certain period to apply for renewal of their driving license anywhere in Japan.

The central government is planning to introduce "e-Government" in 2003, making it possible to use the Internet to apply for government permits, licenses or approvals, or to file tax returns.

5. Laws Concerning Ensuring the Security and Reliability over Advanced Information and Telecommunications Networks

Along with constructing computer networks, appropriate measures have been taken to protect information from unauthorized access and to ensure the reliability, availability, serviceability, integrity and security (RASIS) of the networks. Technological improvements are required in terms of hardware as well as software, to enhance RASIS. The following enactments play a supportive role by making certain acts subject to criminal sanctions:

- The Law on Unauthorized Computer Access (Law No. 128 of 1999) prohibits any person from (1) using another person's ID or password without such other person's consent; (2) attacking security holes and intruding into a computer system; or (3) encouraging unauthorized access by a third party. (According to the National Police Agency (NPA), during the first half of 2002, 42 persons (in 27 cases) were arrested for violation of this Law, which shows an increase by 27 persons (14 cases) compared to the same period in 2001.) Most of the cases involve the misuse of an ID and or password.
- The Amendment to the Criminal Code (Law No. 97 of 2001)—In 1987, various provisions in the Criminal Code were amended to make them applicable to cases where criminal acts such as fraud, destruction or illegal production of

a public or private record or obstruction of business are committed by using or changing an electromagnetic (digital) record.

Under these amendments, a person who, without authority, made an electromagnetic record of a credit card or other card used for payment or who used, transferred, leased or imported such card is subject to imprisonment with forced labour for not more than 10 years or a fine in the amount of not more than JPY 1 million. A person who has such a card in his or her possession is liable to imprisonment with forced labour for not more than 5 years or a fine in the amount of not more than JPY 500,000.

6. Laws Concerning Facilitation of Electronic Commerce

Three kinds of facilitating laws have been enacted:

(1) Laws to adapt existing laws to allow efficient communications through the Internet and other digital networks in place of other means of communications. such as the delivery of documents; for example:

- The Comprehensive Amendments to the Laws that Require the Delivery of Documents and the Like to Allow the Employment of Electronic Media ("IT Comprehensive Law") (Law No. 126 of 2000);
- Amendment to the Commercial Code (Law No. 128 of 2001);
- Amendment to the Securities and Exchange Law and Financial Futures Exchange Law (Law No. 96 of 2000); and
- Amendment to the Patent Law, Etc. (Law No. 41 of 1999).

(2) Laws introducing a digital infrastructure to advance a paperless society and to adapt existing laws to this new infrastructure; including:

- Amendment to Commercial Registration Law (Law No. 40 of 2000);
- Law Concerning Electronic Signatures and Certification Services (Law No. 102 of 2000); and
- Law Concerning Book Entry Transfer of Short-Term Bonds, Etc. (Law No. 75 of 2001) (which was amended by Law No. 65 of 2002, which came into effect from January 6 of 2003, with a title change to "Law Concerning Book Entry Transfer of Bonds, Etc.").

(3) Laws to regulate participants in online business and to protect consumers or users from unfair transactional activities:[9]

- Amendments to the Unfair Competition Prevention Law (Law No. 33 of 1999 and Law No. 81 of 2001);

9 Amendment to the Antique Dealings Act recently passed the Diet for the purpose of regulating Internet auction businesses, under which Internet auction brokers are required to report their names, addresses, method of auction, etc. to the Public Safety Commission.

- Law Concerning Exceptions to the Civil Code Related to Electronic Consumer Contract and Electronic Notice of Acceptance ("Electronic Contract Law") (Law No. 95 of 2001);
- Law on Restrictions on the Liability for Damages of Specified Telecommunications Service Providers and the Right to Demand Disclosure of Identity Information of the Sender (Law No. 137 of 2001);
- Amendment to Specified Commercial Transaction Law (Law No. 28 of 2002);
- Law Concerning Optimisation, Etc. of Transmission of Specified Electronic Mail (Law No. 26 of 2002); and
- Amendments to the Copyright Law (Law No. 86 of 1997; Law No. 77 of 1999).

C. ELECTRONIC TRANSACTIONS AND CONTRACT FORMATION

1. Introduction

Under Japanese law, a contract is formed when two parties declare their intentions to form a contract. Intentions are established by one party's offer and the other's acceptance. In principle, the offer and the acceptance may be made in writing (including through a website or by e-mail) or orally, but in practice, most business contracts are prepared in writing and executed by signatures or seals.[10] In addition, some types of contracts, such as employment or consumer contracts, require delivery of certain documentation prior to their formation.

This section illustrates the legislative adaptation of the existing legal framework concerning contract formation to the new online environment.

2. Timing of Contract Formation—Electronic Contract Law

According to the general principle in the Civil Code of Japan,[11] a contract inter absentees (where the offeror and the offeree do not face each other) comes into effect at the time when the offeree's notice of acceptance is despatched. This principle was adopted more than one hundred years ago (when the common

---

10 In Japan, if a person's seal is affixed on a legal document, even if the person's signature does not appear on the document, the document is presumed to have been executed by that person and to reflect that person's intention, unless this presumption is disproved by other evidence. Therefore, business contracts are usually executed by seals of the parties. In the case of the party being a Japanese company, the seal reported to and registered with the Legal Affairs Bureau is used for that purpose. (Under the Commercial Registry Law, at least one of the representatives of a company is required to report to the Legal Affairs Bureau the seal he or she uses in his or her capacity as the representative, and the seal impression is registered with the Legal Affairs Bureau, which, at the representative's request, issues a certificate of the seal impression.) In practice, one party often requests the other party to execute a contract by affixing the reported seal of its representative and to submit a certificate of the seal impression issued by the Legal Affairs Bureau.

11 Art. 536, para.1. This principle may be modified by the parties' agreement.

method of communication inter absentees was by post or telegraph) in order to accommodate the speedy formation of commercial transactions. However, this reasoning may no longer hold true, since in the present environment of advanced telecommunications, it does not take much time for the offeree's notice to reach the offeror. In addition, since online commerce is trans-national by nature, and because the global standard for contract formation is that a contract is formed when the offeree's notice of acceptance is received by the offeror, it was important to modify the traditional principle to this global standard. Accordingly, in March 2001, the Cabinet submitted the bill of the Electronic Contract Law, which was approved by the Diet in June 2001, and the Law became effective on December 25, 2001. Under the Law, if the offeree's notice of acceptance is made by using any electromagnetic method (including e-mail, facsimile, telex or voice mail), the notice is deemed to have arrived when it becomes possible for the offeror to read or hear it. For example, in the case of e-mail, the notice is deemed to have arrived when it becomes possible for the offeror to get access to the mail server where the e-mail is stored.

3. Electronic Signatures and Certification

The Law Concerning Electronic Signatures and Certification Services (Law No. 102 of 2000) came into force on April 1, 2001. By Article 3 of the Law, a digital document to which a person's electronic signature is attached is presumed to have been duly executed, on the condition that signs or items that are necessary to make the electronic signature are appropriately managed and controlled, and therefore only that person may make the same signature.

A person who receives a digital document with an electronic signature can verify the electronic signature through a certification authority ("CA") that issues an electronic certificate. An electronic certificate is a document with the CA's electronic signature certifying the authenticity of the person's electronic signature.[12]

However, since any person may engage in the business of a CA, in order to inform users of certain objective standards, the Japanese government (Ministry of General Affairs, Ministry of Justice and Ministry of Economy, Trade and Industry) issued a Ministerial Ordinance.[13] If a CA clears the standards under the Ministerial Ordinance, it may apply for an official recognition by the Japanese government by submitting an application form together with supporting documents with one of those three Ministries. Examination of each applicant is con-

---

12 In practice, the public key cryptography method is commonly used in Japan. Under this method, the CA certifies that the public key is owned by the person who executed the relevant document.

13 Ordinance for the Enforcement of the Law concerning Electronic Signatures and Certification Services (issued on March 27, 2001).

ducted by Japan Quality Assurance Organization (JQA), which is licensed as a designated examination institution.[14]

If, as a result of the review by JQA, the applicant is deemed to have satisfied all requirements, it may represent itself as an "Accredited CA," and licensed to use a mark indicating "Accredited under e-Signature Law (Japan)" on its electronic certificate.

An electronic bidding system has been deployed for all public works projects hosted by the Ministry of Land, Infrastructure and Transport since April 21, 2003, and some of those accredited CAs are focusing on business for construction companies.

4. IT Comprehensive Law

By law, a document is required to be delivered to take effect legally. The IT Comprehensive Law was amended to allow for the provision of information by electronic means instead of by physical delivery of the document. The amended laws include:

- Securities and Exchange Law;
- Investment Trust and Investment Corporation Law;
- Investment Advisory Business Law;
- Financial Futures Transaction Law; Insurance Business Law; Asset Securitization Law;
- Act Against Delay in Payment of Subcontract Proceeds, Etc. to Subcontractors;
- Pharmaceutical Affairs Law; Instalment Sales Law; Door-to-Door Sales Law (renamed as Specified Commercial Transaction Law);
- Building Lots and Building Transaction Business Law; and
- Travel Business Law.

For example, in the Investment Advisory Business Law, it is required for an investment adviser to deliver to a client a document stating its name and address, fees, prohibited acts that investment advisers may not conduct, its registration number, the name of the investment analyst, content and method of advice, etc., prior to entering into an investment advisory service contract. With the IT Comprehensive Law, an investment adviser may, in lieu of delivering such a document, transmit such information by sending an e-mail or by delivering a CD-ROM provided, the client agrees to it. It should be noted that the delivery of documentation is still required under those laws, unless the receiver explicitly appears.

---

14 Under the Law, there may be more designated examination institutions, but JQA is the only institution at present (2002). The term of the license as a designated examination institution is five years. JQA is required to conduct the examination in accordance with the guidelines prescribed by the Ministries.

MALAYSIA

by
Michael Raj, Partner
Intellectual Property & Technology Group
Shahrizat Rashid & Lee

A. SOURCES OF LAW AND SYSTEM OF THE COURTS

Malaysia is a multi-racial nation consisting of thirteen states[1] and three Federal Territories[2] forming a federation. Malaysia is a parliamentary democracy headed by a constitutional monarch (called the Yang di Pertuan Agung). Each state is headed by a state ruler and in nine of the thirteen states, the ruler is called the Sultan. Each Sultan by rotation becomes the King for a fixed term of five years.[3] The states of Penang, Malacca, Sabah and Sarawak have Governors. These states were British colonies which were administered directly by the colonial authorities whereas the other states were sultanates under British protection. The government in each state is headed by a Chief Minister, who is an elected member of the State Assembly. The framework of government is determined by two sets of constitutions—the Federal Constitution in respect of the Federation and State Constitutions in respect of the States. These constitutions came into force in their present forms at the grant of independence from Britain in 1957.

Malaysia derives its law pre-dominantly from legislation. Arising from the colonial influence on the country, Malaysia has adopted the English principles of judicial precedence and the rules of equity.

Malaysia is a country with a written constitution ("Federal Constitution") which represents the cornerstone of the legal system. The Federal Constitution is the supreme law of the land and any law which is inconsistent with the Federal Constitution is deemed void to the extent of the inconsistency.

The Federal Constitution encompasses three main concepts.

---

1 Federal Constitution, art. 1 (2).

2 Federal Constitution, art. 1(4), The Federal Territory of Kuala Lumpur, the Federal Territory of Labuan and the Federal Territory of Putrajaya was established under the Constitution (Amendment) Act (No 2) 1973, Constitution (Amendment) (No. 2) Act 1984 and Constitution (Amendment) Act 2001 respectively.

3 Federal Constitution, art. 32(3).

First, an individual has certain fundamental rights, which are entrenched and these rights cannot be encroached upon. The fundamental liberties provided to every citizen in the Federal Constitution are as follows:

- a person shall not be deprived of life or personal liberty save in accordance with the law;[4]
- a person shall not be held in slavery;[5]
- a person shall not be retrospectively punished;[6]
- all persons in Malaysia are equal before the law;[7]
- no citizen shall be banished from Malaysia;[8]
- every citizen has the right to freedom of speech and expression, to assemble peacefully and the right to form associations subject to any restrictions imposed by Parliament in the interest of national security;[9]
- every person has the right to practice his own religion;[10]
- with respect to education, no person is to be discriminated on the grounds of race, religion, descent or place of birth;[11]
- no person shall be deprived of property except in accordance with law.[12]

Second, sovereign power in Malaysia is distributed between the Federation and the States. The State is supreme in matters relating to the individual state and the Federation is supreme in matters, which concern the country as a whole. The respective sovereign jurisdictions of the Federation and the State is laid out in the lists to the Federal Constitution.

Third, no one body is entitled to exercise supreme power. Power is distributed between the Executive, the Legislature and the Judiciary.

1. The Legislature

The legislature in Malaysia is bicameral and consists of a lower house called the Dewan Rakyat (House of Representatives) and an upper house called the Dewan Negara (Senate). The members of the Dewan Rakyat are elected by the public and hold office for a term of five years whilst the members of the Dewan Negara

4 Federal Constitution, art. 5.
5 Federal Constitution, art. 6.
6 Federal Constitution, art. 7.
7 Federal Constitution, art. 8.
8 Federal Constitution, art. 9.
9 Federal Constitution, art. 10.
10 Federal Constitution, art. 11.
11 Federal Constitution, art. 12.
12 Federal Constitution, art. 13.

are appointed by the Yang di Pertuan Agung[13] (the King) and the State Legislative Assemblies. The thirteen individual states possess its own state constitutions. It is by virtue of these state constitutions that the State Legislative Assemblies are established.

2. The Executive

The Executive consists of the Yang di Pertuan Agung, the Prime Minister and his Cabinet, the Civil Service and has the responsibilities of implementing the laws, maintaining order and administering foreign and international policies. The head of the Executive is the Yang di Pertuan Agung who acts upon the advice of the Cabinet.[14]

3. Judiciary and Laws

The Judiciary is independent and determines legal and factual questions in accordance with the laws of the country.

Legislation forms the main body of law in Malaysia. Legislative powers are distributed between the Federation and the State Legislative Assemblies. The matters which are to be legislated by Parliament are contained in the Federal List and include (amongst others) matters relating to external affairs of the country, defence of the Federation, internal security, criminal and civil law procedure and matters pertaining to finance. Those matters which are to be legislated upon by the State Legislative Assemblies are contained in the State Lists and include land matters, local administration of municipal corporations, local government services and state works and water.

Acts of Parliament are applicable to the whole Federation and in addition have extra-territorial effect.[15] The legislature of the State can only make laws, which are applicable to that particular State or part of the State.[16] Whenever there is an inconsistency between the State law and Federal law, the State law is deemed void to the extent of the inconsistency.[17] Parliament may however delegate its powers to legislate to the State Legislative Assemblies subject to certain conditions or restrictions.[18]

Rules and regulations which are enacted under powers which have been conferred by Parliament or the State Legislative Assemblies have the force of law.

Section 3 of the Civil Law Act 1956 allows for the importation of English Law principles, rules of equity and statutes of general application in so far as it ap-

13 Federal Constitution, art. 45.

14 Federal Constitution, art. 40.

15 Federal Constitution, art. 73 (a).

16 Federal Constitution, art. 73 (b).

17 Federal Constitution, art. 75.

18 Federal Constitution, art. 76A.

plies to local circumstances. However the dates of reception of the law differ in West and East Malaysia. East Malaysia consists of the States of Sabah and Sarawak. In West Malaysia the courts will apply the common law and the rules of Equity as administered in England on April 7, 1956. In the state of Sabah the courts will apply the common law, rules of equity and statutes of general application as in force in England on December 1, 1951 and in the state of Sarawak, the courts will apply the common law rules, rules of equity and statutes of general application in force in England on December 12, 1949. In commercial transactions, in the absence of local law, English law is imported by nine states in Malaysia as in force on April 7, 1956. Any laws applied in England after these dates are only of persuasive authority.

Malaysia being previously under the British rule has inherited the doctrine of judicial precedents. Judges are bound by ratio decidendi of earlier cases from superior courts.

The national religion of Malaysia is Islam[19] and as such Islamic law constitutes a source of law applicable to persons professing the religion of Islam. Islamic law is administered by the Syariah Court. The natives of the states of Sabah and Sarawak have native laws applicable only to the natives in those states.

4. The System of the Courts in Malaysia

The Court Structure In Malaysia

Federal Court

- High Court of Malaya
  - Sessions Court
    - Magistrates Court
- High Court of Sabah and Sarawak
  - Sessions Court
    - Magistrates Court

a. Federal Court

The highest court in the country is the Federal Court. Apart from possessing appellate jurisdiction, as the highest court of appeal in the land, it has exclusive jurisdiction to:

(i) determine the validity of any laws made by Parliament or by the Legislature of any State;

19 Federal Constitution, art. 3(1).

(ii) adjudicate on disputes between the States or between the state and the Federation; and

(iii) deal with issues pertaining to provisions of the Federal Constitution.[20]

The Federal Court is also possessed of advisory jurisdiction and the Yang-di Pertuan Agung may refer to the Federal Court any question with reference to any provisions of the Federal Constitution.[21]

b. Court of Appeal

The Court of Appeal was created in 1994.[22] It consists of ten judges and the President. It has the appellate jurisdiction to hear both civil and criminal appeals from any judgement given by the High Court.

c. High Courts

There are two High Courts in Malaysia of co-ordinate jurisdiction[23] the High Court of Malaya and the High Court of Sabah and Sarawak. The High Court judges have the jurisdiction to hear both civil and criminal cases. The High Court has original[24] as well as appellate jurisdiction.

d. Subordinate Courts

The majority of cases are dispensed with by the Subordinate Courts. Three subordinate courts were created by the Subordinate Courts Act 1948: the Sessions Court, the Magistrates Court and the Penghulus Court. The Penghulus Court deals with very minor offences punishable with a maximum fine of RM25. The Sessions Court however, is vested with extensive power. It has the criminal jurisdiction to try all offences other than those punishable by death[25] and may pass any sentence other than the death penalty.[26] The civil jurisdiction of the Sessions Court is provided in section 65 of the Subordinate Courts Act 1948:

(a) unlimited jurisdiction to try all actions and suits of a civil nature in respect of motor vehicle accidents, landlord and tenant and distress, and

(b) jurisdiction to try all other actions and suits of a civil nature where the amount in dispute or the value of the subject matter does not exceed two hundred and fifty thousand ringgit.

---

20 Federal Constitution, art. 128(2).

21 Federal Constitution, art. 130.

22 Constitution (Amendment) Act 1994.

23 Federal Constitution, art. 121.

24 Original jurisdiction refers to proceedings, which are required by law to be commenced in that court. For example in Malaysia, divorce proceedings and child custody cases originate in the High Court as the Subordinate Courts do have jurisdiction to deal with such matters.

25 Subordinate Courts Act 1948, s 63.

26 Subordinate Courts Act 1948, s 64.

The Magistrates Courts in Malaysia have both civil as well as criminal jurisdiction. There are two classes of Magistrates prescribed under the Subordinate Courts Act 1948, the First Class Magistrate and the Second Class Magistrate. A First Class magistrate has the jurisdiction to try all offences which imposes a penalty of a maximum term of ten years imprisonment or those which are only punishable with a fine.[27] A Second Class Magistrate has the jurisdiction to try all offences where the punishment imposed by law is imprisonment for a maximum term of twelve months or those offences punishable with a fine only.[28]

A First Class Magistrate has the civil jurisdiction to hear all actions where the disputed amount does not exceed RM25,000.[29] A Second Class Magistrate has jurisdiction to hear all actions where the amount in dispute does not exceed RM3,000. The Magistrates Court also has appellate jurisdiction to hear appeals from the Penghulus Court.

e. Alternative Dispute Agencies

Apart from the formal courts there are tribunals which have been set up pursuant to various Federal Legislation to settle disputes as to subject matters governed or regulated by such statutes. One such tribunal is the Industrial Court, an established feature in Malaysia and deals with disputes concerning employers and employees.

B. SCHEME OF ONLINE BUSINESS REGULATION

Malaysia has a host of legislation relating to the regulation of business. The following statutes were enacted to specifically govern online business transactions in Malaysia:

(1) Telemedicine Act 1997;

(2) Digital Signatures Act 1997;

(3) Communications and Multimedia Act 1998;

(4) Computer Crimes Act 1997; and

(5) The Copyright (Amendment) Act 1997.

1. Telemedicine Act 1997

Advancement of information technology has made it possible for healthcare to be offered online and over long distances Malaysia is one of the few countries that has telemedicine legislation. The practice of medicine in this manner is beneficial especially to those living in rural areas who do not have access to such services. The Telemedicine Act 1997 provides for the regulation of telemedicine

---

27 Subordinate Courts Act 1948, s 85.

28 Subordinate Courts Act 1948, s 88.

29 Subordinate Courts Act 1948, s 90.

and connected matters. Telemedicine means "the practice of medicine using audio, visual and data communications."[30]

The Act regulates practitioners of telemedicine. A person who wishes to practise telemedicine must be a fully registered medical practitioner who has a valid practising certificate.[31] If that practitioner is licensed outside Malaysia he or she must obtain a certificate to practise Telemedicine from the Malaysian Medical Council.[32] However before a practitioner practises Telemedicine, he or she must obtain the consent in writing of the patient.[33]

In order for the consent to be valid the patient must be informed of the following:

(i) he may withdraw his consent at any time;[34]

(ii the benefits, risk and consequences of the practice of telemedicine;[35]

(iii) that doctor-patient confidentiality exists;[36] and

(iv) that any information used, or uncovered in the course of the treatment may not be used by any other person without the consent of the patient.[37]

The Act also regulates the practice of telemedicine on a minor or a person with mental disability. The consent in this instance must be given by his next friend or guardian ad idem.[38]

Under the Telemedicine Act 1997, the term "practice of medicine" is of uncertain scope. Does it extend to persons selling medication over the internet or to a doctor who attempts to diagnose over the telephone? The definition of telemedicine extends to the practice of medicine using audio, visual and data methods, therefore a diagnosis over the telephone would logically be covered. The Act attempts to guarantee the privacy of patient information . In the traditional face-to-face doctor-patient relationship, the relationship is based on mutual trust and confidence. Where the practice of medicine is conducted using the Internet or other telephony services, third parties such as the network and service providers are involved in the transmission of information and therefore there is always a possibility of interception and patients' confidential information falling into unauthorised hands. The Act does not impose any requirement to obtain a specific licence to conduct such a practice (except where the service

30 Telemedicine Act 1997, s 2.

31 Telemedicine Act 1997, s 3.

32 Telemedicine Act 1997, s 4.

33 Telemedicine Act 1997, s 5(1).

34 Telemedicine Act 1997, s 5(2)a.

35 Telemedicine Act 1997, s 5(2)a.

36 Telemedicine Act 1997, s 5(2)c.

37 Telemedicine Act 1997, s 5(2)d.

38 Telemedicine Act 1997, s 5(5).

is provided from a place outside Malaysia) and neither does it provide any regulations in relation to duties or taxes.

2. Digital Signature Act 1997

The Digital Signatures Act 1997 came into force in on the October 1, 1998, making Malaysia one of the first Asian countries to implement such legislation. The Act is a manifestation of Malaysia's commitment to step into the digital era. It was enacted to promote electronic transactions and to prevent the perpetration of fraud in online business transactions.

The Act addresses three main parties involved in the digital signature certification procedure: the subscriber,[39] the recipient,[40] and the certification authority.[41]

A document which has been signed by the use of a digital signature is valid and binding legally as a document which has been signed with "a hand written signature, an affixed thumb print or any other mark."[42]

The Act provides the framework for the licensing of the Certification Authorities. The Act imposes a penalty on conviction of a fine not exceeding RM500,000 ringgit or imprisonment for a maximum term of ten years or both on those persons who operate (or represent themselves as operating) a certification authority without a licence issued by the Controller of Certification Authorities.[43] The Controller of Certification Authorities, who was first appointed on October 1, 1998, has the responsibility of monitoring and overseeing the activities of the certification authorities.

The Act provides for the establishment of certification authorities which have the duty of issuing certificates and verifying digital signatures. A certificate can only be issued upon the satisfaction of certain requirements under the Act.[44]

3. Communications and Multimedia Act 1998

The Communications and Multimedia Act 1998 came into force on April 1, 1999 and was enacted to regulate the communications and multimedia industries.

---

39 Section 2 of the Digital Signature Act defines a "subscriber" to mean a person who
a) is the subject listed in a certificate
b) accepts the certificate; and
c) hold a private key which corresponds to a public key listed in that certificate.

40 Digital Signature Act 1997, s 2 defines a recipient to mean "a person who receives or has a digital signature and is in a position to rely on it."

41 Digital Signature Act 1997, s 2 defines a certification authority as to mean a person who issues a certificate.

42 Digital Signature Act 1997, s 62(2).

43 Digital Signature Act 1997, s 4(2).

44 Digital Signature Act 1997.

One of the objectives the Act seeks to achieve is to promote the national policy objectives for communications and multimedia. The Government seeks to make Malaysia a regional hub for communications, multimedia information and content service industries. It also seeks to promote the use of the Internet as a primary medium of communication and as such the Act provides that none of the provisions of the Act shall be construed as permitting censorship on the Internet.[45]

The Malaysian Communications and Multimedia Commission was set up to regulate communications and multimedia sectors and to promote national policy objectives for the communications and multimedia industries,[46] to act as an advisor to the Minister responsible for Energy Water and Communications and to implement the laws in relation to communications and multimedia. The Commission is also responsible for the regulatory framework for telecommunications, broadcasting and electronic commerce. As a regulatory body, the functions of the Commission are:

(1) to encourage competition in the communications and multimedia industries in order to prevent anti-competitive conduct. The Commission is also concerned with the development of access codes, standards and licensing.

(2) The Commission has appointed SIRIM Berhad as the certifying agency beginning April 1, 1999. The function of SIRIM is to ensure compliance of technical standards in relation to the provisions of the Communications and Multimedia Act 1998. The management and maintenance of the integrated electronic database is soon to be the responsibility of MIMOS Berhad.

(3) The Commission also seeks to protect the rights of the consumer of communications services.

4. Computer Crimes Act 1997

Information technology and increasing use of the Internet results in the borderless exchange of ideas, information and technology. As such it is essential for Malaysia, a country seeking to achieve the status of a leader in the area of communications and multimedia in the region, to have legislation which seeks to protect the rights and privacy of computer users. The Computer Crimes Act is one of three Acts passed in 1997, which provides a legal framework for the converging communications, multimedia and broadcasting industries. The Act came into force on June 1, 2000 and provides for offences relating to the misuse of computers. There are four main offences created under sections 3, 4, 5 and 6 of this Act: unauthorised access to computer material (commonly referred to as the "hacking offence"); unauthorised access to computer material with the intention of committing or facilitating the commission of a further offence (commonly termed as the "ulterior intent offence"); unauthorised modification of the con-

45 Communications and Multimedia Act 1998, s 3(3).

46 Communications and Multimedia Act 1998, s 3(2).

tents of any computer; and wrongful communication of a code, password or number. The Act also makes it an offence to attempt or abet the commission of any of the offences punishable under this Act.[47]

The Computer Crimes Act creates a statutory presumption that any person who has in his custody or possession any programs or data which he or she is not authorised to have is presumed to have gained unauthorised access in order to procure the same[48] unless he or she is able to prove otherwise.

The provisions of this Act apply to any person regardless of nationality and have effect outside as well as within Malaysia.[49]

5. Copyright (Amendment) Act 1997

The Copyright (Amendment) Act amended the Copyright Act 1987 and came into effect on April 1, 1999. The amended Act makes the unauthorised transmission of works over the Internet an infringement of copyright.

The amended Act has created three new offences:

(i) circumventing or causing any other person to circumvent any effective technological measures that are used by authors in connection with the exercise of their rights under the Act;[50]

(ii) removal or alteration of any electronic rights management information without authority;[51] or

(iii) distributing, importing for distribution or communicating to the public, without authority, works or copies of works knowing that electronic rights management information has been removed or altered without authority.[52]

The commission of any of these offences is punishable on conviction by a maximum fine of RM250,000 or imprisonment for a maximum term of three years or both and for the commission of a subsequent offence, a fine not exceeding RM500,000 ringgit or imprisonment for a term not exceeding five years or both.[53]

The object of the amendments is to provide sufficient protection of intellectual property rights for companies involved in the information technology and multimedia industries.

---

47 Computer Crimes Act 1997, s 7.

48 Computer Crimes Act 1997, s 8.

49 Computer Crimes Act 1997, s 9.

50 Copyright Act 1987, s 41(1)H.

51 Copyright Act 1987, s 41(1)I.

52 Copyright Act 1987, s 41(1)J .

53 Copyright Act 1987, s 41(1)(iii).

C. ELECTRONIC TRANSACTIONS AND CONTRACT FORMATION

Various challenges are posed to the Malaysian legal and regulatory landscape as the nation moves forward into a computer networked environment where the Internet is a tool for commerce. The launch of the Multimedia Super Corridor ("MSC") in 1996 marked the nation's first major step into the information age. As transactions rapidly shift from traditional paper-based means into instantaneous methods of transacting, many of the objectives of the law remain the same. Nevertheless, the law at times falls short of meeting its goals when applied to electronic transactions. Hence, the emergence of new issues under Malaysian contract law will in turn require the exploration of possible solutions to these challenges and the formation of a workable and enforceable framework.

1. Malaysian Law of Contract

The applicability and suitability of existing legal principles in Malaysia vis-à-vis electronic contracts calls for serious examination. The law of contract in Malaysia is governed by the Contracts Act 1950 and the principles are largely derived from English common law and principles of equity. The Contracts Act 1950 is based on the Indian Contracts Act 1872, which itself is a codification of the English common law.

The Contracts Act 1950, which is not a comprehensive statute, does not make any provision for the online environment. The Government of Malaysia has in early 2004 announced its intention of tabling the Electronic Transactions Bill to regulate online commercial transactions. The underlying elements of a valid contract: offer, acceptance and consideration, now raise new concerns when the transaction is consummated in cyberspace.

a. The Validity of Internet Contracts—Offer and Acceptance

An enforceable contract is formed upon an offer being made and clearly and unequivocally accepted. Clearly, in tandem with this would be the furnishing of consideration and the intention of the parties to create legal relations. The last two elements do not pose any difficulties with regard to electronic contacts.

The definition of offer and acceptance is notably different from that used in English law. Section 2(a) of the Contracts Act 1950 provides that "when one person signifies to another his willingness to do or to abstain from doing anything, with a view to obtaining the assent of that other to act or abstinence, he is said to make a proposal"; and "when the person to whom the proposal is made signifies his assent thereto, the proposal is said to be accepted; a proposal, when accepted, becomes a promise."[54]

54 Contracts Act 1950, s 2(b).

The Act labels the person making the proposal as the "promisor" whilst the person accepting the proposal is the "promisee."[55] Hence, what the common law defines as an "offer" is analogous to a "proposal" under section 2 of the Malaysian Contracts Act 1950. The principles of contract law in Malaysia are, nevertheless, quite similar to those under the common law.

Section 2(d) of the Contracts Act 1950 deals with the element of consideration and reads as follows:

> when, at the desire of the promisor, the promisee or any other person has done or has abstained from doing, or does or abstains from doing, something, such as an act of abstinence or promise is called a consideration for the promise.

Section 2(h) of the Contracts Act 1950 goes on to state that a contract is "an agreement enforceable by law" and section 10 provides that "an agreement must be made with the free consent of the parties competent to contract for a lawful consideration and with lawful object." The applicability of the provisions of the Contracts Act 1950 with regard to ascertaining when an offer and acceptance takes place in an online contract is examined next.

b. Offer or Invitation to Treat

The question then arises whether an electronic merchant's offer on a particular website is an offer made to the world at large, *i.e.*, to every person who accesses his site or whether he is merely inviting offers from the public. Advertisements on the websites would, under the Malaysian Contracts Act 1950, be deemed to be proposals and the e-merchants, promisors.[56]

As long as it is the electronic merchant's intention to be contractually bound upon receiving a response in relation to the advertisement, the advertisement on the website will constitute an offer. To hold otherwise would imply that there would never be a contract until the electronic merchant agrees to the offer made by each and every potential purchaser and that the electronic merchant is required to inform each potential purchaser of his intention to perform the contract in order to ensure that there is an enforceable contract. If this is the case, then the advertisement should clearly stipulate that a response from the visitor of the site (the potential customer) constitutes an offer and not the advertisement on the website itself. The test is one of intention.

---

55 Contracts Act 1950, s 2(c).

56 Contracts Act 1950, s 2(a).

c. Communication of Proposal[57]

The applicability of the postal rule,[58] where acceptance takes place at the point of posting, in Malaysia is evidenced in section 4(2) of the Contracts Act 1950.[59] Once an offer is made, the other party is to communicate either his acceptance or rejection. This applies as well to Internet offers and acceptances. The question that surfaces next is whether Malaysian courts will hold electronic mail as instantaneous communication or whether the postal rule would apply.

It is suggested that the provisions in section 4(2) of the Contracts Act 1950 should be applied to online mail. In a Malaysian context, the advertisements by electronic merchants on the website would amount to a proposal and upon the proposal being accepted, the electronic merchants would then become promisors. The communication of an acceptance is complete as against the proposer when it is put in the course of transmission to him, so as to be out of the power of the acceptor,[60] and as against the acceptor, when it comes to the knowledge of the proposer.[61]

Hence, the validity and enforcement of all communication of proposals, acceptances and revocation would be determined in accordance with these rules. Again, however, we await judicial decisions to determine whether the Malaysian courts will view acceptance via e-mail to be analogous to the postal rule or that it, in particular with reference to the click-through mode of acceptance, resembles that of instantaneous communication.

d. Terms of the Contract

The general principle is that once a party has signed a document, he is bound by those terms even if he has not read the terms, applies in Malaysia.[62] Under a transaction via the Internet that uses the "click-wrap" mechanism to draw the customer's attention to the terms and conditions of the contract set out in the dialogue box, the customer is to scroll down the terms in the dialogue box. He may or may not have read or "signed" the agreement, but upon clicking the

---

57 Contracts Act 1950, s 3 provides:

> the communication of proposals, the acceptance of proposals, and the revocation of proposals and acceptances, respectively are deemed to be made by any act or omission of the party proposing, accepting or revoking, by which he intends to communicate the proposal, acceptance or revocation, or which has the effect of communicating it.

58 It must be within the parties' contemplation that the post be utilised for their communication.

59 Contracts Act 1950, s 4(2) reads:

> The communication of an acceptance is complete—
>
> (a) as against the proposer, when it is put in the course of a transmission to him, so as to be out of the power of the acceptor; and
>
> (b) as against the acceptor, when it comes to the knowledge of the proposer.Refer also to the case of *Ignatius v. Bell* [1913] 2 FMSLR 115.

60 Contracts Act 1950, s 4(2)(a).

61 Contracts Act 1950, s 4(2)(b).

62 *Polygram Records Sdn Bhd v. Search & Anor* [1994] 3 MLJ 127.

"OK" or "I Submit" button, he is deemed to have read and will be bound by those terms and cannot allege non est factum. It may be useful to note that section 7(b) of the Contracts Act 1950 provides that. acceptance may be expressed in a manner prescribed by the offeror.

Certain transactions in Malaysia require the inclusion of specific terms and conditions in the contract itself. For instance, Regulation 11(1) of the Housing Developers (Control and Licensing) Regulations 1989 provides that every contract for the sale and purchase of a housing accommodation together with the subdivisional portion of land appurtenant shall be in the form prescribed in Schedules G of the Housing Developers (Control and Licensing) Act 1966 and where the contract of sale is for the sale and purchase of a housing accommodation in a subdivided building, it shall be in the form prescribed by Schedule H of the Housing Developers (Control and Licensing) Act. The Regulations to the Hire Purchase Act 1967 also stipulate that the terms and conditions set out in the relevant schedules of the Regulations must be incorporated into the hire purchase contract.

In the event contracts of this nature (*i.e.*, where the law requires specific terms and conditions to be incorporated into the contract) are conducted over the Internet, then these mandatory terms and conditions must be included in the Online contract.

e. Contractual Capacity

Section 11 of the Contracts Act 1950 states that "every person is competent to contract who is of the age of majority according to the law to which he is subject, and who is of sound mind, and is not disqualified from contracting by any law to which he is subject'.

In Internet contracts, the verification of the identity or capacity of the contracting party is difficult. Contracts, unknown to the merchant, may be entered into with minors.[63] Under the Contracts Act 1950, minors are deemed incompetent to enter into contracts save for necessaries. Hence, electronic merchants will not be able to recover any monies when they enter into transactions with minors and the contract is subsequently found to be void; whilst minors may be able to recover the purchase price from the vendor.

2. Admissibility of Electronic Records and Computer-Generated Records as Evidence

The Evidence Act of 1950 (Act 56) governs the law of evidence in Malaysia. Prior to the amendments to the Evidence Act 1950 in 1993, the traditional legal doctrines, *i.e.*, the "best evidence" rule and the rule against hearsay, prevailed over the admissibility of data found in documents generated by or stored in a

63 The Age of Majority Act 1971 states that a person attain the age of majority at 18.

computer. Only documents authored by a human were recognised to have any legal effect and the party behind the creation of the document would be required to testify as a witness and give evidence as to the facts contained in the said documents. These traditional rules enabled only original documents to be put forth as evidence[64] and precluded documents stored in a computer from being tendered as evidence. Where forms or replies were automatically generated and usually unsigned, the admissibility of that document was uncertain.

The new sections 90A, 90B and 90C were inserted by the Evidence (Amendment) Act 1993 (Act A851) with the objective of addressing the issue of the admissibility of electronic records and computer generated documents. Section 90A in particular was inserted "to bring the "best evidence rule" up to date with the realities of the electronic age."[65] Pursuant to sections 90A to 90C, evidence in the form of electronic data stored in computers that produce or retrieve information, CD-ROM and magnetic diskettes are no longer hearsay and may now be tendered as evidence of any fact stated therein provided that the document was produced by the computer in the course of ordinary use[66] and this may be proven by a certificate to that effect signed by the person normally responsible for the management and operation of the computer.[67] The purpose of the certificate,[68] which is tendered to the court, is to establish that the computer was in good working order at the relevant time, was operating properly in all respects and therefore no reason exists to doubt or suspect the truth or reliability of the output. No certificate, however, would be necessary if the person in charge of the system himself is called to testify in court.[69]

It would appear that in Malaysia the onus of proving the reliability of the computer-generated document lies upon the proponent who intends to admit the computer-generated document as evidence. It is recommended that the common law principle of omnia praesumuntur rite esse acta[70] which is used in criminal law be used to simplify the rule regarding the admissibility of computer evidence.

---

64 The Evidence Act 1950, s 62 provides that a computer print-out is primary evidence.

65 Mahadev Shankar J in *Gnanasegaran a/l Pararajasingam v. Public Prosecutor* [1997] 3 MLJ 1.

66 Evidence (Amendment) Act 1993, s 90A(1).

67 Evidence (Amendment) Act 1993, s 90A(2).

68 The Malaysian case of *Standard Chartered Bank v. Mukah Singh* [1996] 3 MLJ 240 held that a certificate would only be required when the admissibility of the computer evidence is contested. There has not been a local case yet to determine whether a voir-dire will be held should the issue be contested.

69 *Gnanasegaran a/l Pararajasingam v. Public Prosecutor* [1997] 3 MLJ 1.

70 Lord Stephen in *Castle v. Cross* [1984] 1 WLR 1372 stated that "... in the absence of evidence to the contrary, the court will presume that (mechanical instruments) were in order at the material time."

Section 90B[71] further provides guidelines on estimating the weight to be attached to the document or statement admitted by virtue of section 90A. Hence, once a computer-generated document is admitted as evidence, the weight to be attached to such document would have to be ascertained by the courts.

Section 3 of the Evidence Act 1950 defines the word "computer" as "any device for recording, storing, processing, retrieving, or producing any information or other matter, or for performing any one or more of those function, by whatever name or description such device is called." This definition, however, differs somewhat from the definition in the Computer Crimes Act 1997 (Act 563)[72] and may possibly invoke debate as to whether the definitions require reconciliation. In any event, even if a document is said not to have been generated by a "computer" under the definition contained in the Computer Crimes Act 1997, it is submitted that such documents would still be admissible under the Evidence Act 1950 as amended once it satisfies the definition therein. Further, Section 90C provides, inter alia, that the provisions of section 90A shall prevail and have full force notwithstanding anything inconsistent contained in any other provision in the Act, or in the Bankers' Books (Evidence) Act 1949, or in any provision of any written law relating to the certification, production or extraction of documents in any rule of law or practice relating to the production, admission or proof of evidence in any criminal or civil proceeding.

The word "document" in the Evidence Act 1950[73] has been amended as well and is now defined as:

> any matter expressed or described or howsoever represented, upon any substance, material, thing or article, including any matter embodied in a disc, tape, film, sound track or other device whatsoever, by means of:
>
> (a) letters, figures, marks, symbols, signs, or other forms of expression, description, or representation whatsoever;
>
> (b) any visual recording (whether of still or moving images);

---

71 The section states:

> In estimating the weight, if any, to be attached to a document, or a statement contained in a document admitted by virtue of section 90A, the court:
>
> (a) may draw any reasonable inference from the circumstances relating to the document or the statement, including the manner and purpose of its creation, or its accuracy or otherwise;
>
> (b) shall have regard to:
>
> (i) the interval of time between the occurrence of existence of the facts stated in the document or statement, and the supply of the relevant information or matter into the computer; and
>
> (ii) whether or not the person who supplies, or any person concerned with the supply of, such information or the custody of the document, or the document containing the statement, had any incentive to conceal or misrepresent all or any of the facts stated in the document or statement.

72 "Computer" under the Computer Crimes Act 1997 means an electronic, magnetic, optical, electrochemical, or other data processing device, or a group of such interconnected or related devices, performing logical, arithmetic, storage and display functions, and includes any data storage facility or communications facility directly related to or operating in conjunction with such device or group of such interconnected or related devices, but does not include an automated typewriter or typesetter, or a portable hand held calculator or other device which is non-programmable or which does not contain any data storage facility.

73 The same section also provides illustrations on the definition of "document" which, inter alia, states that "a matter recorded, stored, processed, retrieved or produced by a computer is a document."

(c) any sound recording, or any electronic, magnetic, mechanical or other recording whatsoever and howsoever made, or any sounds, electronic impulses, or other data whatsoever;

(d) a recording, or transmission, over a distance of any matter by any, or any combination of the means mentioned in paragraph (a), (b) or (c),

or, by more than one of those means mentioned in paragraphs (a), (b), (c) or (d), intended to be used or which may be used for the purpose of expressing, describing or howsoever representing, that matter."

It is interesting to note that the Malaysian courts in a recent case[74] referred to material on a website when adjudicating the case.[75]

3. Interpretation Act 1948-1967

The Interpretation Act 1948-1967 defines "writing" to include "typewriting, printing, lithography, photography, electronic storage or transmission or any other method of recording information or fixing information in a form capable of being preserved." Hence, applying this definition of "writing" in tandem with the definition of "document" under the Evidence Act 1950, it is clear that electronic records will be deemed as documents in writing.

Section 62A of the Interpretation Act was inserted in 1997 and applies to all statutes in force or revised after 1967. This section provides that where under any written law any information is required or permitted to be given, kept or maintained, and where no means is specified, such information may be given, kept or maintained by electronic means and on electronic medium if firstly, the identity of the person giving the information or the source of any information given by such means is capable of being determined or verified; and secondly, if sufficient precautionary measures have been applied to prevent unauthorised access to any information recorded or fixed by such means or medium. According to this definition, the process of discovery of documents that are in electronic form may be effected in civil litigation.

4. Companies Act 1965

The introduction of section 358A into the Companies Act 1965[76] permitted certain company records and the register to be maintained in an electronic form. This section was inserted by the Companies (Amendment) Act 1992. Reason-

74 *Malaysia Borneo Finance Corp (M) Bhd v. Malayan Produce Co Sdn Bhd & Anor,* [2000] 5 MLJ 352.

75 As per Abdul Malik Ishak J "the website in the internet contains invaluable information that can be tapped at the tip of one's finger and it should be utilised to the core. As I have demonstrated, the website carries the write up about Pengurusan Danaharta Nasional Bhd and it is the best source material of the day."

76 Companies Act 1965, s 358A(1) reads as follows:

> The power conferred on a company by section 358 to keep a register and other records by recording the matter in question otherwise than by making entries in bound books includes the power to keep the register or other record (other than the minute books kept pursuant to Ibid 156) by recording those matters in question otherwise than in legible form, so long as the recording is capable of being produced in a legible form.

able precautions must be taken by the company for guarding against falsification and for facilitating the discovery of any falsification.[77]

The aforementioned statutory provisions, which are by no means exhaustive, illustrate the legislature's recognition of computers as a means of record keeping. At present, there are no statutory requirements that prescribe for records to be kept in an electronic mode and not in the traditional method.

The law, however, mandates that if records are maintained in electronic form, such electronic records must be secure and reasonable precautions should be taken to limit falsification and tampering. Bearing in mind that electronic documents are easily altered without trace, the tendering of such records as evidence in court, must be viewed against the relevant provisions in the Evidence Act 1950.[78]

5. Choice of Law

Electronic commercial transactions have led to a global market place, doing away with traditional geographical boundaries and the necessity for physical attendance of parties. Conflicts in commercial relationships arise in light of the many different customs and legal systems brought together on the Internet. Three main uncertainties surface, namely (i) what law governs the contract; (ii) who should hear the case; and (iii) which judgments should be enforced.

The Malaysian courts have traditionally applied principles derived from the English courts when determining the applicable law for a contract and issues arising from it. In line with the fundamental tenet of freedom of contract, parties contracting on an electronic basis may insert a choice of law clause[79] into the contract. Once the parties determine from the outset which law should apply, which court or arbitrator to decide, who shall enforce the judgment and what assets are seizable to secure judgment, the Malaysian courts will enforce this express clause.

An alternative approach to be considered should the parties fail to express the choice of governing law, would be a practical one which is based on an "interests analysis." The choice of law would then be the law of the country which has the closest nexus to and most significant relationship with the subject matter and "where there is a clear preponderance of such factors."[80] These two traditional principles will apply when determining the law governing an online contract.

There is also the "implied choice" doctrine, which occurs in the event the contracting parties do not express the choice of governing law and where "the court will have to find if there is an implied choice, which is the system of law by reference to which the contract was made, and such implied choice is to be inferred

77 Companies Act 1965, s 358(2)(a).

78 *See* s 90A-90C of the Evidence Act 1950 and previous page.

79 *Elf Petroleum SE Asia Pte Ltd v. Winelf Petroleum Sdn Bhd* [1986] 1 MLJ 177.

80 *Elf Petroleum SE Asia Pte Ltd v. Winelf Petroleum Sdn Bhd* [1986] 1 MLJ 177.

from the terms and/or form of contract or surrounding circumstances."[81] Its suitability for application to online contracts is doubtful, bearing in mind that often a number of countries are involved and varying systems of law are in operation in Internet contracts. It would be an arduous task indeed to ascertain what the implied choice of law is.

Malaysia has yet to take any initiative to resolve this pivotal point by adopting a system of uniform customs, trade and practices[82] and ratifying various model law and international conventions. No legislation has been enacted and no judicial policy has emerged either to resolve this point and to enhance clarity and uniformity of electronic contracts in the international environment.

6. Jurisdiction of Malaysian Courts

A choice of law clause does not oust the jurisdiction of Malaysian courts. A Malaysian party may still seek to enforce an online contract with a foreign party in a Malaysian court provided that any one of the requirements in section 23(1) of the Courts of Judicature Act 1964[83] is met. This section provides extra-territorial jurisdiction to the High Court in cases where foreigners are sued as co-defendants with local residents.[84]

Under Order 11 rule (1) of the Rules of the High Court 1980,[85] the local courts will have extra-territorial jurisdiction over absent or overseas defendants if the defendant is "carrying on a business within the jurisdiction" of the court. Local

---

81 Peh Swee Chin FCJ in *James Capel (Far East) Ltd v. YK Fung Securities Sdn Bhd* [1996] 2 MLJ 1997.

82 For eg the UNIDROIT Principles of International Commercial Contracts issued by the International Institute for the Unification of Private Laws in 1994 and UNCITRAL (United Nations Commission on International Trade Laws) Model Law on Electronic Commerce.

83 Malaysian Courts Judicature Act 1964, s 23 reads as follows:

> Subject to the limitations contained in Article 128 of the Constitution, every High Court shall have jurisdiction to try all civil proceedings—
>
> (a) where the cause of action arose within the local jurisdiction of the court; or
>
> (b) where the defendants or one of the several defendants resides or has his place of business within the local jurisdiction of the court or;
>
> (c) where the facts on which the proceedings are based exist or are alleged to have occurred within the local jurisdiction of the court; or
>
> (d) where any land the ownership of which is disputed is situated within the local jurisdiction of the court.

84 Tan Sri Dato' Mohd Azmi J in *Bank Bumiputra Malaysia Bhd v. International Tin Council & Anor* [1989] 2 CLJ 961. See also Rule 11 of the Rules of the High Court 1980 which widens the jurisdiction of the court beyond the confines of Rule 23 of the Malaysian Courts of Judicature Act 1964 and gives the court the discretionary jurisdiction to allow for process of the court to be served outside it territorial jurisdiction.

85 Order 11 rule 1(1) of the Rules of the High Court 1980 provides that—

> Where a writ does not contain any claim for damage, loss of life or personal injury arising out of—
>
> (i) a collision between ships, or
>
> (ii) the carrying out or omission to carry out a manoeuvre in the case of one or more of two ships; or

case law has held that where the business was carried on is a question of mixed law and fact.[86] In line with English case law, Malaysian courts have taken the approach that the phrase "carry on" implies repetition or a series of acts. Business operated over the Internet making offers to Malaysians would therefore be deemed to be carrying on a business in Malaysia.

7. Enforceability of Foreign Jurisdiction in Malaysia

The enforceability of a foreign judgment in Malaysia and vice versa is governed by the Reciprocal Enforcement of Judgments Act 1958, which is modeled upon the UK Foreign Judgments (Reciprocal Enforcement) Act 1932. Under this Act, only the monetary judgments of the superior courts of countries specified in the Act are enforceable in Malaysia by way of summary procedure.[87] Presently, only the United Kingdom, Hong Kong, India and Singapore are specified. The monetary judgments from the superior courts of all other countries may only be enforced by way of a suit of the judgment. No other similar reciprocal enforcement of judgment agreement has been entered into by Malaysia with any other ASEAN country or any other country.

Arbitration awards, however, will be recognized and enforced by the local courts, as the Arbitration Act 1952[88] does not distinguish domestic from foreign arbitration awards.

The introduction of cyberlaws by legislation and the ongoing amendments to existing legislation is testimony to Malaysia's recognition of the pivotal and pervasive role electronic commerce will play in the future. The versatility, power and frequency of cyberspace contracting will undoubtedly only increase and become standard practice. The law must keep pace with these technological advancements. The amendments and alteration to the existing legislation has thus far been piecemeal in nature. There is no specific statute to date in Malaysia which addresses electronic contracts and their enforceability nor any law to regulate the system or processes required when storing electronic records. Instead, the

---

(iii) non-compliance on the part of one or more of two or more ships, with the collision regulations made under section 251 of the Merchant Shipping Ordinance 1952;

service of notice by writ out of jurisdiction is permissible with the leave of Court in the following cases, that is to say—

(a) if an action begun by the writ is sought against a person domiciled or ordinarily resident or carrying on business within the jurisdiction.

86 Serjen Jemuri CJ (Borneo) in *Arab Malaysian Finance Bhd v. Meridien International Credit Corporation Ltd London* [1993] 3 MLJ 193.

87 Reciprocal Enforcement of Judgments Act 1958, s 3 of the lays down the conditions on which a foreign judgment can be registered:

(a) the judgment must have been that of a superior court of a country to which the Act applies, and not an appeal from a subordinate court;

(b) the judgment must be for a fixed sum of money not being a sum in respect of taxes, or a fine or other penalty; and

(c) the judgment must be "final and conclusive" as between the parties thereto.

88 See section 27 of the Arbitration Act 1952.

law governing electronic contracts consists of various statutes (eg, Digital Signatures Act 1997, Computer Crimes Act 1997, Evidence Act 1950, Contracts Act 1950, Communications and Multimedia Act 1998) read together with general common law principles.

8. Digital Signatures Act 1997

Signatures have been used in paper transactions for centuries. A signature on a document is, among other things, proof of its authenticity. The key aspect of a signature is that only one person is capable of producing it and others are able to verify it.

In order to adapt signature requirements to online commerce, the formal requirements in law need to be updated accordingly. In Malaysia, this requirement is met with the passing of the Digital Signatures Act 1997, which was modeled after the State of Utah of the United States of America Digital Signatures Act. The Malaysian Act establishes a framework for the use of digital signatures for online transactions by Malaysians and those conducting online business with Malaysians. The Act spans the entire range of issues associated with the legal effects of digital signatures, the legal framework for the implementation and operation of a public key infrastructure and the establishment of a regulatory body to oversee and give effect to the provisions of the Act.

The Malaysian Digital Signatures Act is technology specific and recognizes only one form of digital signature technology, namely the asymmetric cryptosystem or Private Key-Public Key Cryptography. It does not provide for, nor anticipate, any other means of electronic authentication such as biometrics and dynamic signature analysis, which some believe will take on equal or even greater importance in the years ahead.

By ignoring other authentication mechanisms and focusing instead on the use of digital signatures for online transactions, the Digital Signatures Act leaves issues raised by other authentication techniques for a later time. The Act, by providing for only one authentication, runs the risk of stunting the development of other authentication methods.

a. The Framework

The Malaysian Digital Signatures Act is regulated by the Ministry of Energy, Water and Communications. The Malaysian Communications and Multimedia Commission is pursuant to the Digital Signatures Act vested with powers and responsibilities include the monitoring and overseeing of the activities of certification authorities,[89] issuing licences to the certification authorities,[90]

89 Digital Signatures Act 1997, s 3(1).

90 Digital Signatures Act 1997, s 8.

maintaining a publicly accessible database of the certification authorities[91] and publishing a list of recognized repositories[92] and date/time stamp service providers.[93] The Commission exercises its powers under the Digital Signatures Act subject to directions by the Minister based on general policy.[94]

The Digital Signatures Act does not provide for a hierarchical structure comprising a web of certification authorities linked together to create a chain of trust where the Commission, as the regulating certification authority, would sit at the root of the structure and issue certificates to one level of certification authorities directly below it whereupon these certification authorities could issue certificates to the next level of certification authorities below them. In that type of structure, the process of verifying the certificates of each certification authority could then be traced up to the regulating authority, which would in effect reduce the licensing function of the Commission and create more certification authorities to undertake that function. Instead, the Malaysian Digital Signatures Act exercises tight control over the digital signature framework wherein the Commission does not act as a certification authority but as the regulating entity and sole body that issues licences to,[95] regulates and controls the certification authorities. The Digital Signatures Act does not provide for licensing of other certification authorities by a certification authority and limits the certification authority's function to the issuance of certificates to subscribers,[96] which are then published in a recognized repository.[97]

The qualification requirements for licensing of certification authorities are prescribed by the Commission[98] under the Digital Signature Regulations 1998. The Act provides that only a trustworthy system must be used by the subscribers and certification authorities[99] and the approved scheme prescribed under the regulations[100] is the public key cryptosystem. The certification authorities are audited for compliance with the Act,[101] the result of which is published by the Commission in the disclosure records,[102] which he maintains for that certification authority.

Under the Digital Signatures Act only licensed certification authorities are allowed to carry on the business of a certification authority.[103] A certification authority that operates without a licence commits an offence under the Digital

91 Digital Signatures Act 1997, s 3(6).

92 Digital Signatures Act 1997, s 68.

93 Digital Signatures Act 1997, s 70.

94 Digital Signatures Act 1997, s 3(4).

95 Digital Signatures Act 1997, s 8.

96 Digital Signatures Act 1997, s 6(1).

97 Digital Signatures Act 1997, s 30.

98 Digital Signatures Act 1997, s 5.

99 Digital Signatures Act 1997, s 27.

100 Digital Signature Regulations 1998, Regulations 28 and 29.

101 Digital Signatures Act 1997, s 20, with exemptions under section 21.

102 Digital Signatures Act 1997, s 20(4).

103 Digital Signatures Act 1997, s 4(1).

Signatures Act[104] and is liable, on conviction, to a fine of RM500,000 or a maximum imprisonment term of 10 years, or both. The Minister may, however, exempt the licensing requirements under the Act to certification authorities within an organization where the certificate and key pairs are for internal use by its members only, or to others that the Minister considers fit.[105]

The first certification authority in Malaysia, Digicert Sdn Bhd, was established in August 1998 and is a joint venture between Pos Malaysia Bhd and MIMOS Bhd. At the time of writing, Malaysia has two other licensed certification authorities, namely, MSC Trustgate.com Sdn Bhd and Bank Negara Malaysia.[106]

There is no specific provision under the Digital Signatures Act for either the Commission or the certification authority to keep the subscriber's private keys in escrow for law enforcement, key recovery services or other purposes. The Act may, however, have facilitated or anticipated this by providing that if a certification authority holds the private key then it would hold it as a fiduciary of the subscriber and may use it only with the subscriber's prior written approval.[107]

b. Validity of Digital Signatures

Four aspects of a digitally signed message are guaranteed, namely its authenticity, integrity, privacy/confidentiality and non-repudiation. The integrity of a message would be enhanced with time/date stamping as it would allow the recipient to verify when the message was actually created and sent.[108] This service is especially useful when a signer's key has been revoked and the recipient needs to prove that the signature was affixed when its certificate is still valid.

The most elemental objective of any electronic authentication legislation is to ensure that electronic signatures are accorded the appropriate legal recognition. Malaysian laws require that certain types of documents are signed or are to be in writing, and a handwritten signature is required by law for such transactions as conveyances of real property, formation of wills, affirmation of affidavits and signing of contracts prescribed by statute. The Digital Signatures Act modifies existing laws with respect to signature requirements and clarifies the effect and legal validity of electronic signatures through the provisions under of Part V of the Act.

This Part V of the Digital Signatures Act provides that where a rule of law requires a signature or provides for certain consequences in the absence of a signature, that rule shall be satisfied by a digital signature which is verified by the public key listed in a valid certificate issued by a licensed certification authority, which was

---

104 Digital Signatures Act 1997, s 4(2).

105 Digital Signatures Act 1997, s 4(3).

106 Bank Negara Malaysia has a restricted license for transactions under the Real Time Electronic Transfer of Funds and Securities (RENTAS)—see section 15 of the Act for the Commission's powers to issue restricted licenses.

107 Digital Signatures Act 1997, s 45.

108 Digital Signatures Act 1997, s 67(d) provides this presumption in adjudicating disputes. See s 70 of the Act for recognition of date/time stamping services by the Commission.

affixed by the signer with intent and which the recipient has no knowledge or notice that the signer has breached a duty as a subscriber or does not rightfully hold the private key used to affix the digital signature.[109] Notwithstanding any written law to the contrary, a digital signature created in accordance with the Act shall be deemed to be a legally binding signature[110] and a digitally signed document shall be as legally binding as a document signed with a handwritten signature, an affixed thumbprint or any other mark.[111]

The Digital Signatures Act defines a message as a digital representation of information.[112] A message that bears a digital signature which is verified by a public key issued by a licensed certification authority and is valid at the time that it was created shall be as valid, enforceable and effective as if it had been written on paper.[113] A copy of that digitally signed message shall be as valid, enforceable and effective as the original message unless it is evident that the signer has designated the digitally signed message to be a unique original in which case only the designated original shall constitute the valid, enforceable and effective message.[114]

Under the Act, a digital signature is authenticated by the certificate that verifies it if the signature was affixed when the certificate was valid.[115] In adjudicating disputes, the court may make certain evidentiary presumptions, namely that the person relying on the digital signature may ascertain and assume the identity of the subscriber and that the signature was affixed with intent once the signature is verified with its corresponding public key. The recipient is also presumed not to have knowledge or notice that the signer has breached any of his duties or does not rightfully hold the private key.[116]

Although the Digital Signatures Act ensures that existing laws do not discriminate against or otherwise discourage the use of electronic signatures, it is important to appreciate that the objective of the Digital Signatures Act is not to override existing laws on signatures but to supplement it for purposes of online transactions. The Act does not preclude the validity of any other forms of signature[117] nor does it preclude any message, document or record from being considered written or to be in writing under other applicable laws.[118]

---

109 Digital Signatures Act 1997, s 62(1).

110 Digital Signatures Act 1997, s 62(2)(b).

111 Digital Signatures Act 1997, s 62(2)(a).

112 Digital Signatures Act 1997, s 2(1).

113 Digital Signatures Act 1997, s 64(1).

114 Digital Signatures Act 1997, s 65.

115 Digital Signatures Act 1997, s 66.

116 Digital Signatures Act 1997, s 67(c).

117 Digital Signatures Act 1997, s 62(3).

118 Digital Signatures Act 1997, s 64(2).

The Digital Signatures Act places strict licensing requirements on certification authorities.[119] The Digital Signatures Act provides that Part 5 of the Act, which accords legal effect and validity to a digital signature, would not apply to digital signatures which are either verified by a certificate issued by exempted certification authorities[120] nor those that cannot be verified by certificates issued by a licensed certification authority.[121] In any other case, however, unless the parties expressly provide otherwise by contract, the licensing requirements under the Digital Signatures Act will not affect the effectiveness, enforceability or validity of any digital signature.[122] This could mean that although an unlicensed certification authority would be prosecuted for operation without a licence, the digital signatures verified by certificates issued by it would still be valid at law.

However, the validity of certificates issued before a certification authority's license is revoked, surrendered or expires are not affected.[123] The Digital Signatures Act allows the Commission to appoint another licensed certification authority to take over such certificates and the certificates shall be deemed to have been issued by that other certification authority.[124]

c. Risks and Reliance Limits

The Digital Signatures Act specifies that, unless otherwise provided for by law or contract, the recipient of a digital signature assumes the risk that the digital signature is forged if his reliance on it is unreasonable under the circumstances.[125] The risk of loss as a result of fraud or forgery is, however, shifted to the subscriber because the subscriber represents to all recipients that he holds the private key corresponding with the certificate and that all representations made to the certification authority, including material ones that were not confirmed by the certification authority in issuing the certificate, are true.[126] This means that the recipient may rely on the certificate as holding out that the subscriber rightfully holds the private key corresponding to the certificate and has digitally signed the message. The certification authority merely represents to

119 Digital Signatures Act 1997, s 4(1).

120 Digital Signatures Act 1997, s 4(6).

121 Digital Signatures Act 1997, s 13(2).

122 Digital Signatures Act 1997, s 13(3).

123 Digital Signatures Act 1997, s 12(5).

124 Digital Signatures Act 1997, s 12(6).

125 Digital Signatures Act 1997, s 63(1). Sub-section (2) provides that if the recipient decides not to rely on the digital signature then he shall promptly notify the signer of this fact and the grounds for his determination.

126 Digital Signatures Act 1997, s 38.

those that reasonably rely on the certificates that the information is accurate;[127] and upon publishing the certificate in a repository, that the certificate has been issued to the subscriber.[128]

The subscriber also indemnifies the certification authority for any loss or damage caused by issuing or publishing a certificate that relied on a false representation or a failure to disclose a material fact, if it was made with the intent to deceive the certification authority or a person relying on the certificate or made with negligence.[129] The representations and indemnification made by the subscriber cannot be disclaimed or contractually limited nor can the subscriber obtain indemnity for its effects if the disclaimer, limitation or indemnity restricts liability for misrepresentation against persons reasonably relying on the certificate.[130]

The Digital Signatures Act further protects the certification authority by providing that it shall not be liable for any loss caused by reliance on a false or forged digital signature if the certification authority has complied with the requirements of the Act.[131] The certification authority's liability is further limited to the amount of reliance limit.[132] In any case, the certification authority shall not be liable for punitive or exemplary damages or for damages for pain or suffering.[133] The provision for recommended reliance limits, however, does not apply to exempted[134] or unlicensed[135] certification authorities.

The private key is the personal property of the subscriber who rightfully holds it[136] and is under a duty to exercise reasonable care to retain control of the private key and prevent its disclosure to any unauthorized person(s).[137] To limit the risk of losing private keys, unless otherwise agreed or contracted against to limit or preclude this ability,[138] the certification authority can suspend certificates for not more than forty-eight hours upon request by a person identifying himself as the subscriber or as a person in a position likely to know that the security of the subscriber's private key has been compromised. These persons include the subscriber's agent, business associate, employee or a member of his or her im-

127 Digital Signatures Act 1997, s 36(a).
128 Digital Signatures Act 1997, s 37.
129 Digital Signatures Act 1997, s 41(1).
130 Digital Signatures Act 1997, s 40.
131 Digital Signatures Act 1997, s 61(a).
132 Digital Signatures Act 1997, s 61(b).
133 Digital Signatures Act 1997, s 61(c).
134 Digital Signatures Act 1997, s 4(6).
135 Digital Signatures Act 1997, s 13(1).
136 Digital Signatures Act 1997, s 44.
137 Digital Signatures Act 1997, s 43.
138 Digital Signatures Act 1997, s 50.

mediate family.[139] However, the certification authority must take reasonable measures to check the identity of the requester. The Commission or the court may also suspend the certificate for 48 hours upon request by any of the persons where the requester represents that the certification authority is unavailable for suspending the certificate.[140]

d. Acceptance of Foreign Certificates

The Digital Signatures Act recognizes that conflicting legal and technical requirements in different jurisdictions may make it difficult or impossible to use digital signatures in cross border transactions. To this end, the Digital Signatures Act permits the Commission to recognize other certification authorities that are licensed or authorized by governmental entities outside of Malaysia that satisfy the prescribed requirements.[141] In this case, the provisions for reliance limits and the validity of digital signatures shall apply to certificates issued by those recognized certification authorities.

139 Digital Signatures Act 1997, s 46.

140 Digital Signatures Act 1997, s 47.

141 Digital Signatures Act 1997, s 19 and Regulations 71–76 of the Digital Signature Regulations 1998.

NEW ZEALAND[1]

by
Mary-Anne Borrowdale and Nicholas S. Wood
Chapman Tripp

A. SOURCES OF LAW

1. Introduction

The central components of the New Zealand legal system were inherited from the United Kingdom at the time of settlement, in the early nineteenth century. These components are:

- the Sovereign;
- the Legislature;
- the Judiciary; and
- the Executive.

A significant feature of New Zealand's constitutional life is the "separation of powers," under which tradition each of the branches of government operates independently of the others. Parliament has supreme law-making authority, and it is the role of the courts to apply the legislation to particular circumstances. In reality, the courts in New Zealand are pro-active in developing the common law as a source of rights and obligations.

2. Constitution

New Zealand is a constitutional monarchy. Under New Zealand law, the Queen is Queen of New Zealand, in addition to being Queen of the United Kingdom of Great Britain and Northern Ireland. The "Crown" is Her Majesty Queen Elizabeth II (who for most purposes is represented in New Zealand by a Governor-General), and her responsible ministers.

---

1 This chapter is based on commentary prepared by Mary-Anne Borrowdale (Chapman Tripp), Mark Smith (Duncan Cotterill), Mellisa Fini, James Davies and Carla Gargiulo (Anthony Harper) and previously published by Oceana Publications Inc. in World Online Business Law.

The office of Governor-General is largely ceremonial, although the role embodies certain wide-ranging "reserve powers" that may be called upon in times of parliamentary crisis.

The authority of the Crown is important both from legal and political perspectives. The Sovereign's powers are exercised in New Zealand through her Ministers. Ministers are appointed to specific portfolios (Health, Social Welfare, Tourism, Justice etc) by the Prime Minister. The Prime Minister is the Member of Parliament who commands the support of a majority of the House. In assenting to the passage of new legislation, the Governor-General acts on the advice of the responsible Minister. Theoretically, however, the Governor-General may refuse the royal assent to legislation if he or she sees sufficient reason to dissent. The Governor-General also has powers to dissolve and prorogue Parliament, and to dismiss a government. Although this latter power has been exercised in Australia,[2] it has never been used in New Zealand.

3. Election of Government

New Zealand has a representative government, elected by voters over the age of 18. Until 1996 the government was elected on the "first past the post" system. Under this system, the country was divided into a number of electorates (99 for the 1993 election), each returning one Member of Parliament. Within each electorate, each elector could cast a single vote for their preferred candidate, and the candidate winning the highest number of votes would be declared the MP for that electorate. The party with the most candidates elected to seats in parliament was then invited by the Governor-General to form a government. The life of each parliament was, and remains, fixed at a maximum of three years. In 1996 the first election was held under the MMP (Mixed Member Proportional Representation) system. Each eligible elector now receives two votes, one for the preferred local candidate and one for the party of their choice.

Two political parties are dominant in New Zealand, the National Party and the Labour Party. Historically, these have been the only parties in the last century which have received enough votes to form governments. The current government is a coalition of the Labour Party and the Progressives, which relies on United Future for support in the House.

The system of government is unicameral, Parliament comprising only a House of Representatives with no upper house. In this respect, it differs from both Australia and the United Kingdom. This characteristic is generally thought to derive from the small population in New Zealand (around 4 million). It commonly re-

2 On 11 November 1975 Australia's Governor-General, Sir John Kerr, dismissed Mr. Gough Whitlam as Prime Minister and appointed opposition leader Mr. Malcolm Fraser as caretaker Prime Minister. The Governor-General's decision was the culmination of events in October 1975 when the Senate refused passage of supply bills until Whitlam called an election. He refused to do so. Following three weeks of constitutional crisis, Whitlam was dismissed and Fraser's coalition government subsequently resoundingly elected.

sults in a faster law-making process than in comparable jurisdictions, labelled by a former Prime Minister as "the fastest law in the west": Palmer *Unbridled Power: An Interpretation of New Zealand's Constitution and Government* (Oxford, 2nd ed., 1987 at 139).

New Zealand is a unitary state, and is not divided into federal and state parliaments. Central government has pre-eminent law-making authority. Elected local councils have recently been given wider powers to make regulations for the administration of their discrete areas, but the councils are still ultimately subject to the central government.

New Zealand lacks a written constitution, which has in recent years been a source of controversy. It does not have a single entrenched legislative instrument that details the powers, duties and obligations of the separate arms of government. However, it does have other documents which are treated as important constitutional sources, including the Treaty of Waitangi (1840), by which the Crown entered into certain pacts with the indigenous Maori population.

4. The Courts

The hierarchy of courts has four tiers, being: in ascending order of importance, the District Court, the High Court, the Court of Appeal and the Supreme Court.

All criminal matters, and most civil disputes, are commenced in the District Court. District Courts are located in all cities, and in many of the smaller towns. Important matters are often transferred from the District Court to the High Court, or are simply commenced in the High Court. Local Disputes Tribunals deal with more minor matters, where the disputed sum is less than $7,500. The specialist Environment Court, Family Court and Youth Court are divisions of, or equivalent to, the District Court.

The High Court sits permanently in the main cities (Auckland, Hamilton, Wellington and Christchurch), and travels regularly to smaller centres. It has exclusive jurisdiction in some matters such as patents, trade marks, admiralty cases and claims for damages exceeding $200,000. The High Court regularly hears appeals from the District Court. Of equivalent jurisdiction to the High Court, although with procedures peculiar to it, is the Employment Court.

The Court of Appeal is in most cases the court of final appeal. This court sits in Wellington, and is comprised of seven permanent members. Decisions may be made by a bench of three, five or more judges, depending upon the significance of the case on appeal.

The jurisdictions of the High Court and the Court of Appeal are set out in the Judicature Act 1908. The jurisdiction of the District Court is derived from the District Courts Act 1947.

A further appeal from the Court of Appeal is available by special leave to the Supreme Court, recently established as New Zealand's highest court. The jurisdiction of this court is derived from the Supreme Court Act 2003. The right of appeal to the Judicial Committee of the Privy Council, sitting in London, has now been abolished except for appeals from decisions in which the Court of Appeal hearing was completed before 1 January 2004.

The courts are run in accordance with the District Court Rules and the High Court Rules, which have the status of legislation. Once quite dissimilar, efforts have been made to model the District Court Rules on those pertaining to the High Court. This consistency has, in most respects, now been achieved, although they remain independent sets of rules.

5. Sources of New Zealand Law

New Zealand inherited from England all of that country's law, including legislation, common law and constitutional conventions, as in force in England on 14 January 1840. Until 1856, the Parliament at Westminster legislated for New Zealand, although the Governor of the Colony had some power to make ordinances. In 1856 New Zealand was given limited legislative powers of its own. Finally in 1947 New Zealand accepted full law-making authority within its own dominions.

New Zealand legislation is inspired by a number of sources, often including English precedents. Other Australian, Canadian and even North American models are now used, particularly in the commercial sphere. The Companies Act 1993, for example, is based a Canadian model. And the much-used Fair Trading Act 1986 is based on Australian trade practices legislation. Although New Zealand contract law is substantially derived from English common law, there has been considerable statutory intervention in this area since the 1970's.

Legislation is proposed by a Member of Parliament, and is passed by the House of Representatives after proceeding through three readings. It becomes law after receiving the Governor-General's assent. Information about the workings of government can be found on the parliamentary website: http://www.govt.nz.

Judge-made law is influenced most commonly by precedents from, and developments in, other Commonwealth jurisdictions. English decisions in particular, whilst not binding in New Zealand, are highly persuasive and are often influential. Reference by the courts to other common law jurisdictions is common, with Australian, Canadian, North American and British decisions being frequently cited.

The doctrine of precedent is strong in New Zealand, with like cases being treated alike. None of the New Zealand courts is bound by its own prior decisions, although lower tiers in the hierarchy are bound by precedent decisions of higher courts.

Future legislative and common law developments are investigated by the New Zealand Law Commission, an independent government-funded body charged with the task of reviewing and improving the country's laws. The Law Commission investigates specific areas of law on its own initiative or as suggested by the Minister of Justice, and not infrequently recommends suitable legislative intervention: http://www. lawcom.govt.nz.

Court hearings in New Zealand are adversarial, in contrast to the procedure of many inquisitorial European jurisdictions.

6. The Legal Profession

New Zealand lawyers are admitted as Barristers and Solicitors of the High Court, and have rights of appearance in all courts. In practice, the majority of lawyers work as solicitors for, or as part of, a legal partnership. Most solicitors have an area of speciality, whether it is commercial law, banking, insurance, tax, litigation or construction law. Some practitioners choose to operate as sole practitioners, in which case their practice is usually general in nature. New Zealand also has an independent bar, at which senior litigators practice independently of any law firm. Their instructions must come from a solicitor, rather than from a client directly.

The New Zealand Law Society oversees the activities of all practising lawyers, and receives and investigates complaints about practitioners: see http://www.nz-lawsoc.org.nz. The Rules of Professional Conduct applicable to all members of the profession may be found on the web-site of the Auckland District Law Society, the country's largest district society: http://www.adls.org.nz.

References:

The Laws of New Zealand

New Zealand Law Journal (Butterworths)

Borrowdale A (ed.) *Butterworths Commercial Law in New Zealand* (4th ed., 1999, Butterworths)

Beck A and Borrowdale A *A Guidebook to New Zealand Companies and Securities Law* (7th ed., 2002, CCH)

Burrows J, Finn J and Todd S (eds) *The Law of Contract in New Zealand* (2nd ed., 2002, LexisNexis)

Todd S (ed) *The Law of Torts in New Zealand* (3rd ed., 2001, Brookers)

B. SCHEME OF ONLINE BUSINESS REGULATION

In New Zealand, online business is regulated by statute (Acts), subordinate legislation (Regulations, etc), case law and the international treaties to which New Zealand is a party and is overseen by a relatively few regulatory agencies (including the Commerce Commission). A large number of Acts, many of which pre-date the Information Age, apply to business conducted online. Consumers are protected by the Fair Trading Act 1986, Consumer Guarantees Act 1993, Contractual Remedies Act 1979, Sale of Goods Act 1908 and relevant industry codes of practice. Online content is regulated by the Films, Videos and Publications Classification Act 1993, the Crimes Act 1961 and the general law of defamation. The Privacy Act 1993 applies to the collection of personal information online by both public and private sector bodies. General commercial laws (the Companies Act 1993, Income Tax Act 1994, Goods and Services Tax Act 1985) affect the operation and taxation of New Zealand entities transacting business online.

Relatively little legislation has been specifically developed for application in the online environment but the Electronic Transactions Act 2002 is a notable exception. The Commerce Committee report to Parliament on the Bill observed:

The bill is based on work carried out by the Law Commission. It closely follows both the Model Law on Electronic Commerce issued by the United Nations Commission on International Trade Law (UNCITRAL) in 1996, and the Australian Electronic Transactions Act 1999 (Commonwealth). It seeks to facilitate the use of electronic technology so as to allow New Zealanders to derive the full benefits of this, particularly in the areas of business and government, and to facilitate the delivery of better government services to citizens through e-government. Objectives include the reduction of compliance and transaction costs for business and the general public; the removal of legislative impediments in dealing with the government electronically; the promotion of consistency between New Zealand law and that of our major trading partners, particularly Australia; and the promotion of the development of electronic commerce. In doing so, the bill aims to achieve two specific objectives: to reduce uncertainty around the use of electronic technology; and to permit certain paper based legal requirements, in particular writing, signature and retention and production of documents, to be met using electronic technology.[3] The Law Commission work referred to by the Commerce Committee has included a series of reports examining the application of New Zealand's laws to electronic commerce.[4] As the Commission noted, "the laws which govern electronic commerce will need to be international rather than domestic in their application," so the Commission intends to continue to monitor international developments in commercial law and practice.[5]

---

3 Report of the Commerce Select Committee on the Electronic Transactions Bill (Wellington, 2000) <http://www.clerk.parliament.govt.nz/content/722/cmetb.pdf>.

4 New Zealand Law Commission *Electronic Commerce Part 1: A Guide for the Legal and Business Community* (Report 50); *Electronic Commerce Part 2: A Basic Legal Framework* (Report 58); *Computer Misuse* (Report 54); and *Electronic Commerce Part 3: Remaining Issues* (Report 68), all available at <http://www.lawcom.govt.nz/>.

5 New Zealand Law Commission *Electronic Commerce Part 1: A Guide for the Legal and Business Community* (Report 50), Preface at x.

C. ELECTRONIC TRANSACTIONS AND CONTRACT FORMATION

1. Introduction

As with other areas of law, the challenge posed by electronic commerce is to adapt existing contract law to regulate the new electronic environment. This section gives a brief overview of common law and statutory provisions regarding contract formation as they apply to electronic commerce.

2. Jurisdiction and the Proper Law of the Contract

Where parties from more than one jurisdiction enter into a contract, an issue arises as to which law should govern that contract. Under New Zealand law, a contract is generally governed by the "proper law" of that contract. The proper law is either the system of law by which the parties intended their contract to be governed, or, if no such intention was expressed or can be inferred, the system of law with which the transaction has its closest and most real connection. If the parties expressly select a foreign system of law to govern their contract, the New Zealand courts will generally give effect to that intention provided it is bona fide, legal and not contrary to public policy. If no system of law is selected by the parties and the transaction is most closely connected with New Zealand, New Zealand law will usually apply.

A separate issue from whether New Zealand law governs a contract is whether the New Zealand courts have jurisdiction to hear disputes arising from the contract. In New Zealand, the jurisdiction of a local court to hear a dispute involving a foreign party depends on whether New Zealand law allows that foreign party to be "served" with the New Zealand court documents initiating the proceeding. Service on a foreign party is generally allowed where the relevant contract was made or entered into in New Zealand, was made by or through an agent trading or residing in New Zealand, was to be wholly or partly performed in New Zealand, or was by its terms or by implication to be governed by New Zealand law. The New Zealand court may also generally assume jurisdiction where there has been a breach in New Zealand of any contract, wherever it was made.[6] Even if service may be validly effected out of New Zealand under these circumstances, the New Zealand courts retain a discretion to refuse to hear the dispute if the foreign party can show that the matter might more appropriately be heard in another country.

3. Fundamental Principles in New Zealand Contract Law

In order to establish that a binding contract has been formed under New Zealand law, the following elements must be established:

- the parties intended to create legal relations;

6 Rule 219, High Court Rules.

- one party to the contract made an offer and the other party or parties accepted that offer;
- the promises contained in that contract were made for valuable consideration; and
- all the essential terms of the contract were certain.

These fundamental principles of New Zealand contract law are based on the common law although a number of statutes have amended this (see, for example, the Illegal Contracts Act 1970, Contractual Mistakes Act 1977, Contractual Remedies Act 1979, Contracts (Privity) Act 1982, Sale of Goods Act 1908, Fair Trading Act 1986, Sale of Goods (United Nations Convention) Act 1994, Minors' Contracts Act 1969 and Consumer Guarantees Act 1993). Generally speaking, there is no requirement that contracts be in writing. Generally, the normal principles of law regarding contract formation and enforcement apply to contracts made in the electronic environment.[7]

4. Intention to create legal relations

A lack of intention to create legal relations will mean that a valid contract does not exist. This most often occurs in domestic arrangements but can also occur in commercial agreements where, for example, a "mere puff" is made or an honourable pledge is given.

In recent years, there has been some discussion about whether autonomous contractual interaction performed by computers gives rise to an intention to create legal relations.[8] The New Zealand Law Commission concludes[9] that ". . . if a computer is programmed to make or accept offers in predetermined circumstances then, plainly, an intention to create legal relations exists on the part of the user of the computer". The Commission supports this view by describing pre-programmed computers as electronic agents. The well-developed rules of principal-agent bind the computer's owner or operator to the computer's autonomous communication. Accordingly, the principal is also responsible for communications sent by an incorrectly programmed computer.

The Electronic Transactions Act 2002 has now largely clarified this area. Section 16 of the Act provides that a person may consent to use, provide or accept information in an electronic form. Such consent may be inferred from a person's conduct. It would appear likely that the owner or operator of a computer which

---

7 See, for example, *Databank Systems Limited v. Commissioner of Inland Revenue* [1990] 3 NZLR 385 (PC) and *Corinthian Pharmaceutical Systems Inc v. Lederne Laboratories* 724 F Supp 605 (1989).

8 See, for example, the New Zealand Law Commission, *Electronic Commerce Part One: A Guide for the Legal and Business Community* (Report 50), October 1998, Wellington, New Zealand at paragraphs 55ff.

9 New Zealand Law Commission, *Electronic Commerce Part One: A Guide for the Legal and Business Community* (Report 50), October 1998, Wellington, New Zealand at paragraph 56.

is pre-programmed to communicate acceptance of offers consents to such communication and, accordingly, is bound by it.

5. Offer and Acceptance

The terms "offer" and "acceptance" are judicial shorthand for the sometimes complex interaction which often precedes contract formation. Much of the considerable body of case law detailing when and whether a contract is formed in, say, a battle of forms or exchange of correspondence, is directly applicable to electronic commerce.

a. Offer

An offer is a promise by one party to another indicating the terms on which it is prepared to deal. An offer must be made with the intention that it will be binding as soon as it is accepted. A number of issues affecting those involved in electronic commerce flow from this.

Whether an offer is merely an invitation to treat is important for those involved in electronic commerce, because acceptance of an offer creates a binding contract between the parties whereas purported acceptance of an invitation to treat does not. Electronic traders in New Zealand should, therefore, carefully consider whether they wish to make an invitation to treat or an offer of their goods or services. In determining whether a statement amounts to an offer or an invitation to treat, courts will consider the offeror's intentions. Indications of a willingness to undertake legal liability on defined terms and a sufficiently clear indication of the terms of prospective conduct will be crucial.[10] This is especially so for New Zealand-based electronic merchants who target both the New Zealand and overseas markets. The Vienna Sales Convention, to which New Zealand is a party,[11] applies to, amongst others, non-domestic contracts between parties in different states.[12] Article 14(2) of the Convention provides that a "proposal" addressed to one or more specific persons is an invitation to treat, unless the contrary is clearly indicated by the offeror. Offerors who wish to avoid making a mere invitation to treat should make it clear that they are making an offer. It may be prudent for entities conducting electronic business which wish to rely on New Zealand law to seek appropriate advice concerning the manner in which goods or services are presented on their website.

Under New Zealand's common law any clauses contained in the offer which will limit the offeror's liability to the offeree, need to be sufficiently drawn to the

10 *Morton–Jones v. R B & J R Knight Ltd* [1992] 3 NZLR 582; *Financings Ltd v. Stimson* [1962] 3 All ER 386; and *Biddle v. Bentley* [1967] NZLR 1047.

11 This has force of law in New Zealand through the *Sale of Goods (United Nations Convention) Act* 1994.

12 Vienna Sales Convention, Articles 1 and 2.

offeree's attention before the offeree communicates acceptance.[13] Notice of a limitation or exclusion of liability must be both timely and adequate. The more onerous or unusual the clause, the more the offeror must do to draw the offending clause to the offeree's attention. Lord Denning, in the Interfoto case,[14] is cited as having suggested that the offeree's attention could only be drawn to some clauses by the addition of a sticker of a large red-hand next to the offending clause. Offerors should consider any clauses in their terms and conditions which are particularly onerous or unusual and consider appropriate electronic "red hands" which sufficiently bring the onerous or unusual terms or conditions to the attention of offerees.

b. Acceptance

Acceptance involves the assent by the offeree to the terms of an offer made by the offeror.[15] This is usually express although it may be inferred from the totality of the parties' conduct.[16] The time of acceptance is important because in most cases it will dictate when the contract was made. Common law rules have been developed regarding the time of communication of acceptance of the offer and the offeror's receipt of this communication to answer specific technological developments, for example the telex.[17] No New Zealand court has considered the application of the existing common law to electronic acceptance. Although much will depend on the facts of individual cases, the following observations are made concerning the likely approach of New Zealand courts where acceptance is made electronically by, say, email.

The offer may dictate the manner of acceptance. The offeror is free to stipulate the manner in which acceptance is to be made and the time of contract formation.[18] Compliance by the offeree to the offeror's stipulation will, in most cases, remove doubt as to when and how acceptance may be successfully communicated.

For electronic communications that were made before the Electronic Transactions Act 2002 came into force, application of the postal acceptance rule is un-

13 *Olley v. Marlborough Court Ltd* [1949] 1 All ER 127.

14 *Interfoto Picture Library Ltd v. Stiletto Visual Programmes Ltd* [1988] 1 All ER 348.

15 *Brinkibon Ltd v. Stahag Stahl und Stahlwarenhandelsgesellschaft mbH* [1983] 2 AC 34 at 41 per Lord Wilberforce.

16 J F Burrows et al, *Law of Contract in New Zealand*, 2nd ed., LexisNexis, Wellington, 2002, at paragraph 3.3.1. See also, *Thomson v. Burrows* [1916] NZLR 223 and *Cavallari v. Premier Refrigeration Co Pty Ltd* (1952) 85 CLR 20.

17 *Entores Limited v. Miles Far East Corporation* [1955] 2 QB 327; *Leach Nominees Pty Ltd v. Walter Wright Pty Ltd* [1986] WAR 244.

18 *Compagnie de Commerce et Commission SARL v. Parkinson Stove Co Ltd* [1953] 2 Lloyd's Rep 487; *Holmell Securities Ltd v. Hughes* [1974] 1 All ER 161.

certain. The postal acceptance rule[19] is an exception to the normal rule[20] that acceptance occurs when it is communicated to the offeror. Assuming that the offeror has not indicated an alternative mode of acceptance in his or her offer and the letter containing acceptance is properly stamped and addressed,[21] the postal acceptance rule provides that acceptance of an offer occurs when the letter is posted. Acceptance may occur even though the offeror does not receive the letter.[22]

It is not clear to what extent this rule applies to electronic communication. Some commentators have suggested that the postal acceptance rule will not apply to email sent and received instantaneously (for example, where an internet service provider is not involved).[23] In this case, acceptance would be effective on receipt and not when the message was sent. More difficult questions are involved where the email is not sent and received contemporaneously. The New Zealand Law Commission has described the application of the postal acceptance rule to this type of e-mail transmission as "debatable" and noted that there are strong reasons for the abolition of the rule in New Zealand.[24] The Commission plans to issue a separate discussion paper dealing with, amongst other things, this issue.[25]

One of the Law Commission's strong reasons for the abolition of the postal acceptance rule is that different rules of acceptance apply depending on whether the contract is domestic or international in nature.[26] The different treatment of acceptance of domestic and international contracts is due to New Zealand being a party to the Vienna Sales Convention.[27] This Convention applies to, amongst others, non-domestic contracts between parties in different states.[28] The Convention provides that communication, including communication of an acceptance, reaches the recipient when it is delivered to him or her personally.[29] The

19 *Adams v. Lindsell* (1818) 106 ER 250; *Sommerville v. Rice* (1912) 31 NZLR 370; *J A Redpath & Sons Ltd v. Melville Ford & Co Ltd* [1950] NZLR 362.

20 *Brinkibon Ltd v. Stahag Stahl und Stahlwarenhandelsgesellschaft mbH* [1983] 2 AC 34 at 41 per Lord Wilberforce.

21 *Getreide-Import-Gesellschaft MBH v. Contimar SA Compania Industrial Commercial y Maritima* [1953] 2 All ER 223.

22 *Byrne v. Van Tienhoven* (1880) 5 CPD 344 at 348 per Lindley J.

23 J F Burrows et al, *Law of Contract in New Zealand*, 2nd ed., LexisNexis, Wellington, 2002 at paragraph 3.4.7.

24 New Zealand Law Commission, *Electronic Commerce Part Two: A Guide for the Legal and Business Community* (Report 58), November 1999, Wellington, New Zealand at paragraph 40.

25 *Ibid.*, at paragraph 41.

26 *Ibid.*, at paragraph 40.

27 This has force of law in New Zealand through the *Sale of Goods (United Nations Convention) Act* 1994.

28 Vienna Sales Convention, Articles 1 and 2.

29 Vienna Sales Convention, Article 24.

Convention overrides the postal acceptance rule.[30] Thus, acceptance occurs when it is received by the offeror.

6. Electronic Transactions Act 2002

Since it came into force on 21 November 2003, the Electronic Transactions Act 2002 has clarified this area.[31] The Act provides default rules about the dispatch and receipt of electronic communications, which apply except to the extent that the parties agree otherwise or an Act provides otherwise.[32] As to the time of receipt, the Act provides that an electronic communication is taken to be received when:

(i) in the case of an addressee who has designated an information system for the purpose of receiving electronic communications, at the time the electronic communication enters that information system; or

(ii) in any other case, at the time the electronic communication comes to the attention of the addressee.[33]

As to the place of receipt, the Act provides that an electronic communication is to be taken as received at the place where:

(i) the addressee has its place of business; or

(ii) if the addressee has more than one place of business, the place of business that has the closest relationship to the underlying transaction (or, if there is no such place of business, the addressee's principal place of business); or

(iii) if the addressee has no place of business, the addressee's ordinary place of residence.[34]

The application of these rules, and particularly those relating to the place of receipt, can have important consequences, because New Zealand law generally recognises a contract as being formed at the place where the offeror receives communication of the offeree's acceptance. Accordingly, if application of the default rules determines that New Zealand is where the relevant contract was made, the New Zealand courts will generally have jurisdiction to hear any dispute relating to that contract.

Since it came into force, the Act has meant that the law regarding acceptance of both domestic and international electronic contracts is the same, that is receipt takes place, in most cases, when it is actually received by the offeror.

---

30 Section 5 of the *Sale of Goods (United Nations Convention) Act* 1994 provides that the Convention operates as a code, that is it has effect in place of the common law.

31 The Act contains no transitional provisions, but the usual principle of New Zealand law is that an enactment does not have retrospective effect: section 7, Interpretation Act 1999.

32 Section 9, Electronic Transactions Act 2002.

33 Section 11, Electronic Transactions Act 2002.

34 Section 13, Electronic Transactions Act 2002.

Where a contract is entered into without the parties communicating by, say, meeting or talking over the telephone, it may be difficult to detect whether the other party has the legal capacity to contract. Electronic traders will be most concerned about the enforceability of contracts made with minors. The Minors' Contracts Act 1969 regulates this area of law. In New Zealand, a minor is any person who has not attained 20 years of age. Contracts made with minors over 18 years of age, or with minors who are or have been married, have effect as if the minor were of full age.[35] Where a minor is under 18 years of age, the contract is unenforceable against the minor, but, as a general rule, a court may order the enforcement of the contract if the contract is fair and reasonable.[36]

a. Consideration

Consideration is something of value provided by one party to the contract in exchange for the other's act, forbearance or promise. The New Zealand Law Commission perceives no need for reform of the doctrine of consideration.[37]

> [t]he need to prove the existence of consideration is essentially unaffected by the advent of electronic communication technology, since the latter represents a revolution in how contracts are formed, rather than the substance of contracts. In the Commission's view, the law relating to consideration does not require any reform in order to respond to the challenges posed by electronic commerce.

b. Certainty

If it appears that the true intention of the parties was not to enter into a binding arrangement until and unless certain unsettled terms of their bargain were settled by agreement then no contract can come into existence until such further agreement is made.[38] But where the courts hold that the parties' true intention was to enter into a binding contract then the courts will do their best to construe the documents[39] and other information[40] that are available so as to give effect to the parties' agreement. This law is well established and its application to the elec-

35 Sections 4 and 5, *Minors' Contracts Act* 1969.

36 Section 6, *Minors' Contracts Act* 1969. However, Parliament currently has before it a proposal to amend the Minors' Contracts Act 1969 to provide that a minor—for the purposes of that Act—is anyone under 18, including a married minor. See the Relationships (Statutory References) Bill, clauses 48-51.

37 New Zealand Law Commission, *Electronic Commerce Part One: A Guide for the Legal and Business Community* (Report 50), October 1998, Wellington, New Zealand at paragraph 76 (emphasis in original).

38 *Attorney-General v. Barker Bros Ltd* [1976] 2 NZLR 495 at 498 per Richmond P. On the certainty requirements, see also, generally, Fletcher Challenge Energy Ltd v. Electricity Corporation of New Zealand [2002] 2 NZLR 433 at 444 per Blanchard J.

39 For example, price lists, *Hillas and Co Ltd v. Arcos Ltd* (1932) 147 LT 503.

40 For example, practice in the relevant market and other objective standards, *Andrews v. Colonial Mutual Life Assurance Society Ltd* [1982] 2 NZLR 556 (this case concerned a renewal of a lease at the "then market rental").

tronic environment would not appear to pose many obvious difficulties. This view is supported by the Law Commission.[41]

7. Documenting Contracts in New Zealand

As a general rule, contracts entered into pursuant to New Zealand law do not have to be in writing to be enforceable. There are, however, a number of exceptions to this principle:

(a) dealings involving land, including contracts for the sale of land and contracts involving the mortgage of land;[42]

(b) assignments of copyright;[43]

(c) hire purchase agreements;[44]

(d) contracts involving the provision of credit;[45]

(e) contracts granting a real estate agency;[46]

(f) assignments of debt and things in action;[47] and

(g) deeds.

a. Deeds

Deeds are similar to contracts in that they are promises which are legally enforceable. However, unlike contracts, they do not require consideration to be enforceable. Deeds have a particular form. The Property Law Act 1952 contains express provisions detailing how a deed is to be executed. In brief, section 4 of the Act requires that the party to be bound by the deed must sign the deed and his or her signature must be attested to by at least one witness. The witness must add his or her place of abode and calling or description.[48]

---

41 New Zealand Law Commission, *Electronic Commerce Part One: A Guide for the Legal and Business Community* (Report 50), October 1998, Wellington, New Zealand at paragraph 81.

42 Section 2, *Contracts Enforcement Act* 1956 and section 49A, *Property Law Act* 1952.

43 Section 114, *Copyright Act* 1994.

44 Section 5, *Hire Purchase Act* 1971. (From 1 April 2005, this Act will be replaced by the Credit Contracts and Consumer Finance Act 2003. Disclosure as required by the 2003 Act must be in writing: see section 32.)

45 Section 20, *Credit Contracts Act* 1981. (From 1 April 2005, this Act will be replaced by the Credit Contracts and Consumer Finance Act 2003. Disclosure as required by the 2003 Act must be in writing: see section 32.)

46 Section 62, *Real Estate Agents Act* 1976.

47 Section 130, *Property Law Act* 1952.

48 Section 4(1), Property Law Act 1952.

b. Companies

Contracts and deeds may be entered into by companies.[49] Briefly, a company may enter into a deed where:

(i) two or more directors of the company sign the deed;

(ii) if there is only one director, that director signs the deed before a witness;

(iii) if the company's constitution so provides, one director (or other person or class of person) signs the deed before a witness; or

(iv) one or more attorneys appointed by the company in accordance with the Companies Act 1993 sign the deed.

Where an obligation is required by law to be in writing, it may be entered into on behalf of a company in writing by a person acting under the company's express or implied authority.[50]

The Electronic Transactions Act 2002 provides that a legal requirement that information be in writing is met by information that is in electronic form if the information is readily accessible so as to be suitable for subsequent reference.[51]

c. Electronic signatures

Electronic signatures are now recognised under New Zealand law. Since 21 November 2003, the Electronic Transactions Act 2002 has provided that a legal requirement for a signature (other than a witness's signature) may be met by means of an electronic signature where the electronic signature adequately identifies the signatory and the electronic signature is as reliable as is appropriate given the purpose for which the signature is required.[52]

49 Section 180(1), *Companies Act* 1993.

50 Section 180(1)(b), *Companies Act* 1993.

51 Section 18, Electronic Transactions Act 2002.

52 Section 22(1), Electronic Transactions Act 2002.

REPUBLIC OF THE PHILIPPINES

by
Vicente B. Amador
SyCip Salazar Hernandez & Gatmaitan

A. SOURCES OF LAW

The 1987 Constitution of the Republic of the Philippines maintains the traditional concept of the doctrine of separation of powers. This separation of powers implements checks and balances among the three branches of government—the executive, legislative, and judicial departments. The legislature—consisting of the Senate and the House of Representatives—enacts laws, the courts interpret them, and the executive department implements them.

1. Constitution

The Constitution is the basic and paramount law to which all other laws must conform and to which all persons, including the highest officials of government, must defer. As the paramount law of the land, the Constitution is supreme; any law that conflicts with the Constitution may be declared unconstitutional by the courts.

2. The Courts

The judicial power is vested in one Supreme Court and in such lower courts as may be established by law. Judicial power includes the duty of the courts of justice to settle actual controversies involving rights that are legally demandable and enforceable, and to determine whether or not there has been a grave abuse of discretion amounting to lack or excess of jurisdiction on the part of any branch or instrumentality of the Government.[1]

The Congress has the power to define, prescribe, and apportion the jurisdiction of various courts, but it may not deprive the Supreme Court of its jurisdiction over cases enumerated in the Constitution itself.[2]

---

1 Section 1, Article VIII.

2 Section 2, Article VIII.

To ensure its independence, the judiciary enjoys fiscal autonomy. Appropriations for the judiciary may not be reduced by the legislature below the amount appropriated for the previous year and, after approval, shall be automatically and regularly released.[3]

All cases involving the constitutionality of a treaty, international or executive agreement, which shall be heard by the Supreme Court *en banc*, and all other cases which under the Rules of Court are required to be heard *en banc*, including those involving the constitutionality, application, or operation of presidential decrees, proclamations, orders, instructions, ordinances, and other regulations, shall be decided with the concurrence of a majority of the Members who actually took part in the deliberations on the issues in the case and voted thereon.[4]

The Supreme Court has the following powers:

(1) Exercise original jurisdiction over cases affecting ambassadors, other public ministers and consuls, and over petitions for certiorari, prohibition, mandamus, quo warranto, and habeas corpus.

(2) Review, revise, modify, or affirm on appeal on certiorari, as the law or the Rules of Court may provide, final judgments and orders of lower courts in:

(a) All cases in which the constitutionality or validity of any treaty, international or executive agreement, law, presidential decree, proclamation, order, instruction, ordinance, or regulation is in question.

(b) All cases involving the legality of any tax, impost, assessment, or toll, or any penalty imposed in relation thereto.

(c) All cases in which the jurisdiction of any lower court is in issue.

(d) All criminal cases in which the penalty imposed is reclusion perpetual or higher.

(e) All cases in which only an error or question of law is involved.

(3) Assign temporarily judges of lower courts to other stations as public interest may require. Such temporary assignment shall not exceed six months without the consent of the judge concerned.

(4) Order a change of venue or place of trial to avoid a miscarriage of justice.

(5) Promulgate rules concerning the protection and enforcement of constitutional rights, pleading, practice, and procedure in all courts, the admission to the practice of law, the Integrated Bar, and legal assistance to the underprivileged. Such rules shall provide a simplified and inexpensive procedure for the speedy disposition of cases, shall be uniform for all courts of the same grade, and shall not diminish, increase, or modify substantive rights. Rules of

---

3 Section 3, Article VIII.

4 Section 4(2), Article VIII.

procedure of special courts and quasi-judicial bodies shall remain effective unless disapproved by the Supreme Court.

(6) Appoint all officials and employees of the judiciary in accordance with the Civil Service Law.[5]

3. Sources of Philippine Law

The sources of Philippine law are, in the following order: the Constitution, the statutes enacted by Congress, and the interpretation of these statutes by the Supreme Court.

The Philippine legal system has a close affinity with that of the United States of America. American jurisprudence therefore has persuasive effect upon Philippine courts.

The Congress recently enacted the Electronic Commerce Act, effective June 14, 2000 (referred to herein sometimes simply as the "Act"), for the purpose of facilitating domestic and international dealings, transactions, arrangements, agreements, contracts and exchanges and storage of information through the utilization of electronic, optical and similar medium, mode, instrumentality and technology. The Act aims to recognize the authenticity and reliability of electronic documents related to such activities, and to promote the universal use of electronic transactions in the government and by the general public. The Act applies to any kind of electronic data message and electronic document used in the context of commercial and non-commercial activities to include domestic and international dealings, transactions, arrangements, agreements, contracts and exchanges and storage of information.

No Philippine case has yet been filed or decided involving the Electronic Commerce Act. However, because of the close affinity of the Philippine legal system with that of the United States of America, decisions of United States courts are of strong persuasive effect upon Philippine courts. Hence, decisions of US courts in cases involving online commerce may be adopted in analogous local cases by Philippine courts.

It is pertinent to point out that in an opinion dated March 19, 1998, the Secretary of Justice stated that the business of an Internet service provider is not considered a "mass media" activity engagement in which is limited to citizens of the Philippines or to corporations wholly-owned by such citizens pursuant to Section 11(1), Article XVI of the 1987 Constitution. Unlike mass media, which "embrace means of communication that reach and influence large numbers of people," an Internet access provider "merely serves as carrier for transmitting messages" and does not "create the messages/information nor transmit them to the general public."

5 Section 5, Article VIII.

B. SCHEME OF ONLINE BUSINESS REGULATION[6]

The regulatory framework in the Philippines is a two-tiered one. An entity that wants to install, operate and maintain networks and provide network services must first have a franchise from Congress. After obtaining the franchise, it can then apply to install, operate and provide specific services or specific networks.

1. Regulated and Deregulated Services

The authorization process for regulated services involves a quasi-judicial procedure. In contrast, deregulated services merely require registration with the appropriate governmental agency to ensure that consumers are protected from fly-by-night operators.

The regulated services pursuant to Republic Act No. 7925 are:

- Local exchange networks and services. These include the basic telephone network or the local network. All services that are offered in the local network are regulated services.
- Domestic long distance or national inter-network exchange long distance services.
- International services, which include overseas international long distance and radio mobile—on the trunk radio, the cellular mobile and other mobile radio services.

The deregulated services under the Act are:

- Radio paging service;
- Network service; and
- Value-added services.

2. Telephones

Philippine telephone companies now have installed 6.7 million lines of which only 2.8 million lines are subscribed. The increase in the number of installed lines is the result of the obligation to install additional lines imposed upon international suppliers of services and cellular mobile telephone services. In contrast, the number of subscribed lines in the cellular business is approximately 2.8 million. It is expected that the cellular phone subscribers will eventually overtake fixed line subscribers and that wireless subscribers will grow faster than fixed line subscribers.

6 "Regulation of ISPs" by Edgardo V. Cabarios, *Building the National Economy Online*, University of the Philippines Law Center (2000).

3. Internet Service Providers

Under the implementing rules of Republic Act No. 7925, Internet services were classified as value-added services and, therefore, deregulated under the law. However this does not include voice over Internet protocol, which is considered a regulated service.

Value added service providers must only register with the National Telecommunications Commission to ensure that consumers are protected. Applications must be acted upon within thirty (30) days to ensure that the service is a liberalized service. Another means of protecting consumers is the requirement to comply with the performance standards set by the National Telecommunications Commission.

Network owners or network providers are not prohibited from offering value-added services. However, they must comply with the following three requirements:

- They must secure prior approval from the commission through a judicial process, not merely through registration.
- They must ensure that the value-added service providers are not discriminated against in rates and access to facilities so that they given the same treatment as the subsidiaries of the owner of the facilities.
- They must maintain several books of accounts to ensure that there is no cross subsidy and to prevent predatory pricing of services.

As a value-added service under Republic Act No. 7925, ISP ownership must at least be 60% Filipino. CATV, which is headed towards convergence, must be 100% Filipino-owned pursuant to Executive Order No. 205. Broadcast media must be 100% Filipino-owned.

Republic Act No. 7925 also prohibits an entity holding one single franchise to engage in both telecommunications and broadcast, which is regarded in the industry as a deterrent to convergence.

C. ELECTRONIC TRANSACTIONS AND CONTRACT FORMATION

The recently enacted Electronic Commerce Act adopts the "functional equivalence principle" so that an electronic document or a digital signature as defined under the Act will have the same legal effect and serve as the functional equivalent under existing laws of a paper document and a manual signature.[7] At the same time, however, the Act leaves it to the parties to agree upon the substantive terms and conditions of their contract[8] so that the question whether a contract exists must still be governed by the provisions of existing laws, principally the Civil Code.[9] In other words, the Electronic Commerce Act does not govern the question as to when a contract is formed online. Section 16 of the Electronic

---

7 Sections 6, 7 and 8.

8 Section 16.

9 Article 1318, Civil Code.

Commerce Act confirms that the offer, acceptance of an offer and such other elements required under existing laws for the formation of contracts shall still apply. The Electronic Commerce Act simply confirms that these contract elements may be expressed and proved by means of electronic data messages and documents.

The following are the essential elements of a contract:

- Consent of the contracting parties;
- Subject matter of the contract; and
- Cause of the contract.[10]

On the existence of consent, the question arises whether "click-through" agreements create an enforceable contact between the parties. This issue has not yet arisen in the Philippines, but United States courts have ruled in favor of the enforceability of such agreements. One court has held that a click-wrap agreement qualifies as a "written contract" because it is automatically stored in the computer's memory when the user agrees to the click-wrap license and there are multiple ways to print the agreement, both from the original version in the click-wrap window and from the stored version.[11] Assuming that the requirements of the Act are satisfied for the application of the "functional equivalence principle," an electronic document or digital signature serves the same purposes as their written counterparts in the following situations:

In instances contemplated by the Stature of Frauds which requires that a contract be in writing and subscribed by the party charged for it to be enforceable against a party sought to be bound, the electronic document and the digital signature satisfy these requirements for purposes of enforcing the contract.

Similarly, since an agreement for the sale of goods at a price not less than five hundred pesos is covered by the Statute of Frauds such a transaction if conducted online must be "in writing" and "subscribed by the party charged" to be enforceable. This makes compliance with the digital signature provision practically mandatory for most electronic commerce transactions. However, the State of Fraud ceases to apply upon partial performance of the parties' obligations, as by the payment of the price or by the delivery of the products.

In situations contemplated by the Rules on Evidence, which requires the production of the original document as the best evidence of its contents, the electronic document is considered an original document and is therefore admissible in evidence.

In situations where the law requires the retention of the original documents like sales invoices which must be kept by sellers under the revenue law, retained copies of electronic documents are sufficient compliance.

---

10 Article 1318, Civil Code.

11 *In Re Real Networks Inc.*, US District Court, Northern District Court of Illinois, May 8, 2000.

The question arises whether the use of digital signatures and electronic documents are mandatory under the Electronic Commerce Act. The Electronic Commerce Act itself says that its provisions apply only in the absence of contrary stipulation by the parties, implying that the parties are free to stipulate what technology other than digital signatures are acceptable to them for the purpose of authenticating their contracts.

However, in situations covered by the Statute of Frauds, such as in transactions involving real property and contracts for the sale of goods at a price not less than five hundred pesos, the use of digital signatures may well be treated as mandatory to ensure that the electronic contract is considered "signed" by the parties and therefore enforceable between them.

The requirements for an electronic signature meeting the functional equivalence standard are:

> An electronic signature on the electronic document shall be equivalent to the signature of a person on a written document if the signature is an electronic signature and proved by showing that a prescribed procedure, not alterable by the parties interested in the electronic document, existed under which—
>
> a) A method is used to identify the party sought to be bound and to indicate said party's access to the electronic document necessary for his consent or approval through the electronic signature;
>
> b) Said method is reliable and appropriate for the purpose for which the electronic document was generated or communicated, in the light of all circumstances, including any relevant agreement;
>
> c) It is necessary for the party sought to be bound, in order to proceed further with the transaction, to have executed or provided the electronic signature; and
>
> d) The other party is authorized and enabled to verify the electronic signature and to make the decision to proceed with the transaction authenticated by the same.[12]

1. Rules Under the Act[13]

To ensure the integrity of electronic documents and digital signatures, the Electronic Commerce Act provides for certain rules that the parties to an electronic transaction must observe:

> **Rules for Equivalence**—Sections 7, 8 and 13 set forth the conditions under which electronic documents, electronic signatures and electronic data messages retained in place of original documents may be treated as the equivalent of paper documents and given legal recognition, validity or enforceability.

12 Section 8. Legal Recognition of Electronic Signatures.

13 The headings are not from the language of the Electronic Commerce Act and are used only for the classification of the Rules.

Rules on Authorship and Attribution—Sections 9 and 18 determine whether and under what conditions an electronic signature or electronic date message may be attributed to a particular person.

Rules on Authentication and Validation—Section 11 specifies the conditions under which a person may be deemed to have approved of the electronic date message or electronic document.

Rules on Admissibility and Evidential Weight—Section 12, in relation to Sections 6 and 7 define the conditions under which an electronic data message or electronic document may be admitted as the best evidence of the agreement and the transaction mentioned in it and how its evidential weight may be assessed. Sections 14 and 15 specify the conditions under which proof of the probative value of an electronic document may be established.

Rules on Repudiation—Sections 18 and 19 provide for the rules by which the person to whom the electronic document is attributed may renounce it.

Rules of Acknowledgment and Receipt—Sections 20, 21, 22 and 23 contain the rules by which receipt of an electronic document may be acknowledged and by which the time and place for their dispatch may be determined.

As a further security safeguard to ensure that the parties to electronic transactions are the actual persons they purport to be, the Electronic Commerce Act recognizes the possibility of using the services of certification authorities. The rules on this point are expected to be issued by the Department of Trade and Industry.

In addition, the Supreme Court also issued the Rules on Electronic Evidence to govern the use of electronic documents and digital signatures as evidence in court proceedings.[14]

Under Section 1 of Rule 4, "an electronic document shall be regarded as the equivalent of an original document under the Best Evidence Rule if it is a printout or output readable by sight or other means, shown to reflect the data accurately." In other words, the printout of the electronic document itself is admissible in evidence as an original document. However, the production and display of the original document itself may be necessary since the printout must be shown to be a true copy of the electronic documents.

14 Resolution A.M. No. 01-7-01 dated July 17, 2002.

ROMANIA

by
Catalin Baiculescu, Partner
Horatiu Dumitru, Ph.D., Senior Associate
Musat & Asociatii

A. SOURCES OF LAW

1. Introduction

The Romanian legal system is part of the Roman law family. It is French influenced, being built on the foundations of the French Civil Code of 1804. The Romanian Civil Code entered into force in 1864.

2. Constitution

Romania is a Republic. The Constitution, approved in 1991, is the fundamental law of the Romanian legislation. It sets forth citizens' basic rights and liberties, as well as the system of public authorities.

a. System of Public Authorities

The Parliament, consisting of the Chamber of Deputies and the Senate, is the supreme representative body of the Romanian people and the sole legislative authority of the State. The Chamber of Deputies and the Senate are elected for a term of office of four years. The Parliament has the power to grant confidence to the Government, based on the latter's program, and to withdraw confidence, by carrying a motion of censure.

The Executive consists of two institutions: the President of Romania and the Government. The President of Romania is the representative of the Romanian State, having the power to safeguard the national independence, unity and territorial integrity of the country. The President of Romania is responsible for guarding the observance of the Constitution and the proper functioning of public authorities. To this effect, he is acting as a mediator between the powers in the State, as well as between the State and society. The President of Romania is elected by universal, equal, direct, secret and free suffrage, for a term of office of four years. The major powers of the President of Romania are:

- appointment of the Government, based on the vote of confidence granted by the Parliament;

- consultation of the Government in major political issues;
- attending Government meetings, at his or her request;
- dissolution of Parliament;
- concluding international treaties in the name of Romania;
- commander-in-Chief of the Armed Forces and Head of the Supreme Council of National Defense; and
- appointment of judges.

The Government (the Cabinet) is the public authority that, in accordance with its government program accepted by the Parliament, ensures the implementation of the domestic and foreign policy of the country, exercising also the general management of the entire public administration. The Government is headed by the Prime Minister, appointed for Cabinet formation by the President of Romania. The Prime Minister has the duty to direct Government actions and to co-ordinate the activities of its members.

The Judicial Authority consists of the courts of law, the Public Ministry and the Superior Council of Magistracy. The courts system is made of the Supreme Court of Justice, Courts of Appeal, Tribunals and Town Courts, in their descending order of importance.

Town Courts have general powers for civil and criminal matters. For some specific matters, Tribunals located in each of the 41 districts of Romania have the power to judge in the first instance. Tribunals are also competent to hear appeals filed against decisions of Town Courts. Appeals brought against Tribunals' decisions have to be judged by Court of Appeals. There are 15 regional Courts of Appeal, having jurisdiction over one, two or even three Tribunals.

The Supreme Court of Justice hears second appeals against lower courts' decisions. It also gives opinions in so-called interest of law appeals filed by the Ministry of Justice, in order to settle a uniform case law in certain legal matters handled by lower courts in different ways.

The Public Ministry is the judicial body comprising prosecutors and its main duty is to represent the legal interests of society and to defend legal order, as well as the citizens' rights and liberties.

The Superior Council of the Magistracy nominates judges for appointment by the President of Romania and acts also as a disciplinary council for judges.

Besides the bodies which form the Legislative, Executive and Judicial branches, the Constitution also refers to the following public authorities:

- the Constitutional Court, mainly in charge of adjudication on the constitutionality of Laws and Government Ordinances;
- the Court of Audit, acting as an oversight body in relation to the formation, administration and use of financial resources of the State and the public sector; and
- the Ombudsman, responsible for defending citizens' rights and liberties.

b. The Legal System

According to the Constitution, primary legislation consists of Laws adopted by the Parliament and Ordinances issued by the Government under certain circumstances. Primary legislation is meant to develop, to implement and to apply constitutional provisions. Consequently, primary legislation provisions cannot be contrary to the Constitution.

Secondary legislation comprises Government Decisions and regulations issued by administrative bodies, according to specific powers set forth within Acts of primary legislation, in order to organize and implement provisions of Laws and Government Ordinances. Accordingly, provisions of secondary legislation cannot be contrary to Laws and Government Ordinances.

2. Laws

Article 72 of the Romanian Constitution states that the Parliament adopts constitutional, organic and ordinary laws. Constitutional laws are those by which Constitution is amended. Organic laws regulate essential areas such as:

a) the election system;

b) the establishment of political parties;

c) organization of the Government and the Supreme Council of National Defense;

d) crimes and punishment regime;

e) the status of public servants; and

f) the general legal property regime.

Organic laws are passed by the majority vote of each Chamber of the Parliament, while ordinary laws may pass by the majority vote of the members present in each Chamber. The legislative initiative belongs to the Government, as well as to the members of the Parliament. After they are passed within the Parliament, the laws are submitted to the President of Romania, in order to be promulgated. Before promulgation, the President of Romania may return the law to Parliament for reconsideration, thought the President may do so only once. After promulgation, laws must be published in the Official Gazette of Romania and will come into force on the day of publication or the date provided within their text.

3. Ordinances

According to Article 114 of the Constitution, Parliament may pass a special law enabling the Government to issue ordinances in areas outside the scope of organic laws. To the extent of such delegation, the ordinance issued by the Government has the same legal effect as a law, upon being published in the Official Gazette of Romania. However, if the enabling law requires it, the ordinances shall be submitted to the Parliament for subsequent approval. In this respect, Parliament may approve, amend or reject the ordinance.

In exceptional circumstances, the Government may adopt emergency ordinances, which shall come into force only after their submission to Parliament for approval. The areas in which emergency ordinances may be issued include those within the scope of organic laws.

4. Government Decisions

Government Decisions are regulations passed in order to organize implementation of laws and ordinances. They are subject to publication in the Official Gazette of Romania.

B. SCHEME OF ONLINE BUSINESS REGULATION

1. Introduction

In Romania, online business has recently been regulated in a comprehensive and uniform manner, covering the main legal aspects that are essential for this area. The relevant legislation on the electronic commerce field is represented by the following acts:

- Law no. 365/2002 electronic commerce (the "Law no. 365/2002");
- Government Ordinance no. 130/2000 on the legal regime of contracts concluded at a distance (the "GO no. 130/2000");
- Law no. 455/2001 on electronic signatures (the "Law no. 455/2001");
- Law no. 676/2001 on the processing of personal data and the protection of private life in the communication sector (the "Law no. 676/2001");
- Law no. 677/2001 for the protection of persons with respect to the processing of personal data and the free circulation of these data (the "Law no. 677/2001");
- Government Ordinance no. 20/2002 on public procurement through electronic auctions, as approved by the Law no. 468/2002 (the "GO no. 20/2002");
- Emergency Government Ordinance no. 79/2002 on the general legal framework on communications (the "EGO no. 79/2002"); and
- Law no.161/2003 Title III regarding the prevention and fighting of cybercrime (the "Law no.161/2003").

2. Scope of Regulations

a. Electronic Commerce

Law no. 365/2002 regulates the main framework in the field of online commerce.

The scope of Law no. 365/2002 consists of:

- the establishment of conditions for providing information society services;
- the legal regime of contracts concluded by electronic means;
- the legal regime of service providers' liability;
- the oversight and control of compliance with legal provisions; and
- the regime of offences and crimes regime, in case of disregarding the provisions of the law.

According to Article 1 of the Law no. 365/2002, an information society service means any activity consisting of service provision that implies the constitution, change, transfer or writing-off of a property right over a tangible or intangible asset, such activity being performed by electronic means and having the following features:

(i) it is performed in consideration of a benefit, usually granted to the offeror by the recipient;

(ii) it is not necessary for the offeror and recipient to be both physically present in the same place; and

(iii) it is made by sending the information at the individual request of the recipient.

The Law no. 365/2002 establishes the main duties of service providers. In this respect, they must make available, to recipients and public authorities, their identification data and tariffs for the services they provide. The service provider must also inform users of the technical procedure for contract conclusion, on the relevant codes of conduct to which the service provider subscribes, as well as of technical means for identification and correction of possible errors.

b. Distance Contracts

GO no. 130/2000 regulates the conditions for execution and performance of contracts concluded at a distance between traders providing products and services, on one side, and consumers, on the other side.

c. Electronic Signatures

Law no. 455/2001 regulates the legal regime of electronic signature and of electronic documents.

"Electronic signature" means a set of data in electronic form, created through software and/or hardware devices, which are used as an identification method. The document bearing an electronic signature recognized by the person to whom it is addressed to, has the same legal effects as an authentic document. Electronic signatures are certified by specialized suppliers of services, which carry out their activity under the control of a national authority.

d. Public Procurement

GO no. 20/2002 sets forth the general framework and the conditions for using online procedures in order to assign public procurement contracts.

According to GO no. 20/2002, "electronic procedure" means the use, in whole or in part, of the technical facilities provided by the Electronic System of Public Procurement, a computer system for public use accessible by the Internet, in the assignment of a public procurement contract.

The contracting authorities which must enforce GO no. 20/2002, as well as the products, services and works to be procured by electronic auction and the value thresholds up to which GO no. 20/2002 is applicable are subject to a Government decision detailed regulation.

The contracting authorities set up by Government decision, as well as the suppliers, executors or providers wishing to participate in the electronic auction procedure, must register in the Electronic System. Within the electronic auction procedure, communications must be made electronically and the documents transmitted must be presented in an electronic form and electronically signed, otherwise they will not be taken into account.

C. ELECTRONIC TRANSACTIONS AND CONTRACT FORMATION

1. General

Contract formation is mainly regulated by the Civil Code and by the Commercial Code. Article 35 par.1 of the Commercial Code comprises a special provision regarding contract formation between absent parties, according to which the contract becomes binding at the moment when the acceptance of the offeree is acknowledged by the offeror.

Generally, these common private law provisions do not require contracts to be concluded in writing. The written form is requested only for matters related to the proof of the legal relationship that has been created by the contract. In a few situations, such as sale and purchase of land, the law expressly requires the contract to be concluded in writing, before a public notary, in order to make it binding between the parties. For the large majority of contracts, however, there is no need to conclude a contract in writing, except to improve certainty and assure clear drafting of terms, preventing litigation that might result from ambiguous clauses.

2. Regulations Applicable to Online Contracting

Online contracting is primarily governed by:

(i) the Law no. 365/2002 regarding electronic commerce;

(ii) the Law no. 455/2001 regarding electronic signatures; and

(iii) the Government Ordinance no. 130/2000 regarding distance contracts.

Similarly to Law no. 365/2002 (harmonized with Directive 2000/31/EC of the European Parliament and of the Council of 8 June 2000 on certain legal aspects of information society services, in particular electronic commerce, in the Internal Market), the Law no. 455/2001 and the Government Ordinance no. 130/2000, have also been based on European Union directives, namely: the Directive 1999/93/EC of 13 December 1999 on a Community framework for electronic signatures and the Directive 97/7/EC of 20 May 1997 on the protection of consumers in respect of distance contracts. While the Law no. 455/2001 regulates the legal regime of digital signatures and digital documents, the Government Ordinance no. 130/2000 completes the set of existing provisions within the Law no. 365/2002, in order to strengthen consumer protection in relation to executing and performing distance contracts between consumers and suppliers.

The Law no. 455/2001 basically provides that an electronic document having an extended electronic signature, based on a certificate issued by a certification authority, has similar legal effects to an ordinary private signature document. The law sets forth the fundamental rules for providing certification services, supervision and liability of certification service providers. Until now, a specific certification authority has not yet been established. Therefore, the powers of such authority are at this moment granted by the law to the Ministry of Communications and Information Technology. Attempts to establish certification service providers have been initiated by the National Association of Internet Service Providers, the National Union of Public Notaries and the Romanian Chamber of Commerce and Industry. None of these projects have been finalized.

The Government Ordinance no. 130/2000 is primarily focused on specific information that must be given by the goods or service provider to the consumer, before the distance contract is executed. Furthermore, the Ordinance regulates the unilateral termination of the contract by the consumer, the terms under which such termination may occur, as well as specific contracts that generally cannot be subject to such termination (except if the parties agree otherwise). Specific provisions refer also to the performance of distance contracts and the duties that have to be fulfilled in relation to such contracts by the goods or service provider.

3. Contracts Concluded by Electronic Means

According to Article 7 par. of the Law no. 365/2002, contracts concluded by electronic means have full legal effects recognized by the law, provided that the legal requirements for contractual effectiveness have been met.

Paragraph 2 of Article 7 further provides that, in order for contracts which have been concluded by electronic means to be binding, the prior consent of the parties with respect to the use of electronic means is not necessary.

Proving the execution of contracts by electronic means, as well as the duties that result from these contracts, is subject to the provisions of the Law no. 455/2001. By enacting these provisions, the Romanian legislators have implemented a new type of contract formation that leads to a fully binding agreement between contracting parties.

An essential and also sensitive issue in online contracting is the proper information of the recipients of information society services. The service provider has the duty—according to Article 8 of the Law no. 365/2002—to provide the recipient, prior to an order being placed by the latter, with the following information:

(i) the technical steps to be followed in order to conclude the contract;

(ii) whether or not the concluded contract will be filed by the service provider and whether it will be accessible;

(iii) the technical means for identifying and correcting input errors in the process of order placement;

(iv) the language in which the contract may be concluded; and

(v) relevant codes of conduct to which the service provider is committed, as well as the electronic means by which these codes may be concluded.

All this information must be made available to the recipient in a clear, comprehensible and unambiguous way. However, the parties may agree to deviate from the duty of providing information, as set forth in Article 8 of the Law no. 365/2002, but only under the condition that none of them is a consumer. Consequently, only in "Business to Business" relationships, where the parties are fully capable to legally protect themselves, is such deviation allowed. Standard contract clauses and general contracting terms must also be provided to the recipient, in a manner able to facilitate their storage and reproduction. However, it is important to stress that these requirements concerning recipient information are not applicable with respect to contracts that are exclusively concluded by e-mail or other similar individual communication means.

Article 9 of the Law no. 365/2002 provides the main rules applicable to electronic contracting. As a general principle, if not otherwise agreed by the parties, a contract shall be deemed to be executed when the offeror becomes aware of the acceptance of the contractual offer. Apart from the general rule, the law grants the parties the possibility to agree between themselves the moment of contract execution, without any interference. However, should such an agreement on contract formation occur, the specific terms must be carefully drafted, in order to avoid litigation.

The law provides for a derogatory solution in the case of contracts that, by their nature or at the request of the beneficiary, require immediate performance of the specific service. Such contracts are deemed to be executed when the provider commenced performance, except for the case when the offeror requested to be previously sent the acceptance. In this last case, the contract shall be deemed to have been executed when the offeror became aware of the acceptance of the contractual offer.

Further, if the recipient sends by electronic means the contractual offer or the acceptance of the firm contractual offer made by the service provider, the service provider must confirm the receipt of the offer, or, as the case may be, the acceptance of such offer, by one of the following methods:

(i) sending an acknowledgment of receipt by electronic mail or by other equivalent individual communications, to the address specified by the recipient, within 24 hours of receipt of the offer or acceptance; or

(ii) confirmation of the receipt of offer or acceptance, by an equivalent means to the one used for sending or accepting the offer, as soon as the offer or the acceptance was received by the service supplier, provided that this confirmation may be stored and reproduced by the recipient.

These legal provisions have been enacted in order to strengthen the recipient's legal position and to always assure him or her of the way the contract has been executed, leaving no doubt that might lead to subsequent legal issues. However, according to a recent study, these provisions do not expressly establish when the actual moment of contract formation occurs; they merely point out the technical steps to be undertaken in order to execute an electronic contract. Still, the duty of confirming the receipt of the offer or acceptance of the offer might lead to the conclusion that contract formation is determined at the moment in which the transmission of the receipt acknowledgement of the acceptance of the offer has been made.[1]

The offer or the acceptance, as well as the confirmation of receiving the offer or the acceptance, made by one of the methods provided under a) or b) above, shall be deemed received when the parties to which they are addressed can access them. Practically, electronic contract formation occurs at the specific moment at which the offeror receives the acceptance, once this can be accessed. The offeror is actually checking the consent of the recipient with respect to the proposed clauses of the contract.[2]

These rules referring to confirmation of receipt of the offer, or of the acceptance of such offer, do not apply to contracts concluded exclusively by electronic mail or by equivalent individual communications.

1 Tiberiu Gabriel Savu, Unele consideratii pe marginea efectelor noii reglementari privind comertul electronic asupra regulilor in materia formarii contractului (Some comments upon effects of the new regulation regarding electronic commerce, on contract formation rules), Revista de drept comercial nr.9/2002, p.108.

2 Ibid., p.109.

SINGAPORE

by
Anne Choo and Chan Yuen Leng
CitiLegal LLC, Advocates & Solicitors

A. SOURCES OF LAW

1. History

The name "Singapore" (meaning "Lion City") was established in the thirteenth century. The Malay Annals ("Sejarah Melayu") relate how Sang Nila Utama, the then ruler of Palembang (now known as Indonesia), named the island after an animal which he mistakenly identified as a lion, hence the term "Singapura."[1] The modern history of Singapore started with the founding of a British East India Company settlement in Singapore by Sir Thomas Stamford Raffles in early 1819. In order to prevent the Dutch from monopolizing trade in the East, he persuaded Governor-General Hastings to establish ports in the vicinity of the Straits of Malacca which was a gateway to China for the Dutch. For this reason, he chose Singapore, a settlement at the southern tip of the Malay peninsula.

Singapore subsequently became part of the Straits Settlements formed by way of the Anglo-Dutch Treaty of 1824. Its territories comprised Penang, Malacca and Singapore. The Straits Settlements' headquarters were later transferred to Singapore, the only profitable settlement amongst the three territories.

In 1851, the Straits Settlements were placed under the administration of the Government of India following the abolition of the East India Company. The Straits Settlements finally became a Crown Colony in 1867.

Singapore continued to prosper in the years leading to the Second World War. On 15 February 1942, the British surrendered Singapore to the Imperial Japanese Army. When the Japanese surrendered in 1945, the Malayan Union (which from 1948 became known as the Federation of Malaya) was formed with, inter alia, Penang and Malacca as its members. Singapore, on its own, became a British Crown Colony.

---

1 <http://www.sg/flavour/profile/pro-history.html>, Ministry of Information and the Arts (MITA).

In 1963, Singapore obtained independence from British rule and merged with the Federation of Malaya and Britain's Borneo territories to form the Federation of Malaysia.

In 1965, Singapore left the Federation of Malaysia and became an independent republic.

2. The Constitution of the Republic of Singapore

The Constitution of the Republic of Singapore establishes the three organs of government namely, the Legislature, the Executive and the Judiciary. The Constitution can only be amended by an Act of Parliament supported by at least two-thirds of the Members of Parliament.

The legislative powers of Singapore vest in the Legislature which consists of the President and Parliament.[2]

The Singapore Parliament consists of only one chamber of elected representatives of the people.

The executive authority vests in the President and the Cabinet.[3] The Cabinet has collective responsibility to the Government,[4] led by the Prime Minister, who is chosen at the discretion of the President.[5]

Cabinet ministers, through the operation of ministerial responsibility, are expected to justify their policies in open debate before Parliament.

The Supreme Court of Judicature Act establishes the Court of Appeal and the Court of Criminal Appeal at the highest level of the hierarchy of the courts followed by the High Court. The Subordinate Courts, on the other hand, are established by virtue of the Subordinate Courts Act and consist of the District and Magistrates' Courts. The Court of Appeal is now the highest court of law in Singapore after the abolition of appeals to the Privy Council in London following the repeal of the Judicial Committee (Repeal) Act in April 1994.

3. Elected Presidency

The President has roles in the Legislature as well as the Executive.

Provisions in the Constitution relating to the elected presidency cannot be amended without the President's concurrence unless it is supported by a two-thirds majority in Parliament. The Presidential Elections Committee decides suitability and eligibility of candidates for presidency.

The elected President has certain veto rights over, inter alia, the expenditure of the country's accumulated reserves and the appointment of top civil servants.

---

2 Constitution of the Republic of Singapore, art. 38.

3 Constitution of the Republic of Singapore, art. 23.

4 Constitution of the Republic of Singapore, art. 24.

5 Constitution of the Republic of Singapore, art. 25(1).

4. Sources of Law

Singapore is a member of the Commonwealth. Its legal system and laws are largely influenced by English common law tradition.

The sources of law in Singapore consist of legislation (viz. statutes, Acts or ordinances encompassing subsidiary legislation such as regulations, bylaws and orders), case law and customary practices.

Reference may be made to laws of other jurisdictions as persuasive authority for various propositions of law, particularly those of other Commonwealth countries. American authorities may also be persuasive authorities, although the United States of America is not part of the Commonwealth.

Historically, the reception of English Law into Singapore can be traced to the Second Charter of Justice of 1826, which is thought to have introduced English law into Singapore. Following the enactment of the Application of English Law Act on 12 November 1993, the reception of English statute law is limited to the statutes specifically incorporated by virtue of the Act. These include for example, the Sale of Goods Act, Supply of Goods and Services Act, Unfair Contract Terms Act and the Partnership Act.

English common law that is part of Singapore law as at 12 November 1993 continues to apply. English common law made after that date will apply insofar as it is applicable to the circumstances of Singapore and its inhabitants and such application is subject to such modifications as those circumstances may require.

5. Common Law and the Doctrine of Stare Decisis

The principle of *stare decisis* or precedent operates both vertically and horizontally, similar to the English position, for reasons of uniformity and consistency. The courts in Singapore require that judges make reference to prior decided cases for guidance and justification of decisions at hand if the immediate case cannot be distinguished from a prior case.

The Court of Appeal is governed by horizontal doctrine of *stare decisis*. It is therefore bound by its own prior decisions subject to departure under the circumstances provided by the rule in *Young v. Bristol Aeroplane Co Ltd*,[6] which was followed in the local decision of *Mah Kah Yew v PP*.[7] However, this doctrine is not applicable to the Singapore Court of Criminal Appeal, which holds itself free to depart from its own prior decisions by virtue of *Chin Seow Noi v PP*,[8] following the English case of *R v Taylor*.[9]

---

6 [1944] 1 KB 718 (Court of Appeal, England).

7 [1971] 1 MLJ 1 (High Court).

8 [1994] 1 SLR 135 (Court of Criminal Appeal).

9 [1950] 2 KB 368 (Court of Criminal Appeal, England).

The Practice Statement on Judicial Precedent issued on 11 July 1994 sums up the position of the courts as follows:

> . . . the Court of Appeal should not hold itself bound by any previous decisions of its own or of the Privy Council, which by the rules prevailing prior to 8 April 1994 were binding on it, . . . where adherence to such particular decisions would cause injustice in a particular case or constrain the development of the law in conformity with the circumstances of Singapore.
>
> Therefore, whilst this Court will continue to treat such prior decisions as normally binding, this Court will, whenever it appears right to do so, depart from prior decisions . . . this power should be exercised sparingly."[10]

The High Court does not consider itself bound by its own prior decisions.[11] Nevertheless, it is bound by decisions of the Court of Appeal.

6. Muslim Law

Article 153 of the Constitution protects the interests of Muslims by compelling the Legislature to provide for the regulation of Muslim religious affairs. The Administration of Muslim Law Act establishes Syariah Courts in Singapore and confers jurisdiction on the Syariah Courts over matters relating to religion, succession, betrothal, payment of dowry, maintenance and consolatory gifts, so long as the parties are Muslims or married under Muslim Law.

The Syariah Courts are presided over by a president appointed by the President of the Republic of Singapore. There is recourse to an Appeal Board over the decisions of the Syariah Courts. The Appeal Board is empowered with revisionary jurisdiction to the exclusion of the High Court. This jurisdiction can be exercised by the President on the recommendation of the Council of the Islamic Religion.

7. Customary Law

Section 3(2) of the Application of English Law Act gives recognition to local customs by subjecting the application of common law in Singapore in certain instances to local circumstances.

In practice, however, there are substantial difficulties in defining the precise nature or ambit of local customs and trade practices. Consequently, while local merchants in Singapore continue to recognise certain customs and trade practices, these customs and practices are not yet an important contributor to the overall development of common law in Singapore.

---

10 [1994] 2 SLR 689.

11 *Wong Hong Toy v PP* [1986] 2 MLJ 336, 338 per Lai J (Court of Appeal).

B. SCHEME OF ONLINE BUSINESS REGULATIONS

1. Background

In recent years, the Singapore government has been aggressively promoting Singapore as a global electronic commerce hub. In 1996, the then National Computer Board introduced the Electronic Commerce Hotbed Programme, which aims to increase electronic commerce in Singapore.

Since then, there have been changes in the existing regulations and enactment of new laws to take into account the development of electronic commerce. The EC Policy Committee was formed in January 1997 to develop the relevant laws and regulations needed for the growth of electronic commerce in Singapore and to ensure that companies felt safe and secure in an environment of predictability and certainty. A significant outcome of the Committee's recommendation was the enactment of the Electronic Transactions Act.

2. Development of Key Statutes & Initiatives

a. Key Statutes

The Electronic Transactions Act and the Computer Misuse Act are two important statutes that have a major impact on the regulation of electronic commerce in Singapore.

The Electronic Transactions Act came into force in July 1998. The Act is mainly modelled after the United Nations Commission on International Trade Law (UNCITRAL) on Electronic Commerce, and the US draft Uniform Transactions Act. The purposes of the Electronic Transactions Act are set out in Section 3 of the Act, which states:

> This Act shall be construed consistently with what is commercially reasonable under the circumstances and to give effect to the following purposes:
>
> (a) to facilitate electronic communications by means of reliable electronic records;
>
> (b) to facilitate electronic commerce, eliminate barriers to electronic commerce resulting from uncertainties over writing and signature requirements, and to promote the development of the legal and business infrastructure necessary to implement secure electronic commerce;
>
> (c) to facilitate electronic filing of documents with government agencies and statutory boards, and to promote efficient delivery of government services by means of reliable electronic records;
>
> (d) to minimise the incidence of forged electronic records, intentional and unintentional alteration of records, and fraud in electronic commerce and other electronic transactions;
>
> (e) to help to establish uniformity of rules and regulations and standards regarding the authentication and integrity of electronic records; and

(f) to promote public confidence in the integrity and reliability of electronic records and electronic commerce, and to foster the development of electronic commerce through the use of electronic signatures to lend authenticity and integrity to correspondence in any electronic medium.

The Computer Misuse Act is a penal statute and deals with offences relating to the use of computers and computer systems including, inter alia, unauthorized access to computer materials, unauthorized use or interception of computer services, unauthorized obstruction of use of computers, and unauthorized disclosure of computer access codes.

The Computer Misuse Act applies to an offence committed outside of Singapore if the computer, programme or data was in Singapore at the material time.

b. Regulatory Regime

The Media Development Authority is the statutory body that regulates the local Internet service providers and Internet content providers.

The key legislative instruments that enable the Media Development Authority to monitor and regulate the Internet are the Broadcasting (Class Licence) Notification and the Internet Code of Practice.

The Class Licence contains the regulatory requirements that apply to Internet service providers and Internet content providers. They are deemed automatically licensed upon registration under the Class Licence (no prior approval from the Media Development Authority is necessary) and are obliged to comply with the Class Licence Conditions and the Internet Code of Practice. Amongst other terms, under the Internet Code of Practice, material that is broadcast by an Internet content provider must not be objectionable on the grounds of public interest, public morality, public order, public security or national harmony.

c. The National Internet Advisory Committee

The National Internet Advisory Committee was appointed by the Ministry of Information and the Arts in August 1996. The National Internet Advisory Committee advises the Media Development Authority on the regulation of electronic information services and assists the Authority in the development of the regulatory framework for the Internet as well.

In 1998, the National Internet Advisory Committee introduced the E-Commerce Code for the Protection of Personal Information and Communications of Consumers of Internet Commerce with the aim of establishing a code relating to the protection of consumers' personal information and communications over the Internet and to build confidence of the public in using the Internet as a medium of communication and business. In February 2002, this code was superceded by the "Model Data Protection Code for the Private Sector" which has not been enacted as law and compliance with it is voluntary.

d. CaseTrust

CaseTrust is a joint project of the Consumers Association of Singapore, Retail Promotion Centre and CommerceNet Singapore Ltd. CaseTrust is an accreditation system encouraging good business practices among store based and web based retailers. A retailer who qualifies under the criteria laid down under CaseTrust's Code of Practice will be allowed to display a logo at its web page. CommerceNet Singapore is a non-profit organisation, which is part of a worldwide consortium represented in various countries with participation of over 660 corporate entities as members. The aim of CommerceNet Singapore is to make electronic commerce easy to use, trusted and to tackle various issues relating to the technological, business, legal and regulatory angles of electronic commerce.

e. E-Commerce Business Policy Helpdesk

In August 1999, the Singapore Government set up an E-Commerce Business Policy Helpdesk to assist businesses seeking clarifications on policies and regulations relating to electronic commerce. The helpdesk aims to create greater awareness among businesses as to the policies and legal framework relating to electronic commerce in Singapore. The then National Computer Board, part of which now forms the Info-communications Development Authority of Singapore, led the implementation of this helpdesk and in the process worked with other relevant regulatory bodies including the Attorney General's Chambers, Economic Development Board, Inland Revenue Authority of Singapore, Monetary Authority of Singapore and the Ministry of Law. One of the functions of the helpdesk is to work with relevant regulatory agencies and international bodies to clarify policy issues and to convey the latest developments in electronic commerce policies and regulations to relevant sectoral agencies.

f. Compliance Requirements

Notwithstanding these initiatives, online businesses are still subject to, and must comply with, the rules, regulations and licensing requirements relevant to their specific business and also such general requirements as relate to any entity (whether individual, partnership or company) wishing to do business in Singapore. For example, persons offering insurance coverage services are required to be licensed in accordance with, inter alia, the Insurance Act. Individuals wishing to retail on the Internet are required to register themselves with the Accounting and Corporate Regulatory Authority either as a partnership, a sole proprietor or a company before commencement of their online business.

g. Regulated Business Activities

A brief description of regulated business activities in Singapore follows.

i. Money Lending, Money Changing and Remittance Business

A money lender residing and carrying on the business of money lending in Singapore is required to take out a licence annually under the Moneylenders' Act.

Similarly a money changer or a person who carries on a remittance business or who advertises himself as carrying on such a business has to obtain a money changer's licence or a remittance licence from the Monetary Authority of Singapore.

ii. Insurance

Under the Insurance Act, no person is allowed to carry on any kind of insurance business or use the word "insurance" to indicate his business unless that person is registered by the Monetary Authority of Singapore in respect of the insurance business.

iii. Appraisers and House Agents

Under the Appraisers and House Agents Act, a person who provides the services of valuing and appraising movable or immovable property of any kind must take out a licence to do so. The same would apply to a person who is a house agent or who advertises himself or herself as such to the public.

iv. Banking and Finance Services

Only banks and finance companies licensed by the Monetary Authority of Singapore pursuant to the Banking Act, the Finance Companies Act, the Securities and Futures Act and/or the Financial Advisors Act may provide banking and/or financial services.

Similarly, share brokers and financial advisers must be registered under the Securities and Futures Act or the Financial Advisers Act before they are entitled to provide share dealing and financial advice and services.

With the growing number of businesses going online, one expects the regulatory framework dealing with electronic commerce matters to be further developed in order to cope with such developments and to maintain its relevance to the business environment. To this end, there already exist various government and quasi-regulatory bodies specifically formed with the aim of ensuring that electronic commerce in Singapore continues to be an efficient and safe method of conducting business.

C. FORMATION OF CONTRACTS IN ELECTRONIC TRANSACTIONS

A preliminary issue regarding the formation of contracts in electronic transactions concerns the validity of contracts formed in an electronic environment. Section 11 of the Electronic Transactions Act[12] ("ETA") removes any uncertainty on this point by providing that a transaction will not be invalidated merely because it took place wholly or partly by way of electronic communication. Electronic records and signatures will also not be denied legal effect, validity or

12 The Electronic Transactions Act was brought into force on 10th July 1998.

enforceability solely on the ground that they exist in the form of an electronic record (Sections 6 and 8 of the ETA).

However, there are exceptions which still require hand-written records and signatures (Section 4 of the ETA). These are:

(a) creation and execution of wills;

(b) negotiable instruments;

(c) creation, performance or enforcement of indentures, declarations of trust and powers of attorney (save for constructive or resulting trusts);

(d) contracts for the sale or other disposition of immovable property, or any interest in such property;

(e) the conveyance or transfer of interests in immovable property; and

(f) documents of title.

1. Formation of Contracts—General Principles

The principles applicable to the formation of electronic contracts are essentially the same as those for normal contracts.

The necessary ingredients for the formation of a contract are:

(a) an offer;

(b) an acceptance of that offer;

(c) the intention of both parties to create legal relations;

(d) consideration (i.e. there must be a benefit) to the promisor or a detriment to the promisee;

(e) legal capacity of the parties; and

(f) sufficiently certain terms of contract.

In electronic transactions, the medium of communication between the offeror and the offeree has changed and it is this change that has raised new issues in two main areas: firstly, when an agreement has been reached between the parties and, secondly, authentication of that contract.

a. What Constitutes an Offer

In Singapore, the test generally applied is whether the offeror's words or conduct are such as to induce a reasonable person to believe that the offeror intends to be bound. Singapore courts have distinguished between that which constitutes an offer and that which is merely an invitation to treat. An invitation to treat invites the other party to make an offer and would not, as opposed to an offer, result in a binding contract upon "acceptance" by the other party. Preliminary negotiations,[13] shop displays[14] and certain advertisements of sale are classic examples of invitations to treat. However, courts will always look at the facts and surrounding circumstances in each case to determine whether an offer has been made.

How should websites on the Internet be treated? One possible view is that they should not be treated any differently from displays in shop windows and should therefore be taken as mere invitations to treat.[15] This would avoid the risk of the online merchant being held to have made an offer to the world at large when he or she was only prepared to sell to a limited class of people, a risk which is exacerbated in Internet transactions due to the great number of potential customers.

On the other hand, such an interpretation would leave consumers who had offered to purchase these Internet services and products without a remedy should the online merchant fail to deliver the service or product as promised. This is because in reality, many websites do not send any notification of their acceptance of the customer's offer to the customer. If so, there would be no legally enforceable contract even though the customer would already have authorised a deduction from his or her credit card account when making the purchase or order.

However, the law has not precluded all displays from constituting an offer[16] but would look at all the circumstances of the case. The online merchant may adequately protect his or her interests by stating clearly on the website any conditions upon which the offer is made. For example, the offer may only be to a limited class of persons or the offer may be subject to the availability of stock.

Before the offer is accepted, the offeror is at liberty to revoke the offer. Offers may also lapse after a specified time or event. The revocation of an offer must be received by the offeree in order to be effective.[17] Section 15 of the ETA deems the recipient to have received the e-mail at the time that the e-mail enters the designated e-mail system or, if the e-mail is sent to an information system of the recipient that is not the designated information system, at such time as the recipient actually retrieves the mail.

b. What Constitutes an Acceptance

Singapore law requires that acceptance must be unequivocal and communicated to the offeror in an agreed or a reasonable manner.

---

13 *Gibson v Manchester City Council* (1979) 1 WLR 294.

14 Fisher v Bell (1960) 3 All ER 731, *Pharmaceutical Society of Great Britain v Boots Cash Chemists (Southern) Ltd* (1953) 1 QB 401.

15 This position is consistent with the US case of *Webber v Jolly Hotels* 1 ECLR 1036, which considered websites as mere advertisements.

16 *Chapelton v Barry UDC* (1940) 1 All ER 356.

17 *Byrne v Van Tienhoven* (1880) 5 CPD 344.

Thus, when an offeree 'accepts' an offer while changing the terms of the original offer, there is no binding contract. Instead, the offeree has rejected the original offer and made a counteroffer which the first party can now accept or reject.

Like the revocation of an offer, there must be communication of the acceptance to the offeror, in the mode prescribed in the offer or, if unspecified in the offer, such other mode as is reasonable in the circumstances. The general rule that acceptance is ineffective until received by the offeror has been applied to most modern methods of communication which are instantaneous, such as telexes. An exception has been made for communications through the post (provided that the terms of the offer have not excluded acceptance by post and it would be reasonable in the circumstances to use the post). It may be taken in such cases that an acceptance sent by letter is effective and binding once the letter is posted. The consequences of this rule are significant. First, a posted acceptance precedes (and therefore prevails) over an uncommunicated revocation of the offer (i.e. where the revocation of the offer may have been sent but has not yet been received)[18] and second, a posted acceptance is effective upon posting even if subsequently lost or delayed.[19]

Which rules on acceptance of offers would apply to electronic transactions? Where the offer is silent, one must look to case law and local legislation. The basis of the court's distinction between acceptances by post and other forms of communication lies in the fact that the other forms of communication contemplated are virtually instantaneous.[20]

At first sight, it appears that online communications are instantaneous. However, they are actually sent to the Internet service provider before arriving at the recipient's server. Although the provider will notify the sender of undelivered e-mail, this may take some time, during which period the sender would not have noticed that the e-mail has not been delivered. This therefore differs from truly instantaneous modes of communication where the sender would almost immediately be aware of whether the communication has been successful. On this basis, one may argue that the postal rule should apply to Internet communications and that acceptance would be valid upon the e-mail being sent. It remains to be seen, however, how Singapore courts will view acceptances via Internet, taking into account s 15 of the ETA which provides that electronic records are deemed sent once they enter an information system outside the control of the sender unless otherwise agreed by the parties.

In this respect, it is to be noted that the provisions in the ETA with regard to formation of contracts may always be varied by agreement of the parties.

---

18 *Harris' Case* LR 7 Ch App 587.

19 Household Fire Insurance Co Ltd v Grant (1879) 4 Ex.D. 216.

20 This distinction was drawn in *Entores Ltd v Miles Far East Corporation* (1955) 2 All ER 493.

c. Contractual Capacity and Authorization

The other main issue in electronic transactions is the authentication of the identity of the parties. A contract is null and void as against a person who is unable to enter into a binding contract, either because that person has no legal capacity or has no legal authority to do so. Generally, parties are able to verify one another's capacity and authority by way of documentary evidence or otherwise. Signatures on contracts are used to bind signatories to the contract as they are presumed to possess the authority to enter into the signed contract. However, in electronic transactions, parties are faceless and verification becomes much harder.

In response to these difficulties, online merchants have taken precautionary measures like including conditions as to capacity in the terms of the offer, which must then be affirmed by the acceptor to be true and correct before the offer can be accepted.

The issue of verifying the identity of the contracting parties is dealt with by the ETA in four main ways:

(1) by giving legal recognition to electronic records and signatures;

(2) by providing a framework to regulate and secure such electronic records and signatures by allowing independent concerns to verify signatures;

(3) by legal presumptions in respect of "secure" electronic records and signatures; and

(4) by providing for sanctions against parties who are in breach of the ETA.

d. Electronic Records and Electronic Signatures

Electronic records are accorded full legal effect and validity (Section 12 of the ETA). Section 13 of the ETA states that an electronic message is deemed to be a party's message if it was sent by that party or by a person who had authority to act on his or her behalf or by an information system programmed by him or his agent. The receiver of the message is also entitled to treat the message as that of a party whose identity is ascertained in accordance with a previously agreed procedure for verification of the source of the electronic message, unless the receiver knows or ought reasonably to have known otherwise. In addition, electronic signatures attached to electronic records may be used to identify the source of that record. Electronic signatures may be proven in any manner.

Since electronic records may be altered and electronic signatures may be forged (just as paper records and handwritten signatures may be), a party is not precluded from proving that an electronic message was either tampered with or had not been sent by him. However, certain presumptions apply under the ETA in relation to secure electronic records and secure electronic signatures.

A "secure electronic record" is defined in s 16 of the ETA as an electronic record to which a prescribed security procedure or a commercially reasonable security procedure agreed to by the parties has been applied to verify that such record has not been altered since a specific point in time.

A "secure electronic signature" is one where a prescribed security procedure or a commercially reasonable security procedure agreed to by the parties has been applied to verify that, at the time it was made, the electronic signature was unique to the person verifying it, capable of identifying the person, created under the sole control of the person using the electronic signature, and linked to the electronic record such that the record could not be tampered with (Section 17 of the ETA).

Under s 18 of the ETA, it is presumed, unless proven otherwise, that a secure electronic record has not been altered since the specific point in time to which the secure status relates and that the secure electronic signature is the signature of the person with whom it correlates and was affixed by that person with the intention of signing or approving the electronic record.

e. Digital Signatures and the Role of Certification Authorities

The security procedure under the ETA prescribes the use of digital signatures and independent third parties known as certification authorities. A digital signature is defined in s 2 of the ETA and is basically an electronic signature which is signed using a "private key" known to the signor which can be verified using a generally available "public key". The sender registers with a certification authority (defined in s 2 of the ETA), who then issues to the sender an electronic key (known only to the sender), which the sender uses to digitally sign his or her messages. A certificate is also produced from this electronic key. The recipient of the signed message then verifies with the certification authority in question whether the public key in the certificate issued matches that of the sender's private key. If so, the recipient is assured that the digital signature was indeed that of the person to whom the signature correlates. A digital signature is secure when 'signed' while the certificate is valid provided the certificate was issued by a licensed (under Part X of the ETA), recognised (under Part VIII of the ETA) or approved certification authority.

The integrity and security of this framework is upheld by regulations and duties prescribed by the ETA in Parts VII, VIII and IX. All certification authorities, whether licensed or unlicensed, are bound by the duties therein.

By adhering to the security framework provided, parties are also legally entitled to rely on the following presumptions:

(1) an electronic record that has been secured within the meaning of the ETA is presumed not to have been altered since it was secured;

(2) the secure electronic signature is presumed to be that of the signatory and to have been applied by the signatory with the intention of authenticating or approving the electronic record; and

(3) where a licensed certification authority issues a certificate, a party may presume that the information published therein is correct, unless it is information identified as subscriber information which has not been verified.

Presumptions (1) and (2) are rebuttable where it would be unreasonable to rely on the digital signature having regard to facts which the person in receipt of the digital signature knows or has notice of, the value or importance of the record in question, the course of dealing between such person and the person who affixed the signature or any indicia of reliability or unreliability apart from the digital signature, and any usage of trade.

To enhance the efficacy of the ETA, the Act contains duties and sanctions additional to those already available at common law or under other statutes. Section 48 of the ETA imposes an obligation of confidentiality on any person who has access to private electronic records. Unpermitted disclosure is a criminal offence punishable by imprisonment for up to twelve months or a fine of up to SGD10,000.00. Unlawful use of a certificate would also render a person liable to criminal prosecution.

2. Terms of the Contract

Singapore law observes a general rule that to bind a party to certain terms and conditions, those terms and conditions must be brought to the party's notice either before or at the time the contract is made. In addition, special attention must be brought to terms which are onerous and oppressive to a party, for example, terms which purport to exclude the liability of the other party. Thus, a person will not be bound if he or she was unaware of such onerous or oppressive terms or conditions even if they are in writing, and it would not have been reasonable for him or her to expect that such terms and conditions should exist.

Conversely, a party's awareness of such terms and conditions which are in writing binds that party, even if he or she failed to read those terms and conditions.

These rules would apply to contracts formed over the Internet and would have to be kept in mind when designing the website display of terms and conditions. Various means of incorporating these rules to online terms and conditions are:

(1) including a single statement that the contract is subject to the terms and conditions of the online business;

(2) including a reference to the terms of the contract by a hyper-link to a webpage displaying the complete terms and conditions;

(3) displaying the terms at the end of the webpage; or

(4) requiring the customer to scroll down a display of the terms and to acknowledge acceptance of those terms before this order can be accepted.

3. Jurisdiction and Governing Law of the Contract

a. Jurisdiction

In Singapore, the courts' jurisdiction is founded primarily on the Supreme Court of Judicature Act in respect of the High Court, and the Subordinate Courts Act in respect of the subordinate courts. Section 16 of the former and s 19 of the latter essentially vest jurisdiction in the courts where:

(1) a defendant is served an originating process whether within or outside Singapore in the manner prescribed by the Rules Of Court 2004 (Revised Edition);

(2) where the defendant submits to the court's jurisdiction; or

(3) where the court has jurisdiction vested in it by virtue of any other written law.

Having established procedural jurisdiction on these bases, one proceeds to establish substantive jurisdiction. This entails a study of the various connecting factors of contract. Where more than one court may lay claim to jurisdiction, a Singapore court will ensure that it is a "proper" forum to adjudicate on the matter. If a more appropriate and convenient forum may be found, the court may decline to adjudicate on the matter.[21]

b. Governing Law

First, in determining the law which governs the contract, (i.e. the law which will determine, amongst other things, the validity and formation of and the rights under the contract), Singapore courts will respect parties' freedom to contract and will not generally overrule the parties' express bona fide choice of governing law.[22]

Secondly, in the absence of an express choice of law by the parties, Singapore courts will try to ascertain the parties' true intentions as to the choice of law as may be inferred from the surrounding circumstances, including the terms, form and nature of the contract as well as other factors (as seen in *James Capel (Far East) Ltd v Y K Fung Securities Sdn Bhd (1996) 2 MLJ 1997).*

Thirdly, if the application of either rule does not give a satisfactory answer, the courts will use an objective test to determine the system of law which has the closest and most real connection with the contract.

In the absence of an express choice of law, the borderless nature of Internet transactions will pose difficulties in the application of the second and third principles above. Thus, it is advisable to always provide expressly in the contract the parties' choice of law governing the contract.

---

21 These principles have been applied in *Bank of Tokyo v Karoon and Anr* (1986) 3 WLR 414.

22 *R v International Trustee for the Protection of Bondholders A/G* (1937) AC 500.

4. Enforcement

Finally, having obtained judgment in the courts, the judgment would be fruitless unless it can be enforced in the jurisdiction of the defendant. Whether this is possible will depend on the reciprocal enforcement treaties to which the particular country is a party.

Singapore has in operation the Reciprocal Enforcement of Commonwealth Judgments Act which facilitates the reciprocal enforcement of judgments in Singapore and other parts of the Commonwealth.

In relation to arbitral awards, Singapore is a party to the New York Convention, which facilitates the reciprocal enforcement of arbitral awards in Singapore and the other countries that are party to the Convention.

SPAIN

by
Enrique Jimenez Batalla
Batalla Abogados

A. SOURCES OF LAW

1. The Historical Development of Spanish Law

The origin of the Spanish legal system might be traced back to both Ancient Roman and Germanic legal systems. Roman Law arrived in the Iberian Peninsula in the first centuries of our Age, through means of the Roman occupation and the subsequent "romanizing" process. Roman Law greatly influenced Visigoth Law and regained strength during the Late Middle Ages, its print is still noticeable nowadays.

Ancient Germanic Law arrived at the time of the fall of the Roman Empire and the Barbarian invasions of the Peninsula, reaching its peak during the Visigoth Kingdom. In addition, Germanic Law has decisively influenced those local sets of rules and rights (in Spanish, Fueros) that were born during the Middle Ages in Spain and still in force in some cases. A very important political and juridical event, that has influenced the development of the Law in Spain, was the breaking down of the whole Peninsula in different Kingdoms, which developed their own private law systems independently, a situation that continues to exist nowadays.[1]

2. Sources of Spanish Law

According to Article 1 of the Spanish Civil Code,[2] the sources of the Spanish legal system are "the law, the custom and the general principles of law", being the 1978 Spanish Constitution as the supreme source of this system. The 1978 Constitution

1 A peculiarity of private law in Spain is the coexistence of several legal systems within the same territory, due to the different kingdoms in which the Peninsula was divided during the Middle Ages, a situation that persisted until the 18th century, when finally Spain might be referred to as a truly united Nation. Nowadays, and as a consequence of this, Spain is divided into seventeen different regions.

2 Except from some small modifications, the same Civil Code has been in operation since 1888.

established Spain as a social and democratic Nation under the rule of Law, and proclaims freedom, justice, equality and political pluralism.

Once the Congress had first approved it and the Spanish people had then ratified it, the Constitution defined the Spanish Nation to be indivisible and indissoluble but simultaneously recognising the autonomy of the constituent regions, an unthinkable possibility under the former dictatorship.

The Constitution recognised the right of autonomy of those adjacent provinces sharing historical, cultural and economic features, as well as to the islands and those single provinces considered to be regional historic entities in themselves. These regions constituted themselves into Autonomous Communities, or Comunidades Autónomas.[3] Another of the fundamental changes introduced by the Constitution was the consideration of Spain as a Parliamentary Monarchy, the monarchy mainly playing a representing role.

Likewise, and in accordance with the majority of democracies nowadays, there is a clear separation of the three branches of government: the Legislative, the Executive and the Judiciary.

The Legislative Power is vested in the Congress (Cortes Generales) that represents the people and consists of two chambers: The Senate (High Chamber) and the House of Representatives (or Congreso de los Diputados, Low Chamber). Among the powers of Congress there are the lawmaking responsibility, the approval of its own Budget and appropriations as well as the control over the Government's acts.

The Executive Power has control over domestic and international affaires, the Civil and Army Administrations and the national defence. This Power is exercised accordingly to the Constitution and the Law. The Government consists of the President, the Vice-presidents, the Secretaries and the members specifically established by Law.

The Judicial Power consists of both Judges and Courts, in charge of administering Justice in the name of the King. In order to accomplish such a task given by the Constitution, the jurisdictional power is vested in the following Judges and Courts:

- Local Judges;[4]
- Original Jurisdiction Judges, in the Criminal, Administrative, Labour, Minors and Penitentiary Supervision branches;[5]

---

3 Translator's note: similarly to the German Länder or the U.S. States.

4 Translator's note: Juzgados de Paz, only when explicitly established by Law and in those cities of less than 5,000 inhabitants.

5 Translator's note: Juzgados de Primera Intancia e Instrucción, de lo Penal, Contencioso-Administrativo, de lo Social, de Menores y de Supervisión Penitenciaria.

- Provincial Courts;[6]
- Superior Courts of Justice;[7]
- National Court;[8] and
- Supreme Court.[9]

3. Lawmaking Initiative in the Spanish Legal System

According to the Constitution and the Rules of the Chambers of Congress, Government, the House of Representatives and the Senate may propose legislation.

The Congress is responsible of the making of the Organic Laws.[10] Their approval, modification or derogations demands absolute majority.

The Congress might delegate on the Government the power of making laws on matters that might not influence fundamental rights nor people's freedom. This act of delegation shall be made explicitly over a certain matter and only temporarily.

Lastly, in accordance with our Constitution, the Government is entitled to produce temporary legislative rules only in cases of extreme urgency. These legislative rules shall never influence the regulation of the Nation's basic institutions, the fundamental rights, duties and people's freedom, the territorial regime or the voting general regime.

The Decree-Laws shall immediately enter debate in the House of Representatives, specially summoned in the event of an off-season decision, within thirty days since its approval by the Government. The House of Representatives must explicitly decide on their approval or repeal.

References

- Act 1/2000, 7 January, Civil Procedure.
- Organic Law 6/1985, 1 July, Judiciary Power.
- Spanish 1978 Constitution.
- Spanish Civil Code.
- Civil Law Institutions, Vol. 1, Díez-Picazo, L. and Gullón, A.

B. SCHEME OF ONLINE BUSINESS REGULATIONS

In view of the constant innovation currently occurring in this field, it is necessary to point out that, despite the strong efforts made by the Spanish legislature

---

6 Translator's note: Audiencias Provinciales.

7 Translator's note: Tribunales Superiores de Justicia.

8 Translator's note: Audiencia Nacional.

9 Translator's note: Tribunal Supremo.

10 Such Organic Laws regulate the development of the fundamental rights and people's freedom.

when trying to establish regulations destined to control electronic commerce, the rules actually existing in the Spanish legislation are fairly divided, which makes it necessary to appeal to several norms depending on the specific matter we are dealing with. Nor is there today sufficient case law[11] on which to ground specific actions.

1. Law 34/2002 Services of the Information Society and Electronic Commerce of 11 July 2002

This law is intended to rearrange EC Directive 2000/31. Its purpose is to regulate the legal system of the services provided by the information society and the contracting through electronic means,[12] as far as the obligations of the service providers are concerned, including those that act as mediators in the transmission of content through communications networks, commercial communications through electronic channels, any previous information, the subsequent subscription of electronic contracts, the conditions concerning their validity and effectiveness and the sanctioning procedures applicable to the services of the information society.

The law itself provided a three month *"vacation legis"* since its publication by the BOE[13] (State's Official Gazette), which means that the enactment, that determines the effective application of the law, took place on 12 October 2002.

The Spanish legislature regulates commercial messages (known as "spam"), as the remittance of such messages is explicitly prohibited when there has not been a previous request by part of the addressee.[14] The purpose of this law, as far as commercial messages are concerned, is to ensure that the addressee of any advertising or commercial messages gives its express and unequivocal authorization to receive such information. The acceptance to receive a specific commercial message, that reflects the addressee's consent, ought to be a specific fact, independent of the purpose intended, which means that the law clearly has excluded any kind of tacit acceptance. The consequences of breaching this provision may be seriously harmful for any business person that decides, despite the legal prohibition, to carry out this kind of conduct.

Article 38 Law of Services of the Information Society classifies as serious fault the transmittal of more than three commercial messages, not requested or not ex-

11 Article 1.6 of the Civil Code: The Jurisprudence shall complement the legal system with doctrine that in a reiterated manner, is established by the Supreme Court when interpreting and applying the law and its general principles.

12 Issue that will be analyzed in detail throughout this article.

13 In Spain a law is only part of the legislation after its full publication by the State Official Gazette.

14 Article 21 Law of Services of the Information Society provides: "It is prohibited to send advertising messages by electronic mail or other equivalent electronic means of communication is not requested or expressly authorized by the addressees of the message".

pressly authorized, in a term of one year to a same addressee. To do so may give rise to the imposition of fines that range from EUR30,001 to EUR150,000.

European Directive 2002/58/EC of the European Parliament and the Council concerns the treatment of personal data and the protection of privacy in the area of electronic communications. On one side, and as already explained, the Spanish Law specifically forbids, under any circumstance, the remittance of commercial messages through e-mail, while the European Directive is more permissive in those circumstances contemplated by the Directive. In particular, Article 13 of the Directive provides that whoever obtains the electronic address of a client to sell a product or service, may use this address to directly sell products or services of similar characteristics. The Directive must deal with these issues in Europe and inevitably has to be fitted into the regulations of all the Member States of the European Union as well. Relevantly, Article 17 of the European Directive provides a maximum term, scheduled for the 31st of October 2003, during which all the Member States[15] must rearrange these dispositions. This situation creates significant legal uncertainty because, on one hand the Spanish legislation presently in force strictly prohibits sending advertising messages through e-mail, while on the other the Directive provides an exception in connection with the using electronic means to send advertising to clients with whom a previous contractual relationship had been established, during the term of one year.

Until the date of transposition of the mentioned Directive, it would be unlawful to send commercial messages not expressly requested, including to usual clients, with the risk for transgressors of incurring sanctions of up to EUR150,000, while the same activity after the incorporation of the Directive by Spanish legislation shall be lawful, as by then the Information Society Law will have been modified in the opposite sense.

Additionally, Spanish companies operating through the Internet will find themselves in a situation of disadvantage in comparison with companies from other European countries, which at the time of transposing the Electronic Commerce Directive decided not to prohibit the remittance of this kind of messages but simply to restrict it, which means they will be able to continue sending such messages while the Spanish companies will be deprived from doing so until at least the 31st of October 2003.

Finally, to comment, as a novelty that is worth mentioning in this matter, Royal Decree 292/2004, of February 20, that creates the public distinguishing sign of trust in the services of the information society and of electronic commerce and that rules the requirements and grant procedure.

15 Spain joined the European Community in 1986 and therefore from that time onwards, undertook to incorporate as is own all Directives approved within the EU.

2. Law 59/2003, of December 19, on Electronic Signature

Law 59/2003, of December 19, on electronic signature, has repealed Royal Decree Law 14/1999, of September 17, on electronic signature, that was approved with the purpose to try to promote the quick incorporation of the new technologies to the Spanish society.

The goal of this new Law is to give a greater security to the communications through the Internet, in order to achieve the citizens to feel more and more confident when carrying out transactions through the net. To achieve this greater confidence appears as something essential to try to avoid, as far as possible, that the prevailing means among the generality of the citizenship retrains the development of the information society. As a reply to this urgent need, the figure of the electronic signature arises as an instrument able to allow a verification of the origin and the integrity of the messages exchanged through the telecommunication nets.

The subjects making possible the use of the electronic signature are those ones called renderers of certification services that are the ones in charge of permanently protecting and managing all the certificates they issue[16].

Likewise, Law makes reference to a specific kind of electronic certificates that are those called recognized electronic certificates. The latter are the ones being granted when all the guarantees required by law have been fulfilled. These certificates constitute a essential piece of the so called recognized electronic signature that is defined following the guidelines provided by Directive 1999/93/CE[17]. The law grants the recognized electronic signature the operative equivalence with the handwritten signature regarding the electronically recorded data.

As previously mentioned, Law 59/2003 on electronic signature has reinforced the juridical framework existing on this matter, including some novelties regarding Royal Decree Law 14/1999, in an attempt to revitalize, as far as possible, this sector as far as the rendering of certification services is concerned.

One the novelties worth mentioning offered by Law regarding Royal Decree Law 14/1999 is the denomination as recognized electronic signature of the electronic signature that is functionally on a level with the handwritten signature. This definition clarifies the fact that the advanced electronic signature is not enough for it to be on a level with the handwritten signature, but, so that this comparison takes place, it is necessary the advanced electronic signature to be based on a recognized certificate and to have been created by a safe creation de-

16 The details of this formality should be contained in the so called declaration of certification practices, that will specify the conditions applicable to the request, issue, use, suspension and expiration of the validity of the electronic certificates.

17 This Directige defines the recognized electronic signature as the advanced electronic signature based on a recognized certificate and generated by a safe device of creation of signature.

vice. All the above in order to give a greater security to all the transactions made through telematic means.

Another novelty of this law is the elimination of the renderers of certification services, and the creation of a simple service for the dissemination of information about the renderers working in the market, the quality certificates as well as the characteristics of the products and services they have for the development of their activity.

The law also modifies the concept of certification of renderders of certification services to grant it a greater liberty degree and provide with a greater protagonism to the participation of the private sector in the certification systems.[18]

Another interesting modification refers to the fact that the law clarifies the obligation to constitute an economic guarantee by the renderers of the certification services that issue recognized certificates, establishing a unique minimum amount of three million euros, making at the same time more flexible the means to constitute the aforementioned guarantee,

Another interesting novelty is that the law reinforces the control measures by the Ministry of Science and Technology on the renderers of the certification services, with the possibility of being assisted by technically qualified independent entities.

We should also outline the regulation established by the law on the electronic ID. This legal text establishes the basic regulation framework of this new tool, outlining its two most characteristic notes, on one hand it serves to prove the identity of its holder at any administrative proceedings, and it also allows the electronic signature of documents.[19]

Another novelty in connection with the Royal Decree Law of 199 is the establishment in the law of the applicable system to the performance of juridical people as signatories, with the purpose of including these entities in the telematic traffic.[20]

In order to give a greater juridical security to the transactions carried out making use of these means, the law requests, on one hand, a special legitimation for the individuals who apply for the issue of certificates, and on the other hand, it obliges the applicants to become responsible for the protection of the data for the creation of electronic signature related to such certificates. Before third parties, it limits the use of these certificates to the acts that comprise the relationship among the entity and the public Administrations and the things or services

18 With this novelty, the law is nearer to the provisions of the Community Directive.

19 As far as the particularities of this system are concerned, its specific regulation will apply.

20 Royal Decree Law of 1999 only allowed the juridical people to be holders of electronic certificates in the scope of the management of taxes.

that constitute the regular traffic of the entity, without detriment to the possible quantitative or qualitative limits that can be added.

Within the reiterated attempts to reinforce the security feeling offered by the telematic means, following the guideline established by Lay 34/2002, of July 11, on services to the information and electronic commerce society, the support containing the electronically signed data is included. Besides, we should outline the novel fact that the law explicitly admits the representation relationships that can underlie in the use of the electronic signature.

Finally, to indicate that this law allows the renderers of the certification services, and in order to improve the trust on their services, to be able to establish coordination mechanisms with the data that should compulsory be at the public Registries, in order to verify the data that appear in the certificates at the moment the same are issued.

3. Order 662/2003, of March 18, Approving the National Plan of Internet Domain Names under the Country Code Corresponding to Spain (".es")

As inferred from the reading of this Order, the good operation of the domain names system is essential for the optimum operation of the Internet, hence the Spanish legislation has specially exerted in ruling this issue.

Thus, since 1996 the Internet began to be used with commercial purposes in Spain, the expansion of this new communication way has been very outstanding, developing almost at the same time as the system for the designation of domain names under ".es", the management of which was assigned in 2000 to a business public company called Red.es[21]. The rules of this entity were later on included in a juridical rule, Order of March 21, 2000[22]; Order that has been repealed by the Order 662/2003, of March 18, that we are analyzing in this point.

The aforementioned Order, already repealed, announced the need to carry out a deeper reform of the system for the assignment of domain names under ".es" to be able to attend the new demands claimed by the increase of Internet users in Spain. This reform was carried out by the Sixth Additional Provision of Law 34/2002, of July 11, on Information and Electronic Commerce Society Services, that rules the general principles of the system for the assignment of domain names under ".es" and through this National Plan of domain names, that develops the existing legal regulation in connection with this assignment system.

One of the most important modifications introduced by this Plan is the reduction of the applicable restrictions to the assignment of domain names under ".es", lightening the prohibitions for the registration foreseen by the previous Orders,

---

21 Formerly called Entidad Publica Empresarial de la Red Técnica Española de Televisión.

22 This Order was modified by Order of July 12, 2001 for the introduction of some technical improvements.

carrying out an extension of the legitimation for the registration and of the types of available domain names. In this latter case, it has created the tirad level domain names.

Regarding the domain names that had been assigned prior to the coming into force of this Plan, the same expressly establishes that they will keep their validity.

4. Constitutional Law for the Protection of Data of Personal Nature 15/1999 of 3 December

The present law is intended to guarantee and protect, as far as the Personal Data treatment is concerned, the public freedom and the fundamental rights of persons, especially their honour and personal and family privacy.[23] In electronic deals when gathering information of a personal nature, the following requirements provided by the mentioned law must be met:

- notification to the Data Protection Agency[24] about the creation of a data bases and as well as their registration;
- security measures required for the correct treatment of information;
- identification of the person responsible for the treatment of information;
- the possibility that user may have access to its information, to modify it or cancel it, provided all the technical means required to do so.

5. Decree 994/1999 of 11 June. Security Measures Applied to Automized Files Containing Information of Personal Nature

This Decree is intended to provide the technical and organizational measures required to guarantee the security standards to be met by the automized files, the centers of information treatment, the premises, equipment, systems, programs and persons involved in the treatment of information of a personal nature. This rule, according to the characteristics of the personal information involved, distinguishes among and requires adoption of:

- **basic level** security measures for files containing personal data;
- **medium level** security measures for the treatment of information concerning the perpetration of administrative or penal infringements, infringements against the Public Treasury and financial services; and

23 Article 18 of the Spanish Constitution guarantees the right to the honour and personal and family privacy, that are conceived as fundamental and ultimate right in the Spanish legislation.

24 *Data Protection Agency.* Its main role is to watch for the compliance of the legislation concerning the protection of personal information, specially with respect to the rights of information, access, opposition, rectification and cancellation of data.

- **high level** security measures for those files containing information about a person's ideology, religion, beliefs, racial origin, health or sexual orientation, as well as any information gathered by the police.

In view of all the above and depending on the nature of the data before which we are, the holder of the file where these data will be stored should take the security measures that may correspond in each case, being subject to the fulfillment of a greater number of requirements, the more the protection level before which we are will be.[25]

C. ELECTRONIC TRANSACTIONS AND CONTRACT FORMATION

1. Introduction

The spread of online commerce has resulted in considerable change in the physical and material patterns of conventional commerce, up to a point where the material support of the contract is losing importance, thus allowing faster contracting. This quick change has often produced a lack of trust in new technologies among consumers, who hesitate to carry out commercial transactions through these means. Regulation has to be adapted to the new circumstances in many countries, in order to provide these transactions with the best possible protection against lawbreaking acts.

Online commerce includes both the purchase of goods or services through the Internet and the transfer of personal data between parties of a certain market sector. Likewise, the exchange of securities between financial establishments, the consultation of data for commercial purposes and many other similar activities might be included in the concept of online commerce as well.

Regarding the means involved, we may differentiate between direct e-commerce, also online e-commerce, and indirect e-commerce, or offline e-commerce. The first refers to the transactions exclusively carried out through electronic means, that is, over the Net.[26] The indirect or offline e-commerce would be those transactions that need some kind of physical support in order to be formal, such as the distribution of a good.

The Act 34/2002, dated 11 July, on the Information Society's Services and E-commerce has been issued to rule all these activities and provide electronic transactions with protection.

2. Validity and Effectiveness

In accordance with article 23 of Act 34/2002, dated 11 July, on the Information Society's Services and E-commerce, contracts carried out by electronic means

25 Due to the "effect 2000", Royal Decree 195/2000, of February 11, extended the term granted by Royal Decree 994/1999 for the implementation of the security measures established for the automated files containing private nature data.

26 Purchase of cinema tickets, flight tickets and many more.

will produce all the effects provided for by the legal system whenever mutual consent and the other legal requirements are fulfilled. Those cases not foreseen by this Act will follow the general legal rules contained in the Civil Code, Commercial Code and the consumers', users' and retail commerce regulation.

The Spanish Civil Code[27] states in this regard that there is a contract only when the following circumstances concur:

- mutual consent;[28]
- the subject matter is identifiable;[29] and
- cause of the consideration.[30]

For the Spanish Civil Code an essential requirement is the concurrence of two declarations of will: the offeror's and the offeree's on the subject matter of the contract and the cause of the consideration. Likewise, the contracting parties must have capacity and authority to enter into a binding agreement, excluding, thus, non-emancipated minors and legally incompetent individuals.

Mutual consent between contracting parties on the use of electronic means is not needed in order for contracts performed in such a way to be formal. However, where the law requires the contract or any other related information to be in a written document, this requirement would be fulfilled where such a contract or information is in electronic format. Specific rules will have to be taken into account where the law provides that the contracts, transactions or legal acts need to be written in a public document to be intervened by a Notary or Real Estate Register Officer.

Lastly, those contracts involving family law and the law of succession will not be valid when carried out through electronic means, in accordance with Article 23 of Act 34/2002.

3. Proof of Contracts Carried Out by Electronic Means

According to Article 24 of Act 34/2002, dated 11 July, on the Information Society's Services and E-commerce, the proof of a contract carried out through electronic means and the duties originated from it will follow the general legal rules and, where appropriate, those established by legislation on the electronic signa-

27 Article 1261 of the Spanish Civil Code.

28 Consent is expressed by the concurrence of the offer and the acceptance of the subject matter and cause of consideration (these last two elements are mandatory elements of the contract).

29 According to article 1271 of the Spanish Civil Code, the subject matter of a contract might be anything within human reach, even the future ones.

30 According to article 1274 of the Civil Code, the cause of valuable consideration will be the provision or promise of a given thing or service: in case of remunerative contracts, the cause will be the service or profit rewarded; in the case of a gratuitous promise, the cause would be the liberality of the rightdoer.

ture.[31] In any case, the electronic support of a contract carried out by electronic means might be used to document it.

In order to understand this Article we may refer to Article 1278 of the Spanish Civil Code, that does not prescribe a single way in which consent might be given. This rule, interpreted in the light of Articles 1261 and 1262 of the same legal text, leads to the conclusion that the contract will be valid no matter the way it was carried out as long as it fulfils the essential conditions for it to be valid.[32]

The Spanish Commerce Code confirms this principle regarding commercial contracts and activities. Article 51 of this legal text states that commercial contracts will be valid and able to serve as proof upon trial no matter the way consent was given and the language used to do so, the category they might belong to and their economic value, as long as they are documented by any means established by Civil Law.

Therefore, a contract will be valid when the following circumstances concur: consent, subject matter and cause of consideration. This means that it makes no difference whether the electronic contracts are electronically signed for them to be valid.

Indeed, electronic contracts not bearing an electronic signature are completely valid despite the lack of such a signature since the user's consent is given by clicking the "acceptance" button. Electronic signature is neither used by the offeror in general terms. The latter usually offers his products online together with some information on the products themselves and his professional activity addressed to the potential consumer. Thus, the potential consumer trusts in the offeror and the truthfulness of the offer, giving his consent without the need of a traditional or electronic signature. Once the contract is carried out in these terms, both parties will have to fulfill the duties originated from it.

In conclusion, contracts carried out through the Net are valid and produce binding effects to the parties to it no matter how the consent has been expressed. In this regard, the fact a contract might be electronically signed does not affect the validity of the transaction itself. It is simply a guarantee that the document has not been manipulated, its authenticity as well as the reserve nature of the information therein contained.

In order to proof the existence of the declarations of will produced by the parties to a contract, according to Article 25 of Act 34/2002 these parties might agree that a third party[33] files the declarations of will contained in the electronic contracts together with the date and time the communication has taken place.[34]

---

31 Ley 59/2003, de 19 de diciembre, de firma electrónica.

32 The consent of both parties validly given, a certain subject matter and a cause of consideration.

33 The authentication bodies will serve this point.

34 This third party must file the declarations that have taken place by telematic means for the period of time previously agreed on. This period might not be longer than five years.

In relation to the moment from when the contract is considered to be valid and to be able to produce its effects, in spite of the different theories on this regard, in the authors' opinion the emission theory is the one nearer to the features of the electronic contracting schemes. According to this theory, the contract is valid from the moment the addressee-accepting party sends his or her declaration of will through electronic means.

4. Rules Applicable to Contracts Carried Out by Electronic Means

Article 26 of Act 34/2002, dated 11 July, on the Information Society's Services and E-commerce, refers to the rules of Private International Law contained in the Spanish legal system. In general terms, the law applicable to a certain contract will be that freely chosen by the parties.[35] A typical example of this freedom of choice could be the contracts between companies. Here, the parties are free to choose between the law applicable to any of the parties or a foreign law. Nevertheless, this rule is not suitable when one of the parties is a consumer. In this case other rules are applicable. Hence, Act 26/1984 on the Consumer's and User's Protection states that in these cases the applicable law will be that of the country in which the consumer has his or her residence.

5. On the Duties Previous to the Beginning the Contracting Procedure

In accordance with Article 27 of Act 34/2002, dated 11 July, on the Information Society's Services and E-commerce, the information-society service provider that carries out activities that involve electronic contracts is due to inform the consumer in a clear, comprehensible and unmistakable way and before starting the contracting procedure about the following:

- The different steps to follow to conclude the contract.
- Whether or not the concluded contract will be filed by the service provider and whether it will be accessible.
- The technical means provided for identifying and correcting errors in the input before placing an order.
- The language or languages offered for the conclusion of the contract.

This duty of information is not needed when both parties have so agreed, as long as any of the parties is not a consumer or the contract has been carried out exclusively by means of e-mail messages or any similar means. Likewise, it is important to underline that previous to the beginning of the contracting procedure, the service provider is due to supply the consumer with the contract terms and general conditions in a way that allows him or her to store and reproduce them.

35 Article 3 of the Rome International Convention on Applicable Law that Governs the Contractual Transactions, dated 19 June 1980.

6. The Information to Be Provided Once the Contract Has Been Carried Out

Article 28 of Act 34/2002 states that the service provider must confirm the acceptance of the recipient upon its reception, either by sending an e-mail message or equal technological method, or by any other means similar to the one used in the contracting procedure. In this regard, the order and the acknowledgement of receipt are deemed to be received when the parties to whom they are addressed are able to access them.

The same article also establishes two exceptions to the duty to confirm the reception of the acceptance of a given offer:

- When both parties agree to do so and none of them might be considered to be a consumer.
- When the contract has been exclusively concluded by exchange of electronic mail or by equivalent individual communications, as long as the use of this method does not involve excluding the aforementioned duty of confirmation.

7. Place Where the Contract Is Concluded

In accordance with Article 29 of Act 34/2002, contracts concluded by electronic means where a party is a consumer will be deemed carried out in the consumer's place of residence. Electronic contracts between companies or professionals might be deemed concluded in the place the service provided is established, when no other conditions have been agreed upon.

The Spanish legal system has exerted itself to favour the electronic arrangement of agreements, strengthening the general contractual principle according to which any contract shall be deemed valid in spite of its exterior appearance,[36] as long as the consent of the parties has been adopted in a proper manner and the contract has a clear subject matter and a fair cause of consideration. Nevertheless, and despite the aforementioned efforts, the electronic conclusion of contracts is delayed where consumers are still suspicious and do not feel comfortable in such a nonmaterial environment.

Legislation

- Act 34/2002, dated 11 July, on the Information Society's Services and E-commerce.
- Law 59/2003, of December 19, on electronic signature.
- Rome International Convention on the Applicable Law that Governs the Contractual Transactions, done on 19 June 1980.
- Act 26/1984 on the Consumers' and Users' Defense.

36 Translator's note: This principle is known by the Spanish juridical doctrine as "espiritualista", or spiritual, since the nonmaterial features of the contract are more important than the material or external ones.

SWITZERLAND

by
Mark A. Reutter and Markus R. Frick
Walder Wyss & Partners Attorneys at Law

A. SOURCES OF LAW

1. Overview

Switzerland is a constitutional democracy with a federal structure and an independent judiciary. The revised *Federal Constitution of the Swiss Confederation of December 18, 1998* came into effect on January 1, 2000.[1] Under the Federal Constitution, the power to enact laws is shared by the Confederation and the 26 sovereign cantons. Swiss federal statutory law is formally enacted by the Federal Parliament. Statutory laws must be submitted to a popular vote (referendum) if a petition with sufficient signatures is presented. A referendum can be mandated by a petition signed by 50,000 citizens. To pass the vote, a simple majority of the votes cast is sufficient.

Amendments to the Federal Constitution must be submitted to a popular referendum; they need to be ratified by a majority of both the voters and the cantons. 100,000 citizens can demand, by means of an initiative, that a proposal to remove or amend a provision of the Federal Constitution, or to insert a new one, be presented for a referendum. While only a few of these initiatives are eventually accepted, they often prompt a milder counter-proposal by the Federal Parliament which has a better chance of being accepted.

Swiss law is primarily statutory. Constitutional provisions take precedence over ordinary statutes and administrative regulations. Such statutory law can be found in the federal and cantonal compilations of the laws.

Switzerland has four national languages: German, French, Italian and Rhaeto-Romanic. The Confederation publishes all its statutes and most of its

1 *Bundesverfassung der Schweizerischen Eidgenossenschaft* of April 18, 1999; available in German, French and Italian at http://www.admin.ch/ch/d/sr/101/index.html.

documents in German, French and Italian.[2] A number of statutes are also available in English through unofficial private translations.[3]

Court decisions are not binding on other courts. Although interpretations of the law by the Swiss Federal Tribunal—Switzerland's Supreme Court—and by the cantonal appellate courts are generally followed, intentional deviation from their decisions is not infrequent and sometimes prompts the higher courts to revise their positions.

Since 1815, Switzerland has adhered to the principle of neutrality in its foreign policy. Switzerland has joined the United Nations only in 2002. Switzerland is neither a member of the European Union ("EU") nor of the European Economic Area. However, in 1999 Switzerland and the EU signed bilateral agreements that came into force on June 1, 2002. The bilateral agreements are sector-specific and cover seven areas: civil aviation, overland transport, the free movement of persons, research, public procurement markets, agriculture and the elimination of technical barriers to trade. In these areas, Swiss law is already, or about to be, harmonized with EU law. In addition, the developments in EU law are closely monitored in Switzerland, and in many areas Euro-compatible Swiss rules have been enacted.

2. Legislation Affecting the Conduct of Business

The lawmaking competence for private law, and hence the most important regulation affecting business undertakings, lies within the Confederation and encompasses primarily civil law. The *Swiss Civil Code ("Civil Code"),*[4] which includes the law of persons (individuals and legal entities), family law (including husband-wife and parent-child relationships), and estate and property law (moveable and immoveable property), was codified in 1907 at the federal level. The *Swiss Code of Obligations ("Code of Obligations")* encompasses the law of contracts, unjust enrichment (quasi contracts), torts, partnerships, corporations and negotiable instruments. It was codified in 1881, passed in 1911, and materially amended in 1936 and 1991.[5] The *Civil Code* and the *Code of Obligations* are the most important Swiss statutes affecting the conduct of business in Switzerland.

Criminal law is principally embodied in the *Swiss Penal Code* ("*Penal Code*").[6]

---

2 Swiss Legislation is available online (in German, French and Italian) through the Official Collection of Swiss Law (AS) at http://www.admin.ch/ch/d/as and through the Systematic Collection of Swiss Law (SR) at http://www.admin.ch/ch/d/sr/sr.html.

3 English translations available will be indicated in the footnotes hereafter.

4 *Schweizerisches Zivilgesetzbuch* of December 10, 1907; available in German, French and Italian at http://www.admin.ch/ch/d/sr/c210.html.

5 *Schweizerisches Obligationenrecht* of March 30, 1911; available in German, French and Italian at http://www.admin.ch/ch/d/sr/22.html.

6 *Schweizersches Strafgesetzbuch* of December 21, 1937; available in German, French and Italian at http://www.admin.ch/ch/d/sr/c311_0.html.

3. Jurisdiction

a. Applicable Rules

The Swiss Jurisdiction Act[7] sets out the jurisdiction rules for domestic civil - litigation matters in Switzerland. As a general rule, a matter is domestic if the parties to the dispute are either domiciled or resident in Switzerland. The *Jurisdiction Act* has replaced the different cantonal jurisdictional rules formerly in place.

In international settings, i.e. in particular if at least one of the parties to a dispute is not domiciled or resident in Switzerland, jurisdiction is primarily governed by international treaties and subsidiary by the *Swiss Private International Law Act ("Private International Law Act").*[8]

The most important international treaty applicable in Switzerland is the *Lugano Convention on the Jurisdiction and Enforcement of Judgments in Civil and Commercial Matters of September 16, 1988 ("Lugano Convention").*[9] The *Lugano Convention* was concluded between the member states of the European Union and the European Free Trade Association. The convention is open to other countries, and, in addition to the current EU and EFTA member states, Poland has joined the convention.[10] The *Lugano Convention* was drafted as a parallel convention with only minor differences to the *Brussels Convention on Jurisdiction and the Enforcement of Judgments in Civil and Commercial Matters of 1968*. The *Lugano Convention* applies between the EU member states on the one hand and Iceland, Norway, Poland and Switzerland on the other. As of March 1, 2002 the *Brussels Convention* was replaced by *Regulation 44/2001 on Jurisdiction and the Recognition and Enforcement of Judgments in Civil and Commercial Matters (the "Brussels I Regulation")*.[11] The *Brussels I Regulation* applies between the EU member states with the exception of Denmark. Since the revision, there are now more noticeable differences between the *Lugano Convention* and the *Brussels I Regulation*. The *Lugano Convention* is currently under review to achieve full parallelism with the *Brussels I Regulation.*

The *Lugano Convention* applies if the defendant in a civil or commercial matter is domiciled in a contracting state.[12] If an agreement contains a jurisdiction clause

---

7 *Bundesgesetz über den Gerichtsstand in Zivilsachen* of March 24, 2000; available in German, French and Italian at http://www.admin.ch/ch/d/sr/c272.html.

8 *Bundesgesetz über das Internationale Privatrecht* of December 18, 1987; available in German, French and Italian at http://www.admin.ch/ch/d/sr/c291.html. An unofficial English translation of the Act can be ordered at http://www.amcham.ch/publications/m_obligations.htm#top.

9 An English text of the Lugano Convention is available at http://www.curia.eu.int/common/recdoc/convention/en/c-textes/_lug-textes.htm.

10 Gibraltar is an also a member by a declaration of extension/ agreement between the UK and Spain.

11 "Official Journal 2001" L 12 p. 1.

12 Article 2 (1) *Lugano Convention*.

that assigns jurisdiction to a court within a contracting state, it is sufficient if one of both parties is domiciled in a contracting state.[13]

b. Jurisdiction Clauses in Online Contracts

In contractual relationships not covered by special or exclusive jurisdiction rules, jurisdiction clauses are generally enforceable under the *Lugano Convention*, provided the form requirements set out in Article 17 *Lugano Convention* are respected. According to this provision, an agreement conferring jurisdiction must either be:

- in writing or evidenced in writing,
- in a form that accords with practices which the parties have established between themselves, or
- in international trade or commerce, in a form that corresponds to a usage of which the parties are or should be aware, and which is widely known and regularly observed by parties to contracts of the type involved in the particular trade or commerce concerned.

While it is likely that jurisdiction clauses exchanged by e-mail meet the form requirements of Article 17 of the *Lugano Convention,* it is not clear how the Swiss courts will apply this provision in connection with a jurisdiction clause posted or communicated over the Internet. The same is true in the case of applicability of the *Private International Law Act*, which provides that the parties may agree on a place of jurisdiction by any "means of communication which may be evidenced by text".

The *Jurisdiction Act* clarifies (for domestic matters) only some of the pertinent issues. It provides in Article 9 that any forms of transmission which allow evidence by text, such as telex, telefax and e-mail, are equal to a jurisdiction clause in writing. The explicit reference to e-mails resolves some of the uncertainties in this respect. Whether clauses merely posted on the Internet comply with the form requirements of the *Jurisdiction Act,* however, is not explicitly addressed.

Apart from form requirements, it remains uncertain whether the mere placement of a clause on a website by one party, in conjunction with a general statement by the other party to agree, e.g. by clicking on the "I accept" button, results in a mutual exchange of declaration of intent as required to conclude a jurisdiction clause.

In the case of contracts which are unrelated to a customer's professional or business activities, (i.e. in consumer matters) the possibilities of the parties to agree on a specific jurisdiction are limited:

- If a consumer is party to a contract listed in Article 13 of the *Lugano Convention,* proceedings under the *Lugano Convention* against the consumer can only be brought in the courts of the state of the consumer's domicile.[14] Article 13 of the *Lugano Convention* covers, *inter alia,* any contract for the supply of

---

13 Article 17 *Lugano Convention.*

14 Article 14 *Lugano Convention.*

goods or services concluded with a consumer, if that contract was preceded by a specific invitation addressed directly to the consumer or by advertising in the state of the consumer's domicile and where the consumer took the necessary steps for the conclusion of the contract in that state.[15] The parties can only agree on a different jurisdiction after the dispute has arisen.[16]

- Both the *Private International Law Act* and the *Jurisdiction Act* provide for similar restrictions to jurisdiction clauses in consumer contracts. A consumer may not validly waive jurisdiction at his or her domicile in advance.[17] Moreover the *Swiss Jurisdiction Act* provides that consumers may not waive (the alternative) jurisdiction to file suit at the domicile of the supplier in advance.[18]

4. Governing Law in International Relationships

a. Applicable Rules and Choice of Law

The determination of the substantive laws applicable to international relationships is governed by the rules of the *Private International Law Act* as well as by international conventions ratified by Switzerland. Switzerland is a member of *The Hague Convention on the Law Applicable to International Sales of Goods and of the United Nations Conventions on Contracts for the International Sale of Goods ("Vienna Convention")*. However, Switzerland has not ratified the *Rome Convention on the Law Applicable to Contractual Obligations.*

If the parties wish to set forth the law applicable to their relationship, they need to enter into a "choice of law" clause. The choice of law must be explicit or result without ambiguities from the terms of an agreement or the relating circumstances. Subject to specific provisions applying to certain contracts, choice of law clauses can be concluded by electronic means.

The scope of application of a substantive law chosen by the parties may be further restricted in exceptional circumstances, such as the infringement of Swiss public policy, or the existence of important mandatory provisions in Swiss law or in a third country law closely connected to the relationship of the parties.

b. Consumer Contracts

The *Private International Law Act* provides in Article 120 that contracts relating to goods and services intended for a consumer's personal use, and not for his or her professional or business activities, are governed by the law of the consumer's habitual residence if:

- the supplier received the order in that country;

---

15 In addition, Article 13 *Lugano Convention* also covers contracts for the sale of goods on installment credit terms and contracts for a loan repayable by installments or for any other form of credit, made to finance the sale of goods. On consumer credits concluded online, see below section "Financial Services" II.J.2.

16 This prohibition does not apply to additional jurisdictions available for the benefit of the consumer. For further cases see Article 15 *Lugano Convention.*

17 Article 114 *Private International Law Act*; Article 21/22 *Jurisdiction Act.*

18 Article 21/22 *Jurisdiction Act.*

- an offer or advertisement in that country preceded the contract and the consumer performed the legal actions required to conclude the contract; or
- the supplier induced the consumer to go abroad and make his or her order there.[19]

No precedents exist as to whether a Swiss consumer's actions accessing a foreign website out of Switzerland and ordering goods or services therefore result in the mandatory application of the Swiss substantive laws under the above provisions. The majority of Swiss authors, influenced by US jurisprudence, consider that the simple accessibility of a website from Switzerland or the mere indication of a toll-free phone number on the website does not constitute a sufficient minimum contact for the application of Swiss law.[20] However, an interactive website combined with an information exchange by e-mail, where address and order forms are available, may constitute sufficient contact to justify both the jurisdiction of Swiss courts and the application of Swiss Law.[21]

B. SCHEME OF ONLINE BUSINESS REGULATION

1. Overview

Online business has only recently come into the focus of the Swiss legislator. A *Federal Act on the Electronic Signature ("Electronic Signature Act")* and a *Federal Act on E-Commerce* ("*E-Commerce Act*") are still in the stages of proposals.[22] The drafts are inspired, to a large extent, by the Electronic Signature Directive and the E-Commerce Directive of the EU.[23] It is likely that Switzerland will follow the current and future European and international trends for a more specific regulation of online business activities.

Today, online business still relies to a great extent on the traditional legal framework under Swiss law. Due to the lack of certified providers, no electronic signatures are available in Switzerland at present. The current situation, however, does not appear to be overly burdensome for online businesses. The Swiss legal frame-

19 Article 120 *Private International Law Act.*

20 With respect to jurisdiction see the similar approach taken by the *Brussels I Regulation.* Under the Regulation, the special consumer jurisdiction is only triggered if a web site is directed towards the country of domicile of the consumer. See section I.A. above (Jurisdiction Clauses in Online Contracts).

21 Oliver Arter/Florian S. Jörg/Urs P. Gnos, *Zuständigkeit und anwendbares Recht bei internationalen Rechtsgeschäften mittels Internet unter Berücksichtigung unerlaubter Handlungen*, St. Gallen, *AJP* 2000, p. 277.

22 Available in German at http://www.ofj.admin.ch/d/index.html, keyword "Rechtsinformatik und Informatikrecht".

23 *Directive 2000/31/EC* of June 8, 2000 on certain legal aspects of information society services, in particular electronic commerce, in the Internal Market (*'Directive on electronic commerce'*), OJ 2000 L 178, p. 1 et seq. (http://europa.eu. int/ smartapi / cgi/sga_doc ?smarta pi!cele xapi! prod! CEL EX numdoc &lg= en& num doc= 32000L0031 &model =guichett); Directive 1999 /93/ECof December 13, 1999 on a Com munity framework for electronic signatures, OJ L 0 13 2000,p.12etseq.(http://europa.eu.int/ur-lex/pri/en/oj/dat/ 2000/l_013/l01320000 119en00120020.pdf).

work is generally liberal and flexible enough to deal with the different interests involved in online business.

2. Legislation

The following legislation relating to or affecting specifically online business has been enacted in Switzerland:

- The *Ordinance on Providing Electronic Certificates*;[24]
- The *Ordinance of the Federal Office of Communications on Providing Electronic Certificates*;[25]
- The revised *Money Laundering Ordinance* which sets out rules on customer identification for opening bank accounts online;[26]
- The *Federal Act on the Surveillance of Postal Services and Telecommunications*[27] and the Ordinance on the Surveillance of Postal Services and Telecommunications[28] set out the conditions required for a surveillance of e-mail communications by the public authorities and the respective responsibilities of Internet Service Providers;
- The *Ordinance on Addressing in the Field of Telecommunications*;[29]
- Certain provisions in the *Penal Code* on Computer Crime, etc;[30]
- The *Swiss Data Protection Act*;[31] and
- The *Circular on Public Advertisement in the Sense of the Investment Fund Legislations*.[32] The circular includes rules on investment services provided over the Internet.

3. Self Regulation

Voluntary self regulation by industry organizations and other private bodies is quite common in Switzerland. Such self regulation may be binding upon mem-

24 *Verordnung über Dienste der elektronischen Zertifizierung* of April 12, 2000; available in German, French and Italian at http://www.admin.ch/ch/d/sr/c784_103.html.

25 *Verordnung des Bundesamtes für Kommunikation über Dienste der elektronischen Zertifizierung* of August 15, 2001; available in German, French and Italian at http://www.admin. ch/ch/d/sr/c784_103_1.html.

26 See section II.J below.

27 *Bundesgesetz über die Überwachung des Post- und Fernmeldeverkehrs* of October 6, 2000; available in German, French and Italian at http://www.admin.ch/ch/d/sr/c780_1.html.

28 *Verordnung über die Überwachung des Post- und Fernmeldeverkehrs* of October 31, 2001; available in German, French and Italian at http://www.admin.ch/ch/d/sr/780_11/index.html.

29 *Verordnung über die Adressierungselemente im Fernmeldebereich* of October 6, 1997; available in German, French and Italian at http://www.admin.ch/ch/d/sr/784_104/index.html.

30 See section below.

31 *Bundesgesetz über den Datenschutz* of June, 19. 1992; available in German, French and Italian at http://www.admin.ch/ch/d/sr/235_1/index.html.

32 See below section II.J below.

bers or appear as mere recommendations. For purposes of online business, the following self regulations merit to be mentioned:

- the Rules on Fairness in Commercial Communications issued by the Swiss Commission for Fairness,[33] which include provisions on direct marketing, including marketing via the Internet; and
- the revised Agreement on the Swiss Banks' Code of Conduct by the Swiss Bankers Association, which also sets out rules on customer identification for opening bank accounts online.[34]

4. Proposals

The following legislation is proposed, but not yet in force:

- Electronic Signature Act, Draft January 2001;[35]
- E-Commerce Act, Draft January 2001.[36]

C. ELECTRONIC TRANSACTIONS AND CONTRACT FORMATION

1. Freedom of the Contractual Form

In order for a contract to be concluded, a manifestation of the parties' mutual assent on all essential points of the contract is required.[37] Since Swiss contract law is based on the principle of freedom of the contractual form, the manifestation of the parties' mutual assent is not subject to the observance of a specific form (such as written form or notarial deed) unless a statutory provision explicitly requires a contract to be in a particular form, or unless the parties reserve the observance of a specific form.[38] Contracts which require being in a particular form under Swiss law are, for example, the sale of real property[39] (notarial deed) and the promise to make a donation[40] (written form). Also an assignment of claims needs to be in writing.[41]

Any contract not subject to statutory or agreed upon form requirements may be concluded through electronic means.

---

33 See section II.G.4. (b) below.

34 See section II.J.2. below.

35 *Bundesgesetz über die elektronische Signatur;* draft available in German at http://www.ofj.admin.ch/d/index.html, keyword "Rechtsinformatik und Informatikrecht".

36 *Bundesgesetz über den elektronischen Geschäftsverkehr;* draft available in German at http://www.ofj.admin.ch/d/index.html, keyword "Rechtsinformatik und Informatikrecht".

37 Article 1 (1) and 2 (1) *Code of Obligations.*

38 Article 11 and 16 *Code of Obligations.*

39 Article 216 (1) *Code of Obligations.*

40 Article 243 (1) and (2) *Code of Obligations.*

41 Article 165 (1) *Code of Obligations.*

2. Rules Applicable to Contracts Concluded by Electronic Means, Manifestation of Assent

The general rules of the *Code of Obligations* in relation to the exchange of the mutual assent,[42] the binding character of an offer,[43] the revocation of an offer[44] and the coming into effect of a contract[45] apply to contracts concluded by electronic means.

In particular, a "click on the mouse" can have the quality of a declaration of intent which can be imputed to the sender.[46] In order to make a potential contractual party aware of the fact that by clicking on the mouse a legally binding declaration of intent can be made (for example as acceptance of an offer), it might be necessary that an explicit indication of the consequences of such a mouse click is made (for example by inserting adequate wording on the web page).[47]

3. Exchange of Mutual Assent

The mutual assent of the parties must cover the essential points of the contract. In the case of commercial contracts, these points are commonly the specification and the price of goods and services. Once the parties have agreed with regard to all essential points, it is presumed that a reservation of ancillary points is not meant to affect the binding nature of the contract.[48]

4. Offer and Acceptance

A contract is concluded if the offer of one party is accepted by the other party within due time.[49]

An important distinction with respect to the conclusion of contracts by electronic means is whether a supplier who posts his or her products and services on the Internet or announces them by e-mail is only inviting the addressee to make an offer[50] or whether he or she is making a binding offer to the addressee.[51] If the latter is the case, the addressee can conclude the contract by unconditionally accepting the offer.[52] Since it is often very difficult to distinguish between a binding offer and an invitation to make an offer, anyone who sells goods or services over a

42 Article 1 and 2 *Code of Obligations.*

43 Article 3 to 5 and 7 *Code of Obligations.*

44 Article 9 *Code of Obligations.*

45 Article 10 *Code of Obligations.*

46 Rolf H. Weber, *E-Commerce und Recht,* Zürich 2001, p. 314 et seq.

47 Rolf H. Weber, *E-Commerce und Recht,* Zürich 2001, p. 314 et seq.

48 Article 2 (2) *Code of Obligations.*

49 Article 3 (1) *Code of Obligations.*

50 In the sense of Article 7 (2) *Code of Obligations.*

51 Article 3 *Code of Obligations.*

52 Article 3 *Code of Obligations.*

website or by e-mail should explicitly clarify whether he or she is making a binding offer to the addressee or not.

Offers made over the Internet or by e-mail are mostly "offers to a person not physically present" in the terms of the Code of Obligations. If such an offer is extended without a time limit being fixed for acceptance, the offer is binding until such moment as one could reasonably expect the receipt of a reply which has been dispatched properly and in due time.[53] An acceptance is considered to have been received once it has arrived in the sphere of control of the offer or, making it possible for the offeror to take notice of the acceptance. If electronic communication is used, this is the case as soon as the acceptance has been saved on the computer or server of the offeror itself, or on the computer or server of a third party (for example the server of the ISP) which the offeror can access at any time.[54] If the declaration of acceptance was dispatched in due time but does not arrive within due time (for example due to Internet or computer problems), the offeror remains bound unless he or she gives notice, without delay, of his of her intent not to be bound.[55]

If an offer is extended to a person physically present (in case of electronic communication, this only applies to offers made with a possibility of immediate communication of dialogue, such as offers made in a chat-room or offers made by phone calls over the Internet) without setting a time limit, the offeror is deemed to be no longer bound if the offer is not accepted forthwith.[56]

In certain exceptional cases, due to the particular nature of a transaction or the circumstances, an express acceptance is not necessary and a contract is deemed to be concluded if the offer is not declined within a reasonable time.[57]

If the offeror revokes the offer, and such revocation reaches the other party prior to, or at the same time as, the offer, or if, in the case of a later arrival, the other party has knowledge of the revocation before he or she has knowledge of the offer, the offer is deemed not to have been made.[58] The same rule applies to the revocation of an acceptance.[59]

5. Coming into Effect of a Contract

If a contract is concluded among persons physically not present, the contract comes into effect at the time when the declaration of acceptance is dispatched.[60]

---

53 Article 5 (1) *Code of Obligations*.

54 Rolf H. Weber, *E-Commerce und Recht*, Zürich 2001, p. 316.

55 Article 5 (2) *Code of Obligations*; Rolf H. Weber, *E-Commerce und Recht*, Zürich 2001, p. 317.

56 Article 4 (1) *Code of Obligations*.

57 Article 6 *Code of Obligations*.

58 Article 9 (1) *Code of Obligations*.

59 Article 9 (2) *Code of Obligations*.

60 Article 10 (1) *Code of Obligations*.

However, if exceptionally an express acceptance is not required, the contract comes into effect when the offer is received.[61]

6. Inclusion of General Terms and Conditions into Online Contracts

General terms and conditions can be included in a contract governed by Swiss law if, prior to the conclusion of the contract, the supplier explicitly and in a manner recognizable to the customer, refers to the general terms and conditions and if the customer has the possibility to take due notice of the content of such general terms and conditions in a reasonable way.[62]

In order for general terms and conditions to become binding in online transactions, they need to be placed on a website or referenced in an e-mail in such a way that the customer can place the offer or declare acceptance only after his or her attention has been sufficiently drawn or even forced to such general terms and conditions. This implies in particular as well that general terms and conditions should be easily readable (size of print, position on the web page), that they have a clear synopsis (important points in bold print), are properly presented and are not excessively long. If general terms and conditions are placed on a website, the customer should technically be in a position to download and store them on his or her own computer. General terms and conditions must be in a language understood by the customer. Even if general terms and conditions have been validly agreed upon, they will be subject to judicial scrutiny as to their validity in the case of a conflict.[63]

The principles outlined above were developed by courts and scholars primarily in connection with the inclusion of general terms and conditions in business-to-consumer contracts. For parties to a business-to-business contract however, a higher degree of experience in the conduct of business can typically be assumed and accordingly, the requirements for general terms and conditions to become binding in business-to-business transactions should in general be less stringent.

7. Mandatory Rules

The *Code of Obligations* sets forth certain mandatory rules for contracts in general as well as for specific contract types. For example, it is not possible to enter an agreement in advance, according to which liability for unlawful intent or gross negligence would be excluded.[64] Such mandatory rules cannot be replaced by mutual agreement of the parties. Contractual provisions which disregard

61 Article 10 (2) *Code of Obligations.*

62 Rolf H. Weber, *E-Commerce und Recht,* Zürich 2001, p. 326 et seq.; Karin F. Schwab, *Die Übernahme von allgemeinen Geschäftsbedingungen in elektronisch abgeschlossene Verträge,* Zürich 2001, p. 66.

63 Rolf H. Weber, *E-Commerce und Recht,* Zürich 2001, p. 327 et seq.

64 Article 100 (1) *Code of Obligations.*

mandatory rules are null and void.[65] This does not affect the validity of a contract as a whole, as long as it cannot be presumed that the parties would not have concluded the contract without such void provisions.[66]

8. Future Developments

The Federal Council has elaborated two drafts of Acts in relation to the conclusion of electronic contracts, the *Electronic Signature Act*[67] and the *Electronic Commerce Act*.[68] These drafts, together with their accompanying reports, have been published in 2001, but have not been adopted by the Swiss parliament and are not yet in force.

The *Electronic Signature Act* would regulate technical aspects regarding the electronic signature and provide that the electronic signature is treated as equivalent with the written signature, according to Article 14 *Code of Obligations*. The proposed Act would also allow the electronic conclusion of those contracts for which Swiss law requires a written signature.

The *Electronic Commerce Act* aims, at the introduction of some clarifications of and changes to the *Code of Obligations* and the *Unfair Competition Act* in relation to the conclusion of contracts by electronic means. In particular, the offer and acceptance by electronic means and the conclusion of certain contracts regarding goods and services for personal or family use by a customer are addressed more specifically.

65 Article 20 (1) *Code of Obligations*.

66 Article 20 (2) *Code of Obligations*.

67 *Bundesgesetz über die elektronische Signatur*; draft available in German at http://www.ofj.admin.ch/d/index.html, keyword "Rechtsinformatik und Informatikrecht".

68 *Bundesgesetz über den elektronischen Geschäftsverkehr*; draft available in German at http://www.ofj.admin.ch/d/index.html, keyword "Rechtsinformatik und Informatikrecht".

UNITED KINGDOM

by
Nick Lockett
DL Legal LLP

A. SOURCES OF LAW

The formal name of the United Kingdom is the "United Kingdom of Great Britain and Northern Ireland." As such the United Kingdom is a denomination for the purposes of international representation comprising England, Wales, Scotland and Northern Ireland. Great Britain includes the United Kingdom, the Isle of Man and the Channel Islands. The Parliament of the United Kingdom meets in Westminster; however in recent years there has been the creation of 'devolved assemblies' for Northern Ireland, Scotland and Wales where certain law-making activities have been devolved to local quasi-parliaments called assemblies.

All four components of the UK have separate legal systems, except for Wales which tends to share the same court structure and body of law as England and the structures of English law are accordingly usually known as Laws of England and Wales, the Law Society of England and Wales, et cetera. Although Scotland and Northern Ireland have their own laws and court structure, there are many points similar to the laws of England & Wales. Accordingly the use of the term "United Kingdom law" has no exact meaning except for a few rare pieces of legislation touching on taxation and social security.

1. Head of State

A hereditary monarchy is in place to occupy the position of Head Of State. The throne descends to the sons of the sovereign in order of age or, if there are no sons, to the daughters, although the male-line descent is under review.[1] The Monarch (Queen Elizabeth II, since February 6, 1952) has no real legislative power although, on paper, she signs off on all important matters such as activating Acts of Parliament (called Royal Assent), appointing ministers of the

1 A law exists for the appointment of a "regent" to temporarily administer the Monarchy's duties if a king or queen is not yet adult or is incapacitated in some way.

Crown, judges and diplomatic representatives and appointing international treaties. Under constitutional custom, the Monarch[2] has virtually no discretion over papers presented for signature and declining a recommendation from the Cabinet would trigger a constitutional crisis. It is said that "the Monarch reigns, she does not rule." The Monarchy however remains a pivotal part of the law-making process in the United Kingdom and an essential feature of the stability of law and the legislature.

2. Parliament

The UK Parliament is one of the oldest representative assemblies in the world. The legislative process involves both Houses of Parliament and the Monarch and technically, the term "Parliament" refers to the House of Commons and the House of Lords presided over by the Monarch. Parliamentary government in the United Kingdom is based on a two-chamber system. The House of Lords (the upper house) and the House of Commons (the lower house) sit separately and are constituted on entirely different principles.

The main functions of Parliament are to:

- examine proposals for new laws;
- provide, by voting for taxation, the means of carrying on the work of government;
- scrutinise government policy and administration, including proposals for expenditure; and
- debate the major issues of the day.

Both assemblies have a role to play in the passing of legislation. Parliament is organized by sessions which are generally conducted by scheduling 160 sitting days in each calendar year. Parliament has a maximum duration of five years. At any time up to the end of this period, a general election can be held for a new House of Commons.

The site of the Houses of Parliament is the Palace of Westminster, a royal palace and former residence of kings. The layout of the Palace is intricate, with its existing buildings containing nearly 1,200 rooms, 100 staircases and well over 3 kilometres (2 miles) of passages. Among the original historic buildings is Westminster Hall, used nowadays for major public ceremonial events.

Control of the Palace of Westminster and its precincts was for centuries exercised by the Queen's representative, the Lord Great Chamberlain. By agreement with the Crown, control passed to the two Houses in 1965. Certain ceremonial rooms continue to be controlled by the Lord Great Chamberlain.

2 The "Monarchy" (or rarely, "Throne") being distinguished from the "Crown," which term includes the organs of government.

While it is possible to distinguish between rules of the constitution which have the force of law and those which do not, it is difficult to classify the law and custom of Parliament under is difficult to place into similar categories. Many rules of constitutional importance are contained in the standing orders of the House of Commons and in the authoritative guide to the procedure of Parliament, Erskine May, as well as in resolutions of the House and in other sources of the practice of the House, such as rulings by the Speaker. As well as the formal powers of each House, there exist numerous informal practices observed by all major parties, for example, agreed pairing between absent MPs of each party.

Although the conduct of a general election is governed by detailed legislation it is only by convention that the government must have the confidence of a majority in the Commons so that when it is clear from the election results that the Prime Minister on whose advice the election had been called has lost the election and another party has been successful, he must resign immediately without waiting for the new Parliament to meet. Where an election gives no overall majority in the Commons, the Prime Minister continues in office for such period as is necessary to discover whether he is able to form a coalition or to govern with the support of other parties.

A detailed breakdown of the history and functioning of Parliament is available at http://www.parliament.uk. Parliament has its own unique language and procedural structure.[3]

3. The Constitution

Surprisingly, there is no written constitution for the United Kingdom. Several important statutes do exists, such as the Magna Carta (1215) and the Bill of Rights (1689), but none of them are any more than regular statutes, susceptible to amendment by Parliament at any time. Although it is often said that the UK has no constitution, this is not strictly true as it has a complex system of government founded on Acts of Parliament and judicial decisions, political practice and law and customs of governmental agencies.

Where there is a written constitution, the legal structure of government assumes a wide variety of forms. Within a federal constitution, the tasks of government are divided into two classes, those entrusted to the federal (or central) organs of government, and those entrusted to the various states, regions or provinces which make up the federation and the federal and state organs of government have limits enforceable as a matter of law. Certain rights of the citizen beyond reach of the organs of government created by the constitution and are entrenched by requiring a special legislative procedure if they are to be amended

3 See: <http://www.parliament.uk/glossary/glossary.cfm>.

or may even be rendering unalterable.[4] Many constitutions also seek to avoid a concentration of power in the hands of anyone organ of government by adopting the principle of separation of powers, vesting legislative power exclusively in the legislature, executive power in the executive and judicial power in the courts.

Within the United Kingdom, there is no written constitution able to secure these objects or serve as the foundation of the legal system. The devolution of the Welsh and Scottish assemblies began to build up the beginnings of a written constitution and unlike the primary positioning of written constitutions in the USA, Canada and other countries, it is unlikely that a formal constitution could ever effectively be written in England as a subsequent assembly would always be entitled to amend the constitution.

The protections which would be found in a permanently established constitution are instead created by the doctrine of the legislative supremacy of Parliament and the rule of law. No formal restraints on the exercise of power exist in the United Kingdom. For example, the Government of Ireland Act 1920 devolved powers of self-government upon Northern Ireland and these powers were subsequently suspended by re-imposing direct rule under emergency powers of Parliament. Limiting the powers of the Parliament would require a written constitution that prevented all future governments from taking back the powers.

The doctrine of the separation of powers

Within a system of government based on law, there are legislative, executive and judicial functions to be performed; and the primary organs for discharging these functions are respectively the legislature, the executive and the courts.

Parliament, courts and central government owe their origin to the monarchy because historically the King governed through his Council, with a mixture of legislative, executive and judicial work. Today these tasks are still carried out in the name of the Crown although judges are independent both of Parliament and government.

The executive function broadly comprises the whole of the authority to govern except the legislative functions of Parliament and the judicial functions of the courts. This includes the maintenance of law and order, the initiation of legislation, the promotion of social and economic welfare, administration of public services, and the conduct of the external relations. Historically the executive was identified with the Sovereign, in whose name many acts are still performed by the Prime Minister, Cabinet and other ministers and overseas by the Ambassadors. Today "the executive" comprises all officials and public authorities through which functions of government are exercised, including the civil service, armed forces, police, local authorities and many statutory bodies.

---

4 Federal Republic of Germany.

4. Acts and Bills

A draft law takes the form of a parliamentary Bill. It must go through the necessary stages in both Houses of Parliament. The Act enters into force on the day the Bill receives the Royal Assent, unless the Act provides for other dates.

Before Bills are introduced into Parliament, there has often been consultation or discussion with interested parties such as professional bodies and voluntary organisations. Proposals for legislative changes may be contained in government White Papers. These may be preceded by consultation papers, sometimes called Green Papers, which set out government proposals that are still taking shape and seek comments from the public. There is no requirement for there to be a White or Green Paper before a Bill is introduced into Parliament. Once a Bill has become law it is called an Act of Parliament.

The two main sources of constitutional law in England are:

a) *Formal legislation* (including Acts of Parliament; legislation enacted by ministers and other authorities upon whom Parliament has conferred power to legislate and exceptionally, legislative instruments issued by the Crown under its prerogative powers (Although since 1973, legislation enacted by organs of the European Community has priority over the powers of Parliament; and

b) *Judicial precedent* (known as case-law). In the United Kingdom, there is a reserved power for a court to exercise the function of interpreting and applying the constitution in disputed cases and these decisions are an authoritative indication of the meaning of law (and which since 1973 has included decisions of the European Court of Justice in Luxembourg in relation to Community law and where a House of Lords decision is subject to the European Court of Justice rulings).[5] Interpretation of UK legislation can also refer to the statements, committee reports and discussions which took place in Parliament and which are reported in the official parliamentary report Hansard.[6]

A secondary source of legal rules is "custom" or rules of conduct-based upon social or commercial custom. Custom of this kind is not an important source of constitutional law although the trade custom may be recognised by judicial decision as lawful and expected business practice and may then be deemed to having binding force of law. Many rules of the constitution that do not have the force of law are based on the customary usages of various organs of government.

Thus the "common-law constitution" has allowed judges to protect citizens from general warrants for the arrest for publishing seditious papers,[7] freedom from seizure of property taken in the exercise of prerogative powers without com-

5 Similarly for cases affecting human rights, the European Court of Human Rights interpretations are paramount.

6 The courts also have authority to rule on validity of subordinate legislation but have no authority to rule on the validity of an Act of Parliament.

7 *Entick v Camngton.*

pensation,[8] freedom from Crown Privilege against production of documents in evidence in criminal proceedings,[9] and the authority of the Court to make a Home Secretary subject to its orders in the absence of express legislative immunity.[10] Despite such rulings having full binding effect, they are not binding for all time since they may be set aside by express Parliamentary Act.[11]

Development and Process of Law

The British constitution ensures flexibility because its principles and rules can be changed by an Act of Parliament and this flexibility has served to avoid revolutionary tendencies despite the numerable changes in the system of government and the complete change from personal rule by the monarch to the collective ascendancy of the Government through the Prime Minister and Cabinet.

As the legislature must be free to make new laws, if the legislature wishes to alter a law previously enacted, it is convenient if the new Act expressly repeals the old law or states the extent to which the old law is amended. Therefore where two Acts conflict with each other, as exists in most jurisdictions, the courts apply the Act which is later in time, and any earlier Act inconsistent with the later Act is taken to have been repealed by implication. In Britain, the operation of implied repeal (legislative supremacy) may have special constitutional significance as it is impossible for Parliament to enact that in a subsequent statute dealing with the same subject-matter will be void, although in theory, with sufficient mandate,[12] a supreme Parliament could make fresh constitutional arrangements for the future which preclude revocation of the Act.

The legislative function involves the enactment of general rules determining the structure and powers of public authorities and regulating the conduct of citizens and private organisations. In the United Kingdom, legislative authority is vested in the Queen in Parliament: new law is enacted when, usually on the proposal of the government, it has been approved by Commons and Lords and has received the royal assent. Under the Parliament Acts of 1911 and 1949, legislation may be enacted even though it has been rejected by the House of Lords. While the House of Lords remains part of the legislature, its power to amend measures passed by the Commons is limited; and it is politically subordinate to the elected House of Commons.

Government Bills predominate in Parliament, with ministers being responsible for supervising their passage through each House and for implementing new Acts once they have received the Royal Assent.

---

8 *Burmah Oil v Lord Advocate.*

9 *Conway v Rimmer.*

10 *M v Home Office.*

11 Even retrospectively where expressly stated in the Act.

12 At least 51% of those *entitled* to vote.

While supreme legislative authority of Parliament can be qualified by devolution of power onto executive bodies by Act of Parliament (which allows, for example, ministers and government departments to make subordinate legislation and the authority of the European Community under the European Communities Act 1972 to legislate in respect of the UK.

Law is created in three stages:

(a) pre-publication of the Bill;

(b) passage of the Bill through Parliament;

(c) Implementation of the Act after Royal Assent.

5. Delegated Legislation

In order to reduce pressure on parliamentary time, Acts of Parliament often give government ministers or other authorities the power to regulate administrative details by means of 'delegated' or secondary legislation. This mostly takes the form of Orders in Council, Regulations and Rules known as Statutory Instruments (SIs). These are as much the law of the land as are Acts of Parliament. SIs are normally drafted by the legal department of the ministry concerned and may be subject, when in draft, to consultations with interested parties. About 3,000 SIs are issued each year.

To minimise any risk that delegating powers to the executive might undermine the authority of Parliament, such powers are normally only delegated to authorities directly accountable to Parliament. The relevant Acts sometimes provide for some measure of direct parliamentary control over proposed delegated legislation, by giving Parliament the opportunity to affirm or annul it. Parliament always has the right to consider whether the SI is made in accordance with the powers that it delegated.

The House of Lords has established procedures whereby all Bills with delegating powers are examined before they begin their passage through the House. The Delegated Powers Scrutiny Committee (established in 1992) keeps under constant review the extent to which legislative powers are delegated by Parliament to government ministers. There is an informal understanding in the Lords that, when the Committee has approved provisions in a Bill for delegated powers, the form of those powers should not normally be the subject of debate during the Bill's subsequent passage.[13]

6. Devolved Assemblies

Devolution is the transfer of powers from a central body to subordinate regional bodies. The UK Parliament at Westminster has devolved different powers to three bodies: the Scottish Parliament, The National Assembly for Wales and The Northern Ireland Assembly.

---

13 The House of Commons has no equivalent committee.

B. SCHEME OF ONLINE BUSINESS REGULATION

1. DirectGov (formerly the Office of the E-Envoy)

The e-Government Unit is responsible for leading the work on Directgov. This unit was launched in March 2004 as a new electronic service designed around the needs of the government user-interface and has the express intention of making it much easier to find and access government information and services electronically. It brings together information from across many Whitehall departments in one place, making it easier for people to find what they want from government, rather than having to search across several departmental sites.

In the Cabinet Office Douglas Alexander, Minister for the Cabinet Office of which e-Government Unit is part of, has responsibility for e-government issues.

The Rt. Hon. Patricia Hewitt MP, Secretary of State for Trade and Industry, is the e-Minister with overall responsibility for the Government's e-agenda. Stephen Timms MP, Minister of State for Energy, e-Commerce and Postal Services, takes the day-to-day lead on e-commerce issues.

The Office of the e-Envoy was set up in September 1999 as part of the Cabinet Office The functions of the Office of the E-Envoy have been assumed into the e-Government unit. The unit also has responsibilities across the whole e-agenda, notably e-commerce and e-government including e-Policy, Service Transformation, e-Delivery and e-Communications.

The e-Policy team focuses on operational and infrastructure strategies. It ensures that the infrastructure for the new economy is delivered; transforming government for improved services to citizens and business; ensuring best use of the enabling technology to support Government goals and seeking to make the UK the best environment to do business by building the infrastructure for the "new" economy. In particular it focuses on Security and Resilience, e-Government Strategy and modernisation, e-Democracy and Europe and Markets, Technologies and Innovation.

It also carries out critical work in formulating common policies, frameworks and guidelines to underpin the development of e-government and in comparing the UK government to other countries in the development of e-government services to ensure that e.UK remains a competitive environment.

2. Department of Trade and Industry

The DTI is committed to ensuring that UK businesses are in the best position to be able to exploit the immense potential of the Information Age. It houses the Communications and Information Industries Directorate (CII) which works with industry and the science base to improve the global competitiveness of the UK's communications, information and electronics businesses, thereby enhancing the competitiveness of the UK economy and improving the quality of life in the UK. The CII works closely with industry in developing the Information Society including links to "UK Online for Business" and also provides information and resources on online commerce for UK telecommunications, IT and software, electronics, and the content industries engaged in domestic and European strategies and benchmarking projects. It works closely with other e-regulators to provide co-ordination with UK, European and International regulation and policy in all areas of the communications and information industries and a new group particularly focuses on all aspects of data security.

3. OFCOM

The Communications Reform White Paper proposed the creation of a new unified Super-Regulator, the Office of Communications (OFCOM), responsible for the entire communications sector. This new super-regulator is independent and acts at arm's length from the Government but works closely with the DTI, DCMS and other relevant departments and agencies at national European and international level. OFCOM combines the existing functions of the Broadcasting Standards Commission, Independent Television Commission, OFTEL, the Radio Authority, and the Radiocommunications Agency. The Communications Act 2003 (UK) defines and confers on OFCOM its powers and duties, including in relation to managing radio spectrum. The acting Chief Executive of OFCOM, Mike Goddard, gave evidence to the Committee on 27 May and the Committee heard further evidence on spectrum management aspects of the Bill on 17 June 2002.

Lord Currie was announced to be OFCOM's chairman in September 2002 and the Board, comprising nine members, was appointed in December 2002. The Board was initially responsible for overseeing the subsumption of the functions of the five regulatory bodies referred to above into OFCOM and for development of the new regulatory regime, as set out in the Act.

A Content Board was appointed by OFCOM,[14] to advise on content issues, focusing on broadcasting, and to encourage the development of media literacy and effective self-regulation. OFCOM also established a Consumer Panel,[15] to represent consumers' interests.

The functions, powers, obligations and property of the five former regulators have been transferred to OFCOM, which continues to exercise their functions in accordance with the provisions of the *Communications Act* and which will develop and maintain new regulation. The relevant responsibilities include:

- administration and enforcement of telecommunications operators' licences (OFTEL);
- broadcasting standards and fairness (Broadcasting Standards Commission);
- licensing and regulation of the independent television services (Independent Television Commission);
- licensing and regulation of the independent radio broadcasters (Radio Authority); and

14 Communications Act 2003 s 12.

15 Communications Act 2003 s 16(2).

- allocation, maintenance and supervision of non-military radiofrequency spectrum (Radiocommunications Agency).

OFCOM also exercises in the communications sector powers deriving from the *Competition Act 1998* and the *Enterprise Act 2002*. OFCOM must have regard when exercising its powers and discharging its functions to the principle that "regulatory activities should be transparent, accountable, proportionate, consistent and targeted only at cases in which action is needed;" and to "the opinions of consumers in relevant markets and of members of the public generally and the different interests of persons in the different parts of the United Kingdom and of those living in rural and urban areas."[16]

OFCOM's duties are subject to certain overarching European Community obligations, including to promote competition in relation to electronic communications networks and electronic communications services; to contribute to the development of the European internal market; and to promote the interests of all persons who are citizens of the European Union. It is anticipated that OFCOM will increasingly rely on general competition law (i.e. antitrust) powers, rather than sector-specific powers. In relation to communications matters, it is likely that OFCOM will exercise the relevant powers of enforcement.

4. Data Protection

The Office of the Information Commissioner (formerly the Data Protection Registrar) headed by the Information Commissioner enforces and oversees the Data Protection Act 1998 and the Freedom of Information Act 2000. The Commissioner is a UK independent supervisory authority reporting directly to the UK Parliament and she has an international co-ordination role to ensure that the UK and other European Member States treat data protection and freedom of information equally and fairly. In the national role, she is supervisor and prosecutor of all Data Protection and Freedom Of Information matters.

In the UK the Commissioner has a range of duties including the promotion of good information handling and the encouragement of codes of practice for data controllers (i.e., anyone who decides how and why personal data—information about identifiable, living individuals—are processed). The Commissioner has a range of duties including the promotion of good information handling and the encouragement of codes of practice for data controllers.

5. Home Office Encryption Co-Ordination Unit

The purpose of the Encryption Co-ordination Unit is to ensure that the development of security systems protecting online commerce and the telecommunications infrastructure are, as far as possible, compatible with the needs of law enforcement for a continuing flow of intelligence and evidence. It works closely with the

16 Communications Act 2003 s 3(4).

Regulation Of Investigatory Powers Act Unit which provides details on and advises on the implementation of the Regulation Of Investigatory Powers Act.

6. The Office of Government Commerce (OGC)

The Office of Government Commerce (formerly CCTA) is civil government's centre of excellence in e-procurement (which concerns the whole life cycle of an asset or service) and works with departments, their executive agencies and NDPBs to achieve best value in online commercial activities.[17]

7. The Office of Fair Trading

The OFT's job is to regulate markets to ensure that they work appropriately for consumers in an open, fair and vigorous manner and that competition is fostered. It has three main operational areas—Competition Enforcement, Consumer Regulation Enforcement, Markets and policies initiatives.

The OFT looks at any allegation of anti-competitive behaviour, including cartels and the abuse of market power. It will advise referral to the Competition Commission (CC) of all mergers that might substantially lessen competition and, where appropriate, will refer to the CC markets where competition may not be working well. It also takes court action to protect consumers against unfair trading practices and as well as business behaviour, investigations will cover government laws and regulations to ensure a competitive environment for business and consumers. It also receives complaints from trading standards officers working at local level.

The Competition Enforcement (CE) Division of the OFT plays a key role in UK regulators in enforcing current legislation including The Competition Act 1998, stopping cartels and other damaging anti-competitive agreements, stopping any abuse of a dominant market position, promoting a strong competitive culture across a wide range of markets, informing business, through a widespread education programme, about changes in legislation and working with the European Commission on EC anti-trust and cases of anti-competitive practice.

8. The Competition Commission

This is an independent public body established by the Competition Act 1998 and which replaced the Monopolies and Mergers Commission (MMC) on 1 April 1999. The Commission has two distinct functions. On its reporting side, the Commission has taken over the former MMC role of carrying out inquiries into matters referred to it by the other UK competition authorities concerning monopolies, mergers and the economic regulation of utility companies. Secondly, the newly established Appeal Tribunals hear appeals against decisions of the Director General of Fair Trading and other regulators of utilities in respect of infringements of

17 <http://www.ogc.gov.uk/>.

the prohibitions contained in the Act concerning anti-competitive agreements and abuse of a dominant position.

The Commission consists of members and staff, headed by a Chairman, Dr. Derek Morris. A President of the Appeals Tribunal is responsible for the Commission's appeal functions. The Chairman and President are also members of the Commission. With the exception of the Chairman and the President, members are part-time.

Members are appointed by the Secretary of State for Trade and Industry following an open competition. They are appointed for their diversity of background, individual experience and ability, not as representatives of particular organisations, interests or political parties. They are normally appointed for an initial term of three years and are subsequently eligible for re-appointment.

The Commission comprises an appeals panel, a reporting panel and specialist panels for Utilities (Electricity and Gas) Panel, telecommunications, water and newspapers. Members of the appeals panel will hear appeals against prohibition decisions; members of the reporting panel will conduct inquiries into merger, monopoly and regulatory references; and members of the specialist panels for electricity, telecommunications and water will assist in some of the regulatory inquiries. Members can be appointed to all three types of panel. Newspaper panel members deal only with newspaper inquiries.

The Chairman appoints a group of members for individual reporting inquiries. The President appoints members of the appeals panel to Tribunals. The Secretary of State may appoint members for newspaper merger references.

9. Inland Revenue and Customs and Excise

Taxation of online business is governed by the Inland Revenue and HM Customs and Excise. The Inland Revenue governs corporate and individual tax whilst the Inland Revenue governs the treatment of VAT. A combined E-Commerce site is operated to provide advice on the treatment of Electronic Commerce for UK tax, the Government's agenda and to provide guidance on tax consequences of trading over the Internet and information about the Electronic Commerce Consultation Forum. It also provides useful information about taxation proposals for digitised products and for the treatment of Internet services in the future.

10. The Gaming Board for Great Britain

This is the regulatory body for casinos, bingo clubs, gaming machines and the larger society and all local authority lotteries in Great Britain. It was given its statutory functions under the 1968 Gaming Act and 1976 Lotteries and Amusement Act. Its role is to ensure that those involved in gaming and lotteries are fit and proper to be so and to keep gaming free from criminal infiltration; to ensure that gaming and lotteries are run fairly and in accordance with the law; and to advise the Secretary of State on developments in gaming and lotteries so that the law can respond to change. In carrying out its statutory duties, the Board seeks to ensure, so far as possible, that licence and certificate holders know what is required of them and that applicants, licence and certificate holders are treated impartially and with equal fairness. The Board consists of a part-time Chairman and four other part-time members appointed by the Secretary of State for Culture, Media and Sport. It has a staff and Inspectorate of some 75 persons.

Those who wish to organise gaming or run lotteries must have the necessary permissions. In this respect, the Board determines applications for certificates of consent from those who wish to provide casino or bingo gaming, without which an application cannot be made for a licence from the appropriate licensing authority. The Board also has powers to object to the grant or renewal of a licence, determines applications for certificates of approval which are required by those who wish to be employed to operate, supervise or manage casino gaming or to manage bingo gaming, determines applications for the grant of certificates which are needed by those who wish to sell, supply or maintain gaming machines and determines applications for the registration of societies who wish to run larger lotteries and of local authority lottery schemes.[18]

11. UK Online

A Government site designed to provide an extensive resource for UK companies to find out how information and communication technologies can improve competitiveness.

12. The Internet Watch Foundation

The Internet Watch Foundation (IWF) was launched in late September 1996 by PIPEX founder Peter Dawe to address the problem of illegal material on the Internet, with particular reference to child pornography. It is an independent organisation to implement the proposals jointly agreed by the government, the police, the two major UK service provider trade associations, ISPA and LINX, and Mr Dawe. Up to March 1997, IWF was overseen by a steering group from the two associations, the DTI, the Home Office and the IWF Chief Executive with funding from the Dawe Charitable Trust.

From April 1997, IWF has been funded by the UK industry on a subscription basis and is controlled by a Board which includes representatives from the ISP industry and from a wide range of stakeholders in the Internet including industry, child and education, consumer, libertarian and other media organisations.

---

18 Larger Lotteries are defined as those where the proceeds of a single lottery exceed GBP20,000 or where a series of lotteries has cumulative proceeds of more than GBP250,000. Societies wishing to run smaller lotteries must register with the relevant local authority. Lotteries cannot be run for commercial profit or gain. (The Board has no responsibility for the National Lottery which is regulated by the Director General of the National Lottery.)

13. The Internet Service Providers' Association

This represents 95% of the ISP dial-up market in the UK and all members have signed up to the ISPA Code of Conduct.

Resources:

http://www.competition-commission.org.uk/about/index.htm

http://www.dti.gov.uk/cii/cii/index.shtml

http://www.dti.gov.uk/insight_information_age.html

http://www.itc.org.uk

http://www.radio.gov.uk

http://www.ukonlineforbusiness.gov.uk

www.bsc.org.uk

www.communicationsbill.gov.uk

www.datprotection.gov.uk

www.inlandrevenue.gov.uk/e-commerce

www.ispa.org.uk

www.iwf.org.uk

www.ofcom.gov.uk

www.oft.gov.uk

www.oftel.gov.uk

www.radioauthority.org.uk

C. ELECTRONIC TRANSACTIONS AND CONTRACT FORMATION

1. Introduction

English law requires no particular form for the creation of contractual rights and obligations and therefore a contract can be created, providing that the necessary elements are in place, orally or in writing. It also recognizes both unilateral and bilateral contracts. Conflicts usually arise around the question of evidential proof about establishing that a contract has been entered into and defining the terms of the contract.

There is no doubt that it is easily possible to contract online under English Law by means of a website, SMS or electronic mail in the same way that it is possible to contract by use of fax, EDI, telex or letter.[19]

19 Therefore rules about capacity, contracts with minors, consideration follow normal English law contract rules, estoppel and acceptance by conduct will continue to apply online and are therefore not specifically covered.

Although there are various international treaties and initiatives such as the UNCITRAL[20] Model Law on Electronic Commerce and the OECD Guidelines on Electronic Commerce, these have no binding force under English Law, as most of the law is promulgated from the European Commission or the United Kingdom Government. The legislation is often supplemented by industry guidelines, which are non-binding but are given effect by being adopted as industry best practice.

Drafting considerations

A lawyer's drafting practice involves a skilful blend of art and science. The art of draftsmanship is about writing what the parties have agreed in such a way that the lawyer's client obtains everything he wishes whilst the counterparty obtains those parts that the lawyer's client wishes him to obtain whilst believing that he obtains everything he wishes.

Although contracts are often internationally drafted in the English language, a brief look at the internet will show how many of them are drafted by non-native speakers of English and using a non-native speaker in relation to contacts can sometimes allow a skilled draftsman on the other side of a negotiation to achieve significant advantages by appearing to draft the agreed principles. Subtle changes by the use of one word rather than another may however open the contract to a different interpretation in the future.

If the draftsman does not understand the difference in the meaning of the terms "reasonable endeavours", "reasonable commercial endeavours", and "all reasonable endeavours" then they should not be drafting the contract in English. For example a change from "no significant change" to "no material changes" or simply to "no change" can create a real opportunity for one party to claim that a termination right or a breach of contract has occurred. Many a distribution argument has turned on the interpretation of the word "promote" where one party has considered this is the same as the word "exploit".

The lawyer's science in the use of language is that skill in writing what his client wishes in such a way that his client's obligations remain open to favourable interpretation regardless of the circumstances prevailing at any time.

Pre-contractual considerations for contracts

The pre-contract stage of a transaction is one of the least thought about steps but often plays a vital role in shaping the nature of the final deal that is entered into. At pre-contract stage, it is important to ascertain how a deal will be structured, financed and operated and these points are often agreed between the parties without legal advice and by the time the lawyers are brought in at a later stage, it is too late to re-shape the deal or positions are too set in concrete. The ideal solution, therefore, is to seek legal advice at the outset, although the fact that a company is doing so may not be disclosed to the other side.

20 UN Commission on International Trade Law.

Commercial and legal approaches often differ most acutely at the pre-contract stage and companies are often reluctance to instruct lawyers early in the proceedings because of a preference not to incur the expense of legal advice until go-ahead of a proposed deal is reasonably certain. The nature of creating a commercial deal involves looking at the successful goal and difficult points that arise early on are often either ignored or overlooked.

More mature companies have standard confidentiality and NDA pre-deal letters although few have a pre-deal list of regulatory issues that need to be considered. The lawyer's pre-contractual role is to advise their client in relation to the advantages and disadvantages of the proposed deal, and the pitfalls that they may encounter.

Deals should always be protected by binding non-disclosure agreements between the parties in order to protect confidential information on both sides whether or not the deal goes forward.

Any initial Memorandum of Understanding or other similar non-binding document should only be signed, after legal clearance on the pitfalls and regulatory issues that may apply and it may be appropriate in some cases for the technical difficulties and regulatory impact issues to be initially discussed between the legal counsel leaving the commercial directors free to continue negotiations and to come back to the pitfalls and regulatory issues later in the main negotiations. Ideally, a revised Memorandum of Understanding in more detail should be discussed and agreed as quickly as possible and is often achieved by two senior principals, each advised by a senior lawyer, being tasked with this. Any "undoing" of commercial discussions already reached must be done sensitively and stated to be necessary due to the legal background.

The question of whether parties trust people or documents also varies from culture to culture. Middle East negotiations typically place the most importance on the people they are negotiating with. Those from Anglo-Saxon backgrounds, such as the United Kingdom and the United States, place a heavy reliance on written agreements and a Memorandum of Understanding is often used to bridge the gap between these divergent approaches. Such a document gives comfort to both sides because in the absence of trust of the person, there will be a refusal to enter into the Memorandum of Understanding where it is not binding and in the Anglo-Saxon mindset where there is no trust, the reliance on a non-binding Memorandum of Understanding is meaningless and will be so stated.

Duty of good faith

Although many aspects of company commercial law have been harmonised throughout the European Union, there remains a large divergence between European Union countries as to the extent to which parties may be liable for pre-contractual behaviour and information. Most civil law countries (which encompasses most of continental Europe), there is a well developed concept of pre-contractual liability.

This "pre-contractual liability" doctrine imposes a legal obligation on both parties to negotiate in good faith. If one party withdraws from the negotiations without good reason, they may be liable to the other for bad faith and end up compensating the non-withdrawing parties for the cost of the lost business time, advisers' fees and associated costs and expenses.

Indeed in Germany, Switzerland, Italy, Spain, Belgium, France, Netherlands, Poland and Portugal there is a particularly high duty of good faith negotiations, "*culpa in contrahendo*", which requires a party to inform the other side of all the important points that they could not discover alone and the courts in these countries have even gone so far as to take the concepts and terms negotiated in pre-contract discussions and then to fill in the missing details of the bargain (including specifying reasonable prices or terms).

"culpa in contrahendo" examples

Each party also has a duty to exercise reasonable diligence in performing their obligations and must behave morally and ethically. Examples of where the breach of "*culpa in contrahendo*" duties arise can include:

The non-disclosure of a secret contract race,

The use of an unfair tender process,

The non-disclosure of information known by one party which is material to the deal where that party is aware the other side does not know about these facts and would materially alter its position if it knew;

The introduction of a significant modification to a term.

This last requirement of good faith, moral and ethical behaviour, effectively prevents a party from withdrawing from negotiations that are quite well developed without reasonable justification. Thus where civil law applies to the negotiations (normally where one of the parties operates in a civil law country and the discussions take place there without any binding pre-agreement for negotiations to be under English law, regardless of the law of the final contract) parties cannot simply pull out of the deal without incurring a liability to the other side.

In order to ensure that contracts are enforceable in any circumstances, the parties often agree a "break fee" clause which states that, in the event that any compensation for withdrawal arises, this is limited to a particular sum as liquidated damages (a genuine pre-estimate of liquidated damages) recognising that the parties agreed expenses during negotiations.

The other thing to note is that although the duty of good faith exists at the start of negotiations in most civil law countries, the duty grows with time and the entering into of a contractual document, albeit non-binding, crystallises the duty and provides the necessary evidence. A claim for breach of duty of good faith as a result of withdrawal from negotiations is more likely to succeed the further the negotiations have developed, and in particular, will be easier to prove if the parties have entered into a Memorandum of Understanding or other similar document.

This doctrine of pre-contractual liability does not exist in common law jurisdictions and although English common-law protects parties from fraudulent and negligent misrepresentations in relation to a proposed transaction, it permits either party, except in very limited circumstances, to withdraw without liability from negotiations at any stage before the contract is signed and without any need to give reasons.

English businesses are often unaware of the existence of this "good-faith" doctrine overseas and can incur liability where they unreasonably withdraw from initial discussions without a sound reason to explain withdrawal. Similarly continental European businesses are often surprised to find they have no recourse against an English counterpart when their discussions have been made subject to English law and the negotiations are subsequently terminated.

Culpa Damages

The aggrieved party may seek to bring a claim in pre-contractual liability and to recover damages that represent their loss of opportunity, loss of opportunity to pursue other proposals, and wasted professional and other management time and expense.

By comparison, common law countries such as England, Wales and Ireland have a very limited duty of good faith. There is no duty in law to continue negotiations and indeed the common law protects the parties' freedom to contract or not as the case may be, subject to the final document excluding prior representations. Limited pre-contractual liability may arise for information supplied because although mere opinions are not actionable, statements inducing one party to enter into a contract are actionable in tort under principles of misrepresentation. Statements that are specifically incorporated into a contract or warranties that can be shown to be collateral to the contract are therefore actionable for breach of contract.

For this reason, main agreements frequently contain clauses that specifically exclude all reliance on, and liability arising in respect of, information, representations and warranties made during or before negotiations and which have not been repeated in the contract.

Avoiding pre-contractual liability

Parties operating in England and who have met the doctrine of precontractual liability will wish to avoid it. Equally, they may wish to be alert to instances when a counterpart from a civil law jurisdiction seeks to exclude precontractual liability as this may indicate that there could be non-disclosure of a secret contract race, use of an unfair tender processes or non-disclosure of information which would cause it to materially alter its position if it knew.

A party may seek to exclude pre-contractual liability by specifically including a limitation in the Memorandum of Understanding and where this is done, the clause needs to be legally binding. Some Common Law countries including

France and Portugal do not permit the exclusion of pre-contractual liability to be excluded and in any event, most common law countries will not consider a pre-contractual liability clause to be valid to exclude liability for fraud or gross negligence. It is usual to make all pre-negotiations subject to English law and this must be done in writing and signed by both parties, however this does not entirely exclude civil law application in all countries in Europe.

Private International law considerations however should also be brought into play, since they may impact upon the extent to which the parties can agree to make the negotiations subject to English law. The reason why London has grown up as a major legal centre for Europe, particularly during the era of very cheap flights, is that it allows meetings to take place and conducted in England which as far as possible excludes application of civil jurisdiction laws. Many meeting room centres have for this reason grown up around major London airports such as Gatwick and Heathrow. Essentially, if one of the parties is English, the meetings are in England and correspondence is in English, it is likely that a submission to English law will be upheld. Where there is also an exclusory clause excluding pre-contractual liability and applying English law there would have to be exceptional circumstances for civil law remedies to apply.

Non-binding documents

There are a number of types of non-binding documents and the mere use in a title of the statement of non-binding will not guarantee that it is, as a matter of law, non-binding. It is important to ensure that it is drafted so as to be non-binding.

Typical non-binding documents are:

- Letter of Intent—a unilateral letter sent from one party to the other stating heads of agreement or contract.
- Memorandum of Understanding—a bilateral document signed by both parties (sometimes referred to as Heads of Agreement, Deal Memorandum or Term Sheet).
- Intention to proceed (ITP)—this is used largely in building or manufacturing contracts and operates as an instruction for one party to proceed with the construction pending legal documents operating via concept of unjust enrichment which allows the party who has performed the contract to receive payment to the extent that the work has been largely performed.

Drafting non-binding documents

The typical contents of a non-binding document will include a statement of the terms agreed to be binding (lock-out, non-solicitation, confidentiality, publicity) and those which are non-binding together with a timetable for the progress of discussions and the transaction and the obligations of the parties during negotiation such as requirements of due diligence and disclosure.

Pre-contractual liability can be prevented by applying English law to all negotiations although in certain civil law countries, private international law may apply the domestic law irrespective of the chosen English law and it is therefore common that communications from UK companies including initial interest letters are marked:

> "Except for clauses 23, 34, 36 and 38 which shall be binding, neither the clauses of this document nor any related negotiations shall be legally binding nor shall constitute any offer to sell or otherwise participate in any business arrangement and they are not intended to give rise to legal rights or obligations. This document and any negotiations relating to it is subject to the exclusive jurisdiction of English Courts and subject to English Law. Negotiations and this document are, except for the above binding clauses, only an expression of the current intention of the parties which may change form time to time and negotiations are indicative only & will only become binding upon entry by the parties into a subsequent written and duly executed contract incorporating the terms intended and stated to be binding upon the parties. Either party shall be free to cease negotiations or withdraw from negotiations without penalty or liability for compensation and if no contract is entered into, no liabilities are incurred by any party involved in the negotiations surrounding this document, save for liabilities arising under the aforementioned binding clauses."

If it is intended that certain binding obligations are created, the document itself must be legally recognised as being a contract under its native putative law.[21] Under English law, a contract is validly formed if there is offer, acceptance, an intention to create legal relations and consideration or value passed or exchanged between the parties.[22]

It is therefore necessary to consider whether the content of a document is capable of being binding as, under English law, an agreement to agree or an agreement to negotiate to reach an agreement between the parties is not enforceable. Thus enforceability will arise only where there is certainty (even where that certainty is created by a determinable third party).

- An undertaking to buy a company's assets at a price to be agreed—Non-binding.
- An undertaking to buy a company's assets at a price to be fixed by an independent third party to be agreed between the parties is non-binding as it constitutes an agreement to agree on an independent third party to determine the value of company's assets—Non-binding
- An undertaking to buy a company's assets at a price to be fixed by a named independent third party (whether named individually or by position held)—Binding

21 The law that would apply if it were to be a contract.

22 If no consideration passes between the parties, the document should be made a deed to ensure that it is binding. A deed may be executed by a company if it is signed by any two directors or by one director and the secretary of the company and the wording of the document makes it clear that it is being executed as a deed by the company. This is fulfilled if the document is called a "deed" and the signature contains the words "Signed as a Deed by".

- An undertaking to buy a company's assets at a price to be fixed by an independent third party to be agreed and, where if not agreed by a given date, to e determined by a named 3rd party—Binding.

Exclusivity Agreements and Lock-Out Agreements

Where a purchaser wants to ensure that a seller does not negotiate with anyone else during a specified period of time, they may enter into a "lock out" agreement although such an agreement is generally only enforceable for a reasonable time in the circumstances of the contract. A typical lock out clause might state that one or both parties must terminate all discussions currently taking place with any other parties, must instruct their agents to cease communications and discussions, and that one or both parties shall not open, re-open or continue discussions until a given date and that during the exclusive negotiation period, the parties will advise of any approach by another party. Non-dealing will usually be defined as not soliciting, initiating or responding to any approach (whether direct or indirect) with a view to carrying out similar or competing deals or negotiations with any other party. The caselaw on the area of lock-out agreements is complex so legal advice is essential to ensure binding lock-out agreements and in most circumstances, a seller who wishes to deal with an alternative purchaser can simply delay during the lock-out period so that the exclusive period for the transaction expires.

Under English law, a penalty clause is unenforceable. Liquidated pre-estimate damages clauses are therefore usually drafted for breach of any period of exclusivity or for break fees in terms such as

> "Without prejudice to any rights the parties may have in the event of a breach of undertakings or promises of exclusivity, the non-breaching party shall be entitled to recover by way of liquidated damages for such breach the sum of £2,500 + VAT which the parties have agreed is a good faith estimate of the costs likely to be incurred by each party in relation to fees and disbursements of professional advisers."

Offers

A contract is made by offer and acceptance with the intention of creating a legally enforceable relationship. An offer must be communicated to the other party (the offeree) and can be revoked at any time before its acceptance, but notice of the revocation must be communicated to the offeree and is operative only upon receipt by him. Acceptance must be unequivocal and strictly in accordance with the terms of the offer but can be implied from conduct. Acceptance of an offer can be withdrawn before it has been communicated to the offerer. In the case of acceptance by letter or telegram, it is operative on dispatch in the ordinary course of mailing, but acceptance by telex or facsimile is operative only on receipt by the offerer.

There is no basic difference in English Law between a commercial contract and any other type of contract although special provisions relate to contracts for the sale of goods and to contracts involving consumers. A contract is made up from 4 elements. An offer, an acceptance, due consideration and an intention to create legal relations. When all four elements are present the contract represents a legally enforceable agreement between two or more parties. It is the consideration or core promises made by the parties which define the rights and obligations of the parties of most contracts is a set of mutual promises called "consideration." Confusion often arises from the advertising of goods or services and confusion with the possibility that this may be an offer. Advertising goods can constitute either an offer to sell or an invitation to treat (i.e. an invitation to make an offer) and which category an advert falls within will depend upon the exact nature of the display and surrounding circumstances. In most cases, a display of goods will be an invitation to treat which will give rise to an offer to purchase the goods when the consumer selects them. For the advertisement to constitute an offer would expect the retailer to fulfil an unlimited number of orders within the delivery time objectives stated in the advert.

In many cases there is difficulty in establishing where and when a contract is actually concluded. The terms and conditions should state this although consumer laws may require observance of certain consumer rights.

The offer will usually be concluded when one party communicates its unconditional acceptance to the other party. Any counter-offer constitutes a rejection of the first offer and a new offer to the receiving party.

The advertising of goods or services on a website is clearly an invitation to treat as it cannot be reasonable to expect that the online supplier could fulfil an unlimited number of orders within the delivery time objectives stated on the website.

A visitor to the site makes an offer to purchase goods either at the invited price or at another price and this can be rejected or accepted by the visitor. The website terms and conditions must be provided to the visitor at the time of the visitor's offer, in the absence of which a later communication that goods can be supplied with terms added will constitute a counter-offer. Unfortunately in many cases there is difficulty in establishing where and when a contract is actually concluded. The terms and conditions should state this although consumer laws may require observance of certain consumer rights.[23] The offer will usually be concluded when one party communicates its unconditionally acceptance to the other party.

Acceptance

Under English law, the usual rule for determining acceptance is the 'postal rule'. This provides that a contract accepted by mail is deemed to have been concluded at the moment the acceptance is placed into the postal system. The main rationale for such an approach was that, once the message has been posted, it moves out of the sender's control and because it was developed to cope with early reliable postal services which were closer to today's courier standards, the letter could be

23 At the time of writing, the UK Government is seeking views on the EU proposals on the future options for ensuring the safety of services provided to consumers following the publication in August 2002 of a European Commission consultation paper on the future options for ensuring the safety of services provided to consumers. Views are also being sought on a proposed Sales Promotion regulation which will create a harmonised regime for sales promotions involving offers of discounts, free gifts, premiums, and promotional competitions and games. Views are similarly being sought on the Sale of Consumer Goods Directive.

guaranteed to be delivered to the sender. Thus a contract accepted by post will be concluded before the offeror is aware of the fact of acceptance.

Once acceptance has been posted, an acceptance cannot be withdrawn, even though an intention to withdraw is brought to the attention of the offeror prior to delivery of the acceptance letter. As telegraph, telex, telephone and fax were developed, the law had to consider new approaches. Responding to the emergence of the telex and telephone systems, the courts developed another "'instantaneous communications" rule of contract formation.

In Entores Ltd v Miles Far East Corp [1995] 2 All ER 493, plaintiffs, who were located in London, had made an offer which had been accepted by the defendants in Amsterdam. The question for the court was where a contract made using communications by telex should be regarded as having been concluded. The court concluded that the contract was made when the acceptance was received by the plaintiffs in London because:

> "where . . . parties are in each other's presence or, though separated in space, communication between them is in effect instantaneous, there is no need for any such rule of convenience. To hold otherwise would leave no room for the operation of the general rule that notification of the acceptance must be received. . . An acceptor could say: '1 spoke the words of acceptance in your presence, albeit softly, and you did not hear me'; or '1 telephoned to you and accepted, and it matters not that the telephone went dead and you did not get my message' . . . So far as Telex messages are concerned, though the despatch and receipt of a message is not completely instantaneous, the parties are to all intents and purposes in each other's presence just as if they were in telephonic communication, and I can see no reason for departing from the general rule that there is no binding contract until notice of the acceptance was received by the offeror."

This view was later endorsed by the House of Lords in Brinkibon Ltd v Stahag Stahl und Stahlwarenhandel GmbH [1982] 1 All ER 293, although the court stated that where it could be established that there was:

> "some error or default at the recipient's end which prevents receipt at the time contemplated and believed in by the sender. . . . No universal rule can cover all such cases; they must be resolved by reference to the intentions of the parties, by sound business practice and in some cases a judgement where the risks should lie."

Most commercial contracts are now dealt with via e-mail, either expressly accepting the terms of an attached or agreed document with the use of a digital signature or via a confirmation by fax. Despite the arguments that e-mail is unreliable, there is little evidence that e-mails go astray when properly addressed. E-mails are sometimes not delivered because the recipient's mail box is full or the size of the file exceeds the box limits, but this is a matter controllable by the recipient and is the equivalent of the failure to collect a recorded delivery envelope or having a letter that is too big to fit through the letterbox. The similarities of e-mail to postal mail are closer than the similarities of fax or telex where the recipient machine sends to the sending machine a confirmation of good receipt. The so-called e-mail receipt being a controllable feature which the recipient can turn off or which can be sent by the recipient's server even though the mail is undeliverable to or unreadable by the recipient.

Under the Commerce Directive it is stated that "*the order . . .will be deemed to be received when the parties to whom they are addressed are able to access them*". This is a difficult provision which has led to many uncertainties because it refers to the "order" and not the "acceptance". The starting point is that e-mail is instantaneous or very nearly so. As the requirement for a receipt does not apply to e-mail or similar e-communications,[24] this means that the acceptance is concluded the millisecond it enters the recipient's e-mail box on the recipient' server as that is the point that the party to whom it is addressed is able to access the message. The burden of proof is unclear but where the sender of the acceptance can show that it has not received a delivery failure message, the burden is likely to move to the recipient to show delay or technical inability access the mailbox. Thus for contracts by e-mail under English law the contract is concluded when the e-mail acceptance is received and when the webpage acknowledges the acceptance on the order. In other words, the sending party will be entitled to show that the mail was sent by them and that no delivery failure message was received and then the burden of proof will shift to the intended recipient to show some error or default at the recipient's end which prevents receipt at the time contemplated and believed in by the sender. In order to introduce certainty into many E-commerce transactions, it is common for a transaction specific or negotiation specific e-mail to be set up which is set to automatically reply to any incoming message.[25]

Consideration

There are no formalities or adequacy tests for consideration and as long as a valuable consideration passes to one party whether a right interest, profit, benefit or a forebearance, obligation loss or responsibility is given, suffered or undertaken by the other, then the consideration test is passed. Thus a payment of a lesser sum already falling due is not a discharge of a greater sum as it cannot form consideration.

Under the Family Law Reform Act 1969, s 1, a person is deemed to attain full contracting age on attaining the age of eighteen (previously twenty-one). and they are therefore accountable as an adult under (a) any civil statutory provision, any deed, will or other instrument of whatever nature. Capacity to buy and sell goods is regulated by the general law concerning capacity to contract and to transfer and acquire property (i.e. 18 years) and no contract will be valid to mi-

24 Regulation 11(3).

25 This usually states that "the message sent has been received but not yet reviewed. Normal hours when messages are reviewed are [ ].

nors (infants) except where necessaries are sold and delivered to a person. This is the same whether the contract is made online or under conventional fora.[26]

In the case of a company, it is advisable to examine its charter, memorandum and articles of incorporation or other documents covering its corporate powers in relation to its capacity to contract although the *ultra vires* rule as it affects a third party dealing with a company was abolished by the Companies Act 1989.

Performance of Contracts

Some classes of contracts are declared illegal or void by statute or law, such as gaming and wagering, lotteries, sale of public offices and certain trade restriction agreements. Some others are illegal under common law, or as being contrary to the public policy, such as those which involve commission of a criminal or unlawful act, are immoral in nature, or are in general restraint of trade.

A contract may be discharged by performance which must, in principle, be regarded as the essence of the contract in the absence of an agreement to the contrary, but where no time limit is fixed, a reasonable time will be implied. In commercial contracts, however, time limits must he strictly observed, particularly in the case of delivery of goods, unless otherwise agreed or unless the time limit is extended. The place of performance, if not specified will be inferred from the contract and the circumstances in accordance with the intentions of the parties.

Performance may be excused by tender, rescission, a new agreement, cancellation, impossibility of performance, frustration of the purpose of performance or by breach of a condition as opposed to a breach of warranty. The latter gives rise only to a right of action for damages. A breach is failure to perform the contract without sufficient cause and an anticipatory breach may occur before the completion date by the other party.

In cases of repudiation, there must be definite evidence of an intention not to fulfill the contract. To be effective, a repudiation must be accepted by the other party and if not accepted, the contract remains in force until the time comes for performance. A breach gives rise to a right of action for damages or, in some special cases as, for instance, contracts for the sale of unique articles of personal property, for a decree of specific performance, or in other cases, for an injunction to restrain the breach.

Generally, the party committing the breach is not released from his obligation to perform the contract. Part performance prior to breach may create a separate cause of action; it can be discharged by payment in accordance with the contract, by set-off of debts due, by counterclaim, by giving a release under seal, by an agree-

26 There are limitations regarding bankrupts, mentally incapacitated persons and persons under 18 years. Where "necessaries" are delivered to a minor or to a person who by reason of mental incapacity or drunkenness is incompetent to contract because they do not intend to create legal relations or do not understand the bargain then the person must pay a reasonable price for them. "Necessaries" means goods suitable to the condition in life of the person concerned and to his actual requirements at the time of the sale and delivery. An infant's contract is voidable at his option on attaining 18, except as regards contracts for necessaries or contracts for the infant's benefit.

ment between the parties, or by the award of a judgment. Payment must be in cash, coin, or notes unless the creditor accepts a bill or check in lieu thereof.

The law on the subject of mistake, misrepresentation and fraud in the context of contractual relationships is subject to very fine distinctions which can perplex even a trained lawyer.

To have legal effect, a mistake must be one of fact. Mutual mistake which lies at the root of the contract (for example, as to the existence, but not the quality of the subject matter) or unilateral mistake as to the nature of the offer made or as to the nature of the transaction concerned, renders a contract void and property transferred may be recovered.

Where the formation of a contract is induced by an innocent or fraudulent misrepresentation of fact, the contract is voidable at the option of the injured party. The right to exercise this option will be lost if property transferred under the contract has been subsequently transferred to a purchaser for value in good faith and may also be lost after such a lapse of time that the court considers it would be unjust to allow the contract to be declared void. A misrepresentation whether innocent or fraudulent, may give rise to a claim for damages. In the case of a fraudulent misrepresentation, such damages will include all the consequences of the fraud. Innocent misrepresentation gives a right to damages in the discretion of the court, if made without negligence, and damages as of right if made negligently. Fraudulent misrepresentation, as to the identity of a contracting party or as to the nature of the transaction concerned, may render the contract void on the grounds of mistake.

Fraud is defined as an untrue representation of fact made willfully or without honest belief in its truth, or recklessly careless whether it be true or false.

Remedies for Failure to Perform

The general rule as to the measure of damages or breach of contract is that they must reasonably be considered as arising naturally from the breach, or may reasonably be supposed to have been in the contemplation of the parties at the time they made the contract. If there were special circumstances which are known at the time and which were in fact communicated by the parties to each other, then damages resulting from such special circumstances are included. Damages resulting from breaches of contracts for the sales of goods are subject to certain rules under the Sales of Goods Act. The Law of Property (Miscellaneous Provisions) Act 1989 abolished an archaic principle of English Law under which the amount of damages payable in cases of breach of contracts relating to the sale of land were extremely limited. Now damages for breach of contracts relating to land are measured on the same basis as for other contracts.

Generally the starting point is that damages are adequate compensation although for certain contracts, such as non-disclosure contracts and confidentiality contracts, injunctive relief will be available where damages are not an adequate remedy.

Commercial Contracts often contain provisions whereby the title to the goods does not pass to the buyer until payment and can also contain further provisions enabling an unpaid seller to take back goods delivered to a buyer. Generally the unpaid seller's rights are not affected by any sale or disposition by the buyer unless the same is assented to by the seller but such rights may be defeated or affected by a disposition of a document of title by a buyer or of the goods themselves by a buyer in possession of those goods, in each case, to a third party who takes it in good faith for value and without notice.

Intentional neglect or failure by the buyer to pay for the goods entitles the seller either to sue for the price or for damages, the amount of which is governed by the ordinary rules unless otherwise agreed. The *prima facie* measure of damages, when there is an available market, is the difference between the contract price and the market or current price at the time of failure to accept the goods.

With an appropriately worded contract it is sometimes possible to transfer a right of action for the recovery of the goods to the proceeds of sale of those goods.

It is always the duty of the seller to mitigate the damages, which usually involves a resale of the goods at the best available price. Intentional neglect or failure by the seller to deliver the goods entitles the buyer to sue for damages for non-delivery. The loss of anticipated profit on a sub-contract for the sale of the goods is not recoverable unless the intention to re-sell before delivery is known to both parties at the time of the contract. Delivery dates may be extended by agreement, but where late delivery is accepted the damages are basically the differences in value of the goods at the two respective dates. Where the contract itself fixes the damages they are recoverable, unless they amount to a penalty or forfeiture in which case they will be reduced to the sum recoverable under the usual rules. A breach of warranty by the seller does not by itself entitle the buyer to reject the goods; the remedy lies in damages which may be set off wholly or partly against the price of the goods and any excess damages may still be recovered.

There is no basic difference in English Law between a general commercial contract and an online contract.

Incorporation of Terms

Website design has the unenviable task that it must make a site attractive and easy to use whilst effectively incorporating disclaimers, terms, conditions and other items which required by law. Unless effectively incorporated, the terms will not be binding between the parties and it is a generally accepted principal that the party providing and relying on the terms must show that the terms were brought to the other party's notice prior to the conclusion of the contract.[27] There are a number of ways of incorporating contract terms on a website:

(a) Referring to the terms with a hypertext link so that a customer can click on the link if he or she wishes to read the terms and usually placed next to the order or log-in button.

27 Unusual or important terms should be highlighted or placed in a prominent colour on the website.

(b) Displaying the terms on the web page where they must be seen and accepted as a mandatory part of the order process prior to conclusion of the contract. Usually the customer needs to scroll past the terms and conditions before they can proceed onto the next screen in the order process and often they must also click a "tick-box" expressly stating that they accept the terms and conditions. Therefore the consumer is required to scroll through the terms and conditions and can be expected to read them.

Displaying the terms in a pre-sale contractual web page with the express acceptance tick-box is the best method of incorporating terms and conditions. The E-Commerce Directive required the Member States of the European Union to recognise such online actions as click-wrap acknowledgment of the terms and conditions.

It is still open to a consumer to argue that the terms and conditions were not displayed in full or were displayed in an unreadable format and therefore they were not bound by these. Upon the website owner showing that the site is adequately set up and no faults were reported, the burden of proving this failure will shift to the consumer. (This is the advantage of the "next step" button being below the terms, as it is highly unlikely that terms would fail to display but the button would display.)

A number of websites of major operators are in fact designed in such a way that the terms and conditions are not incorporated but use method a) above. The terms are supposed to open in a separate browser window but regularly fail so that a blank console window is loaded. In such cases, the consumer may not be bound by the terms and conditions, although there is indicative caselaw that a non-consumer may have acceded to whatever the terms were because they chose to ignore the obvious failure. In the case of consumers, it is unclear whether the terms apply. It should also be remembered that the Unfair Terms in Consumer Agreements Regulations will apply to the consumer terms and that unfair and blacklisted terms will be void.

It is sensible, therefore, to require the programmers to put into place a check-sum sequence so that the order will automatically terminate if the terms and conditions pages are not loaded and displayed properly.

Terms should state that the purchase is an offer by the buyer which is conditional upon the seller clearing the credit-card details and not being requested to take anti-fraud steps. In early 2002, a number of online retailers refused to accept a number of credit cards because the card providers' anti-fraud steps were inadequate. Even where the credit card purchase is checked online, the terms and conditions should allow the seller to cancel the order upon e-mail notice at any time where the seller's anti-fraud checks reasonably indicate that this is an appropriate course of action and without liability.

Terms should also include the Errors and Omissions Excluded (E&OE) marking so that the contract is not valid where errors and omissions arise.[28]

---

28 Although in practice it may be difficult to show that both parties were aware of the error or omission.

The conditional acceptance nature of any confirmation given at the end of the online ordering process should also provide that the order is subject to separate confirmation by e-mail about stock levels. It should also be conditional upon the availability of goods by the supplier from stock at the indicated price. The seller should reserve the right to withdraw the offer at any time before the order is dispatched upon notice to the buyer and without liability where a price error occurs on the website or where goods are no longer available from the suppliers stock at the indicated price. Where a higher price is notified to the buyer, the buyer will need to confirm that they are willing to purchase the goods at the higher price. This notification of a higher price will constitute a withdrawal of the conditional offer and a new counter-offer.

This simple and somewhat obvious step would have prevented the arguments which arose in the UK about price-error offers such as the Argos televisions which were accidentally offered for GBP1.99 instead of GBP199. Care will, of course, have to be taken to ensure that any e-mail confirmation does not contain a lower pricing error.

Where a clear pricing error does occur, then the online retailer will not be bound by the order. In some cases such as the Argos case, there is clearly a mistake and it is well established in such cases that an error of significant magnitude which is or should be clearly obvious allows either party to rescind the contract prior to fulfilment.

In some rare cases, however the error may not be obvious, for example where a online retailer sells bicycles for GBP199 instead of GBP299. Where the conditional order confirmation shown above is not followed, then there may be a binding offer as the buying party is unlikely to be aware of the mistake. This is a matter of consideration in each case and the result may vary on the evidence.

Where a consumer with no industry knowledge buys a computer printer online because it is marked at GBP199 when competitors are offering it at GBP299, the consumer may suspect that there is a mistake. Where the offer is marked as a special offer or promotion, the consumer may be entitled to state that they believed this was a special deal only available from that supplier and may be able to show a binding contract. Where the consumer buys multiple units, this argument is weakened as it is indicated that the consumer may be aware of the mistake. In the case of a knowledgeable computer professional, even if buying as a consumer, the professional may be expected to know that a retailer is unlikely to be making a 30% mark-up on a computer printer as margins in the industry are smaller and therefore that the price is a mistake.

In many cases of dispute, the first port of call of the aggrieved party will be the local Trading Standards authorities operated by local government or in relation to unfair consumer practice, the Office of Fair Trading.

The sequence of purchase should include:

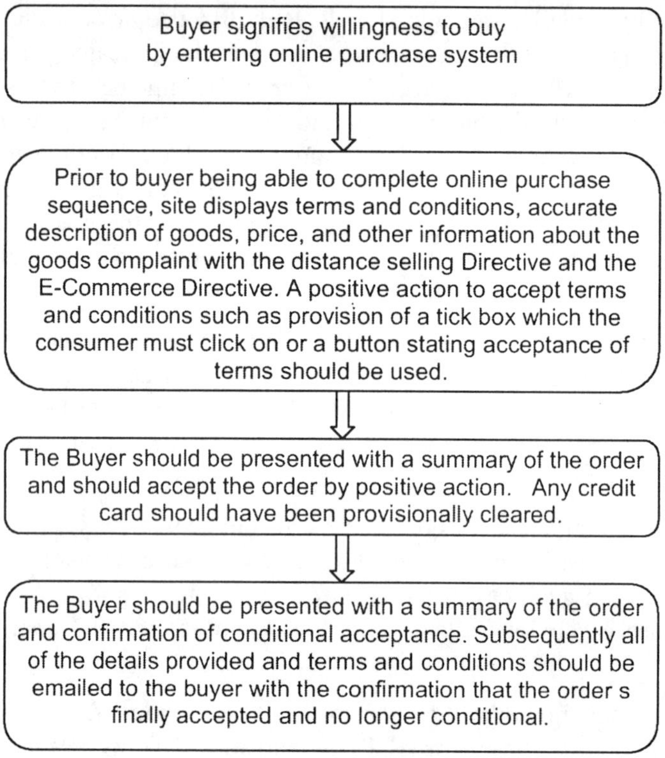

It is also important that the terms and conditions make it clear when the contract is deemed to be concluded and this will depend on the business of the website owner. Most terms and conditions provide that the contract is only concluded when there is an e-mail confirmation to the ordering party.[29]

It is important that a company can retrieve a full picture of the transaction including all the relevant terms and conditions at the time of conclusion of the online contract and it is therefore necessary for companies to keep a record of all changes in their terms and conditions.

It is also vital that the e-retailers can track and record any non-delivery receipts so that they can demonstrate that on the balance of probability the confirmatory e-mail was sent to and received by the buyer's server.[30]

---

29 This creates a problem where the ordering party does not have an e-mail address.

30 E-mail "delivery-receipts" may not be sufficient evidence as they are not usually sent from the recipient's computer.

The Sale of Goods Act 1979

The Sale of Goods Act 1979 applies to any contract for the sale of goods unless its provisions are excluded wholly or partially or varied by express agreement between the parties or by custom or usage (as is the case of C.I.F., F.O.B. or ex-ship contracts). Certain conditions and warranties are implied under the Act in any contract subject to the Act, unless a contrary intention appears: (1) a condition that the seller has, or will have, at the time when the property in the goods passes, a right to sell the same; (2) a warranty that the buyer shall have and enjoy undisturbed possession of the goods; (3) a warranty that the goods shall be free of encumbrances or charges to a third party not declared or known to the buyer at the time of the contract. When there is a sale of goods by description, the Act implies a condition that the goods shall correspond with the description and when the buyer expressly or by implication makes known to the seller the particular purpose for which the goods are required in order to show that the buyer relies upon the seller's skill or judgment and when the goods are of a description which it is in the course of the seller's business to supply, there is an implied condition that the goods shall be reasonably fit for such purpose. However, in the case of the sale of a specified article under its patent or trade name, there is no such implied condition.

When goods are bought by description from a seller who deals in goods of that description, there is an implied condition under the Act that the goods shall be of satisfactory quality and where goods are sold by sample, there are implied conditions that the bulk shall correspond to the same in quality, that the buyer shall have a reasonable opportunity to compare bulk with the sample and that the goods shall be free from any defect rendering them unsatisfactory which would not be apparent on reasonable examination of the sample. An implied condition as to quality or fitness for a particular purpose may be annexed by usage of the trade. In the case of the sale of an article bearing a trademark, there is an implied warranty that the mark is genuine and has been properly applied.

The Unfair Contract Terms Act 1977

The Unfair Contract Terms Act of 1977 provides that clauses purporting to exclude the liability of either of the contracting parties will have no effect in certain types of contract. The Act mainly applies to contracts in which one party is a consumer and the other party is a business. However, regardless of the capacities in which the parties are contracting, all exemption clauses purporting to exclude or restrict liability from death or personal injury are void. Other clauses which are void, *ab initio*, are those which seek to exclude or limit the liability of a manufacturer under a guarantee or strict liability under the terms of the Consumer Protection Act of 1987. Other clauses will generally be subject to a reasonableness test. The test of whether the clause is reasonable is a question of fact for the court. There are various guidelines provided by the Act to assist the court in assessing reasonableness and these are based on such factors as the bargaining positions of the parties and any inducements offered to the consumer as an incentive to contract. The main types of contracts which are exempted from the Act are international sales contracts, all contracts of insurance, contracts relating to interests in real property, contracts relating to patents and trademarks, contracts relating to the dissolution and constitution of a company and contracts for the transfer of securities.

As a general rule, it is possible to exclude liability for breach of these implied conditions unless the sale is to a consumer or is on the basis of one party's standard terms and conditions in which case (unless one of the parties is resident outside the U.K.), the attempt to exclude liability will be void (but see Unfair Contract Terms Act 1977 below).

The Sale of Goods Act declares that the property or title to the goods passes where the terms of the contract show a clear intention that it shall pass and provides rules for ascertaining the intention of the parties as to the time at which the title is to pass, when the contract is silent on this point. Goods must be specifically ascertained before the title can pass. The title to goods can be passed by delivery of bills of lading properly endorsed if drawn to order, but, if accompanied by a bill of exchange, the buyer must accept or pay for the goods if the title is to pass to him. An unpaid seller has a lien on the goods while in his possession; a right to stop goods in transit if the buyer becomes insolvent; and a right to resell the goods (subject to some limitations). In addition, if the title to the goods has not passed, he has a special right to withhold delivery. However, an unpaid seller has no right of lien if he sells the goods on credit with two exceptions: (i) if the goods have been sold on credit, but the term of credit has expired; (ii) if the buyer becomes insolvent.

Unfair Terms and Consumer Contracts Regulations 1994

These apply to all business contracts with consumers for the sale and supply of goods and services and cover all terms, not just limitations of liability and exclusions and the regulations to cover terms which have not been individually negotiated or terms which have been drawn from a general pool of terms so that although a contract may have been negotiated if it has been negotiated from a pool of terms then it will not be treated as individually negotiated.

Unfair terms are automatically void and can not be enforced against consumers and there is an exhaustive black list of terms which are considered to be automatically unfair.

2. The E-Commerce Directive

The E-Commerce Directive was adopted on 8 June 2000 and published in the Official Journal of the European Union on 17 July 2000. It entered into force in

England and Wales on 21st August 2002.[31] The Directive[32] ensures that all Information Society services benefit from the Internal Market principles of free movement of services and freedom of establishment and that Information Society services can be provided throughout the European Union if they comply with the law in their home Member State. It permits specific harmonised rules only where strictly necessary to ensure that businesses and citizens can supply and receive Information Society services throughout the EU, irrespective of frontiers.[33] Member States are precluded from imposing special authorisation schemes for ISPs which are entitled to operate from other EU states.[34]

a. Transparency and Certainty under the E-Commerce Directive

The Directive is now in force and provides a method by which it is possible to determine where operators are established, creates transparency requirements for commercial online communications and specific requirements for inclusion of detail within electronic contracts. As a measure to promote confidence in online commerce, certain consumer opt-outs will be invalid. It also provides limitations to the liability of Information-society Service Providers (ISPs)[35] as well as requirements regarding online dispute settlement facilities. Regulation 3(1) sets out those matters excluded from the scope of the Regulations. Regulation 3(2) provides that the Regulations do not have prospective effect.

The DTI conducted a second public consultation between 7 March and 2 May 2002, and invited comments on the implementing regulations and the interim guide for business.

---

31 Except for s16 which comes into force on 23rd October 2002. Regulation 16 amends the Stop Now Orders (E.C. Directive) Regulations 2001.

32 The Regulations should be read with the Electronic Commerce Directive (Financial Services and Markets) Regulations 2002 (S.I. 2002/1775), the Financial Services and Markets Act 2000 (Regulated Activities) (Amendment) (No. 2) Order 2002 (S.I. 2002/1776), The Electronic Commerce Directive (Financial Services and Markets) (Amendment) Regulations 2002 (S.I. 2002/2015) and the Financial Services and Markets Act 2000 (Financial Promotion) (Amendment) (Electronic Commerce Directive) Order 2002 (which is expected to be made shortly and to come into force on 21st August 2002). They make parallel provisions in those areas subject to regulation by the Financial Services Authority under the Financial Services and Markets Act 2000.

33 Most of the provisions of the regulations have effect in addition to any other information requirements in Community law including those contained in the Consumer Protection (Distance Selling) Regulations 2000 (S.I.2000/2334).

34 Directive Article 4.

35 Confusingly the Directive and EU guidance papers talk about ISPs which previously meant Internet service providers of connectivity. Since the EU Directive was published, the term ISP is now commonly used to mean Information-society Service Providers. The term ISP is therefore now considerably wider and catches all providers of a service using communications protocols of the information society.

The Directive covers all European-established Information-society Services whether business to business (B2B) or business to consumer (B2C).[36] It also catches services provided free-of-charge to the recipient where they are funded by advertising or sponsorship revenue. The sectors and activities covered include on-line newspapers, online databases, online financial services, online professional services (such as lawyers, doctors, accountants, estate agents), online entertainment services (such as video on demand) online direct marketing, online advertising and other online services, but only applies only to ISPs (Information-society Service Providers) established within the EU.

Under Article 2(c) of the Directive, an ISP will have a place of establishment where the operator actually pursues an economic activity using a fixed establishment.[37] The establishment of a service provider is therefore irrespective of where websites or servers are situated. It is also irrespective of any mail-drop facilities which are provided to the ISP in a particular country. This means that a US web-hosted operation will not be caught by the establishment rule unless it operates a branch office or subsidiary within the EU (or in some cases if it appoints an agent). ISPs will be subject to the laws of the Member State in which they are established.[38]

Regulations 4 and 5 allow an enforcement authority[39] to take measures in respect of a given information society service in derogation from the general principle that another Member State information society service cannot be subject to restrictions where these are necessary for reasons of public policy (including the protection of minors, the fight against hatred on grounds of race, sex, religion or nationality), public health, public security, and the protection of consumers and proportionate to those objectives. These must be considered on a case by case basis, however, any such restrictions will have to be proportionate to the stated objective, and can only be imposed after the Member State in which the service provider is established has been asked to take adequate measures and has failed to do so.

Transparency of information society service provider operations is covered by Article 6 which requires Member States to oblige information society service

36 Including tele-shopping, SMS-shopping and online shopping malls etc.

37 The Regulations state that the presence and use of the technical means and technologies required to provide the information society service do not, in themselves, constitute an establishment of the provider. In cases where it cannot be determined from which of a number of places of establishment a given service is provided, that service is to be regarded as provided from the place of establishment where the provider has the centre of his activities relating to that service. It is unclear exactly how this establishment rule will work, but it is expected that the if there is any establishment in Europe then the ISP will become subject to the Directive in which case the test of whether an entity with number of places of establishment is established in England for the purposes of the Regulations will depend upon whether the service is regarded as provided from a place of establishment in England in which the ISP has the centre of his activities.

38 Article 3 (subject to certain exeptions).

39 Or, where no enforcement authority is a party to the proceedings, a court.

providers to make available to customers and competent authorities basic information concerning their activities including:

- name of the Service Provider;
- geographic address of establishment;
- e-mail address;
- rapid contact and communication methods;[40]
- trade (or similar) register (including any registration number and how to identify the service provider in the register);
- if subject to any authorisation scheme, details of the supervisory authority;
- if a regulated professional, details of the professional body or similar institution, professional title and member state in which the title is granted, reference to the professional rules and how to access them;
- membership details of professional bodies where applicable;
- VAT number (if applicable); and
- if prices are shown then these must be clear and unambiguous and must indicate whether tax and delivery costs are included.

The Regulations require Member States to remove any prohibitions or restrictions on the use of electronic contracts. Therefore, any restrictions in law which have meant that click-wrap and similar techniques are not acceptable are likely to be invalid. Regulation 9 imposes a duty on a service provider to provide certain information about how and where contracts are concluded by electronic means (unless parties who are not consumers have agreed otherwise). They also impose certain information requirements for the conclusion of electronic contracts, in particular in order to help consumers to avoid technical errors.[41] These must clearly and unambiguously identify the different technical steps to follow to conclude the contract and whether or not the concluded contract will be filed (retained) by the service provider[42] and whether it will be accessible to the consumer at a later date, the technical means for identifying and correcting input errors prior to the placing of the order and the languages offered for the conclusion of the contract. Any codes of conduct must be identified.

With regard to regulated professions (such as lawyers or accountants), the underlying Directive required online provision of services to be permitted and required changes in national rules on advertising so that professions were not prevented from operating websites. However, the online activities of regulated

40 These must be direct and effective contact details and a facility for a reply by e-mail some days later will not be considered rapid.

41 Regulation 9.

42 Note required for e-mail orders see Regulation 9(4).

professions will have to respect certain rules of professional ethics which should be reflected in codes of conduct to be drawn up by professional associations.

b. Liability of Intermediaries

Article 12 requires Member States to ensure that service providers are not liable for the content of communications in cases where they play a passive role as a "mere conduit" of information from third parties. Articles 13 and 14 limit service providers' liability for other intermediary activities such as the storage of information.[43]

As regards the "mere conduit" function, Article 12 of the Directive excludes transmission providers from damages liability provided that they do not modify the content transmitted except for manipulations of a technical nature enabling the transmission of the information.

Article 13 deals with the caching function. In particular, it establishes that information society service providers engaging in caching will not be liable for the damages unless they have actual knowledge either that the information at the initial source of the transmission has been removed, that access to it has been disabled, or that a competent authority has ordered such removal and they fail to remove or disable access to the information upon obtaining this knowledge.

Article 14 states that providers that store third party content on their servers may not be held liable for damages, unless they fail expeditiously to block access to the information upon obtaining actual knowledge of the illegal activity or information or upon becoming aware of facts or circumstances from which illegal activity or information is apparent. Article 15 stresses that a duty to monitor may not be imposed upon online intermediaries; however Member States may impose upon intermediaries a *"duty of care, which can reasonably be expected from them and which are specified by national law, in order to detect and prevent certain types of illegal activities."* The duty of care could require intermediaries to implement and operate filtering and control mechanisms if required by Government. Service providers who fail to implement such mechanisms may then be held liable for failure to comply with the mentioned duty of care.

c. Junk Mail and Commercial Communications

The Regulations impose a duty on a service provider to ensure that any commercial communications constituting or forming part of an information society service which are provided complies with certain requirements. This is in the interests of transparency requirements to ensure consumer confidence and fair trading. This means that such communications must:

- be clearly identifiable as a commercial communication;

43 See Intellectual Property chapter of this commentary.

- clearly identify the person on whose behalf commercial communications are made;
- clearly identify any promotional offer (including discount, premium or gift) and the conditions to qualify, which must be easily accessible, clear and unambiguous; and
- clearly identify as such any promotional competition or game and the conditions for participation, which must be easily accessible, clear and unambiguous.

In addition, Regulation 8 imposes a duty on an information society service provider to ensure that any unsolicited commercial communication sent by him or her is clearly and unambiguously identifiable as such as soon as it is received. This will probably mean that it will need to be identified in the subject header and not buried somewhere in the text of the message.[44] For telephone calls and SMS, this will immediately have to be disclosed.

Article 2(f) of the Directive (UK Regulation 2) defines "commercial communication" as any means of communication, in any form, designed to promote, directly or indirectly, the goods, services or image of any person pursuing a commercial, industrial or craft activity or exercising a regulated profession, other than a communication either (a) consisting only of information allowing direct access to the activity of that person including a geographic address, a domain name or an electronic mail address; or (b) relating to the goods, services or image of that person provided that the communication has been prepared independently of the person making it.[45]

d. Order Confirmation

Regulation 11 imposes requirements on the service provider in relation to the placing of an order unless parties have agreed otherwise. Under the regulations when a recipient of an information society service places his or her order through technological means, an information society service provider is required to acknowledge receipt of the order to the recipient of the service without undue delay and by electronic means and make available to the recipient of the service appropriate, effective and accessible technical means allowing him or her to identify and correct input errors prior to the placing of the order.[46]

e. Penalties for Not Providing Rectification Possibilities

Where a person enters into a contract to which these Regulations apply and the information society service provider has not made available means of allowing

44 In the case of someone reading only headers in e-mail, any identification in the body of the text would not be identified immediately.

45 For this purpose, a communication prepared without financial consideration is to be taken to have been prepared independently unless the contrary is shown.

46 No opt-out is permitted for consumers.

him or her to identify and correct input errors in compliance with regulation 11(1)(b), then he or she shall be entitled to rescind the contract.[47]

f. Mere Conduit Connectivity Providers, Caching and Hosting Liabilities

The E-Commerce Regulations establish a liability regime for online intermediary activities and clarify the liability standards applicable to online intermediaries as a result of their involvement with illegal or infringing material hosted or re-transmitted by them. It limits the liability for damages of Information-society Service Providers when they act in an intermediary role as mere conduit[48], cache provider, or hosting provider.[49] Nothing in the regulations prevents injunctions from being imposed upon online intermediaries and Member States courts can impose *all types of injunctions* upon online intermediaries, instead of merely prohibitory injunctions.

As such Regulations 17 to 19 create a defence for intermediary information society service providers from any liability incurred from the activities of mere conduits, caching and hosting, providing the circumstances set out in the Regulations are closely followed.

The Regulations do not preclude the agreement of different contractual terms or affect the rights of any party to apply to a court for relief or the power of any administrative authority to prevent or stop the infringement of any rights.

Where any intermediary information society service provider is charged with a criminal offence under Regulations 17-19, the burden of proof in proceedings lies with the intermediary information society service provider to show a prima-facie defence and thereafter the burden transfers to the prosecution beyond reasonable doubt.

It provides a solution that prevents online intermediaries from being held liable *without knowledge* of the existence of the illegal or infringing content, while at the same time providing protection to properly aggrieved parties. Certain important issues are however unclear because the E-Commerce Directive does not establish circumstances and requirements under which "notice" is to be given to ISPs alerting them of the existence of unlawful material in their facilities are reliable enough for online intermediaries to act on. The Directive threatens ISPs with liability for damages, having acquired knowledge of the existence of un-

47 Unless any court having jurisdiction in relation to the contract in question orders otherwise on the application of the service provider. This is expected only to be allowed in rare cases.

48 "Mere conduit activity" includes both transmitting information by way of providing cables, servers and routers and the provision of access to communication networks (including the Internet) as well as proxy caching and the storing on a local server of copies of high demand material that originates from remote servers. This may include the cache copies of search engines although the position is not entirely clear.

49 The limitations apply to all kinds of illegal material provided by third parties, including copyright, trademark, defamatory statements, pornography, etc.

lawful material, for example through the receipt of notices, they do not remove it immediately.

As a result, online intermediaries have an incentive to systematically take down material, without considering the position of the party whose material is removed, thus preventing such a party from its right to evidence its lawful use of the material. ISPs have the catch-22 position that the removal of material may infer incorrect use of the system or unlawful content and, in some cases, the removal may be defamatory. It is therefore likely that ISPs will consult external lawyers to establish that they acted on the advice of those lawyers and that therefore their actions were objectively reasonable in the circumstances. It is also likely that ISPs will ask for certification in a similar manner to that required under the Digital Millennium Copyright Act in the USA. Obviously, there will also need to be a balance between freedom of expression and freedom of contract and the use of notice-and-takedown within competition law.

Regulation 22 does, however, make provision in relation to matters which a court should have regard to when determining whether a service provider has actual knowledge for the purposes of regulations 18(b)(v) and 19(a)(i) and requires a court to take into account all matters which appear to it in the particular circumstances to be relevant, including whether a service provider has received a notice through a means of contact made available in accordance with regulation 6(1)(c), and the extent to which any notice includes the full name and address of the sender of the notice, details of the location of the information in question and details of the unlawful nature of the activity or information in question.

The E-Commerce Directive requires member States to ensure the setting-up of effective, alternative cross-border online dispute settlement systems, provision of fast, efficient legal redress appropriate to the online environment and require effective proportionate and dissuasive sanctions for violations of the rules established under the Directive. No provision exists under the Regulations for this although further amendments are expected.

The Directive does not deal with the application of the Brussels Convention on jurisdiction, recognition and enforcement of judgements in civil and commercial matters nor does it interfere with the Rome Convention as regards the law applicable to contractual obligations in consumer contracts or with the freedom of the parties to choose the law applicable to their contract.

Regulation 16 amends the Stop Now Orders (E.C. Directive) Regulations 2001.[50] The Stop Now Orders (EC Directive) Regulations came into force on 1

50 Transposing the Injunctions Directive. The E-Commerce Directive adds that Directive to the list of Directives annexed to the Injunctions Directive.

June 2001.[51] This means that an application can now be made under those Regulations for a court order to stop an infringement of the Directive which harms the collective interests of consumers and the extension of the Stop Now Orders Regulations is consistent with the enforcement of other EC Directives which protect consumers.

The Stop Now! Regulations allow the Director General of Fair Trading and other consumer-protection bodies[52] to apply to the courts for a Stop Now Order where there is an infringement of the law of a member State which implements any of the Directives covered by the Injunctions Directive. The courts can make Stop Now! "Community infringements" Orders to require traders to cease such infringements which harm the collective interests of consumers and can also order traders to publish corrective statements with a view to eliminating the continuing effects of past infringements. The courts can also make a pro-active order if they find that it is likely that a trader will commit a Community infringement.[53]

Applications for a Stop Now Order can also be made by a number of other persons (public bodies with responsibility for protecting consumer interests in the UK) listed in Schedule 3 to the Regulations. The Secretary of State can also, under regulation 4, designate organisations whose purpose is to protect consumer interests and which meet criteria set out to be parties so entitled. Applications can also be made by bodies having equivalent powers in other member States under the equivalent legislation and which are listed in the Official Journal of the European Communities.

3. Codes of Practice

In the UK, there is a wide reliance on Codes of Practice which are adopted or promoted as industry standards to help to protect consumers' rights and offer a faster and more responsive solution than can be set down in law. Recent private sector and Government online commerce initiatives include TrustUK (http://www.trustuk.og.uk) a private sector led scheme launched in July 2000 to approve codes of practice for retail e-commerce allowing online businesses that meet the TrustUK criteria display an "e-hallmark" on their websites. As part of its e-confidence initiative, the European Commission is working with business and consumer partners to develop an EU scheme for online commerce codes based on the TrustUK approach.

The UK also plays a leading role in the OECD Consumer Policy Committee on developing a range of online commerce issues including codes of practice and

---

51 Giving effect in the UK to Directive 98/27/EC of the European Parliament and of the Council of 19 May 1998 on injunctions for the protection of consumers' interests.

52 For example, Trading Standards authorities.

53 The Regulations contain a non-exhaustive list of UK law which is to be regarded as transposing the Directives in Schedule 1 (regulation 2(3)).

continuing work on the OECD Guidelines for Consumer Protection in the Context of Electronic Commerce. The Guidelines advise governments, businesses, consumers and their representatives on the core characteristics of effective consumer protection for online commerce. They cover information provision, advertising and marketing, transaction procedures, payment security, data privacy, dispute resolution and redress.

4. Electronic Signatures

a. The EU Electronic Signatures Directive

The origins of the proposals for the UK's Electronic Communications Act 2000 can be found in the E.U. Electronic Signatures Directive[54] which was due for implementation by not later than 19 July 2001. The Directive applies to signatures used in any application including all major contracts, intellectual property registrations, and other signature uses but does not require the use of particular electronic signatures (e-Signatures) and is technologically neutral and does not require any specific technology. It introduces a uniform standard for legal recognition of electronic signatures regardless of their origin in the EU and facilitates the legal recognition of electronic writing and sets uniform standards for trusted service providers certifying e-Signatures and issuing qualified certificates supporting the advanced e-Signatures protocols (known as Certification Service Providers or CSPs) and the secure signature creation devices used to create advanced e-Signatures.

The Commission reached the tentative conclusion that any regulation for the purposes of fighting crime should be as minimal as possible, but that free trade requires a common system of encryption regulation and rejected the idea of a compulsory key escrow system for state security purposes, proposing instead that there should be legal compulsion to decrypt communications under a judicial warrant. At the beginning of 1999, the European Parliament proposed a number of amendments, which include changing references to 'digital signatures' to 'electronic signatures', and strengthening data protection and privacy provisions, but not including any detailed technological requirements. It also wanted the Commission to review the Directive before 2003 to ensure that technological or legal changes do not mean that the Directive ceases to fulfill its intended objects.

Under the European Proposals, e-Signatures constitute "data appended to other data that performs similar functions to a hand written signature and which may indicate the source of the data" and are formally designated as "any data in electronic form which is attached to or logically associated with other electronic data and which serve as a method of authentication of the content or authorship

---

54 Directive 1999/93/EC of the European Parliament and of the council of 13 December 1999 on a Community framework for electronic signatures, adopted and dated 13 December 1999, published in the OJ of l9 January 2000 (OJ L 13, 19.01.2000, p.12).

of the message." This allows a "digital signature" to include a typed-in name, a scanned-in signature, an electronic representation of a hand written signatures, a unique sequence of characters, a digital representation of a biological aspect[55] and a signature created by cryptographic means.

The Commission sought to achieve by the Directive a regulatory scheme which allowed for effective electronic signatures and which permitted an advanced cryptographic signatures. The Commission required that advanced electronic signatures be given the same legal status as handwritten signatures on paper documents whilst other forms of electronic signature are merely subject to the principle of non-discrimination.[56] Advanced signatures would need to be:

(a) created by a means which the signatory retains under their sole control;

(b) capable of uniquely identifying the signatory and uniquely linked to them;

(c) linked to the related data in such a manner that any subsequent data changes were detectable; and

(d) utilising technologically secure methods.

To encourage the development of certification services there is an absolute prohibition from requiring Certification Service Providers (CSP) to obtain prior authorisation although the EU Directive permits Member States to set up voluntary accreditation schemes. It also provides for the legal recognition of electronic signatures as equivalent to hand-written signatures and establishes liability rules for CSP.

The Directive does not aim to regulate systems, which are governed by private law agreements so that electronic signature systems "governed by voluntary private law agreements between a defined number of participants" will not be affected nor denied legal effectiveness and admissibility. Multilateral agreements with third countries on mutual recognition of certification services are also permitted to ensure interoperability in the global marketplace and the Commission is preparing a mutual recognition system Directive in due course.

Certification Service Providers will be liable for the accuracy of all information included in a qualified certificate and for the completeness of all information required in a certificate although CSPs are not liable for damage arising from the use of a qualified certificate which exceeds the limit on the value of transactions for which the certificate can be used.[57]

55 *E.g.*, eye retina, fingerprint scans.

56 The principle of non-discrimination requires that Member States national laws cannot automatically deny legal effectiveness or admissibility for such signatures.

57 This envisages that the only acceptable qualified certificates will be those checked online at the time of verification and that certain certificates may have a per-transaction limit but no limit to the number of transactions which can be made.

The Directive imposes a requirement for national law to determine how Member States domestic law allows electronic documents and electronic signatures to be used.[58] The Digital Signatures Directive also sought to permit but not obligate Member States of the EU to establish voluntary non-mandatory domestic licensing regimes for CSPs.[59] Thus the Directive will achieve, in the whole of Europe, through the advanced digital signature implementation, a uniform system to offer authentication of the message originator, to guarantee integrity of the information and non-repudiation of messages which will be fully admissible in Court and will ensure that a digital signature was authentic and valid at the time of signature of a document electronically.

Certificates will be used to link the owner to the signature and contain useful information about the trust service provider, the nature of the guarantee and the certificates will need to be compliant with Annex 1 of Directive[60] and created and managed within a Public Key Infrastructure (PKI). A PKI is a combination of software, encryption technologies and services that provide a high level of trust and creates a security architecture[61] covering certification, public key cryptography and the management process

b. Digital Signatures in the UK

The first consultation on most of the matters covered by Parts I and II was undertaken by the previous conservative Government in March 1997 and was widely criticised.[62] The criticism coupled with the publication in October 1997 of the European Commission policy document entitled "Towards a European Framework for Digital Signatures and Encryption" (http//www.ispo.cec.be/eif/policy) led to

58 This was the result of a compromise wording in order to mitigate the impact of the requirement that Member States "shall ensure that advanced electronic signatures satisfy the legal requirements of a signature in the same manner as a hand-written signature."

59 In the UK, this is likely to be implemented by schemes such as "tScheme" (http://www.fei.org.uk/fei/news/tscheme.html).

60 Certificates which comply with Annex II of the Directive are termed Qualified Certificates.

61 Risk management with the British Standard on Information Security Management, BS 7799, is a business-led approach to best practice on information security management; risk assessment is at the heart of BS 7799

62 Additional documents about the Government's general policy towards electronic communications and information technology can be found at http://www.iagchampions.gov.uk/strategy.htm—the Cabinet Office "E-Government—A strategic framework for public services in the Information Age"—April 2000; http://www.cabinet-office.gov.uk/innovation/1999/ecommerce—the Performance and Innovation Report "e-commerce@its.best.uk"; http://www.cabinet-office.gov.uk/moderngov/1999/whitepaper/index.htm—the Cabinet Office Modernising Government White Paper (Cm 4310); http://www.dti.gov.uk/com/competitive—the DTI Competitiveness White Paper (Cm 4176) published in December 1998 and http://www.number-10.gov.uk/public/info/index.html—"Our Information Age: The Government's Vision" (URN 98/677; 4-98) and bulletins at http://www.number-10.gov.uk/public/info/index.html. The websites of the e-envoy (http://www.e-envoy.gov.uk), the Cabinet Office Central IT Unit (http://www.citu.gov.uk) and the DTI (http://www.dti.gov.uk).

a significant re-write of the proposals which were then overtaken by a general election in the UK.[63]

In 1999, the new UK labour Government produced a draft Electronic-Commerce Bill which was put out to Public Consultation in July 1999.[64] This was again subject to criticism and underwent significant review in light of that criticism. Although the Bill originally started life as the Electronic Commerce Bill, the electronic commerce sections were heavily criticised as were the e-signature key escrow provisions. As a result of the widespread criticisms, the Government withdrew many of the contentious provisions in the re-drafted document and added a much needed section for modification of telecommunications licences. As a result, the Bill was more related to e-Communications than e-Commerce and accordingly was renamed the Electronic Communications Bill.[65] In particular the Government has retreated from the very contentious proposals for a national key escrow infrastructure and a very complex approved cryptography system.

Although the system in the UK is technologically neutral, it is widely believed that an asymmetrical system is the more secure basis and amongst the digital signature cryptography systems, this is widely used as the preferred system. Asymmetrical systems use one key to encrypt or sign a message and a different key to decrypt or verify the data or communication.[66]

The resulting Electronic Communications Act 2000 implements the EU Directive on e-Signatures and is also compatible with the Cryptography Guidelines, published by the Organisation for Economic Co-operation and Development

63 The Government announced its response to the consultation and its amended policy on the provision of licensed cryptography services in April 1998 by a parliamentary statement by Mrs Barbara Roche(Parliamentary Under Secretary of State at the Department of Trade and Industry (DTI) at the time. Reference: Hansard, HoC, c27 and available at http://www.parliament.uk/commons.htm.

64 A broader consultation was published in March 1999called "Building Confidence in Electronic Commerce: A Consultation Document" (URN 99/642) http://www.dti.gov.uk/cii/elec/elec_com.html > which invited various responses(summaries of which are available at http://www.dti.gov.uk/cii/elec/conrep.htm. This was followed quickly with the Trade and Industry Select Committee of the House of Commons report "Building Confidence in Electronic Commerce: The Government's Proposals," May 1999, HC 187 http://www.parliament.uk/commons/selcom/t&ihome.htm and resulted in a newly drafted Electronic Communications Bill being published for consultation on 23 July 1999 as part of the Government's "Promoting Electronic Commerce" scheme (Cm 4417) (see http://www.dti.gov.uk/cii/elec/ecbill.html which also invited responses form the public and industry).

65 This Act which now relates to the future of the communications networks is likely to be subject to significant amendments in due course to take into account EU proposals on access to digital communications networks etc.

66 "Communication" includes a communication comprising sounds or images or both and a communication effecting a payment. "electronic communication" means a communication transmitted (whether from one person to another, from one device to another or from a person to a device or vice versa) by means of a telecommunication system (within the meaning of the Telecommunications Act 1984) or by other means but while in an electronic form.

(OECD) on 19 March 97,[67] and the United Nations Commission on International Trade Law (UNCITRAL) Model Law on Electronic Commerce.[68]

c. Cryptography Service Providers

The Secretary of State is required to establish or make arrangements for the establishment and maintenance of a register of approved providers of cryptography support services and specifies what information[69] is to be contained in the register and to make arrangements for the public to have access to the register and any changes.[70] In the UK, the Alliance for Electronic Business (AEB) has drawn up an industry led scheme (known as the "tScheme") and the Government has indicated that it will not set up the register or otherwise commence Part I of the Act[71] if it continues to be satisfied that the tScheme meets the Government's objectives.[72]

The main purpose of the voluntary register is to ensure that providers on the register have been independently assessed for quality standards. Cryptographic Service Providers are not obliged to apply for approval under scheme although any approved CSPs must comply with any rules made under the approval as well as rules for the handling of complaints and disputes and the modifying or withdrawing of approval.

Although the aim of the Act is to be technologically neutral, the Secretary of State is given the power to set requirements at his discretion to assist the effectiveness of the approvals scheme[73] e.g. by regulation, and also to impose conditions on the approval. Approval can be granted either in respect of all the services in respect of which it is sought or in respect of only some of them.

Approved persons are required to comply with such technical and other requirements as may be prescribed by the Secretary of State from time to time and must continue to be able and willing to comply with any future requirements and a fit and proper person to be approved in respect of those services.[74] Before making any changes to the general scheme of the approvals system, however, the Secretary of State must consult appropriate persons.

---

67 Available on the OECD website at: <www.oecd.org/subject/e_commerce>.

68 Available on the UN website at <www.un.or.at/uncitral/english/texts/electcom/ml-ec.htm>.

69 Such as name and address, including appropriate electronic addresses, services for which the person is approved and any conditions of approval.

70 In particular the Secretary of State is required to ensure that sufficient publicity is given to any withdrawal or modification of an approval as will bring it to the attention of persons likely to be interested in it.

71 Power to delegate the functions to tScheme exist under s3 of the Act.

72 Further details are available at <http://www.fei.org.uk/fei/news/tscheme.html>.

73 Such as relating to the technology provided, to the person providing the service, their background and experience, and the way they provide the technology to the public.

74 Relevant factors include any known contraventions of provisions of this legislation, and convictions for offences involving fraud or dishonesty, or engaging in discriminatory practices, or engaging in deceitful, oppressive, unfair or improper business practices.

A limitation in the Act protects from excessive use of powers to impose authorisation conditions because any requirement for the provision of information in excess of matters mentioned in subsection (3)(a) to (d) of the Act or for the maintenance of a procedure for handling complaints or disputes are invalid.

Cryptography Support Services will be deemed provided in the United Kingdom if they are provided from premises in the United Kingdom, are provided to a person who is in the United Kingdom when he or she makes use of the services or are provided to a business carried on in the UK.[75]

The Act protects the information obtained under Part I[76] and sets out the purposes for which it may be disclosed[77] and makes improper disclosure a criminal offence. As such, it safeguards individual privacy and commercially confidential information unless the disclosure is justifiable under the provisions set out.

Although the Secretary of State can make substantive additional provisions,[78] any such regulations will be subject to affirmative resolution procedure in both Houses of Parliament on the first occasion that the Secretary of State exercises the powers to make regulations and thereafter subject to negative resolution procedures.[79]

The cryptography support services that may be approved by the Secretary of State include those services relating to confidentiality[80] and securing the authenticity or integrity of communications and data.[81]

The approval scheme includes only those services primarily involving a continuing relationship between the supplier of the service[82] and the customer and are not intended to cover the supply of an item[83] unless such supply is integral to the provision of the cryptographic service itself.

d. Enforceability of Electronic Signatures

The Act facilitates electronic commerce and electronic communications by providing that in any legal proceedings, an electronic signature incorporated into any

---

75 This includes any part of a business which is operated from premises in the UK or a business carried on in the UK.

76 Electronic Communications Act 2000, s4.

77 In order to carry out the approvals functions, for a criminal investigation or for those civil proceedings specified in subsection (2)(e).

78 The Secretary of State is not empowered to make any order which relates to matters managed by the Commissioners of Inland Revenue or the Commissioners of Customs and Excise.

79 Electronic Communications Act 2000, s5.

80 I.e., securing that such electronic communications or data can be accessed, or can be put into an intelligible form (defined in section 15(3)), only by certain persons.

81 "Authenticity" and "integrity" are defined in section 15(2).

82 Cryptography support services would include registration and certification in relation to certificates, time-stamping of certificates or documents, key generation and management, key-storage and providing directories of certificates.

83 Whether hardware or software.

particular electronic communication or data when that signature is certified by a person is admissible in evidence to prove the authenticity[84] of the communication or data or its integrity.[85] Thus it will be for the court to decide in a particular case whether an electronic signature has been correctly used and what weight it should be given (e.g. in relation to the authentication or integrity of a message) against other evidence. Some businesses in the UK have already contracted with each other about how they are to treat each other's electronic communications and those arrangements will remain valid.

The definition of an electronic signature under the Act mirrors the definition in the EU Directive[86] and an electronic signature is incorporated into a communication or into data if it is certified by a person if they have made a statement confirming that the signature, its means of producing, communicating or verifying the signature, or any procedure applied to the signature is a valid means of establishing the authenticity or integrity of the communication or data.

The Appropriate Minister[87] has the power to modify legislation as deemed appropriate for the purpose of authorising or facilitating the use of electronic communications or electronic storage, whether this is something which is required to be or may be:

(a) done or evidenced in writing or otherwise using a document, notice or instrument;

(b) done by post or other specified means of delivery;

(c) carried out under signature or seal or delivered as a deed or witnessed;

(d) done by the making of any statement or declaration made under oath or contained in a statutory declaration;

(e) kept, maintained or preserved for the purposes of recording data in any account, record, notice, instrument or other document; or

(f) authorisation to make any payment.

---

84 Authenticity of any communication or data means any method of proving that the communication or data comes from a particular person or other source, whether it is accurately timed and dated and whether it is intended to have legal effect.

85 Integrity of any communication or data is any method of by which it is sought to show whether there has been any tampering with or other modification of the communication or data.

86 Anything in electronic form which (a) is incorporated into or otherwise logically associated with any electronic communication or electronic data; and (b) purports to be so incorporated or associated for the purpose of being used in establishing the authenticity of the communication or data, the integrity of the communication or data, or both.

87 Where an "Appropriate Minister" is empowered under section 8 of the Act then in relation to any matter with which a department of the Secretary of State is concerned, the "Appropriate Minister" is the Secretary of State, in relation to any matter with which the Treasury is concerned, the "Appropriate Minister" is the Treasury and for any other Government department where there is no Secretary of State, then the Appropriate Minister is the Minister in charge of that department.

However an order under this section authorising the use of electronic communications or electronic storage for any purpose may not be made unless the creation of authorisation for electronic signatures will be no less satisfactory that in cases of conventional signatures.

The Secretary of State can however make provision as to the electronic form to be taken for any use authorised or can impose conditions for the use of e-Signatures and can provide that where the conditions are not satisfied then the e-Signature will be invalid or can be refused.

Additionally regulations can be made to provide for services to be provided or proved by intermediaries, for conditions in relation to the data storage facilities or record-keeping, proof in legal proceedings, the provision for different fees or charges to apply where use is made of communications or storage signed by e-Signatures and the provision for criminal or civil liability arise in respect of the making of false or misleading statements in connection with anything electronically signed where conventional signature would incur similar liability.

The Secretary of State is also empowered to make rules requiring the production of the contents of any records kept which are digitally signed but may not require the use of electronic communications or electronic storage for any purpose.

Section 14 mirrors the EU Directive's prohibition on key escrow, providing that no power exists to impose a requirement on any person to deposit a key[88] for electronic data with another person although this does not cover a) provision of a key for electronic data with the intended recipient of electronic communications or b) arrangements made to put the information in an intelligible form, where no third-party key deposit arrangements exist, upon the loss or corruption of a key.[89]

There is a power to modify legislation to remove restrictions arising from other legislation which prevent the use of electronic communications or storage in place of paper. The power can be used selectively to offer the electronic alternative to those who want it. There are a large number of provisions in statutes on many different topics, which require the use of paper or which might be interpreted to require this.[90] The power can be used in any of these cases and is not limited to the provision of written information.

88 "Depositing a key" with a person includes references to doing anything that has the effect of making the key available to that person.

89 "Key" means any code, password, algorithm, key or other data the use of which (with or without other keys) which allows access to the electronic data, or facilitates the putting of the electronic data into an intelligible form.

90 Such as communication with Government Departments, submissions of information, applications for licences or permits and communications between businesses and individuals where there is a statutory requirement that the communication should be on paper.

For example the power has already been used in relation to filings under the Companies Act 1985.[91] Under the Companies Act 1985 (Electronic Communications) Order 2000[92] the legal obstacles in the Companies Act 1985 to companies communicating electronically with their shareholders were removed and the scope of information that can be delivered electronically to Companies House widened. Companies can now communicate with shareholders and auditors electronically (by fax, e-mail or website)[93] to if they seek the agreement of shareholders to the distribution of annual reports, accounts and other information on a website, or through other electronic communications and to allow shareholders to use e-communications to appoint proxies, and give them voting instructions, although neither companies nor their shareholders will be obliged to use electronic communications. By the end of 2001, it is expected that incorporation of companies will be permitted electronically.

Government co-ordination of the changes needed for e-Signatures will be needed and the role has been assigned to the Central IT Unit in the Cabinet Office.

e. Certification Authorities and Trusted Third Parties

The UK Government widely recognised the necessity that, in any successful digital economy, there was a need for secure and verifiable signature protocols and that if a person creates a message, then recipients must be able to rely upon the authenticity and accuracy of that message.

Using asymmetric key (dual-key) protocols, a message encrypted (encoded) with a person's private key can be read by anyone with that person's public key and this guarantees that the holder of the private key was the message author.

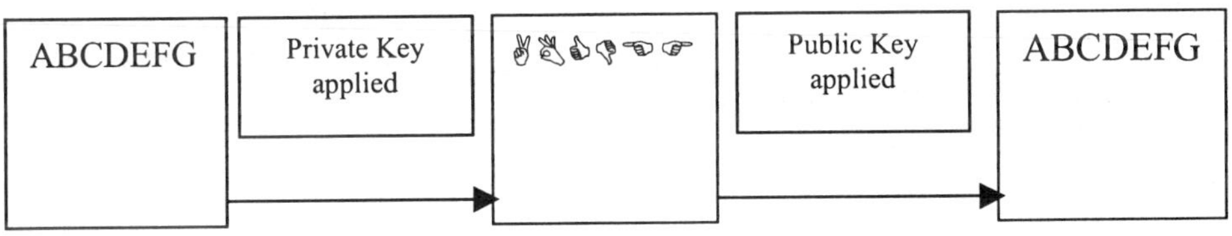

91 On 5 March 1999 the DTI consulted about whether the Act should be changed to enable companies to use electronic means to deliver company communications, to receive shareholder proxy and voting instructions and to incorporate. The consultation letter "Electronic Communication: Change To The Companies Act 1985" is available from DTI's Company Law and Investigations Directorate, telephone 020 7215 0409.

92 (2000/3373) came into force on 22 December 2000.

93 Best practice guidance on "Electronic Communications with Shareholders" is available from the Institute of Company Secretaries and Administrators (ICSA) at 16 Park Crescent, London, W1B 1AH and a summary of key recommendations can be accessed on the ICSA website at www.icsa.org.uk.

A 'digest' of a message is a unique value that relates to that message and that message alone and if the owner of the private key 'signs' the message by encrypting the digest with the private key, then even though the message itself can be sent unencrypted, if the digest decodes with that person's public key then the recipient knows that message came from the owner of the private key and that the message has not been altered.

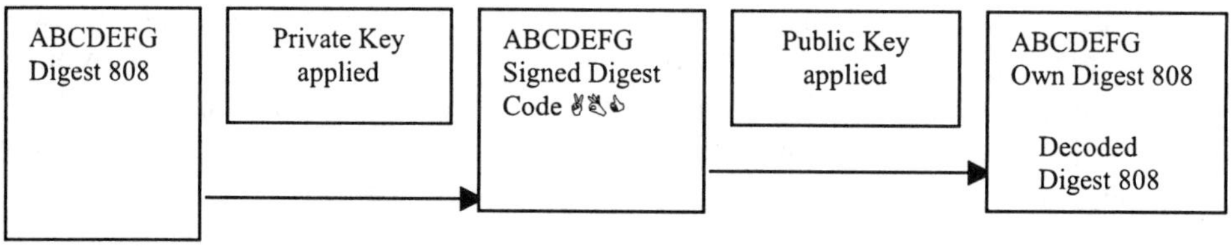

This system can also be used to ensure privacy due to the 2-way nature of dual-key systems because if a message is encoded with the person's public key, then interception becomes pointless as only the owner of the private key can read the message. It was the concern of government enforcement agencies that criminal elements and tax evaders would use these systems to secure documents and messages in the knowledge that interception of the message will not lead to disclosure of the contents.

Certification Authorities (CAs) and Certification Service Providers (CSPs) are trusted organisations who signs a person's public key and provide information about them within a 'digital certificate'. Anyone receiving the digital certificate can then check it by using the public key of the CA or CSP which will confirm the identity of the public key holder. It can be expected for example that banks and national post-offices will become CSPs and that the Bank's public key will be widely available on cheque book covers, plastic cards and smart-cards issued by banks etc.[94]

94 For example, a pilot is currently underway by a UK bank which provides the bank's public key on all plastic cards issued by the bank. The cards are readable by any computer equipped with a magnetic card reader costing GBP49. It is expected that digital signatures will be also available on flash memory cards as uded in digital cameras and PDAs etc.

For example:

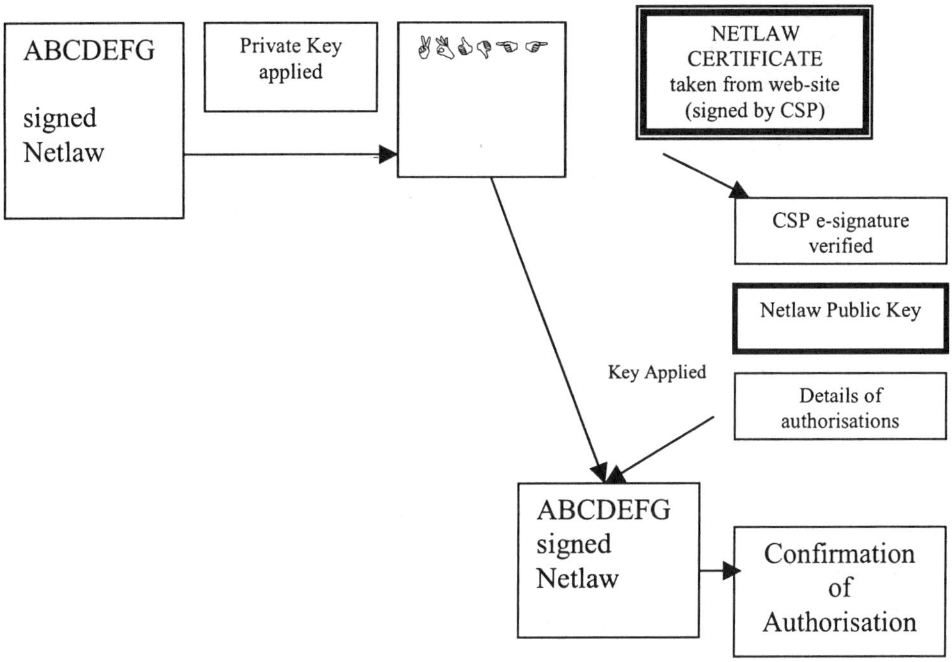

The UK Government's preferred option for certification is that it will be optional to obtain a Certification licence. As an incentive for a CA or CSP to become licensed, the UK Government has suggested limitations of liability to the relying parties for licensed CAs and CSPs. It is however difficult to see how any limitation of liability is commercially consistent with the widespread adoption and trust needed for such schemes to be accepted and many industry operators considered that the benefit of a licensing scheme should be a government funded insurance scheme for liabilities in excess of a given amount in relation to any particular certificate.[95]

f. Key Escrow

The discussion so far has been around the use of a digital signature—the encryption of only a digest of a message which is attached to the message. If the entire message is encrypted then law enforcement and revenue authorities are likely to be well displeased. Why don't I just encrypt the whole message? Then no one else can read it. Firstly, it takes up a lot of resources (it is much quicker to encrypt only the digest) and government authorities will want to gain access to the

95 The critical part of any certification scheme is the certification policy (certification practice statement CPS) of the CA or CSP and the requirement to comply with the policy or statement.

private keys of users of encryption, even though they may not care about the users only of digital signature.

The policy of the US government is that the private key should be handed over to the government or stored somewhere safe by the CA and handed over to law enforcement officials if they request it. That way, if the law enforcement officials wish to have access to a particular encrypted message, they can demand the key and decrypt the message. This practice is called "key escrow." There is a variation of key escrow which involves chopping the private key up into pieces and having each piece given to a different person (called key recovery). When the key, or any part of it, is kept by a person other than the government, that person is described as a Trusted Third Party (TTP). All users are expected to trust the trusted third party.

Some method for letting police get hold of a person's private key was also the policy of the Conservative government. This policy was the subject of a consultation paper released in March 1997, but nothing was ever done about it. The present Labour government has not yet decided on its policy, and the DTI is apparently set to have another round of public consultation at any moment. The Germans have introduced a law which requires a CA to be licenced, but which prohibits the storage of a private key by the CA. The EU has been rumoured to reject escrow (or certainly the type of escrow which would place the private keys in the hands of the government ab initio) sufficiently to be willing to trade away some of the privacy issues surrounding the Data Protection Directive in order to reject escrow.

g. The Logic of Key Escrow?

The first question which must be asked is why would any self-respecting criminal or terrorist actually use a key escrow system? Even if it is a punishable offence not to escrow the key, it would be a pathetic criminal who delivered the private key to the TTP and then used the system to send 'You meet me outside the bank with the motor running' messages which could be so easily read by law enforcement. However, as an FBI delegate at an encryption conference once retorted, 'we meet some pretty stupid criminals, let me tell you'.

The second challenge to the logic of an escrow system is that it takes away what it seeks to help. Company, commercial and banking systems which promise to be extremely secure using encryption (and therefore far less susceptible to fraud and forgery than current systems) will have some (unquantifiable measure) of that promise taken away by making the keys aggregate in one place as prime target. To some extent this concern is addressed by distributing the keys in pieces around a set of TTPs. This makes penetration of the TTP system harder (perhaps exponentially harder) but even so it is a technical fix to a logical flaw.

h. Authorising Electronic Communications under the Companies Act 1985

The Companies Act 1985 (Electronic Communications) Order 2000 (2000/3373) came into force on 22 December 2000 to remove the legal obstacles in the Companies Act 1985 that prevent to companies communicating electronically with their shareholders and to widen the scope of information that can be delivered electronically to Companies House.[96]

Companies will therefore no longer have to rely solely on company information being sent by post and therefore may communicate with shareholders and auditors electronically (by fax, e-mail or website).

Under the amendments to the Companies Act[97] most companies are now able to both distribute annual reports, accounts and other information on a website, or through other electronic communications (with the agreement of shareholders) and to allow shareholders to use e-communications to appoint proxies, and give them voting instructions,[98] although nothing will require companies nor their shareholders, under present rules, to use electronic communications. In addition to the information that can already be sent to the Registrar electronically, it will be possible later in 2001 to incorporate companies electronically and thereafter to file annual returns electronically.

The Companies Act Order was one of the first made under sections 8 and 9 of the Electronic Communications Act 2000 and modified various provisions of the Companies Act 1985 to allow the use of electronic communications between companies and their members, debenture holders and auditors, and between companies and the registrar of companies.

The Order also removes the requirement with respect to memorandum and articles of association for attestation of the signatures of subscribers to the memorandum where the memorandum and articles are delivered to the registrar of companies electronically and permits the electronic delivery of statements, in-

---

96 For further details see "Electronic Communications with Shareholders: A Guide to Recommended Best Practice" and the accompanying guidance notes obtainable from The Policy Unit, The Institute of Chartered Secretaries and Administrators, 16 Park Crescent, London W1B 1AH. A Regulatory Impact Assessment of this Order is available from the Department of Trade and Industry, Company Law and Investigations Directorate, Room 507, 1 Victoria Street, London SW1H 0ET.

97 Best practice guidance on "Electronic Communications with Shareholders" is available from the Institute of Company Secretaries and Administrators (ICSA) at 16 Park Crescent, London, W1B 1AH and a summary of key recommendations can be accessed on the ICSA website at www.icsa.org.uk.

98 Companies will be able to choose what type of electronic communications medium best serves their purposes, such as publication of information on a website, or sending information by e-mail, fax or other methods.

stead of delivery of a sworn statutory declaration in writing, to the registrar in relation to:

Section	Effect
12	Duty of registrar on incorporation of a company
30	Exemption from requirement of "limited" as part of company name
43, 47	Re-registration of private company as public
49	Re-registration of limited company as unlimited
155, 156	Relaxation for private companies of prohibition against financial assistance
403	Entries of satisfaction and release of charges: England and Wales
419	Entries of satisfaction and release of charges: Scotland
685	Registration of joint stock company as public company
686	Other requirements for registration under Chapter II of Part XXII
691	Documents to be delivered to registrar by oversea company establishing place of business

The Order permits people to receive copies of amounts and reports electronically as accounts and reports can be sent directly to an electronic address supplied expressly for that purpose by the recipient. The accounts and reports can also be published on a website and the recipient notified of their availability in a manner agreed with him although any web-publication must be continuously available on the website for at least 21 days before the general meeting before which they are to be laid.

UNITED STATES

by
John S. "Chip" Rainey
Locke Liddell & Sapp LLP

A. FEDERALISM IN THE UNITED STATES AND ITS ROLE IN JURISDICTION

1. Federal Laws and the Doctrine of Preemption

In the United States, there is a true federal system,[1] with 52 jurisdictions imposing laws, and operating separate court systems.[2] These are the 50 states, the District of Columbia, and the federal government. In the U.S. federal system, there is a division of power between the states and the central government, so that, at least in theory, with respect to most matters involving business and domestic trade, the states are free to adopt individual legal regimes. In general, while solely the federal government may regulate interstate commerce, intrastate commerce theoretically remains the exclusive domain of the respective states. The U.S. Constitution provides that the federal government is a limited government, having only those powers specifically given to it under the Constitution and

1 In a federal system, the national government holds significant power, but the smaller political subdivisions also hold significant power. The United States, Canada, Australia, and Brazil are examples of federal systems.

2 Although each of the countries *within* the European Union would be characterized as being a unitary state, in which most power is held by the central government, in fact, the European Union, in and of itself, is developing into a federated system, much like the United States (*see Power and Interdependence: World Politics in Transition.* Keohane, R. O., & Nye, J.S., p.260, 3rd ed. 2001), except that the purposes of the federal government at the inception of the United States—common defense and international trade—are not part of the EU's purpose. Instead, the EU has been formed primarily for economic and business purposes, including harmonized regulations, free flow of persons, goods and services among the various members, and a single monetary system. *See* Treaty on European Union (commonly known as the Maastricht Treaty), Title 1, Article B (which lists five goals for the European Union, of which only one mentions foreign affairs and defense, and then only in language expressing the hope for the development in the future of a common defense), found at http://europa.eu.int/en/record/mt/top.html (last visited July 1, 2004).

their logical extensions.[3] As the U.S. Supreme Court stated in *United States v. Butler*:

> It hardly seems necessary to reiterate that ours is a dual form of government; that in every state there are two governments—the state and the United States. Each State has all governmental powers save such as the people, by their Constitution, have conferred upon the United States, denied to the States, or reserved to them. The federal union is a government of delegated powers. It has only such as are expressly conferred upon it and such as are reasonably to be implied from those granted. In this respect,' we differ radically from nations where all legislative power, without restriction or limitation, is vested in a parliament or other legislative body subject to no restrictions except the discretion of its members.[4]

Despite this notion of federal government powers limited to those expressly enumerated in the Constitution, there remains considerable room within the scope of such enumerated powers for federal regulation over many aspects of business and consumer activities in the United States, especially with respect to the Internet. Much of that power devolves from the interplay of the U.S. Constitution's Commerce Clause, and its Supremacy Clause.

a. General Notions of Pre-emption under the Supremacy Clause

The preemption doctrine derives from the Supremacy Clause of the U.S. Constitution. Article VI, Clause 2 of the United States Constitution provides that:

> This Constitution, and the Laws of the United States which shall be made in Pursuance thereof; and all Treaties made, or which shall be made, under the Authority of the United States, shall be the supreme Law of the Land; and the Judges in every State shall be bound thereby, any thing in the Constitution or Laws of any State to the Contrary notwithstanding.[5]

This means, of course, that *any* constitutionally-valid federal law—even a regulation issued by a federal agency pursuant to an express delegation of regulatory power to such agency by the U.S. Congress—trumps *any* state law if there is an express conflict between the state law and the federal law.[6] This is known as *express preemption*. When Congress chooses to expressly preempt state law, the only question for courts becomes determining whether the challenged state law is one that the federal law is intended to preempt. An example of express preemption in the Internet context is the federal E-SIGN Act.[7]

---

3 U.S. V. Butler, 297 U.S. 1 (1936).

4 *Id.* at 63.

5 U.S. Const. Art. VI.

6 When enacting a federal law, Congress may explicitly define the extent to which it intends such law to pre-empt state law. e.g., *Shaw vs. Delta Air Lines, Inc.*, 463 U.S. 85,95-96 (1983).

7 Electronic Signatures in Global and National Commerce Act (E-SIGN), 15 U.S.C. §§ 7006(9).

Just as importantly, state law is trumped by federal law in several other circumstances, as well, which collectively are known as *implied preemption*.[8] In the first circumstance of implied preemption, Congress may evidence by statute intent to occupy an entire field of regulation, even in the absence of express preemptive language, in which case the states must leave all regulatory activity in that area to the Federal Government.[9] In the second circumstance, even if Congress has not displaced state regulation entirely, a federal statute may nonetheless be found to have pre-empted state law to the extent that such state law actually conflicts with federal law. Such a conflict arises when compliance with both state and federal law is impossible,[10] "or when the state law stands as an obstacle to the accomplishment and execution of the full purposes and objective of Congress".[11]

Implied preemption presents more difficult issues than express preemption. The most important question in determining if federal law has preempted a state law is Congressional intent.[12] There are three recognized fundamental principles of analyzing Congressional intent with respect to implied preemption: (a) when the federal law has "occupied the field" in which the state law purports to regulate; (b) when a state law—even if it has the same ultimate goal as a federal law—stands as an obstacle to the *full implementation* of a federal law and therefore be preempted, if it interferes with the methods by which the federal statute was designed to reach this goal;[13] and (c) state common law damage claims are a form of state regulation that are also subject to the Supremacy Clause.[14] In short, even if statutory language is unclear, federal law will still act to preempt a state law if "the ordinary application of the two laws create a conflict."[15]

The Court has to look beyond the express language of federal statutes to determine whether Congress has "occupied the field" in which the state is attempting

---

8 See *Hodges v Delta Airlines*, 44 F.3d 334, 336 (5th Cir. *En banc* 1995*)* State law is displaced by federal law where (1) Congress expressly preempts state law; (2) Congressional intent to preempt is inferred from the existence of a pervasive regulatory scheme; or (3) state law conflicts with federal law or interferes with the achievement of federal objectives (citing to Hillsborough County, Florida v. Automated Medical Laboratories, Inc., 471 U.S. 707, 713, 105 S.Ct. 2371, 2375, 85 L.Ed.2d (1985); Shaw v. Delta Airlines, Inc., 463 U.S. 85, 95, 103 S.Ct. 2890, 2899, 77 L.Ed.2d 490 (1983); Rice v. Santa Fe Elevator Corp., 331 U.S. 218, 230, 67 S.Ct. 1146, 1152, 91 L.Ed. 1447 (1947); Silkwood v. Kerr-McGee Corp., 464 U.S. 238, 248, 104 S.Ct. 615, 621, 78 L.Ed.2d 443 (1984)).

9 *See, e.g.*, *Fidelity Federal Savings & Loan Assoc. vs. De La Cuesta*, 458 U.S. 141,153 (1982); *Rice vs. Santa Fe Elevator Corn*., 331 U.S. 218, 230 (1947).

10 *Florida Lime & Avocado Growers, Inc., v. Paul*, 373 U.S. 132, 142-43 (1963).

11 *Hines v. Davidowitz*, 312 U.S. 52, 67 (1941) and *Fidelity Federal Savings & Loan Assoc.* Supra, at 153, *Michigan Canners & Freezers Assoc. Inc. v. Agricultural Marketing & Bargaining Bd*, 467 U.S. 461, 469 (1984.)

12 *Papas v Upjohn Co.*, 926 F.2d 1019, 1022 (11th Cir. 1991).

13 926 F.2d at 1021, citing *International Paper Co. v. Ouelette*, 479 U.S. 481,494(1987).

14 926 F.2d at 1022.

15 Id, citing *Taylor v. General Motors Corp.*, 875 F.2d 816,828 (11th Cir. 1987).

to regulate, or whether a state law directly conflicts with federal law, or whether enforcement of the state law might frustrate federal purposes. Federal "occupation of the field" occurs, according to the Court in *Pennsylvania v Nelson*,[16] when there is "no room" left for state regulation. In that case, a court is to determine the pervasiveness of the federal scheme of regulation, the federal interest at stake, and the danger of frustration of federal goals in making the determination as to whether a challenged state law can stand. For example, in *Silkwood v Kerr-McGee*,[17] the Court, voting 5-4, found that a $10 million dollar punitive damages award against a nuclear power plant was not impliedly pre-empted by federal law. Even though the Court had recently held that state regulation of the safety aspects of a federally-licensed nuclear power plant was preempted, the Court drew a different conclusion with respect to Congress's desire to displace state tort law—even though the tort actions might be premised on a violation of federal safety regulations.

Along the same lines, the Supreme Court permitted some types of tort actions to proceed in *Cipollone v Liggett Group*, a closely-watched case concerning the extent of an express preemption provision in two cigarette labeling laws of the 1960s.[18] The case was a wrongful death action brought against tobacco companies on behalf of Rose Cipollone, a lung cancer victim who had started smoking cigarettes in the 1940s. The Court considered the preemptive effect on state law of a provision that stated "No requirement based on smoking and health shall be imposed under state law with respect to the advertising and promotion of cigarettes." The Court concluded that several types of state tort actions were preempted by the provision, but refused to find that the labeling law preempted all tort actions against the cigarette manufacturers and allowed other types to go forward. Perhaps the most interesting aspect of the case, from a constitutional standpoint, is the debate between justices over whether express preemption provisions should be read narrowly (a view adopted by seven justices) or read normally (a view favored by Justices Thomas and Scalia).

Most recently, in *American Insurance Association v Garamendi*, the Supreme Court considered the constitutionality of a California law, the Holocaust Victim Insurance Relief Act of 1999 (HVIRA), designed to help California Holocaust survivors collect on unpaid insurance claims from German insurance companies. In its decision, a bare majority of the Justices held that HVIRA was preempted and thus unenforceable because it interfered with the federal government's conduct of foreign affairs, despite the absence of any clear statement in any executive agreement preempting state laws. Specifically, the Court found that the state Act conflicted with national policy and "stands in the way of [the President's] diplomatic objectives." However, in a strongly worded dissent, the

16 350 U.S. 497 (1956).

17 464 U.S. 238 (1984).

18 505 U.S. 504 (1992).

minority argued that "Courts step out of their proper role when they rely on no legislative or even executive text, but only on inference and implication, to preempt state laws on foreign affairs grounds."

b. Commerce Clause Pre-emption

The Supreme Court has ruled that instruments of commerce can be regulated under the Commerce Clause of the Constitution. This is because virtually all Internet access occurs over telephone lines on the public access switched system, which has been ruled to be regulated by the federal government because it is so inextricably linked with interstate commerce. Even when a substantial portion of an Internet transaction is over private, leased lines, there remains the substantial possibility that some portion of the communications necessary for the transaction will involve the public telephone lines.[19]

2. Personal Jurisdiction

In order for a person or legal entity to be subject to defend a lawsuit, whether brought in state court or in a federal court, the person must be amenable to lawsuit in the location where the suit is brought. This is known as personal jurisdiction. In the United States, there are two types of personal jurisdiction: general and specific. Specific jurisdiction means that a defendant is amenable to defend the lawsuit in the subject forum because of the circumstances surrounding the particular conduct that is in question in the lawsuit. General jurisdiction means that a defendant is amenable to defend the lawsuit in the subject forum because the defendant has sufficient nexus with that forum such that it would not be unfair to expect him to have to answer in that forum, even if the circumstances surrounding the particular conduct that is in question in the lawsuit occurred principally, or even exclusively, in another jurisdiction.

A court determines the existence of personal jurisdiction over a nonresident defendant by examining the "(1) assertion of jurisdiction by the law of the forum;" and "(2) conformity of the law with the Constitution."[20] A defendant is amenable to the personal jurisdiction of a federal court to the same extent that he or she would be amenable to the jurisdiction of a state court in the same forum.

Until the mid 1980s the primary analysis of a court in determining personal jurisdiction was focused on actions of the defendant *directed* towards the forum state. We now understand that the *effects* of the defendant's actions in the forum state, even where the defendant's causal actions were committed in or directed to another state, can form the basis of sufficient contacts. The case most often

19 Public, in this case, does not imply owned by the federal or any state government. Instead, virtually all telecommunications in the United States occur via privately held telephone companies. But many of these companies are "common carriers" providing service to anyone who wants it and is willing to comply with the rules of service. These common carriers have come under the regulation of the government.

20 *Panda Brandywine Corp. v. Potomac Elec. Power Co.*, 253 F.3d 865, 867 (5th Cir. 2001).

cited for the effects of a defendant's action being a basis for personal jurisdiction is *Calder v. Jones*.[21]

> [I]n that case the Supreme Court determined that jurisdiction was proper in California over nonresident defendants because the defendants' "intentional conduct" in Florida injured the plaintiff in California. The suit involved an allegedly libelous article prepared by newspapermen in Florida about the respondent/plaintiff Jones, a resident of California, that was calculated to cause injuries to Jones. The Calder "effects test" examines whether the nonresident defendant "intended to and did cause tortious injury" in the forum. Jurisdiction is then based on the "effects" of the defendant's conduct in the forum state. The rationale behind the effects test is that courts will not require the injured party to travel to the nonresident defendant's forum to seek redress when the defendant "knowingly caused the injury" in the injured party's forum.[22]

In contrast to specific personal jurisdiction, "general jurisdiction" exists when a court may try *any* claims against a defendant, regardless of whether the claims relate to the defendant's contacts or not. For individuals, general jurisdiction always exists in the state where the defendant is domiciled. For corporate defendants, general jurisdiction exists both in the state of incorporation and state of principal place of business. However, general jurisdiction also arises when a non-resident defendant has contacts with the forum state unrelated to the cause of action, but that are "continuous and systematic."[23]

Jurisdiction based upon online activities: *the Zippo Sliding Scale*

With few exceptions, most cases involving the exercise of jurisdiction over out-of-state and international websites are analyzed in terms of specific jurisdiction. Under most states, specific jurisdiction is determined under a three-part test: The nonresident defendant must purposely avail itself of the forum state; the claim must arise out of the defendant's forum-state activities; and the exercise of jurisdiction must be reasonable. *See, e.g., Jewish Defense Org. Inc. v. Superior Court*.[24]

Although no Internet jurisdiction case has yet reached the U.S. Supreme Court, a number of the Circuit Courts of Appeal have heard such cases, and many, including the 9th, 7th, 2nd, and 5th Circuits[25] have elected to follow the "sliding scale" jurisdictional approach, which was outlined by the District Court in *Zippo*

---

21 465 U.S. 783 (1984).

22 G. Peter Albert, Jr. & Laff, Whitesel & Saret, Ltd., *Intellectual Property Law in Cyberspace* 216 (Supp. 2002).

23 *Mink v AAAA Dev. LLC*, 190 F.3d 333, 336 (5th Cir. 1999).

24 72 Cal.App.4th 1045 (1999) (citing *Panavision Int'l L.P. v. Toeppen*, 141 F.3d 1316 (9th Cir.1998)).

25 The Fifth Circuit expressly adopted *Zippo*, but declined to assert jurisdiction over a defendant using the *Zippo* analysis in *Mink v AAAA Dev. LLC*, 190 F.3d 333, 337 (5th Cir. 1999).

Manufacturing Co. v. Zippo Dot Com Inc.[26] Under this test, the "likelihood that personal jurisdiction can be constitutionally exercised is directly proportionate to the nature and quality of commercial activity that an entity conducts over the internet."[27]

The *Zippo* court analyzed the cases that had been published to date involving specific jurisdiction exercised or refused where the Internet was the basis by which the plaintiff in the particular case was attempting to establish the necessary minimum contacts. These cases through the time the Zippo decision was announced, while having some degree of variability,[28] usually fell within a sliding scale of jurisdiction. At one end of the sliding-scale spectrum are those defendants who conduct business transactions over the Internet with residents of the forum state. When the defendant enters into contracts with residents of a foreign jurisdiction that involve the knowing and repeated transmission of computer files, jurisdiction is proper.[29] In these cases, the exercise of jurisdiction "is almost always proper" because the defendant has made actual commercial contact with a forum resident.[30] For example, in *Zippo Manufacturing*, the court held that jurisdiction was properly exercised because the defendant contracted with approximately 3,000 individuals and seven Internet service providers in Pennsylvania.[31]

Most courts that have adopted the Zippo sliding scale, however, would hold that the mere posting of copyrighted or trademarked information on a website generally will not be sufficient to confer jurisdiction over the infringing party.[32] Thus, in *Desktop Technologies Inc. v. Colorworks Reproduction & Design Inc.*,[33] a Canadian defendant registered a website using the plaintiff's trademark. The court declined to assert jurisdiction solely on the basis of the existence of the defendant's site. The court held that "there must be something more" than merely use of a trademark on the Internet to subject the defendant to jurisdiction in the fo-

26 952 F. Supp. 1119 (W.D. Pa. 1997).

27 See also *Cybersell v. Cybersell Inc.*, 130 F.3d 414 (9th Cir. 1997).

28 For instance, before *Zippo*, there were a fair number of cases where personal jurisdiction was found despite contacts that appear to be based almost exclusively on the basis of the accessibility of the defendant's web site to citizens of the forum state. See, e.g., *Inset Systems, Inc. v. Instruction Set, Inc.*, 937 F. Supp. 161 (D. Conn. 1996) (sustaining exercise of jurisdiction over defendant where defendant's only contacts with Connecticut were an Internet web site and an 800 telephone number, both of which advertised defendant's services, with the court making particular note that the web site and 800 number were accessible to anyone with Internet access or a telephone including Connecticut residents).

29 *Panavision*, 141 F.3d at 1319.

30 *See e.g. Millennium Enters v. Millennium Music*, 33 F.Supp.2d 907 (D. Or. 1999).

31 See also *Thompson v. Handa-Lopez Inc.*, 998 F. Supp. 738 (holding that personal jurisdiction could be exercised over California defendant who operated Internet casino because defendant entered into contracts with casino players in California knowing it would receive immediate financial gain).

32 *Panavision*, 141 F.3d at 1319.

33 1999 WL 98572 (E.D. Pa. 1999).

rum state.[34] However, if the use of the copyrighted material is for the purpose of soliciting business of residents of the forum state, then such use will subject a defendant to jurisdiction. In *Colt Studio Inc. v. Badpuppy Entertainment*,[35] the defendant operated a members-only area of its Web site, which contained the plaintiff's copyrighted photos. Due to the fact that 12 percent of the defendant's subscribers were California residents, and the defendant had, therefore, established continuing contractual obligations with California residents, jurisdiction over the defendant was held to be proper.[36]

Even a relatively insignificant amount of commercial activity may be sufficient to satisfy the purposeful-availment prong of personal jurisdiction. The critical inquiry in determining whether there is a purposeful availment of the forum state is the quality, not the quantity, of the contacts. In *Stomp Inc. v. NeatO LLC*,[37] the court held that the defendant was subject to jurisdiction in California, even though only two sales had been consummated with forum residents.

At the other end of the Zippo sliding scale are "passive websites," where the defendant merely posts advertisements or informational material. The majority of courts that have confronted this issue have held that such sites do not subject the defendant to jurisdiction. In one of the leading cases after *Zippo*, *Cybersell Inc. v. Cybersell, Inc.*,[38] the 9th Circuit held that an Internet advertisement standing alone was insufficient to subject an advertiser to jurisdiction.[39]

An application of this principle can be seen in the case of *Black & Decker Inc. v. Pro-Tech Power Inc.*,[40] where the court held that even though the Taiwanese defendant operated a website that advertised its potentially infringing products, jurisdiction was not proper because the defendant did not actually engage in any commercial contact with the forum state. Websites have been characterized as passive even when they contain allegedly defamatory material specifically targeted at residents of the forum jurisdiction. In such cases, the courts have held that jurisdiction is not proper in the forum unless the defendant takes additional

---

34 *Id.*

35 75 F. Supp.2d 1104 (C.D. Cal. 1999).

36 *Id.* But see, *McDonough v. Fallon McElligott, Inc.*, 1996 U.S. Dist. LEXIS 15139, No. 95-4037, slip op. (S.D. Cal. Aug. 6, 1996), where in another case centered around copyright material, the court refused to exercise personal jurisdiction over the defendant solely on the basis of its maintenance of a website, explaining that just because the Web enables easy world-wide access, allowing computer interaction via the Web to supply sufficient contacts to establish jurisdiction would eviscerate the personal jurisdiction requirement as it currently exists; so the mere presence of defendant's website used by Californians cannot establish jurisdiction by itself.

37 61 F. Supp.2d 1074 (C.D. Cal. 1999).

38 130 F.3d 414 (9th Cir. 1997).

39 See also *CFOs To Go Inc. v. CFO 2 Go Inc.*, 1998 WL 320821 (N.D. Cal. 1998) (holding that website with description of defendant's business and contact information was insufficient to confer jurisdiction).

40 26 F. Supp.2d 834 (E.D. Va. 1998).

steps—"something more"—to direct the defamatory material toward the forum state.[41] However, the "something more" requirement can be satisfied by relatively insignificant contact with the forum state. For instance, in *Nicosia v. De Rooy,*[42] the court held that sending only eleven e-mails to California residents inviting them to view the allegedly defamatory articles was sufficient to confer jurisdiction over the defendants.[43]

Although the majority of courts addressing the issue have declined to exercise jurisdiction over "advertisement" websites, several courts have rejected the idea that advertisement sites are merely passive. In *Inset Sys. Inc. v. Instruction Set Inc.*,[44] the defendant operated a website that advertised its business and provided a toll-free number for inquiries. The court held that the minimum-contacts test was satisfied because this advertisement constituted a repeated solicitation of business in the forum state.[45] In contrast, in *Ty v. Clark*, a defendant in Great Britain was sued for operating an interactive website that utilized the plaintiff's famous "beanie baby" trademark.[46] The defendant's site contained information about ordering beanie babies through mail or by phone, but consumers could not actually engage in online purchases. The court held that this was merely an informational use of the Internet and was not enough to exercise personal jurisdiction.[47]

A final category of cases that may be more difficult to properly analyze involves the circumstance where the websites at issue are not passive and yet do not actively engage in commercial transactions with forum residents, at least as of the date of the lawsuit. Since *Zippo*, most courts that have dealt with the issue have concluded that the mere fact that a website is capable of interacting with residents of the forum is not a proper basis for exercising jurisdiction. Unless there is specific evidence that the defendant has conducted business with residents of the forum, the defendant has not "purposely availed itself" of the benefits of the forum state and is not subject to jurisdiction.[48]

It is important for persons who live or operate a business outside the United States to understand that pursuant to the current state of U.S. jurisdictional anal-

---

41 See *Jewish Defense Org.*, 72 Cal.App.4th 1045 (1999).

42 72 F. Supp.2d 1093 (N.D. Cal. 1999).

43 See also *Blumenthal v. Drudge*, 992 F. Supp.44 (D. D.C. 1998) (posting of allegedly defamatory material about a resident of the District of Columbia, when combined with contacts and e-mail solicitations to D.C. residents, was sufficient to confer jurisdiction).

44 937 F. Supp. 161 (D. Conn. 1996).

45 See also *Telco Communications v. An Apple A Day*, 977 F. Supp. 404 (E.D. Va. 1997) (holding that mere maintenance of advertisement Web site was equivalent to "regularly" soliciting business in Virginia).

46 *Ty v. Clark*, 2000 WL 51816 (N.D. Ill. 2000).

47 *Id.*

48 *See e.g., Origin Instruments Core. v. Adaptive Computer Sys. Inc.*, 1999 WL 76794 (N.D. Tex. 1999).

ysis, they too can be brought before U.S. courts based on minimum contacts, including Internet contacts. Federal courts in particular abide by the "rule of aggregation" under Rule 4k of the Federal Rules of Civil Procedure. It addresses personal jurisdiction in cases where the defendant has sufficient minimum contacts with the United States as a whole, or in "aggregate," but not with any one particular state. In this case, the rule allows any federal court in any state to exercise personal jurisdiction over the defendant. In *Quokka Sports, Inc. v. Cup International, Ltd., N.D.*,[49] the rule was used against a foreign defendant whose only contacts with the U.S. were through its website. The New Zealand-based defendant operated a website that "incorporated a portion of the [plaintiff's trademark] AMERICA'S CUP in its domain name, *americascup.com*, and actively competed with the plaintiff's site."[50] The site targeted the U.S. market as a whole, but not any one state in particular.[51] Accordingly, the U.S.-based plaintiff was able to use Rule 4(k) and the sliding scale test of *Zippo* to sue the foreign defendant in the forum state of California.[52]

As we have seen, the "sliding scale" analytical framework obviously is not restricted to the exercise of jurisdiction over out-of-state but U.S. resident defendants. However, courts do not mechanically apply this scheme to international defendants without concern for the additional burden on such defendants. The court in *Euromarket Designs Inc. v. Crate & Barrel Ltd.*[53] held that when a court contemplates exercising jurisdiction over a foreign defendant, "particular importance" must be placed on the determination of the reasonableness prong.

The expansive reach of domestic courts will make it increasingly likely that conduct that is lawful in one forum may subject the defendant to liability in a foreign jurisdiction. In *Playboy Enterprises Inc. v. Chuckleberry*, 939 F. Supp. 1032 (S.D.N.Y. 1996), the defendant was sued for unlawfully utilizing the plaintiff's trademarks over the Internet. Because the defendant actively solicited customers in New York through its website, the court held that jurisdiction was proper. In fact, the court issued an injunction requiring the defendant to either shut down its site or adopt a method of access that would screen out users residing in the United States.

3. Venue

Establishing personal jurisdiction over a defendant is a necessary first step to a court finding it proper to permit the case against an out-of-state party to proceed. Nonetheless, even if a court were to find that personal jurisdiction were proper over a defendant, the court might still refuse to exercise such jurisdiction and

---

49 1999 U.S. Dist. LEXIS 21000 (N.D. Cal. Dec. 13, 1999).

50 *Id.* at 228.

51 *Id.*

52 *Id.* at 229.

53 96 F. Supp.2d 824 (N.D. Ill. 2000).

dismiss the case, because another jurisdiction was a better forum in which the case should be tried. In the United States, this is based upon the doctrine of the inconvenient forum.

For example, for lawsuits in the federal courts, the general federal venue statute, 28 USC §1391, provides that lawsuits may be brought only in "(1) a judicial district where any defendant resides, if all defendants reside in the same State, (2) a judicial district in which a substantial part of the events or omissions giving rise to the claim occurred, or a substantial part of property that is the subject of the action is situated, or (3) a judicial district in which any defendant is subject to personal jurisdiction at the time the action is commenced, if there is no district in which the action may otherwise be brought" whenever the court's *subject matter jurisdiction* is founded on "diversity of citizenship"—*i.e.,* where the court's jurisdiction is founded on the constitutional grant (see note 5) allowing federal courts to hear cases "between Citizens of different States." In all other cases, the suit may be brought in "(1) a judicial district where any defendant resides, if all defendants reside in the same State, (2) a judicial district in which a substantial part of the events or omissions giving rise to the claim occurred, or a substantial part of property that is the subject of the action is situated, or (3) a judicial district in which any defendant may be found, if there is no district in which the action may otherwise be brought." There are specialized venue rules for particular kinds of federal actions that override these general venue rules in federal court; for example, 28 USC §1400 provides special venue rules in copyright and patent cases, requiring copyright cases to be brought "in the district in which the defendant or his agent resides or may be found" and patent cases to be brought "in the judicial district where the defendant resides, or where the defendant has committed acts of infringement and has a regular and established place of business."

B. CONTRACT FORMATION IN THE OFF-LINE WORLD

Before considering the transacting of business via the Internet or other online methods, to understand how the law of such transactions in the United States, one must first understand the law of contract formation in the off-line world. The United States is a country where the legal heritage began with the development of the common law, that is, judge-made law. While statutes enacted by Congress, if constitutionally valid, will supercede the common law, most law affecting contracts in the United States is either common law, or statutes based upon the common law that are designed to make the law uniform among the states. The common law and uniform statutes based upon the common law tend to evolve relatively slowly over time, based upon prior decisions that have the effect of legal precedence. Because of this, courts tend to apply existing law to new situations, with only incremental evolution of the law.

Interestingly, despite the fact that the Internet has been hyped as resulting in a paradigm shift in the way business will be done, the existing law (common law and uniform statutes) actually adapts quite well to the Internet. In part, this is because for more than a hundred years, people have conducted business at a distance, without having first known, or previously done business with, each other. Much of the law now being applied to the Internet comes from the law of contract and the formation of contracts using telegrams, mail or telephone. The difficulty with electronic commerce has always been wrestling with the absence of paper in the formation of the contract. The traditional definition of a "writing," however, is not limited to ink on paper. Rather, the essence of the requirement is that the communication be reduced to a tangible form. As early as 1869, a New Hampshire court found a telegraphed contract to be a sufficient writing under the statute of frauds, stating:

> [i]t makes no difference whether that operator writes the offer or the acceptance . . . with a steel pen an inch long attached to an ordinary penholder, or whether his pen be a copper wire a thousand miles long. In either case the thought is communicated to the paper by use of the finger resting upon the pen; not does it make any difference that in one case common record ink is used, while in the other case a more subtle fluid, known as electricity, performs the same office.[54]

This does not mean that in many regards the Internet does not require substantial shifts in legal thinking. Jurisdictional issues take on greater importance,[55] content becomes immortal, and time frames are dramatically compressed.

1. Elements of Contract Formation

a. Offer

An offer is an expression by a person or entity about the intent of the offeror to be bound to an agreement. It is "a display of willingness to enter into a contract on specified terms, made in a way that would lead a reasonable person to understand that an acceptance, having been sought, will result in a binding contract."[56] The expression must be about some promise to do or refrain from doing something which is obviously not in jest (as in "sure, I'll sell you my house for $500, free and clear of debt" would not, in almost every circumstance, constitute a valid offer, since the reasonable person would know that the offer was not seriously made), and the offeror must be in a position to make that offer (they legally own or can provide what they're offering, and are of full age and capacity).

An advertisement usually is not an offer—it's merely an invitation to the public to come in and make an offer to the store, or to call and make an offer to the person who ran the ad. The price may be fixed in the ad, but other terms are usually open: how will you pay? how and when will you take delivery? However, if an ad is more specific, stating details like "first twenty-five people" and "at our

54 *Howley v. Whipple*, 48 N.H. 487 (1869).

55 If a website is a public site, then it can be accessed from anywhere in the world.

56 *Black's Law Dictionary*, 1111 (7th ed. 1999).

Main Street location" and "Feb. 28, 2004 only", that advertisement might be an offer, acceptable by the first 25 people that show up at that place on that day.

An offeror may revoke the offer if it has not yet been accepted, or if there were no independent consideration to make the offer nonrevocable for a period of time. Even in the absence of revocation, an offer can also expire after a reasonable time, or if the offeror or offeree dies, or the subject matter of the agreement is destroyed.

b. Acceptance

Acceptance is "[a]n agreement, either by express act or by implication from conduct, to the terms of an offer so that a binding contract is formed."[57] Once a party receives an offer, they (and only they) are in a position to accept or reject it. If the offer specifies a method of acceptance (other than silence), that is generally how assent is made. If the offer does not specify the mode of acceptance, then any reasonable means of notifying the offeror may be used. The "reasonable means" must be at least as fast and as legally dependable as the means used by the offeror. For example, if the offer came by mail, the offeree can accept by mail, by fax, or by telegram.

i) Counteroffer

If the offeree sends back a response which is not an expression of acceptance of the offer, but instead contains something like "I won't pay you $20,000. Will you consider $18,000?" then the legal effect of the offeree's statement is two-fold: it constitutes a rejection and termination of the original offer, and it constitutes a counter-offer. When an "acceptance" comes back with new or different terms, it is considered a counter-offer. Usually this takes the original offer off the table.

ii) Acceptance by Performance

Until the Uniform Commercial Code was adopted, in the United States, silence did not constitute assent even when the offeror included self serving statements in the offer like "your failure to reject this offer within three days constitutes your acceptance of all of its terms."[58] When two parties are negotiating an agreement for goods, there may be a point in their negotiations where one party starts to perform their part of the agreement. In this case, performance may indicate acceptance of the offer to date. The UCC (governing law for sale of goods) of-

57 *Id.* at 11.

58 Note, however, that the parties in a prior contract or a master contract may agree that silence will be deemed assent. A classic example of this is with respect to derivatives and other financial agreements, such as those promulgated by the International Swaps and Derivatives Association (ISDA).

fers a method of interpretation for these cases (sometimes called "the battle of the forms"):

1. Was the latest offer expressly conditional on assent to those terms (as in "we have a contract only if you agree to these terms")?

- If yes, acceptance agrees to those terms
- If no:

2. If last offer was not expressly conditional, the writings form a contract. The latest additional or different terms become mere proposals unless both parties are merchants. Between merchants:

- does the latest offer expressly limit acceptance to the new terms?
- do the new terms materially alter the agreement (like adding an arbitration agreement)?
- has objection to new terms been given, or will be given within a reasonable time (like 10 days)?

3. If writings do not yet form a contract, or the offer was expressly conditional but the acceptance was not to those terms and one party starts performance:

- The agreed-upon terms are included,
- The additional or materially different terms are "knocked out," (the minority view is that the offeree's new terms fall away)
- other open terms in the contract are determined by using UCC gap fillers.[59]

While the UCC specifies many gap fillers, open terms are generally filled by determining what's reasonable for that market and time.

c. Consideration

Consideration is bargained-for legal detriment. Often it's an exchange of money for goods or services. Consideration is "[s]omething of value (such as an act, a forbearance, or a return promise) received by [one party to the agreement from the other]."[60] Each party must give consideration to the other to make the agreement binding as a contract.[61]

Sometimes we have a situation where two parties agree to do business conditional on something occurring before they can form a contract. Such a situation might include obtaining financing before buying a house, or working together on a project for someone else, or an offer to buy goods at a special price for only a limited time. In these cases, consideration may be in the form of an option contract.

59 See UCC § 2-207.

60 *Black's Law Dictionary*, at 300.

61 *Id.*

2. A move towards uniformity

Although contract law is primarily a function of state, not federal, law there is significant uniformity among the fifty states on commercial contracts due to the efforts of the National Conference of Commissioners on Uniform State Laws ("NCCUSL"). The NCCUSL is a body of legal experts, consisting of lawyers, judges, and law professors that proposes model statutes in various fields of law, which the states are free to adopt or reject at will.[62] In the 1940s, the NCCUSL began work on a model code known as the Uniform Commercial Code ("UCC") in the interest of harmonizing state law on the enforcement of commercial contracts. The most recent version of the code was published in 1958[63] and has since been adopted, either wholly or partially, by forty-nine states.[64]

The Statute of Frauds provision of the UCC, section 2-201(1), has been the source of great controversy in the legal community in its application to Internet transactions. "Section 2-201(1) says that contracts for the sale of goods for a price of $500 or more generally must be memorialized in a signed writing to be enforceable."[65] The writing and signature serve an evidentiary function, enabling the contracting parties to prove in a court of law the existence of the contract.[66] More specifically, the writing and signature facilitate "attribution," prove "intent," and prevent "repudiation."[67] Attribution is the identification of a person as a party to a contract.[68] A signature performs this function due to its uniqueness to each person. Requiring a written signature of a contracting party prevents the signer from later denying that he is a party to the contract, that, for example, someone else signed it instead. The act of signing also proves a party's intent to be bound by a contract's terms.[69] Like the wax seal required in days of old, a signature is an affirmative act that focuses the mind of the contracting party, impressing on the signer the binding nature of the agreement. Finally, a written and signed document that memorializes the exact terms of an agreement prevents contracting parties from later denying or "repudiating" its terms.[70]

For contracts formed over the Internet for goods priced at $500 or more, literal compliance with the Statute of Frauds is impossible. A typical consumer purchase over the Internet, for example, requires the buyer to choose the items he or

---

62 Gregory E. Maggs, *The Waning Importance of Revisions to U.C.C. Article 2*, 78 Notre Dame L. Rev. 595, 595 n.1 (2003).

63 James J. White & Robert S. Summers, *Uniform Commercial Code* at 600 (4th ed. 1995).

64 *Id.* at 596.

65 Maggs, *supra* note, at 613.

66 Jennifer L. Koger, *You Sign, E-SIGN, We All Fall Down: Why the United States Should Not Crown the Marketplace as Primary Legislator of Electronic Signatures*, 11 Transnat'l L. & Contemp. Probs. 491, 498-99 (2001).

67 *Id.* at 499.

68 *Id.*

69 *Id.*

70 *Id.*

she is interested in, give credit-card and shipping information, and click on an "OK" or "I Agree" button to consummate the deal. Neither the consumer nor the merchant signs a written contract. Thus, under the UCC, if the sale was for goods totaling $500 or more, the contract could not be enforced if one party breaches. Fortunately, this and other shortcomings of traditional contract law and its application to Internet transactions have been filled by state and federal statutes as well as by judge-made law.

Owing to the adaptability of our legal system, U.S. courts will generally enforce online contracts that do not comport with traditional requirements of contract law. But while a court will typically enforce such a contract as a whole, it may not necessarily enforce each of its specific terms.

C. CONTRACT FORMATION IN THE ONLINE WORLD

Like any except the most casual transaction in the off-line or physical world, electronic transactions involve documents (referred to as "records" in the electronic context)[71] and signatures (electronic signatures, in cyberspace).[72] The difference is that the medium through which the documents may be created, stored, communicated, executed, or retrieved will be an electronic one.[73]

To say that a contract is enforceable is a statement about four conditions regarding its execution:

(1) A*uthorization*. Is the type of transaction one which can be conducted electronically?

(2) *Signature*. Is there a valid signature or other manifestation of assent—that is, was the electronic signature affixed to the document or record made by the person purporting to make such signature, or by someone with authority to sign on behalf of the purported signer; and were all of the formalities necessary for such electronic signature to be recognized as binding followed by the parties (e.g., the requirement that, on certain documents, signatures must be notarized)?

(3) *Consent*. Have the parties mutually consented to conducting the transaction electronically?

---

71 See Electronic Signatures in Global and National Commerce Act (E-SIGN), 15 U.S.C. §§ 7006(9), stating that a record "means information that is inscribed on a tangible medium or that is stored in an electronic or other medium and is retrievable in perceivable form;" Uniform Electronic Transactions Act (UETA) § 2(13), defining an electronic record as a "record created, generated, sent, communicated, received or stored by electronic means."

72 See E-SIGN, 15 U.S.C. § 7006(5), stating that an electronic signature "means means an electronic sound, symbol, or process, attached to or logically associated with a contract or other record and executed or adopted by a person with the intent to sign the record." See also, UETA § 2(8).

73 E-SIGN clarifies that *electronic* is to be read expansively and "means relating to technology having electrical, digital, magnetic, wireless, optical, electromagnetic, or similar capabilities." 15 U.S.C. § 7006(2).

(4) *Recordation and Accessibility.* Are the records that document the transaction retrievable and generally available to all parties to be bound by the agreement?

While virtually anything that could be contracted for in the physical world can also be contracted for in the online world, most of the case law so far, as one would expect, has centered around the formation of agreements for software, hardware and other things related directly to the online world. The quintessential online agreement is a license to permit the downloading of software. However, the line of cases in the United States most often cited as the progenitor of most online contracting actually involved an order for computer hardware that was not made over the Internet. And most of these cases involved one company, Gateway 2000.

Before the Internet became a more universal distribution channel, a body of law was already developing for contracting at distances. In some instances, the case law centered around electronic transmissions of offer and assent; in other circumstances, the case law was concerned with the notion of assent by conduct. The electronic transmission cases, some dating back to the early days of the telegraph, have given us the basis for law involving the formation of contracts via click-wraps and e-mail. The assent-by-conduct cases have given us the basis for law involving the formation of contracts via more passive means, such as via shrink-wrap and browse-wrap agreements.

1. The Software License

Today, the Internet is the medium through which more than USD2 trillion in goods and services have been bought. To achieve the explosive growth in the Internet, millions of users have each consented to somewhere between a few and hundreds of contracts over the Internet. That is, the Internet is the medium through which we learn about products and services, contract to acquire those items, and also contract for the very right to use the medium itself. Therefore, before anything else is sold in e-commerce, the average user would first use the Internet contract for the downloading of software applications, consent to a license to view electronic information, and consent to the terms and conditions of use of the e-commerce site.

a. Shrink-wrap Agreements

One of the earliest of the modern cases whereby the court found a assent to contract by conduct between persons who did not otherwise know each other, and who did not deal with each other on a negotiated, face-to-face basis, was the case of *Carnival Cruise Lines, Inc. v. Shute.*[74] In that case, Mr. and Mrs. Shute, a couple living in Washington State, purchased a cruise to Puerto Vallarta, Mexico from Carnival Cruise Lines. The contract terms that were printed on the back of

74 499 U.S. 585 (1991).

the ticket specified that all disputes arising out of the ticket purchase or the cruise would be litigated in Florida under Florida law. Mrs. Shute was injured when she slipped and fell on a mat during a galley tour on the boat during the cruise. Alleging negligence on the part of Carnival Cruise Lines, Mrs. Shute sued in federal district court in Washington State. The United States Supreme Court held that Shute's suit could not be heard in Washington as the Court held the choice of forum clause was enforceable. The Court stated that it rejected the notion that:

> ". . . a nonnegotiated forum-selection clause in a form ticket contract is never enforceable simply because it is not the subject of bargaining. Including a reasonable forum clause in a form contract of this kind may well be permissible for several reasons: first, a cruise line has a special interest in limiting the fora in which it potentially could be subject to suit. Because a cruise ship typically carries passengers from many locales, it is not unlikely that a mishap on a cruise could subject the cruise line to litigation in several different fora . . . [A] clause establishing ex ante the forum for dispute resolution has the salutary effect of dispelling any confusion about where suits arising from the contract must be brought and defended, sparing litigants the time and expense of pretrial motions to determine the correct forum, and conserving judicial resources that otherwise would be devoted to deciding those motions . . . [P]assengers who purchase tickets containing a forum clause like that at issue in this case benefit in the form of reduced fares reflecting the savings that the cruise line enjoys by limiting the fora in which it may be sued.[75]

Before the *Gateway* cases, the Seventh Circuit established substantial precedents when it decided the case of *ProCD, Inc. v. Zeidenberg*.[76] It is not an exaggeration to say that through the date of this monograph, *ProCD* is the most important case in the United States on shrink-wrap, was the progenitor of the *Gateway* cases, and has set the foundation for contracting over the Internet. The facts of this case illuminate U.S. law with respect to copyright law, protection of databases and contract formation by conduct.

ProCD had constructed a database of names and telephone numbers from some 3,000 telephone directories, and then sold a version of this database on a five CD-ROM set of discs. The database was packaged with application software that allowed access to the information on the CD-ROMs under the name "SelectPhone." There was both a consumer and commercial version of the database. The consumer version of this package sold for approximately USD150, included five CD-ROM discs, and could be bought off the shelf in retail stores.[77]

Each box sold of the consumer version of the software stated that the software was restricted according to the terms of the enclosed license. In addition, the

75 Id at 593-94.

76 86 F.3d 1447 (7th Cir. 1996).

77 *Id.*

user's manual contained the license and the license appeared on the user's screen every time the program was run.[78]

The 7th Circuit, in reversing the district court's dismissal of the complaint against court noted that it would be impossible to print the entire license terms on the exterior of the box to be viewed before sale. The court found " notice on the outside, terms on the inside, and a right to return the software for refund if the terms are unacceptable . . . may be a means of doing business valuable to buyers and sellers alike."[79] The court found that these licenses were important to mass marketing and distribution in the software industry and analogized the transaction to concert tickets, sporting events where the purchaser pays money up front and later receives the tickets with the terms included. If the terms are objectionable the purchaser has the option to return the tickets for refund. Under the 7th Circuit's analysis, Zeidenberg was the offeree, not the offeror. ProCD, through the retail store, was the offeror, and had proposed a contract that the buyer would accept by using the software after having an opportunity to read the license. When Zeidenberg used the software he accepted, creating a contract including the terms of the shrink-wrap license.[80]

Since ProCD, there has been a shifting tide of cases in relation to consumers being bound to terms inside a box. Seven months after ProCD, the 7th Circuit applied its reasoning from that case to the case of *Hill v Gateway 2000, Inc.*[81] According to the reported decision, the Hills ordered a computer from Gateway over the telephone. Included in the box in which the computer was delivered was Gateway's Standard Terms And Conditions Agreement. Under these terms buyers were permitted thirty days to return the computer at Gateway's expense. The terms also required the Hills to submit any disputes with Gateway to arbitration. The Hills say the arbitration clause did not stand out from other terms, but conceded they did not read the terms closely enough to discover the arbitration clause. The Hills kept the computer beyond thirty days before complaining about defects in the computer. Eventually the Hills brought a class-action suit against Gateway. Gateway defended by asking the court to enforce the arbitration clause.[82]

The Seventh Circuit's decision emphasized the similarities between the circumstances in its earlier ProCD case and the instant case. Gateway shipped the computers to the Hills with an "accept or return offer". While the arbitration clause was not discussed in the telephone conversation, neither was the inclusion of application programs or Gateway's warranty, upon which the Hills relied. The court found that these valuable promises bound Gateway just as the arbitration

78 *Id.*

79 *Id.*

80 *Id.*

81 105 F. 3d 1147 (7th Cir. 1997), *cert. denied*, 522 U.S. 808 (1997).

82 *Id.*

clause bound the Hills. The court found that consumers could protect themselves by requesting a copy of the terms before purchase, consulting public sources such as computer magazines and websites and inspecting the documents and returning the computer if they found the terms unacceptable.[83] Both the *ProCD* case and the Gateway case are frequently cited as supporting the notion of the enforceability of contracts where acceptance occurred by conduct, rather than an express rendition of assent.[84] While neither of these cases involved the on-line world, they were progenitors to cases where the contracts were created—or not—based solely on conduct occurring on-line.

b. Click-wrap Agreements

Click-wrap agreements came into use when software vendors began distributing software by means other than disks, such as when the software is pre-installed on a computer for the user, or when the software is downloaded over the Internet. Upon downloading, installation or first use of the application, a window containing the terms of the license opens for the user to read. The user is asked to click either "I agree" or "I do not agree". If the user does not agree, the process is terminated. These "click-wrap" agreements often remove many factual questions whether the user had adequate notice of the license terms and manifested assent to them. With respect to software downloads, the click-wrap terms often are displayed at the very start of the contract formation process, although often the terms are contained in a scrollable window that requires the user to scroll down to read all of the terms. This positioning often eliminates U.C.C. Section 2-207 issues regarding agreement to additional or different terms.

In one of the first click-wrap cases, *i.Lan Systems, Inc. v. Netscout Service Level Corp.*,[85] the court held that a plaintiff was bound by the terms of a license agreement that appeared on its computer screen when it loaded the defendant's software, because the plaintiff indicated its assent to be bound thereby by clicking on an "I agree" icon at the foot of the license agreement. The *i.Lani Systems* Court reached this conclusion despite the fact that the plaintiff had ordered the

83 *Id.*

84 That is not to say that these cases are universally accepted as being valid. For instance, in *Klocek v. Gateway 2000 Inc.*, 104 F. Supp. 2d 1332 (D. Kan. 2000), the court rejected the notion of ProCD that held that the vendor was the master of the offer. The Klocek found that Klocek could have as easily been deemed under traditional UCC analysis to have made an offer to buy, as Gateway was deemed to have made an offer to sell, particularly since Kolcek initiated the transaction by placing the call to Gateway. Since Klocek was a consumer, the Gateway Terms and Conditions included in the box were deemed to have been additional terms under a UCC 2-207 analysis, that would only be deemed accepted by the consumer upon an express statement that was conspicuously made that conditioned Klocek's acceptance and use of the computer upon the acceptance of the terms and conditions sought by Gateway. The *Klocek* court held that Gateway failed to make its delivery of the computer so conditioned, and found the arbitration clause embedded in the terms and conditions to be unenforceable due to the failure of Klocek to have expressly assented to its applicability.

85 183 F. Supp. 2d 328 (D. Mass 2002).

software in a purchase order it sent to the defendant before clicking on the "I agree" icon. The purchase order in question did not contain the limitation of liability clause found in the license agreement. Nonetheless, the court enforced the limitation of liability clause, holding such a result was appropriate under UCC Section 2-204, which provides that "a contract for sale of goods may be made in any manner sufficient to show agreement, *including conduct* by both parties which recognizes the existence of such a contract." (Emphasis added). The court further held that such a result was also appropriate under UCC Section 2-207, which permits the addition of additional terms to a contract, here the purchase order, either on explicit or implicit consent. The court found the requisite explicit consent present in the plaintiff's act of clicking on the "I agree" icon. The necessary implicit consent was also present because the additional terms in the license agreement came as no surprise to, and caused no hardship for, the plaintiff.[86]

Recently, the American Bar Association conducted a project under the auspices of the Joint Working Group on Electronic Contracting Practices, within the Electronic Commerce Subcommittee of the Cyberspace Law Committee, and also within the Uniform Commercial Code Committee of the Business Law Section of the ABA to analyze validity of assent issues regarding electronic contracts. The result of this project has been the publication of an article designed to give practitioners guidance on how to make it more likely that manifestations of assent of their click-wrap agreements will be upheld by the courts.[87] Attached to this chapter is a short checklist of actions that may be taken to enhance the possibility of such a finding.

c. Browse-wrap Agreements

Beginning in 2000, a new term crept into the literature to describe an agreement purportedly formed by the conduct of a visitor to a website: "Browse-wrap."[88] This agreement is more like the shrink-wrap agreement discussed previously, and less like the click-wrap agreement, despite the fact that both browse-wrap and click-wrap agreements involve the online world. Like the shrink-wrap agreement held enforceable in *Hill v. Gateway 2000, Inc.*,[89] whereby the acceptance of the manufacture's offer occurred strictly through the conduct of the consumer, the visitor to the website is deemed to have accepted the website owner's offer by continuing to browse that website. Click-wrap agreements, conversely, require affirmative conduct on the part of the accepting party to complete the formation of a contract.

---

86 *Id.*

87 Christina L. Kunz, Maureen F. Del Duca, Heather Thayer, & Jennifer Debrow, *Click-Through Agreements, Strategies for Avoiding Disputes on Validity of Assent*, 57 Bus. Law 401 (2001).

88 *Pollstar v. Gigmania Ltd.*, 170 F.Supp 2d 974 (E.D. Cal. 2000).

89 105 F. 3d 1147 (7th Cir. 1997).

Typically, U.S. law favors express assent to an agreement, versus assent implied by conduct, in order to find that the parties have entered into an enforceable agreement.

Many websites contain agreements accessible through a "terms of use" link or a "terms of sale" link. It is, for example, typical for a "legal terms and conditions" hyperlink to be placed close to the "submit" button one clicks on to send credit card payment information. Typically, below the "submit" button, one finds language to this effect: "This sale is governed by the contract accessible through this link. By clicking on this button you agree to these terms and conditions."

Courts routinely enforce these contracts. *Caspi v. Microsoft*[90] compares such contracts to the situation encountered in the *Carnical Cruise Lines* case, finding no relevant difference between Caspi's situation and the one in *Carnival Cruise Lines*:

> "The scenario presented here is different because of the medium used, electronic versus printed; *but, in any sense that matters, there is no significant distinction.* The plaintiffs in *Carnival* could have perused all the fine-print provisions of their travel contract if they wished before accepting the terms by purchasing their cruise ticket. The plaintiffs in this case were free to scroll through the various computer screens that presented the terms of their contracts before clicking their agreement." (emphasis added)

This approach is well-grounded in traditional contract doctrine. The agreement behind the hypertext link is an offer. An *offer* is a manifestation of willingness to enter into a bargain so made as to justify another in understanding that his or her assent will conclude the bargain.[91] Clicking on the "submit" button is an acceptance. An acceptance is a manifestation of a willingness to enter the bargain proposed by the offer. One who clicks on the "submit" button will be deemed to have accepted even if he or she did not read the contract as long as there was an adequate opportunity to read and understand the agreement. This is an application of the so-called "duty to read": If one has an adequate opportunity to read and understand an agreement, and enters into the agreement without reading it, the law will, within broad limits, treat one as if one had read and understood the agreement.

Section 19 of the Restatement of Contracts states that, in order to be effective, assent to a contract and its terms must be manifested. This need not necessarily take the form of saying "I agree" or signing one's name; however, one must intend to manifest assent, and it must be accomplished through an intentional, voluntary act.[92] An act which appears to manifest consent will be construed as indicating assent regardless of the actor's intent, but only if the actor knew or had reason to know that the act would be taken as a manifestation of his or her

90 732 A.2d 528 (1999).

91 See Restatement (Second) of Contracts, Section 24.

92 *Restatement (Second) of Contracts*, § 19; Arthur L. Corbin, *Corbin on Contracts*, § 3.28 (Joseph M. Perillo ed., rev. ed., West 1993); *see* UCC 2-206(a).

assent.[93] It is not the actor's subjective intent to be bound, but rather the action he or she takes to manifest assent that binds him.[94] While manifestations of assent are necessary to establish contract formation, it is not necessary that the offer and acceptance be specifically identified in order to establish the existence of a contract.[95] However, the manifestations of assent provided must be made with reference to one another.[96] All of this implies, then, that one must know of an offer in order to accept it and be bound by its terms. In the context of website user agreements, then, a threshold question is whether the user was ever made aware of the existence of the contract such that he or she could assent to it or its terms. If the user is unaware of the offer, he or she cannot, under this analysis, accept it, and therefore cannot be bound by its terms.

Moreover, while silence may be inferred as assent in the context, silence, without more, is insufficient by itself to establish assent.[97] For instance, an offeror cannot force an offeree to assent through silence by unilaterally imposing a requirement that the offeree must respond negatively in order to manifest a *lack* of assent.[98] In fact, forty-five states have passed laws stating that when a merchant sends an individual unsolicited merchandise, it must be identified as a gift.[99] Nor can an offeror exempt himself or herself from such strictures by writing an exemption into the contract.[100]

In contrast, the *Restatement (Second) of Contracts* section 69(1)(b) provides to the contrary that "Where the offeror has stated or given the offeree reason to understand that assent may be manifested by silence or inaction, and the offeree in remaining silent and inactive intends to accept the offer." It also provides that assent by silence can be effective in the following situations: 1) where the offeree accepts the benefit offered with the knowledge the offeror expects to be compensated for it; 2) where, due to a previous course of dealings, the offeree

93 *Restatement (Second) of Contracts* § 19.

94 *Restatement (Second) Contracts* § 21.

95 *Restatement (Second) of Contracts* § 22; UCC § 2-204.

96 *Restatement (Second) of Contracts* § 23.

97 *Corbin on Contracts*, §§ 3.18-3.19.

98 *Id.*; *Cook v. The MV Wasborg*, 189 F. Supp 464, 468 (Dist. Or. 1960) ("It is an accepted rule of law that silence and inaction do not amount to an acceptance of an offer."); *Bowley v. Fuller*, 115 A. 466, 467 (Maine 1921) ("A mere failure to respond cannot be converted into an acceptance unless the offeree has agreed in advance that such silence should be so construed or there was some legal duty to that effect ... Even if the plaintiff had attempted in his offer to make silence on the defendant's part a constructive acceptance, the law would not permit it."); *Albrecht Chem. Co., Inc. v. Anderson Trading Corp.*, 84 N.E. 2d 625, 626 (N.Y. Ct. of Appeals 1949) ("'A party cannot be held to contract where there is no assent. Silence operates as an assent, and creates an estoppel, only where is has the effect to mislead. . . . When a party is under a duty to speak, or when his failure to speak is inconsistent with honest dealings, and misleads another, then his silence may be deemed to be acquiescence.'").

99 James J. White, *Autistic Contracts*, in *Perspectives on Contract Law* 158, 161 (Randy E. Barnett, ed., 2d ed. Aspen 2001).

100 *Restatement (Second) of Contracts* § 196.

knows that his or her silence will be presumed to be an acceptance; 3) where the offeree acts inconsistently with the offeror's rights in property offered.[101] Finally, where the parties, though their actions, indicate their belief that a contract has been formed, the contract will be presumed to exist even if the writings supporting it are insufficient alone.[102]

2. Recent Moves Towards Uniformity

a. The Federal E-Sign Act and its state Counterpart, UETA

While the basic elements of contract formation date to long before the development of the Internet, the fact that e-commerce means, almost invariably, that parties unknown to each other will be contracting at a distance does present legal difficulties, despite the fact that the issues are not entirely novel. The biggest issue concerns enforceability of such agreements. In the United States, enforceability of electronic contracts is governed by two different regimes: at the national level the Electronic Signatures in Global and National Commerce Act (E-SIGN),[103] and for most states, the Uniform Electronic Transactions Act (UETA).[104] The next section will examine UETA in more depth.

E-SIGN was passed to make it clear that a record does not fail to become an enforceable agreement (i.e. a binding contract) merely because it was entered into, in part or in whole, using electronic means.[105] Coming less than a year after the endorsement of UETA by the National Conference of Commissioners on Uniform State Laws at their 1999 annual convention, E-SIGN was passed amid concerns that UETA might be slow to be adopted and that the states might adopt divergent state laws. At the time of E-SIGN's passage, a great deal was being made in the press about the need for the United States to maintain its lead in the digital economy, and many commentators felt that the failure to have national legislation clarifying that electronic transactions were as valid as paper-based transactions would cause the United States to cede the lead in the new economy to Europe or East Asia. E-SIGN made it clear that online agreements were con-

---

101 *Restatement (Second) of Contracts* § 69.

102 *Restatement (Second) of Contracts* § 4; UCC §§ 2-204, 2-207; *but see Restatement (Second) of Contracts* § 110 (statute of frauds); UCC § 2-201(1) (statute of frauds).

103 15 U.S.C. §§ 7001 *et seq.* (2004) (Signed in to law by President Clinton on June 30, 2000, and effective October 1, 2000).

104 UETA was formerly approved by the National Conference of Commissioners on Uniform State Laws (NCCUSL) on July 23, 1999, at its national convention. A copy of the model version of this act is available at <http://www.law.upenn.edu/bll/ulc/fnact99/1990s/ueta99.htm>, last visited on July 2, 2004.

105 Section 101(a) of E-SIGN provides that "(1) a signature, contract, or other record relating to such transaction may not be denied legal effect, validity, or enforceability solely because it is in electronic form; and (2) a contract relating to such transaction may not be denied legal effect, validity, or enforceability solely because an electronic signature or electronic record was used in its formation." 15 U.S.C. § 7001(a) (2004).

sidered to be "in writing" whenever a law, such as the statute of frauds, requires that the contract between the parties be in writing to be enforceable.[106]

E-SIGN has no effect on many substantive rights of contracting parties. For example, it does not purport to alter any requirement under a statute, regulation or law, state or federal, except for any requirement that to be enforceable the contract must be in writing, manually or mechanically signed or in non-electronic form.[107] If a law requires that certain disclosures must be made to a consumer, or that a warning, notice or recordation occur in a certain manner and at a certain time, then E-SIGN does not disturb such obligations.[108] Nor can E-SIGN be used to compel a person to use electronic records or signatures.[109] For non-users of the Internet, E-SIGN has no compulsory effect. However, for Internet users, E-SIGN permits electronic commerce to proceed with less risk that the agreement will be found unenforceable.

b. UETA

UETA has been enacted in forty-five states and the District of Columbia.[110] Interestingly, New York, long considered to be the state with the most developed commercial law, and Washington, home of Microsoft and a state that is purportedly quite sophisticated about electronic commerce, are two of the five states that have yet to enact UETA.[111] UETA is a model code, like the UCC, that was created and published by NCCUSL in July 1999 "in an effort to prepare state law for transactions through electronic commerce."[112]

---

106 *Specht v Netscape Comm.*, 306 F.39 17, __ (2d Cir 2002).

107 15 U.S.C. § 7001(b)(1).

108 15 U.S.C. § 7001(f). Note, however, that a consumer may elect to receive all such notices or disclosures electronically, in which event statutory requirements for the delivery of the notice or disclosure are satisfied. 15 U.S.C. § 7001(c)(1)(A).

109 15 U.S.C. § 7001(b)(2), which states that E-SIGN does not "(2) require any person to agree to use or accept electronic records or electronic signatures, other than a governmental agency with respect to a record other than a contract to which it is a party." Of course, a party to a proposed transaction may insist on the use of electronic contracting, but this leaves the other party free to refuse to enter into the contract. The parties are free to choose the method of documenting their agreement, and E-SIGN may not be used as a bludgeon to force those who are not online into electronic agreements.

110 See <http://www.bakernet.com/ecommerce/uetacomp.htm> for an up-to-date list of states that have enacted UETA.

111 Both of those states also have some form of electronic signature law, but in those cases, the requirements are more stringent than under the UETA or the federal E-Sign Act. See *Electronic Signatures and Records Act* (Chp 57A, N.Y. Consolidated Laws 2004) and *Washington Electronic Authentication Act* (Chp 19.34, Wash. Rev. Code).

112 F. Lawrence Street, *Law of the Internet* § 1.10 ¶1 (Mathew Bender Release No. 004, 2002).

UETA and ESIGN effectively promulgate the same rule on the writing and signature requirements of the Statute of Frauds.[113] Section 7 of UETA makes explicit exemptions for these requirements:

1. "A [ ] signature may not be denied legal effect or enforceability solely because it is in electronic form.

2. A contract may not be denied legal effect or enforceability solely because an electronic record was used in its formation.

3. If a law requires a record to be in writing, an electronic record satisfies the law.

4. If a law requires a signature, an electronic signature satisfies the law."[114]

E-SIGN, Title I, accomplishes the same result by more general terms, in stating that, "notwithstanding any previously existing statute of frauds, 'a signature, contract, or other record relating to such transaction may not be denied legal effect, validity, or enforceability solely because it is in electronic form.'"[115] Therefore, while contracts formed over the Internet for goods totaling USD500 or more are typically not memorialized on paper, nor actually signed by either party, they are still enforceable under E-SIGN and UETA (depending on the state).

It is important to note that E-SIGN and UETA apply to commercial contracts only and have no effect on the preexisting laws governing real property, trusts and estates (e.g. wills, codicils, trust documents), court filings, or any other body of law with writing or signature requirements or both.[116]

c. UCITA

The Uniform Computer Information Transactions Act (UCITA) is an Act adopted, with a great deal of controversy, by the NCCUSL to serve as a uniform Act and model for the contracting of "computer information".[117] Computer information is defined rather broadly in UCITA to include software, multimedia products and access to databases, including online content.[118] The drafters of UCITA felt that it was a necessary law, that was significantly different from the

---

113 Maggs, *supra* note, at 614.

114 Street, *supra* note, at § 1.10 ¶2 (citing U.E.T.A. § 7 (1999)); *id.*, at § 1.11[1] ¶1 (stating that ESIGN has the same provisions for e-contracts).

115 Maggs, *supra* note, at 614 (citing 15 U.S.C. 7001(a)(1)).

116 Street, *supra* note, at §§ 1.10[1], 1.11[2] (addressing the scope of UETA and E-SIGN respectively).

117 The UCITA, as obtainable from the University of Pennsylvania web page, is approximately 114 pages long, excluding the official comments. Those comments add up to an additional 116 pages. Accordingly, it would make for an exceedingly long (and boring) paper to attempt to recap and interpret each of those provisions here, and the reader is referred to the University of Pennsylvania Law School web page, located at *http://www.law.upenn.edu/bll/ulc/ucita/citam99.htm*.

118 UCITA § 102.

UETA. In fact UETA and UCITA are designed to be mutually exclusive. The Introductory comments to the Official Version of UCITA express succinctly the differences between the scope of UCITA, which is exclusively concerned with the licensing of digital content, either with or without the associated intellectual property rights, and other laws that deal primarily in goods:

> Software, multimedia, digital databases, artificial intelligence systems, and other computer information products are governed by an intellectual property law dominated by copyright law. A copyright owner has the *exclusive right* to reproduce and distribute copies of a work, engage in public display or performances of the work, and modify the work. This intellectual property law is much different from property law for goods. In law, software and most other digital products are treated more like books, than like cars. A purchaser that acquires a copy of computer information remains subject to the fact that the copyright holder retains control over most uses of the copy of information, unless it licenses or sells some or all of its rights.
>
> Because the transactions focus on computer information, important transactional issues commonly exist in reference to what rights to use are to be conveyed. These issues are not present when goods are sold. In a sale of goods, the buyer owns the subject matter (e.g., the toaster); ownership creates exclusive rights in the item purchased. In contrast, when the subject matter is computer information, a person who acquires a copy may own the diskette, but does not own the information or rights associated with it. Instead, the person's rights to use the information depend on contract terms and intellectual property rights. Terms of the agreement determine what the purchaser obtains beyond the diskette.[119]

In late 1999, it was expected that UCITA would become an important piece of legislation, with much support from the software industry. However, since that time, despite an early adoption by Virginia and Maryland, UCITA has virtually gone nowhere, and, in fact, several states have adopted anti-UCITA legislation.[120] It has frequently been characterized by its detractors as the tool by which behemoths such as Microsoft will attempt to take even further advantage of the unsuspecting consumer. Such perceptions were not disabused by the fact that immediately prior to its passage by the NCCUSL, the general counsel for eighteen software companies came out strongly in favor of the proposed law,[121] while the Attorneys General for some twenty-four states and the Federal Trade

119 UCITA Introduction.

120 UCITA has been adopted in Maryland and in Virginia. Iowa, North Carolina, and West Virginia have adopted anti-UCITA "bomb shelter" legislation, which denies enforcement of contracts governed by UCITA against residents of those states. Sections 208 and 209 of UCITA address the formation of contracts using shrink-wrap and click-through mechanisms with respect to transactions in computer information. See <http://www.bakernet.com/ecommerce/ucitacomp.htm> for a more current listing of the status of UCITA legislation.

121 See letter dated July 13, 1999 from Colleen M. Pouliot, *et al.*, to Gene N. LeBrun, available at website <http://www.2Bguide.com> visited on November 1, 1999. Ms. Pouliot is Senior Vice President and General Counsel for Adobe Systems Incorporated, and the letter was also signed, inter alia, by the general counsels of Microsoft, Intuit, Lotus, Symantec, Novell and Visio. Mr. LeBrun is President of the NCCUSL.

Commission have opposed the law on the basis that it substantially reduces the rights of ordinary consumers.[122]

Much of the criticism directed towards UCITA actually seems to be directed at earlier drafts. Originally, the NCCUSL had proposed drafting a new Uniform Commercial Code article, Article 2B, to deal with the issues now covered by UCITA. NCCUSL had proposed issuing the draft Article 2B in conjunction with the American Law Institute ("*ALI*"), asking the fifty states and the District of Columbia to enact the change as a part of each state's UCC. However, in the Spring of 1999, the ALI withdrew its support of the project and the NCCUSL decided that UCITA was better offered to the states as a separate uniform law, and not as part of the UCC. Substantial sections of UCITA were rewritten in the last two months prior to presentation to the NCCUSL annual meeting to try to ensure its passage.

One of the things that made UCITA controversial was that it attempted to do some things that copyright law does not accomplish. The official comments clarify that information includes data, even if informational property rights do not attach. In *Feist Publications, Inc. v. Rural Telephone Serv. Co.*,[123] the United States Supreme Court reaffirmed that facts were not copyrightable,[124] hence no informational property rights would attached to a mere compilation of facts such as telephone numbers.[125] Despite the fact that no informational property rights attach, the UCITA adopted the approach of the Seventh Circuit in *ProCD, Inc. v. Zeidenberg*, and provides that the provisions of the Act apply to all information.

---

122 The Act is also actively opposed by the trade association, the Motion Picture Association of America. *See E-Commerce Plan Faces Tough Fight*, published on the CalLaw web page (August 4, 1999), located at <http://www.callaw.com/stories/edt0804e.htm>, visited on November 2, 1999.

123 499 U.S. 340 (1991).

124 *Id.* At 348. *See also Harper & Row, Publishers, Inc. v. Nation Enterprises*, 471 U.S. 539, 556 (1985).

125 *Feist Publications*, at 350. Justice O'Connor, writing for the majority, noted that "[a]s applied to a factual compilation, assuming the absence of original written expression, only the compiler's selection and arrangement may be protected; the raw facts may be copied at will. This result is neither unfair nor unfortunate. It is the means by which copyright advances the progress of science and art." *Id.*

VIETNAM

by
Ngo Ngoc Thu, Of Counsel
Russin & Vecchi, LLC

A. GENERAL INTRODUCTION TO SOURCES OF LAW

1. The National Assembly

In Vietnam, the National Assembly has authority to make laws under the Constitution.[1] The only body with constitutional and legislative powers is the National Assembly,[2] which is the highest and most powerful representative body of the people of Vietnam. It has the power to amend the Constitution and existing laws, as well as to plan a program for drafting and promulgating new laws and ordinances.[3]

The National Assembly determines fundamental external and domestic policy, socio-economic affairs, matters of national defense and security, the structure and functions of governmental organizations and social relationships among the people.[4] These issues are regulated in the laws passed by the National Assembly.

2. National Assembly Standing Committee

The National Assembly meets twice a year, and between sessions the business of the National Assembly is undertaken by the National Assembly Standing Committee ("NASC"). The NASC is a permanent body of the National Assembly. At each congress the National Assembly elects a new NASC and delegates work to it. The NASC consists of the Chairman and Deputy Chairmen of the National Assembly and some other members.[5] This committee is responsible for explaining and interpreting the Constitution, laws and ordinances.

1 Vietnam Constitution, 1992, art. 12.

2 Vietnam Constitution, 1992, art. 83.

3 Vietnam Constitution, 1992, art. 84.1.

4 Vietnam Constitution, 1992, art. 83.

5 Vietnam Constitution, 1992, art. 90.

An ordinance is a legal instrument issued by the NASC which regulates issues delegated to the NASC by the National Assembly. After a period of implementation, an ordinance is submitted to the National Assembly for consideration and ultimately the National Assembly will decide if the ordinance will become a law.[6] To introduce an ordinance, more than half of the NASC's members must vote in favor.[7] With respect to the ranking of legal instruments of Vietnam, an ordinance is lower than a law.

3. The President

After a new Constitution, laws, and ordinances have been introduced by the National Assembly or the NASC, they must be announced by the President. The President, who is the head of State in terms of domestic and foreign affairs, announces a law or an ordinance by means of an order.[8] The date of the order will be the effective date of the law or ordinance, unless otherwise stated in the law or ordinance.[9]

4. The Government

The government is responsible for providing guidance for the implementation of legal instruments passed by the National Assembly or NASC. This guidance is issued in the form of decrees. There are two types of decree:

- a decree which regulates in detail the implementation of a law or an ordinance, or regulates the duties, powers and structure of ministries or other governmental bodies or regulates the duties and powers of the government; or
- a decree which regulates an essential matter which did not qualify to be included in a law or ordinance. Such a decree will normally govern social and economic affairs, and its promulgation must be approved in writing by the NASC (e.g, the draft decree on e-commerce discussed at Part I.B).

Ministers and chiefs of ministerial level bodies may issue decisions, circulars and instructions in order to provide guidance on implementing laws, ordinances, decrees and Prime-ministerial decisions within their jurisdiction. In the event that one matter involves several ministries, those ministries may get together to issue joint circulars to ensure uniformity.

5. The Prime Minister

The Prime Minister is the head of the government. Based on the Constitution, laws, ordinances and decrees, the Prime Minister decides programs and measures to manage the activities of the government and central and local adminis-

6 Law on the promulgation of legal instruments, 1996, art. 21.1.

7 Law on the promulgation of legal instruments, 1996, art. 47.2.

8 Law on the promulgation of legal instruments, 1996, art. 50 and 51.

9 Law on the promulgation of legal instruments, 1996, art. 75.1.

trative bodies. He also issues instructions to guide, hasten and supervise the activities of governmental bodies in the implementation of policies, programs and laws of the State and decisions of the government.[10]

6. The Order of Priority of Legal Instruments

In general, legal instruments issued by a lower government body must be consistent with those issued by a superior governing body. The Constitution is the basic law of the State and is also the highest legal instrument. Therefore, other legal instruments must be issued in accordance with the Constitution. If a legal instrument is contrary to the Constitution or other legal instruments issued by higher governmental bodies, such instrument must be revoked by the issuing body or implementation must be prevented. Specifically, the National Assembly may revoke legal instruments issued by the President, NASC and Prime Minister if those instruments are contrary to the Constitution and laws. Similarly, the Prime Minister may revoke decisions, instructions and circulars issued by ministers, chiefs of ministerial level bodies or lower administrative bodies if those instruments are not consistent with the Constitution, laws and other higher instruments.[11]

Laws, ordinances and other legal instruments must be detailed so that they can be implemented immediately after coming into force. If a law or ordinance contains a provision which needs to be further elaborated on by other implementing documents, such provision must determine the time frame and the competent authority responsible for providing this detailed elaboration.[12] In practice, a vast majority of laws and ordinances need to be clarified by other implementing documents. In addition, a decree also needs to be detailed by one or more circulars. Therefore, many laws and ordinances which have been issued and become legally effective cannot be implemented because their implementing decrees have not been issued or even, if their implementing decree has been issued, a circular may also required to be promulgated.

7. The Court System

The power to try cases is vested in courts of various levels. In Vietnam there is no system of precedent. Except for the military court, the system of courts in Vietnam consists of the Supreme People's Court, provincial People's Courts and district People's Courts. Trials may have two stages: the first instance trial and the appeal. Depending on the particular case, a first instance trial may be heard at a district or provincial court. An appeal will be heard by a higher court than the one which heard the first instance trial. Provincial courts are responsible for hearing foreign-related cases in the first instance. Hearings are held in accor-

10 Law on the promulgation of legal instruments, 1996, art. 57.

11 The Constitution, 1992, art. 114.4.

12 Law on the promulgation of legal instruments, 1996, art. 7.1.

dance with statutory rules. To encourage consistency between the courts, the council of judges under the Supreme People's Court may issue resolutions, which are signed by the chief of the Supreme People's Court.

B. REGULATION OF ONLINE BUSINESS

The Internet is relatively new to Vietnam. Its application is not very popular. However, the government acknowledges the important role of the Internet in developing the country's economy and society as a whole, and considers the Internet an important part of the national communication infrastructure, which is protected by law.[13]

The key regulation on the Internet is Decree 55/2001/ND-CP of the government, dated August 23, 2001 regarding the management and provision of Internet services ("Decree 55"). As defined in Decree 55, Internet services include services to access, connect to and apply the Internet.[14] Internet services are provided by companies which are Internet service providers ("ISPs"), Internet exchange service providers ("IXPs") and Online service providers ("OSPs"). A company providing Internet services may:

- set up its own network at its main office and other places to provide services to users in Vietnam and abroad in accordance with the provisions of its license and business conditions, except for Internet services forbidden to be provided or not yet licensed to be provided as required by law;
- provide services to overseas users, provided it complies with the law of Vietnam and the country to which services are provided; and
- lease its network to organizations and other companies providing Internet services.

Such a company must refuse to provide services to those whose use of Internet services violates the law on the Internet.[15]

Companies must be responsible for the quality of the services they provide in order to ensure the rights of users. In doing so, companies have the following obligations:

- to register and announce criteria for their services in accordance with regulations on the management of the quality of services required by the State;
- ensure that the quality of services provided to users conforms with standards which the companies have registered and announced; and

13 Decree 55/2001/ND-CP of the government on August 23, 2001, art. 2.2.

14 Decree 55/2001/ND-CP of the government on August 23, 2001, art. 12.

15 Decree 55/2001/ND-CP of the government on August 23, 2001, arts. 18.1, 18.2 and 9.

- report their activities to the relevant State authorities.[16]

The Ministry of Post and Telecommunications is the State authority responsible for licensing IXPs and ISPs.[17] Different State authorities are responsible for other Internet-related activities. For example, the Ministry of Culture and Information is responsible for issuing licenses to OSPs and the Ministry of Trade manages activities related to electronic commerce. Since Internet services in Vietnam are not widespread yet, only a limited number of IXPs, ISPs and OSPs have been licensed. It is estimated that by 2005 there will be about five licensed IXPs, 40 ISPs and many OSPs due to the opening up of the Internet service market to non-State sectors.[18]

One application of the Internet involves electronic commerce. At the time of this article, no regulations had been made on this issue, although the promulgation of regulations is essential in forming a legal framework for electronic commerce development. A decree on electronic commerce is expected to be issued in the near future. Since electronic commerce is still a new issue and is at an experimental stage, there is much work to be done and much to be learnt. In addition, an ordinance on electronic commerce will be promulgated once electronic commerce in Vietnam has developed and after the relevant authorities have comprehensively studied this issue. The provisions of this ordinance will be based on the results of implementing the decree. The government is taking an active role in developing Internet application services and electronic commerce with a view to familiarizing people with buying and selling via the Internet. Therefore, it is hoped that in future most commercial transactions will be carried out electronically.[19]

If companies are to do business by way of electronic commerce, they need to be able to introduce and advertise their products and services. The provision of such information via the Internet is governed by a regulation on the management and licensing of information and websites on the Internet.[20] According to this regulation, any organization or company which wishes to publish information about its services or products on the Internet or set up its own website in Vietnam must first obtain approval from the Ministry of Culture and Information.[21]

---

16 Decree 55/2001/ND-CP of the government on August 23, 2001, art. 26.

17 Decree 55/2001/ND-CP of the government on August 23, 2001, art. 13.1 and 13.2.

18 Decision 33/2002/QD-TTg of the Prime Minister on February 8, 2002, art. 1.I.2b.

19 Decision 33/2002/QD-TTg of the Prime Minister on February 8, 2002, art. 1.II.3b.

20 Decision 27/2002/QD-BVHTT of the Ministry of Culture and Information on October 10, 2002.

21 Decision 27/2002/QD-BVHTT of the Ministry of Culture and Information on October 10, 2002, art. 8.

This applies equally to both local and foreign invested companies.[22] Information published on the Internet or on a website must not:

- negatively affect the independence and sovereignty of Vietnam;
- encourage people to fight against the State of Vietnam nor damage the unity of the people;
- provoke violence nor advocate wars creating hostility among peoples and countries;
- incite sexual or criminal activities; or
- disclose national or military secrets, security information, economic information, foreign affairs and other secrets as required by law.

Applications by foreign entities and central-level organizations are considered by the Ministry of Culture and Information. The Department of Culture and Information of each province is responsible for evaluating applications submitted by local organizations and companies and then makes a recommendation to the Ministry of Culture and Information as to whether to issue a license.[23] The license issued by the Ministry of Culture and Information to an organization or company must be announced on the homepage of such organization or company's website.

Business is booming at Internet cafés throughout Vietnam, and the Internet is being accessed by growing numbers of people. Demand for electronic business can only increase. Regulation of the use of the Internet in Vietnam is in the early stages, and comprehensive laws on the Internet and electronic commerce have yet to be promulgated but a draft decree on electronic commerce, which will form the legal basis for doing business over the Internet, is expected to be issued soon. The government is aware of the importance of the Internet and its potential for developing Vietnam's economy, and it is encouraging that it is beginning to take steps to promote the use of the Internet by businesses.

C. ELECTRONIC TRANSACTIONS AND CONTRACT FORMATION

A transaction for the sale and purchase of goods, especially an electronic transaction, normally starts with an offer by the seller. An offer is a proposal to enter into a contract for the sale and purchase of goods within a definite time. The proposal is sent to a particular person and the offer must contain the main points of the contract.[24]

---

22 Decision 27/2002/QD-BVHTT of the Ministry of Culture and Information on October 10, 2002, art. 3.

23 Decision 27/2002/QD-BVHTT of the Ministry of Culture and Information on October 10, 2002, art. 9.

24 Commercial Law 1997, art. 51.1.

A contract may be made verbally, in writing or by conduct. If required by law, certain kinds of contracts for the sale and purchase of goods must be made in writing. Usually, a contract is deemed to be formed when all the parties have signed. The parties may sign on a different date, but must sign on the same contract. The Commercial Law of Vietnam states that a contract for the purchase and sale of goods is deemed to be formed at the time that all present parties sign it. However, with respect to electronic transactions, it is not feasible for all parties to be present. Therefore, if the parties cannot sign in person, the contract is deemed to be signed at the time the offeror receives a notice of acceptance of the offer from the offeree. This notice of acceptance must be received by the offeror during his liability period, which commences when the offer is delivered to the offeree and lasts until the end of the period during which it is specified that the offer must be accepted. In the absence of any indication, the liability period of the offer maker is 30 days from delivery of the offer.[25]

An offer or notice of acceptance may be made by telex, fax, e-mail and other electronic means. All are considered forms of documents by law.[26] These documents may be considered as contracts if they contain the following principal information:

- name of goods;
- quantity of goods;
- quality and specification of goods;
- price;
- mode of payment; and
- place and date of delivery of goods.[27]

In addition to the above principal information, parties may agree on other provisions to be included in the contract.

Further, Vietnam has promulgated a regulation on the establishment, issuance, use and control of electronic signatures on electronic documents for electronic payment through banks.[28] This regulation applies to organizations providing payment services through provincial branches of the State Bank and conducting electronic payment transactions through the State Bank. The regulation permits the chief of the organization providing payment services to make agreements with customers on the use of electronic signatures. This means that electronic

25 Commercial Law 1997, art. 53.1.

26 Commercial Law 1997, art. 49.3.

27 Commercial Law 1997, art. 50.

28 Decision 543/2002/QD-NHNN of the State Bank dated May 29, 2002.

signatures can be used widely. The important thing is that an electronic signature is considered as valid as a real signature on paper.[29]

Where a transaction for the sale and purchase of goods involves foreigners, to constitute a valid contract the following conditions must be fulfilled:

- the seller and purchaser must have legal status. The foreign party must be a merchant whose legal status is specified by the law of his country. The Vietnamese party must also be a merchant and allowed to engage directly in commercial activities with foreigners;
- the transacted goods must be permitted to be bought and sold under the laws of the countries of the two parties;
- the contract must contain the necessary information; and
- the contract must be made in writing.[30]

D. CONSUMER PROTECTION IN ONLINE BUSINESS

The legitimate rights of consumers are protected by law. This protection is closely related to the advertising activities of producers and service providers. True advertising enables consumers to select the product or services of their choice whereas false advertising can mislead.

There are several laws protecting the rights of consumers such as the Commercial Law, Ordinance on Protection of the Rights of Consumers, Ordinance on Advertising and Decree No.32/1999 ND-CP on Promotion, Commercial Advertising and Exhibitions. The common point of these laws is that they require honesty in advertising activities. Information provided when advertising goods and services must be accurate, truthful and clear and must harm neither producers nor consumers.[31] Information on specification, quality, price, usage, warranty, packaging and expiry which is advertised, must be consistent with the respective factors of the goods sold and services provided.[32]

Consumers may require producers and service providers to ensure the quality and standards of their products and services regarding essential needs such as accommodation, clothing, travel, education, health, environment and other products and services advertised by them.[33] Consumers may claim compensation if the quality or standard of products and services do not comply with those advertised or agreed in the contract. In addition, a seller has the following responsibilities:

- ensuring the quality and specification of the product to be sold;

29 Decision 543/2002/QD-NHNN of the State Bank dated May 29, 2002, art. 1.

30 Decision 543/2002/QD-NHNN of the State Bank dated May 29, 2002, art. 81.

31 Ordinance on Advertising 2002, art. 6.2.

32 Decree 32/1999/ND-CP of the government dated May 5, 1999, art. 18.

33 Ordinance on Protection of Consumers 1999, art. 10.

- ensuring that the quality of the product to be sold is the same as described on the packaging or as selected by the purchaser;
- ensuring the ownership of the product sold to the purchaser; and
- providing warranty services as agreed between the parties or as required by law.

Based on the above responsibilities, if the quality of products does not conform to that in the contract, the seller will be fully responsible for damage (if any) whether or not the seller is aware of such damage.[34] Upon the delivery of goods, if the purchaser discovers that goods are defective or damaged, he or she may delay payment, in full or in part, to the seller until the seller remedies the problem. The purchaser may also retain full or partial payment for the goods if there is proof that the seller has cheated the purchaser, the seller does not deliver the goods, or the goods are in dispute, until remedies have been agreed.[35]

The law prohibits merchants from:

- increasing prices resulting in loss to producers and consumers;
- misleading consumers;
- selling false goods;
- selling bad quality goods or goods of the wrong specification;
- lying in advertising; and
- promoting goods illegally.[36]

The above factors may be negotiated and agreed in an online contract.

34 Commercial Law 1997, art. 68.

35 Commercial Law 1997, art. 72.2.

36 Commercial Law 1997, art. 9.3.

PART 2
SAMPLE FORMS AND AGREEMENTS

WEBSITE DEVELOPMENT AGREEMENT CHECKLIST

submitted by John S. "Chip" Rainey of
Locke Liddell & Sapp LLP (United States)

Note: This checklist is designed to guide the attorney in drafting a Website Development Agreement. It is a list of things to be considered in drafting the agreement, but not everything mentioned in this checklist will be appropriate for each agreement. The checklist is neither developer nor customer oriented, as it is merely a list of things to consider, and if it is appropriate to include a clause addressing a particular item on the checklist, then the attorney may draft that clause to favor the customer, favor the developer, or to be neutral. Terminology used in this checklist is as follows:

"Customer" means the person or organization that would be considered the owner of the site or the sponsor of the site by third-parties, notwithstanding that the server actually publishing the site to the web may be operated by the developer or a third party.

"Sponsor" is an alternative word used to refer to the customer, and is used primarily when distinguishing the customer/owner of the site from a third party host.

"Host" refers to the organization or person that actually owns the server on which the website resides and is responsible for maintaining a connection between the server and the Internet. As used in this checklist, the "host" may or may not be the customer, depending on who is taking responsibility for owning, maintaining and connecting to the Internet the website server computer.

"Developer" means the person or organization that is undertaking for a fee the obligation of developing some or all of the text, images, graphics, sound, colors or other visible and invisible aspects of the website, for the benefit of the customer. The developer could also be the host of the website. Generally, the content is owned by the customer, and the developer owns certain programs, scripts, routines that cause that content to be published in a specific way on to the Internet, but in some circumstances, the developer may actually owned some of the content, and has merely given permission to the customer to republish that content, with or without attribution, as the parties may agree.

Checklist

1. Timetable for development activities

a. Deadline for completion of design specifications

b. Deadline for development of site plan

c. Deadline for development of design elements, including:

i. Site themes consisting of colors, borders, font, banner placement and navigation aids

ii. Logos, trademarks, service marks

iii. Decisions regarding incorporation of graphics, Photos, video, audio

d. Deadline for submission of web prototype page and content site to client

e. Deadline for client to approve prototype

f. Deadline for submission of beta site to client

g. Deadline for client to provide comments on web beta site

h. Deadline for responding to client comments in writing

i. Deadline for development of back office or active server page capabilities

j. Deadline for development and publishing of initial content into test website

k. Deadline for client testing of test website

l. Deadline for publication of live website

Note: If the website is to be published in stages with increasing functionality over time contemplated in the initial website development agreement, then for each functional area or stage of the website, a separate timeline should be developed.

2. Scope of services—Allocate responsibility among developer and client

a. Responsibility for initial content

b. Responsibility for design elements

c. Responsibility for programming and script development

d. Responsibility for updating and maintaining content

i. Will training manuals be provided to customer

ii. How frequently will content be updated

iii. Will maintenance responsibilities be split among developer and sponsor

iv. Will there be a web host separate from either sponsor and developer, who will maintain some or all of the content

v. Will developer deliver a task list organized web page by web page to serve as a tickler for content maintenance

e. Responsibility for linking to external sites and clearing of intellectual property rights

f. Responsibility for training

i. Customer's webmaster

ii. Host's IT personnel

iii. Call center personnel

g. Responsibility for mounting website or individual web pages to host server and maintaining visibility on the Internet of web pages

i. Monitoring of website post-development

1. ensuring against accidental or viral corruption

2. ensuring against unauthorized posting to site by hackers

ii. Publishing new pages and content to host

iii. Verifying availability and download speeds

iv. Verifying security

h. User call center maintenance

Note: If a user of the website has a problem, either with access to the site or the interpretation of content, or if a user has a question regarding an online transaction, the agreement may address who will maintain the call center to handle such questions. Frequently this is handled in a separate document.

3. Base Content

a. Copyright notice

i. Bottom of each web page

ii. In terms of use, provide address of agent registered with U.S. Copyright Office for limitation of liability on online service provider under the Digital Millennium Copyright Act

iii. File designation of copyright agent with U.S. Copyright Office for limitation of liability on online service provider under the Digital Millennium Copyright Act

b. Terms of access to website

i. If website is solely informational, passive Terms of Access will probably suffice (i.e., mere access to website is tacit approval of such terms)

ii. If website actively delivers something to the user, or initiates a transaction—such as E-commerce—then a separate Terms of Use agreement, requiring either a click-through, or a written signature on file, should be considered

c. Privacy policy

d. Disclaimer of rendition of legal advice

e. Disclaimer of rendition of medical advice

f. Contact information

i. Webmaster

ii. Marketing personnel

iii. Investor relations

iv. Mailing and delivery address

4. Functionality

a. Definition of functional use of website

i. Marketing and general public relations

1. most common use of websites

2. frequently represents a portion of a website that also delivers other functionality

ii. Regulatory compliance; e.g.

1. Replacement of EBB for interstate natural gas pipelines

2. Simultaneous disclosure required by SEC under new Fair Disclosure standards

iii. Information delivery (non-profit motive) to:

1. general public

2. target audience

3. authorized users only

iv. Information delivery (profit motive)

1. Will it follow the network broadcast model, relying on advertising revenue

2. subscription basis

3. research for a fee based upon either hourly or per-search cost

v. E-commerce

1. B-2-B (business to business)

a) Sale of goods

1) Online catalogue

2) Order entry

3) Order tracking

4) Invoicing—bill presentment

5) Online payment

b) Financial services

c) Sale of "Computer Information" as that term is defined in the proposed Uniform Computer Information Transaction Act, including access to database information or software downloads

d) Initiation of a sale of services

2. Retail

a) Sale of goods

b) Financial services

c) Sale of "Computer Information" as that term is defined in the proposed Uniform Computer Information Transaction Act, including access to database information or software downloads

d) Initiation of a sale of services

vi. Portal

1. General purpose, à la Yahoo.com or How2.com

2. tailored to a specific audience, such as lawyers, investors or physicians

vii. Recruiting and employment matters

1. Targeting to new graduates

2. posting of openings and how to contact HR personnel

3. disseminating benefit information to current employees and retirees, with proper security

b. FTP

i. Refers to File Transfer Protocol

ii. Used to download files onto the user's computer, including software, or copies of documents

iii. May also be used to upload files from user to server for certain permitted transactions, such as posting a schedule of natural gas transportation nominations.

c. Telnet—VPN

i. Using the Internet to establish a direct link into the systems of the customer or host

ii. Similar to historical dial-up systems

iii. May be used anywhere dial-up systems were used in past, with appropriate security—for example, a board of realtors may maintain its multiple listing service via the Internet, instead of by dial-up telephone, but only realtors with an approved password and user i.d. may access portions, or even all, of the system.

iv. Through tunneling method, may be used to establish a virtual private network (VPN) through a service provider for conducting EDI transactions

d. News—usenet

i. Access to the worldwide bulletin board used to broadcast articles of importance to a specific group of users, known as newsgroups

5. Site-specific content

This may be the guts of the agreement, but is so specific to the individual circumstance that it is impossible to contemplate all of the issues that may arise. On the other hand, usually this is the one area where the customer has the most responsibility. If the developer is not offering specific content to the customer, but is merely consulting as to the website, then all of the site specific content would be the customer's responsibility. The developer may have the obligation in the agreement, however, to inform the customer as to any requirements or restrictions inherent to publishing the content. For instance, the developer may need to specify that all test be published in HTML, or that graphics be in a certain format so as to meet performance requirements, but this may cause the page to present differently on different browsers—probably not a consideration when delivering only text or delivering graphics that do not need to be positioned precisely with respect to the margins of the page. Alternatively, the content may need to be delivered in a page description language, such as Adobe Acrobat, whereby the precise layout of the page is maintained, but which will require the user to have client-side software to interpret the file properly, such as the ubiquitous Adobe Acrobat Reader.

6. Security

a. During development

b. Credit cards or other payment methods

c. Access to databases where customer financial information or personal identifying information is maintained

d. Encryption of secured transactions

  i. Minimum of 48 bit encryption

  ii. Most newer browsers support 128 bit encryption, which is recommended standard, unless site is directed to mass market

e. Password protection

  i. Applies whenever a user is seeking access to either:

    1. back-office systems of customer—such as into a database or other sensitive area;

    2. A subscription-only area; or

    3. User identifying or personnel information

  ii. Protection over access to passwords

f. Backup

g. Use, content and placement of cookies on the user's computer

h. Disaster recovery

7. Performance Standards

a. Uptime

  i. Will site be maintained as a 24/7 site

  ii. Is it likely that the customer will experience any sales or lost revenue resulting from downtime

  iii. How many hits are expected on average

  iv. Maximum sustained hit rate

v. Must consider effect that advertising occurring on other media might have on peak hit rate

Reference the infamous Victoria's Secret situation, when the company advertised an online fashion show during the Super Bowl in 1999, causing such a jam trying to get onto the site that the site crashed, thereby causing exactly the opposite effect of that which was intended—lost sales and diminished reputation.

b. Load times

i. Should be based upon most-common connect speeds to the site

ii. With graphics, generally should not exceed 30 seconds at most-common connect speeds

iii. Offer the user a text-only version of page, if connect speeds too slow, or if graphics are not essential to the full use of the website by the average user.

c. Tracking visitor information

8. Fees and expenses and payment

a. Fees

b. Reimbursement of expenses

i. Travel

ii. Licensing of third-party software

iii. Other out-of-pocket expenses

iv. Right of audit

c. Additional work

i. Most favored client status

ii. Period for which fees for additional work is fixed at current prices

iii. Maximum dollar or percentage amount that fees may increase in future

d. Payment

i. At project completion

ii. Based upon milestones

iii. Upon submission of invoice

iv. When past due

v. Interest on past due amounts

9. Indemnification

a. By vendor/consultant

i. For breach of certain warranties

ii. For actions taken by employees or subcontractors while on customers premises

iii. Responsibility for client to cooperate with developer regarding any claim, including promptness of notification

iv. For customer's own actions or omissions

1. For ordinary negligence

2. Express negligence standard in applicable jurisdiction

b. By sponsor/customer

i. For content provided by customer

ii. For operation of website (if developer will not be host or have responsibility for content)

iii. For damages suffered by vendor's employees while on customer's premises

iv. Responsibility of developer to cooperate with client for any claims

c. Insurance supporting indemnification

10. Warranties and limitation of liability

a. Developer warranties

i. Non-infringement warranty

1. Owns all code and other products, or

2. Has right to sublicense customer, without any additional cost to customer other than as specified in contract

ii. No surreptitious code warranty

iii. No virus warranty

iv. Performance according to performance standards warranty

v. Adequate training and staffing of personnel

vi. Compliance with all laws

vii. Authority to execute agreement

viii. No violation of agreements with any third party

ix. If client is paying any amounts in advance, warranty of solvency

b. Customer warranties

i. Authority to execute agreements

ii. No violation of agreements with any third party

iii. Compliance with all laws

iv. Non-infringement of any content or other customer-supplied material on intellectual property rights of any third-party.

c. Disclaimer of Warranty

i. Disclaimer of implied warranties

1. Merchantability

2. Fitness for particular purpose

ii. Client disclaims warranty as to accuracy or completeness of content

iii. Express warranties given are not for any third party's benefit

d. Limitation of Liability

11. Confidentiality, Non-solicitation and Non-competition

a. Provisions protecting confidential information

i. Include ability to obtain injunctive relief to enforce confidentiality, even if other disputes are to be settled non-judicially

ii. Injunction should be obtainable without bond or other security

b. Provisions limiting the rights of a party to solicit the employees of the other party

c. Provisions prohibiting the developer from using the information or business know-how gained in performing the consulting/development work for customer to go into a competing business or to sell capabilities to persons intending to directly compete with customer

12. Ownership of developed products and intellectual property

a. Ownership of copyright to content

b. Ownership of trademarks, graphics, logos

c. If new software, Java applet, script developed that performs specific function, who will own such software, applet or script

d. Work made for hire v. assignment of interest in intellectual property right

e. Patent of business process or software

f. Perpetual license to use developer's intellectual property even if developer not used for maintenance or future development

g. Consideration of moral and termination rights, particular where complex or artistic graphics are used

h. Rights of publicity clearance for video

i. Use of public domain or royalty free pictures and audio clips

j. Clearance of all intellectual property rights of third parties

13. Breach, default and termination

a. Breach of warranty by Developer is default

b. Failure to achieve milestones or other breach of contract is default

c. Failure to pay for services rendered when due is a default

d. Grace Periods

e. Notification

f. Remedies
    i. Of customer, for developer's breach
        1. Termination
        2. Refund
        3. Damages
        4. Specific performance
    ii. Of developer, for customer's breach
        1. For costs incurred
        2. For damages
        3. For specific performance
g. Survivability of provisions

14. Dispute Resolution

a. Appointment of client representative and developer project manager
b. Graduated escalation of dispute resolution
c. Mandatory mediation
d. Binding arbitration
e. Waiver of jury
f. Exclusive forum designation/choice of venue

15. General

a. Notice provision
b. Waiver
c. Amendment
d. Governing Law
e. Severability
f. Assignability
g. No prior agreements
h. Independent contractor status
i. Battle of the forms resolution
j. Force majeure conditions

WEBSITE HOSTING AGREEMENT CHECKLIST

submitted by John S. "Chip" Rainey of
Locke Liddell & Sapp LLP (United States)

Note: This checklist is designed to guide the attorney in drafting a Website Hosting Agreement. It is a list of things to be considered in drafting the agreement, but not everything mentioned in this checklist will be appropriate for each agreement. The checklist is neither host nor sponsor oriented, as it is merely a list of things to consider, and if it is appropriate to include a clause addressing a particular item on the checklist, then the attorney may draft that clause to favor the sponsor of the website, favor the host, or to be neutral.

1. Services

a. Procurement of hardware

b. Storage space

c. Access to server

d. Interface to Internet on-ramp, including telecommunications

  i. 56 kbs lines

  ii. ADSL lines

  iii. Fractional or full T1 lines

  iv. Fractional or full T3 lines

e. Creation or maintenance of firewall

2. Fees, Expenses and Payments

a. Fees

b. Reimbursement of expenses

  i. Travel

  ii. Licensing of third-party software

  iii. Other out-of-pocket expenses

  iv. Right of audit

c. Additional work

  i. Most favored client status

ii. Period for which fees for additional work is fixed at current prices

iii. Maximum dollar or percentage amount that fees may increase in future

d. Payment

i. At project completion

ii. Based upon milestones

iii. Upon submission of invoice

iv. When past due

v. Interest on past due amounts

3. Content and grant of license

a. Sponsor responsible for all content, unless expressly provided by host

b. Sponsor will promptly remove any content found to:

i. Violate others rights to privacy

ii. Be defamatory

iii. Violate third party's intellectual property rights

c. Will discussion pages be maintained?

i. Monitoring of content of discussions or chat rooms

ii. Storage of messages

iii. Tracking of IP address or other identifying information of persons posting on message boards, in discussion forums or on chat pages

d. Sponsor grants temporary, limited license giving host the right to post content on host computer, ending on termination of hosting—the later of the termination of the agreement or the end of transition assistance

e. No use of content by host except as expressly permitted in agreement or as mandated by applicable law

4. Intellectual property rights

a. Ownership of copyright to content

b. Cooperation in obtaining any patent from the USPTO for software or business process

5. Confidentiality, Non-solicitation and Non-competition

a. Provisions protecting confidential information

b. Provisions limiting the rights of a party to solicit the employees of the other party

c. Provisions prohibiting the host from using the information or business know-how gained in performing the hosting and maintenance work for sponsor to go into a competing business or to sell capabilities to persons intending to directly compete with sponsor

6. Privacy rights and collection of personally identifiable information

a. Access to user's information limited to persons with need to know

b. Double firewall to access credit card information—reverify every transaction and store information off-line only until collected from credit card company

c. No use of personally identifiable information for any purpose by host not expressly permitted by agreement

d. No use of personally identifiable information for any purpose by host not permitted by privacy policy of sponsor.

7. Security

a. Maintenance of firewall

b. One-way FTP sites

c. Password protection to publish new content remotely

d. Physical restriction on access to server

e. Protection of personal identifying information

f. Protection of credit card information

g. Nightly backup

h. Monitoring activity to detect virus or hacker intrusion even if firewall breached

i. Redundant systems

j. Disaster recovery

8. Warranties and limitations of liability

a. host's warranties

i. Performance according to performance standards warranty

ii. No virus warranty

iii. Non-infringement warranty

iv. Adequate training and staffing of personnel

v. Compliance with all laws

vi. Authority to enter into agreement

vii. No violation of agreements with any third party

b. Sponsor's warranties

i. Non-infringement of any content or other sponsor-supplied material on intellectual property rights of any third-party.

ii. Authority to enter into agreement

iii. Compliance with all laws

iv. No violation of agreements with any third party

c. Disclaimer of warranties

i. Disclaimer of implied warranties

1. Merchantability

2. Fitness for a particular purpose

d. Limitation of liability

9. Performance standards

a. Uptime guarantees

b. Access speeds

c. Download speeds

d. Express statement of number of simultaneous users or hits per minute/hour

e. Tracking of user profiles

10. Indemnification

a. By host

i. For any claims against sponsor that any content of the site provided by host violates the intellectual property rights of any person, or is defamatory or violates the privacy rights of any person, or is inflammatory or inciting others to commit crimes or other bad acts, or violates federal export controls

ii. For any cost, loss or damages suffered by sponsor or by employees of host for such employees negligent or wrongful acts while at the facilities of sponsor

b. By sponsor

i. For any claims against host that content of site provided by sponsor violates the intellectual property rights of any person, or is defamatory or violates the privacy rights of any person, or is inflammatory or inciting others to commit crimes or other bad acts, or violates federal export controls

ii. For any cost, loss or damages suffered by host or by employees of sponsor for such employees negligent or wrongful acts while at the facilities of host

11. Term

a. Fixed term

b. Renewal periods

i. Terminates automatically unless expressly renewed in writing

ii. Renews automatically unless expressly terminated by a specified time prior to renewal date

c. Termination for convenience

d. Transitional services from date of termination until a new host is arranged

e. Cooperation with new host and sponsor on transferring website

12. Breach, default and termination

a. Breach of warranty by host is default

b. Other breach of contract is default

c. Failure of sponsor to pay for services rendered when due is a default

d. Grace Periods

e. Notification

f. Remedies

g. Survivability of provisions

13. Dispute Resolution

a. Appointment of sponsor representative and developer project manager

b. Graduated escalation of dispute resolution

c. Mandatory mediation

d. Binding arbitration

e. Waiver of jury

f. Exclusive forum designation/choice of venue

14. General

a. Notice

b. Waiver

c. Amendment

d. Governing Law

e. Severability

f. Assignability

g. No prior agreements

h. Independent contractor status

i. Battle of the forms resolution

j. Force majeure conditions

CONTENT AGREEMENT CHECKLIST FOR PORTAL PROJECTS

submitted by Andrew F. Simpson of
Arculli and Associates (Hong Kong)

Note: This checklist is intended to provide guidance in respect of the issues that should be considered when preparing or negotiating a content agreement for an Internet project. It is neutral as between the content provider and portal operator, raising issues for each party's consideration rather than proposing positions on those issues.

CHOICE OF MODEL

There are a number of models that might be adopted for Internet content projects and the choice of model will have strategic implications for the parties and their negotiations:

- Content Provider Agreement—the portal operator sources content from an upstream provider, for which it might pay a monthly fee or a reduced fee plus a share of advertising revenue. The portal operator is the supplier of the content at the retail-level.
- Co-Marketing Agreement—the retail service is hosted by the portal operator and the content provider is the retail supplier of the service (contracting directly with the customer). Users might pay a subscription for access to premium content. Often there is a revenue sharing arrangement between the portal operator and the content provider.
- Merchant Agreement—content is aimed at the promotion of the merchant's goods or services. The merchant might pay some combination of a subscription fee, design fees, hosting fees and a share of revenues.
- On-site Co-Marketing and Merchant Agreements—content is hosted (and viewed) on the portal operator's own servers.
- Off-site Co-Marketing and Merchant Agreements—content is located on a third party's servers but viewed by users through the portal operator's platform.
- Associated Hardware and Software—particular content may require the addition of particular hardware and software elements, which should be identified

and separately specified, as those are important to the operation of the arrangements.

STRATEGIC OBJECTIVES

- Consider each party's strategic objectives in providing and acquiring the content—to what uses will it be put?
- How critical is the content to each party's broader activities?
- Where will the portal operator position the content on its site(s)?

PARTIES

- Full names and business addresses of each party.
- Full details of the contact for the other party.
- Verify the background of the other party (size, reputation, local assets, corporate affiliation).
- Confirm other party's ownership of intellectual property rights in relation to the content in question.

TERM AND TERMINATION

- When will the agreement commence?
- When will the Internet service launch?
- After what initial term can the parties terminate the agreement?
- In what particular circumstances can each party terminate the agreement early (e.g. breach, insolvency)?
- What renewal rights will each party have?
- Can the portal operator continue to use content after termination of the agreement?

CONTENT

- Is the content unusual or novel?
- Is the content likely to have any special legal character (gambling, financial, indecent)?
- Does the content provider have examples of how the content should appear?
- Does the portal operator have details (diagram) of the technical configuration that is proposed?
- What material will the content provider furnish (e.g. data feeds, text, images, video, audio, downloadable software, server software)?

- In what format will the content be provided (e.g. HTML, hard copy, JPEG, source code, object code, etc.)?
- When and how will the content be provided?
- How often will content be updated?
- How will updates be provided?
- What server space limits (if any) apply in relation to the content?
- What quality standards must the content meet?
- What service levels must the portal operator meet?
- What happens if content falls short of quality standards?
- What happens if service falls short of service levels?
- Can the portal operator select content from among a range to be offered?
- Is there to be a trial period?

Note that misdescription of the content to be provided (including its format, specifications and origins) is a very common problem in content agreements. It is important that the content in question should be clarified at an early stage and specified exactly in the agreement.

INTELLECTUAL PROPERTY AND EXCLUSIVITY

- Will the portal operator gain ownership of all or part of the content or merely a licence to use it?
- If the portal operator is merely licensed to use the content, what is the scope of its rights: exclusive or non-exclusive; perpetual or terminable; worldwide or restricted geographically; any right to modify, adapt or create derivative works; any right to sell, distribute or sublicense?
- What rights will the content provider have in respect of any modification or customization or coding of the content?
- What trademarks, if any, are to be used and how?
- Is the content provider to be restricted from providing the content to third parties and, if so, how?
- Is the content already hosted elsewhere and, if so, will that change?
- Is the portal operator to be restricted from hosting competing content providers' content and, if so, how?

LINKING, FRAMING AND CUSTOMISATION

- Will the portal operator be required to do anything to the content before it can be used?

- Will the portal operator be permitted to do anything to the content before it is used?
- Will all of the content be hosted on the portal operator's site or will the site link to another on which some of the content is to be hosted?
- Are any hyperlinks to be inserted in the content and, if so, who will do this and who will be responsible for updating them?
- Which party will be able to insert links in the content?
- Will the portal operator be able to modify or edit the content?
- Will the portal operator be able to "frame" the content?

DOCUMENTATION AND SUPPORT

- What documentation must the content provider furnish to the portal operator?
- What support must the content provider give the portal operator?
- What service levels must the content provider meet in rectifying faults in the content?
- What training must the content provider give to the portal operator's personnel?

END-USERS

- What information will be collected from end-users?
- Which party will collect end-users' information and what rights will the other party have in relation to that information?
- Which party will be responsible for preparation of retail terms and conditions?
- Who is responsible for billing and collection of retail charges?
- What telephone or e-mail support will be provided to end-users and by which party?
- What marketing is proposed by each party?
- What joint marketing is proposed by the parties?
- Who bears the cost of marketing activities?
- What advertising will the portal operator provide and at what charges?
- Where on the portal operator's site will advertising appear?
- What restrictions, if any, apply in relation to advertising (e.g. in relation to competing content)?

CHARGES

- Is the content provider liable to pay a joining fee, hosting fees or content processing fees?

- Is the portal operator liable to pay for its licence to use the content, modification of the content, staff training or support by the content provider?
- How is revenue to be allocated between the parties?
- Which party will be responsible for invoicing and bad debts?

OTHER

- Are there any other relevant obligations not included among the points above?

CHECKLIST FOR WEBSITE COUNSEL

by Joseph F. Ruh, Jr., Eastman Kodak Company,
June M. Besek, Executive Director and Director of Studies, Kernochan Center for Law, Media, and the Arts, Columbia University
Susan E. Colman, Attorney at Law, Washington, DC
Joost J. Linnemann, Kennedy Van Der Laan, Amsterdam
Oliver R. Smoot, Jr., Information Technology Industry Council

CONTENTS

4. Document Retention
5. Formation of Contracts
6. Unsolicited Submissions / Suggestions
7. Tax Issues
8. Data Privacy
9. Notices and Disclaimers
10. Protection against misuse / online theft
11. Jurisdiction

Part C: Issues Arising in Particular Areas of the Website

1. Marketing information related to Company products
2. Shareholder Information
3. Product finder / dealer locator
4. Customer service / technical support information
5. Chat Rooms and Newsgroups
6. Online distribution
7. E-commerce capability
8. Information customizable to individual
9. Educational information related to Company's business
10. Entertainment
11. Links to / from other websites
12. Display of awards / certifications
13. Display of advertising

Introduction

This Checklist provides a framework for discussions between website administrators and their legal counsel. Its purpose is to help the client and the lawyer better understand the way in which the company websites are being used, and the way in which the legal risks presented by the websites are being managed.

The Checklist is directed toward a generic business website, but covers many issues that arise in personal or specialized websites. It should be particularly helpful to the thousands of business websites that are used by their owners primarily as extensions of the existing company marketing, sales, and communication channels.

With that audience in mind, the Checklist assumes that the website is associated with an established business that has addressed many of these issues in a non-website context. For example, most businesses have processes in place to approve advertising and marketing material before publication, to review form agreements before use, and to handle inquiries from current and prospective customers.

The key assumption of the Checklist is that whenever an existing company policy or practice can be applied to the website, it will usually be more efficient to extend the existing policy or practice to include the website, rather than inventing new or separate policies or practices specifically for the website.

For example, a company's existing practices for having advertising material reviewed and approved before use could be expanded to include the use of that material, or new material, on the website. Similarly, the company's existing customer service practices could be expanded to include the delivery of those services through the website.

It follows from that assumption that company policies and practices must be reviewed and adapted to deal with the existence and evolution of the website. As the website develops, the company must continuously identify and communicate the impact of that development on the other parts of the company. It is our hope that this Checklist will make that process easier for all concerned.

A. Collecting the Facts

1. How many websites are there?

a. Intentional websites

b. Unintentional websites

- Intranet sites accessible from outside the Company
- Employee sponsored websites
- Websites of parent or subsidiaries
- Websites of dealers
- Websites of trade organizations
- Websites of customers
- Parody / commentary sites
  - "McSpotlight" http://www.mcspotlight.org/
  - "Distorted Barbie" http://users.rcn.com/napier.interport/barbie/barbie.html

2. Why does each website exist?

a. What is its purpose?

Is there an established / formal purpose, approved by management?

Who approves expansion of or changes to the website?

Who coordinates expansion with other parts of the Company?

b. Who is its audience?

Who is the intended audience?

- shareholders

- suppliers
- existing customers
- potential customers
- selected constituencies (political / charitable / cultural / religious)
- general public
- competitors
- business partners
- other

Is there an unintended audience? How are they restricted from access?

Where (in what geographies) is its audience?

c. What information or services are available to the audience?

- Marketing information on Company goods and services
- Product descriptions, specifications, or prices
- Shareholder Information
- Company fact book—names, addresses, subsidiaries, divisions
- Press releases, annual reports, financial results (SEC filings)
- Product finder / dealer locator
- Customer service / technical support information
- Online order placement / order status
- Technical reference information or publications
- Online access to Company customer service / technical employees
- Access to other customers or suppliers (chat rooms, newsgroups)
- Updated software / data files
- E-commerce capability
- Online product / software distribution
- Information customizable to individual (e.g.—financial website online portfolio tracker)
- Features or testimonials about customers using Company products
- Educational information related to the Company's business
- Entertainment
- Other information
- Links to other websites of interest

d. What information does website collect from its audience?

Customer registration information

Customer feedback / suggestions

Information needed to customize the website (preferences / products owned by customer)

Transaction information

3. Infrastructure—How is the website equipment, software, and administration organized?

a. Servers

Who owns / operates the servers? Company or third party service provider?

If third party, consider what data gets collected about Company website, who owns it, and who controls its reuse and distribution.

Where are the servers located?

Consider the impact on jurisdiction and tax liability of physical location of equipment and personnel.

Are mirror sites used?

Mirror sites are servers that hold duplicate copies of the master sites, but are located in different geographies to make access easier for users in different parts of the world.

Who owns / operates the mirror sites?

Consider who has rights to the data generated by those sites.

Consider the implications on jurisdiction.

b. Administration

Who updates / edits the website? Who acts as webmaster? Company or third party service provider?

Consider whether appropriate editorial discretion & management supervision is available.

c. Connections to the Net

How does the website connect to the internet?

Who is the Internet Access Provider?

d. Security

What are the security measures in place?

Consider both prevention of access from the outside (firewalls / passwords), and prevention of distribution of information from the inside (gateways / usage tracking systems / employee education)?

Who operates / monitors these security devices—Company or third party service provider?

Is website security integrated with other Company security personnel and policies?

e. Third Party Support

Who is helping Company with the website? Possible third parties include:

- internet access providers
- internet service providers
- E-commerce service providers
- E-commerce fulfillment companies
- website developers
- consultants
- advertising agencies
- customers
- suppliers
- business partners
- others

Contracts with third parties should (i) exist and (ii) deal with the relevant issues identified in this checklist.

E.g. If name of website designer appears on Company website (usually at the bottom: "site designed by xxxx"), consider economic value to third party of that advertising space. Is that value fairly reflected in the financial relationship between the parties?

f. Use of Encryption

Does Company use / support encryption in connection with the website, or its e-mail systems?

Consider the laws / regulations of countries that regulate the use of encryption. E.g.—can customers / suppliers / employees located in countries that restrict use of encryption take advantage of website / e-mail facilities that require the use of encryption?

B. Issues Common to Entire Website

1. Website management

a. Who is in charge of the website?

Is there a manager of sufficient rank in the Company paying attention, or is the website the work of the technical community, proceeding without substantial direction?

b. How are responsibilities for legal compliance on the website allocated?

Who is responsible for content submission? Is it the organization submitting the content, or the website managers, that are required to maintain the documentation concerning rights and clearances?

What are responsibilities of third party contributors (website developers / ad agencies) for obtaining and keeping records of clearances?

Is there a clear communication process between website management and legal advisors?

2. Licensing of Content For Use on Website

a. Identification of Content

Identify each piece of copyrightable content (e.g., text, picture, graphic, audio clip embodying a musical work and sound recording, etc.).

What is the source of the material?

Is there any basis from which to conclude the material is not protected by copyright (or other rights)?

b. Potential Licensees

All copyright-protected content must be licensed for use on the website by either the Company (as website owner/operator) or by a third party acting on behalf of the Company (e.g., ad agency may obtain rights on behalf of Company).

c. Potential Licensors

Anyone with rights to material that Company wants to publish on/distribute through the website is a potential licensor, including

- customers
- suppliers
- developers
- agencies
- employees (for personally owned material—i.e., not materials created in the course of their employment)
- every member of the audience invited to contribute to/communicate through the website.

Potential licensor must have

- rights that are broad enough to encompass the desired use (copyright rights are separable and a license may cover some uses and not others) and
- the right to license or sublicense to the Company.

d. License Terms: Scope of use/Limitations on use

For "original material" (i.e., material created for the website), or pre-existing material the Company licenses specifically for use on its site:

Is scope of use broad enough to permit current and future uses, including the creation of derivative works (who will own?), and does it provide worldwide rights?

If any limitations on use do exist, consider what administrative process exists for preventing material from being re-used outside of those limitations.

For "re-purposed material" (i.e., material originally created for the Company in one medium, that is later reproduced on the website, such as annual reports, or product literature):

What rights did the owner convey?

What rights were retained?

Do the original license rights permit the use of that material on the website?

Does it permit the creation of derivative works?

Are there any restrictions on media, mode of distribution, geographical scope, term?

Watch out in particular for re-use of television and print advertising (advertisers assume they own the rights to the ad, but the agency may only have negotiated with the models for TV rights, not all media or broadcast rights).

e. License Terms: Assignment rights/sublicensing rights/third party usage rights

Can Company move entire website to new host server (may be an issue if some material was provided by the third party currently hosting the website)?

Can ownership/control of entire website be transferred to new owner in the event of merger, acquisition or divestiture?

Can Company establish mirror websites if required (same content hosted on different server)?

Can Company sublicense portion of its website to a third party (e.g., national non-profit A wants to sublicense portion of its website to local non-profit B)?

Can Company grant third parties rights to reproduce or to publicly distribute, perform or display portions of the website (e.g., church group requests permission to use an image in church publication; researcher requests permission to reproduce a chart in a book being prepared for publication; teacher asks permission to use portions of website in interactive training CD-ROM; dealer asks permission to use content from website to create trade show brochure, etc.)?

f. License Terms: Indemnification

Do licensors provide appropriate indemnification to Company against risk of infringement?

Is the licensor financially able to satisfy the indemnity if necessary?

Is the indemnity applicable in all jurisdictions where material may be displayed?

Consider the value of an indemnity provision in an online click-wrap agreement where licensor (i.e., person contributing material to website) is identified only by a credit card, or an e-mail address, or a screen name?

Do what you can to lessen your risk—find out how your licensor obtained its rights, whether there are relevant limitations on scope, whether rights are subject to renewal, termination, etc.

g. License Terms: Term and termination

Do the rights expire after a set time?

Is the license terminable upon breach by the website?

h. Administrative issues

Is there a way to match up the subject matter with the applicable license terms?

Test:
(i) Given the license, can all copies/derivatives of the subject matter be located?
(ii) Given an element of content (e.g., text, picture, graphic, audio clip, etc.) can the applicable license terms be located?

Does Company have process in place to accept and respond to inquiries concerning reproduction and distribution of material on its website?

Termination:

If license terminates (by expiration or breach) is there a process for removing the material from the website and preventing its reuse by removing it from, or isolating it within, the website archives?

i. Rights of publicity and model releases

Who has obtained, and kept on file, the model releases for each image or video clip that contains a recognizable individual?

Are those releases broad enough to permit the intended use on the website?

E.g., assume image of a face is intentionally distorted for effect on the website—does scope of model release permit/prohibit that distortion?

3. Trademarks & domain names

a. Trademarks

What Company trademarks are used on the website?

Are they used correctly? (i.e. color / graphic design / placement)?

Does the Company provide a distinctive icon for others to use to link to the Company website? Is that icon the same as a Company trademark?

If the Company doesn't provide an icon for others to use, is a Company trademark being misused by others as a link to Company website?

Does the Company display the trademarks of others on its website? Does it have a right to display those trademarks?

Does Company include hidden meta-tags in its website, with the trademarks or product names of third parties, to cause Web search engines to retrieve Company website when audience conducts a search for competitor's product?

b. Domain Names

See *Applying The Trademark Misuse Doctrine To Domain Name Disputes*, S. Davidson & N. Engisch, available online at: http://www.cla.org/trademark%20misuse.pdf

Is Company domain name the same as a federally registered trademark of a third party? Consider InterNIC and other registrar policies for resolving domain name disputes.

Are third parties confusing Company customers with confusingly similar domain names?

Is Company website confusing to customers of third parties? (e.g. Acme.com, Acme.org, Acme.net, Acme.co.uk, Acme.se, AcmeOnline.com, AcmeInc.com).

Domain names are used for more than websites. Consider possibility of e-mail with customer information being sent to wrong generic e-mail address at a confusingly similar domain: info@acme.org or webmaster@acme.org or postmaster@acme.org instead of @acme.com.

Have domain names been registered under the top-level domains of those jurisdictions where Company has trademarks (e.g. acme.co.uk, acme.de, acme.fr)?

Consider tradeoff between the cost of registering domain names in those jurisdictions, versus the cost of fighting domain name grabbers. Consider the impact of slightly different domain names (e.g. acme.de, acme1.de, acme_online.de, acmeUSA.de).

Note that some registrars require actual use of the domain name as a condition of registration.

4. Document Retention

a. What is the Company's document retention / document destruction policy? How is it applied to the information on the website?

Consider the implication of "dynamically generated" web pages—pages that are created by the combination of multiple elements that change over time or based on audience input or other variables. If necessary, could Company reproduce a dynamically generated page if the content of that page became an issue?

5. Formation of Contracts

a. Online contract vs. EDI relationship

Company's prior experience with EDI relationships (online data transfer and transactions usually governed by signed, written agreements), may provide management with false sense of security when Company undertakes E-commerce. Management needs to be educated about the differences.

b. Issues in online contract formation

See generally, *A Cryptography Primer*, C. Merrill, [online] at http://cla.org/RuhBook/chp_Hlt798985072BM_4_.htm

Confidentiality—are the communications leading up to the formation of the contract, and the contract itself, free from risk of disclosure to third parties?

At the website: does it use a secure server, or encrypted e-mail?

Authentication—are both parties to the contract really who they say they are? Is one party (i) an impostor (posing as some other real person), or (ii) fictitious (posing as a non-existent person)?

At the website: what process is used to verify the identity of the other party (e.g. confirmation by return e-mail, mail, telephone, credit check, etc.)?

What process is used to confirm Company identity to potential customers? Consider possibility of fraudulent websites trading off of the Company name.

Message Integrity—are the contents of all the communications, and the contract itself, free from changes caused by computer glitch or malicious tampering?

At the website: does it use a secure server or encrypted e-mail?

Non-Repudiation—can each party prevent the other party from denying the communications and contract formation took place?

At the website: what is the process for recording & storing data about the formation of an online contract?

What data / reference information about the contract is communicated to the other party (e.g. confirming e-mail, reference number, invoice, etc.)?

Time Date Stamping—if date and time of the communications is important, can it be irrefutably established?

At the website: Is date and time of formation (i) stored in Company records and (ii) included on confirmation back to other party?

Consider implications of error in a computer generated time / date stamp on customer's computer because of faulty system clock. Consider implications of stating the time without stating a reference time zone.

c. Offer and acceptance

Is a link in small print at the bottom of a web page to an online "terms of service" sufficient to establish the offer?

Does use of the website by the audience, with or without knowledge of the "terms of service," constitute acceptance?

Does the answer apply in both jurisdiction of the website, and jurisdiction of the audience participant?

d. Statute of frauds

Does the online contract satisfy the requirement of the statute of frauds?

If not, will the statute of frauds be satisfied if a confirming copy of the contract is printed in hard copy and mailed to the other party?

e. Age & competence to contract

Can Company form an online contract with (i) a minor, (ii) a minor with a parent's credit card, (iii) a legal incompetent (e.g. person under legal supervision of a guardian) with access to a computer.

If not, what is the Company due diligence obligation concerning the competence of the other party before Company is entitled to rely on the contract?

f. Warranty of non-infringement, and claims under indemnity provisions

Of what value is the other party's warranty / indemnity?

Two issues: (i) ability to collect damages from licensor, and (ii) impact on defense in third party suit.

Consider—if Company accepts material (music, text, images) from audience for publication on its website, and the material infringes third party rights, is Company's defense of an infringement claim affected by the quality of its efforts to confirm the identity, age & competence of its contributors?

Digital signatures

Consider what constitutes an adequate signature for the type of contract being formed. Specific laws or regulations (banking / consumer protection / securities) may impose requirements different from general contract law.

Jurisdiction for enforcement and resolution of disputes

Have choice of law and choice of venue clauses been specified in the contract?

Most jurisdictions honor a choice of law provision in a contract. The law selected in the contract may also apply to the question of whether or not a valid contract was formed in the first place.

Formation of contract

Alternatives for confirming online contracts come in varying shades of gray: Click-wrap / web wrap, simple online notice, e-mail confirmation, etc.

Consider proposed revisions to UCC Article 2B for guidance.

Consider tiers of formality—less important contracts may use less cumbersome / less intrusive form of online contract.

Contracts with Consumers

Consider additional requirements if the other party is (or could be) a consumer. Specific laws or regulations may impose requirements different from general contract law. In transactions between parties in different countries, where one party is a consumer, the law of the consumer's country may take precedence over otherwise applicable law.

6. Unsolicited Submissions / Suggestions

a. Does Company have a process for receiving and responding to unsolicited suggestions from the public? Has that process been adapted to deal with electronic submissions.

Consider the implications of receiving suggestions through e-mail, through a suggestion box on the website, or through a customer service online chat room or newsgroup.

What is the process for receiving suggestions, responding to them, and keeping them isolated from the rest of the Company until the proper clearance or waiver has been obtained from the contributor?

7. Tax Issues

a. Has Company considered how its website, and its activities on that website, affect Company's exposure to various taxing jurisdictions for income, sales, and use taxes?

E.g. server farms in some jurisdictions may constitute a "permanent establishment" of Company in those jurisdictions for tax purposes.

8. Data Privacy

What data about the audience is collected?

- automatically (without knowledge of the audience) e.g. through the use of cookies, or other automatic means?
- by voluntary submission (with knowledge of the audience)?

Is data collected from audience members who are located in other jurisdictions?

If so, is the data stored and processed in those other jurisdictions, or does the data cross international borders? Consider the application of data privacy rules / regulations in the jurisdiction of the audience member.

E.g. in England, consider that the use of a "cookie" without the user's consent may violate data privacy legislation in that it may be used to communicate information deemed "personal", and may also implicate England's *Computer Misuse Act 1990* which prohibits a person from causing a computer to function in a way which is unauthorized by the user. *Contributed by* Jeremy Newton, Cameron McKenna, Mitre House, 160 Aldersgate St, London UK EC1A 4DD

Are children targeted as sources of data?

Is data collected from children handled differently?

Is the information verified? (See discussion about online contracting, above).

How is that data used?

- by website?
- by others in Company?
- by third parties?

What is the website privacy policy?

Examples:

http://www.dell._Hlt79898527_Hlt79898528cBM_5_BM_6_om/policy/privacy.htm (Dell Privacy Policy)

http://www.ford.com/en/support/privacyStatement.htm (Ford Motor Company Privacy Policy)

Is website policy consistent with the Company's general data privacy policies?

Consider if website policy provides that "customer data is not used for any purpose other than the website", but if website data is subsequently integrated into Company's data warehouse?

What privacy policy elements are incorporated into the Company policy?

- accountability for control of data
- identified purposes for use of data
- opt-in or opt-out by audience member for use of its data
- limitations on collection
- limitations on use, disclosure, and length of retention
- accuracy, and method by which audience can verify accuracy
- safeguards
- openness concerning data protection policies
- access to data
- redress

Is data privacy policy communicated to the website audience?

Can audience member provide comment, or complain, or seek redress concerning use of personal data? Are the communications from the audience properly managed?

Consider the following guidelines when establishing data privacy policies:

Electronic privacy laws, medical privacy laws, consumer credit laws. *Electronic Privacy Information Center*, [online] at http://www.epic.org

European Communities Directive on the protection of individuals with regard to the processing of personal data, [online] at http://europa.eu.int/eur-lex/pri/en/oj/dat/2002/l_201/l_20120020731en00370047.pdf

Information Technology Industry Council *Privacy Policy and Guidelines* http://www.itic.org

Interactive Services Association *Privacy Policies* [online] at http://www.ftc.gov/bcp/privacy/wkshp97/comments2/isa039.htm

Center for Media Education: *Online Advertising Targeting Children*

Better Business Bureau Children's Advertising Review Unit *1997 Self Regulatory Guidelines for Children's Advertising* [online] at http://www.caru.org/guidelines/index.asp

Federai Trade Commission Staff Report: *Public Workshop on Consumer Privacy on the Global Information Infrastructure* [online] at http://www.ftc.gov/reports/privacy/privacy1_Hlt79899418.BM_7_htm

9. Notices and Disclaimers

Does the Company website have a user agreement or disclaimer? Should it?

How should consent to the user agreement / disclaimer be obtained? Click-wrap? Optional hyperlink? Passive? (see Online Contracting discussion, above)

What subjects should be covered in the user agreement and disclaimer?

- uploading of content (text / graphics / images / software programs) by audience
- submission of suggestions / new ideas
- disclaimers relating to quality of content or availability of website
- disclaimers related to implied endorsement of links to other websites
- limited license for permitted use of content by audience
- choice of law and venue

Sample Disclaimers / Agreements

http://www1.us.dell.com/content/topics/global.aspx/policy/en/policy?c=us&cs=&l=en&s=gen&~ck=lf&~section=007 (Dell website terms of use)

http://www.intel.com/sites/corporate/tradmarx.htm?iid=HPAGE+footer_legal& (Intel)

10. Protection against misuse / online theft

Types of misuse

Infringement of copyrights

- simple infringement
- framing
- linking

Infringement / dilution of trademarks

- misuse of trademark
- domain name grabbing
- confusingly similar domain names
- misrepresentation—acting improperly in the name of a third party

  e.g. fake notice that Nike was providing free replacement shoes in exchange for mail in of old shoes

Interference with existing contractual relationships

Interception of data in transit

Theft of data stored on Company or intermediary server

Disruption of E-commerce activities / overloading of server

Preventive Measures / Due Diligence

Audit existing website. Remove sensitive information that should not be accessible, or establish password control system. Consider technical solutions:

- encryption
- digital watermarking

Establish policy providing guidelines for publication of new material on website.

Consider need for enforcement in other jurisdictions when establishing online contracts and licenses.

Establish criteria for linking from Company website to third party site.

Identify someone responsible for survey / audit / monitoring of the Internet for purposes of spotting potentially damaging activity of others.

Consider combination of internal resources, and external services (e.g. web clipping services, web security services)

Undertake proactive, periodic surveys / reviews of internet.

competitors
related industries
trade associations
suppliers
customers
dealers
newsgroups / forums

general key word searches on key terms and issues

Segment / target search activities to focus on most sensitive Company issues.

11. Jurisdiction

What law is applicable?

In contracts, most problems can be addressed by a choice of law in the contract. International law may also be applicable (e.g. Convention on the International Sale of Goods).

Applicable law for other legal issues depends on the importance that various private international law systems award to factual circumstances. These other areas include: tax, criminal, regulatory (consumer protection / cultural preservation / local language), contractual, obscenity, defamation, infringement, rights of publicity, rights of privacy, data privacy.

What courts can be addressed?

In cases that involve the internet, the competence of courts can be (and has been) based upon a number of factual circumstances:

- where the server is located
- where the website can be accessed
- where the subject of personal data resides
- where the effects of a defamatory statement are felt

Where, and how, can a decision be enforced

Consider

- international scope of decisions
- enforcement treaties between countries
- rules of arbitration

C. Issues Arising In Particular Areas of the Website

1. Marketing information related to Company products

Product specifications, photographs, descriptions

Consider whether Company has sufficient rights to reproduce existing printed / other media advertising on the website.

Consider how product information on website affects scope of warranty. Does information on website differ from other product information? Could it be construed as amending the warranted specifications? Does it get updated consistently with product information that ships with the product?

What if some products are not available in all countries, or differ, by country, in function, features or branding? Is information about the product on the website accurate in all countries in which the website is accessible?

Consider whether dealers / distributors should be able to copy product information from manufacturer's website and redistribute on dealer website, or link back to manufacturer website.

Consider (i) how information would be kept current on dealer sites, and (ii) whether manufacturer has sufficient rights to permit redistribution by others.

Prices

Consider implication of price information on the website on Company's other distribution channels, especially where product and service pricing historically varies by region or channel of distribution.

Information for suppliers and dealers, or other special audience segments

Does website have private / secure areas that contain information only accessible to special classes of audience, such as suppliers or dealers?

Consider how the passwords are issued and maintained. Is sharing of passwords permitted?

Consider how access is controlled, monitored and recorded. How are access violations dealt with?

If access is provided to some, but not all, dealers, consider antitrust implications.

2. Shareholder Information

Press releases

Consider how timing and distribution of press releases to the media, or filing of information with the government, is coordinated with the timing of posting the information on the website. If Company establishes practice of posting news releases on website, consider implication of failing to post a significant press release that is distributed through other media outlets.

Annual reports

Does Company have all of the rights necessary to publish the annual report on the website? Annual reports are usually not prepared by same people who do advertising, so releases and licenses may be insufficient if they do not contemplate publication on the website.

3. Product finder / dealer locator

Consider competition law implications of (i) identifying some, but not all, dealers, or (i) linking to some, but not all dealer websites, or (iii) causing the automated dealer locator to display certain dealers favored by the Company always at the top of the list of local dealers (vs. random, alphabetic, or geographic sort order).

4. Customer service / technical support information

How are customer inquiries managed?

Who responds to online inquiries—the webmaster, or the customer service personnel?

Do inquiries via the website get integrated into other customer service databases?

Does website provide online / automated customer service information? How is that database of information maintained? If it contains excerpts of questions submitted by customers, or names of customers, has the customer's consent been obtained?

5. Chat Rooms and Newsgroups

Does website provide facilities for audience to share information with other members of audience (chat rooms / newsgroups / customer forums)?

Have participants given their consent to the original use, and the reuse, of their contributions?

Is the use of the website by the audience monitored by the Company?

> Consider (i) derogatory statements about Company products, (ii) derogatory statements about competitor's products, (iii) defamatory statements about anyone, (iv) obscene and other inappropriate use.
>
> Consider the product liability implications of a product complaint being posted on a Company sponsored newsgroup / chat room, but overlooked by the Company, and having no action taken on it. Will the Company be considered to be on notice of the defect?

6. Online distribution

Does Company distribute products or product updates / bug fixes online?

> Consider how the online distribution is coordinated with the Company's other distribution methods, to be sure that intent of licensing and warranty provisions are preserved regardless of method of distribution. (e.g. Is online update covered by original shrink-wrap license? Or is new, online license required for the update?)

7. E-commerce capability

If Company is new to E-commerce, consider that management may not have anticipated all the issues that an E-commerce capability will present, including:

- consumer protection laws in various jurisdictions
- distribution of pricing information globally

- ability of existing MIS systems to accept payment or grant credit (credit cards, credit checks)
- requirement for robust back room operations (order processing, shipping, returns, customer service)
- worldwide marketing skills (language laws, advertising regulations, differing warranty obligations)
- worldwide shipping & receiving capability, and need to comply with export / import laws, tariffs, and customs regulations
- export issues for products distributed online
- tax implications (income and sales tax)

8. Information customizable to individual

If website tracks individually identifiable data (investment portfolio, areas of interest, products ordered, credit card, e-mail address, last date visited) consider data privacy and website security issues.

9. Educational information related to Company's business

What are the sources of the information distributed?

Have sufficient rights been obtained?

How is the information kept current?

> Consider implications of information that was accurate when it was posted online becoming inaccurate through the passage of time.

Does Company have a means to purge or update information that is obsolete or no longer accurate?

10. Entertainment

Online entertainment is frequently special content obtained from a third party (unless the website belongs to an entertainment company).

> Consider whether sufficient rights to the content have been obtained. The key issue in online entertainment is anticipating great success for the content—if content is a hit, how are re-use rights allocated?
>
> Consider the possibility of reusing the material on mirror sites, licensing it to other sites, licensing it in other media, and extending the term of use online.

If entertainment is targeted at children, be aware of public interest in issues related to marketing to children. See *Data Privacy*, above.

11. Links to / from other websites

Does Company have a policy concerning to whom it will, and will not, provide links?

Consider antitrust implications of a popular website providing links to some, but not all, of its dealers.

Consider implications of having links to some, but not all, suppliers.

Does Company obtain consent of other website before initiating the link?

Is there a record of consents that were granted?

Does Company require / request that other websites obtain Company's consent before links are established to the Company website?

Does Company take any action to identify and discourage those sites who have not received consent?

12. Display of awards / certifications

Does Company display any third party certifications or awards on its website (e.g. NetCensor / BBB Online)?

If so, have the conditions of the third party relating to the display of that information been satisfied?

How does the website monitor that it continues to comply with those requirements over time?

13. Display of advertising

Does the company display any advertising of third party products or services on Company website?

Who has control of what material gets advertised?

Does Company approve each ad? Or has Company contracted with online ad broker, and delegated supervision to the broker?

Consider possibility of ads that run on Company websites that promote competitors, or that promote products or services offensive to Company's target audience.

B2B WEBSITE USER AGREEMENT

submitted by John S. "Chip" Rainey of
Locke Liddell & Sapp LLP (United States)

Form Note: The following terms and conditions are for access to a website where the intended users are commercial concerns, and not individual consumers. These terms and conditions do not require an active click-through acceptance of their terms, since they may change frequently, and are usually only associated with demonstration portions of the website. Typically, if the website offers anything of commercial value, registration and some sort of validation of the end user is required to access the most useful parts of the website (frequently accompanied by an access charge, either on a "per occurrence" basis or a subscription basis). To be allowed to access such restricted portions of the site, a click-wrap agreement would also be required.

B2B Portal Inc.

Please read these online terms and conditions (the "*Agreement*") carefully. By accessing, using or downloading materials from this website, you agree to be bound by these terms and conditions just as if you had signed this Agreement. If you do not agree to be bound by this Agreement, do not use this website.

B2B Portal Inc., a Delaware corporation (the "*Company*") is the owner of this website (the "*Web Site*"). This Web Site contains information, including all text, graphics, photographs, graphs, sounds, data, images, audio, page headers, software (including HTML and other scripts), buttons, video, and other icons, and the arrangement and compilation of this information (collectively, the "*Information*"), that is either owned or licensed by the Company. The Web Site contains both public and restricted areas. Only persons who have executed a Membership Agreement with the Company and who have been issued a UserID and password ("*Members*") have a license to access the restricted areas of this Web Site (the "*Member Area*"). Areas of the Web Site that are accessible by non-members are called the "*Public Area.*" Your use of this Web Site and access to the Information is expressly conditioned upon your agreement that all such access and use shall be governed by all of the terms and conditions set forth in this Agreement. In addition, access to certain areas of the Web Site may also be governed by other terms and conditions. In the event of a conflict between the terms and conditions set forth below and those necessary to access the Member Area of the Web Site, the ones governing the Member Area of the Web Site will govern your access to such areas and any transactions conducted while in such Member Areas, and these terms and conditions will apply to the public portions of the Web Site or any in any area where there is not a conflicting provision. You hereby acknowledge and agree as follows:

1. License Grant. The Company grants you a worldwide, non-exclusive and non-transferable license to use this Web Site. You may download, view, copy and print the Information incorporated into this Web Site solely for your use, and the Information may not be transferred, shared with or disseminated to any one for any purpose which is inconsistent with the business purpose of the Web Site, or to facilitate unfair competition with the Web Site, or which is inappropriate under applicable US or international law.

2. Use Restrictions. Notwithstanding the foregoing license grant, you may not resell, redistribute, broadcast or transfer the Information or use the Information in a searchable, machine-readable database or file except through the authorized access to the Web Site. Unless separately and specifically authorized in writing by the Company, you may not rent, lease, sublicense, distribute, transfer, copy, reproduce, publicly display, publish, adapt, modify, create derivative works, store or time-share the Web Site, any part thereof, or any of the Information received or accessed via the Web Site to or through any other person or entity. Access to the Member Area without the authorization of the Company is strictly prohibited. You agree to use the Member Area, Web Site, and Information for lawful purposes only. You agree not to post or transmit any information through the Web Site which (1) infringes the rights of others or violates their privacy or publicity rights, (2) is unlawful, threatening, abusive, defamatory, libelous, vulgar, obscene, profane, indecent or otherwise objectionable, (3) is protected by copyright, trademark or other proprietary right without the express written permission of the owner of such right, or (4) which is used to unlawfully collude against another person in restraint of trade and competition. You shall be solely liable for any damages resulting from any infringement of copyright, trademark or other proprietary right, or any other harm resulting from your use of the Web Site or Information.

3. Submissions. You hereby grant to the Company and its affiliates a worldwide, royalty-free, perpetual, irrevocable, non-exclusive right and license to use, reproduce, modify, adapt, publish, translate, create derivative works from, distribute, perform and display any message posted on the Web Site or any e-mail or other materials or Information sent by you to the Company and to incorporate it (in whole or in part) in other works in any form, media or technology now known or later developed.

4. Linking. You may not utilize logos, marks, or other distinctive graphics, video, or audio material in your links, without the Company's express written permission, which the Company may withhold in its discretion. You may not link in any manner reasonably likely to 1) imply affiliation with or endorsement or sponsorship by the Company; 2) cause confusion, mistake, or deception; 3) dilute the Company's trademarks or service marks; or 4) otherwise violate state or federal law. In addition, you may only link to the home page of the Web Site.

5. Modification. The Company reserves the right to modify the terms and conditions of this Agreement. Such modifications may include, without limitation, changes in prices, implementation of user priorities, implementation of rules for use by you, and discontinuance of functional aspects of the Web Site. The Company may also add, withdraw or modify Information within the Web Site or services provided through the Web Site at any time in its sole discretion. All such modifications shall be displayed online, and such display shall constitute effective notice under this Agreement on the day the Company places them on the Web Site. You agree to review the terms and conditions of this Agreement periodically to be aware of such revisions.

6. Password Disclosure. If at any time you are issued a UserID and/or password and you learn or suspect that such identifiers have been disclosed or otherwise made known to any person other than yourself, you agree to immediately notify the Company and to confirm such notice in writing within seventy-two (72) hours. Upon receiving such notice, the Company will assign a new UserID and/or password to you within a reasonable period of time. If your negligence contributed to the disclosure of your UserID or password, then re-issuance and reactivation of such identifiers may be subject to the Company's standard charges.

7. Delays in Services. Neither the Company nor any of its licensors (including its and their officers, directors, employees, affiliates, agents, representatives or subcontractors) shall be liable for any loss or liability resulting, directly or indirectly, from delays or interruptions due to electronic or mechanical equipment failures, telephone interconnect problems, defects, weather, strikes, walkouts, fire, acts of God, riots, armed conflicts, acts of war or other like causes. The Company shall have no responsibility to provide you access to the Web Site while interruption of the Web Site due to any such cause shall continue.

8. Termination. Termination or cancellation of this Agreement shall not affect any right or relief to which the Company may be entitled, at law or in equity. Upon termination of this Agreement, all rights granted to you will terminate and revert to the Company. This Agreement and the license rights granted hereunder shall remain in full force and effect unless terminated or canceled for any of the following reasons; 1) upon thirty (30) days written notice by either party of its intent to terminate this Agreement; 2) immediately by the Company if you fail to make any payment when due; 3) immediately by the Company for any unauthorized access or use by you, including: (i) concurrent access of the Member Area with identical UserIDs; (ii) permitting another person or entity to use your UserID or password to access the Member Area; or (iii) any other access or use of the Member Area except as expressly provided in this Agreement; 4) immediately by the Company if you assign or transfer (or attempt the same) any rights granted to you under this Agreement; 5) immediately by the Company if you fail to abide by the rules and regulations relating to the use of, or tamper with or alter any of the Information contained in, or accessed through, the Web Site; 6) immediately by the Company if you transmit or receive any Information using the Web Site (or cause the same) in violation of this Agreement (the Company, at its sole discretion, shall determine whether any information transmitted or received violates this provision); or 7) immediately by the Company if you violate any of the other terms and conditions of this Agreement.

9. Monitoring. You acknowledge that the Company reserves the right to, and may from time to time, monitor any and all Information transmitted or received through the Web Site. The Company, at its sole discretion and without further notice to you, may (but is not obligated to) review, censor or prohibit the transmission or receipt of any Information which the Company deems inappropriate or that violates any term or condition of this Agreement. During monitoring, Information may be examined, recorded, copied, and used for authorized purposes. Use of the Web Site, authorized or unauthorized, constitutes consent to such monitoring.

10. Equipment and Operation. You shall provide and maintain all telephone and other equipment necessary to access the Web Site, and the costs of any such equipment and/or telephone connections or use, including any applicable taxes or similar fees or charges, shall be borne solely by you. You shall reimburse the Company for any such costs incurred by the Company due to use of the Web Site by you. You are responsible for operating your own equipment and for familiarity with the Information used with or available through the Web Site. The Company reserves the right to refuse assistance or to charge additional fees if you seek assistance from the Company with respect to such Information or any other matters not directly relating to the operation of the Web Site.

11. Limited Warranty. You acknowledge that the Information and links provided through the Web Site are compiled from sources which are beyond the control of the Company. Though such Information is recognized by the parties to be generally reliable, the parties acknowledge that inaccuracies may occur, and that the Company and its licensors do not warrant the accuracy or suitability of the Information. **For this reason, you acknowledge that the Web Site and information are provided to you on an "as is, with all faults" basis. B2B Portal and its licensors expressly disclaim any and all warranties, whether express, oral, implied, statutory or otherwise, including any implied warranty of fitness for a particular purpose or merchantability, any warranties arising by virtue of custom of trade or course of dealing and any implied warranties of title or non-infringement. Further,** B2B Portal and its licensors do not represent or warrant that the Web Site or information will meet your requirements or are suitable for your needs. Under this Agreement, you assume all risk of errors and/or omissions in the Web Site and Information, including the transmission or translation of Information. You hereby assume all responsibility (and thereby hold B2B Portal harmless), by whatever means you deem most appropriate for your needs, for detecting and eradicating any virus or program with a similar function.

12. Limitation of Liability. You assume full responsibility for implementing sufficient procedures and checks to satisfy your requirements for the accuracy and suitability of the Web Site and Information, and for maintaining any means that you may require for the reconstruction of lost data or subsequent manipulations or analyses of the Information provided under this Agreement. **You agree that B2B Portal and its licensors (including its and their officers, directors, employees, affiliates, agents, representatives and subcontractors) shall not in any event be liable for any special, incidental or consequential damages arising out of the use or inability to use the Web Site and information for any purpose whatsoever. If the above limitations of liabilities should fail in their essential purpose for any reason, such liability is and shall be limited to a sum equal in amount to ten (10%) percent of the sums paid to B2B Portal by you under the terms of this Agreement or $100.00, whichever is greater, as limited damages and not as a penalty even if B2B Portal or its affiliates have been advised of the possibility of such damages. This liability shall be complete and exclusive. The provisions contained in this section shall survive termination of this Agreement.**

13. Indemnification. You agree to release, indemnify, defend and hold harmless B2B Portal its licensors and their affiliates, officers, directors, employees, agents and representatives from and against any and all losses, damages, claims, demands, suits, liabilities, fines, penalties and expenses (including reasonable attorney's fees and expenses) (collectively, "claims") of whatever kind, character or nature brought by or on behalf of any person that arise out of, are related to or in connection with this Agreement or your access or use of the Web Site or information, even if caused, in whole or in part, by the joint, sole, or concurrent negligence, willful misconduct, strict liability or other fault, whether passive or active, of any person or entity, including any of the indemnified parties.

14. Privacy. The Company Web Site does not collect any personally identifying information about you except when you expressly provide it. You agree that the Company can use your personal identifying information for editorial, promotional, or marketing purposes, unless you request that your information not be used in such manner. The Company may place a "cookie" in the browser files of your computer. Such cookie does not contain any personally identifying information. Please see our Privacy Policy for more details.

15. No Conflicting Terms. If there is any conflict between this Agreement and any help text, manuals, or other documents, this Agreement shall govern, whether such other documents are prior to or subsequent to this Agreement, or are signed or acknowledged by any employee or representative of the Company; however, this does not apply to any Membership Agreement executed between you and the Company. The terms of executed Membership Agreements will prevail in the event of any conflicting terms.

16. Attorney's Fees. If the Company takes action (by itself or through its representatives) to enforce any of the provisions of this Agreement, including collection of any amounts due hereunder, the Company shall be entitled to recover from you (and you agree to pay), in addition to all sums to which it is entitled or any other relief, at law or in equity, reasonable and necessary attorney's fees and any costs of any litigation.

17. Governing Law; Limitations; Venue. The laws of the State of New York, excluding any rule or principle that would refer to and apply the substantive law of another state or jurisdiction, shall govern this Agreement. To the extent allowed by applicable law, any claims or causes of action arising from or relating to your access and use of the Web Site or Information contemplated by this Agreement must be instituted within two (2) years from the date upon which such claim or cause arose or was accrued. Further, any such claim or cause of action may only be brought in the state or federal courts located in Houston, Harris County, Texas, and you agree to submit to the exclusive personal jurisdiction of such courts and hereby appoint the Secretary of State of Texas as your agent for service of process.

18. Severability. Whenever possible, each provision of this Agreement shall be interpreted in such manner as to be effective and valid under applicable law, but if any provision of this Agreement shall be prohibited or invalid under applicable law, such provision shall be ineffective to the extent of such prohibition or invalidity without invalidating the remainder of such provision or the remaining provisions of this Agreement. Any unenforceable provision will be replaced by a provision that comes closest to the intention of the parties at the time the original provision was agreed upon.

19. U.S. Government Restricted Rights. The Information on this Web Site is provided with "RESTRICTED RIGHTS." Use, duplication or disclosure by the Government is subject to restrictions as set forth in applicable laws and regulations. Use of the materials by the Government constitutes acknowledgement of the Company's proprietary rights in them.

20. Copyright, Patent and Trademark Notice. All rights reserved. The Web Site and Information is the valuable, exclusive property of the Company or its licensors and nothing in this Agreement shall be construed as transferring or assigning any such ownership rights to you or any other person or entity. Contract law and various intellectual property laws protect the Information, including domestic and international copyright laws. Except as permitted in this Agreement, you may not copy, adapt, distribute, commercially exploit, or publicly display the Information or any portion thereof in any manner whatsoever without the Company's prior written consent. You may not remove, alter or obscure any copyright, legal or proprietary notices in or on any portions of the Information. The Company, and its associated logos, and all page headers, custom graphics, buttons, and other icons are service marks, trademarks, registered service marks, or registered trademarks of B2B Portal Inc. All other product names and company logos mentioned on the Web Site or Information are trademarks of their respective owners.

21. Notice and Procedure for Copyright Infringement Claim. The Company, pursuant to 17 U.S.C. Section 512 as amended by Title II of the Digital Millennium Copyright Act (the "Act"), reserves the right, but not the obligation, to terminate your license to use the Web Site or Information if it determines in its sole and absolute discretion that you are involved in infringing activity, including alleged acts of first-time or repeat infringement, regardless of whether the material or activity is ultimately determined to be infringing. The Company accommodates and does not interfere with standard technical measures used by copyright owners to protect their materials. In addition, pursuant to 17 U.S.C. Section 512(c), the Company has implemented procedures for receiving written notification of claimed infringements and for processing such claims in accordance with the Act. The Company's designated agent to receive notification of claimed infringement is:

Grace Note
contactus@b2bportal.com
B2B Portal Inc.
600 Travis Street,
Suite 3400,
Houston, TX 77042, USA,
Phone: (+1) 888-555-1111

In addition, any written notice regarding any defamatory or infringing activity, whether of a copyright, patent, trademark or other proprietary right, should be sent to the Company-designated agent, listed above, and must include the following information:

A. A physical or electronic signature of a person authorized to act on behalf of (1) the owner of an exclusive right that is allegedly infringed or (2) the person defamed.

B. Identification of the copyrighted work claimed to have been infringed, or, if multiple copyrighted works at a single online site are covered by a single notification, a representative list of such works at that site. Similarly, for other types of infringing materials, a list of such materials.

C. Identification of the material that is claimed to be infringing, to be the subject of infringing activity, or that is claimed to be defamatory and that is to be removed or access to which is to be disabled, and information reasonably sufficient to permit the Company to locate the material.

D. Information reasonably sufficient to permit the Company to contact you, such as your address, telephone number, and/or electronic mail address.

E. A statement that you have a good faith belief that use of the material in the manner complained of is not authorized by the copyright or other proprietary right owner, its agent, or the law.

F. A statement that the information in the notification is accurate, and under penalty of perjury, that you are authorized to act on behalf of the owner of an exclusive right that is allegedly infringed or on behalf of the person defamed.

22. Assignments. You may not assign any of your rights, obligations, privileges, or performance hereunder without the prior written consent of the Company, which the Company may withhold or grant in its sole discretion. Any assignment by you other than as provided for in this Section 22 shall be null and void, *ab initio*.

23. Entire Agreement. This Agreement is complete and effective at the time you agree to it by accessing or using the Web Site or information. This Agreement constitutes the entire agreement between the parties, and no other agreement, written or oral, exists between you and the Company.

PASSIVE TERMS OF USE

submitted by John S. "Chip" Rainey of
Locke Liddell & Sapp LLP (United States)

Note: The following terms of service are designed for use on websites where access is provided to the public without charge (although for certain services there may be a requirement for registration or fee). These terms of service do not require an active click-through acceptance of the terms, since they may change frequently, and no attempt is made to verify the identity of the person registering on the site. These terms of service are for consumer-oriented websites and are not for use on B2B websites.

USER AGREEMENT

1. ACCEPTANCE OF TERMS

You may use any of the Services of DotComCo accessed through this website upon your completion of a registration (see Section 3), but your use of any of these Services are subject to the following terms of this agreement (the "*User Agreement*"), which may be updated by us from time to time without notice to you, by our posting the changes in a special section of our website, and us providing a link to the changes on the home page of the website. You can review the most current version of the User Agreement at any time at: http://docs.DotComCo.com/info/terms/. In addition, when using particular DotComCo owned or operated services, you and DotComCo will be subject to any guidelines or rules applicable to such services which are then in effect, as posted on this website from time to time. All such guidelines or rules are hereby incorporated by reference into the User Agreement. Your use of any Service on any day constitutes an acceptance of all of the terms in the User Agreement posted on the website on such day.

2. DESCRIPTION OF SERVICES

DotComCo provides through this website access to [description of information content or transactional capability, expressed generally] for registered users (the "*Services*"). The Services may include advertisements and you agree that such advertisements are necessary for DotComCo to provide the Services cost effectively. You also agree that the Services may, from time to time, include electronic communications from DotComCo, such as infrequent service announcements and administrative messages. You agree to accept such communications as part of DotComCo membership and you will not be able to opt out of receiving them, in part because they may contain information necessary for your continued effective use of the website. There also may be other electronic communications such as newsletters regarding specific topics that you may be able to opt out of their receipt. Unless explicitly stated otherwise, any new features that augment or enhance the current Services, including the release of new functionality, shall be subject to this User Agreement.

The Services may require use of data and information compiled from sources whom DotComCo does not control and whose information has not been independently investigated or verified. As more fully explained in Section 17, You agree that all Services are and will be provided "**AS-IS**" and that DotComCo shall have no responsibility for the timeliness, deletion, or misdelivery of any communications, for the failure to store any user communications or personalization settings, or to investigate the accuracy of the content obtained from third parties. You are solely responsible for obtaining access to the Internet to access the Service and such Internet access may involve third party fees (such as Internet service provider or airtime charges). Unless we have agreed in a separate agreement to obtain access for you to the Internet, DotComCo will not be responsible for any of those fees, including any fees based on the volume of content delivered or airtime, notwithstanding that some or a substantial part of such content or airtime may be used for the display or delivery of advertisements. In addition, you must provide and are responsible for all equipment and software necessary to access the Service.

If any area is designated by a warning that is an adult area or contains mature content, you must be at least 18 years of age to access and view such areas.

3. REGISTRATION

By using the Service and completing the registration profile, you represent that you are of legal age to form a binding contract and are not a person barred from receiving services under the laws of the United States or other applicable jurisdiction. You also agree to: (a) provide true, accurate, current and complete information about yourself as prompted by the Service's registration form (such information being the "Registration Data") and (b) maintain and promptly update the Registration Data to keep it true, accurate, current and complete. If you provide any information that is untrue, inaccurate, not current or incomplete, or DotComCo has reasonable grounds to suspect that such information is untrue, inaccurate, not current or incomplete, DotComCo has the right to suspend or terminate your account and refuse any and all current or future use of the Service (or any portion thereof).

4. MEMBER ACCOUNT, PASSWORD AND SECURITY

You will receive a UserID and password once you register for the Services. You will also be required to click through an agreement that will show your agreement to be bound by the terms and conditions of the registration process. You are responsible for maintaining the confidentiality of the UserID and password, and you will be fully responsible for all activities that occur under your UserID or password. You agree to (a) immediately notify DotComCo of any unauthorized use of your UserID or password, and (b) exit from your account at the end of each session. You will solely be liable for any loss or damage arising from your failure to comply with this Section 4.

5. MEMBER CONDUCT

All text, graphics, photographs, graphs, sounds, data, images, audio, page headers, software (including HTML and other scripts), buttons, video, and other icons, and the arrangement and compilation of this information (collectively, the "***Information***"), whether publicly posted or privately transmitted, are the sole responsibility of the person from which such Information originated. This means that you, and not DotComCo, are entirely responsible for all Information that you upload, post, e-mail, transmit or otherwise make available via the Service. DotComCo does not control the Information posted via the Service and, as such, does not guarantee the accuracy, integrity or quality of such Information. You understand that by using the Service, you may be exposed to Information that is offensive, indecent or objectionable. Under no circumstances will DotComCo be liable in any way for any Information, including, but not limited to, for any errors or omissions in any Information, or for any loss or damage of any kind incurred as a result of the use of any Information posted, e-mailed, transmitted or otherwise made available via the Service.

You agree to not use the Service to:

a. upload, post, e-mail, transmit or otherwise make available any Information that is unlawful, harmful, threatening, abusive, harassing, tortuous, defamatory, vulgar, obscene, libelous, invasive of another's privacy, hateful, or racially, ethnically or otherwise objectionable;

b. harm minors in any way;

c. impersonate any person or entity, including, but not limited to, a DotComCo official, or falsely state or otherwise misrepresent your affiliation with a person or entity;

d. forge headers or otherwise manipulate identifiers in order to disguise the origin of any Information transmitted through the Service;

e. upload, post, e-mail, transmit or otherwise make available any Information that you do not have a right to make available under any law or contract (including anything that would be considered to be inside information under securities law, or that is the proprietary and confidential information of anyone else);

f. upload, post, e-mail, transmit or otherwise make available any Information that infringes any patent, trademark, trade secret, copyright, likeness, personality or other proprietary rights ("Intellectual Property Rights") of any party;

g. upload, post, e-mail, transmit or otherwise make available any unsolicited or unauthorized advertising, promotional materials, "spam," "pyramid schemes," or any other form of solicitation, except in those areas that are designated for such purpose;

h. upload, post, e-mail, transmit or otherwise make available any material that contains software viruses or any other computer code, files or programs designed to interrupt, destroy or limit the functionality of any computer software or hardware or telecommunications equipment;

i. interfere with or disrupt the Service or servers or networks connected to the Service, or disobey any requirements, procedures, policies or regulations of networks connected to the Service;

j. violate any applicable local, state, national or international law, including, but not limited to, US or state securities law or any regulations promulgated under such laws, any rules of any national or regional stock or other securities exchange, and any other regulations having the force of law;

k. "stalk" or otherwise harass another; or

l. collect or store personal data about other users.

You acknowledge that DotComCo and its designees shall have the right (but not the obligation) in their sole discretion to pre-screen, refuse, or move any Information that is available via the Service. Without limiting the foregoing, DotComCo and its designees shall have the right to remove any Information that violates the User Agreement or is otherwise objectionable. You bear all risks associated with the use of any Information, including any reliance on the accuracy, completeness, or usefulness of such Information.

You acknowledge, consent and agree that DotComCo may access, preserve, and disclose your account information and any Information you post via the Services if required to do so by law or in good faith to: (a) comply with legal process; (b) enforce the User Agreement; (c) respond to claims that any Information violates the rights of third-parties; (d) respond to your requests for customer service; or (e) protect the rights, property, or personal safety of DotComCo, its users and the public.

You understand that the technical processing and transmission of the Service, including your Information, may involve (a) transmissions over various networks; and (b) changes to conform and adapt to technical requirements of connecting networks or devices.

You understand that the Service and software embodied within the Service may include security components that permit digital materials to be protected, and use of these materials is subject to usage rules set by DotComCo and/or content providers who provide Information to the Service. You may not attempt to override or circumvent any of the usage rules embedded into the Service. Any unauthorized reproduction, publication, further distribution or public exhibition of the materials provided on the Service, in whole or in part, is strictly prohibited.

6. DOTCOMCO PRIVACY POLICY

Registration Data and certain other information about you are subject to our Privacy Policy. For more information, see our full privacy policy at http://docs.DotComCo.com/privacy/. DotComCo is particularly concerned about the safety and privacy of children. For this reason, parents or legal guardians of children under the age of 18 who wish to allow their children access to the Service must create a separate DotComCo Family Account. When you create a DotComCo Family Account and add your child to the account, you certify that you are at least 18 years old and that you are the parent or legal guardian of the child/children listed on the DotComCo Family Account. By adding a child to your DotComCo Family Account, you are giving DotComCo permission to allow your child to access all of the Services including, e-mail, message boards, instant messages and chat (among others). Please remember that the Service is designed to appeal to a broad audience. Accordingly, as the parent legal guardian, it is your responsibility to determine whether any of the Services and/or Information (as defined in Section 6 below) is appropriate for your child. Not all portions of the Services that may be accessed via a DotComCo Family Account are appropriate for all children

7. SPECIAL ADMONITIONS FOR INTERNATIONAL USE

Recognizing the global nature of the Internet, you agree to comply with all local rules regarding online conduct and acceptable Information. Specifically, you agree to comply with all applicable laws regarding the transmission of technical data exported from the United States or the country in which you reside.

8. INFORMATION SUBMITTED OR MADE AVAILABLE BY YOU

DotComCo does not claim ownership of Information you submit or make available for inclusion on the Service. However, with respect to Information you submit or make available for inclusion on publicly accessible areas of the Service, you grant DotComCo the following worldwide, royalty free and non-exclusive license(s), as applicable:

> With respect to photos, graphics, audio or video you submit or make available for inclusion on publicly accessible areas of the Service, the license to use, distribute, reproduce, modify, adapt, publicly perform and publicly display such Information on the Service. This license exists only for as long as you elect to continue to

include such Information on the Service and will terminate at the time you remove or DotComCo removes such Information from the Service.

With respect to Information other than photos, graphics, audio or video you submit or make available for inclusion on publicly accessible areas of the Service, the perpetual, irrevocable and fully sublicensable license to use, distribute, reproduce, modify, adapt, publish, translate, publicly perform and publicly display and make derivative works of such Information (in whole or in part) in any format or medium now known or later developed.

9. INDEMNITY

You agree to indemnify and hold DotComCo, and its subsidiaries, affiliates, officers, agents, co-branders or other partners, and employees, harmless from any claim or demand, including reasonable attorneys' fees, made by any third party due to or arising out of Information you submit, post, transmit or make available through the Service, your use of the Service, your connection to the Service, your violation of the User Agreement, or your violation of any Intellectual Property Rights of another.

10. NO RESALE OF SERVICE

You agree not to reproduce, duplicate, copy, sell, trade, resell or exploit for any commercial purposes, any portion of the Service (including your DotComCo I.D.), use of the Service, or access to the Service.

11. GENERAL PRACTICES REGARDING USE AND STORAGE

You acknowledge that DotComCo may establish general practices and limits concerning use of the Service, including without limitation the maximum number of days that e-mail messages, message board postings or other uploaded Information will be retained by the Service, the maximum number of e-mail messages that may be sent from or received by an account on the Service, the maximum size of any e-mail message that may be sent from or received by an account on the Service, the maximum disk space that will be allotted on DotComCo's servers on your behalf, and the maximum number of times (and the maximum duration for which) you may access the Service in a given period of time. You agree that DotComCo has no responsibility or liability for the deletion or failure to store any messages and other communications or other Information maintained or transmitted by the Service. You acknowledge that DotComCo reserves the right to log off accounts that are inactive for an extended period of time. You further acknowledge that DotComCo reserves the right to modify these general practices and limits from time to time.

12. MODIFICATIONS TO SERVICE

DotComCo, at any time and from time to time, may modify or discontinue, temporarily or permanently, the Service (or any part thereof) with or without notice.

You agree that DotComCo shall not be liable to you or to any third party for any modification, suspension or discontinuance of the Service.

13. TERMINATION

You agree that DotComCo may, immediately terminate your DotComCo account, any associated e-mail address, and access to the Service for Cause without any notice. Cause for such termination shall include, but not be limited to, (a) breaches or violations of the User Agreement or other incorporated agreements or guidelines, (b) requests by law enforcement or other government agencies, (c) a request by you (self-initiated account deletions), (d) discontinuance or material modification to the Service (or any part thereof), (e) unexpected technical or security issues or problems, and (f) extended periods of inactivity. You agree that all terminations for cause shall be made in DotComCo's sole discretion and that DotComCo shall not be liable to you or any third-party for any termination of your account, any associated e-mail address, or access to the Service.

14. DEALINGS WITH ADVERTISERS

Your correspondence or business dealings with, or participation in promotions of, advertisers found on or through the Service, including payment and delivery of related goods or services, and any other terms, conditions, warranties or representations associated with such dealings, are solely between you and such advertiser. You agree that DotComCo shall not be responsible or liable for any loss or damage of any sort incurred as the result of any such dealings or as the result of the presence of such advertisers on the Service.

15. LINKS

The Service may provide, or third parties may provide, links to other World Wide websites or resources. Because DotComCo has no control over such sites and resources, you acknowledge and agree that DotComCo is not responsible for the availability of such external sites or resources, and does not endorse and is not responsible or liable for any Information, advertising, products, or other materials on or available from such sites or resources. You further acknowledge and agree that DotComCo shall not be responsible or liable, directly or indirectly, for any damage or loss caused or alleged to be caused by or in connection with use of or reliance on any such Information, goods or services available on or through any such site or resource.

16. DOTCOMCO'S PROPRIETARY RIGHTS

You acknowledge and agree that the Service and any necessary software used in connection with the Service ("Software") contain proprietary and confidential information and embody the Intellectual Property Rights of DotComCo that is protected by applicable intellectual property and other laws. You further acknowledge and agree that Information contained in sponsor advertisements or copyrights, trademarks, service marks, patents or other proprietary rights and laws protect information presented to you through the Service or advertisers. Except as expressly authorized by DotComCo or advertisers, you agree not to modify, rent, lease, loan, sell, distribute or create derivative works based on the Service or the Software, in whole or in part.

DotComCo grants you a personal, non-transferable and non-exclusive right and license to use the object code of its Software on a single computer; provided that you do not (and do not allow any third party to) copy, modify, create a derivative work of, reverse engineer, reverse assemble or otherwise attempt to discover any source code, sell, assign, sublicense, grant a security interest in or otherwise transfer any right in the Software. You agree not to modify the Software in any manner or form, or to use modified versions of the Software, including (without limitation) for the purpose of obtaining unauthorized access to the Service. You agree not to access the Service by any means other than through the interface that is provided by DotComCo for use in accessing the Service.

17. DISCLAIMER OF WARRANTIES

YOU AGREE THAT:

a. YOUR USE OF THE SERVICE IS AT YOUR SOLE RISK. THE SERVICE IS PROVIDED ON AN "AS IS" AND "AS AVAILABLE" BASIS. DOTCOMCO EXPRESSLY DISCLAIMS ALL WARRANTIES OF ANY KIND, WHETHER EXPRESS OR IMPLIED, INCLUDING, BUT NOT LIMITED TO THE IMPLIED WARRANTIES OF MERCHANTABILITY, FITNESS FOR A PARTICULAR PURPOSE, TITLE AND NON-INFRINGEMENT.

b. DOTCOMCO MAKES NO WARRANTY THAT (i) THE SERVICE WILL MEET YOUR REQUIREMENTS, (ii) THE SERVICE WILL BE UNINTERRUPTED, TIMELY, SECURE, OR ERROR-FREE, (iii) THE RESULTS THAT MAY BE OBTAINED FROM THE USE OF THE SERVICE WILL BE ACCURATE OR RELIABLE, (iv) THE QUALITY OF ANY PRODUCTS, SERVICES, INFORMATION, OR OTHER MATERIAL PURCHASED OR OBTAINED BY YOU THROUGH THE SERVICE WILL MEET YOUR EXPECTATIONS, AND (V) ANY ERRORS IN THE SOFTWARE WILL BE CORRECTED.

c. ANY MATERIAL DOWNLOADED OR OTHERWISE OBTAINED THROUGH THE USE OF THE SERVICE IS DONE AT YOUR OWN DISCRETION AND RISK. DOTCOMCO MAKES NO WARRANTY THAT ANY MATERIAL DOWNLOADED IS FREE OF ANY VIRUS, WORM, SPYWARE OR OTHER HARMFUL SOFTRWARE. YOU WILL BE SOLELY RESPONSIBLE FOR ANY DAMAGE TO YOUR COMPUTER SYSTEM OR LOSS OF DATA THAT RESULTS FROM THE DOWNLOAD OF ANY SUCH MATERIAL. OBTAIN AND MAINTAIN EFFECTIVE ANTI-VIRUS SOFTWARE.

d. NO ADVICE OR INFORMATION, WHETHER ORAL OR WRITTEN, OBTAINED BY YOU FROM DOTCOMCO OR THROUGH OR FROM THE SERVICE SHALL CREATE ANY WARRANTY NOT EXPRESSLY STATED IN THE USER AGREEMENT.

SOME JURISDICTIONS DO NOT ALLOW THE EXCLUSION OF IMPLIED WARRANTIES, SO THE ABOVE EXCLUSION MAY NOT APPLY TO YOU.

18. LIMITATION OF LIABILITY

YOU EXPRESSLY UNDERSTAND AND AGREE THAT DOTCOMCO SHALL NOT BE LIABLE TO YOU FOR ANY DIRECT, INDIRECT, INCIDENTAL, SPECIAL, CONSEQUENTIAL OR EXEMPLARY DAMAGES, INCLUDING BUT NOT LIMITED TO, DAMAGES FOR LOSS OF PROFITS, GOODWILL, USE, DATA OR OTHER INTANGIBLE LOSSES (EVEN IF DOTCOMCO HAS BEEN ADVISED OF THE POSSIBILITY OF SUCH DAMAGES), RESULTING FROM: (i) THE USE OR THE INABILITY TO USE THE SERVICE; (ii) THE COST OF PROCUREMENT OF SUBSTITUTE GOODS AND SERVICES RESULTING FROM ANY GOODS, DATA, INFORMATION OR SERVICES PURCHASED OR OBTAINED OR MESSAGES RECEIVED OR TRANSACTIONS ENTERED INTO THROUGH OR FROM THE SERVICE; (iii) UNAUTHORIZED ACCESS TO OR ALTERATION OF YOUR TRANSMISSIONS OR DATA; (iv) STATEMENTS OR CONDUCT OF ANY THIRD PARTY ON THE SERVICE; OR (v) ANY OTHER MATTER RELATING TO THE SERVICE.

SOME JURISDICTIONS DO NOT ALLOW THE LIMITATION OR EXCLUSION OF LIABILITY FOR INCIDENTAL OR CONSEQUENTIAL DAMAGES, SO THE ABOVE LIMITATION OR EXCLUSION MAY NOT APPLY TO YOU.

19. NOTICE

DotComCo may provide you with notices, including those regarding changes to the User Agreement, by either e-mail, regular mail, or postings on the Service. You expressly agree to accept notice by any of those methods, and that you will keep DotComCo informed of your current valid e-mail address. **CHECK YOUR E-MAIL ADDRESS FREQUENTLY SO YOU DO NOT MISS ANY NOTICES FROM DOTCOMCO OR CHANGES TO THIS AGREEMENT**.

20. TRADEMARK INFORMATION

The DotComCo logo, trademarks and service marks and other marks that are, from time to time, used by DotComCo as a logo or for product and service names are trademarks of DotComCo Inc. (the "*DotComCo Marks*"). Without DotComCo's prior permission, which DotComCo is under no obligation to provide, you agree not to display or use in any manner, the DotComCo Marks.

21. NOTICE AND PROCEDURE FOR MAKING CLAIMS OF COPYRIGHT OR INTELLECTUAL PROPERTY INFRINGEMENT

DotComCo respects the Intellectual Property Rights of others, and we ask our users to do the same. DotComCo may, in appropriate circumstances and at its discretion, disable and/or terminate the accounts of users who appear to be infringers. If you believe that your work has been copied in a way that constitutes copyright infringement, or your intellectual property rights have been otherwise violated, please provide DotComCo's Copyright Agent the following information:

1. an electronic or physical signature of the person authorized to act on behalf of the owner of the copyright or other intellectual property interest;
2. a description of the copyrighted work or other intellectual property that you claim has been infringed;
3. a description of where the material that you claim is infringing is located on the site;
4. your address, telephone number, and e-mail address;
5. a statement by you that you have a good faith belief that the disputed use is not authorized by the copyright owner, its agent, or the law;
6. a statement by you, made under penalty of perjury, that the above information in your Notice is accurate and that you are the copyright or intellectual property owner or authorized to act on the copyright or intellectual property owner's behalf.

DotComCo's Agent for Notice of claims of copyright or other intellectual property infringement can be reached as follows:

By mail:
[Name:]
c/o DotComCo Inc.
1000 Main Street
Anywhere, State 99999
By phone: (xxx) xxx-xxxx
By fax: (xxx) xxx-xxxx
By e-mail: copyright@DotComCo.com

22. GENERAL INFORMATION

No Third Party Beneficiaries. Except as otherwise expressly provided in this User Agreement, this User Agreement is intended solely for the benefit of You and Dotcom Co, and no third party is intended to be able to enforce or otherwise be considered a beneficiary to this User Agreement.

Entire Agreement. The User Agreement constitutes the entire agreement between you and DotComCo and governs your use of the Service, superceding any prior agreements between you and DotComCo. You also may be subject to additional terms and conditions that may apply when you use or purchase certain other DotComCo services, affiliate services, third-party content or third-party software.

Choice of Law and Forum. The User Agreement and the relationship between you and DotComCo shall be governed by the laws of the State of ________________ without regard to its conflict of law provisions. You and DotComCo agree to submit to the personal and exclusive jurisdiction of the courts located within the county of ________________________. This is true even if you live in a different state or country. **DO NOT USE THE SERVICES OR ACCESS THE WEBSITE IF YOU CANNOT AGREE TO THIS CHOICE OF LAW AND FORUM**.

Waiver and Severability of Terms. The failure of DotComCo to exercise or enforce any right or provision of the User Agreement shall not constitute a waiver of such right or provision. If any provision of the User Agreement is found by a court of competent jurisdiction to be invalid, the parties nevertheless agree that the court should endeavor to give effect to the parties' intentions as reflected in the provision, and the other provisions of the User Agreement remain in full force and effect.

No Right of Survivorship and Non-Transferability. You agree that your DotComCo account is non-transferable and any rights to your DotComCo I.D. or Information within your account terminate upon your death. If DotComCo receives a copy of your death certificate, your account may be immediately terminated and all contents therein permanently deleted.

Statute of Limitations. Any claim or cause of action arising out of or related to use of the Service or the User Agreement must be filed within one (1) year after such claim or cause of action arose or be forever barred.

Titles. The section titles in the User Agreement are for convenience only and have no legal or contractual effect.

SAMPLE SHRINK-WRAP LICENSE

submitted by John S. "Chip" Rainey of
Locke Liddell & Sapp LLP (United States)

DEVCO. SHRINK-WRAP LICENSE

IMPORTANT!! READ BEFORE OPENING SOFTWARE ENVELOPE

Note: The Software inside this box is sealed inside a separate envelope. PLEASE READ THIS LICENSE CAREFULLY BEFORE opening that envelope or USING THE SOFTWARE. BY opening that envelope, you are presumed to have used the software, and **by USING THE SOFTWARE, YOU ARE AGREEING TO BE BOUND BY THE TERMS OF THIS LICENSE. This License contains an obligation for you to arbitrate any disputes you have with DevCo.** IF YOU DO NOT AGREE TO THE TERMS OF THIS LICENSE, PROMPTLY RETURN THE UNUSED and unopened SOFTWARE TO THE PLACE WHERE YOU OBTAINED IT with your receipt AND YOUR MONEY WILL BE REFUNDED, if you purchased the software within the last thirty days If you purchased the software more than thirty (30) days ago, but you have not opened the sealed envelope, you may still return the software and receive a credit against the purchase of other software from DevCo.

1. *License.* The software accompanying this License (hereinafter "*Software*"), regardless of the media on which it is distributed, are licensed to you by DevCo Software Company, Inc. ("*VENDOR*"). You own the medium on which the Software is recorded, but VENDOR and VENDOR's Licensors (referred to collectively as "*VENDOR Parties*") retain title to the Software and all related documentation. This license lets you do only the following things:

- Use the Software on a single computer (but if you own for your own use both a desktop and lap top and no other person will be using either machine, you may call us at (888) 555-1111 to register the right to use the software for both machines).
- Make one copy of the Software in machine-readable form for backup purposes only. You must reproduce on such copy the VENDOR's copyright notice and any other proprietary legends that were on the original copy of the Software.
- Transfer all your license rights in the Software, the backup copy of the Software, the related documentation and a copy of this License to another party, provided the other party reads and agrees to accept the terms and conditions

of this License. If you registered a copy for both a lap top and a desktop machine that are personal to you, and you transfer your license rights to the Software, you must stop using and delete the extra copy. **Once you transfer your rights I the software to another person, you may keep no copies.**

2. *Limitations on Use.* The Software contains the copyrighted material of the VENDOR PARTIES, as well as their trade secrets and other proprietary material. In order to protect them, and except as permitted by law, you may not:

- Decompile, reverse engineer, disassemble or otherwise reduce the Software to a human-perceivable form
- Modify, rent, lend, loan, distribute, provide access to (via a network or any type of peer-to-peer arrangement) or create derivative works based upon the Software in whole or in part
- Electronically transmit the Software from one computer to another or over a network.

3. *Termination.* This License is effective until terminated. You may terminate this License at any time by destroying the Software, related documentation and all copies thereof, provided you have not transferred any copy of the software to anyone else. This License will terminate immediately without notice from VENDOR if you fail to comply with any provision of this License. Upon termination, you must destroy the Software, related documentation and all copies thereof.

4. *Export Law Assurance.* You agree that neither the Software nor any other technical data received from VENDOR, nor the direct product thereof, will be exported outside the United States except as authorized and as permitted by the laws and regulations of the United States. If the Software has been rightfully obtained by you outside of the United States, you agree that you will not reexport the Software nor any other technical data received from VENDOR, nor the direct product thereof, except as permitted by the laws and regulations of the United States and the laws and regulations of the jurisdiction in which you obtained the Software.

5. *Government End Users.* If you are acquiring the Software on behalf of any unit or agency of the United States Government, the following provisions apply. The Government agrees:

(i) if the Software is supplied to the Department of Defense (DoD), the Software is classified as "Commercial Computer Software" and the Government is acquiring only "restricted rights" in the Software and its documentation as that term is defined in Clause 252.227-7013(c)(1) of the DFARS; and

(ii) if the Software is supplied to any united or agency of the United States Government other than DoD, the Government's rights in the Software and its documentation will be as defined in Clause 52.227-19(c)(2) of the FAR or, in the case of NASA, in Clause 18-52.227-86(d) of the NASA Supplement to the FAR.

6. *Limited Warranty on Media.* VENDOR warrants the tangible media on which the Software is recorded to be free from defects in materials and workmanship under normal use for a period of ninety (90) days from the date of purchase as evidenced by a copy of the receipt. VENDOR's entire liability and your exclusive remedy will be replacement of the media not meeting VENDOR's limited warranty and which is returned to VENDOR or an VENDOR authorized representative with a copy of the receipt. VENDOR will have no responsibility to replace any media damaged by accident, abuse or misapplication that occurs after the packaging in which the Software is contained leaves the retailer where it was purchased. ANY IMPLIED WARRANTIES ON THE TANGIBLE MEDIA, INCLUDING THE IMPLIED WARRANTIES OF MERCHANTABILITY AND FITNESS FOR A PARTICULAR PURPOSE, ARE LIMITED IN DURATION TO NINETY (90) DAYS FROM THE DATE OF DELIVERY. THIS WARRANTY GIVES YOU SPECIFIC LEGAL RIGHTS, AND YOU MAY ALSO HAVE OTHER RIGHTS WHICH VARY BY JURISDICTION.

7. *Disclaimer of Warranty on Software.* You expressly acknowledge and agree that use of the Software is at your sole risk. The Software and related documentation are provided "AS IS" and without warranty of any kind and VENDOR EXPRESSLY DISCLAIMS ALL WARRANTIES, EXPRESS AND IMPLIED, INCLUDING, BUT NOT LIMITED TO, THE IMPLIED WARRANTIES OF MERCHANTABILITY, TITLE, NONINFRINGEMENT AND FITNESS FOR A PARTICULAR PURPOSE, EVEN IF VENDOR OR VENDOR'S RETAILER OR OTHER AUTHORIZED REPRESENTATIVE KNEW OR HAD REASON TO KNOW OF THE USE YOU INTENDED FOR THE SOFTWARE. VENDOR DOES NOT WARRANT THAT THE FUNCTIONS CONTAINED IN THE SOFTWARE WILL MEET YOUR REQUIREMENTS, OR THAT THE OPERATION OF THE SOFTWARE WILL BE UNINTERRUPTED OR ERROR-FREE, OR THAT DEFECTS IN THE SOFTWARE WILL BE CORRECTED BY VENDOR. THE ENTIRE RISK AS TO THE RESULTS AND PERFORMANCE OF THE SOFTWARE IS ASSUMED BY YOU. FURTHERMORE, VENDOR DOES NOT WARRANT OR MAKE ANY REPRESENTATIONS REGARDING THE USE OR THE RESULTS OF THE USE OF THE SOFTWARE OR RELATED DOCUMENTATION AS TO THEIR CORRECTNESS, ACCURACY, RELIABILITY, CURRENTNESS, OR OTHERWISE. NO ORAL, WRITTEN OR ELECTRONICALLY-POSTED INFORMATION GIVEN BY VENDOR OR VENDOR'S AUTHORIZED REPRESENTATIVE SHALL CREATE A WARRANTY OR IN ANY WAY INCREASE THE SCOPE OF THIS WARRANTY. SHOULD THE SOFTWARE PROVE DEFECTIVE, YOU (AND NOT VENDOR OR VENDOR'S AUTHORIZED REPRESENTATIVE) ASSUME THE ENTIRE COST OF ALL NECESSARY SERVICING, REPAIR OR CORRECTION. SOME JURISDICTIONS DO NOT ALLOW THE EXCLUSION OF IMPLIED WARRANTIES, SO THE ABOVE EXCLUSION MAY NOT APPLY TO YOU.

8. *Limitation of Liability.* UNDER NO CIRCUMSTANCES INCLUDING NEGLIGENCE, SHALL VENDOR, OR ITS DIRECTORS, OFFICERS, EMPLOYEES OR AGENTS, BE LIABLE TO YOU FOR ANY INCIDENTAL, INDIRECT, SPECIAL OR CONSEQUENTIAL DAMAGES (INCLUDING DAMAGES FOR LOSS OF BUSINESS PROFITS, BUSINESS INTERRUPTION, LOSS OF BUSINESS INFORMATION, AND THE LIKE) ARISING OUT OF THE USE, MISUSE OR INABILITY TO USE THE SOFTWARE OR RELATED DOCUMENTATION, EVEN IF VENDOR OR VENDOR'S AUTHORIZED REPRESENTATIVE HAS BEEN ADVISED OF THE POSSIBILITY OF SUCH DAMAGES. SOME JURISDICTIONS DO NOT ALLOW THE LIMITATION OR EXCLUSION OF LIABILITY FOR INCIDENTAL OR CONSEQUENTIAL DAMAGES, SO THE ABOVE LIMITATION OR EXCLUSION MAY NOT APPLY TO YOU. In no event shall VENDOR's total liability to you for all damages, losses, and causes of action (whether in contract, tort (including negligence) or otherwise) exceed the amount paid by you for the Software.

9. *Controlling Law and Severability.* This License shall be governed by and construed in accordance with the laws of the United States and the substantive laws of the State of Texas as if the entire agreement was to be entered into and performed in Texas, regardless of where you acquired the Software. If for any reason a court of competent jurisdiction finds any provision of this License or portion thereof, to be unenforceable, that provision of the License shall be enforced to the maximum extent permissible so as to effect the intent of the parties, and the remainder of this License shall continue in full force and effect.

10. *Arbitration.* Should any dispute ever arise between you and VENDOR arising out of or related to this Agreement, including any dispute regarding the enforceability of this arbitration provision, you agree that you will submit all such disputes, and any claims, causes of action or demands for damages to binding, mandatory arbitration before a single arbitrator, pursuant to the Federal Arbitration Act, or any applicable state law in the event the Federal Arbitration Act is held not to govern the arbitration in question. If you reside in the United States, the arbitration will occur in the city nearest to where you live that has an office of the American Arbitration Association (AAA), but the AAA shall not administer this arbitration, unless the parties are not able to agree on an arbitrator. If you reside outside the United States, then the arbitration shall be conducted in New York City. VENDOR shall pay for the cost of the arbitrator and other administrative costs of the arbitration, unless the arbitrator finds that you brought the demand for arbitration in bad faith or just to cause VENDOR to incur such costs, in which case, the arbitrator shall assess all of the administrative costs of the arbitration against you. Each Party shall pay the costs of its own attorneys and any witnesses presented. The parties agree to work together in good faith to nominate a neutral retired judge living in or near the appropriate city to serve as the arbitrator. The parties agree that (a) the arbitration will be conducted in accordance with the rules of the AAA, and the supplemental procedures to be

used in consumer disputes, (b) the arbitration will be conducted in English, (c) the arbitrator's decision and any award shall be I writing and (d) all results of the arbitration shall be kept confidential by all parties.

11. *Complete Agreement.* This License constitutes the entire agreement between the parties with respect to the use of the Software and the related documentation, and supersedes all prior or contemporaneous understandings or agreements, written or oral, regarding such subject matter. No amendment to or modification of this License will be binding unless in writing and signed by a duly authorized representative of VENDOR.

STRATEGIES FOR EFFECTIVE ASSENT TO CLICK-WRAP AGREEMENTS

submitted by John S. "Chip" Rainey of
Locke Liddell & Sapp LLP (United States)

Obtaining Valid Assent: Practice Tips and Checklist

1. Make sure that the agreement is fair.—the more onerous the terms, the more likely a court is to require clear evidence of assent.

2. Permit and encourage the entire agreement to be read before requiring the user to register assent:

   a. Do not put the agreement in a pop-up window that may be difficult for the user to retrieve, especially if the pop-up window is separate from the box or button clicked that evidences assent

   b. In large print, include the words,

      YOU MUST READ OUR USER AGREEMENT AND CLICK THAT YOU AGREE TO ITS TERMS BEFORE CONTINUING

   c. Make sure the website is engineered so that the user may not continue, or make the purchase, unless they have actually clicked the required assent.

3. Permit a mechanism for the user to indicate no assent. Sometimes, users get confused if the only button displayed is one that says "I Agree" or similar words, and do not realize that they still retain the option of leaving the website in question without clicking the assent. Do not design the website so that the user is precluded from leaving the site without accepting the terms and conditions of the agreement. Preferable would be two buttons, one that says "I Agree" and one that says "I Don't Agree." Avoid ambiguous terms on the button like "Continue" or "Next Page."

4. Make certain that the language immediately above or next to the button to be clicked to register assent is unambiguous—that by clicking the assent, the user is bound by all of the terms of the agreement. This language should be set off from the terms and conditions and the other language on the page.

5. If the document contains a requirement for mandatory arbitration, this should also be noted in unambiguous language in bold or enlarged print, immediately above or next to the button to be clicked for assent.

6. Permit the user to print a copy of the agreement to which they are assenting. An effective way to do this is to use three buttons at the bottom of a page, such as:

[I Agree] [Print] [I Decline]

7. Make certain that your database of end users includes the following fields: date of assent; method of assent; version of contract assented to.

8. Send e-mail confirmation after assent, with a copy of the terms and conditions and a reminder that the use of the website or the software is subject to such terms and conditions.

9. If the click-wrap is for the download of software, include a splash screen each time the software is booted reminding the user that its use is subject to the Terms and Conditions. Better yet, require the user to click "OK" each time before preceding.

10. If the click-wrap is for the use of a non-public website (or non-public portions of a website), include a reminder on the first screen that the user sees that use fo the website is subject to the Terms and Conditions.

11. If the click-wrap is for the use of a non-public website (or non-public portions of a website), prevent any ability to access such location except through a page that contains the above reminder and a hyperlink that permits the user to see the terms.

12. If the terms are ever amended, require full assent again before allowing the user to proceed. Alternatively, you may use e-mail notice *if* your terms and conditions expressly allow for the agreement to be amended by e-mail notice, you provide the end user an adequate time to read the new terms before their effective date, and your agreement expressly provides that continued use after such amendment constitutes acceptance of the terms.

13. Make certain that the website is internally consistent, so that there is not any information in an FAQ or otherwise on the website that contradicts the Terms and Conditions set out in the user agreement.

GUIDELINES FOR ONLINE CLICK AGREEMENTS

submitted by Vicente B. Amador of
SyCip Salazar Hernandez & Gatmaitan (Philippines)

The following procedure on click-through agreements will help ensure compliance with applicable legal requirements in the Philippines.

1. The text of the online Agreement should be displayed to the user;

2. The user should not be permitted to click on the accept button without affording him the opportunity to review the entire agreement;

3. The font size should be readable;

4. All substantive terms should be visible and complete without hyperlinks to access additional terms;

5. The user should read the agreement at his own pace and should have the ability to browse through and to view all the terms of the agreement;

6. The wordings of all notices and disclaimers should be conspicuous to the user;

7. Accept/Decline buttons must be at the end of the agreement;

8. The buttons should clearly state "Accept/Decline" ;

9. The customer must accept the agreement by clicking on the "Accept" button before being given access to the subject product or service;

10. The customer's clicking on the "Decline" button should immediately deny him access to the product or service;

11. The customer should be have an online form confirmation page of his Order and an opportunity to correct any errors prior to clicking the "Accept" or "Decline" buttons;

12. Records retained by the Provider of the product or service must include: (1) the procedure the user had to express his assent; (2) the version of the agreement in effect at the time of the transaction; (3) the customer's identifying personal information; (4) his electronic assent; and (5) full-text copies of each version.

13. Directly above the Accept/Decline buttons, there should be a standard notice of consequences of accepting/declining the terms:

> PLEASE READ THE TERMS AND CONDITIONS OF THIS AGREEMENT CAREFULLY. BY CLICKING ON THE "ACCEPT" BUTTON, BELOW, YOU ACCEPT THE TERMS AND CONDITIONS OF THIS AGREEMENT WHEN YOU CLICK THE "ACCEPT" BUTTON. IF YOU DO NOT ACCEPT ALL THESE TERMS, CLICK ON THE "DECLINE" BUTTON AT THE END OF THIS AGREEMENT. IF YOU CLICK ON THE "DECLINE" BUTTON, YOU WILL HAVE NO ACCESS TO PRODUCT OR SERVICE.

I Accept

I Decline

COMMERCIAL DISPUTE RESOLUTION PROCEDURES

submitted by John S. "Chip" Rainey of
Locke Liddell & Sapp LLP (United States)

(Administered Arbitrators)

A. *Exclusive Dispute Resolution Procedures*. The procedures specified in this Annex shall be the sole and exclusive procedures for the resolution of any controversy, dispute, disagreement or claim between the Parties arising out of or relating to this Agreement, including any question concerning the Agreement's existence, validity, termination, interpretation, performance or enforcement ("Dispute") for the validity and enforceability of these dispute resolution procedures.

B. *Interim Relief.* Nothing herein shall prohibit a Party from obtaining temporary injunctive relief or other provisional judicial relief from the arbitral panel, a referee appointed by [organization administering the arbitration] ("Organization") or any court of competent jurisdiction if necessary to avoid irreparable harm or to preserve the status quo. The arbitral tribunal or referee shall have the authority to award such relief, and any award of such relief shall be enforced as an award final as to its terms until the arbitrators vacate, modify or make permanent such relief.

C. *Rules*. Any arbitration shall be conducted according to the Organization's Commercial Rules of Arbitration (the "Rules"), subject to the provisions set forth in this Annex. In the event of a conflict between the Rules and the provisions of this Annex, this Annex shall govern.

D. *Procedural Law*. The validity of this Annex, the conduct of the arbitration proceedings, and the enforcement of any award shall be determined under, conducted in accordance with and governed by The United States Federal Arbitration Act, Title 9 USC Section 1 et seq.

E. *Submission to Jurisdiction*. Each Party irrevocably submits to the jurisdiction of the Organization with respect to any Dispute, including any action related to this Annex or any award rendered pursuant to this Annex, and the parties expressly waive any defense in such action based on lack of personal jurisdiction, improper venue or forum nonconveniens.

F. *Language*. Negotiations, mediations and arbitrations shall be conducted in the English language.

G. *Negotiation*. Any Dispute shall first be discussed in good faith between senior executives of each Party who shall have authority to settle such Dispute ("Senior Executives"), who shall meet in New York, New York, U.S.A. or other mutually agreed place in order to attempt in good faith to find an amicable solution within thirty (30) days after receipt of notice from either Party that a Dispute exists.

H. *Binding Arbitration*. If the Parties are unable to resolve the Dispute through mediation under the procedure described in Paragraph H, then such Dispute shall be referred to the Organization, through its officers located in ___________________________.

I. *Consolidation*. If any Dispute is submitted to arbitration, all then current Disputes (including counterclaims) between the Parties shall be consolidated in a single arbitration proceeding. Any party to the arbitration shall be entitled to join in any arbitration initiated under this Annex any Person who is not a Party to this agreement if (a) the Person agrees to resolve the specified dispute pursuant to the procedures set forth in this Annex, and (b) the arbitral panel determines, upon application of the Party seeking joinder, that the joinder of such Person will promote efficiency, expedition, and consistency of the result and will not unfairly prejudice any other Party.

J. *Notices*. With respect to the initial appearance of the Parties in the arbitration proceeding and with respect to the arbitral awards, notification thereof shall be made to the Parties by personal delivery at the addresses indicated in the Notices provision of the Agreement, unless the law of the place of notification permits another form of notification. All other notifications and communications arising from the arbitral proceedings may be made to the Parties in the manner (including electronic notification) and to the address specified in the Notices provision of the relevant agreement.

K. *Arbitrators*. The number of arbitrators shall be three (unless the Parties agree upon a single mutually acceptable arbitrator) and the arbitrators shall be appointed as follows:

1. The arbitrators shall be fluent in English.

2. Each Party (including its Affiliates joined in such arbitration) shall nominate one independent, impartial and disinterested arbitrator for confirmation by the Organization. If the Organization shall determine that the person nominated by a Party would not be independent, impartial or disinterested according to its rules and criteria, then the Manager of the Organization for its officers located in ___________________________ shall appoint an arbitrator for that Party. If a Party (including its Affiliates joined in such arbitration) fails to nominate an arbitrator within the time period specified by the

Rules, the Manager of the Organization for its officers located in __________________________ shall appoint an arbitrator for that Party.

3. The arbitrators nominated by the Parties shall agree on a third arbitrator, who will act as Chairman of the Arbitral Tribunal. If the two arbitrators fail to reach an agreement on the third arbitrator within thirty (30) days of their confirmation by the Organization, the Manager of the Organization for its officers located in __________________________ shall appoint the third arbitrator, who will act as Chairman of the arbitral tribunal.

L. *Discovery and Experts*. Discovery in any arbitration proceeding shall be conducted in accordance with the then-current Supplementary Rules Governing the Presentation and Reception of Evidence in International Commercial Arbitration of the International Bar Association. At the request of either Party or by the arbitrators, technical issues of fact shall be submitted for resolution in accordance with the Rules by a neutral expert appointed by the Organization after consultation with the Parties.

M. *Duration of Arbitration*. The Parties shall use their best efforts to conclude any arbitral proceeding within one hundred eighty (180) calendar days from the date that the last arbitrator accepts his or her appointment; provided that if the arbitral award is not issued within such one hundred eighty (180) calendar days, then the arbitration proceeding shall continue until an award is made.

N. *Record*. The arbitral tribunal shall arrange for a transcribed record of the arbitral proceedings upon the request of either Party.

O. *Decisions and Awards*. The arbitrators shall issue a reasoned written decision and award based on the terms of the relevant agreements and the governing law specified in the relevant agreement, including any statutes of limitations, but without regard to any provisions of such law respecting choices of laws.

The arbitrators shall have the authority to award specific performance or an injunction to the prevailing Party, and to make an award of damages and interest thereon. **The arbitrators shall have no right to grant, and the Parties hereby waive any right to seek or receive, special, punitive or exemplary damages, or indirect or consequential damages (including lost profit, revenue and prospective business opportunity, even if the losing Party knew of the possibility of such damages) or any damages other than direct damages**. Awards of damages and interest shall be paid in US Dollars, increased by any tax applicable to such award, and made without deduction or offset. All of the expenses that arise from the arbitral proceedings, as well as the fees of the arbitrators, shall be paid by the losing Party, if any, as determined by the arbitrators or otherwise shall be paid as allocated by the arbitrators.

Any award rendered by the arbitrators shall be final, conclusive and binding on the Parties (including their Affiliates and third parties joined in such arbitration) and may be entered and enforced by any court of competent jurisdiction. The Parties agree to exclude, to the fullest extent permitted by law, any right of application or appeal to any court in connection with any question of law arising in the course of the arbitration proceedings or out of any decision or award by the arbitrators. If a decision by the arbitrators is vacated for any reason, the Parties shall submit to a new arbitration of the Dispute in accordance with the procedures set forth in this Annex.

SIMPLIFIED CONSUMER ARBITRATION CLAUSE

submitted by John S. "Chip" Rainey of
Locke Liddell & Sapp LLP (United States)

Arbitration

Should any dispute ever arise between you and VENDOR arising out of or related to this Agreement, including any dispute regarding the enforceability of this arbitration provision, you agree that you will submit all such disputes, and any claims, causes of action or demands for damages to binding, mandatory arbitration before a single arbitrator, pursuant to the Federal Arbitration Act, or any applicable state law in the event the Federal Arbitration Act is held not to govern the arbitration in question. If you reside in the United States, the arbitration will occur in the city nearest to where you live that has an office of the American Arbitration Association (AAA), but the AAA shall not administer this arbitration, unless the parties are not able to agree on an arbitrator. If you reside outside the United States, then the arbitration shall be conducted in New York City. VENDOR shall pay for the cost of the arbitrator and other administrative costs of the arbitration, unless the arbitrator finds that you brought the demand for arbitration in bad faith or just to cause VENDOR to incur such costs, in which case, the arbitrator shall assess all of the administrative costs of the arbitration against you. Each Party shall pay the costs of its own attorneys and any witnesses presented. The parties agree to work together in good faith to nominate a neutral retired judge living in or near the appropriate city to serve as the arbitrator. The parties agree that (a) the arbitration will be conducted in accordance with the rules of the AAA, and the supplemental procedures to be used in consumer disputes, (b) the arbitration will be conducted in English, (c) the arbitrator's decision and any award shall be in writing and (d) all results of the arbitration shall be kept confidential by all parties.

PART 3
GENERAL COMMENTARIES

EFFECTIVE FORMATION OF CONTRACTS BY ELECTRONIC MEANS AND DISPUTE RESOLUTION IN THE NEW E-CONOMY: STILL MORE QUESTIONS THAN ANSWERS[1]

by
Karen Mills, Chartered Arbitrator
J.D., F. C.I.Arb., F. S.I.Arb., F. H.K.I. Arb.
KarimSyah Law Firm

Introduction

As electronic technology evolves it will give rise to as many legal questions as it will solve business problems. Regardless of the extent to which the "new *e-conomy*" really does change the way we do business, it will certainly require the world to seek new paradigms in many facets of the law.

Of course transactions themselves, and the substantive commercial provisions embodied in transactional contracts, have not changed in any material way. What has changed, and will continue to evolve, are primarily the means by which the parties, and their counsel, will communicate in establishing those contracts. There still are, and will continue to be, buyers, sellers, lenders and borrowers just as there will continue to be contracts negotiated and concluded for the purchase of goods and services, financing of assets and projects, issuance and transfer of stocks and bonds, provision and perfection of security, and payment and repayment of principal, interest and other compensation, as well as the failure to make such payments, thereby requiring rights and obligations to be pursued through legal means.

1 Paper prepared for and delivered at the Third Asian Financial Law Conference of the International Bar Association, Asia Pacific Forum at Sydney, Australia, 18-21 November, 2000. [Reproduced with permission.]

In e-commerce, not only are contracting parties not necessarily situate within, or subject to the jurisdiction of, the courts of a single geographical area, but there may be no way to determine exactly WHERE one or more of the parties are situate. Communication through the internet can take any form the transmitting party desires. Letterheads can be created and any name can be affixed to an electronic message so how can one ascertain with certainly WHO is the originator of a communication? Documents transmitted electronically can be edited and revised seamlessly by a recipient, or anyone else having access to such document. How does one determine or, more importantly, prove WHEN an agreement has been reached and WHAT are the terms of that agreement? And what law will apply to that agreement? Or, put another way, what governing body has jurisdiction over that agreement and/or the parties thereto? These are some of the questions which arise when we consider the first of the topics which our illustrious conference organisers have assigned to this writer: how can a contract effectively be formed by electronic means? And one answer will inevitably emerge: electronic commerce can be regulated smoothly, safely and consistently only if there is a single universal framework within which all legal systems will operate.

The Contract

The first question that must be examined is: what constitutes a "contract"?

The basic definition of a contract has generally been considered to be a "meeting of minds".

From a legal point of view, by "contract" we must assume we mean a legal, binding and enforceable contract. The legal force of a contract depends upon the law that governs the contract itself and its enforceability depends upon the law of the place in which one is attempting to enforce it. Although some jurisdictions may require contracts to be in writing to be binding, others, such as Indonesia, theoretically, and subject to certain exceptions, do not.

As Indonesia is the jurisdiction in which I practice, where an issue is discussed in reference to a specific law, I will refer to the law of Indonesia. Setting aside what one reads in the press these days about how law is implemented, or not implemented, in Indonesia, the basic law of obligations is virtually identical to mid-twentieth-century Dutch law[2] and thus is typical of civil law and, for many purposes, not totally unlike common law.

Article 1338 of the Indonesian Civil Code (the "Civil Code") is the basic provision of Indonesian law affording freedom of contract. The Article provides, inter alia, that a contract has the force of law as between or among the parties who have validly and legally entered into it.

---

2 Dutch Laws in force at the time of Indonesia's independence, in 1945, were adopted and, except to the extent subsequently repealed or superseded by new laws, remain in effect.

A contract is legally concluded when it fulfills the required conditions set out in Article 1320 of the Civil Code. Those conditions[3] are:

a. The parties must each have the legal capacity to conclude a contract. All persons are deemed to have such legal capacity except: (i) minors (under 21 years old, unless married[4]) and (ii) persons under official custody[5].

b. The subject matter must be clearly defined. If possible the quality and quantity thereof should be specified[6]. The obligations of each of the parties must be clear.

c. The contract must be for a permissible legal purpose; i.e. no obligation or performance may be contrary to the law, public order or public morality.

d. There must be a meeting of minds, by free consent, without any coercion, error or deceit.

Where there is lack of legal capacity, or of free consent on the part of a party, the contract is voidable and annulment may be requested from the court. In cases of ambiguity about the subject matter or illegal cause, the contract is null and void *ab initio*, and the court must, ex officio, so declare.

A contract which fulfills the requirements mentioned above comes into existence as a legally binding obligation the moment there is an agreement between or among the parties[7] (whether or not the same is in writing) and cannot be terminated unilaterally[8] without judicial intervention.[9] Every contract must be performed in good faith.[10]

Let us, then, examine the questions that arise when a contract is concluded through electronic means, primarily through the internet.

a. Legal Capacity

With traditional contract negotiation the parties are generally known to each other, at least sufficiently for each to determine the approximate age and mental capacity of the other(s). But how does one determine that the person who is making a commitment through the internet does have legal capacity? How does one even determine what constitutes such legal capacity in the jurisdiction to which such party is subject or, in many cases, even what jurisdiction that may

3 Note: these are enumerated here in a different order from that provided in the Civil Code.

4 Article 330 Civil Code.

5 Article 433 Civil Code.

6 Article 1333 Civil Code.

7 Article 1338 Civil Code.

8 Or in some case even bilaterally, such as ante-nuptial settlements.

9 Article 1266 Civil Code.

10 Article 1338 Civil Code.

be? A contractual commitment might easily be made over the internet by an underage child or even, for that matter, an insane person or incarcerated criminal. At least in Indonesia, a court should rule that an underage child will not be held liable for breach of contract.

A mechanism to determine exactly with whom one is contracting is clearly in order. Asking for such information as a preliminary measure may suffice, provided the responding party provides accurate information. But how can one even determine that?

b. Certainty of obligations

In simple internet-based sales of goods, where a purchaser orders from a clear description of the goods, and enters credit card details, neither this, nor many of the other questions discussed herein are likely to present much of a problem. Not only can the seller ascertain through the credit card company whether the party's credit is current and the billing address corresponds with the requested shipping address (thus, for the most part, eliminating the capacity difficulty), but normally a mechanism of order confirmation will be applied, whereby a "click" to order an item is followed by a request for a second confirming click, and in some cases even a third. Goods will normally not be shipped until the credit is authorised.

However, most more complicated contractual obligations assumed through electronic commerce will be embodied in a series of negotiating correspondences sent through e-mail, or through a combination of telephone conversations, e-mail, telefax and perhaps other means as well. Where drafts are exchanged through the internet and, when all of the terms are finally agreed upon, a hard copy is produced for execution, we can be reasonably secure that the terms set out in that hard copy will correctly represent the agreement of the parties, particularly where, as in Indonesia and some other civil law jurisdictions, such as France, the parties initial each page. But what of contracts that are constituted by the exchange of e-mails only? How does one determine at what stage the contract has been concluded and which of the set of e-mails constitute the final terms?

And what about integrity of content? How does one ensure that the electronically created document which one party has sent to another is not edited and revised. How do we prove that the terms of the contract which are negotiated through the internet and finally agreed upon will not be adjusted just that little bit when presented as evidence, or for enforcement?

c. Legal purpose

There are certain activities which would be legal in some jurisdictions but are contrary to law and/or public policy in others, such as Indonesia. Gambling is one example, which concept is deemed to extend to the holding of raffles, sweepstakes or lotteries. How the prohibition against an Indonesian resident entering, and winning, for example, a foreign state lottery, could be put into effect is difficult to contemplate. But it is clear that any action submitted to an Indonesian court to enforce a gambling obligation would almost certainly be rejected on the basis of illegality. This would apply regardless of how the obligation were incurred—in person or electronically.

There are other essential issues to be considered relating to computer fraud and crime, but these are well beyond the scope of this paper and we shall leave them to others to discuss.

d. Free Consent—"signing" a contract

As mentioned above, under Indonesian law, the contract is deemed to come into existence the moment both parties have come to agreement on their respective rights and obligations. So we need to ensure not only that such rights and obligations are clear, but that they have in fact been agreed to. Traditionally this would be indicated by the parties affixing their signature to the end of the agreement (and, as mentioned above, their initials to each page, in jurisdictions where the same is either the law or the practice.)

Probably the major difficulty faced by the legal profession in ensuring effective formation of contracts through electronic means stems from the requirements of most jurisdictions that contracts need be in writing and signed by the parties if they are to be enforceable. This requirement differs in common law and civil law jurisdictions. Common law jurisdictions normally have strict requirements of writing through legislation such as statutes of frauds[11]. Civil law jurisdictions vary. Normally the requirement of a signed writing is not as stringent as in common law jurisdictions and is a matter of evidentiary value rather than one of validity.

Under Indonesian law, although theoretically a contract need not be committed to writing so long as the formal requirements as met, as a practical matter where there is no writing the compliance with these requirements will be difficult to prove if contested. Furthermore, the requirements under Indonesian law and practice for proving the authenticity of a signature are quite stringent, normally requiring two witnesses or a notarial legalisation.

Electronic Signatures

How does one prove that a party sought to be bound by an electronically generated contract really agreed to it? To this question we are beginning to see solutions emerge through the advances of technology. An example is the "electronic signature", which has already been approved by U.S. President Clinton, who signed the Act—electronically of course—that gave full legal effect to electronic signatures. But exactly what will constitute an electronic signature?

---

11 See, *inter alia*, Section 2 of the UK Law of Property Act of 1989, and Article 2-201 of the U.S. Uniform Commercial Code.

A suggested mechanism of how electronic signatures might be arranged is contained in *General Usage for International Digitally Ensured Commerce* (known as "GUIDEC"), issued by the International Chamber of Commerce ("ICC"). GUIDEC applies the term "ensure" to indicate the method by which a sender of a message may authenticate, or ensure, the message. An ensured message is one that is: *"(1) intact and unaltered since ensured, and (2) identified with its ensurer."*[12] The method suggested by which parties may ensure involves a combination of a private and a public key, with third-party certification, and is described in some detail in the GUIDEC. GUIDEC is not intended for use in simple internet sales, but only for negotiated contractual legal documentation and other instruments by which a party may be bound.

Technology companies are already offering encription software, usually bundled with internet browsers, which can legally certify a signatory. But how is fraud to be avoided? Does the electronic signature stay with the computer in which the software is installed, or can a person apply it from any computer? In either case, how can one protect it against hacker, or even co-worker, break-in? GUIDEC refers to this problem and provides that a sender of an ensured message is not to be held responsible for such message if the same is forged. It does not advise how to avoid hacking and forgery, however, nor could it be expected to do so.

We understand that another solution will soon be offered by a Japanese company which is preparing to launch a device to enable electronic documents to be signed with a fingerprint. This is a field that will certainly continue to evolve in the near future. But each time a "foolproof" system is developed, will it only be a very short matter of time before the code is broken?

Some contracts require a higher standard of execution. Under Indonesian law, for example, certain contracts must be taken as notarial deeds thereby being entitled to official status or force of law. Examples are contracts for the sale of land or seagoing vessels, establishment of companies and the creation of certain security interests over property. The contracting parties to such deeds must appear before the notary, who reads out to them the deed and certifies their acknowledgement that those are the terms to which they have agreed. Such a deed is then be executed in the presence of the notary. Can this type of contract be consummated through electronic means? It seems clear that it cannot, at least not unless and until a jurisdiction with authority over such deeds adopts an entirely new paradigm for such authentic government-regulated documentation.

And at least for the foreseeable future, regardless of what facilities are being offered for electronic contracts, if the legal profession wishes to ensure the integrity and enforceability of negotiated contracts, and be sure that such contracts will meet the test for validity and enforceability in any jurisdiction in which it

12 See Article 2, Section VII, GUIDEC, available at: www.iccwbo.org/home/guidec/guidec.asp.

may be disputed, it would still be wise to commit the final copy to paper and have each party sign it in the traditional way.

UNCITRAL Model Law

As mentioned above, although the formal requirements for a contract do not necessarily require it be committed to writing, a verbal contract can create innumerable evidentiary difficulties whenever the obligations of the parties are disputed. Thus, for all practical purposes, we must assume that a "writing" is required to establish contractual obligations.

The United Nations Commission on International Trade Law ("UNCITRAL") has been prescient enough to provide a suggested solution to this problem in their Model Law on Electronic Commerce of 1996 (as supplemented in 1998, the "Model Law"). As with their model arbitration law and their rules of procedure for *ad hoc* arbitrations, UNCITRAL offers the Model Law to all jurisdictions to adopt in support of the commercial use of international contracts in electronic commerce. Article 11 of the Model Law states:

> "In the context of contract formation, unless otherwise agreed by the parties, an offer and the acceptance of an offer may be expressed by means of data messages. Where a data message is used in the formation of a contract that contract shall not be denied validity or enforceability on the sole ground that a data message was used for that purpose."

"Data message" is defined as:

> ". . . information generated, sent, received or stored by electronic, optical or similar means including, but not limited to, electronic data interchanges. (EDI), electronic mail, telegram, telex or telecopy."

Generally the solutions offered by the Model Law provide that documents, instruments, or other units of information will not be denied legal effect, validity or enforceability solely on the grounds that the same is in the form of a data message.

Thus jurisdictions which have adopted, or which will adopt, the Model Law will now have a basis for recognition and admissibility of electronically created and/or transmitted contractual and other documentation. This will mean, among other things, that within such jurisdictions, where a regulatory authority does not wish to recognise electronic "data messages", it will have to take affirmative action, i.e. promulgate legislation which specifically and categorically excludes it. Requirement of execution as a deed before a notary would certainly constitute such legislation. Otherwise, the mere fact that the messages are contained in electronic media will not cause such message to be viewed as being inferior to a written document.

Governing Law

UNCITRAL and the ICC, through the Model Law and GUIDEC respectively, are already laying the basis for a uniform international standard of recognition and application of electronic contractual data. The Model Law addresses validity of electronic messages while GUIDEC addresses protection of their integrity. Jurisdictions that do not adopt the Model Law nor apply the system offered by GUIDEC will have to find their own way in navigating across these troublesome shoals. But it is clear that because electronic commerce can cut across any number of jurisdictional borders, consistent regulation can only be effected if all countries apply the same, or at least a similar, regulatory framework. And, of course, this leads us to another of the major questions: how are international electronic contracts to be interpreted where the laws of each relevant jurisdiction (to the extent such jurisdictions can be determined) differ?

Certainly it is to be recommended that parties clearly designate their choice of governing law in any electronic contract. However, in simple sales and other contracts in which the parties are unlikely to use counsel and thus even less likely to consider the issue, how does one establish what law is to govern the electronic transaction? In traditional paper contracts, where the governing law is not clear, general principles of private international law would apply the law of the place where the contract is concluded and/or the law of the place in which the contract is performed. In a transaction contracted electronically neither of these factors may be able to be ascertained and thus neither of such general rules can be applied. The contract may be concluded in cyberspace and/or may be performed in more than one, or in indeterminable, jurisdictions.

Legal control—the right to make and enforce laws—has always been based upon the territorial control of the geographical area so governed. If the internet is either domiciled everywhere, or nowhere, what laws can effectively govern activities conducted within or through it: transactions which occur in cyberspace. Is this not the great metaphysical question of our age: Just where is cyberspace located?

There is no government with the jurisdiction to govern or regulate cyberspace. Only if all governments adopt the same laws to govern e-conomic transactions will there be the possibility of an even playing field and effective, transparent, flow of business through the internet. Otherwise a transaction may be subject to too many, conflicting, laws, or perhaps to none at all.

New Paradigms

Let us take the example of the right to tax. Most countries tax on a combination of the bases of: (i) source of income (where the activity giving rise to the income takes place), and (ii) destination of income (where the recipient of the income is domiciled or resident). How then do we determine which taxing authority may tax any given electronic transaction? A product may be produced, or service rendered, in one or more countries through a facility owned by a resident of another but under license from the IPR owner located in a third country, marketed by a marketing company located in one or more 4th countries through the internet and purchased by buyers in any number of 5th countries. The goods are stored in warehouses in one or more 6th countries and shipped to all buyers from there, but the purchase price is paid by credit card to a bank in a 7th country and credited to the account of a subsidiary of the seller located in an 8th country. What taxing authority determines the taxes that are due and payable; who is responsible to pay them; and to which taxing authority must they be paid? This question was posed by Indonesia's Director of Income Tax, Gunadi, in his recent paper for the International Fiscal Association's compilation of national reports on Taxation of Electronic Commerce. Gunadi concluded, as we must also conclude, that electronic commerce forces us all to seek new paradigms in the legal regulation of business transactions. But no country can do this alone. It will require co-operation among all countries for the questions, posed in this conference and those questions yet to emerge, meaningfully and consistently to be answered.

DISPUTE RESOLUTION

The second topic assigned to this writer is resolution of disputes in electronic commerce. There are different aspects from which one might discuss this topic and we shall try to take a summary overview of these.

The first question to be addressed in any dispute resolution matter is: have the parties agreed in their contract to a certain method for resolution of any disputes that may arise thereunder? As the primary criterion in removing resolution of disputes from the jurisdiction of the courts is consent of the parties, most laws on arbitration and alternative dispute resolution ("ADR") require that the agreement to arbitrate, or to employ another means of ADR, be in writing and signed by both, or all, parties. Where the Model Law has been adopted, the writing requirement should be satisfied if such agreement is clear in the electronic messages. If not, it will depend upon the attitude of the court in the jurisdiction in which the agreement is contested, whether such court will accept jurisdiction over the dispute or order the parties to follow the terms of their dispute resolution clause.

In common law countries, it would seem more likely that courts, following recent trends, will decline jurisdiction if the weight of the evidence shows that the parties did agree to arbitrate. In Indonesia, however, it is less likely because in a civil law country court decisions are not considered as precedent for others, and up to the present, courts have tended to accept jurisdiction where any doubt can be thrown on the scope of the arbitration clause. Indonesia's new Arbitration Law, Law No. 30 of 1999, states categorically that where the parties have entered into a valid agreement to arbitrate their disputes the courts do not have, and must decline, jurisdiction. Article 4 (2) requires that the agreement to arbitrate be in writing. And although Article 4 (3) recognises e-mail as a form of writing, it requires at the minimum a record of receipt. Article 4 of Law No. 30 of 1999 states as follows:

> "Article 4
>
> "(1) In the event the parties have previously agreed that disputes between them are to be resolved through arbitration and have granted such authority, the arbitrators are competent to determine in their award the rights and obligations of the parties if these matters are not regulated in their agreement.
>
> "(2) The agreement to resolve disputes through arbitration, as specified in paragraph (1), shall be contained in a document signed by the parties.
>
> "(3) In the event the agreement for resolution of disputes by arbitration is contained in an exchange of correspondence, including letters, telexes, telegrams, telefaxes, e-mail, or any other form of communication, the same shall be accompanied by a record of receipt of such correspondence by the parties."[13]

The newly revised rules of Indonesia's national arbitral institution, BANI (*Badan Arbitrase Nasional Indonesia*) mirrors the requirement of Law No. 30 of 1999 so that the designation of BANI as the body competent to hear the dispute must be in writing. But the new BANI rules follow the concept embodied in the Model Law and specifically include electronically generated documents in the definition of "writing".

So far there has not, to our knowledge, been any case in which an agreement to arbitrate contained in an electronically concluded contract has been contested in the Indonesian courts. However, judging from past experience, it is very possible that should one arise in the near future, unless BANI rules have been agreed upon, the benefit of any doubt as to the validity of the arbitration clause and/or whether the electronic contractual agreement to arbitrate meets the "writing" requirement, may well be decided in favor of the party seeking to invalidate the agreement to arbitrate and to litigate the dispute. As Indonesia's program of judicial reform progresses, it is hoped that agreements to arbitrate will be honored regardless of the form they may take.

Jurisdiction

Where it cannot be established that parties to an electronically concluded contract have agreed to a specific method of dispute resolution, such as arbitration, and the parties do not subsequently agree to such, one must look to the courts for resolution of any dispute which may arise. But the question is then what court? If the place of domicile or residence of a party is known, the other party may bring an action in the court which has in personam jurisdiction over the party to be claimed against. If not, whether the court of the domicile of the complaining party has jurisdiction over the subject matter will depend upon the laws of the complainant's jurisdiction.

---

13 From an unofficial translation of Law No. 30 of 1999, prepared by the writer.

Most arbitration rules and some laws enabling arbitration make it clear that an arbitral tribunal has the jurisdiction to decide upon its own jurisdiction over the subject matter of and parties to a dispute. This is the principle known as "*competenz competenz*". Where this principle is recognised, if one party submits a dispute to arbitration and the other party contests jurisdiction of the tribunal on the grounds of an alleged defect in the agreement to arbitrate or inapplicability of such agreement to the subject dispute, or for any other reason, that objection must be submitted to and decided by the arbitral tribunal itself.

Venue

Many arbitration laws require that in order to be valid an arbitral award must state where the award was rendered and must be signed by all arbitrators. Both of these requirements can cause difficulties where the arbitration is held in cyberspace and rendered electronically. Some arbitration rules and laws have different requirements for procedures, registration and/or enforcement, depending upon whether the arbitration is domestic or international. Where the arbitrators do not hold hearings in a single location but sit in different places, as do the parties, where can the arbitration be deemed to be held and where is the award rendered? Only if the parties can agree that the arbitral reference will be deemed to be held, and/or the award rendered, in a specific geographic location will cyber-arbitrations be feasible where either of the parties resides or maintains assets in a jurisdiction with such requirements.

Where the award is required to be signed by the arbitrators, unless the Model Law has been adopted in the jurisdiction in which the award is sought to be enforced and unless such jurisdiction recognises electronic signatures or ensured signatures as provided in the GUIDEC, the original award will have to be printed out in hard copy and sent around to the full tribunal for signature. For the present, this is a precaution which it is probably wise to take in any arbitration unless the parties have specifically agreed, in a signed writing, to the contrary.

Cyber-Arbitration/Mediation

Where the parties to an electronically concluded contract have agreed to a specific form of dispute resolution, such as arbitration, and have designated the institution or rules applicable, then such arbitral body or ad hoc tribunal so designated will have jurisdiction. The arbitration should proceed in the normal manner according to the chosen rules of procedure. Many traditional arbitral institutions and centres are currently reviewing their procedures in order to accommodate electronic transmission of documents and many both accept and encourage submission of documents, as well as deliberation of the arbitrators, through the internet. As mentioned above, Indonesia's BANI has included electronically created instruments in the definition of "writing" and specifically allows submissions and notices by e-mail. Singapore is one of the most advanced jurisdictions in embracing electronic commerce, with both the courts and tax office now requiring submissions through the internet.

Video conferencing is also being adapted for arbitral hearings and some forward looking tribunals have commenced holding entire arbitral references in cyberspace.

Many senior arbitrators—and it is that generation that dominates the arbitration field, like no other—may try the electronic or video medium once or twice out of curiosity. But is its likely to be quite some time, if ever, before we shall see most experienced arbitrators opt out of sitting together, for hearings and/or deliberations, particularly in complex cases.

Cyber-arbitration, by which let us assume we may include arbitration through video-conferencing, has been criticised by some traditionalists for a number of reasons. One of the more noted drawbacks is that where witnesses are to be heard and cross-examined the traditional interaction between the witness and the questioner is lacking, thus eliminating the ability of the arbitrators to judge the credibility and comprehension of a witness through his or her demeanor.

Nonetheless there is a trend towards holding cyber-arbitrations and we see demonstrations of these in virtually every major international conference on dispute resolution over the past few years. The medium is still young and technology is still developing. Some arbitral institutions are considering preparing special rules for cyber-arbitrations, while for the most part existing rules can be adapted to the medium.

Mediation

As outlined above, most of the problems associated with cyber-arbitration relate to enforcement of the award eventually rendered in light of the relevant governing law. But the internet may be more suitable for other forms of ADR which, not being binding, need not be evaluated from the enforcement viewpoint. On the other hand, mediation, the most common form of non-binding ADR, may be difficult to hold electronically with any great success. Certainly documents can be transmitted by the parties to the mediator electronically, but normally the success of mediation is dependent upon the mediator establishing a personal relationship of trust with each of the parties to the dispute, which will be difficult without face-to-face meetings or, at the very least, extended telephone conversations. Thus unless parties are very sophisticated, and involved, in electronic commerce, and rather dispassionate as to their dispute, the internet may still prove too cold and impersonal for successful mediation of most disputes.

Dispute Resolution Relating to Electronic Commerce

There are certain disputes which relate specifically to electronic commerce and internet use, and these are eminently suitable for resolution through electronic means. The most common of these would be intellectual property issues, and in particular disputes as to ownership and use of domain names on the internet. Because of the nature of disputes relating to domain names, being very similar to disputes relating to trademark registration and infringement, these can often be adjudicated without the necessity of hearings or witness cross-examination. And there are many such disputes arising recently primarily due to the practice of "cybersquatting", whereby opportunistic fledgling entrepreneurs register well-known trade names, or even names of persons, as internet domain names, and then sell the name to the company or person with the rightful ownership of that name, for considerable profit. Before there was any control over this practice millions of dollars were made by some of these cybersquatters.

But in the past few years a number of organisations have set up procedures specifically for the resolution of domain name disputes. The International Corporation for Assigned Names (ICANN) and the World Intellectual Property Organisation (WIPO) both have adopted special administrative procedures specifically designed for the purpose.[14] More than 1,000 cases were submitted to ICANN within less than a year. Various arbitration centres, such as the Hong Kong International Arbitration Centre ("HKIAC"), as well as some independent groups are also in the process of setting up such mechanisms. The HKIAC has already contracted to resolve all domain name disputes arising in China and plans to expand to English-language-based international domain-name disputes very soon.

Electronic and internet technology is a relatively new medium for the dispute resolution practitioner. In order to fall into place with the increasing cyberisation of the business world, some old concepts will need to be discarded and new ones adopted.

Conclusion

Concurrent with, although not arising out of, the economic chaos which reigned in the last few years of the twentieth century came the rise of electronic commerce. As financial markets struggle to restructure debt obligations and rebuild ailing economies, a new universal internet e-conomy is emerging which pays no heed to geographical borders or long-established commercial traditions. The job of the legal practitioner has changed, and is changing, all around us and we find we must establish new paradigms in order to address the myriad of questions and pitfalls we are encountering every step of the way. Because there is no single governing body with the power and authority to regulate borderless commerce, we can no longer expect business practices to comply with the laws and regulations established in any one jurisdiction or by any one government. International organisations such as UNCITRAL and ICC are seeking to offer global solutions. It is up to each government individually, as well as all governments collectively, to remove the stumbling-blocks which its old regulatory framework may have, over the years, set in the way of new business trends. And it is up to the legal profession to help our governments in this effort for are we not, after all, the bridge which connects those lawmakers with the constituency which must follow their laws in the proper conduct of business and the growth of the world's economies?

---

14 See John P. Gaffney's note, *Domain Name Dispute Resolution*, in the September, 2000 IBA Committee D Newsletter, Arbitration And ADR, for a discussion of these procedures.

BASIC CONTRACTUAL ISSUES[1]

by
George W. Thompson
Neville Peterson LLP

Introduction: Issues to Address in a Contract

Contracts may be negotiated in various ways: face to face, by telephone, telefacsimile, or e-mail or by exchange of offer and acceptance documents, such as a purchase order. Similarly, contracts can be called a number of different things besides contracts, such as purchase orders or invoices. The parties may agree to a single transaction, involving a one-time sale and payment; they may have a series of identical transactions; or they may enter into a supply contract, whereby the buyer agrees to purchases all of its needs from the seller, or the seller agrees to provide all of its production to the buyer.

Although each of these situations calls for unique language in the final agreement between the parties, there are a number of points that should always (or almost always) be covered in a contract for the sale of goods in international commerce. This chapter will address those points, and will provide sample language which can be adapted for use in a contract.

In discussing the various issues and drafting language to address them, we have paid particular attention to the requirements of the Uniform Commercial Code (UCC) and the United Nations Convention on Contracts for the International Sale of Goods (the U.N. Convention). The discussion in this chapter touches on many of the points raised in Commentary Chapter I.2, which covered the U.N. Convention and contrasted its approach with that of the UCC on topics of contract formation, performance, breach and damages.

Identifying the Names and Places of Business of the Parties

The contract should always specify the names of the parties and their business addresses. Doing so is not only a matter of common sense, but can determine

1 This chapter was originally published in TRANSNATIONAL CONTRACTS, eds. Lawrence J. Bogard & George W. Thompson (1997-current) by George W. Thompson, as part of Booklet B.1 "Basic Contractual Issues" (Release 2004-2, March 2004).

whether a specific "gap filler" code applies to the transaction. As discussed in Commentary Chapter I.2 to this treatise, the U.N. Convention applies to sales contracts between parties whose places of business are in different Convention signatory countries. U.N. Convention, Article 1.1. The business addresses listed in the contract will help determine whether businesses from two signatory states are involved, and hence whether the Convention applies.

Similarly, section 1-105(1) of the UCC provides that a particular state's version of the UCC applies to "transactions bearing an appropriate relation to [such] state", in the absence of a contrary choice of law provision in the contract. The business addresses set forth in the contract will help indicate whether the transaction has "an appropriate relation to" a particular state.

Identifying the Merchandise and the Price

Again, it is a common sense proposition that the contract should identify the merchandise covered, its quantity, and either the price or a reference for determining the price. Under the U.N. Convention, providing such information is the *sine qua non* for establishing a contract in the first place. U.N. Convention, Article 14.2. The UCC has a more flexible standard under which a contract may be formed "[e]ven though one or more terms are left open", UCC § 2-204. However, failing to specify such fundamental terms in the contract merely invites misunderstandings and disputes between the parties.

If the seller has provided the buyer with a model or sample of the merchandise to be sold, the contract should specifically reference this fact, by stating (for example): "Seller represents that the goods will conform to, and possess the qualities of, the [sample/model of the merchandise] that seller provided to buyer in connection with this agreement."

Transportation Terms and Risk of Loss

In all sales transactions, one of the parties is going to be responsible for transporting the goods from here to there. "Responsible" means contractually bound to arrange and pay for transportation to a specified point and bear the risk of loss if the goods disappear, or are destroyed or damaged, *enroute*. Also, the point at which the responsibility for the goods passes from the seller to the buyer is, in most circumstances, the point at which the seller has performed its obligation to deliver the goods to the buyer. Thus, the issue of transportation terms determines not only the party that will have to bear certain costs and obligations, but also determines the point at which the seller has completed its major obligation under the contract.

Obviously, as a general rule, the costs, complexity, and potential for things to go wrong are relatively greater in a sale involving international transportation than in a strictly domestic transaction. The parties should, accordingly, pay close attention to the division of responsibility for transporting the goods. To assist them, there are two different, widely recognized guidelines that provide common definitions of the buyer's and seller's responsibilities, and have reduced the allocation of responsibilities to a commonly-recognized shorthand: the UCC, and the International Commercial Terms (INCOTERMS). Although either regime may be used in international contracts, INCOTERMS are more likely to be acceptable to non-American parties.

Unfortunately, many traders are insufficiently familiar with the details of these resources to make an informed choice in negotiating and performing their contracts. Adding to the potential confusion is the fact that both the UCC and INCOTERMS use identical acronyms (such as "F.O.B.") for completely different substantive requirements. Parties that are used to placing the UCC terminology in their domestic sales contracts, and who simply incorporate those terms into their international contracts, run a considerable risk of agreeing to something other than what they thought they had agreed to, or at least of getting into a dispute concerning what the contract term really meant. To avoid possible mistakes, it is imperative that traders and their counsel familiarize themselves with INCOTERMS, in cases where these will be used in a contract, and that the contractual language they use reflects the proper use of INCOTERMS.

We have provided a discussion of INCOTERMS, followed by a section on UCC terms that compares and contrasts both. Each section includes sample provisions for inclusion in contracts.

INCOTERMS

The INCOTERMS are a set of sixteen trade terms, each of which establishes a different point at which the responsibility for transporting the goods, and the risk of loss, changes hands from the seller to the buyer. These points range from the seller's facility to buyer's facility, and can include virtually any place in between. The INCOTERMS spell out quite clearly each party's responsibility to arrange and pay for transportation, insurance, and ancillary charges such as customs clearance fees, as well as the actions each must take to effect or receive delivery of the goods. They thus provide an objective, readily-understandable, and commonly accepted protocol for allocating costs and responsibilities.

The INCOTERMS are published by the International Chamber of Commerce. They are neither a law nor an international agreement, and have no official government sanction. The INCOTERMS are a strictly private, voluntary set of rules with no basis in legislation. *Guide to INCOTERMS 2000* (Int'l Chamber of Commerce) at 12. The INCOTERMS are included in a contract only upon agreement of the parties, and there is no requirement that they be used at all.

If adopted in a contract, the INCOTERMS qualify as a "usage . . . which in international trade is widely known to, and regularly observed by, parties to contracts" for the sale of merchandise, as set forth in Article 9.2 of the U.N. Convention. As such, "[t]he parties are considered, unless otherwise agreed, to have impliedly made" the INCOTERMS "applicable to their contract". Recent federal court decisions have concluded as much. *St. Paul Guardian Ins. Co. v. Neuromed Med. Sys. & Support, GmbH*, 2002 U.S. Dist. LEXIS 5096 (S.D.N.Y.); *BP Oil International v. Empresa Estatal Petroleos de Ecuador*, 332 F.3d 333 (5th Cir. 2003)("Even if the usage of Incoterms is not global, the fact that they are well known in international trade means that they are incorporated through article 9(2))"(citing *St. Paul Guardian*). At a minimum, Article 9.2 permits the parties to use the shorthand INCOTERMS provision (*e.g.*, F.O.B.) without the need for restating the paragraphs-long explanation for what this means. *St. Paul Guardian, supra* (use of the INCOTERM acronym demonstrates parties' agreement to the term's substantive requirements). It thereby permits the parties to a contract, and a reviewing tribunal, to refer to the specified term as defined by the INCOTERMS to determine what it was that the parties agreed to. A buyer or seller would, therefore, face little chance of success if it were to argue that the referenced term meant something other than what the INCOTERMS specify. Attempts to do just that were rejected in both *St. Paul Guardian* and *BP Oil*.

The INCOTERMS are divided into four separate groups: "E", "F", "C" and "D", each of which includes one or more specific trade terms. Each group provides a different point at which the costs of transportation and risk of loss changes from the seller to the buyer. Under the "E" group, that point is at the seller's facility; under the "F" group, it is when the goods are placed on the conveyance for international transportation; under the "C" group, risk also passes when the goods are placed on the conveyance, but the seller bears the costs of international transportation; and under the "D" group, the risk passes at the point of delivery. Each term within a group provides a variation in detail, but reflects the group's common requirement.

The goods' transfer point also serves at the point at which the seller has met its delivery obligations under a contract of sale. Thus, when we speak of risk of loss, we are addressing two separate, related concepts. The first is the INCOTERMS sense: if the goods are lost, destroyed, or otherwise compromised, the INCOTERMS provision tells us which party bears the financial burden for this event. The second is the contractual sense. If something happens to the goods before the risk of loss has passed to the buyer, the seller will potentially be in breach of the contract for failing to deliver the goods as required. The longer the portion of the journey for which the seller is responsible, the greater the possibility that an untoward event will occur to the seller's detriment. Of course, even after the risk has passed from the seller to the buyer, if the goods are non-conforming or late, the seller may have liability under the contract.

INCOTERMS have undergone decennial revisions since 1980, which have resulted in changes to the details of specific trade terms and the addition or removal of certain terms. The most recent revision was issued in 2000. There is no apparent restriction on using an earlier version of INCOTERMS in a contract. Both in planning a transaction and drafting a contract, the parties should reference the specific version of INCOTERMS on which they have relied. Simply stating, for example, "F.O.B. port of Los Angeles" is too ambiguous, for several reasons. First, it fails to specify that the INCOTERMS provision is meant, rather than the UCC provision. Second, it fails to state which version of INCOTERMS is being used. Whenever a trade terms from INCOTERMS is used on, the full reference should be provided: "F.O.B. port of Los Angeles (INCOTERMS 2000)".

Parties to a sales contract may alter the "official" INCOTERMS to meet the requirements of their particular agreement. If they decide to vary the terms, they should do so explicitly in the contract. For example, if they decide to use the Free On Board term but agree that the seller shall pay all costs of placing the goods aboard the vessel, they could provide as follows: "The merchandise will be sold F.O.B. New York [named vessel and steamship company], except that seller shall pay all costs of placing the merchandise aboard the named vessel." Keep in mind that most contractual modifications to an INCOTERM have been limited to shifting relatively minor costs or clarifying the party to bear a cost when the INCOTERM is ambiguous, as opposed to effecting a fundamental alteration of the term.

We turn now to the specific INCOTERMS. This discussion covers the terms of each group and specific term, sets forth their financial, documentation and risk of loss responsibilities, and provides sample contract language to reflect each trade term.

The "E" Group

Ex Works [named place] and the New Export Regulations

There is only one trade term within the "E" group: Ex Works, abbreviated EXW. Under the Ex Works term, the seller is required to make the goods available to the buyer at its named facility, *e.g.*, a factory or warehouse, on or by the date specified in the contract. It is the seller's responsibility to obtain the goods at the named place, load, transport and insure them, and pay for these. The seller has no responsibility to arrange or pay for loading, transportation or insurance. Risk of loss passes from the seller to the buyer at the time and place the goods are made available to the buyer. The seller is required to provide a commercial invoice, but is otherwise not required to obtain documents needed clear the goods for export (*e.g.*, an export license) although it must, if requested, provide the buyer with assistance in obtaining such documents. Thus, a buyer would use Ex Works only if it has access to a transportation provider that can pick up the goods in a timely manner and undertake their transportation to the country of destination.

Practically speaking, from the seller's viewpoint an Ex Works sale is, or at least has been until recently, similar to a domestic sale, as the seller is not required by the INCOTERMS to transport the merchandise (with the attendant risk and cost) or obtain the export documentation. From the INCOTERMS standpoint, sellers that wished to avoid export control responsibilities often insisted on Ex Works terms, thereby placing the burden of acting as exporter on the buyer.

While the INCOTERMS 2000 continues this approach, parties to an agreement using the Ex Works term should be aware that revisions to the Census Bureau's Foreign Trade Statistical Regulations (FTSRs) and the Bureau of Industry and

Security's (BIS, formerly Bureau of Export Administration) Export Administration Regulations (EARs) in 2000 now require the seller's involvement in the export regulatory process. The new regulations provide specific obligations on the U.S. seller for both statistical reporting and export control compliance purposes. These new requirements may entail the adoption of new contractual provisions, to insure that each party complies with the rules, provides necessary information to the other, and maintains the confidentiality of information it receives.

The BIS Regulations

The new regulations define a sale where the buyer is not physically or legally present in the United States, and its agent takes delivery of the goods in the U.S. for subsequent exportation as a "routed transaction". The following description of a routed transaction, taken from the Federal Register notice announcing the EAR amendments, encompasses virtually all Ex Works contracts:

> For export control purposes the exporter has generally been the seller. An export transaction, however, has two principal parties in interest: a U.S. party and a foreign party—usually the seller and the buyer. (The terms are used interchangeably in our discussion.) In a "routed export transaction," the foreign principal party in interest agrees to terms of sale that may include assuming responsibility for export licensing. This rule provides that when the foreign principal party expressly assumes responsibility in writing for determining license requirements and obtaining necessary authorization, that foreign party must have a U.S. agent who becomes the "exporter" for export control purposes. Without such a written undertaking by the foreign principal, the U.S. principal is the exporter, with all attendant responsibilities.

Parties to a Transaction and Their Responsibilities, Routed Export Transactions, Shipper's Export Declarations, the Automated Export System (AES), and Export Clearance; *Final Rule*, 65 Fed. Reg. 42565 (Dep't Comm. 2000). The rule requires the foreign "principal party in interest"—in most cases, the foreign buyer—to appoint an agent that is physically present in the United States to act as the exporter for control compliance purposes. If the foreign principal party in interest is unable or unwilling to appoint a U.S. agent, the United States principal party in interest—generally, the seller—must assume such responsibilities itself. Thus, unless the U.S. seller is willing to assume the responsibility for export control compliance, or the foreign buyer can find a U.S. agent to take on that responsibility, the transaction cannot proceed. Note that the adoption of responsibility for export licensing entails meeting related regulatory obligations, such as record keeping.

Also, if the foreign principal party in interest does appoint an agent for export control compliance purposes, the U.S. seller is required to provide certain information to that agent:

> (c) *Information sharing requirements.* In routed export transactions where the foreign principal party in interest assumes responsibility for determining and obtaining licensing authority, the U.S. principal party in interest must, upon request,

> provide the foreign principal party in interest and its forwarding or other agent with the correct Export Control Classification Number (ECCN), or with sufficient technical information to determine classification. In addition, the U.S. principal party in interest must provide the foreign principal party in interest or the foreign principal's agent any information that it knows will affect the determination of license authority, see § 758.1(g) of the EAR.

65 Fed. Reg. at 42572.

This new requirement may pose practical problems for both parties to a transaction. The seller in an Ex Works transaction now faces the novel experience of complying with export control regulations, unless the foreign principal party in interest appoints a U.S. agent for this purpose. In the latter event, the seller will have to provide certain information to the foreign buyer's agent. Unless the seller wishes to adopt this role, the foreign buyer is now obligated to appoint an agent who takes on the legal role of exporter for export control compliance purposes, with the attendant responsibility and potential liability.

The foreign principal party in interest's appointment of an agent must be in writing, and should be accepted in writing by the appointed agent. In addition, the U.S. principal party in interest should get copies of both documents: "While the EAR[s] do not require the U.S. principal party in interest to obtain a writing from the agent to establish its export compliance role, it would be a good business practice to confirm the agent's responsibilities." 65 Fed. Reg. at 42566.

The Census Bureau Regulations

The Census Bureau regulations also address the division of responsibilities in routed transactions. One noteworthy aspect of the Census Bureau rule is its definition of the "exporter" as the "U.S. principal party in interest". Under this definition, unless the foreign purchaser has a presence in the United States to take possession of the goods here and arrange their outbound shipment, the U.S. seller is considered to be the exporter:

> The FTSR defines the term exporter (U.S. principal party in interest) as the person in the United States that receives the primary benefit, monetary or otherwise, of the export transaction. Generally, that person is the U.S. seller, manufacturer, order party, or foreign entity. The foreign entity must be listed as the U.S. principal party in interest on the SED or AES record, if it is in the United States when the items are purchased or obtained for export. The foreign entity must then follow the provisions for preparing and filing the SED or AES record specified in Secs. 30.4 and 30.7 of the FTSR, pertaining to the U.S. principal party in interest. In most cases, the forwarding or other agent is not a principal party in interest.

Foreign Trade Statistics Regulations; Shipper's Export Declaration or Filing Export Information Electronically Using Automated Export System; Clarification; Final Rule, 65 Fed. Reg. 42555, 42558 (Comm. Dep't 2000).

The new Census Bureau rule also allows either the U.S. seller or the foreign buyer's U.S. agent to take the responsibility of filing the paper version of the

Shipper's Export Declaration (SED) or the electronic Automated Export System (AES) record in a routed transaction. In this regard, it resembles the BIS rule concerning responsibility for export license applications. As with the BIS rule, the Census Bureau rule requires the foreign principal party in interest to provide its agent with a written authorization to perform these responsibilities on the principal's behalf, if the foreign principal decides to undertake them. If either the foreign party or designated agent is unwilling to take on this responsibility, the obligation remains with the seller. Of course, if neither party is willing to perform the FTSR-required reporting, the transaction cannot proceed.

Even if the foreign principal party in interest designates an agent, under the Census Bureau rule the U.S. principal party in interest must always be identified on the SED or AES record, and will be required to provide certain information to the foreign party's U.S. agent:

> In a routed export transaction, the exporter (U.S. principal party in interest) is only responsible for providing basic commodity information and their Internal Revenue Service (IRS), Employer Identification Number (EIN) to the forwarding or other agent. The forwarding or other agent is responsible for obtaining a power of attorney or written authorization from the foreign principal party in interest and preparing, signing, and filing the SED or AES record based on the information obtained from the exporter (U.S. principal party in interest) and other parties to the transaction. The exporter (U.S. principal party in interest) is only responsible and liable for the information it is required to provide the forwarding or other agent in Sec. 30.4(c)(2) of the FTSR.

65 Fed. Reg. at 42557. This means that the U.S. seller is almost always required to be involved in compliance with the Census Bureau requirements:

> In a routed export transaction, the forwarding or other agent may be the exporter for compliance purposes under the EAR. However, the forwarding or other agent is never the "U.S. principal party in interest" on the paper SED or in the "U.S. principal party in interest" field of the AES record, except when the forwarding or other agent acts as an "order party."

65 Fed. Reg. at 42558.

The U.S. principal party in interest (which as noted will in most circumstances be the seller) in a routed transaction has the following information-reporting requirements to the foreign principal's agent:

> In a routed export transaction, where a foreign principal party in interest designates a U.S. forwarding or other agent to act on its behalf to prepare and file the SED or AES record, the exporter (U.S. principal party in interest) must provide the forwarding or other agent with the following information to assist them in preparing the SED or AES record: (1) Name and address of the U.S. principal party in interest; (2) U.S. principal party in interest's IRS, EIN; (3) Point of origin (State or Foreign Trade Zone (FTZ)); (4) Schedule B description of commodities; (5) Domestic (D), foreign (F), or Foreign Military Sale (FMS) (M) code; (6) Schedule B Number; (7) Quantity/unit of measure; (8) Value; (9) Upon request by the foreign principal party in interest or its agent, the Export Control Classification Number (ECCN) or

> with sufficient technical information to determine the ECCN; and (10) Any information that it knows will affect the determination of license authority.

65 Fed. Reg. at 42559, codified at 15 C.F.R. § 30.4(c)(1). The U.S. seller has an obvious interest in maintaining the confidentiality of this information, and should require that information it conveys be kept in confidence by the buyer's agent. By the same token, the buyer has an interest in assuring that the seller actually provides the listed information, and should mandate in the contract that the seller does so.

The new regulations place new responsibilities on each of the parties to a routed transaction, and it is fair to predict that they will change the way that U.S. sellers and foreign buyers do business such transactions.

Parties using Ex Works terms should also take into account that the absence of a "delivery" by the seller may complicate the transaction's timing (delivery consists of simply making the goods available at the seller's facility). If the contract requires that goods are to be made available on a specified date, the buyer should be aware of that date and consequently make arrangements to pick up the goods then. However, if under the contract the goods will be made available during a range of dates, *e.g.*, at some point in a specified week, then the contract should require the seller to notify the buyer when they have actually been placed ready for pickup. (Such notification is a good idea even if the goods are to be made available on a specified date.) Otherwise, the buyer may not take custody of the merchandise in a timely manner. Because the risk of loss would have transferred to the buyer at the time the goods were made available to it, the passage of time increases the possibility that the goods will be damaged; in that event, INCOTERMS places the liability on the buyer, even though the damage occurred in the seller's facility.

➤SAMPLE LANGUAGE:

> The goods will be sold Ex Works (INCOTERMS 2000) [seller's named facility]. Seller will notify buyer by telephone when the goods have been delivered by the seller for buyer's disposal.

This language should be customized to meet the parties' needs, for example, by providing if appropriate a different form of notification that the goods have been made available. As discussed above, some form of immediate notification is highly advisable.

In addition, the parties should address issues arising from the revised EARs and FTSRs. The following provision mandates that the U.S. seller provide information required under the regulations, and that the foreign purchaser and its U.S. agent maintain the confidentiality of the information provided. Note that two points of information required from the seller—the quantity/unit of measure and value—may be required for transportation and insurance documentation purposes, and thus cannot be maintained in strict confidence. The same may be true of the seller's name and address.

➤*SAMPLE LANGUAGE:*

The parties share the understanding that this transaction is considered a "routed transaction" under the Export Administration Regulations (EARs), 15 C.F.R. Part 732 *et seq.*, and the Foreign Trade Statistics Regulations (FTSRs), 15 C.F.R. Part 30. Buyer hereby agrees to undertake to meet the information reporting requirements of the FTSRs by appointing a qualified agent in the United States for such purposes, and will provide Seller with documentation of such appointment. Seller agrees to provide the agent appointed by the buyer with such information as is required under 15 C.F.R. § 30.4(c)(1) and/or other provisions of the FTSRs to comply with the information reporting requirements of the FTSRs. Buyer agrees that its agent designated under this provision shall use the information received from Seller solely for purposes of complying with the information reporting requirements of the FTSRs, and will not otherwise disclose any such information to any person except as may be needed for transportation or insurance of the merchandise.

The FTSRs require a power of attorney or other authorization from the foreign buyer to its designated U.S. agent. The following document should serve that purpose. Note that it contains the agent's acceptance of the power conferred by the foreign buyer.

➤*SAMPLE FORM:*

LIMITED POWER OF ATTORNEY

KNOW ALL MEN BY THESE PRESENTS, THAT

Acme S.A., a corporation organized and doing business under the laws of the country of ___________ and with a business address of ________________, hereby appoints Jimmy's Forwarding, with a business address of ________ ______________ as a true and lawful agent and attorney for Acme S.A., with power and authority defined and limited as follows:

Jimmy's Forwarding is authorized and empowered to act as the agent for Acme S.A., within the meaning of the applicable Census Bureau regulations, 15 C.F.R. § 30.4(a)(2), to perform services required to facilitate certain routed export transactions between a United States principal party in interest and Acme S.A., and to retain or appoint other parties to perform some or all of those services. The scope of Jimmy's Forwarding's authority under this instrument is as follows:

Jimmy's Forwarding is authorized and empowered to prepare and file the Shipper's Export Declaration or Automated Export System record on Acme S.A.'s behalf, in any and all routed export transactions within the meaning of applicable Census Bureau and Bureau of Export

Administration regulations, between a United States principal party in interest as defined in those regulations, and Acme S.A. Jimmy's Forwarding is authorized and empowered to seek and obtain all information needed from third parties, including the United States principle party in interest, providers of transportation services, and others, necessary to properly prepare and file the Shipper's Export Declaration or Automated Export System record in these circumstances.

Jimmy's Forwarding is authorized and empowered to retain or appoint other entities, including freight forwarders, to perform some or all of the services referenced in the preceding paragraph 1.

Jimmy's Forwarding is authorized and empowered to take all actions required to comply with the requirements of the Census Bureau and Bureau of Export Administration regulations applicable to routed export transactions in which Jimmy's Forwarding performs services pursuant to this power of attorney.

This limited power of attorney shall remain in effect until revoked in writing.

____

NAME

POSITION, Acme S.A.

Dated

CORPORATE SEAL

On behalf of Jimmy's Forwarding, I hereby accept the Limited Power of Attorney provided to Jimmy's Forwarding by Acme, S.A. Pursuant to this instrument, Jimmy's Forwarding will act as a true and lawful agent and attorney for Acme S.A., with power and authority defined and limited as set forth herein.

____

NAME

POSITION, Jimmy's Forwarding

Dated:

CORPORATE SEAL

____

The "F" Group

The essential element of the "F" group is that the seller makes the goods available to the buyer for international transportation at a named point in the country of exportation. The seller bears the responsibility, costs and risks of transportation to that point, and has fulfilled its contractual obligation to deliver the goods when they have been turned over to the specified carrier at the named place. By the same token, the buyer assumes the obligation of arranging and paying for international transportation. The parties can "customize" the "F" term chosen so that, for example, the seller arranges for international transportation on the buyer's behalf, even though the attendant costs and risks are borne by the buyer. The parties are free to vary from the stated requirements of the term in this manner, and should do so through a specific statement in their contract: "The merchandise will be sold F.O.B. New York, with seller to arrange ocean transportation on buyer's behalf on a carrier to be chosen by [buyer/seller]."

However, unlike the Ex Works term, the seller is generally considered the exporter under each of the "F" terms, even though the goods are handed over to the buyer prior to exportation. The responsibility for complying with export regulations in such cases thus falls on the seller.

Free Alongside Ship [named port of shipment]

The Free Alongside Ship or FAS term requires the seller to delivery the goods to the buyer alongside the carrying vessel in the country of exportation and within the delivery period specified in the contract. According to the *Guide to INCOTERMS 2000*, "alongside" can mean on the dock next to the vessel, "or in lighters at the named port of shipment." In practice, delivery is often effected when the seller transfers the goods to the ocean shipping line's custody. Thus, the seller is responsible for the goods' inland movement to the port of exportation. The seller is also required to obtain and provide a receipt evidencing delivery.

The buyer is responsible for arranging and paying for the ocean transportation, although by mutual agreement the seller may make the actual transportation arrangements. Of course, if the buyer arranges the transportation, it must notify the seller of the port and carrier to permit timely, accurate delivery. The buyer also is responsible for the goods from the point of delivery alongside the vessel, *i.e.*, must pay for, and bear the risk of, placing the goods on board the vessel and moving them to the point of delivery in the country of importation. Under the INCOTERMS 1990, the buyer's obligations included export clearance, including export control compliance and statistical reporting; such an arrangement would qualify as a routed transaction under the revised Bureau of Industry and Security and Census Bureau export regulations. The allocation of responsibilities was reversed in the INCOTERMS 2000, under which the seller must take care of export clearance.

If the parties to a transaction decide to use the INCOTERMS 1990 FAS provision in their agreement, they must take account of the routed transaction regulations discussed previously.

Finally, as specified by the term's name, FAS is appropriate only for vessel transportation, and should not be used for transportation by means other than vessel.

➤*SAMPLE LANGUAGE:*

The goods will be sold FAS (INCOTERMS 2000) [named port/named vessel/named shipping line].

Free on Board [named port of shipment]

The Free on Board ("FOB") term requires the seller to deliver the goods to the buyer aboard the ocean vessel. Delivery is effected when the goods have passed over the ship's rail. The seller is, therefore, responsible for inland transportation to the port of exportation, and must split with the buyer the costs of placing the goods on the vessel. The buyer must arrange and pay for ocean transportation and insurance (although the seller may make such arrangements on the buyer's behalf), and of course bear some costs of loading the goods aboard the vessel. The seller's and buyer's share of such costs may vary depending on the customary allocation of costs in the particular port of loading; such allocation may vary from port to port.

Under the FOB term, the seller is considered the exporter and has the responsibility for effecting export clearance.

One often-overlooked point is that FOB, in INCOTERMS usage, is suitable only for vessel movements. Indeed, it is appropriate only for cargo that is loaded over the ship's rail, and should not be used for containerized cargo. A frequent contract drafting error is to use the INCOTERMS FOB term in connection with non-vessel transportation forms. The error apparently arises through a combination of unfamiliarity with INCOTERMS and drafters' assumption that the INCOTERMS version of FOB is as broad in scope as the Uniform Commercial Code's version.

Another frequent drafting error involves the use of the term "FOB" without specifying whether the INCOTERMS or UCC version is meant. Potential confusion is easily avoided simply by specifying in parentheses which source is meant.

➤*SAMPLE LANGUAGE:*

The goods will be sold FOB (INCOTERMS 2000) [named port/named vessel/named shipping line].

Free Carrier [named place]

Under the Free Carrier (FCA) term, the seller is required to transport and deliver the merchandise to the carrier chosen by the buyer and at the place specified by the buyer. The seller's responsibilities, which include any necessary licenses, will be discharged when the goods are delivered as required by the contract. The buyer's responsibilities include arranging and paying for the international transportation and insurance (if desired) and notifying the seller of the place for delivery.

FCA is appropriate for any means of transportation. It provides the parties with considerable flexibility in determining the place for delivery. The "named place" need not be a seaport, or even an airport or rail depot, although (depending on the mode of transportation) delivery to one of the three is most common. Rather, it could be any place where the buyer's named carrier can take delivery and control of the goods from the seller, such as a freight forwarder's warehouse or a trucking company's receiving station.

The flexibility available under FCA makes it more akin in many respects to the UCC's FOB term than to the other two INCOTERMS "F" terms. Delivery can be made at any point within the country of exportation. If delivery is made at a point other than the port of exportation, the buyer should be aware that it is assuming the costs and risks involved in internal transportation to the actual place of export. Also, depending on whether the internal delivery point is the port of exportation, *e.g.*, an airport or river port, the FCA term may be considered a "routed transaction" under the BIS and Census Bureau regulations. The parties to an FCA contract should discuss their understanding of which will be responsible for export clearance, both to avoid potential contractual disputes and possible regulatory violations.

➤*SAMPLE LANGUAGE:*

The goods will be sold FCA (INCOTERMS 2000) [named place/named carrier].

The "C" Group

The "C" group of INCOTERMS requires the seller to bear certain costs of the goods' transportation, while placing on the buyer the risk of loss during such transportation. The "C" group is unique in dividing costs and risks in this manner. Under all terms in the "C" group the seller is responsible for export clearance. Thus, there should be no concern that a "C" group sale will be considered a routed transaction.

Cost and Freight [named port of destination]

The Cost and Freight (CFR) terms requires the seller to arrange and pay for international transportation to the named port of destination. The seller also bears the risks and costs of bringing the goods to the point of international transport and placing them aboard the means of carriage. The seller has met its delivery obligations once the goods are aboard. Use of the CFR term is limited to water transportation.

The buyer bears the risk of loss from the point at which the goods are placed aboard the means of carriage for transportation. The responsibility for obtaining and paying for insurance for the carriage is placed on the buyer.

➤*SAMPLE LANGUAGE:*

The goods will be sold CFR (INCOTERMS 2000) [named port of destination].

Cost, Insurance and Freight [named port of destination]

The requirements of the Cost, Insurance and Freight (CIF) term are similar to those of CFR, except that the seller is responsible for obtaining and paying for insurance. As with CFR, CIF should be used only for transportation on a water-going vessel.

➤*SAMPLE LANGUAGE:*

The goods will be sold CIF (INCOTERMS 2000) [named port of destination].

Carriage Paid To [named place of destination]

The Carriage Paid To (CPT) term requires the seller to arrange and pay for the goods' international transportation, as well as the goods' inland movement in the country of exportation to the international carrier. The risk of loss transfers from the seller to the buyer at the point when the goods are handed over to the first carrier. That point may be anywhere within the country of exportation, *e.g.*, a freight forwarder's warehouse. Note that CPT (like CFR) does not require the seller to obtain insurance for the transportation of the merchandise. The CPT term is usable for any form of transportation.

➤*SAMPLE LANGUAGE:*

The goods will be sold CPT (INCOTERMS 2000) [named place of destination].

Carriage and Insurance Paid To [named place of destination]

The seller and buyer have the same obligations under the Carriage and Insurance Paid To (CIP) term, with the exception that the seller must obtain and pay for insurance covering the transportation. CIP is appropriate for any mode of transport.

➤*SAMPLE LANGUAGE:*

The goods will be sold CIP (INCOTERMS 2000) [named place of destination].

The "D" Group

The "D" group of INCOTERMS places both the costs and risks of international transportation on the seller. The seller will not fulfill its contract until the goods are delivered at some point following the main international carriage, either in the country of unloading from the international carrier, an intermediate country, or the country of final destination (to the extent that these may vary). Thus, the seller faces potential contractual liability for international shipping delays, as well as the possibility that the goods will be lost, damaged, or stolen before arrival. In such an event, the seller bears the costs (or is responsible for obtaining insurance to cover them), and also faces a potential breach of contract claim for failing to deliver merchandise of the quantity and/or quality required under the agreement.

Delivered at Frontier [named place]

The Delivered at Frontier (DAF) term envisions that the merchandise will be brought to a specified point at the frontier of a country, which may be (but does not have to be) the country of exportation. The merchandise thus delivered will almost always undergo subsequent transport through the territory of the adjacent country. The seller's major obligation is to deliver the merchandise to the named frontier point. Note that the delivery point should be beyond the customs border of the second country. The buyer is obligated to assume the costs and risks of transportation, including customs clearance at the adjacent country, following delivery.

Although DAF may be used for any mode of transport, its utility would be primarily for merchandise moving by ground transport.

➤*SAMPLE LANGUAGE:*

The goods will be sold DAF (INCOTERMS 2000) [named point of delivery on the frontier].

Delivered Ex Ship [named port of destination]

Under the Delivered Ex Ship (DES) term, the seller is responsible for the costs and risks of delivering the merchandise by vessel to a specified port of destination. The seller's delivery obligation is met when the ship reaches the named port. Thereafter, the buyer is responsible for removing the goods from the vessel and their subsequent transportation.

A DES contract places the seller at the mercy of the vessel line's adherence to its schedule. If the vessel is late, the seller may be found in breach of its contract. To avoid this possibility, the parties may consider including a limited extension of the delivery date in the event the carrying vessel does not arrive on time, or else establish a range of dates going several days beyond that of the vessel's scheduled arrival in which delivery may be timely effected.

As the name indicates, DES is applicable only for water transport by vessel.

➤*SAMPLE LANGUAGE:*

The goods will be sold DES (INCOTERMS 2000) [named port of destination]. *Optional "delayed delivery" language*: In the event the vessel on which the merchandise has been placed is delayed in arrival at [the named port of destination], delivery of the merchandise shall be considered timely under this contract if made within [seven] days after the date specified herein.

Delivered Ex Quay (Duty Paid) [named port of destination]

The Delivered Ex Quay (Duty Paid) (DEQ) term makes it the seller's responsibility to deliver the goods to the named port of destination and have them removed from the arriving vessel and placed dockside. In addition, the seller is responsible for customs clearance and payment of duties. The buyer's responsibilities commence with taking delivery at dockside.

DEQ places greater costs and responsibilities on the seller. Not only does it face the potential delays in delivering the goods to the foreign port by the contractually-specified date, but it also has to take into account the uncertainties of customs procedures and costs in a foreign country. If a seller decides to accept DEQ terms in its contract, it should verify the amount of duty liability it will incur, and determine the complexities of customs procedures in the country of unloading. One preliminary point for consideration is whether a foreign seller can legally effect customs clearance in that country.

As the *Guide to INCOTERMS 2000* points out, the terms of DEQ may be altered by agreement of the parties. The responsibility for customs clearance and duty payment may be shifted to the buyer by stating "DEQ (not cleared for import)" in the contract, dropping the reference "Duty Paid". In addition, the seller should consider adding the "delay" language suggested above in the discussion of DES.

Once again, DEQ is appropriate only for water transport by vessel.

➤*SAMPLE LANGUAGE:*

The goods will be sold DEQ (INCOTERMS 2000) [named port of destination].

Delivered Duty Unpaid [named place of destination]

Delivered Duty Unpaid (DDU) requires the seller to deliver the goods at a specified place in the country of importation or a third country. The seller is liable for international transportation, removal of the goods from the means of carriage, and subsequent inland transportation to the named place. The buyer is liable for customs clearance, duties and taxes.

DDU is appropriate for all means of international transport.

➤*SAMPLE LANGUAGE:*

The goods will be sold DDU (INCOTERMS 2000) [named place of destination].

Delivered Duty Paid [named place of destination]

The Delivered Duty Paid (DDP) term requires the seller to deliver the goods at a specified point in the country of importation (or a third country), and clear customs and pay applicable duties in the country of delivery. The cautions provided above concerning similar obligations under DEQ are equally applicable for DDP.

One point to consider is which party will be responsible for paying internal taxes (such as Value Added Tax). The *Guide to INCOTERMS 2000* suggests that the seller can avoid responsibility for VAT payment through contract language stating "DDP, VAT unpaid". This language may, of course, be modified to address any other taxes with which the seller might otherwise be charged.

DDP is appropriate for all forms of international transport.

➤*SAMPLE LANGUAGE:*

The goods will be sold DDP (INCOTERMS 2000) [named place of destination].

Trade Terms Under the Uniform Commercial Code

The UCC also sets forth trade terms that allocate the costs and risks of delivery. Pursuant to UCC § 1-105(1), these terms may be used in international sales. Thus, with the UCC established as a possible competitor to INCOTERMS, the parties should specify which of the two applies to their contract. Making this choice is even more crucial in light of the UCC's use of several acronyms that are identical to those used in INCOTERMS, but that impose substantially different responsibilities on the parties. Misunderstandings may arise when the parties use the same trade term acronym. If one of the parties is in the U.S., it may be more familiar with the UCC and simply assume the UCC's application, while a non-U.S. party may have no knowledge of the UCC and simply assume that INCOTERMS is referenced. As suggested in the preceding discussion of INCOTERMS, a parenthetical reference following the trade term acronym should avoid any confusion.

Free on Board

The UCC's version of Free on Board (FOB), UCC § 2-319(1), has substantial differences from the INCOTERMS' version. The UCC permits the parties to specify a place of shipment or a place of delivery in the contract using this term. If a place of shipment is specified, it means that the seller is obligated to make the goods available to the buyer at the named place, and bear the risks and costs of putting them into the buyer's possession. If a place of delivery is specified, the seller bears the risks and costs of transporting them to that point. The term may be used for any mode of transport, not just vessels. In addition, the seller bears all costs of loading the goods on board the vessel, vehicle, or other conveyance.

The UCC's version of FOB encompasses many more possible delivery points, and attendant divergences in the allocation of costs and risks, than that of INCOTERMS. In fact, depending on whether and where a shipment or delivery point is named, FOB in UCC parlance can embrace any one of a number of INCOTERMS, ranging from Ex Works through the "D" group. For example, a contract stating "FOB (UCC) seller's warehouse" is analogous to an INCOTERMS Ex Works contract, although the UCC term appears to require the seller to pay for loading while the INCOTERMS places this responsibility on the buyer. The UCC would permit an FOB delivery point of anywhere within the country of exportation (as would FCA) or in the country of arrival/importation (as would a "D" term). Because the UCC's FOB does not divorce transportation risks and costs, it does not have an analog to the "C" terms.

Under the UCC, FOB may be used for any mode of transportation, unlike INCOTERMS. Although FOB in a UCC sense may be used for placement of goods on a vessel, it diverges from its INCOTERMS counterpart by making the seller responsible for all costs of loading, rather than dividing the costs as under the INCOTERMS' FOB.

Note also that the UCC term does not address responsibility for export clearance. Thus, if the goods are made available at a named place in the country of exportation, a routed transaction may be involved, and the BIS and Census Bureau regulations discussed previously would be applicable.

Free Alongside Vessel

The UCC's version of Free Alongside Vessel (FAS), UCC § 2-319(2), requires the seller to bear the risks and costs of placing the goods alongside the designated vessel at a named port. It thus resembles FAS under the INCOTERMS, except that it does not provide that the seller is responsible for export clearance. As a result, if the UCC's version of FAS is used, the sale may be considered a routed transaction for export control and statistical reporting purposes.

Cost, Insurance and Freight

Cost, Insurance and Freight (CIF) in UCC terminology requires the seller to arrange and pay for transportation by "a carrier at the port for shipment", and arrange and pay for insurance covering such transportation. UCC § 2-320(1). This may encompass the international movement of goods, although this is not necessarily the case, as the port for shipment may be a point at which the goods are loaded for inland transportation in the country of exportation. In an important divergence from CIF under the INCOTERMS, the UCC version places the risk of loss during transportation on the seller instead of the buyer.

Cost & Freight

Cost & Freight (C&F) for UCC purposes has the same meaning as CIF, except that the seller is not obligated to obtain insurance covering the transportation of the goods. UCC § 2-320(1), (3). It too places the risk of loss during transportation on the seller.

Delivery "Ex-Ship"

The term Delivery Ex-Ship, for UCC purposes, requires the seller to pay for, and bear the risk of loss for, the merchandise until it is unloaded from the vessel. The UCC term is more akin to DEQ under the INCOTERMS, although it makes no provision for customs clearance and duty payments.

Passage of Title

Although the INCOTERMS establish the point at which possession and control of the goods transfers from seller to buyer, they specifically do not govern passage of title to the merchandise. J. Ramberg, *ICC Guide to Incoterms 2000* (1999) 11, 12. Nevertheless, as a general rule there is a relationship between the physical delivery of merchandise and the passage of title, as set forth in national laws concerning title transfer. In the United States, for example, title transfer is determined under the UCC. Thus, even if the parties to a contract have agreed to rely on INCOTERMS to define the place and method of delivery, if they agree that U.S. law governs the contract they would look to the UCC to determine title transfer questions. (Note that the United Nations Convention on Contracts for the International Sale of Goods explicitly avoids coverage of title transfer matters, leaving them to national law for resolution. Convention Article 4(b); *see St. Paul Guardian, supra*).

Under the UCC, both delivery and transfer of title occur at the point of delivery, unless the parties have agreed to a different arrangement. The Code provides that delivery is the point at which the seller makes merchandise available to the buyer in accordance with the contract, thereby fulfilling its contractual obligation. *See* UCC § 2-301: "The obligation of the seller is to transfer and deliver and that of the buyer is to accept and pay in accordance with the contract." Also, once delivery has been made, the risk of loss for the merchandise shifts from the seller to the buyer under the UCC. *See* UCC §§ 2-319-322 concerning points at which delivery and passage of risk take place.

Section 2-401 of the UCC establishes the relationship between delivery of merchandise and passage of title. It provides that title passes at the time of delivery, unless otherwise agreed between the parties. Thus, as a general rule, the seller will fulfill its contractual obligation to deliver the goods covered by a contract simultaneously with passage of title to those goods from the seller to the buyer. *MEI International, Inc. v. Schenkers International Forwarders, Inc.*, 1992 WL 176657 (S.D.N.Y. 1992)("[u]nder U.C.C. § 2-401(2), title to goods passes at the time and place that the seller completes performance with respect to the physical delivery of the goods"); *The Hong Kong and Shanghai Banking Corp. v. HFH USA Corp.*, 805 F. Supp. 133 (W.D.N.Y. 1992).

Section 2-401 provides:

> § 2-401. Passing of Title; Reservation for Security; Limited Application of This Section.
>
> Each provision of this Article with regard to the rights, obligations and remedies of the seller, the buyer, purchasers or other third parties applies irrespective of title to the goods except where the provision refers to such title. Insofar as situations are not covered by the other provisions of this Article and matters concerning title become material the following rules apply:
>
> > (1) Title to goods cannot pass under a contract for sale prior to their identification to the contract (Section 2-501), and unless otherwise explicitly agreed the buyer acquires by their identification a special property as limited by this Act.

> Any retention or reservation by the seller of the title (property) in goods shipped or delivered to the buyer is limited in effect to a reservation of a security interest. Subject to these provisions and to the provisions of the Article on Secured Transactions (Article 9), title to goods passes from the seller to the buyer in any manner and on any conditions explicitly agreed on by the parties.
>
> (2) Unless otherwise explicitly agreed title passes to the buyer at the time and place at which the seller completes his performance with reference to the physical delivery of the goods, despite any reservation of a security interest and even though a document of title is to be delivered at a different time or place; and in particular and despite any reservation of a security interest by the bill of lading.
>
> (a) if the contract requires or authorizes the seller to send the goods to the buyer but does not require him to deliver them at destination, title passes to the buyer at the time and place of shipment; but
>
> (b) if the contract requires delivery at destination, title passes on tender there.
>
> (3) Unless otherwise explicitly agreed where delivery is to be made without moving the goods,
>
> (a) if the seller is to deliver a document of title, title passes at the time when and the place where he delivers such documents; or
>
> (b) if the goods are at the time of contracting already identified and no documents are to be delivered, title passes at the time and place of contracting.

This provision means that title passes on delivery. *Bank of New York v. Margiotta*, 416 N.Y. Supp. 2d 146 (1979). Note, however, that the UCC's provision only applies if the parties have not reached a contrary agreement; if the parties agree to passage of title under a circumstance other than delivery, the agreement of the parties will control. *S&H Communications, Inc. v. Senscor Technologies, Inc.*, 633 N.Y. Supp. 2d 146 (1995).

Application of the general rules concerning delivery and title transfer that are set forth in the UCC and court cases hinges on when delivery occurs. UCC § 2-401(2) covers delivery that is effected when the goods are transported to the buyer by the seller. Section 2-401(2)(a) provides that, when the seller's responsibility is limited to sending but not delivering the goods, delivery occurs at the time and place of shipment. Under § 2-401(2)(b), by contrast, when the contract requires the seller to deliver the goods to the buyer, delivery occurs when the goods have been brought to the buyer's facility.

Section 2-401(3) covers transfer of title where the goods will not be moved as part of the contract, *i.e.*, where the merchandise is made available for the buyer to pick up at the seller's facility and the buyer will have sole responsibility for transporting the merchandise from that point. Under § 2-401(3)(a), title transfer is made when and where any required document of title is delivered to the buyer; this may occur at the seller's facility or elsewhere. However, implicit in this provision is that delivery occurs at the seller's facility.

As we have seen, the UCC delivery provisions differ in important respects from those of INCOTERMS, although each UCC provision has a more or less analogous INCOTERM. To avoid any potential ambiguity in the determination of when delivery and title transfer have occurred, a sales contract using INCOTERMS should specify that title to the goods passes when deliver under the chosen INCOTERM takes place, or at some other point if the parties so agree.

Under the UCC, upon agreement of the parties, delivery of the merchandise and passage of title may occur at different points. Although the seemingly broad "[u]nless otherwise explicitly agreed" prefatory language of Section 4-201(2) would appear to permit the parties to agree to title transfer after delivery has occurred, the UCC elsewhere curtails their ability to do so. Section 2-401(1) provides that "[a]ny retention or reservation by the seller of the title (property) in goods shipped or delivered to the buyer is limited in effect to a reservation of a security interest."

Courts have reached different conclusions concerning whether this limitation may be bypassed by agreement of the parties. The divergent interpretations were noted in *Northwestern Flyers, Inc. v. Olson Bros. Mfg. Co., Inc.*, 679 F.2d 1264, 1271 (8th Cir. 1982): "[c]ompare *Bowman v. American Home Assurance Co.*, *supra*, 213 N.W.2d at 448 (explicit agreement can prevent passage of title beyond time of delivery) with *In re Bosson*, 432 F. Supp. 1013, 1020 n.24 (D. Conn. 1977) (parties by agreement cannot delay passage of title beyond date of final delivery)." *See also The Hong Kong and Shanghai Banking Corp. v. HFH USA Corp.*, 805 F. Supp. at 144 ("U.C.C. § 2-401 provides that a title retention agreement such as the one in this case operates to reserve a security interest in the seller"); *Usinor Industeel v. Leeco Steel Products, Inc.*, 209 F. Supp.2d 880 (D. Ill. 2002)(same).

The fact that § 4-201(2) does not contain a proviso specifically permitting the parties to delay title passage beyond delivery supports the view that the seller's title retention beyond this point would not be permitted. This was the analysis followed in *In re Bosson*, 432 F. Supp. at 1020 n.24:

> Although § 2-401(2) begins with the phrase '[unless] otherwise explicitly agreed,' the prior subsection places limits on the parties' contractual freedom. Specifically, § 2-401(1) negates any attempt to forestall passage of title beyond the moment of final delivery; contract language purporting to do so merely results in a security interest being retained. Similarly, § 2-401(1) prohibits the passage of title prior to the identification of the goods in question to the contract. In between these extremes, however, the parties may by contract specify the point at which title passes.

Other countries' laws may permit the seller to maintain unreserved title to merchandise after delivery if the contract so provides. *Usinor*, *supra* ("{u}nder French law, the seller of goods has an absolute right to contract for title until payment"); *St. Paul Guardian*, *supra* ("it is standard 'practice under German law to agree that the transfer of title will only occur upon payment of the entire purchase price, well after the date of passing of risk and after receipt of the goods by the buyer.'") Consequently, the choice of national law governing the contract will determine this issue.

Notices and Waiver

To facilitate communication between the parties, the contract should address the form and recipients of notices. The drafter of such a provision should take into account the need to get notice to responsible persons in an expeditious manner. The parties may consider using such means as telephone or e-mail communication, followed up by a written notice that is sent *via* a means such as registered mail or an express courier service, that allows tracking and proof of delivery.

➤*SAMPLE LANGUAGE:*

> **Notices.** All notices under this agreement shall be in English, and shall be in writing and given by registered airmail or private courier, cable, or telex (acknowledged by answer back) or telefax confirmed by a copy sent by airmail or private courier, addressed to the parties at the addresses immediately below their respective signatures hereto, or to such other address of which either party may advise the other in writing. Notices will be deemed given when sent.

We note that cable and telex are no longer favored means of communication in international business, and a party that considers using one or both of them should determine whether the other party has the capability to receive such messages.

➤*SAMPLE LANGUAGE:*

> **Notices.** Any notices or other communications between the parties provided for or issued in connection with this agreement shall be made by any reasonable means in writing, with postage or other delivery costs prepaid by the sender, to the parties at the following addresses to the attention of the person designated. A party may require that notices be sent to a different address and/or different designated party upon notice to the other party. [Designate names and addresses below.]

During the course of a contract that covers an extended period of time and/or involves multiple shipments of goods, the parties' conduct often varies from the written terms of their contract. For example, the buyer may accept a later shipping date than is called for under the contract, or the seller may accept payment later than the contract specifies. While such accommodations may allow the parties to get along in a pragmatic and cooperative manner, their prolonged use may have an adverse consequence in the event one of the parties later attempts to enforce the letter of the contract. Article 9.1 of the U.N. Convention binds the parties to "any practices which they have established between themselves." If, in practice, one party waives a contractual requirement, this article may prevent it from reasserting the written requirement.

To avoid this potential problem, the contract should contain a provision that expressly subordinates informal practices to the letter of the agreement. The following paragraph addresses this issue.

➤*SAMPLE LANGUAGE:*

Waiver. Any waiver(s) of a requirement or provision of this agreement by one or both parties shall neither be considered to constitute a future waiver of such requirement or provision nor an alteration of any requirement or provision of this contract.

➤*SAMPLE LANGUAGE:*

Waiver. The parties agree that the failure of either party at any time to require performance by the other party of any of the terms and conditions of this agreement shall not operate as a waiver of the right of such party to request and require strict performance of the same or like provisions, or any other provisions hereof, at a later time.

Renegotiation, Alteration and Amendment

The parties to a contract frequently decide to alter or amend its terms. In anticipation of one party or the other, or both, deciding to seek a change, the contract should include a renegotiation, alteration and amendment clause. This clause should require that any change be made in writing, and be signed on behalf of each party by persons in a position of responsibility. An example follows.

➤*SAMPLE LANGUAGE:*

Alteration or Amendment. Neither this agreement nor any provision thereof may be altered, amended, varied, changed or modified in any manner, except by means of a written agreement executed on behalf of a party by the person who executed this agreement or his delegate or successor.

Indemnification

The buyer often requires the seller to indemnify it against damages resulting from claims brought by third parties. Typically, the buyer could be found liable in contract, for defects in goods that it purchased from the seller and resold or for late delivery of resold goods due to the seller's breach. In addition, the buyer may be subject to tort liability for death or personal injury caused by the resold merchandise.

The parties may consider including an indemnity provision to address such occurrences. A sample is provided below.

➤*SAMPLE LANGUAGE:*

Indemnification. The seller agrees to indemnify and hold the buyer, its officers, directors, employees, successors, and assigns harmless against all claims, charges, causes of action, losses, damages, judgments or costs or expenses of whatever form or nature, including attorneys' fees and other costs of legal defense, whether direct or indirect, that they, or any of them, may sustain or incur as a result of any acts or omissions of the seller or any of its directors, officers, employees, or agents, including but not limited to (1) breach of any of the provisions of this agreement, (2) negligence or other tortious conduct, (3) liability arising from the sale of the merchandise covered by this agreement, or (4) violation by the seller or any of its directors, officers, employees, or agents of any applicable law, regulation, or order in [the country of importation or exportation].

Insurance

As a related concern, the buyer may also require the seller to maintain insurance coverage that includes both parties and is sufficient to indemnify both in the event of a third party claim resulting from the merchandise. The following model language addresses the seller's responsibility to obtain and maintain a general liability policy for a specified period. This provision is premised on a continuing sales relationship between the seller and buyer for a specified period.

➤*SAMPLE LANGUAGE:*

Insurance. Seller agrees that it will procure and maintain at its own expense for the entire term of this agreement and a [two year] period thereafter comprehensive general liability insurance [including product liability insurance] in an amount not less than $[5,000,000] single limit coverage. Seller shall contract for such insurance from responsible insurance carriers.

Confidentiality of Proprietary Information

Occasionally, the sale of merchandise also requires the seller to provide related "know how" to the buyer; such knowledge is often considered by the seller to be business proprietary information. As a general matter, such occasions are more common when the contract involves providing a mix of goods and services, a made to order product, and/or a longer-term relationship with a series of successive transactions. Information confidentiality concerns are less frequent in contracts involving "off the shelf" articles. Also, the buyer may provide the seller with confidential information when the goods are to be built to the buyer's specification.

A confidentiality provision should define the covered information, protect against either party's disclosure or misuse of the other's proprietary information, and where appropriate provide guidelines for the proper use of the information.

➤*SAMPLE LANGUAGE:*

Confidentiality of Technical Information. The buyer shall hold in strict confidence the technical information supplied to it by the seller and shall not divulge the same to any other person, firm, or corporation without the prior written permission of the seller, except as reasonably required to perform its obligations under the agreement. The buyer, its agents, directors, officers, and employees shall use their best efforts to maintain such technical information secret and confidential and shall exercise the same degree of care for such purpose as the buyer desires to keep secret and confidential. The obligation of the buyer to keep the technical information secret and confidential shall survive termination of this agreement for any reason.

➤*SAMPLE LANGUAGE:*

Use of Technical Information and Proprietary Rights. The buyer shall not, without the seller's prior specific written consent, use for any purpose other than implementation of this agreement any portion of the technical information supplied by the seller hereunder or any patent, trademark, or other industrial property right of the seller, copy any of seller's designs of any of the products that are the subject of this agreement. Acknowledging that the damages sustainable by the seller as a consequence of any breach of the buyer's obligations under this Section 6.2 may be difficult to measure in monetary terms, the buyer hereby agrees that the seller shall be entitled to have the continuation of any such breach permanently enjoined.

➤*SAMPLE LANGUAGE:*

Confidential Information

A. The buyer shall not, either directly or indirectly, in whole or in part, except as authorized in writing by the seller, use or disclose to any person, firm, corporation, or any other entity, any information of a proprietary nature ("trade secrets") owned by the seller or any of its affiliated companies including, but not limited to, records, customer lists, data, formulae, documents, drawings, specifications, inventions, processes, methods and intangible rights.

B. Any information regarding the products which, during the term of this agreement is divulged by either party to the other is confidential and shall be protected from disclosure.

C. The prohibited use or disclosure, as used herein, shall be for the term of the Agreement and at any time within five (5) years of the termination of this Agreement.

➤*SAMPLE LANGUAGE:*

Protection of Confidential Information. The parties acknowledge that, during the course of negotiations leading to, and performance following, the entry into force of this contract, each may have been given access to or knowledge of certain proprietary information concerning the business of the other, including business plans, financial information, product development, specifications, and performance requirements, and customer lists and account records. Each party agrees that all such confidential information will only be provided to, and used by, those personnel who are responsible for the performance of this agreement, and that such provision and use shall be solely for purposes relating to the performance of this agreement.

Protection of Intellectual Property

Occasionally, a sale of merchandise involves the use of intellectual property: for example, the sale involves merchandise bearing a trademark owned by the seller, or the seller grants permission to the buyer to use a trademark in connection with the marketing and advertising of the goods. In these circumstances, the contract should address the nature and scope of the seller's grant of authority to the buyer to use the intellectual property.

Below are several examples of intellectual property provisions adapted for contracts for the sale of goods. The first provides a "bare bones" reference covering all common forms of intellectual property, while the second and third address trademarks and trade names only. Following these three examples is a paragraph requiring the buyer's assistance in protecting the seller's intellectual property in the country of importation.

➤*SAMPLE LANGUAGE:*

Trademarks, Patents, Copyrights and Brand Names

A. Any and all trademarks, patents, copyrights and brand-names now in effect, created, applied for or received in the future, of the Product, shall always be and remain the property of the seller.

B. The buyer shall not under any circumstances acquire any rights whatsoever in any trademark, patent, copyright, brand name or other proprietary right of the seller.

➤*SAMPLE LANGUAGE:*

Trademarks and Trade Names. The buyer shall not directly or indirectly use any of the seller's trademarks or part thereof, or any mark or name confusingly similar thereto, as part of its corporate or business name or in any other manner, except that on the seller's written consent the buyer may use the seller's trademarks relating to the products for purposes of advertising the products, and in any other manner previously approved by the seller in writing. In addition, the buyer shall not register any of the seller's trademarks or any mark or name closely resembling them, unless requested to do so by the seller in writing, nor shall the buyer remove or deface any of the seller's trademarks affixed to the products.

➤*SAMPLE LANGUAGE:*

Rights in Trademarks and Trade Names. Buyer expressly recognizes and acknowledges that all right, title and interest in and to the [identify trademarks/trade names relating to products subject to the sales contract] are vested in seller. Buyer further recognizes that nothing herein shall be construed to give buyer any right, title or interest in or to the [trademarks/trade names] nor shall buyer claim any such right, title or interest.

➤*SAMPLE LANGUAGE:*

Protection of Proprietary Rights. The buyer agrees to cooperate with and assist the seller, at the seller's expense, in the protection of trademarks, trade names, patents, or copyrights owned by or licensed to the seller, and shall inform the seller immediately of any infringements or other improper action with respect to such trademarks, trade names, patents, or copyrights that shall come to the attention of the buyer.

Compliance With Laws

Each party may wish to have a contractual guarantee that the other has complied with all applicable laws and regulations. For example, both the buyer and seller have an interest in the other's assurance that export control requirements have been met, the former to be sure either that there are no export control impediments to timely and full delivery or that the goods have not been shipped in violation of export control requirements, and the latter to be certain that the buyer has not reexported or otherwise used the goods in a proscribed manner. If the goods are subject to health, safety, or other requirements in the country of importation, the buyer will likely seek a contractual provision that they do conform to the requirements.

➤*SAMPLE LANGUAGE:*

Compliance With Laws. Seller shall comply with all applicable [name of jurisdiction] [federal/provincial/state/local] laws, rules, regulations and orders in performing this agreement.

The buyer may seek specific guarantees and an indemnification that the seller has met certain specified legal requirements, such as payment of customs duties when the seller also acts as the importer, as in the following example.

Seller warrants that it has complied with all requirements of [customs authorities] concerning the articles that seller has imported. Seller further warrants that articles that it has imported are not subject to assessment or collection of additional duties, taxes, fees, fines, penalties or other claims by [customs authorities] or any other agency or ministry of the Government of [country] or of any [state/provincial/local] government. Seller further warrants that any exports of articles from [country] are in compliance with export control laws, rules and regulations imposed by the Government of [country]. Seller agrees to indemnify buyer for any additional duties, taxes, fees, fines, penalties or other claims assessed by or any other agency or ministry of the Government of [country] or of any [state/provincial/local] government for any breach of the warranties provided in this paragraph.

Warranties, Defects and Returns

In crafting a provision concerning warranties, and notice of defects, the parties should be cognizant of the relevant requirements of the UN Convention and the UCC. As discussed in Commentary Chapter I.2, UCC §§ 2-313 through 2-316 provide detailed warranty requirements. In a contract governed by the UCC, these requirements will apply unless there is an express derogation from them in the contract. Article 35 of the U.N. Convention, on the other hand, has fewer and less explicit warranty requirements.

The following paragraph should be considered as a complement to the warranty provisions of the UCC and the U.N. Convention.

➤*SAMPLE LANGUAGE:*

Warranties

A. The seller shall, at its discretion, repair or replace any Product at its own expense found by the buyer to be defective, provided that:

(1) In the case of visible and apparent defects, immediate written notice is given by buyer to the seller of such defects and the defective products are returned to the seller within ___ weeks of the date of their receipt by the buyer;

(2) In the case of functional or non-apparent defects, written notice is given by the buyer to the seller within ___ months of the date of their shipment by the seller;

B. The seller shall pay [fifty (50)] percent of the round-trip cost of transportation for merchandise covered by validated warranty claims.

The above limited warranty is subject to the following restrictions:

(1) That the Product not be used for any purpose other than the normal purpose for which it was manufactured;

(2) The observance by the user of all operation instructions and recommendations provided by the seller;

(3) the buyer's cooperation in and with any investigation by the seller with respect to defects.

Excusable Non-Performance

The parties should consider including a provision setting forth the reasons for which performance of a contractual requirement may be excused for unforeseen or unavoidable events such as natural disasters or government action. Several sample provisions follow.

➤*SAMPLE LANGUAGE:*

Force Majeure. Neither party shall be in default hereunder by reason of any failure or delay in the performance of any obligation under this agreement where such failure or delay arises out of any cause beyond the reasonable control of the party and without the fault or negligence of such party. Such causes shall include, without limitation, storms, floods, other acts of nature, fires, explosions, riots, war or civil disturbance, strikes or other labor unrest, embargoes and other governmental actions or regulations that would prohibit either party from ordering or furnishing products or from performing any other aspects of the obligations hereunder, delays in transportation, and inability to obtain necessary labor, supplies, or manufacturing facilities. In the event that any such events prevent or delay either party from performing hereunder, the parties will cooperate with each other to minimize and mitigate any potential damages that one or both parties may suffer as a result of such failure or delay in performance and to assist each other in overcoming the causes for the failure or delay in performance.

➤*SAMPLE LANGUAGE:*

Excusable Failure or Default. The parties shall be relieved of liability for failure to perform any obligation or requirement under this agreement if such performance is made impossible by act of God, labor dispute, government action, regulation or prohibition, or any circumstance of any nature that is reasonably beyond the control of the parties.

Choice of Law

Most parties to commercial agreements doubtless do not anticipate a falling out with their contracting partner, and in the vast majority of transactions the terms of the sales agreement are fulfilled without a dispute. Nevertheless, the possibility of a disagreement, or (short of that) the need to interpret ambiguous contract language or fill gaps left by the contract, requires the parties to designate a jurisdiction whose laws will govern the contract's construction.

If the parties do not make a choice and a dispute arises, a choice will be made for them. The U.N. Convention will perforce apply to contracts between parties located in Convention signatories unless they specifically "opt out" of its coverage. U.N. Convention, Article 6. Similarly, the UCC as codified in a specific state will apply to international "transactions bearing an appropriate relation to" that state, unless the parties have specifically provided that another law will apply. UCC § 1-105(1). Even if the parties are content to have the UCC govern their transaction, they should specify the state whose version of the UCC shall apply.

The following choice of law clause provides a straightforward approach to the issue.

➤*SAMPLE LANGUAGE:*

> **Applicable Law.** This agreement shall be construed, enforced, and performed in accordance with the laws of the State of New York.

The choice of forum and means of dispute resolution are closely related to the choice of governing law. Unless the parties specify the jurisdiction in which a dispute will be heard, they are inviting a "race to the courthouse" in one of the countries in which a party resides or which otherwise has jurisdiction to resolve disputes arising from the contract. The parties are free to choose a forum, and that choice should be respected by the court that was chosen, and other courts potentially having jurisdiction, unless the choice was "unreasonable".

United States courts will generally defer to choice of forum provisions in international sales contracts. The U.S. Supreme Court set forth the fundamental rule in *The Bremen v. Zapata Off-Shore Co.*, 407 U.S. 1, 12-13 (1972): "a freely negotiated private international agreement, unaffected by fraud, undue influence, or overweening bargaining power, such as that involved here, should be given full effect." In reaching this conclusion, the Court considered that "[t]he choice of . . . forum was made in an arm's-length negotiation by experienced and sophisticated businessmen, and absent some compelling and countervailing reason it should be honored by the parties and enforced by the courts." *Id.* at 12. In short, in normal circumstances the judiciary must respect the express agreement of the parties even if, as in *The Bremen*, doing so means the U.S. court must divest itself of jurisdiction over the dispute.

The Supreme Court mentioned several possible bases for U.S. courts to disregard the contractual provision: "fraud, undue influence, or overweening bargaining power". *Id.* In addition, "[a] contractual choice-of-forum clause should be held unenforceable if enforcement would contravene a strong public policy of the forum in which suit is brought, whether declared by statute or by judicial decision. See, e.g., *Boyd v. Grand Trunk W. R. Co.,* 338 U.S. 263 (1949)." *Id.* at 15. On the other hand, the Court largely rejected the forum's supposed inconvenience to one of the parties as a basis for disregarding a choice of forum clause in an international contract, as the clause itself evidenced the parties' agreement that the chosen forum was convenient:

> Courts have also suggested that a forum clause, even though it is freely bargained for and contravenes no important public policy of the forum, may nevertheless be "unreasonable" and unenforceable if the chosen forum is seriously inconvenient for the trial of the action. Of course, where it can be said with reasonable assurance that at the time they entered the contract, the parties to a freely negotiated private international commercial agreement contemplated the claimed inconvenience, it is difficult to see why any such claim of inconvenience should be heard to render the forum clause unenforceable. We are not here dealing with an

> agreement between two Americans to resolve their essentially local disputes in a remote alien forum. In such a case, the serious inconvenience of the contractual forum to one or both of the parties might carry greater weight in determining the reasonableness of the forum clause. The remoteness of the forum might suggest that the agreement was an adhesive one, or that the parties did not have the particular controversy in mind when they made their agreement; yet even there the party claiming should bear a heavy burden of proof. Similarly, selection of a remote forum to apply differing foreign law to an essentially American controversy might contravene an important public policy of the forum. For example, so long as Bisso governs American courts with respect to the towage business in American waters, it would quite arguably be improper to permit an American tower to avoid that policy by providing a foreign forum for resolution of his disputes with an American towee.
>
> This case, however, involves a freely negotiated international commercial transaction between a German and an American corporation for towage of a vessel from the Gulf of Mexico to the Adriatic Sea. As noted, selection of a London forum was clearly a reasonable effort to bring vital certainty to this international transaction and to provide a neutral forum experienced and capable in the resolution of admiralty litigation. Whatever "inconvenience" Zapata would suffer by being forced to litigate in the contractual forum as it agreed to do was clearly foreseeable at the time of contracting. In such circumstances it should be incumbent on the party seeking to escape his contract to show that trial in the contractual forum will be so gravely difficult and inconvenient that he will for all practical purposes be deprived of his day in court. Absent that, there is no basis for concluding that it would be unfair, unjust, or unreasonable to hold that party to his bargain.

Id. at 16-18. The Court specifically noted the "uncertainty and possibly great inconvenience to both parties could arise if a suit could be maintained in any jurisdiction in which an accident might occur or if jurisdiction were left to any place" where jurisdiction over the case might arise. *Id.* at 13-14.

Although *The Bremen v. Zapata* arose in the relatively narrow context of federal admiralty jurisdiction, the Supreme Court has relied on it to posit a general rule of deference to the choice of forum clause chosen by the parties in disputes arising under federal statutes as a general matter. For example, in *Scherk v. Alberto-Culver Co.*, 417 U.S. 506 (1974), the Court considered whether a dispute concerning alleged securities law violations could be adjudicated in a United States federal district court in the face of a contractual provision requiring that disputes be resolved by arbitration before the International Chamber of Commerce in Paris, France. Applying the Federal Arbitration Act, 9 U.S.C. § 1 *et seq.*, the Court concluded that the district court lacked jurisdiction, notwithstanding that the dispute involved the defendant's alleged violation of a federal statute.

The Court emphasized that a choice of forum provision was advisable in international contracts to avoid uncertainty about dispute resolution:

> In this case, by contrast, in the absence of the arbitration provision considerable uncertainty existed at the time of the agreement, and still exists, concerning the law applicable to the resolution of disputes arising out of the contract.

> Such uncertainty will almost inevitably exist with respect to any contract touching two or more countries, each with its own substantive laws and conflict-of-laws rules. A contractual provision specifying in advance the forum in which disputes shall be litigated and the law to be applied is, therefore, an almost indispensable precondition to achievement of the orderliness and predictability essential to any international business transaction. Furthermore, such a provision obviates the danger that a dispute under the agreement might be submitted to a forum hostile to the interests of one of the parties or unfamiliar with the problem area involved.
>
> A parochial refusal by the courts of one country to enforce an international arbitration agreement would not only frustrate these purposes, but would invite unseemly and mutually destructive jockeying by the parties to secure tactical litigation advantages.

417 U.S. at 517 (footnotes omitted). Citing uncertainty and possibly great inconvenience to both parties could arise if a suit could be maintained in any jurisdiction in which an accident might occur or if jurisdiction were left to any place" where the defendant party might be found, *The Bremen*, 407 U.S. at 13, the Court held "that the agreement of the parties in this case to arbitrate any dispute arising out of their international commercial transaction is to be respected and enforced by the federal courts in accord with the explicit provisions of the Arbitration Act", 417 U.S. at 520-21.

Scherk also provided guidance concerning the circumstances in which a forum selection clause or arbitration clause could be disregarded for fraud:

> In The Bremen we noted that forum-selection clauses "should be given full effect" when "a freely negotiated private international agreement [is] unaffected by fraud . . . ." 407 U.S., at 13, 12. This qualification does not mean that any time a dispute arising out of a transaction is based upon an allegation of fraud, as in this case, the clause is unenforceable. Rather, it means that an arbitration or forum-selection clause in a contract is not enforceable if the inclusion of that clause in the contract was the product of fraud or coercion. Cf. *Prima Paint Corp. v. Flood & Conklin Mfg. Co.*, 388 U.S. 395 .

417 U.S. at 519 note 14. Thus, a mere allegation of fraud in the formation, performance, or non-performance of the contract will not suffice to block enforcement of the clause. Rather, the party seeking non-enforcement will have to allege and prove that the clause was fraudulently included in the contract; on its face, this would appear to be a tall order in most circumstances.

Interestingly, the Court indicated that the choice of forum could be construed as also indicating the parties' choice of law applicable to the contract, or at least to any dispute arising from the contract: "Under some circumstances, the designation of arbitration in a certain place might also be viewed as implicitly selecting the law of that place to apply to that transaction." 417 U.S. at 519 note 13. The Court did not delve further into this issue, as in the contract before it the parties had agreed in the arbitration clause that "[t]he laws of the State of Illinois, U.S. A. shall apply to and govern this agreement, its interpretation and performance", *id.* at 508 note 1.

The rule of deference to the parties' contractual choice of arbitration was later amplified in *Mitsubishi Motors v. Soler Chrysler-Plymouth*, 473 U.S. 614 (1985)(ordering arbitration of alleged violation of antitrust laws).

The Bremen arose out of an admiralty action in which federal courts have exclusive jurisdiction. Both *Scherk* and *Mitsubishi Motors* involved the interpretation of federal statutes, over which federal courts have exclusive jurisdiction, and hinged on application of the federal Arbitration Act. Thus, it appears quite well-settled that forum selection and arbitration clauses will be enforced by federal courts hearing cases arising from their exclusive jurisdiction.

However, federal courts also have diversity jurisdiction over cases arising out of non-federal laws where the parties are "citizens of a State and citizens or subjects of a foreign state" and "the matter in controversy exceeds the sum or value of $75,000, exclusive of interest and costs." 28 U.S.C. § 1332(a)(2). The Arbitration Act would require federal courts sitting in diversity jurisdiction to honor an arbitration agreement to the same extent they would in a federal question case. 9 U.S.C. §§ 2-4. On the other hand, the federal court's enforcement of a forum selection clause will be determined by the laws of the state in which the court sits. *Klaxon Co. v. Stentor Electric Mfg. Co.*, 313 U.S. 487, 497 (1941); *Hartford Fire Insurance Co. v. Orient Overseas Containers Lines (UK) Ltd.*, 230 F.3d 549 (2d Cir. 2000).

To the extent the parties agree to Federal jurisdiction over a dispute, they should be certain that a federal district court would have jurisdiction over the matter.

If the parties agree that a dispute should be resolved through arbitration, they should specify this in the contract, and name the arbitration service to be used and the place where arbitration will take place.

The first following paragraph provides a judicial choice of forum, while the next two paragraphs provide for arbitration.

➤*SAMPLE LANGUAGE:*

Forum. The parties agree to resolve any and all disputes arising from this contract in United States District Court for the Southern District of New York.

➤*SAMPLE LANGUAGE:*

Dispute Resolution. Any dispute between the parties regarding the interpretation or performance of this agreement shall be decided by binding arbitration in New York, New York, under the auspices, and in accordance with the applicable rules for commercial disputes, of the American Arbitration Association (AAA). The dispute will be heard before one arbitrator. The parties hereby agree to forego dispute resolution by any other means. The decision of the arbitrator shall be final and conclusive. Each party will pay its own costs of arbitration. Arbitral awards may be entered before any court of competent jurisdiction.

➤*SAMPLE LANGUAGE:*

Arbitration. Any dispute concerning or arising from this agreement shall be heard, settled and decided under the Rules of the American Arbitration Association (the "Rules") in effect as of the date hereof (and those Rules with respect to matters not regulated by them shall incorporate the UNCITRAL Arbitration Rules) by three (3) arbitrator(s) appointed in accordance with the Rules. Such arbitration shall be conducted in English, shall be subject to the substantive and procedural rules of the AAA, and shall be held in New York City, New York, unless the parties shall otherwise mutually agree. The award in such arbitration shall be final and enforceable in any court of competent jurisdiction.

➤*SAMPLE FORM:*

"One Time" Sales Agreement

The following sales agreement is designed for a single, non-recurring sale of merchandise.

AGREEMENT

The undersigned parties hereby enter into the following sales agreement.

1. The Seller is [full name and address]. The Buyer is [full name and address]. The Buyer has appointed [full name and address] to act as its buying agent in negotiating and performing this Agreement.

2. The Seller has agreed to sell to the Buyer ___ quantity "Primadonna" widgets (hereinafter "the merchandise") for a total price of $_______. The merchandise shall be more specifically described in an addendum to this Agreement to be provided by the Seller.

3. The Buyer will deposit $_______ to the Seller's account on or before ____________, 2002, and will pay the $________ balance of the sales price on or before ___________, 2002. Payment shall be in the form of wire transfer or cashier's check to the Seller, with the Seller's account information to be separately provided to the Buyer.

4. The terms of sale are DES (INCOTERMS 2000) [named vessel and port of arrival.] Pursuant to the specified INCOTERM, the Seller shall be responsible for the costs and risks of transportation and insurance, and attendant services, until the carrying vessel's arrival in the port of ________. The Seller shall provide the Buyer with such commercial documentation as will be necessary to clear customs in the country of importation and obtain possession of the merchandise from the carrier.

5. The Seller shall retain title to the merchandise until the merchandise arrives in the port of _________.

6. The Seller will deliver the merchandise to the ocean carrier on or before _________, 2002, with the understanding that the merchandise will arrive in

the port of ____________ on or before __________, 2002. The Seller and the Buyer agree that the aforementioned arrival date may vary depending on the ocean carrier's shipping schedule.

7. The Seller and the Buyer agree that the merchandise is sold "as is", and the Seller provides no warranty, express or implied, concerning the merchandise.

8. This Agreement may be modified or terminated upon the mutual assent of the parties.

9. This Agreement shall be governed by the laws of the State of Montana, U.S.A. Any dispute between the parties shall be resolved through arbitration under the Rules of the American Arbitration Association, with the place of arbitration to be Billings, Montana U.S.A.

Signed:

INTERNATIONAL JURISDICTION IN EUROPEAN UNION E-COMMERCE CONTRACTS*

by
Norel Rosner
Assistant Professor, Department of Private and Notarial Law
University of Groningen, The Netherlands

* Published May 1, 2002. Reproduced with permission.

I. Introduction

"These changes, the most significant since the Industrial revolution, are far-reaching and global. They are not just about technology. They will affect everyone, everywhere."[1] This is the language used by European Commission's president in order to describe the impact of Information and Communication Technology ("ICT") on the society as a whole. However, one cannot overlook the fact that this impact *will* occur in the future and has yet to reach our surroundings. Indeed, if we were to have a quick look at the statistical data, we may notice that the total worth of European e-commerce markets in 1999 was only 18 billions Euro, a modest 17% from the 104 billion Euro, the value of the worldwide e-commerce market.[2]

The current situation is in need, therefore, of immediate improvement. Otherwise, one may only wonder if the new revolution "will affect everyone, everywhere". The tackling of this issue necessitates an approach directed to three separate aspects: Firstly, efficient measures should be taken in order to make *technology accessible*. Secondly, the current *business-consumers practices have* to be adapted to the requirements of a virtual market. Finally, in order to ensure the certainty and uniformity of laws regulating this new environment, which in turn will promote the public trust needed for progress in this area, a framework of efficient legal rules should be adopted.

1 See Romano Prodi, Introductory remarks for "eEurope", a European Commission program designed at speeding up the uptake of digital technologies across Europe, at http://europa.eu.int/comm/information_society/eeurope/index_en.htm.

2 See Booz-Allen & Hamilton and the Ministry of Economic Affairs of the Netherlands, The Competitiveness of Europe's ICT Markets-The crisis amid the growth, p. 24, at http://www.minez.nl/.

It comes almost without saying that the current article will focus only on the latter issue, namely legislative aspects. At the same time, it might be of relevance to mention that while e-commerce posses a number of legal problems, the space available for this analysis does not allow, unfortunately, to treat all these aspects. Indeed, one has to differentiate between three important issues related to e-commerce: Firstly, there are intellectual property matters. Secondly, one can encounter issues related to privacy. Finally, there are important considerations about choice of law and choice of forum to be taken into account, of course mainly in contracts involving international elements.

The purpose of this article is to consider the latter important aspect of international contracts concluded through electronic means, namely the question which forum has jurisdiction to try potential conflicts that may arise from such contracts. When attempting to supply an answer to the above-mentioned question, I shall first try to define the term e-commerce. Subsequently, several specific issues for e-commerce contracts will be identified and then possible solutions will be offered in the light of two recent legislative developments at the European level. Finally, the concluding thoughts will suggest possible solutions based on a recently adopted legislative act.

II. What is e-commerce?

It is a rather difficult task to provide a precise definition of the term e-commerce. The literature on this subject contains various descriptions, ranging form broad and extensive to rather concise and simple formulations. In the following lines I will mention a number of such definitions with a view to provide an as accurate as possible picture.

In a paper published by the European Commission in order to describe the nature of e-commerce and to identify several issues on this area, the definition used includes:

> "any form of business transaction in which the parties interact electronically rather than by physical exchanges or direct physical contact."[3]

Meanwhile, the Ministry of Economic Affairs of the Netherlands published in 1998 a policy paper designed at expanding and improving the use of e-commerce. This plan refers in its turn to electronic commerce as covering:

> "all business transactions that are carried out electronically with a view to improving the efficiency and effectiveness of market and business processes."[4]

One of the most concise definitions for e-commerce, specific for the dynamic world of business, has been suggested by Mr. A.P. van Kerckhoven, product de-

3 See European Commission, Electronic Commerce-An Introduction, at http://www.ispo.cec.be/ecommerce/answers/introduction.html.

4 See the Ministry of Economic Affairs of the Netherlands, Electronic Commerce Action Plan, The Hague, March 1998, p. 7, at http://www.minez.nl/.

velopment-manager at World Online International, formerly a leading Dutch Internet provider:

> "E-commerce is the use of telecommunication and computers in order to support trade."[5]

From the aforementioned definitions we may infer a number of factors that seem to appear on more than one occasion: Firstly, e-commerce presupposes the existence of a business transaction. Secondly, the parties to such a transaction will maintain contact through electronic means rather than conventional ways of communication. Lastly, e-commerce is designed at creating a more efficient business environment.

Having established that, it is quite obvious that e-commerce is not limited to Internet. It rather includes all business transactions carried out through electronic means; Such is the case, for instance, with the so-called Electronic Data Interchange transactions ("EDI"), developed in the 1980's in order to support transactions between suppliers and customers, or with teleshopping and pay television. Nevertheless, e-commerce has known a remarkable expansion only with the establishment of the Internet as a communication protocol available on a large scale. This article is thus limited in scope to jurisdictional issues arising out of contracts concluded through Internet, indeed one of the fastest growing environments where e-commerce is being conducted. In fact, in a definition of e-commerce recently used in a working paper of the European Commission, it is only the Internet that is mentioned as the medium where transactions are being concluded:

> "E-commerce, the buying and selling of goods and services using the Internet."[6]

III. Categories of e-commerce

Electronic transactions may be concluded between various parties: Private enterprises, consumers or public authorities. Depending on the parties participating in the transaction, e-commerce can be subdivided in four distinct categories:[7]

- Business to business transactions involving performance against payment or performance against performance (for example when one party supplies statistical data in exchange for the results of a market research).
- Business to consumer transactions involving the purchase of products by individuals outside their trade or profession. An additional term used to describe this category is *electronic retailing*.

  These first two categories may also be classified under the heading electronic trading.

5 From a presentation held with the occasion of the conference entitled "*De invloed van informatietechnologie op het recht*", Rotterdam, 23 March 2000.

6 See European Commission, working paper eEurope, an Information Society for All, at http://europa.eu.int/comm/information_society/eeurope/objectives/area03_en.htm.

7 On this issue see also note 3, supra., at p. 3.

- Business to administration transaction is a category that finds itself in an incipient stage. It involves commercial relations between companies and public bodies, for example following a government procurement contract.
- The consumer to administration category has only recently emerged and is of a rather limited application. However, one can imagine that a certain degree of efficiency and effectiveness can be added to government activities if a number of such operations will be concluded online (for example in welfare payments or tax matters).

At this stage of its development, the most important categories of e-commerce are the first two above mentioned. The share of the other two categories is negligible in the larger context of global e-commerce. However, with the emergence of the World Wide Web and the relative easy accessibility to its services, the proportion between the share of business to business and business to consumer transactions has been dramatically shifted in the past three years. If this proportion was of ten to one[8] in 1996 at a global scale, it reached in 1999 40%/60% in the United States and 31%/69% in the European Union.[9]

It is due to these fast changes that the newly spotted legal issues in these respective areas should be treated with priority. In particular, in contracts involving consumers, steps should be taken to allow for the protection of this rather exposed category. Henceforth, the remarks to follow are to describe choice of forum issues in this category, as well as in business to business transactions.

IV. Jurisdiction in business-to-consumer e-commerce contracts

As noted above, approximately one third of today's world e-commerce is conducted between businesses and consumers. Due to the rapid growth of the numbers of private households connected to Internet, one can reasonably expect that this percentage will continue to increase. Under these circumstances, the question arises which court has jurisdiction to try international conflicts arising from consumer contracts concluded through Internet. Will the same rules applicable to conventional consumer contracts apply? Or should other considerations be taken into account?

A necessary distinction

In answering this question, it is my intention to first explain one legal peculiarity posed by e-commerce. To be more precise, a basic distinction has to be made according to the nature of the obligation to be performed. As a consequence, we may identify two categories of electronic commerce: On one hand there is the trade with *physical goods and services* and, on the other hand, the trade with *electronic materials* (software, images, voice, text etc.). This basic distinction

8 See note 4, *supra*, at p. 8.

9 See note 2, *supra*, at p. 24.

leads to a further division of e-commerce contracts: In the former case, the Internet is being used as the medium to communicate and sometimes to even conclude a contract, while in the latter event the Internet represents the place where *the performance takes place.* In other words, while in the first case the contract is concluded by using electronic means but the performance takes place outside the electronic environment, in the second instance the whole transaction, from the moment an offer is being made and until the obligation in question is being performed, can be located on the same network.

The solution upheld by the Brussels I regulation

Having established this basic distinction specific to e-commerce, I shall now proceed to describe some jurisdictional rules as established in the recently adopted Council Regulation on Jurisdiction and the Recognition and Enforcement of Judgements in Civil and Commercial Matters[10] (hereinafter the "Brussels I regulation")*. This is a revised version of the 1968 Convention on Jurisdiction and the Enforcement of Civil and Commercial Judgements[11] (hereinafter the "Brussels Convention"), due to enter into force on 1st of March 2002 between all Member States of the European Union with the exception of Denmark.[12] This step is being pursued as a result of the inclusion[13] of the subject-matter of this instrument, namely recognition and enforcement of foreign judgements in civil and commercial matters, in the home and justice affair pillar of the European Union. Besides the interests in more uniformity of law, the reason that prompted the adoption of an updated version of the Brussels Convention has to do also with the appearance of new forms of commerce non existent in 1968, one of them being of course e-commerce.

The regulation maintains in article 2 the general jurisdictional rule according to which defendants domiciled in one of the Contracting states shall be sued at the

---

10 See Council Regulation (EC) No. 44/2001, 22 December 2000, Official Journal L 012, 16.01.2001, p. 1, available online at: http://europa.eu.int/eur-lex/pri/en/oj/dat/2001/l_012/l_01220010116en00010023.pdf.

*European legislation hereby cited in this article may be retrieved online from http://www.lexis.com, http://www.westlaw.com, http://europa.eu.int/celex/, http://europa.eu.int/eur-lex/en/index.html or other EU law portals. For a detailed overview see http://www.law.nyu.edu/library/foreign_intl/european.html.

11 See EC Bulletin 1969, Supplement No. 2, p. 17, available online at http://europa.eu.int/eur-lex/en/lif/dat/1968/en_468A0927_01.html.

12 In case of the Kingdom of Denmark the 1978 version of the Brussels Convention will be applicable, as published in Official Journal L 304, 30/10/1978 p. 0001—0073, available online at http://europa.eu.int/eur-lex/en/lif/dat/1978/en_478A1009_01.html.

13 See Article 65, Treaty of Amsterdam, Official Journal C 340, 10.11.1997, p. 145-308, available online at http://europa.eu.int/eur-lex/en/treaties/dat/eu_cons_treaty_en.pdf (the consolidated version of the Treaty on European Union) and at http://europa.eu.int/eur-lex/en/treaties/dat/ec_cons_treaty_en.pdf (the consolidated version of the Treaty establishing the European Community).

place of their domicile. However, just like the initial Brussels Convention, the act contains special jurisdictional rules for consumer contracts, that is to say for contracts concluded outside a trade or profession. Therefore, according to article 16 of the regulation, a consumer domiciled in a Contracting state has the choice of suing the other party either before the court of the place of his or her domicile or in the Contracting State where the other party is domiciled. The question that arises is whether e-commerce contracts, whereby the offer is not directed specifically to the country of the consumer but rather to a global audience, can be included in this category. In other words, can a company from the Netherlands selling products through an interactive website reasonably expect to be sued in any of the Contracting states where consumers are domiciled?

The solution offered by the new Brussels regulation does not leave place for any doubts; Accordingly, the drafters of this legal act have chosen to allow for the prevalence of consumers' interests at the detriment of the industry. The language used in article 15 (1)c is thus very clear in stating that jurisdiction is covered by this section when:

> ". . . the contract has been concluded with a person who pursues commercial or professional activities in the Member State of the consumer's domicile or, by any means, directs such activities to that Member State or to several countries including that Member State, and the contract falls within the scope of such activities."

Moreover, the former condition included in article 13(3)b of the original Brussels Convention according to which the consumer has to take the necessary steps for the conclusion of the contract in the State of his or her domicile has been omitted from the new text. As a result, one could reasonably expect that, as long as a consumer has his or her permanent domicile on the territory of a Contracting state, the e-commerce contract can be concluded not only from this domicile in one of the Union states, but also while the person in question is on a business trip to, let us presume, Japan. Of course, in such a case one condition is that the website where the goods or materials are being advertised would be available in the Contacting State where the consumer has his or her domicile.

It should be also noted that in order to trigger the protection of these jurisdictional rules the fact whether the object of transaction is physical goods or services or electronic materials is irrelevant. The only two conditions that make article 15 applicable are domicile in one of the Contracting States and conclusion of the contract outside the trade or profession.

As a consequence, the answer to the above mentioned hypothetical question would be that, indeed, an Internet company based in the Netherlands could reasonably expect to be sued in any of the Contracting states where its website is available. The only way to avoid such a situation is to clearly state that the products are not intended for a certain market.

Criticism on the new Regulation

The solution adopted in the Brussels regulation has given rise to a certain amount of criticism from the European computer industry.[14] The main criticism relates to the uncertainty that this provision will trigger. As a result, a European company trading through the Internet will face even lesser protection with the adoption of the new regulation, a result certainly not in line with the general interest in promoting e-commerce throughout the European Union.

This solution conflicts with the opinion expressed by some authors[15] according to whom the consumers should be afforded protection only when they are the passive factor, i.e. they do not employ any effort to reach the other party. In this instance, the consumer is being rather sought in the country of his or her domicile and, according to the same authors, the rules of the legal system most closely connected to that consumer, in this case those of the place of domicile, should be applicable. According to the same opinion, consumers parties to e-commerce contracts cannot be considered passive since the very fact that they surfed the Internet in search for a certain product makes them active. As a consequence, following this rationale, the protection afforded by article 15 above described is not to cover consumers in e-commerce contracts.

The opinion is, of course, open to criticism. Some authors simply name it "bad law".[16] I would tend to consider that such a consumer is entitled to special protection. We cannot compare a consumer in an Internet contract with someone who travels to another country and, for example, purchases an automobile because of the lower price. This is my idea of an active consumer. Someone surfing on the Internet sitting comfortable at home may, at best, be called a curious person, but certainly not an active consumer. I would therefore be of opinion that such a consumer is entitled to receive the protection of his home forum.

Of course nobody denies that in such a case problems will arise due to the uncertainty that this solution will cause for Internet companies. They are running indeed the risk of being sued in each Contracting State where they sell their products. However, this issue can be tackled by using other methods than denying consumers' protection. One solution would be to mention on the website in question that the offer of products or services is not intended for sale in certain countries.[17] Another viable solution would be to insert in the contract a provision for choice of forum combined with a provision for choice of law. However,

---

14 See Explanatory Memorandum, Council Regulation on Jurisdiction and the Recognition and Enforcement of Judgements in Civil and Commercial Matters, Commission Proposal COM (1999), 348 final, Brussels, 14.07.1999, at p. 17, OJ No C266 p. 2, 21.09.1999.

15 See for example Katharina Boele-Woelki, *De functie van het IPR bij Internet-geschillen*, NJB 5 June 1998, at p. 1028.

16 See Herbert Kronke, Applicable Law in Torts and Contracts in Cyberspace, in Katharina Boele-Woelki and Catherine Kessedjian, *Internet Which Court decides? Which Law applies? Quel tribunal decide? Quel droit s'applique*, The Hague, 1998, at p. 83.

17 See also the Explanatory Memorandum, at p. 17.

such a step can be taken only after the dispute has arisen (article 17(1) Brussels regulation).

The complexity of establishing domicile

Another issue to be discussed in this context is connected with the establishment of the domicile of the defendant. According to article 15 of the Brussels regulation, the provision of this article shall not interfere with the application of article 4. This last provision establishes the rule according to which if the defendant is domiciled in a third country the Jus Commune of the plaintiff's Contracting State is applicable. Accordingly, we may infer that article 15 is applicable only if the defendant is domiciled in a Contracting state. For the defendants domiciled outside the European Union article 4, thus national jurisdictional rules, will apply. At the same time, the domicile of a company or a legal person is established, according to the newly introduced article 60, either where "it has its statutory seat, central administration, or principal place of business." The problem with Internet companies is that often these co-ordinates are very difficult to be established. There are countries, the so-called Internet-paradises, where the identity of the owner of an Internet site is treated in the same manner as the bank or the correspondence secrecy. Moreover, sometimes the principal place of business of such a company, especially if it sells electronic materials, is rather difficult, if not impossible, to be established.

In such a case one cannot cite any legal rules that can govern such a relationship. A court seized with such a case may establish the domicile of such a company using other elements such as the extension of the domain name, for example .nl (Netherlands) or .de (Germany). If, however, this extension does not bring any clarification (it might also be .com or .net) then other elements can become relevant such as the language of the Internet site or the currency in which the prices are mentioned.

The updated version of the Brussels Convention will undoubtedly bring necessary adjustments to the original text. However, while consumers are afforded a necessary protection, the European legislator should reach in the future a balance between the interests of the latter category and the legitimate concerns of the industry.

V. Jurisdiction in business-to-business e-commerce contracts

If consumers enjoy a privileged status, the rules applying to contracts concluded in the framework of a trade or profession, the so-called business-to-business contracts, are of a different nature. In fact, the revised version of the Brussels Convention does not provide specific jurisdictional rules to be applied when concluding an e-commerce business-to-business contract. As a consequence, I shall attempt in the following lines to provide several solutions based on the already existing rules.

Remarks on the Brussels I regulation

Accordingly, the main jurisdictional rule of the Brussels Convention, preserved in the recently adopted EC Council regulation, states that defendants domiciled in a Contracting state, whatever their nationality, shall be sued in the courts of their place of domicile (art. 2). If, however, the defendant is domiciled in a third country, then the respective national rules of each of the Contracting states will apply (art. 4). Since business-to-business contracts are concluded mainly by companies or legal persons, the act refers us to the new article 60 for the definition of the term "domicile" as applicable to these parties. In accordance to this latter provision, the domicile is to be established having due regard, alternatively,[18] to the place where the company or the legal person "has its statutory seat, central administration, or principal place of business."

The problem that appears when dealing with e-commerce is that seldom these co-ordinates are rather difficult to be established. Since these three criteria are alternative, the finding of any of the above will suffice to conclude that a company or a legal person is domiciled in a certain territory. However, as it has been stated above in the previous section, Internet companies can, at times, be difficult to locate. They might either have their statutory seat and central administration in a so-called Internet-paradise country, whereas the principal place of business may be in the electronic environment, especially if they focus on trade in electronic materials. In this case, the court seized with such an issue may use a number of other criteria in order to establish the domicile of such a company or legal person: The extension of the domain name, the language of the website and the currency used to express the prices of their offer. The problem would appear, of course, if the extension would be, for example .com, the language of the site English and the prices stated in US Dollars and/or Euro. In such a case, one should turn to the alternative jurisdictional rules contained in article 5 of the Brussels I regulation.

Nevertheless, it should be noted that the alternative jurisdictional grounds apply only to the extent that the defendant is domiciled in one of the Contracting states. If the solution provided above for the establishment of the domicile of a company or a legal person in Contracting State or in a third country will not suffice, than probably the only remaining solution is to turn to the national rules of private international law. Alternatively, one would expect that an interpretation judgement on this issue would be rendered sooner rather than later by the European Court of Justice at Luxembourg.

Forum Solutions

Turning to the provisions of article 5, the first paragraph establishes the general jurisdictional rule in matters related to contracts according to which the courts of the Contracting states of the place of performance are competent to adjudicate in

18 *Ibid.*, at p. 24.

such conflicts. Further in the same paragraph it is stated that in a contract for the sale of goods or the provision of services jurisdiction belongs to the courts of the place where the goods were delivered or should have been delivered or, in case of service provision, in the courts of the Contracting state where the services were provided or should have been provided. This seems to be a satisfactory provision, able to clarify, to a certain degree, the above-mentioned dilemma. In other words, provided that the contract is for the supply of physical goods or provision of services, the article under analysis in this paragraph is applicable to business-to-business e-commerce contracts.

However, if the contract is for the sale of electronic materials (software, images, voice, text, etc.), the foregoing provision can be hardly applicable. In such a contract, the place where the performance takes place, or, to be more specific, where the materials are being delivered, may be located only after considerable efforts. Even when attempting to construe article 5(1)b in an extensive manner, thus considering electronic materials as being assimilated to goods[19] or services, the place of delivery is quite difficult, if not impossible, to be established: Is it the place where the supplier enters the data in the hardware or the place where the data is downloaded. What if, in a contract between two companies, one Dutch and the other English, the electronic material is being downloaded from a laptop while the person responsible for this activity is on a business trip to Greece? Will this mean that the court of the latter state can try a conflict arising from such a contract? The scarcity of rules in this area causes the answer to such questions to be open for interpretation. In particular, the problem arises because such materials can be downloaded anywhere in the world.

In other words, the place of performance in such a case is difficult to be established. If, let us presume, the difficulties encountered when attempting to establish the domicile of a company or a legal person occur when the contract in question stipulates the delivery of electronic materials, then the solutions are not to be found in the above analyzed provisions. Instead, in such complicated cases, the most viable solution would be to introduce a choice of forum clause, in accordance to article 23 of the new Brussels I regulation.

If at least the domicile of one party can be established in a Contracting state, than a choice of forum clause can be included in the contract. The jurisdiction established in accordance to article 23 might be exclusive, unless the parties agree otherwise. In addition, the EC regulation contains specific provisions aimed at according the same legal value to agreements on choice of forum concluded in writing and the ones agreed upon through electronic means.[20]

19 See K. Boele-Woelki, *Conflictenrechtelijke aspecten van Internet-koop-overeenkomsten*, in Molengrafica, 1997, at p. 139-165.

20 Article 23, Paragraph 3 of the Brussels I regulations reads as following:

"Any communication by electronic means which can provide a durable record of the agreement shall be deemed to be in writing."

Indeed, many of the problems analyzed above can be easily avoided if such a clause is being included in a contract for the sale of physical goods, electronic materials or provision of services. Such a choice may express preference for the courts of a Contracting state, thus in accordance to the Brussels I regulation, or for an out-of-court dispute settlement arrangement, in accordance with the recently adopted European Parliament and Council Directive on certain legal aspects of electronic commerce in the internal market[21] (hereinafter the "Directive on electronic commerce").

VI. Out-of-court jurisdiction

Possible benefits

Compared to other categories of trade, e-commerce presents a number of specific features: Perhaps one of the most evident is the speed with which transactions are being concluded. Especially when electronic materials are being purchased, the simple downloading of the software in question can last for only a few moments. Another feature, of course, is that due to Internet's global accessibility, a company or legal person offering goods, services or electronic materials by using this medium can reasonably expect to sell products worldwide. At the same time, companies or legal persons active on the Internet may at times be difficult to trace according to traditional criteria, i.e. statutory seat, central administration or principal place of business.

Considering these special features presented by e-commerce, settlements of disputes in courts might not constitute always the most suitable option. It is a well known fact that court procedures last very often for quite a long time, even when the issues concern conventional contracts. One could hardly imagine that for a contract in which the performance has been completed in a few minutes the parties will tolerate having to wait for a few months, or sometimes even longer, for a judgement to be rendered.

Likewise, besides the importance of the rapidity of conflict resolution, companies or legal persons trading on the Internet might prefer to save the costs which any court dispute, especially in a foreign country, entails. This statement is even more valid if we take into account the fact that the probability to be sued in a foreign country is quite high in these cases. Finally, regular courts might not be always the most competent forum to assess and decide in certain issues strictly connected to this category of commerce (for instance when establishing the domicile of a company or a legal person).

---

21 See Directive 2000/31/EC of the European Parliament and of the Council of 8 June 2000 on certain legal aspects of information society services, in particular electronic commerce, in the Internal market ("Directive on electronic commerce"), *Official Journal L 178, 17/07/2000, p. 0001-0016*, available online at http://europa.eu.int/eur-lex/pri/en/oj/dat/2000/l_178/l_17820000717en00010016.pdf.

Under these circumstances, perhaps out-of-court dispute settlement would constitute a valid alternative to the conventional court system. In this manner, the issues discussed above may be successfully tackled; especially in the event these bodies would be specialized in e-commerce transactions, the issue of time-consuming procedures could come to a sound solution. For instance, one can imagine that in this case the proceedings will be conducted through electronic mail, thus saving time and costs. The efficiency of this solution will be expressed also in terms of reduced costs for the parties and certainty as to where in the world can a distributing company be sued, regardless of the fact that it conducts businesses on a global scale. Likewise, being a specialized body, issues such as the domicile of a company or a legal person can be tackled through the development of clear case-law based rules, thus adding to the certainty of law in the area of e-commerce.

The Virtual Magistrate Project

Such an out-of-court dispute settlement body specialized in computer-related conflicts does not represent a completely new idea; The Virtual Magistrate Project (hereinafter VMP)—available online at http://www.vmag.org/—was established in 1996 in a joint effort of the Villanova Center for Law and Information (part of the Villanova University School of Law, Pennsylvania, USA), the American Arbitration Association, the Cyberspace Law Institute, while the funds were provided by the National Center for Automated Information Research. As this article is being written, in early 2002, the project is being run by the Chicago-Kent College of Law, itself part of the Illinois Institute of Technology. The aim of this pilot initiative is to provide quick arbitration solutions for disputes arising out of the use of computer networks.

The proceedings before this arbitration body are conducted in the following manner (See also the table on the left): The complaint is being submitted to the VMP via e-mail or a special form designed for this purpose. Subsequently, one or three arbitrators are randomly chosen from a pool of professional magistrates. The dispute is then referred to his or her judgement and, after hearing from the parties, a decision is rendered in a maximum of 72 hours from the moment the complaint has been accepted. The magistrate can issue, if need be, interim decisions. Interestingly enough, the concept paper of this project (http://www.vmag.org/docs/concept.html) states that:

> "In making a decision, the Virtual Magistrate Project will not automatically apply the law of any specific legal jurisdiction. It will consider the circumstances of each complaint, the views of the parties about applicable legal principles and remedies, and the likely outcome in any ultimate litigation or dispute resolution."

In other words, very important is to introduce a choice of law clause in the initial contract, of course alongside a choice for the dispute settlement of VMP. Otherwise, the magistrate will take into account various criteria that despite the fact that might lead to a sound decision, do not contribute to the interests of the parties in legal certainty.

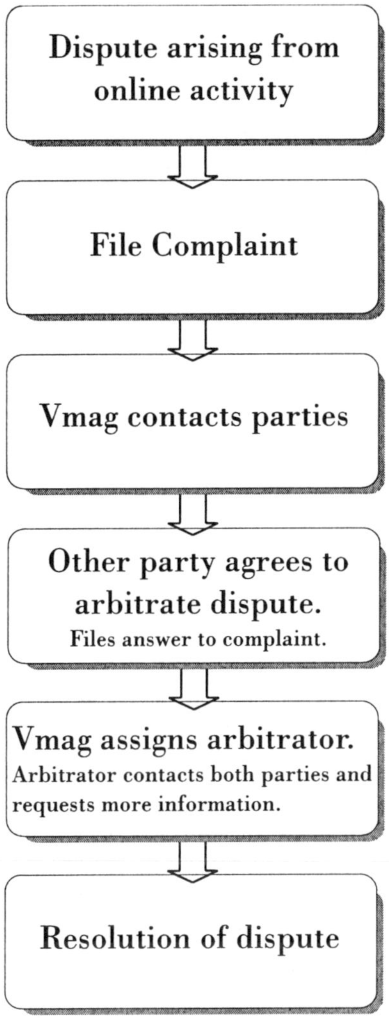

Table I: Proceedings in the framework of the VMP
Source: http://www.vmag.org/started.html (printed with permission)

The decisions so rendered can be reconsidered but are not subject to appeal. Likewise, they are enforceable as any other decisions issued by private arbitrators.

Worth mentioning in this context is the fact that, being a cyberspace service, it can be accessed anywhere in the world. Therefore, for instance, one can imagine the situation whereby the supplier of software is domiciled in Brazil, the buyer in Belgium and the conflict is settled before a dispute settlement body such as the Virtual Magistrate Project.

Out-of-court dispute settlement in Europe

Having been aware of the importance of such mechanisms for the settlement of legal conflicts, particularly in cases the amount under dispute is of low value and the parties involved are of negligible size,[22] the European Commission chose to refer to this matter in its draft proposal for a directive on electronic commerce:[23]

> "Member States shall ensure that, in the event of disagreement between an Information Society service provider and its recipient, their legislation allows the effective use of out-of-court schemes for dispute settlement, including appropriate electronic means."

This legislative act has been recently adopted. However, the provision establishing the framework for the functioning of out-of-court dispute settlement bodies has been the subject of several modifications. It now reads as following:

> "Member States shall ensure that, in the event of disagreement between an information society service provider and the recipient of the service, their legislation does not hamper the use of out-of-court schemes, available under national law, for dispute settlement, including appropriate electronic means."[24]

Comparison between the two versions

Even though the change in the wording of the provisions seems quite marginal, it is the opinion of the author of this article that the amendment is more than a matter of language; If, in the first case, the directive lays down the obligation for the Member States to allow the existence of such out-of-court dispute settlement bodies, the adopted version merely prohibits Member States from limiting the jurisdiction of already available schemes as to exclude e-commerce disputes. Under these circumstances, it might have been more appropriate for the furtherance of such out-of-court arrangements had the initial wording been retained. Nevertheless, one may find it difficult to deny that the intention of the European legislator to promote the use of such out-of-court bodies is rather obvious. The explanatory memorandum makes it clear that the aim behind this provision is to facilitate "the setting up of effective cross-border alternative dispute resolution systems".[25] It is

---

22 On this issue see the Financial Times, Move to Resolve Net Disputes, 21-Feb-2000 and Brussels Seeks Net Dispute System, 22-Feb-2002, online at http://www.ft.com.

23 See Article 17, paragraph 1, Proposal for a European Parliament and Council Directive on certain legal aspects of electronic commerce in the internal market, Commission Proposal COM (1998), 585 final, Brussels, 18.11.1998, at p. 5, OJ No C030 p.4, 05.02.1999. See also the amended Proposal for a European Parliament and Council Directive on certain legal aspects of electronic commerce in the internal market, Commission Proposal COM (1999), 427 final, Brussels, 17.08.1999, available online at http://europa.eu.int/eur-lex/en/com/pdf/1999/en_599PC0427.pdf.

24 See Article 17, paragraph 1, Directive on electronic commerce, *Official Journal L 178, 17/07/2000*, p. 0014, online at http://europa.eu.int/eur-lex/pri/en/oj/dat/2000/l_178/l_17820000717en00010016.pdf.

25 See Explanatory Memorandum, Proposal for a European Parliament and Council Directive on certain legal aspects of electronic commerce in the internal market, Commission Proposal

however for the national law to prescribe the precise conditions under which such schemes may be mandated to try conflicts arising out of e-commerce contracts.

The second paragraph

Paragraph 2 of the same provision, as enshrined in the proposal submitted by the Commission, makes it clear that Member States have to subject these bodies to several fair trail principles, among other independence and transparency, adversarial techniques, procedural efficacy, legality of the decision, freedom of the parties and their representation. The main difference between the text of Commission's proposal and the one eventually adopted has to do mainly with the extension of these principles to cover especially, but not limited to, proceedings in consumer disputes:

> "Member States shall encourage bodies responsible for the out-of-court settlement of, in particular, consumer disputes to operate in a way which provides adequate procedural guarantees for the parties concerned."[26]

At the same time, instead of enumerating the principles which have to be abided by, the final version makes reference only to "adequate procedural guarantees", a term that leaves more freedom for Member States to apply whatever principles otherwise available under their own national laws. One may therefore reasonably conclude that any suspicion that such bodies will not respect basic principles of due process is unfounded.

Moreover, probably concerned with the rapidity with which a decision should be rendered the drafters of this directive state in the explanatory memorandum that, specifically for Internet disputes, the settlement of such conflicts could take place electronically.

According to the information available at this stage, only a limited number of such specialized out-of-court dispute settlement bodies are currently functioning in Europe. Once established, such schemes will be able to operate on a larger scale than the territory of the European Community. Indeed, such a body will be capable of reaching a global audience. As a consequence, one may reasonably claim that the more established such a dispute settlement system is, the more global reach will enjoy. One may only hope that in a world where geographic boundaries can hardly be noticed, the so-called cyberspace, the use of such dispute settlements arrangements will facilitate the development of e-commerce as a viable alternative for conducting international transactions.

COM (1998), 585 final, Brussels, 18.11.1998, at p. 5, OJ No C030 p.4, 05.02.1999. See also the amended proposal at http://europa.eu.int/eur-lex/en/com/pdf/1999/en_599PC0427.pdf.

26 See Article 17, paragraph 2 of the Directive on electronic commerce, as cited in note 21, supra.

VII. Conclusive remarks

The Internet was first developed in 1970's as a communication mean between universities and research schools in North America. From this point of view, it can be easily assimilated to the 17th century Republiek der Letteren,[27] an academic network developed among European scholars. The significant difference is, however, that the exchange of information system used in the past remained at the stage of a strictly academic-oriented network, whereas the Internet has evolved to entail a preponderantly commercial character.

This article has sought to shed some light in the area of international jurisdictional rules, analyzed from a European point of view, in conflicts arising out of e-commerce contracts. For this purpose, I have looked at an important legislative development at the European Community level, namely the Council Regulation (EC) on Jurisdiction and the Recognition and Enforcement of Judgements in Civil and Commercial Matters. While providing a reasonable protection standard for consumers concluding e-commerce contracts, the regulation fails to address the issue of domicile of companies and legal persons conducting business activities exclusively through electronic means. This omission is even more evident in the business-to-business contracts, especially when it is difficult to establish the place of performance of the obligation in question.

One possible way to avoid these problems would be the inclusion of a forum choice clause in the initial contract. While being able to apt for the jurisdiction of a certain court, the parties may at the same time choose to solve their future dispute before an out-of-court panel. In this last case, the main peculiarity of e-commerce, namely efficiency in terms of time, may be preserved. In this context, the Virtual Magistrate Project may provide a viable model to be looked at when implementing article 17 of the Directive on electronic commerce.

Finally, allow me to add a final word on the law applicable by such dispute settlement bodies: Of course the will of the parties is in this case very important, and the panel will be bound by the choice of law agreed among the parties. If such a choice of law clause is missing, the body might look at the law of the forum or of another country, in accordance to the private international law rules applicable in that respective state. However, one can imagine the situation whereby an independent body of rules and regulations would be developed to apply only to legal relationships connected to the cyberspace. Such a development would not be entirely surprising; After all, it would be something in the spirit of the *Mare Liberum*[28] theory developed by Hugo Grotius in the 17th century for the Law of the High Seas.

---

27 See Dr. J.A.H.G.M. Bots, *Republiek der Letteren Ideal en Werhlijkheid*, Amsterdam, 1977.

28 See C.G. Roelofsen, The sources of Mare Liberum; The Contested Origins of the Doctrine of the Freedom of the Seas, in W.P. Heere (ed.), International Law and its Sources; Liber Amicorum maarten Bos, Deventer, 1988.

PERSONAL JURISDICTION IN INTERNET-RELATED LITIGATION[1]

by
George W. Thompson
Neville Peterson LLP

Introduction

The electronic commerce "revolution" has given business enterprises vastly expanded opportunities to buy and sell products and services across national and international political boundaries. Parties looking for new business opportunities can seek trading partners through Internet website access, and can communicate instantaneously through electronic mail (e-mail).

With these expanded business opportunities, courts have been presented with disputes arising from one or more parties' electronic presence on the Internet. Resolving these disputes has required, as a preliminary matter, that the defendant(s) be found susceptible to personal jurisdiction in the forum chosen by the plaintiff to resolve a dispute. In conducting their analyses of whether electronic activities conducted outside a particular jurisdiction suffice to confer personal jurisdiction, courts have applied rules developed in the pre-electronic age. The results have not always been consistent, to put it mildly.

This chapter examines the leading cases concerning personal jurisdiction arising from electronic commerce in federal courts in the United States. Most such cases arise in "diversity" actions, *i.e.*, disputes involving citizens of different states in the United States, or a citizen of one state and a foreign country. To have jurisdiction over the defendant in such actions, the defendant either must be "doing business" in the forum state, or must have sufficient "contacts" with that state to warrant being called to court there.

For companies engaged in electronic commerce, or anticipating doing so, these cases may serve as a useful planning tool, for they provide guidance as to the types

1 This chapter was originally published in TRANSNATIONAL CONTRACTS, eds. Lawrence J. Bogard & George W. Thompson (1997-current) by George W. Thompson, as part of Booklet C.2 "Personal Jurisdiction in Internet-Related Litigation" (Release 2003-2, February 2003).

of Internet presence that may result in being brought into court in a given state in the United States. Although this chapter examines contract dispute cases, it goes beyond them to consider other types of Internet-related disputes, including alleged intellectual property infringement, defamation, and negligence. These non-contract cases are included for two reasons. First, as part of its planning process, a business should be aware of whether its electronic presence could result in legal liability; such potential liability goes well beyond that associated with breach of contract. Second, similar rules govern courts' consideration of personal jurisdiction for both contract and non-contract disputes, so an understanding of the latter is germane to the former.

The chapter focuses on federal court decisions in the United States. Although federal tribunals are the *fora*, the applicable substantive law is usually that of a state. As a general matter, the federal courts are sitting in place of state courts under "diversity" jurisdiction. To provide the necessary background for those readers who did not undergo the joys of first year civil procedure classes in an American law school, as well as those who did but do not recall the details, we have provided a **brief** synopsis of the bases for jurisdiction in diversity cases.

Federal Court Jurisdiction in the Federal System

Under 28 U.S.C. § 1332, federal district courts are given jurisdiction over certain disputes in which the parties are citizens of different states in the U.S., or one of the parties is a citizen of a country other than the U.S.

> Sec. 1332. Diversity of citizenship; amount in controversy; costs
>
> (a) The district courts shall have original jurisdiction of all civil actions where the matter in controversy exceeds the sum or value of $75,000, exclusive of interest and costs, and is between—
>
> (1) citizens of different States;
>
> (2) citizens of a State and citizens or subjects of a foreign state;
>
> (3) citizens of different States and in which citizens or subjects of a foreign state are additional parties; and
>
> (4) a foreign state, defined in section 1603(a) of this title, as plaintiff and citizens of a State or of different States. For the purposes of this section, section 1335, and section 1441, an alien admitted to the United States for permanent residence shall be deemed a citizen of the State in which such alien is domiciled.

In adjudicating a diversity action, the federal court will, as a general matter, apply state law. As a preliminary matter, the federal court will look to the law of the state in which it is located to determine whether that law permits the exercise of personal jurisdiction over the defendant. *PDK Labs, Inc. v. Friedlander*, 103 F.3d 1105, 1108 (2d Cir. 1997). Each state has enacted "long-arm statutes" that specify the circumstances in which an out of state defendant may be brought before the state's courts, so the federal court will look to the state's long-arm statute for guidance. Typically, such statutes provide jurisdiction over an out of state defendant for torts committed in-state, out of state torts having an in-state impact, and for contract disputes where goods or services were to be provided to or from the state, as well as over an out of state defendant who conducts business in the state.

A state's exercise of long-arm jurisdiction is also subject to the requirements of constitutional due process. Briefly, the defendant must have some connection with the forum state sufficient to provide it with the reasonable expectation that its activities could result in its being sued there. Federal courts exercising diversity jurisdiction are equally subject to this mandate.

The requirements of due process in these situations were summarized by the Supreme Court in *Burger King Corp. v. Rudzewicz*, 471 U.S. 462, 475 (1985). We have quoted from this opinion at length, as it ties up the relevant constitutional points in a single concise package.

> The Due Process Clause protects an individual's liberty interest in not being subject to the binding judgments of a forum with which he has established no meaningful "contacts, ties, or relations." *International Shoe Co. v. Washington*, 326 U.S., at 319. By requiring that individuals have "fair warning that a particular activity may subject [them] to the jurisdiction of a foreign sovereign," *Shaffer v. Heitner*, 433 U.S. 186, 218 (1977) (STEVENS, J., concurring in judgment), the Due Process Clause "gives a degree of predictability to the legal system that allows potential defendants to structure their primary conduct with some minimum assurance as to where that conduct will and will not render them liable to suit," *World-Wide Volkswagen Corp. v. Woodson*, 444 U.S. 286, 297 (1980).
>
> Where a forum seeks to assert specific jurisdiction over an out-of-state defendant who has not consented to suit there, this "fair warning" requirement is satisfied if the defendant has "purposefully directed" his activities at residents of the forum, *Keeton v. Hustler Magazine, Inc.*, 465 U.S. 770, 774 (1984), and the litigation results from alleged injuries that "arise out of or relate to" those activities, *Helicopteros Nacionales de Colombia, S. A. v. Hall*, 466 U.S. 408, 414 (1984). Thus "[t]he forum State does not exceed its powers under the Due Process Clause if it asserts personal jurisdiction over a corporation that delivers its products into the stream of commerce with the expectation that they will be purchased by consumers in the forum State" and those products subsequently injure forum consumers. *World-Wide Volkswagen Corp. v. Woodson, supra*, at 297-298. Similarly, a publisher who distributes magazines in a distant State may fairly be held accountable in that forum for damages resulting there from an allegedly defamatory story. *Keeton v. Hustler Magazine, Inc., supra*; *see also Calder v. Jones*, 465 U.S. 783 (1984) (suit against author and editor). And with respect to interstate contractual obligations, we have emphasized that parties who "reach out beyond one state and create continuing relationships and obligations with citizens of another state" are subject to regulation and sanctions in the other State for the consequences of their activities. *Travelers Health Assn. v. Virginia*, 339 U.S. 643, 647 (1950). *See also McGee v. International Life Insurance Co.*, 355 U.S. 220, 222-223 (1957).
>
> * * *
>
> Notwithstanding these considerations, the constitutional touchstone remains whether the defendant purposefully established "minimum contacts" in the forum

State. *International Shoe Co. v. Washington*, *supra*, at 316. Although it has been argued that foreseeability of causing injury in another State should be sufficient to establish such contacts there when policy considerations so require, the Court has consistently held that this kind of foreseeability is not a "sufficient benchmark" for exercising personal jurisdiction. *World-Wide Volkswagen Corp. v. Woodson*, 444 U.S., at 295 . Instead, "the foreseeability that is critical to due process analysis . . . is that the defendant's conduct and connection with the forum State are such that he should reasonably anticipate being haled into court there." *Id.*, at 297. In defining when it is that a potential defendant should "reasonably anticipate" out-of-state litigation, the Court frequently has drawn from the reasoning of *Hanson v. Denckla*, 357 U.S. 235, 253 (1958):

> The unilateral activity of those who claim some relationship with a nonresident defendant cannot satisfy the requirement of contact with the forum State. The application of that rule will vary with the quality and nature of the defendant's activity, but it is essential in each case that there be some act by which the defendant purposefully avails itself of the privilege of conducting activities within the forum State, thus invoking the benefits and protections of its laws.

This "purposeful availment" requirement ensures that a defendant will not be haled into a jurisdiction solely as a result of "random," "fortuitous," or "attenuated" contacts, *Keeton v. Hustler Magazine, Inc.*, 465 U.S., at 774; *World-Wide Volkswagen Corp. v. Woodson*, *supra*, at 299, or of the "unilateral activity of another party or a third person," *Helicopteros Nacionales de Colombia, S. A. v. Hall*, *supra*, at 417. Jurisdiction is proper, however, where the contacts proximately result from actions by the defendant himself that create a "substantial connection" with the forum State. *McGee v. International Life Insurance Co.*, *supra*, at 223; *see also Kulko v. California Superior Court*, *supra*, at 94, n. 7. Thus where the defendant "deliberately" has engaged in significant activities within a State, *Keeton v. Hustler Magazine, Inc.*, *supra*, at 781, or has created "continuing obligations" between himself and residents of the forum, *Travelers Health Assn. v. Virginia*, 339 U.S., at 648, he manifestly has availed himself of the privilege of conducting business there, and because his activities are shielded by "the benefits and protections" of the forum's laws it is presumptively not unreasonable to require him to submit to the burdens of litigation in that forum as well.

Jurisdiction in these circumstances may not be avoided merely because the defendant did not physically enter the forum State. Although territorial presence frequently will enhance a potential defendant's affiliation with a State and reinforce the reasonable foreseeability of suit there, it is an inescapable fact of modern commercial life that a substantial amount of business is transacted solely by mail and wire communications across state lines, thus obviating the need for physical presence within a State in which business is conducted. So long as a commercial actor's efforts are "purposefully directed" toward residents of another State, we have consistently rejected the notion that an absence of physical contacts can defeat personal jurisdiction there. *Keeton v. Hustler Magazine, Inc.*, *supra*, at 774-775; *see also Calder v. Jones*, 465 U.S., at 788-790; *McGee v. International Life Insurance Co.*, 355 U.S., at 222-223. *Cf. Hoopeston Canning Co. v. Cullen*, 318 U.S. 313, 317 (1943).

Once it has been decided that a defendant purposefully established minimum contacts within the forum State, these contacts may be considered in light of

> other factors to determine whether the assertion of personal jurisdiction would comport with "fair play and substantial justice." *International Shoe Co. v. Washington,* 326 U.S., at 320. Thus courts in "appropriate case[s]" may evaluate "the burden on the defendant," "the forum State's interest in adjudicating the dispute," "the plaintiff's interest in obtaining convenient and effective relief," "the interstate judicial system's interest in obtaining the most efficient resolution of controversies," and the "shared interest of the several States in furthering fundamental substantive social policies." *World-Wide Volkswagen Corp. v. Woodson*, 444 U.S., at 292. These considerations sometimes serve to establish the reasonableness of jurisdiction upon a lesser showing of minimum contacts than would otherwise be required. *See, e. g., Keeton v. Hustler Magazine, Inc., supra*, at 780; *Calder v. Jones, supra*, at 788-789; *McGee v. International Life Insurance Co., supra*, at 223-224. On the other hand, where a defendant who purposefully has directed his activities at forum residents seeks to defeat jurisdiction, he must present a compelling case that the presence of some other considerations would render jurisdiction unreasonable. Most such considerations usually may be accommodated through means short of finding jurisdiction unconstitutional. For example, the potential clash of the forum's law with the "fundamental substantive social policies" of another State may be accommodated through application of the forum's choice-of-law rules. Similarly, a defendant claiming substantial inconvenience may seek a change of venue. Nevertheless, minimum requirements inherent in the concept of "fair play and substantial justice" may defeat the reasonableness of jurisdiction even if the defendant has purposefully engaged in forum activities. *World-Wide Volkswagen Corp. v. Woodson, supra*, at 292; *see also* Restatement (Second) of Conflict of Laws 36-37 (1971).

Personal jurisdiction may be either general or specific. As described in *Zippo Manufacturing Co. v. Zippo Dot Com., Inc.*, 952 F. Supp. 1119, 1124 (W.D.Pa. 1997):

> The Constitutional limitations on the exercise of personal jurisdiction differ depending upon whether a court seeks to exercise general or specific jurisdiction over a non-resident defendant. *Mellon*, 960 F.2d at 1221. General jurisdiction permits a court to exercise personal jurisdiction over a non-resident defendant for non-forum related activities when the defendant has engaged in "systematic and continuous" activities in the forum state. *Helicopteros Nacionales de Colombia, S.A. v. Hall*, 466 U.S. 408, 414-16, 80 L. Ed. 2d 404, 104 S. Ct. 1868 (1984). In the absence of general jurisdiction, specific jurisdiction permits a court to exercise personal jurisdiction over a non-resident defendant for forum-related activities where the relationship between the defendant and the forum falls within the 'minimum contacts' framework of *International Shoe Co. v. Washington*, 326 U.S. 310, 90 L. Ed. 95, 66 S. Ct. 154 (1945) and its progeny. *Mellon*, 960 F.2d at 1221.

In a specific jurisdiction scenario, the claim before the court must arise out of the defendant's contacts with the forum state, and it must be reasonable for that court to hear it. *3D System, Inc. v. Aarotech Laboratories, Inc.*, (1Fed. Cir. 1998).

Finally, from both a statutory and constitutional standpoint, the determination of whether personal jurisdiction over an out of state defendant is proper is the same regardless of whether the defendant is located in another state of the United States, or is located outside the U.S.

Types of Internet Jurisdiction Cases

The underlying jurisdictional problem arising from electronic commerce is that the Internet is an electronic entity without boundaries. It can be accessed from anywhere, and information placed on it is immediately made available anywhere in the world. A person in location A may post information on the Internet that is contained in a server in location B and accessed by parties in location C, or, more realistically, A, B and C through Z.

The cases addressing Internet jurisdiction can be divided into three categories, depending on the "interactivity" of the website involved and the extent of the defendant's Internet and non-Internet related contacts with the host forum. As discussed in *Blackburn v. Walker Oriental Rug Galleries, Inc.*, 999 F. Supp. 636, 638-639 (E.D. Pa. 1998), these categories are (1) extensive business contacts between defendant and forum, (2) defendant's websites involving some interactivity with persons in the forum, and (3) "passive" websites, to which persons in the forum may gain access, but with limited or no capacity for two-way communication.

> In analyzing a defendant's contacts through the use of the Internet, the probability that personal jurisdiction may be constitutionally exercised is "directly proportionate to the nature and quality of commercial activity that an entity conducts over the Internet." *Zippo Manufacturing Co. v. Zippo Dot Com., Inc.*, 952 F. Supp. 1119, 1124 (W.D.Pa. 1997). Three types of contacts have been identified in order to determine the existence of personal jurisdiction. *Weber v. Jolly Hotels*, 977 F. Supp. 327, 333 (D.N.J. 1997). The first type of contact is when the defendant clearly does business over the Internet. *Id.* "If the defendant enters into contracts with residents of a foreign jurisdiction that involve the knowing and repeated transmission of computer files over the Internet, personal jurisdiction is proper." *Zippo*, 952 F. Supp. at 1124 (citing *CompuServe, Inc. v. Patterson*, 89 F.3d 1257 (6th Cir. 1996)). The second type of contact occurs when "a user can exchange information with the host computer. In these cases, the exercise of jurisdiction is determined by examining the level of interactivity and commercial nature of the exchange of information that occurs on the Website." *Zippo*, at 1124 (citing *Maritz, Inc. v. Cybergold, Inc.*, 947 F. Supp. 1328 (E.D.Mo. 1996)); *Weber*, 977 F. Supp. at 333. The third type of contact involves the posting of information or advertisements on an Internet website which is accessible to users in foreign jurisdictions. *Zippo*, 952 F. Supp. at 1124; see *Weber*, 977 F. Supp. at 333; *Bensusan Restaurant Corp. v. King*, 937 F. Supp. 295 (S.D.N.Y. 1996). Personal jurisdiction is not exercised for this type of contact because "a finding of jurisdiction . . . based on an Internet website would mean that there would be nationwide (indeed, world wide) personal jurisdiction over anyone and everyone who establishes an Internet website. Such nationwide jurisdiction is not consistent with personal jurisdiction case law. . ." *Weber*, 977 F. Supp. at 333 (quoting *Hearst Corp. v. Goldberger*, 1997 WL 97097, at *1 (S.D.N.Y. 1997)).

In each scenario, in general the court will also consider the existence and extent of non-electronic contacts between the defendant and the host.

The *Blackburn* formulation of the analytic approach first set forth in *Zippo* provides a useful basic framework for considering whether a given set of contacts will result in a finding of jurisdiction, and we will follow it (in reverse order) in reviewing the relevant caselaw. However, the *Blackburn/Zippo* approach does have several important limitations. First, it does not, and likely could not, provide definitive guidance concerning the definitions or boundaries of each category. Application of the overall approach must necessarily take place on a case by case basis; as we shall see, different courts may reach different conclusions when presented with similar fact patterns. Second, while the *Blackburn/Zippo* approach has found fairly wide acceptance, it is not universally followed. Several relatively early cases reached results directly at odds with those obtaining under the *Blackburn/Zippo* approach, and companies considering the extent of their electronic presence in the states where those cases were decided should be particularly aware of the split in authority.

"Passive" Website Cases

Cases Finding No Jurisdiction

The first *Blackburn/Zippo* scenario is the passive website, where the defendant has created a home page that advertises its products or services but does not permit online negotiations or ordering. Such sites may allow for limited electronic communication between the defendant and the world at large.

The first major "no jurisdiction" case decided was *Bensusan Restaurant Corp. v. King*, 937 F. Supp. 295 (S.D.N.Y. 1996), cited in both *Zippo* and *Blackburn*. The plaintiff in *Bensusan* filed a trademark infringement complaint in the Southern District of New York, alleging that the Missouri defendant's webpage included a logo similar to that of plaintiff's. Both the plaintiff and defendant operated jazz nightclubs, both of which were called "The Blue Note." The server hosting defendant's web page was located in Missouri.

Defendant's webpage was generally accessible. It contained information about defendant's club, a schedule of events, and ticket purchasing information. Tickets could not be purchased electronically from defendant, but could be obtained either through outside ticketing services or from defendant by telephone. The telephone number for ordering tickets directly from defendant was included on the web page. Defendant would not deliver tickets to purchasers, but rather required that they be picked up in person.

The court applied New York's long-arm statute to determine whether jurisdiction over defendant was proper. It first found inapplicable C.P.L.R. § 302(a)(2), which permits "personal jurisdiction over any non-domiciliary who 'commits a tortious act within the state' as long as the cause of action asserted arises from the tortious act." The court considered whether the mere creation of a web page with a telephone number to place an order amounted to a sale or offer to sell the allegedly infringing product in New York. Even though a New York resident could access defendant's web page, he would have to undertake several additional affirmative steps before engaging in business contact with defendant, including calling the ticket office to reserve tickets and personally obtaining the tickets at defendant's location. Thus, any act of infringement would have occurred in Missouri, not New York. In the absence of any tickets being sent to New York, or other allegedly infringing activity being directed to New York, the court was unable to find tortious conduct in the forum state.

The court's comment concerning this arrangement merits quotation: "The mere fact that a person [in New York] can gain information on the allegedly infringing product is not the equivalent of a person advertising, promoting, selling or otherwise making an effort to target its product in New York."

The court next considered "C.P.L.R. § 302(a)(3)(ii), which permits a court to exercise personal jurisdiction over any non-domiciliary for tortious acts committed outside the state that cause injury in the state if the non-domiciliary 'expects or should reasonably expect the act to have consequences in the state and derives substantial revenue from interstate or international commerce.'" It rejected plaintiff's argument that defendant participated in interstate commerce by virtue of hiring nationally-known bands failed to address the statutory requirement that defendant have substantial revenue from interstate commerce; "mere participation in it" was not enough. In light of defendant's claim that the overwhelming percentage of its revenues was obtained from local patrons, and plaintiff's failure to demonstrate (or even allege) that defendant obtained substantial revenue from interstate commerce, the court concluded that defendant could not have reasonably foreseen that its allegedly infringing acts would have consequences in New York.

Bensusan also concluded that the requirements of due process would be violated by asserting jurisdiction over defendant. Defendant did "nothing to purposefully avail himself of the benefits of New York. . . . Creating a site, like placing a product into the stream of commerce, may be felt nationwide—or even worldwide—but, without more, it is not an act purposefully directed toward the forum state." Nor did defendant target New York residents to view its website or conduct any business in New York. For due process purposes, it was insufficient to argue that defendant "should have foreseen that users could access the site in New York and be confused as to the relationship of the two Blue Note clubs."

Bensusan thus declined jurisdiction over a truly passive website: one with no interactivity between the defendant and a site user. Moreover, defendant had no non-Internet contacts with New York. *Bensusan* would seem to be as pure a "passive website" fact pattern as one could imagine. Note that the court did not separately consider general and specific jurisdiction in its discussion.

The decision was affirmed, 126 F.3d 25 (2d Cir. 1997), emphasizing that the long-arm statute's requirement that a defendant either commit a physical act in New York, or that if it commits an out of state tort with New York consequences it must derive substantial revenue from interstate commerce. The appellate court agreed that defendant met neither requirement. Interestingly, the appellate opinion did not delve into the passive website analysis considered by the trial court. It also pointed out that New York's long-arm statute provides lesser coverage than would be permitted under the due process clause, in that it requires that an defendant who commits an out of state tort that has effects in New York must derive substantial income from interstate commerce, and accordingly "'exclude[s] non-domiciliaries whose business operations are of a local character.'" Thus, in part, the result in *Bensusan* may be considered a creature of an idiosyncratic New York statute, and may not be reflective of the outcome of an identical case in a state that has a more expansive long-arm statute.

A similarly passive website was at issue in *Hearst v. Goldberger*, 1997 U.S. Dist. LEXIS 2065 (S.D.N.Y. 1997). Defendant, located in New Jersey, was sued in New York for trademark infringement for placing the allegedly infringing mark on its home page. Although defendant planned to market certain legal services over the Internet, at the time of the lawsuit it had not commenced business operations, much less sold or contracted to sell services in New York or elsewhere.

In an impeccably well-reasoned opinion, the court found that defendant's website "is, at most, an announcement of the future availability of his services for attorneys," and "thus is most analogous to an advertisement in a national magazine." Although, like an advertisement, the website could be viewed throughout the United States, it was not targeted to New York residents. Under New York law, "advertisements in national publications are not sufficient to provide personal jurisdiction under Section 302(a)(1)," even if they target the New York market.

The court opined that jurisdiction might have been proper had plaintiff waited to file its action until defendant actually contracted to sell its services to New York, but noted that waiting could have given rise to a laches defense.

The court also dismissed plaintiff's argument that defendant's e-mails to New York residents conferred jurisdiction. These communications occurred after the lawsuit was commenced, and thus were irrelevant for jurisdictional purposes. In any event, the court considered the e-mails to be "analogous to letters to or telephone communications with people in New York," and found they "are not sufficient to establish personal jurisdiction under CPLR §§§§ 302(a)(1) or the due process clause."

The court specifically noted New York State court precedent that "negotiating and concluding goods contracts by telephone and mail did not provide personal jurisdiction."

Nor did defendant commit a tortious act in New York within the meaning of CPLR § 302(a)(2), which requires that the cause of action asserted must arise from the tortious act. The alleged tort, defendant's passing off of its service using an infringing trademark, could be considered to take place in New York through an offer to sell the services in that state, as long as defendant was located in New York when the offer was made. However, because defendant had not yet commenced offering services for sale, and was not itself located in New York, jurisdiction under this provision was improper.

Finally, the court considered jurisdiction under CPLR § 302(a)(3), which covers a tortious act outside New York that causes injury in New York. Because defendant neither regularly transacted business in New York nor derived substantial revenues from interstate commerce, this provision was inappropriate was well.

In *Weber v. Jolly Hotels*, 997 F. Supp. 327 (D.N.J. 1997), the New Jersey plaintiff sued an Italian hotel company in New Jersey for personal injury occasioned by defendant's alleged negligence. Plaintiff had stayed at the hotel as a guest, and had arranged her travel through a travel agent located in New Jersey. New Jersey's long-arm statute, N.J. Sup. Ct. R. 4:4-4(c)(1), "permits the exercise of personal jurisdiction over a non-resident defendant to the full extent permitted by the Due Process Clause of the Fourteenth Amendment of the Constitution." Consequently, the court combined its statutory and constitutional analyses to conclude that it could not exercise personal jurisdiction over defendant.

The court first rejected plaintiff's argument that the travel agent was defendant's exclusive independent contractor, so that the court consequently had specific jurisdiction over defendant to the same extent it would have over the travel agent. Plaintiff could not take advantage of this argument because the travel agent did not have an exclusive relationship with defendant, and the services offered were in Italy, not New Jersey.

The court then turned to plaintiff's argument that defendant's website gave rise to general jurisdiction. The website included information about defendant's hotels as an advertisement, rather than to conduct business over the Internet. The court followed the reasoning in *Hearst* that "advertising on the internet falls under the same rubric as advertising in a national magazine," and concluded "that exercising jurisdiction over a defendant who merely advertises its services or product on the Internet would violate the Due Process Clause of the Fourteenth Amendment."

The reasoning and result in *Bensusan* were followed in *Cybersell, Inc. v. Cybersell, Inc.*, 130 F.3d 414 (9th Cir. 1997), wherein the appellate court upheld a dismissal for lack of personal jurisdiction in a service mark infringement case involving an Arizona plaintiff and Florida defendant. Defendant offered various Internet consulting services, which it advertised on its own website using the name "Cybersell." The website invited e-mail inquiries from readers.

The applicable Arizona long-arm statute, Rule 4.2(a) of the Arizona Rules of Civil Procedure, conferred Arizona court jurisdiction over defendants "to the maximum extent permitted by the Constitution of this state and the Constitution of the United States," and had been interpreted as being coterminous with the federal constitution's due process requirements. Thus, the court's inquiry was whether exercising jurisdiction over the defendant "comports with due process." There was no need to first conduct an analysis under state law.

The court characterized defendant's website as passive. It noted that defendant had not conducted or sought to conduct business in Arizona:

> No Arizonan except for [plaintiff] 'hit' [defendant's] website. There is no evidence that any Arizona resident signed up for [defendant's] web construction services. It entered into no contracts in Arizona, made no sales in Arizona, received no telephone calls from Arizona, earned no income from Arizona, and sent no messages over the Internet to Arizona. The only message it received over the Internet from Arizona was from [plaintiff]. [Defendant] did not have an '800' number, let alone a toll-free number that also used the 'Cybersell' name. The interactivity of its web page is limited to receiving the browser's name and address and an indication of interest—signing up for the service is not an option, nor did anyone from Arizona do so. No money changed hands on the Internet from (or through) Arizona.

Consequently, defendant had not purposefully availed itself of the privilege of conducting business in Arizona. Because this prerequisite under the due process clause had not been met, jurisdiction in Arizona was improper.

The court's discussion centered around specific jurisdiction, as plaintiff had conceded that there was no general jurisdiction over defendant.

In *Soma Medical Int'l v. Standard Chartered Bank*, 96 F.3d 1292 (10th Cir. 1998), the Utah plaintiff sued defendant, a Hong Kong bank, in Utah alleged breach of contract, negligence, breach of implied covenant, and civil conspiracy due to the bank's disbursement of funds that were deposited in plaintiff's account to an unauthorized party.

The court first dismissed plaintiff's argument for general jurisdiction, finding that defendant was not "conducting substantial and continuous local activity in" Utah. Defendant had not undertaken any of the specified indicia for such activity, such as being licensed to do business in the state or generating a substantial percentage of its revenue there. That defendant had filed several Uniform Commercial Code financing statements in Utah was considered insufficient to qualify as substantial and continuous in-state activity.

Moreover, the bank's website was characterized as "passive," limited to having information posted on it. Relying on the three-category *Zippo* analysis, the court concluded that a passive website did not constitute the type of activity required for assertion of jurisdiction over defendant.

Turning to the question of specific jurisdiction, the court applied Utah's long-arm statute, Utah Code Ann. §§ 78-27-24.

> Any person . . . who in person or through an agent does any of the following enumerated acts, submits himself . . . to the jurisdiction of the courts of this state as to any claim arising out of or related to:
>
> (1) the transaction of any business within this state;
>
> (2) contracting to supply services or goods in this state;
>
> (3) the causing of any injury within this state whether tortious or by breach of warranty . . .

The reach of this law is long enough "'so as to assert jurisdiction over nonresident defendants to the fullest extent permitted by the due process clause of the Fourteenth Amendment to the United States Constitution.'" Utah Code Ann. §§ 78-27-22.

The court considered the correspondence between defendant and plaintiff concerning plaintiff's account, the bank's other contacts with Utah, and the fact that defendant maintained a website accessible in Utah. As to the former, it pointed out that the available evidence indicated that plaintiff had approached defendant to open an account, not the other way around, and the correspondence concerning a relationship instigated by plaintiff would not provide sufficient contacts between defendant and the forum state. The bank's other contacts with Utah had nothing to do with plaintiff in the case at hand, and therefore were irrelevant in analyzing personal jurisdiction. Finally, the court could not conclude that defendant's "maintenance of a passive website, merely providing information to interested viewers, constitutes the kind of purposeful availment of the benefits of doing business in Utah, such that [defendant] could expect to be haled into court in that state."

Although the court did not directly address plaintiff's contention that the website "solicit[s] business from all over the planet," including Utah, it appears that plaintiff may not have provided evidentiary proof on this point, as indicated by the court's statement that defendant "has failed to carry even its relatively light burden of making a prima facie showing that the website is anything more than such a passive informational site."

Barrett v. Catacombs Press, 64 F. Supp. 2d 440 (E.D.Pa. 1998), was a defamation action filed by a Pennsylvania plaintiff against defendants from several states, one of whom (from Oregon) moved to dismiss for lack of personal jurisdiction. Allegedly defamatory material was posted on the Oregon defendant's website and thereafter circulated among several "list-serv" discussion groups. Oregon defendant and plaintiff also exchanged e-mail correspondence containing the allegedly defamatory statements.

Applying Pennsylvania's long-arm statute, the court determined that it did not have jurisdiction over the defendants. First, the absence of any "systematic and continuous" contacts between defendants and Pennsylvania precluded a finding of general jurisdiction. The posting of information on a nationally-accessible website, like the placement of material in a national publication, does not amount to such contacts.

Second, in the absence of any non-Internet related contacts between Oregon defendant and Pennsylvania, the court had to consider whether the electronic contacts conferred specific jurisdiction. Following the reasoning set forth in *Zippo* and refined in *Blackburn*, it found that the websites on which the material was posted were passive in nature. It reiterated that posting material on a nationally-accessible website did not mean that a particular state was targeted for receipt of the information. It acknowledged that list-serve and discussion groups were "technically" different than a website, but found that they are "akin to a 'passive' Web site and insufficient to trigger this court's jurisdiction," primarily because they similarly did not target a specific state. Finally, the two e-mail communications between plaintiff and Oregon defendant were limited in volume and did "not occur in a context of a 'substantial connection'" between Oregon defendant and Pennsylvania.

The court also rejected plaintiff's argument that the alleged tort had an "effect" in Pennsylvania, as they did not specifically note plaintiff's connections in that state, but rather his national reputation. It characterized the analysis thusly: "Unless Pennsylvania is deliberately or knowingly targeted by the tortfeasor, the fact that harm is felt in Pennsylvania from conduct occurring outside Pennsylvania is never sufficient to satisfy due process."

Personal jurisdiction was likewise declined in *Grutkowski v. Steamboat Lake Guides & Outfitters, Inc.*, 1998 U.S. Dist. LEXIS 20255 (E.D.Pa. 1998), a wrongful death action filed by a Pennsylvania plaintiff against, *inter alia*, a defendant in Colorado. Plaintiff had asserted jurisdiction over the Colorado defendant because of the latter's website and its use of a Colorado booking agent. The Colorado defendant's motion to dismiss was granted, and the action against it was transferred to the district court in Colorado. The court's discussion was limited to general jurisdiction.

Citing *Blackburn*, the court found that the Colorado defendant's website was passive. It contained "information and photographs describing the various tours and services" defendant offered and a map showing defendant's location. It also permitted "an interested reader to send an e-mail message to" defendant, but did "not permit a reader to purchase or reserve tours over the Internet and thus, does not permit [defendant] to 'transact business' over the Internet." The website provided a telephone number at which defendant could be contacted. The court found that this amounted "to no more than passive advertisements, and though commercial in nature," did not establish "either systematic or continuous contacts with Pennsylvania through their maintenance."

The limited interactivity offered by the option of sending e-mail to defendant provided "the electronic equivalents of advertisements' response cards" and was "insufficient to make these pages more than advertisements. On strikingly similar facts, *Blackburn* held that a website which permitted a reader to send e-mail to the site's sponsor did not establish jurisdiction over the site's sponsor in the reader's forum. *See Blackburn,* 999 F. Supp. at 639."

Accordingly, the court declined to find general jurisdiction over the Colorado defendant.

Similarly, that defendant's use of a booking agent did not confer jurisdiction, as the agent merely responded to inquiries from interested persons, including those in Pennsylvania, but did not direct its advertising to that state.

In *Mink v. AAAA Development LLC*, 190 F.3d 330 (5th Cir. 1999), the appellate court affirmed the trial court's dismissal of a patent and copyright infringement case filed in Texas by a Texas plaintiff against a Vermont defendant. The Texas long-arm statute permitted jurisdiction to the extent authorized by the U.S. constitution, so the court addressed the matter strictly from a constitutional due process standpoint. The analysis followed that set forth in *Zippo*.

Defendant's website had the following features: product information, a printable mail-in order form, a toll-free telephone number, and mailing and e-mail addresses. However, orders were not taken through the website, leading the court to characterize it as "passive" as it offered nothing more than advertisement. "There was no evidence that [defendant] conducted business over the Internet by engaging in business transactions with forum residents or by entering into contracts over the Internet." Consequently, the court concluded that defendant neither was conducting business over the Internet nor had sufficient interactivity with Texas to support personal jurisdiction.

Remick v. Manfredy, 52 F. Supp. 2d 452 (E.D.Pa. 1999), another defamation action, involved a Pennsylvania plaintiff, individual defendants from Illinois and Indiana, and a law firm defendant from Illinois. The individual defendants' only possible contacts with Pennsylvania were through the Internet. They maintained a website containing information about one of the defendants, a professional boxer. The site offered memorabilia for sale and an order form that had to be mailed. No orders had been placed from Pennsylvania. Electronic purchases were not possible. The law firm website provided information about the firm's practice and attorneys.

Following *Blackburn*, the court found that websites containing nothing "other than general information and advertising" failed to provide such "continuous and substantial contacts" with the forum state as would be needed for general jurisdiction. The court then addressed specific jurisdiction solely in the context of non-Internet contacts.

No jurisdiction was found in *Wildfire Communications, Inc. v. Grapevine, Inc.*, 2001 U.S. Dist. LEXIS 18238 (D. Mass. 2001), a trademark infringement case involving a Massachusetts plaintiff and Illinois defendant. Defendant marketed certain "internet service provider" (ISP) services in an area of Illinois, operated three websites accessible from anywhere, entered into a domain name sales contract with plaintiff, and marketed a product called an internet business card to plaintiff in Massachusetts.

In the court's view, defendant had not "purposefully availed" itself of Massachusetts law to the extent needed to sustain jurisdiction. Defendant's websites did not specifically solicit business in Massachusetts; its ISP services were unavailable there; and there was no evidence that it had any customers or business in the state.

The passive nature of defendants' website led to a finding of no jurisdiction in *Lofton v. Turbine Design, Inc.*, 100 F. Supp. 2d 404 (N.D. Miss. 2000), a defamation action. Defendants, located in Florida, had posted on the site the allegedly defamatory material, leading to plaintiffs' assertion that publication and hence injury had taken place in the forum state Mississippi. The website also advertised defendants' business by providing information about their products and services, but did not set forth prices or permit site users to obtain quotes or enter into contracts online.

The court concluded with little discussion that there was no specific jurisdiction over defendants, merely noting that "defendants have not established [with Mississippi] any contacts directly related to the cause of action." The court also rejected plaintiffs' argument that the injurious effect of the defamatory material's publication was felt in Mississippi, on the grounds that the website was not specifically directed toward that state and that a contrary conclusion would permit jurisdiction to arise from a passive website. The court rested its analysis on *Zippo* as followed by the Fifth Circuit in *Mink*.

Cases Finding Jurisdiction

A relatively early decision, *Inset Systems, Inc. v. Instruction Set, Inc.*, 937 F. Supp. 161 (D. Conn. 1996), found personal jurisdiction arising from a passive website in a trademark infringement and unfair competition action. Defendant, a Massachusetts corporation that provided computer consulting services, maintained a website whose domain name allegedly infringed plaintiff's registered trademark. Although the opinion is not entirely clear on the point, it appears that the website was informational only, and simply advertised defendant's service. Defendant also maintained a toll-free telephone number, but did not maintain an office or employees in Connecticut, nor did it regularly conduct business there.

The court looked to the Connecticut long-arm statute, C.G.S. §§ 33-411(c)(2), which provides jurisdiction over "any cause of action arising . . . out of any business solicited in this state . . . if the corporation has repeatedly so solicited business, whether the orders or offers relating thereto were accepted within or without the state. . . ." It concluded that defendant advertised continuously and repetitively over the Internet by virtue of its website; in doing so, it analogized to cases involving printed advertisements circulated in Connecticut, and found that Internet advertising was more repetitive than its hard-copy counterpart: "unlike hard-copy advertisements . . . which are often quickly disposed of and reach a limited number of potential consumers, Internet advertisements are in electronic printed form so that they can be accessed again and again by many more potential consumers."

The court also found that the constitutionally-required minimum contacts with the forum were present. Because defendant had "directed its advertising activities via the Internet and its toll-free number toward not only the state of Connecticut, but to all states," it had "purposefully availed itself of the privilege of doing business within Connecticut" and "it could reasonably anticipate the possibility of being hailed into court here."

Inset Systems was cited with approval in *Maritz, Inc. v. CyberGold, Inc.*, 947 F. Supp. 1328 (E.D. Mo. 1996), a case involving alleged trademark infringement and unfair competition by defendant, a California resident. Missouri's long-arm statute, Mo. Rev. Stat. §§ 506.500, provided for jurisdiction as follows:

> Any person or firm, whether or not a citizen or resident of this state, or any corporation, who in person or through an agent does any of the acts enumerated in this section, thereby submits such person, firm, or corporation, and, if an individual, his personal representative, to the jurisdiction of the courts of this state as to any cause of action arising from the doing of any of such acts:
>
> (1) The transaction of any business within this state . . .
>
> (3) The commission of a tortious act within this state . . .

The court noted that this provision has been interpreted to subject non-residents to jurisdiction in Missouri to "the extent permissible under the due process clause."

As described by the court, defendant's website provided information about the company and an Internet service it planned to offer in which it would forward advertisements to interested readers by e-mail. Readers were invited to sign up for the forwarding service by sending their e-mail addresses to defendant using an option on the website. Any Internet user could participate. The service was not yet in operation at the time of the lawsuit.

The court looked first to the "nature and quality of contacts provided by the maintenance of a website on the internet" and found them to be more extensive than mass mailings of material or advertising a toll-free telephone number. A website is accessible to all users, wherever located, on a continuing basis.

The court disagreed with defendant's characterization of its website as "passive" both because it provides advertising accessible by all Internet users and because defendant responded "automatically and indiscriminately responds to each and every internet user who accesses its website."

Next, the court looked to the quantity of defendant's contacts with Missouri, and found "that defendant has transmitted information into Missouri regarding its services approximately 131 times," based on the number of times a Missouri resident other than plaintiff had visited the website. In the court's view, this indicated "that defendant is purposefully availing itself to the privilege of conducting activities in Missouri."

Third, the court found that the litigation before it "results from alleged injuries that, at least in part, arise out of or relate to [defendant's] website and the information posted at the website."

Accordingly, the court held that it had personal jurisdiction over defendant.

The approach taken by *Inset Systems* was also followed in *Telco Communications v. An Apple A Day*, 977 F. Supp. 404 (E.D. Va. 1997), an action asserting defamation and other torts arising from statements allegedly posted on the Internet by defendants, residents of Missouri. The state long-arm statute, Virginia Code Section 8.01-328.1(A)(4), "permits personal jurisdiction to be exercised over a defendant who caused a tortious injury in Virginia by an act or omission outside Virginia if the defendant 'regularly does or solicits business, or engages in any other persistent course of conduct, or derives substantial revenue from goods used or consumed or services rendered' in Virginia." It has been interpreted to "extend[ ] personal jurisdiction to the fullest extent permitted by due process."

Defendants had allegedly posted several defamatory press releases on the Internet. The court, citing *Inset Systems*, found that this was "conducting business" in Virginia for long-arm purposes. "Because they conducted their advertising and soliciting over the Internet, which could be accessed by a Virginia resident 24 hours a day, the Defendants did so regularly for purposes of the long-arm statute. Accordingly, the Court finds that posting a website advertisement or solicitation constitutes a persistent course of conduct, and that the two or three press releases rise to the level of regularly doing or soliciting business, thus satisfying subsection 4." The court distinguished *Bensusan* on the ground that, unlike New York, Virginia does not require that a "nonresident defendant must be physically present in a state in order for jurisdiction to attach."

Moreover, the court stated, the posted press releases were analogous to defamatory letters sent to a forum state. Like such letters, although the press releases were not directed at plaintiff's actions in the forum state, they had their primary injurious effect there.

The complaint in *Heroes, Inc. v. Heroes Foundation*, 958 F. Supp. 1 (D.D.C. 1996), alleged trademark infringement and unfair competition by defendants, one of which, a New York charitable corporation, moved to dismiss. The court denied the motion based on its application of the District of Columbia's long-arm statute, which provides for personal jurisdiction over:

> a person who acts directly or by an agent as to a claim for relief arising from the person's (1) transacting any business in the District of Columbia; or (2) causing tortious injury in the District of Columbia by an act or omission outside the District of Columbia if he regularly does or solicits business, engages in any other persistent course of conduct, or derives substantial revenue from goods used or consumed, or services rendered, in the District of Columbia.

The New York defendant had advertised for contributions in a District newspaper, and also maintained a website that "provides information about the organization and its members," solicits donations, and invites readers to send e-mail communications to defendant. Donations could not be made electronically using the website, but had to be made by other means.

The court concluded that it had personal jurisdiction. Its decision did not hinge solely on defendant's maintenance of a website. Indeed, the court sidestepped the question of whether the website alone would confer jurisdiction, but strongly hinted that it would reach an affirmative answer on the question:

> Because the defendant's home page is not the only contact before the Court, see above, the Court need not decide whether the defendant's home page by itself subjects the defendant to personal jurisdiction in the District. In weighing the importance of this particular contact, however, the Court notes that the defendant's home page explicitly solicits contributions, and provides a toll-free telephone number for that purpose. The home page also contains the defendant's allegedly infringing trademark and logo, the subject of the plaintiff's underlying claims. And the home page is certainly a sustained contact with the District; it has been possible for a District resident to gain access to it at any time since it was first posted.

The court noted but did not explicitly choose between the reasoning in *Bensusan*, on the one hand, and *Inset Systems* and *Maritz*, on the other. However, its *dicta* indicated, at the least, that defendant's passive website provided a "contact," and can be read as providing a strong indication of the court's inclination in a website-only case.

In short, the finding of jurisdiction rested on the combination of the newspaper advertisement and the website. "By soliciting donations on the Internet on a home page which is always available to District residents, and by soliciting donations in the District's local newspaper, the defendant has purposefully availed itself of the privilege of conducting activities within the District, and could reasonably anticipate the possibility of being haled into court there." The decision may be criticized (from the *Blackburn/Zippo* standpoint) for including a passive website as a contact to be weighed to any extent in determining personal jurisdiction. The opinion does not address whether the newspaper advertisement alone warranted a finding of jurisdiction, and the result perhaps could be sustained on that contact alone without departing from *Blackburn/Zippo*.

The *dicta* in *Heroes* implying that a passive website alone may give rise to personal jurisdiction is questionable in light of the District of Columbia Circuit's decision in *GTE New Media Services Inc. v. Ameritech Corp.*, 199 F.3d 1343 (D.C. Cir. 2000), a case arising from accusations that defendants conspired to monopolize the market in Internet business directories. The court dismissed the notion that a party's website, in and of itself, could provide a sufficient basis for personal jurisdiction:

> [P]ersonal jurisdiction surely cannot be based solely on the ability of District residents to access the defendants' websites, for this does not by itself show any persistent course of conduct by the defendants in the District. Access to a website reflects nothing more than a telephone call by a District resident to the defendants' computer servers, all of which apparently are operated outside of the District. And, as this court has held, mere receipt of telephone calls outside the District does not constitute persistent conduct "in the District" within the meaning of the long-arm statute.

The district court had described the websites in question as "highly interactive," so, at a minimum, *GTE* casts substantial doubt on a passive website operator's susceptibility to jurisdiction in the District of Columbia solely by virtue of the website.

Hasbro, Inc. v. Clue Computing, Inc., 994 F. Supp. 34 (D. Mass. 1997) involved alleged trademark infringement resulting from the Colorado defendant's use of the word "Clue" on its website. The Massachusetts long-arm statute authorized personal jurisdiction over a non-resident whose out-of-state actions cause tortious injury in Massachusetts if the non-resident "regularly does or solicits business, or engages in any other persistent course of conduct, or derives substantial revenue from goods used or consumed or services rendered, in" Massachusetts.

The court determined that there was harm in Massachusetts resulting from the alleged infringement, and concluded that defendant was doing business in the state within the meaning of the long-arm statute simply by virtue of maintaining a website that was continuously available to state residents. The website was analogous to a nationally published advertisement. The website also states that defendant will provide its consulting services to any visitor to the site (including, presumably, those in Massachusetts), and also mentions a Massachusetts company as one of defendant's clients. Thus, the court concluded, "[b]y maintaining a website which can be continuously accessed by Massachusetts residents, combined with the actions discussed above, [defendant] does regularly solicit business in Massachusetts through its website, and therefore satisfies the jurisdictional requirements of 3(d)."

Comment

Although the majority of reported opinions have adopted *Blackburn/Zippo*-type analysis that passive websites in and of themselves do not give rise to personal jurisdiction, several cases have found passive jurisdiction based solely on a defendant's operation of a passive website. For the most part, the analyses and results in these cases cannot be reconciled with the *Blackburn/Zippo* approach. Thus, even an operator of a passive website should beware that, in some states, it may be subject to personal jurisdiction solely by virtue of its home page.

Interactive Website Cases

These cases fall under the second *Blackburn/Zippo* category, in which the visitor and host of a website can exchange information to a certain extent. As elucidated in *Blackburn*, "the exercise of jurisdiction is determined by examining the level of interactivity and commercial nature of the exchange of information that occurs on the Website." Thus, the results in these cases are more likely to hinge on specific attributes of the websites in question.

Cases Finding No Jurisdiction

In *Morantz v. Hang & Shine Ultrasonics, Inc.*, 79 F. Supp. 2d 537 (E.D.Pa. 1999), the court found it did not have personal jurisdiction in a trademark infringement action; the case was then transferred to the district court where the New York defendant was located. The Pennsylvania plaintiff asserted that personal jurisdiction arose from defendant's use of an allegedly infringing image on its website. Defendant also maintained a toll-free telephone number, which it apparently listed on its website.

The court noted that the limited degree of interactivity might even qualify the site as "passive" as defined by *Blackburn/Zippo*, but in any event it declined to exercise personal jurisdiction. First, it held that "there must be 'something more' than a mere website to justify the exercise of personal jurisdiction over a non-resident corporation," and that the simple existence of a website and a toll-free number operated by a defendant would not confer jurisdiction over that party.

In search of the "something more," the court considered the website's attributes:

> [T]hese website features are not interactive enough to justify the exercise of personal jurisdiction by this Court. The presence of an e-mail link or a form for placing orders on a website does not create the kind of minimum contacts required to establish personal jurisdiction.

The fact that defendant sold a "promotional videotape over the Internet does not increase the interactivity of the website or transform it into a site through which [defendant] does its business," because this was simply another means for defendant to advertise itself.

Moreover, defendant's website was not targeted at the forum state, nor did defendant actively seek business there. In addition, there was no evidence that the website resulted in significant levels of contacts with Pennsylvania. Although defendant had received several e-mail contacts from that state through its website, the level of activity was too small to support a finding of jurisdiction. Defendant did not have any non-Internet indicia of business in Pennsylvania, such as maintaining a bank account or place of business in the state.

The court also ruled that the maintenance of a toll-free telephone number was insufficient to confer personal jurisdiction on an out-of-state resident, although it implicitly acknowledged that other courts have ruled differently.

The discussion in *Molnlycke v. Dumex*, 1999 U.S. Dist. LEXIS 13678 (E.D.Pa. 1999) addressed only general jurisdiction, as plaintiff had conceded that specific jurisdiction was unavailable. The patent infringement action was filed in Pennsylvania by a Swedish company against a Canadian defendant; plaintiff's asserted tie with the forum was that its wholly-owned subsidiary was located there. Plaintiff's assertion of personal jurisdiction was premised on the defendant's maintenance of two websites, which not only advertised defendant's products but also permitted site visitors to purchase them.

However, the court concluded that "the establishment of a website through which customers can order products does not, on its own, suffice to establish general jurisdiction. To hold that the possibility of ordering products from a website establishes general jurisdiction would effectively hold that any corporation with such a website is subject to general jurisdiction in every state." These websites were akin to a general advertising campaign that was not aimed at Pennsylvania in particular. They failed to constitute the kind of "prolonged, targeted advertising campaign and presence in Pennsylvania [that] justified general jurisdiction."

Additionally, plaintiff had "failed to demonstrate that the websites are 'central' to the defendant's business," or that Pennsylvania sales were an essential part of defendant's business. Thus, the fact that a small volume of sales had been made in Pennsylvania through the websites would not suffice to confer general jurisdiction.

Decker v. Circus Circus Hotel, 49 F. Supp. 2d 743 (D.N.J. 1997) also involved New Jersey residents bringing a personal injury action against an out of state hotel, this time in Nevada.

Because defendant's website was configured to permit a visitor to reserve a room electronically, the court found that defendant had placed its hotel and services into the stream of commerce to an extent sufficient to support long-arm jurisdiction. The court declined to exercise general personal jurisdiction, however, because the "Internet site contains a forum selection clause requiring that by making a reservation over the Internet, customers agree to have their disputes settled in Nevada state and federal courts. This forum selection clause ought to be enforced." Therefore, it determined that it would "not exercise personal jurisdiction over the defendant based on the maintenance of its Internet site."

The remaining jurisdictional contacts urged by plaintiff—television and magazine advertisements and mailing of promotional materials to state residents upon their request—were also insufficient to support a finding of general personal jurisdiction.

The court next rejected specific personal jurisdiction, which required that the action arise out of defendant's contacts with New Jersey, on the ground that plaintiffs had failed to provide evidence concerning their initial contacts with defendant.

A "middle"-type website did not provide personal jurisdiction over a defendant located in the United Kingdom in *Ty Inc. v. Clark*, 2000 U.S. Dist. LEXIS 383 (N.D. Ill. 2000), an action for trademark infringement and other unfair competition claims arising from the site. Citing *Zippo*, the court considered the website to be moderately interactive: it permitted e-mail communications with prospective buyers but did not permit order placement or contract formation and expressly stated that defendant would not sell through the site. Rather, it provided a printable form for buyers to send to defendant. The court considered the facts to resemble those of *Mink*, and concluded that it lacked personal jurisdiction.

Cases Finding Jurisdiction

VP Intellectual Properties, LLC v. Imtec Corp., No. 99-3136 (D.N.J. 1999) involved a patent infringement action between a New Jersey plaintiff and an Oklahoma defendant. Defendant maintained a website that included:

(1) company and product descriptions;

(2) distributor information;

(3) ordering information; and

(4) a catalog request form that can be filled out and electronically transmitted to the company.

Although a customer could obtain product information, it could not order products through the website, which led the court to describe it as a "middle category" case, in *Blackburn's* parlance. The court concluded that the website was insufficiently "active" to support general jurisdiction.

The court found specific jurisdiction over defendant for those of the allegedly-infringing products that had been sold in New Jersey, based on the rule that specific personal jurisdiction over a patent infringement claim will lie in a state where such sales have occurred. However, because the sales were not made through defendant's website, the finding of specific jurisdiction concerning certain products did not implicate defendant's Internet activities.

In *Christian Science Bd. v. Nolan*, 259 F.3d 209 (4th Cir. 2001), a trademark infringement case, the court affirmed a finding of specific jurisdiction over Arizona defendants that had contributed material to a website in North Carolina. The website operator, resident in North Carolina, also was sued there.

There were sufficient contacts between defendants and North Carolina to find specific jurisdiction. Defendants had sought the website's creation in North Carolina and sent text materials there for inclusion on the website; such materials underlay the trademark infringement claim. They thus had purposefully availed themselves of the privilege of conducting activities in North Carolina. It made no difference that defendant did not compensate the North Carolina website operator for his services.

The jurisdictional contacts arose not from the website *per se*, but from defendants' activities in seeking its establishment and providing materials to it. Defendants entered into a "collaborative enterprise" with a party in North Carolina, knowing that the consequence of their activities would be the placement of material on a website. Thus, the court did not address whether the site itself sufficed to confer jurisdiction, despite defendants' invitation to do so. The Fourth Circuit did note the district court's characterization of the website as active, without indicating whether it agreed with it.

"Doing Business" Cases

Cases Finding Jurisdiction

In *CompuServe, Inc. v. Patterson*, 89 F.3d 1257 (6th Cir. 1996), the plaintiff was an Internet service provider located in Ohio. As part of its service, it contracted with software providers to offer software products to its subscribers. Defendant, located in Texas, entered into one such agreement with plaintiff. Defendant electronically sent the software to plaintiff, which in turn offered the software to its subscribers. Plaintiff thereafter began offering its subscribers a similar software product of its own, prompting defendant to claim that plaintiff's product infringed his trademark, and defendant to file a declaratory judgment action in Ohio to adjudicate the trademark issue.

The appellate court reversed the trial court's dismissal of the action for lack of personal jurisdiction over defendant. The court acknowledged that defendant's contacts with Ohio were "almost entirely electronic in nature," but found that they nevertheless fit within the traditional concept of "doing business" in the state. Defendant had "purposefully availed" himself of the privilege of doing business in Ohio by subscribing to plaintiff's services, entering into an agreement to permit plaintiff to distribute his software, and electronically sending his software to plaintiff per the agreement.

In the court's view, these contacts were substantial. The court particularly emphasized the fact that defendant had "entered a written contract with [plaintiff] that called for the application of Ohio law, and he then purposefully perpetuated the relationship with [plaintiff] via repeated communications with its system in Ohio." Although "merely entering into a contract with [plaintiff] would not, without more, establish that [defendant] had minimum contacts with Ohio," the fact of a contract, plus defendant's placing his products in the stream of commerce along with his other "deliberate and repeated" contacts with the state would suffice for personal jurisdiction purposes.

Compuserve predated *Zippo* and *Blackburn*, and indeed was cited in both cases as an example of a "doing business" scenario. *Compuserve* is noteworthy in that it considered electronic contacts as similar to non-electronic contacts; the opinion did not appear to see anything unique about the Internet for purposes of analyzing jurisdiction. It treated an electronic contract and course of dealing no differently than it would their dead tree and snail mail counterparts.

Zippo Mfg. Co. v. Zippo Dot Com, 952 F. Supp. 1119 (W.D. Pa. 1997), first set forth the three-category mode of analysis that was restated and refined in *Blackburn*. *Zippo* was a trademark infringement, dilution, and false designation action involving a Pennsylvania plaintiff and a California defendant. Defendant maintained a website on which placed information about itself, advertisements for its services, and an application to subscribe to its Internet news services that included an electronic payment feature. A subscriber that completed the application would be issued a password allowing it to gain access to information contained on defendant's server.

The court noted that defendant's contacts with Pennsylvania were almost exclusively over the Internet; defendant did not maintain offices or employees in Pennsylvania, nor did it engage in non-Internet promotion there. Approximately 3,000 Pennsylvania residents, or two percent of defendant's subscriber base, were located in Pennsylvania. All of these subscribers would have contracted with defendant exclusively through the Internet, by accessing defendant's web page. In addition, defendant had "entered into agreements with seven Internet access providers in Pennsylvania to permit their subscribers to access [defendant's] news service."

Defendant used the allegedly infringing name on its website, in its domain name, and on electronic messages that it sent to subscribers.

The court found that it was presented with a "doing business" case, like *Compuserve*, in that defendant "has done more than create an interactive website through which it exchanges information with Pennsylvania residents in hopes of using that information for commercial gain later. . . . Dot Com has contracted with approximately 3,000 individuals and seven Internet access providers in Pennsylvania. The intended object of these transactions has been the downloading of the electronic messages that form the basis of this suit in Pennsylvania."

Defendant's contacts with the state were too extensive to be considered "fortuitous;" defendant "repeatedly and consciously chose to process Pennsylvania residents' applications and to assign them passwords" and "knew that the result of these contracts would be the transmission of electronic messages into Pennsylvania. The transmission of these files was entirely within its control." Because defendant had made a "conscious choice to conduct business with the residents of" Pennsylvania, its claim that its contacts were fortuitous was rejected.

Similarly, the court found that the large number of transactions that defendant had entered into with Pennsylvania residents were sufficient to pass the minimal contacts requirement.

The court concluded that the cause of action arose from defendant's Pennsylvania-related conduct, as Pennsylvania was the place where defendant's alleged trademark infringement and plaintiff's consequent injury had occurred due to defendant's substantial contacts with the state.

The Washington state defendant's website in *Standard Knitting, Ltd. v. Outside Design, Inc.*, 2000 WL 804434 (E.D. Pa. 2000), was described by the court as "fully interactive" and as "one through which business is conducted with residents of foreign jurisdictions, including Pennsylvania." However, the court did not provide details concerning the website's capabilities. Interestingly, although the website was sufficiently interactive for personal jurisdiction purposes, the court concluded that venue was proper in the district court where defendant resided.

The District of Columbia Circuit found that plaintiff had sufficiently demonstrated that defendant was doing business in the District to warrant jurisdictional discovery in *Gorman v. Ameritrade Holding Corp.*, 293 F.3d 506 (D.C. Cir. 2002). This breach of contract action arose from the Nebraska defendant's alleged failure to honor an agreement by a corporation it acquired to maintain a front-page link on its website to the Virginia plaintiff's website. The appeals court reversed the district court's dismissal for lack of jurisdiction, but dismissed on the alternative ground that service had not been properly effected.

The court first dismissed defendant's contention that jurisdiction would not lie anywhere because electronic transactions it conducts with District residents occurred in cyberspace. Analogizing the internet to mail and telephone transmissions, it stated that it would rely on the traditional approach of determining whether defendant's contacts with the District were "'continuous and systematic.'"

Defendant maintained an interactive website that permitted it to conduct electronic transactions with District residents, allowing the latter to open accounts and transmit funds to them, purchase and sell securities, and pay for those transactions. Defendant electronically transmitted trading confirmations, account statements, and other information to account holders in the District. These electronic transactions resulted in the formation of stock brokerage contracts between defendant and District residents, and defendant's receipt of revenues from such contracts. Indeed, defendant also offered these services through telephone and postal transactions.

The court distinguished the facts in *Gorman* from those in *GTE*, in that in the latter case District residents "did not engage in business transactions with the defendants" by using the defendant's website.

The court affirmed the district court's dismissal solely because of the defective service of process on defendant, and stated that, but for that defect, it would have reversed and remanded for jurisdictional discovery.

The rationales of *Compuserve* and *Zippo* were cited in *Intercon, Inc. v. Bell Atlantic Internet Solutions, Inc.*, 205 F.3d 1244 (10th Cir. 2000), a tort action stemming not from defendant's operation of a website but from the unauthorized routing of its customers' e-mail traffic through plaintiff's server. Such activity sufficed for jurisdiction even though defendant argued that it conducted no business in Oklahoma, the site of plaintiff's server. However, the court found that defendant had purposefully directed its activities toward the state by continuing to route e-mail traffic there after having been informed of the problem by plaintiff. Such continued activity following notice was deliberate and intentional, rather than fortuitous; the court implied that a different result might obtain had notice not been given.

"Internet Plus" Cases

A number of decisions have focused on both the Internet-related and non-electronic contacts that a defendant has with the forum state. Although they did not found personal jurisdiction arising solely from a defendant's Internet activities, they nevertheless provide guidance concerning the nature and extent of a company's overall business operations that may give rise to personal jurisdiction over the company. We have treated these cases outside of the *Blackburn/Zippo* passive/interactive categories, even though the courts may have looked to these categories in reaching their conclusions, because it of their explicit focus on non-electronic contacts.

In *Digital Equipment Corp. v. AltaVista Technology, Inc.*, 960 F. Supp. 456 (D. Mass. 1997), a trademark dispute, defendant had entered into a written, non-electronic agreement with plaintiff conveying its trademark rights in the term "AltaVista" and licensing back the limited use of that term. Defendant maintained a website that was accessible in Massachusetts, and which allegedly used the term in an infringing manner. The court concluded that the website, coupled with the licensing agreement, sufficed to provide personal jurisdiction over defendant.

The court found that defendant had successfully solicited sales of both advertising and software in Massachusetts through its website. Although acknowledging that general advertising on a website may not confer jurisdiction, the court pointed out that such advertising in this case was related to both the contract between plaintiff and defendant and the cause of action, and thus provided sufficient contacts for jurisdictional purposes.

In addition, defendant's website was accessible in Massachusetts on a continuous basis and solicited business there, and software purchased on it could be electronically transmitted to a computer in Massachusetts. Therefore, the court found that jurisdiction was alternatively present under the state long-arm statute covering "a tort committed in Massachusetts based on acts committed elsewhere, coupled with either regular solicitation of business, or continuing contacts, or the derivation of substantial revenue from Massachusetts."

Although the opinion did not discuss defendant's website in terms of the *Blackburn/Zippo* passive/interactive analysis, and did not reveal whether software or advertising could be purchased on the website itself, it indicated that such capability was irrelevant to its discussion:

> Ultimately, it does not matter for jurisdictional purposes whether these sales were made because a computer user clicked while accessing [defendant's] Website, or by calling a toll-free telephone number, or by answering mail. The reality is that a Website is accessible by people in Massachusetts, they have accessed [defendant's] Website, and [defendant's] actions resulted in purchases being made by Massachusetts citizens.

Thus, *Digital* falls in line with the *Inset/Maritz/Telco* reasoning that operation of a passive website would confer jurisdiction simply by being accessible by residents of a state, with the apparent added requirement that state residents must have effected purchases of the goods and/or services advertised on the website.

Blumenthal v. Drudge, 992 F. Supp. 44 (D.D.C. 1998), a defamation case, concluded that jurisdiction over the defendant Internet personality was proper in the District of Columbia. Defendant as doing business in the District by virtue of his "interactive" website, as well as specified non-electronic contacts. The indicia of website interactivity included its feature allowing visitors to send e-mail communications to defendant and to subscribe to e-mailed subscriptions to defendant's writings, resulting in a "constant exchange of information and direct communication" between defendant and residents of the District. Additionally, defendant had solicited donations through his website, and received positive responses from several District residents. The subject of defendant's website, political gossip, was in the court's view of particular interest to residents of the District.

Defendant's non-electronic contacts included in-person, telephone, and postal contacts with the District and its residents.

The *Blumenthal* court interpreted precedential decisions concerning Internet jurisdiction to require not only an interactive website, but non-electronic contacts between a defendant and the forum state. Although the cases cited in *Blumenthal* may have involved non-electronic contacts, they do not appear to require that such contacts are a *sine qua non* for personal jurisdiction. In this regard, *Blumenthal* and *Compuserve* would appear to be inconsistent, as the latter specifically hinged on Internet-only contacts.

Although *Blumenthal's* result was explicitly premised on a finding of both net and non-electronic contacts, its conclusion concerning the interactive nature of defendant's website alone probably would have supported a finding of personal jurisdiction under the *Blackburn/Zippo* approach.

An out-of-state alleged "cyber pirate's" registration of and attempt to sell domain names to a party that held the trademarks in those names gave rise to jurisdiction in *Panavision Int'l v. Toeppen*, 141 F.3d 1316 (9th Cir. 1998), affirming 938 F. Supp. 616 (C.D. Cal. 1996). Defendant had established websites using the disputed names. Such sites were indisputably "passive". The court found that they nevertheless gave a basis for specific jurisdiction under California's long-arm statute, which considered whether the out-of-state tort had the purpose or effect of causing harm in California. Defendant had not only registered the domain names—an action which the court noted would not in itself give rise to jurisdiction—but engaged in a scheme to extort money from the California plaintiff, thereby causing injury in the state. Thus, defendant's activity beyond the maintenance of a website underlies the jurisdictional discussion. The court distinguished its prior *Cybersell* decision finding no jurisdiction because the defendant there had not purposefully directed its activity to the forum state.

By contrast, jurisdiction could not be founded on an alleged cyberpiracy scheme in *K.C.P.L., Inc. v. Nash*, 1999 U.S. Dist. LEXIS 18464 (S.D.N.Y. 1998). The parties had engaged in fruitless discussions for defendant to convey rights to the domain name in exchange for money, and these provided the grounds for plaintiff's assertion that defendant was engaged in extortion.

Defendant never established a website using the allegedly infringing trademark, and the allegedly infringing domain name had an arguably valid connection to the name of the enterprise that defendant sought to establish, undercutting the claim that defendant was an extortionist. The court declined to follow *Toeppen* based on these factual differences, as well as the more restrictive reach of the New York long-arm statute. The statutory requirements that defendant regularly conduct or solicit business in New York or derive substantial revenue from interstate or international commerce were not present, warranting dismissal of the action.

The Court of Appeals for the Federal Circuit addressed the issue of personal jurisdiction in diversity cases arising from patent claims in *3D System, Inc. v. Aarotech Laboratories, Inc.*, 60 F.3d 1373 (Fed. Cir. 1998). The court's conclusion regarding jurisdiction arising from a website is probably the least noteworthy aspect of the decision. Citing *Cybersell*, the court found that a defendant's mere operation of a passive website would not provide district court jurisdiction over it. The site in question could receive e-mail communications, but these were forwarded to a corporate subsidiary of defendant. Thus, defendant did not purposefully direct its activity to the forum state through the website and could not be sued there.

In addition to addressing internet-related jurisdiction, *3D System* discusses the test which district courts should apply in patent cases that are subject to appeal to the Federal Circuit, and confirms that the standard is that of the Federal Circuit, rather than that of the circuit court in which the district is located. Finally, it holds that a patent infringement claim may result from an offer to sell, and that a price quotation may suffice as an offer despite a statement contained on it that it is not an offer.

A series of back and forth e-mail messages, coupled with non-electronic communications between the parties, warranted a finding of specific jurisdiction in *Resuscitation Technologies, Inc. v. Continental Health Care Corp.*, 1997 U.S. Dist. LEXIS 3523 (S.D. Ind. 1997). The plaintiff and various individual defendants had conducted electronic, telephone, and postal correspondence, as well as held face in-person meetings, to negotiate a potential combination of the plaintiff and defendant corporations. After termination of the negotiations, plaintiff sought a declaratory judgment that no contract had been formed to combine the two enterprises, and seeking damages for alleged breach of a confidentiality agreement in place between the parties.

Defendants moved to dismiss, on the ground that they had insufficient contacts with Indiana to support personal jurisdiction. The court looked solely at specific jurisdiction, as plaintiff had conceded the absence of general jurisdiction over defendants.

The court considered the large-scale exchange of e-mail correspondence was particularly important, because these went to the heart of the dispute—"whether or not a contract was formed between two parties by reason of their use of the Internet or other electronic transmissions." The messages exchanged were "numerous and continuous over a period of months," and indicated that defendants had "reached beyond the boundaries of their own states to do business in Indiana." However, the court also emphasized that the parties had held face to face meetings that, although conducted out of state, "were directed towards setting in motion a business operation that would have a significant commercial impact in Indiana." Thus, the finding of personal jurisdiction appears to rest on both the electronic and non-electronic contacts that defendants had with the forum state.

The Sixth Circuit approvingly cited *Zippo* in looking to the interactive nature of a website in *Neogen Corp. v. Neo Gen Screening, Inc.*, 282 F.3d 883 (6th Cir. 2002), a Michigan company's appeal of the dismissal of its trademark infringement and unfair trade practices action against a Pennsylvania corporation that performed "diagnostic testing of blood samples from newborn infants." The court reversed the trial court's dismissal and remanded the action.

The court noted that a defendant's maintenance of a passive website would alone be insufficient to confer jurisdiction. However, although the defendant's website in *Neogen* consisted "primarily of passively posted information", it had features indicating the defendant's "purposeful availment" of contacts with Michigan: the issuance of passwords to Michigan residents so they could check test results on the website, the site's inclusion of data collected from Michigan residents, and its welcoming of business from Michigan residents (and those of all other states) by providing a printable form that a viewer could use to contact defendant. The court acknowledged that the latter two features were passive, but nevertheless viewed them as indicating that defendant courted business in Michigan through the website.

While the *Neogen* court considered the question of jurisdiction arising from defendant's website to be a "close" one, it did not reach a conclusion specifically on that question. In addition to the website, defendant had other, non-internet contacts with Michigan that, in conjunction with the website, sufficed to confer specific jurisdiction. These consisted of defendant's performance of fourteen tests for Michigan residents in 1999, its anticipation that an equal number would be performed in 2000, and its performance of an undisclosed number of tests for Michigan residents in previous years. The performance of such tests and acceptance of payment therefor indicated defendant's intentional performance of business in Michigan.

The court emphasized that its analysis was conducted under Federal Rule of Civil Procedure 12(b), so that it deemed all facts in the complaint to be true and interpreted them in the light most favorable to plaintiff, and acknowledged that defendant could again challenge personal jurisdiction following completion of discovery.

By contrast, the court found insufficient jurisdictional contacts with Maryland in *Robbins v. Yutopian Enterprises, Inc.*, 205 F. Supp. 2d 426 (D. Md. 2002), an action pleading copyright infringement and state unfair competition law violation. Plaintiff was a Pennsylvania resident, and defendant was located in California. Defendant's website offered for sale the software underlying the copyright claim, and permitted users to engage in other unspecified transaction. Defendant had conducted 46 transactions in Maryland by internet or telephone in a ten and one-half month period, although it was not stated that any of these involved the software in question. Plaintiff provided evidence that at least one user in Maryland purchased items from defendant's website, and also received mailed and telephoned solicitations from defendant.

The court first noted that there were insufficient contacts "among the defendant, the forum, and the litigation" to warrant finding specific jurisdiction—the lawsuit did not involve a specific activity by defendant in Maryland.

It then found that defendant's activities in Maryland were not "sufficiently continuous or systematic" to trigger general jurisdiction. In the court's view, 46 transactions fell short of this standard. While acknowledging the *Zippo* "active" website criterion and finding that defendant's website qualified as active, that fact was not significant in the absence of a specific transaction between a Maryland resident and the alleged copyright infringement. Under these facts, the court considered that defendant had "a mere presence on the Internet" and was not amenable to jurisdiction in Maryland. The case was consequently transferred to the district court in defendant's district.

The court found specific jurisdiction based on the parties' contractual relationship, but rejected general jurisdiction based on defendant's moderately interactive website, in *Westcode, Inc. v. RBE Electronics, Inc.*, 2000 U.S. Dist. LEXIS 815 (E.D. Pa. 2000). Although the mere existence of a contract between the parties would not automatically result in jurisdiction, defendant's numerous shipments of substantial numbers of items to plaintiff, coupled with extensive communications between them, established the requisite contacts. These contacts related to the contract whose alleged breach underlay the lawsuit. Consequently, the requirements for finding specific jurisdiction were met.

Despite this finding, the court went on to consider whether defendant's website provided the basis for general jurisdiction and looked to *Zippo* for its approach. The site was "little more than a promotional resource" that "passively displayed" information and did not permit the execution of orders online. The court rejected plaintiff's argument that the website's inclusion of hyperlinks, e-mail addresses, and a "click-wrap" agreement made it interactive, noting that these could not give rise to a contractual relationship online and did not "constitute systematic and continuous' activity within Pennsylvania."

In *The Winfield Collection, Inc. v. McCauley*, 105 F. Supp. 2d 746 (E.D. Mich. 2000), the court dismissed a copyright infringement action concerning craft patterns brought against a Texas defendant by a Michigan plaintiff. Defendant's non-internet contacts with Michigan included purchasing several patterns by post from plaintiff, and selling crafts made with those patterns to several Michigan resident through "E-bay", an online auction service. Defendant also maintained a website that the court characterized as interactive.

The court found first that defendant's purchases from plaintiff did not constitute doing business in Michigan. Nor did the E-bay sales: the choice of successful bidder was outside of defendant's control, and therefore did not constitute purposeful availment of the privilege of doing business in Michigan but rather were "random" and "attenuated".

Next, although defendant maintained a website that could "send and receive messages, including responding to purchase orders," the mere fact of her website's "interactivity" was insufficient to establish minimum jurisdictional contacts in the absence of evidence that she had developed a Michigan customer base. An interactive site in and of itself was analogous to "an isolated advertisement in a nationally-distributed magazine," and would not open the site operator to jurisdiction anywhere in the United States.

The Winfield Collection's discussion is noteworthy in several respects. In holding that sales made on an electronic auction service's website could not provide minimum jurisdictional contacts, the court appears to exclude a popular category of internet transactions from giving rise to out-of-state jurisdiction. The holding hinged not on the small number of sales in Michigan, but instead on the lack of predictability and seller control over the buyer's location. The implication of this view is that the number of auction sales is immaterial for jurisdictional purposes, as they all would be random due to the unpredictability of the successful bidder's location.

The decision also critiques *Zippo*'s three-tier analytic framework because it considered that "the distinction drawn by the Zippo court between actively managed, telephone-like use of the internet and less active but 'interactive' websites is not entirely clear," and that "the proper means to measure the site's 'level of interactivity' as a guide to personal jurisdiction remains unexplained." The court nevertheless appeared to accept *Zippo*'s passive/interactive distinction, at least as a way of describing a website's operation.

The Winfield Collection's critique is misplaced, to the extent it construed *Zippo* as holding that interactive websites are *per se* subject to jurisdiction. *Zippo* considered a website's capability of doing business with other *fora* as a step to determine whether such business had in fact been conducted with the forum hearing a lawsuit. *The Winfield Collection*'s concern with identifying the dividing line between a site that is "clearly doing business," and one that is in the "middle ground" in *Zippo*'s parlance, is a valid one, but simply identifies an issue likely to arise every time jurisdiction is in question.

PART 4
PRIMARY SOURCE MATERIAL

Electronic Signatures in Global and National Commerce Act (USA)

Uniform Electronic Transactions Act of 1999 (USA)

Uniform Law Conference of Canada: Uniform Electronic Commerce Act

UNCITRAL Model Law on Electronic Signatures (2001)

UNCITRAL Draft Convention on Electronic Contracting

ELECTRONIC SIGNATURES IN GLOBAL AND NATIONAL COMMERCE ACT[1]

PUBLIC LAW 106-229
JUNE 30, 2000

An Act

To facilitate the use of electronic records and signatures in interstate or foreign commerce.

Be it enacted by the Senate and House of Representatives of the United States of America in Congress assembled,

SECTION 1. SHORT TITLE.

This Act may be cited as the "Electronic Signatures in Global and National Commerce Act".

TITLE I—ELECTRONIC RECORDS AND SIGNATURES IN COMMERCE

SEC. 101. GENERAL RULE OF VALIDITY.

(a) IN GENERAL.—Notwithstanding any statute, regulation, or other rule of law (other than this title and title II), with respect to any transaction in or affecting interstate or foreign commerce—

(1) a signature, contract, or other record relating to such transaction may not be denied legal effect, validity, or enforceability solely because it is in electronic form; and

(2) a contract relating to such transaction may not be denied legal effect, validity, or enforceability solely because an electronic signature or electronic record was used in its formation.

---

1 Editors note: On June 30, 2000 President Clinton signed into law the Electronic Signatures in Global and National Commerce Act (ESIGN). ESIGN is quite similar to "electronic signature" acts already approved in several states (known as Uniform Electronic Transactions Act—'UETA'). ESIGN validates electronic signatures, records and contracts that would otherwise be held invalid because of their electronic format.

(b) PRESERVATION OF RIGHTS AND OBLIGATIONS.—This title does not—

(1) limit, alter, or otherwise affect any requirement imposed by a statute, regulation, or rule of law relating to the rights and obligations of persons under such statute, regulation, or rule of law other than a requirement that contracts or other records be written, signed, or in nonelectronic form; or

(2) require any person to agree to use or accept electronic records or electronic signatures, other than a governmental agency with respect to a record other than a contract to which it is a party.

(c) CONSUMER DISCLOSURES.—

(1) CONSENT TO ELECTRONIC RECORDS.—Notwithstanding subsection (a), if a statute, regulation, or other rule of law requires that information relating to a transaction or transactions in or affecting interstate or foreign commerce be provided or made available to a consumer in writing, the use of an electronic record to provide or make available (whichever is required) such information satisfies the requirement that such information be in writing if—

(A) the consumer has affirmatively consented to such use and has not withdrawn such consent;

(B) the consumer, prior to consenting, is provided with a clear and conspicuous statement—

(i) informing the consumer of (I) any right or option of the consumer to have the record provided or made available on paper or in nonelectronic form, and (II) the right of the consumer to withdraw the consent to have the record provided or made available in an electronic form and of any conditions, consequences (which may include termination of the parties' relationship), or fees in the event of such withdrawal;

(ii) informing the consumer of whether the consent applies (I) only to the particular transaction which gave rise to the obligation to provide the record, or (II) to identified categories of records that may be provided or made available during the course of the parties' relationship;

(iii) describing the procedures the consumer must use to withdraw consent as provided in clause (i) and to update information needed to contact the consumer electronically; and

(iv) informing the consumer (I) how, after the consent, the consumer may, upon request, obtain a paper copy of an electronic record, and (II) whether any fee will be charged for such copy;

(C) the consumer—

(i) prior to consenting, is provided with a statement of the hardware and software requirements for access to and retention of the electronic records; and

(ii) consents electronically, or confirms his or her consent electronically, in a manner that reasonably demonstrates that the consumer can access information in the electronic form that will be used to provide the information that is the subject of the consent; and

(D) after the consent of a consumer in accordance with subparagraph (A), if a change in the hardware or software requirements needed to access or retain electronic records creates a material risk that the consumer will not be able to access or retain a subsequent electronic record that was the subject of the consent, the person providing the electronic record—

(i) provides the consumer with a statement of (I) the revised hardware and software requirements for access to and retention of the electronic records, and (II) the right to withdraw consent without the imposition of any fees for such withdrawal and without the imposition of any condition or consequence that was not disclosed under subparagraph (B)(i); and

(ii) again complies with subparagraph (C).

(2) OTHER RIGHTS.—

(A) PRESERVATION OF CONSUMER PROTECTIONS.—Nothing in this title affects the content or timing of any disclosure or other record required to be provided or made available to any consumer under any statute, regulation, or other rule of law.

(B) VERIFICATION OR ACKNOWLEDGMENT.—If a law that was enacted prior to this Act expressly requires a record to be provided or made available by a specified method that requires verification or acknowledgment of receipt, the record may be provided or made available electronically only if the method used provides verification or acknowledgment of receipt (whichever is required).

(3) EFFECT OF FAILURE TO OBTAIN ELECTRONIC CONSENT OR CONFIRMATION OF CONSENT.—The legal effectiveness, validity, or enforceability of any contract executed by a consumer shall not be denied solely because of the failure to obtain electronic consent or confirmation of consent by that consumer in accordance with paragraph (1)(C)(ii).

(4) PROSPECTIVE EFFECT.—Withdrawal of consent by a consumer shall not affect the legal effectiveness, validity, or enforceability of electronic records provided or made available to that consumer in accordance with paragraph (1) prior to implementation of the consumer's withdrawal of consent. A consumer's withdrawal of consent shall be effective within a reasonable period of time after receipt of the withdrawal by the provider of the record. Failure to comply with paragraph (1)(D) may, at the election of the consumer, be treated as a withdrawal of consent for purposes of this paragraph.

(5) PRIOR CONSENT.—This subsection does not apply to any records that are provided or made available to a consumer who has consented prior to the

effective date of this title to receive such records in electronic form as permitted by any statute, regulation, or other rule of law.

(6) ORAL COMMUNICATIONS.—An oral communication or a recording of an oral communication shall not qualify as an electronic record for purposes of this subsection except as otherwise provided under applicable law.

(d) RETENTION OF CONTRACTS AND RECORDS.—

(1) ACCURACY AND ACCESSIBILITY.—If a statute, regulation, or other rule of law requires that a contract or other record relating to a transaction in or affecting interstate or foreign commerce be retained, that requirement is met by retaining an electronic record of the information in the contract or other record that—

(A) accurately reflects the information set forth in the contract or other record; and

(B) remains accessible to all persons who are entitled to access by statute, regulation, or rule of law, for the period required by such statute, regulation, or rule of law, in a form that is capable of being accurately reproduced for later reference, whether by transmission, printing, or otherwise.

(2) EXCEPTION.—A requirement to retain a contract or other record in accordance with paragraph (1) does not apply to any information whose sole purpose is to enable the contract or other record to be sent, communicated, or received.

(3) ORIGINALS.—If a statute, regulation, or other rule of law requires a contract or other record relating to a transaction in or affecting interstate or foreign commerce to be provided, available, or retained in its original form, or provides consequences if the contract or other record is not provided, available, or retained in its original form, that statute, regulation, or rule of law is satisfied by an electronic record that complies with paragraph (1).

(4) CHECKS.—If a statute, regulation, or other rule of law requires the retention of a check, that requirement is satisfied by retention of an electronic record of the information on the front and back of the check in accordance with paragraph (1).

(e) ACCURACY AND ABILITY TO RETAIN CONTRACTS AND OTHER RECORDS.—Notwithstanding subsection (a), if a statute, regulation, or other rule of law requires that a contract or other record relating to a transaction in or affecting interstate or foreign commerce be in writing, the legal effect, validity, or enforceability of an electronic record of such contract or other record may be denied if such electronic record is not in a form that is capable of being retained and accurately reproduced for later reference by all parties or persons who are entitled to retain the contract or other record.

(f) PROXIMITY.—Nothing in this title affects the proximity required by any statute, regulation, or other rule of law with respect to any warning, notice, disclosure, or other record required to be posted, displayed, or publicly affixed.

(g) NOTARIZATION AND ACKNOWLEDGMENT.—If a statute, regulation, or other rule of law requires a signature or record relating to a transaction in or affecting interstate or foreign commerce to be notarized, acknowledged, verified, or made under oath, that requirement is satisfied if the electronic signature of the person authorized to perform those acts, together with all other information required to be included by other applicable statute, regulation, or rule of law, is attached to or logically associated with the signature or record.

(h) ELECTRONIC AGENTS.—A contract or other record relating to a transaction in or affecting interstate or foreign commerce may not be denied legal effect, validity, or enforceability solely because its formation, creation, or delivery involved the action of one or more electronic agents so long as the action of any such electronic agent is legally attributable to the person to be bound.

(i) INSURANCE.—It is the specific intent of the Congress that this title and title II apply to the business of insurance.

(j) INSURANCE AGENTS AND BROKERS.—An insurance agent or broker acting under the direction of a party that enters into a contract by means of an electronic record or electronic signature may not be held liable for any deficiency in the electronic procedures agreed to by the parties under that contract if—

(1) the agent or broker has not engaged in negligent, reckless, or intentional tortious conduct;

(2) the agent or broker was not involved in the development or establishment of such electronic procedures; and

(3) the agent or broker did not deviate from such procedures.

SEC. 102. EXEMPTION TO PREEMPTION.

(a) IN GENERAL.—A State statute, regulation, or other rule of law may modify, limit, or supersede the provisions of section 101 with respect to State law only if such statute, regulation, or rule of law—

(1) constitutes an enactment or adoption of the Uniform Electronic Transactions Act as approved and recommended for enactment in all the States by the National Conference of Commissioners on Uniform State Laws in 1999, except that any exception to the scope of such Act enacted by a State under section 3(b)(4) of such Act shall be preempted to the extent such exception is inconsistent with this title or title II, or would not be permitted under paragraph (2)(A)(ii) of this subsection; or

(2)(A) specifies the alternative procedures or requirements for the use or acceptance (or both) of electronic records or electronic signatures to establish the legal effect, validity, or enforceability of contracts or other records, if—

(i) such alternative procedures or requirements are consistent with this title and title II; and

(ii) such alternative procedures or requirements do not require, or accord greater legal status or effect to, the implementation or application of a specific technology or technical specification for performing the functions of creating, storing, generating, receiving, communicating, or authenticating electronic records or electronic signatures; and

(B) if enacted or adopted after the date of the enactment of this Act, makes specific reference to this Act.

(b) EXCEPTIONS FOR ACTIONS BY STATES AS MARKET PARTICIPANTS.—Subsection (a)(2)(A)(ii) shall not apply to the statutes, regulations, or other rules of law governing procurement by any State, or any agency or instrumentality thereof.

(c) PREVENTION OF CIRCUMVENTION.—Subsection (a) does not permit a State to circumvent this title or title II through the imposition of nonelectronic delivery methods under section 8(b)(2) of the Uniform Electronic Transactions Act.

SEC. 103. SPECIFIC EXCEPTIONS.

(a) EXCEPTED REQUIREMENTS.—The provisions of section 101 shall not apply to a contract or other record to the extent it is governed by—

(1) a statute, regulation, or other rule of law governing the creation and execution of wills, codicils, or testamentary trusts;

(2) a State statute, regulation, or other rule of law governing adoption, divorce, or other matters of family law; or

(3) the Uniform Commercial Code, as in effect in any State, other than sections 1-107 and 1-206 and Articles 2 and 2A.

(b) ADDITIONAL EXCEPTIONS.—The provisions of section 101 shall not apply to—

(1) court orders or notices, or official court documents (including briefs, pleadings, and other writings) required to be executed in connection with court proceedings;

(2) any notice of—

(A) the cancellation or termination of utility services (including water, heat, and power);

(B) default, acceleration, repossession, foreclosure, or eviction, or the right to cure, under a credit agreement secured by, or a rental agreement for, a primary residence of an individual;

(C) the cancellation or termination of health insurance or benefits or life insurance benefits (excluding annuities); or

(D) recall of a product, or material failure of a product, that risks endangering health or safety; or

(3) any document required to accompany any transportation or handling of hazardous materials, pesticides, or other toxic or dangerous materials.

(c) REVIEW OF EXCEPTIONS.—

(1) EVALUATION REQUIRED.—The Secretary of Commerce, acting through the Assistant Secretary for Communications and Information, shall review the operation of the exceptions in subsections (a) and (b) to evaluate, over a period of 3 years, whether such exceptions continue to be necessary for the protection of consumers. Within 3 years after the date of enactment of this Act, the Assistant Secretary shall submit a report to the Congress on the results of such evaluation.

(2) DETERMINATIONS.—If a Federal regulatory agency, with respect to matter within its jurisdiction, determines after notice and an opportunity for public comment, and publishes a finding, that one or more such exceptions are no longer necessary for the protection of consumers and eliminating such exceptions will not increase the material risk of harm to consumers, such agency may extend the application of section 101 to the exceptions identified in such finding.

SEC. 104. APPLICABILITY TO FEDERAL AND STATE GOVERNMENTS.

(a) FILING AND ACCESS REQUIREMENTS.—Subject to subsection (c)(2), nothing in this title limits or supersedes any requirement by a Federal regulatory agency, self-regulatory organization, or State regulatory agency that records be filed with such agency or organization in accordance with specified standards or formats.

(b) PRESERVATION OF EXISTING RULEMAKING AUTHORITY.—

(1) USE OF AUTHORITY TO INTERPRET.—Subject to paragraph (2) and subsection (c), a Federal regulatory agency or State regulatory agency that is responsible for rulemaking under any other statute may interpret section 101 with respect to such statute through—

(A) the issuance of regulations pursuant to a statute;

(B) to the extent such agency is authorized by statute to issue orders or guidance, the issuance of orders or guidance of general applicability that are publicly available and published (in the Federal Register in the case of an order or guidance issued by a Federal regulatory agency). This paragraph does not grant any Federal regulatory agency or State regulatory agency authority to issue regulations, orders, or guidance pursuant to any statute that does not authorize such issuance.

(2) LIMITATIONS ON INTERPRETATION AUTHORITY.—Notwithstanding paragraph (1), a Federal regulatory agency shall not adopt any regulation, order, or guidance described in paragraph (1), and a State regulatory agency is

preempted by section 101 from adopting any regulation, order, or guidance described in paragraph (1), unless—

(A) such regulation, order, or guidance is consistent with section 101; or

(B) such regulation, order, or guidance does not add to the requirements of such section; and

(C) such agency finds, in connection with the issuance of such regulation, order, or guidance, that—

(i) there is a substantial justification for the regulation, order, or guidance;

(ii) the methods selected to carry out that purpose—

(I) are substantially equivalent to the requirements imposed on records that are not electronic records; and

(II) will not impose unreasonable costs on the acceptance and use of electronic records; and

(iii) the methods selected to carry out that purpose do not require, or accord greater legal status or effect to, the implementation or application of a specific technology or technical specification for performing the functions of creating, storing, generating, receiving, communicating, or authenticating electronic records or electronic signatures.

(3) PERFORMANCE STANDARDS.—

(A) ACCURACY, RECORD INTEGRITY, ACCESSIBILITY.—Notwithstanding paragraph (2)(C)(iii), a Federal regulatory agency or State regulatory agency may interpret section 101(d) to specify performance standards to assure accuracy, record integrity, and accessibility of records that are required to be retained. Such performance standards may be specified in a manner that imposes a requirement in violation of paragraph (2)(C)(iii) if the requirement (i) serves an important governmental objective; and (ii) is substantially related to the achievement of that objective.

Nothing in this paragraph shall be construed to grant any Federal regulatory agency or State regulatory agency authority to require use of a particular type of software or hardware in order to comply with section 101(d).

(B) PAPER OR PRINTED FORM.—Notwithstanding sub-section (c)(1), a Federal regulatory agency or State regulatory agency may interpret section 101(d) to require retention of a record in a tangible printed or paper form if—

(i) there is a compelling governmental interest relating to law enforcement or national security for imposing such requirement; and

(ii) imposing such requirement is essential to attaining such interest.

(4) EXCEPTIONS FOR ACTIONS BY GOVERNMENT AS MARKET PARTICIPANT.—Paragraph (2)(C)(iii) shall not apply to the statutes, regulations, or other rules of law governing procurement by the Federal or any State government, or any agency or instrumentality thereof.

(c) ADDITIONAL LIMITATIONS.—

(1) REIMPOSING PAPER PROHIBITED.—Nothing in subsection (b) (other than paragraph (3)(B) thereof) shall be construed to grant any Federal regulatory agency or State regulatory agency authority to impose or reimpose any requirement that a record be in a tangible printed or paper form.

(2) CONTINUING OBLIGATION UNDER GOVERNMENT PAPERWORK ELIMINATION ACT.—Nothing in subsection (a) or (b) relieves any Federal regulatory agency of its obligations under the Government Paperwork Elimination Act (title XVII of Public Law 105-277).

(d) AUTHORITY TO EXEMPT FROM CONSENT PROVISION.—

(1) IN GENERAL.—A Federal regulatory agency may, with respect to matter within its jurisdiction, by regulation or order issued after notice and an opportunity for public comment, exempt without condition a specified category or type of record from the requirements relating to consent in section 101(c) if such exemption is necessary to eliminate a substantial burden on electronic commerce and will not increase the material risk of harm to consumers.

(2) PROSPECTUSES.—Within 30 days after the date of enactment of this Act, the Securities and Exchange Commission shall issue a regulation or order pursuant to paragraph (1) exempting from section 101(c) any records that are required to be provided in order to allow advertising, sales literature, or other information concerning a security issued by an investment company that is registered under the Investment Company Act of 1940, or concerning the issuer thereof, to be excluded from the definition of a prospectus under section 2(a)(10)(A) of the Securities Act of 1933.

(e) ELECTRONIC LETTERS OF AGENCY.—The Federal Communications Commission shall not hold any contract for telecommunications service or letter of agency for a preferred carrier change, that otherwise complies with the Commission's rules, to be legally ineffective, invalid, or unenforceable solely because an electronic record or electronic signature was used in its formation or authorization.

SEC. 105. STUDIES.

(a) DELIVERY.—Within 12 months after the date of the enactment of this Act, the Secretary of Commerce shall conduct an inquiry regarding the effectiveness of the delivery of electronic records to consumers using electronic mail as compared with delivery of written records via the United States Postal Service and private express mail services. The Secretary shall submit a report to the Congress regarding the results of such inquiry by the conclusion of such 12-month period.

(b) STUDY OF ELECTRONIC CONSENT.—Within 12 months after the date of the enactment of this Act, the Secretary of Commerce and the Federal Trade Commission shall submit a report to the Congress evaluating any benefits provided to consumers by the procedure required by section 101(c)(1)(C)(ii); any burdens imposed on electronic commerce by that provision; whether the benefits outweigh the burdens; whether the absence of the procedure required by section 101(c)(1)(C)(ii) would increase the incidence of fraud directed against consumers; and suggesting any revisions to the provision deemed appropriate by the Secretary and the Commission. In conducting this evaluation, the Secretary and the Commission shall solicit comment from the general public, consumer representatives, and electronic commerce businesses.

SEC. 106. DEFINITIONS.

For purposes of this title:

(1) CONSUMER.—The term "consumer" means an individual who obtains, through a transaction, products or services which are used primarily for personal, family, or household purposes, and also means the legal representative of such an individual.

(2) ELECTRONIC.—The term "electronic" means relating to technology having electrical, digital, magnetic, wireless, optical, electromagnetic, or similar capabilities.

(3) ELECTRONIC AGENT.—The term "electronic agent" means a computer program or an electronic or other automated means used independently to initiate an action or respond to electronic records or performances in whole or in part without review or action by an individual at the time of the action or response.

(4) ELECTRONIC RECORD.—The term "electronic record" means a contract or other record created, generated, sent, communicated, received, or stored by electronic means.

(5) ELECTRONIC SIGNATURE.—The term "electronic signature" means an electronic sound, symbol, or process, attached to or logically associated with a contract or other record and executed or adopted by a person with the intent to sign the record.

(6) FEDERAL REGULATORY AGENCY.—The term "Federal regulatory agency" means an agency, as that term is defined in section 552(f) of title 5, United States Code.

(7) INFORMATION.—The term "information" means data, text, images, sounds, codes, computer programs, software, databases, or the like.

(8) PERSON.—The term "person" means an individual, corporation, business trust, estate, trust, partnership, limited liability company, association, joint venture, governmental agency, public corporation, or any other legal or commercial entity.

(9) RECORD.—The term "record" means information that is inscribed on a tangible medium or that is stored in an electronic or other medium and is retrievable in perceivable form.

(10) REQUIREMENT.—The term "requirement" includes a prohibition.

(11) SELF-REGULATORY ORGANIZATION.—The term "self-regulatory organization" means an organization or entity that is not a Federal regulatory agency or a State, but that is under the supervision of a Federal regulatory agency and is authorized under Federal law to adopt and administer rules applicable to its members that are enforced by such organization or entity, by a Federal regulatory agency, or by another self-regulatory organization.

(12) STATE.—The term "State" includes the District of Columbia and the territories and possessions of the United States.

(13) TRANSACTION.—The term "transaction" means an action or set of actions relating to the conduct of business, consumer, or commercial affairs between two or more persons, including any of the following types of conduct—

(A) the sale, lease, exchange, licensing, or other disposition of (i) personal property, including goods and intangibles, (ii) services, and (iii) any combination thereof; and

(B) the sale, lease, exchange, or other disposition of any interest in real property, or any combination thereof.

SEC. 107. EFFECTIVE DATE.

(a) IN GENERAL.—Except as provided in subsection (b), this title shall be effective on October 1, 2000.

(b) EXCEPTIONS.—

(1) RECORD RETENTION.—

(A) IN GENERAL.—Subject to subparagraph (B), this title shall be effective on March 1, 2001, with respect to a requirement that a record be retained imposed by—

(i) a Federal statute, regulation, or other rule of law, or

(ii) a State statute, regulation, or other rule of law administered or promulgated by a State regulatory agency.

(B) DELAYED EFFECT FOR PENDING RULEMAKINGS.—If on March 1, 2001, a Federal regulatory agency or State regulatory agency has announced, proposed, or initiated, but not completed, a rulemaking proceeding to prescribe a regulation under section 104(b)(3) with respect to a requirement described in subparagraph (A), this title shall be effective on June 1, 2001, with respect to such requirement.

(2) CERTAIN GUARANTEED AND INSURED LOANS.—With regard to any transaction involving a loan guarantee or loan guarantee commitment (as those terms are defined in section 502 of the Federal Credit Reform Act of 1990), or involving a program listed in the Federal Credit Supplement, Budget of the United States, FY 2001, this title applies only to such transactions entered into, and to any loan or mortgage made, insured, or guaranteed by the United States Government thereunder, on and after one year after the date of enactment of this Act.

(3) STUDENT LOANS.—With respect to any records that are provided or made available to a consumer pursuant to an application for a loan, or a loan made, pursuant to title IV of the Higher Education Act of 1965, section 101(c) of this Act shall not apply until the earlier of—

(A) such time as the Secretary of Education publishes revised promissory notes under section 432(m) of the Higher Education Act of 1965; or

(B) one year after the date of enactment of this Act.

TITLE II—TRANSFERABLE RECORDS

SEC. 201. TRANSFERABLE RECORDS.

(a) DEFINITIONS.—For purposes of this section:

(1) TRANSFERABLE RECORD.—The term "transferable record" means an electronic record that—

(A) would be a note under Article 3 of the Uniform Commercial Code if the electronic record were in writing;

(B) the issuer of the electronic record expressly has agreed is a transferable record; and

(C) relates to a loan secured by real property.

A transferable record may be executed using an electronic signature.

(2) OTHER DEFINITIONS.—The terms "electronic record", "electronic signature", and "person" have the same meanings provided in section 106 of this Act.

(b) CONTROL.—A person has control of a transferable record if a system employed for evidencing the transfer of interests in the transferable record reliably establishes that person as the person to which the transferable record was issued or transferred.

(c) CONDITIONS.—A system satisfies subsection (b), and a person is deemed to have control of a transferable record, if the transferable record is created, stored, and assigned in such a manner that—

(1) a single authoritative copy of the transferable record exists which is unique, identifiable, and, except as otherwise provided in paragraphs (4), (5), and (6), unalterable;

(2) the authoritative copy identifies the person asserting control as—

(A) the person to which the transferable record was issued; or

(B) if the authoritative copy indicates that the transferable record has been transferred, the person to which the transferable record was most recently transferred;

(3) the authoritative copy is communicated to and maintained by the person asserting control or its designated custodian;

(4) copies or revisions that add or change an identified assignee of the authoritative copy can be made only with the consent of the person asserting control;

(5) each copy of the authoritative copy and any copy of a copy is readily identifiable as a copy that is not the authoritative copy; and

(6) any revision of the authoritative copy is readily identifiable as authorized or unauthorized.

(d) STATUS AS HOLDER.—Except as otherwise agreed, a person having control of a transferable record is the holder, as defined in section 1±201(20) of the Uniform Commercial Code, of the transferable record and has the same rights and defenses as a holder of an equivalent record or writing under the Uniform Commercial Code, including, if the applicable statutory requirements under section 3±302(a), 9±308, or revised section 9±330 of the Uniform Commercial Code are satisfied, the rights and defenses of a holder in due course or a purchaser, respectively. Delivery, possession, and endorsement are not required to obtain or exercise any of the rights under this subsection.

(e) OBLIGOR RIGHTS.—Except as otherwise agreed, an obligor under a transferable record has the same rights and defenses as an equivalent obligor under equivalent records or writings under the Uniform Commercial Code.

(f) PROOF OF CONTROL.—If requested by a person against which enforcement is sought, the person seeking to enforce the transferable record shall provide reasonable proof that the person is in control of the transferable record. Proof may include access to the authoritative copy of the transferable record and related business records sufficient to review the terms of the transferable record and to establish the identity of the person having control of the transferable record.

(g) UCC REFERENCES.—For purposes of this subsection, all references to the Uniform Commercial Code are to the Uniform Commercial Code as in effect in the jurisdiction the law of which governs the transferable record.

SEC. 202. EFFECTIVE DATE.

This title shall be effective 90 days after the date of enactment of this Act.

TITLE III—PROMOTION OF INTERNATIONAL ELECTRONIC COMMERCE

SEC. 301. PRINCIPLES GOVERNING THE USE OF ELECTRONIC SIGNATURES IN INTERNATIONAL TRANSACTIONS.

(a) PROMOTION OF ELECTRONIC SIGNATURES.—

(1) REQUIRED ACTIONS.—The Secretary of Commerce shall promote the acceptance and use, on an international basis, of electronic signatures in accordance with the principles specified in paragraph (2) and in a manner consistent with section 101 of this Act. The Secretary of Commerce shall take all actions necessary in a manner consistent with such principles to eliminate or reduce, to the maximum extent possible, the impediments to commerce in electronic signatures, for the purpose of facilitating the development of interstate and foreign commerce.

(2) PRINCIPLES.—The principles specified in this paragraph are the following:

(A) Remove paper-based obstacles to electronic transactions by adopting relevant principles from the Model Law on Electronic Commerce adopted in 1996 by the United Nations Commission on International Trade Law.

(B) Permit parties to a transaction to determine the appropriate authentication technologies and implementation models for their transactions, with assurance that those technologies and implementation models will be recognized and enforced.

(C) Permit parties to a transaction to have the opportunity to prove in court or other proceedings that their authentication approaches and their transactions are valid.

(D) Take a nondiscriminatory approach to electronic signatures and authentication methods from other jurisdictions.

(b) CONSULTATION.—In conducting the activities required by this section, the Secretary shall consult with users and providers of electronic signature products and services and other interested persons.

(c) DEFINITIONS.—As used in this section, the terms "electronic record" and "electronic signature" have the same meanings provided in section 106 of this Act.

TITLE IV—COMMISSION ON ONLINE CHILD PROTECTION

SEC. 401. AUTHORITY TO ACCEPT GIFTS.

Section 1405 of the Child Online Protection Act (47 U.S.C. 231 note) is amended by inserting after subsection (g) the following new subsection:

> "(h) GIFTS, BEQUESTS, AND DEVISES.—The Commission may accept, use, and dispose of gifts, bequests, or devises of services or property, both real (including the use of office space) and personal, for the purpose of aiding or facilitating the work of the Commission. Gifts or grants not used at the termination of the Commission shall be returned to the donor or grantee.".

Approved June 30, 2000.

UNIFORM ELECTRONIC TRANSACTIONS ACT OF 1999[1]

Drafted by the
NATIONAL CONFERENCE OF COMMISSIONERS ON UNIFORM STATE LAWS
and by it
APPROVED AND RECOMMENDED FOR ENACTMENT IN ALL THE STATES
at its
ANNUAL CONFERENCE
MEETING IN ITS ONE-HUNDRED-AND-EIGHTH YEAR IN DENVER, COLORADO
JULY 23-30, 1999

WITH PREFATORY NOTE AND COMMENTS

UNIFORM ELECTRONIC TRANSACTIONS ACT (1999)

PREFATORY NOTE

With the advent of electronic means of communication and information transfer, business models and methods for doing business have evolved to take advantage of the speed, efficiencies, and cost benefits of electronic technologies. These developments have occurred in the face of existing legal barriers to the legal efficacy of records and documents which exist solely in electronic media. Whether the legal requirement that information or an agreement or contract must be contained or set forth in a pen and paper writing derives from a statute of frauds affecting the enforceability of an agreement, or from a record retention statute that calls for keeping the paper record of a transaction, such legal requirements raise real barriers to the effective use of electronic media.

One striking example of electronic barriers involves so called check retention statutes in every State. A study conducted by the Federal Reserve Bank of Boston identified more than 2500 different state laws which require the retention of canceled checks by the issuers of those checks. These requirements not only impose burdens on the issuers, but also effectively restrain the ability of banks handling the checks to automate the process. Although check truncation is validated under the Uniform Commercial Code, if the bank's customer must store the canceled paper check, the bank will not be able to deal with the item through electronic transmission of the information. By establishing the equivalence of an electronic

---

record of the information, the Uniform Electronic Transactions Act (UETA) removes these barriers without affecting the underlying legal rules and requirements.

It is important to understand that the purpose of the UETA is to remove barriers to electronic commerce by validating and effectuating electronic records and signatures. It is NOT a general contracting statute—the substantive rules of contracts remain unaffected by UETA. Nor is it a digital signature statute. To the extent that a State has a Digital Signature Law, the UETA is designed to support and compliment that statute.

A. Scope of the Act and Procedural Approach. The scope of this Act provides coverage which sets forth a clear framework for covered transactions, and also avoids unwarranted surprises for unsophisticated parties dealing in this relatively new media. The clarity and certainty of the scope of the Act have been obtained while still providing a solid legal framework that allows for the continued development of innovative technology to facilitate electronic transactions.

With regard to the general scope of the Act, the Act's coverage is inherently limited by the definition of "transaction." The Act does not apply to *all* writings and signatures, but only to electronic records and signatures relating to a transaction, defined as those interactions between people relating to business, commercial and governmental affairs. In general, there are few writing or signature requirements imposed by law on many of the "standard" transactions that had been considered for exclusion. A good example relates to trusts, where the general rule on creation of a trust imposes no formal writing requirement. Further, the writing requirements in other contexts derived from governmental filing issues. For example, real estate transactions were considered potentially troublesome because of the need to file a deed or other instrument for protection against third parties. Since the efficacy of a real estate purchase contract, or even a deed, between the parties is not affected by any sort of filing, the question was raised why these transactions should not be validated by this Act if done via an electronic medium. No sound reason was found. Filing requirements fall within Sections 17-19 on governmental records. An exclusion of all real estate transactions would be particularly unwarranted in the event that a State chose to convert to an electronic recording system, as many have for Article 9 financing statement filings under the Uniform Commercial Code.

The exclusion of specific Articles of the Uniform Commercial Code reflects the recognition that, particularly in the case of Articles 5, 8 and revised Article 9, electronic transactions were addressed in the specific contexts of those revision processes. In the context of Articles 2 and 2A the UETA provides the vehicle for assuring that such transactions may be accomplished and effected via an electronic medium. At such time as Articles 2 and 2A are revised the extent of coverage in those Articles/Acts may make application of this Act as a gap-filling law desirable. Similar considerations apply to the recently promulgated Uniform Computer Information Transactions Act ("UCITA").

The need for certainty as to the scope and applicability of this Act is critical, and makes any sort of a broad, general exception based on notions of inconsistency with existing writing and signature requirements unwise at best. The uncertainty inherent in leaving the applicability of the Act to judicial construction of this Act with other laws is unacceptable if electronic transactions are to be facilitated.

Finally, recognition that the paradigm for the Act involves two willing parties conducting a transaction electronically, makes it necessary to expressly provide that some form of acquiescence or intent on the part of a person to conduct transactions electronically is necessary before the Act can be invoked. Accordingly, Section 5 specifically provides that the Act only applies between parties that have agreed to conduct transactions electronically. In this context, the construction of the term agreement must be broad in order to assure that the Act applies whenever the circumstances show the parties intention to transact electronically, regardless of whether the intent rises to the level of a formal agreement.

B. Procedural Approach. Another fundamental premise of the Act is that it be minimalist and procedural. The general efficacy of existing law in an electronic context, so long as biases and barriers to the medium are removed, validates this approach. The Act defers to existing substantive law. Specific areas of deference to other law in this Act include: (1) the meaning and effect of "sign" under existing law, (2) the method and manner of displaying, transmitting and formatting information in Section 8, (3) rules of attribution in Section 9, and (4) the law of mistake in Section 10.

The Act's treatment of records and signatures demonstrates best the minimalist approach that has been adopted. Whether a record is attributed to a person is left to law outside this Act. Whether an electronic signature has any effect is left to the surrounding circumstances and other law. These provisions are salutary directives to assure that records and signatures will be treated in the same manner, under currently existing law, as written records and manual signatures.

The deference of the Act to other substantive law does not negate the necessity of setting forth rules and standards for using electronic media. The Act expressly validates electronic records, signatures and contracts. It provides for the use of electronic records and information for retention purposes, providing certainty in an area with great potential in cost savings and efficiency. The Act makes clear that the actions of machines ("electronic agents") programmed and used by people will bind the user of the machine, regardless of whether human review of a particular transaction has occurred. It specifies the standards for sending and receipt of electronic records, and it allows for innovation in financial services through the implementation of transferable records. In these ways the Act permits electronic transactions to be accomplished with certainty under existing substantive rules of law.

UNIFORM ELECTRONIC TRANSACTIONS ACT (1999)

SECTION 1. SHORT TITLE. This [Act] may be cited as the Uniform Electronic Transactions Act.

SECTION 2. DEFINITIONS. In this [Act]:

(1) "Agreement" means the bargain of the parties in fact, as found in their language or inferred from other circumstances and from rules, regulations, and procedures given the effect of agreements under laws otherwise applicable to a particular transaction.

(2) "Automated transaction" means a transaction conducted or performed, in whole or in part, by electronic means or electronic records, in which the acts or records of one or both parties are not reviewed by an individual in the ordinary course in forming a contract, performing under an existing contract, or fulfilling an obligation required by the transaction.

(3) "Computer program" means a set of statements or instructions to be used directly or indirectly in an information processing system in order to bring about a certain result.

(4) "Contract" means the total legal obligation resulting from the parties' agreement as affected by this [Act] and other applicable law.

(5) "Electronic" means relating to technology having electrical, digital, magnetic, wireless, optical, electromagnetic, or similar capabilities.

(6) "Electronic agent" means a computer program or an electronic or other automated means used independently to initiate an action or respond to

electronic records or performances in whole or in part, without review or action by an individual.

(7) "Electronic record" means a record created, generated, sent, communicated, received, or stored by electronic means.

(8) "Electronic signature" means an electronic sound, symbol, or process attached to or logically associated with a record and executed or adopted by a person with the intent to sign the record.

(9) "Governmental agency" means an executive, legislative, or judicial agency, department, board, commission, authority, institution, or instrumentality of the federal government or of a State or of a county, municipality, or other political subdivision of a State.

(10) "Information" means data, text, images, sounds, codes, computer programs, software, databases, or the like.

(11) "Information processing system" means an electronic system for creating, generating, sending, receiving, storing, displaying, or processing information.

(12) "Person" means an individual, corporation, business trust, estate, trust, partnership, limited liability company, association, joint venture, governmental agency, public corporation, or any other legal or commercial entity.

(13) "Record" means information that is inscribed on a tangible medium or that is stored in an electronic or other medium and is retrievable in perceivable form.

(14) "Security procedure" means a procedure employed for the purpose of verifying that an electronic signature, record, or performance is that of a specific person or for detecting changes or errors in the information in an electronic record. The term includes a procedure that requires the use of algorithms or other codes, identifying words or numbers, encryption, or callback or other acknowledgment procedures.

(15) "State" means a State of the United States, the District of Columbia, Puerto Rico, the United States Virgin Islands, or any territory or insular possession subject to the jurisdiction of the United States. The term includes an Indian tribe or band, or Alaskan native village, which is recognized by federal law or formally acknowledged by a State.

(16) "Transaction" means an action or set of actions occurring between two or more persons relating to the conduct of business, commercial, or governmental affairs.

Sources: UNICTRAL Model Law on Electronic Commerce; Uniform Commercial Code; Uniform Computer Information Transactions Act; Restatement 2d Contracts.

Comment

1. **"Agreement."**

Whether the parties have reached an agreement is determined by their express language and all surrounding circumstances. The Restatement 2d Contracts ' 3 provides that, "An agreement is a manifestation of mutual assent on the part of two or more persons." See also Restatement 2d Contracts, Section 2, Comment b. The Uniform Commercial Code specifically includes in the circumstances from which an agreement may be inferred "course of performance, course of dealing and usage of trade . . ." as defined in the UCC. Although the definition of agreement in this Act does not make specific reference to usage of trade and other party conduct, this definition is not intended to affect the construction of the parties' agreement under the substantive law applicable to a particular transaction. Where that law takes account of usage and conduct in informing the terms of the parties' agreement, the usage or conduct would be relevant as "other circumstances" included in the definition under this Act.

Where the law applicable to a given transaction provides that system rules and the like constitute part of the agreement of the parties, such rules will have the same effect in determining the parties agreement under this Act. For example, UCC Article 4 (Section 4-103(b)) provides that Federal Reserve regulations and operating circulars and clearinghouse rules have the effect of agreements. Such agreements by law properly would be included in the definition of agreement in this Act.

The parties' agreement is relevant in determining whether the provisions of this Act have been varied by agreement. In addition, the parties' agreement may establish the parameters of the parties' use of electronic records and signatures, security procedures and similar aspects of the transaction. See Model Trading Partner Agreement, 45 Business Lawyer Supp. Issue (June 1990). See Section 5(b) and Comments thereto.

2. **"Automated Transaction."**

An automated transaction is a transaction performed or conducted by electronic means in which machines are used without human intervention to form contracts and perform obligations under existing contracts. Such broad coverage is necessary because of the diversity of transactions to which this Act may apply.

As with electronic agents, this definition addresses the circumstance where electronic records may result in action or performance by a party although no human review of the electronic records is anticipated. Section 14 provides specific rules to assure that where one or both parties do not review the electronic records, the resulting agreement will be effective.

The critical element in this definition is the lack of a human actor on one or both sides of a transaction. For example, if one orders books from Bookseller.com through Bookseller's website, the transaction would be an automated transaction because Bookseller took and confirmed the order via its machine. Similarly, if Automaker and supplier do business through Electronic Data Interchange, Automaker's computer, upon receiving information within certain pre-programmed parameters, will send an electronic order to supplier's computer. If Supplier's computer confirms the order and processes the shipment because the order falls within pre-programmed parameters in Supplier's computer, this would be a fully automated transaction. If, instead, the Supplier relies on a human employee to review, accept, and process the Buyer's order, then only the Automaker's side of the transaction would be automated. In either case, the entire transaction falls within this definition.

3. **"Computer program."** This definition refers to the functional and operating aspects of an electronic, digital system. It relates to operating instructions used in an electronic system such as an electronic agent. (See definition of "Electronic Agent.")

4. "**Electronic.**" The basic nature of most current technologies and the need for a recognized, single term warrants the use of "electronic" as the defined term. The definition is intended to assure that the Act will be applied broadly as new technologies develop. The term must be construed broadly in light of developing technologies in order to fulfill the purpose of this Act to validate commercial transactions regardless of the medium used by the parties. Current legal requirements for "writings" can be satisfied by almost any tangible media, whether paper, other fibers, or even stone. The purpose and applicability of this Act covers intangible media which are technologically capable of storing, transmitting and re-

producing information in human perceivable form, but which lack the tangible aspect of paper, papyrus or stone.

While not all technologies listed are technically "electronic" in nature (e.g., optical fiber technology), the term "electronic" is the most descriptive term available to describe the majority of current technologies. For example, the development of biological and chemical processes for communication and storage of data, while not specifically mentioned in the definition, are included within the technical definition because such processes operate on electromagnetic impulses. However, whether a particular technology may be characterized as technically "electronic," i.e., operates on electromagnetic impulses, should not be determinative of whether records and signatures created, used and stored by means of a particular technology are covered by this Act. This Act is intended to apply to all records and signatures created, used and stored by any medium which permits the information to be retrieved in perceivable form.

5. **"Electronic agent."** This definition establishes that an electronic agent is a machine. As the term "electronic agent" has come to be recognized, it is limited to a tool function. The effect on the party using the agent is addressed in the operative provisions of the Act (e.g., Section 14).

An electronic agent, such as a computer program or other automated means employed by a person, is a tool of that person. As a general rule, the employer of a tool is responsible for the results obtained by the use of that tool since the tool has no independent volition of its own. However, an electronic agent, by definition, is capable within the parameters of its programming, of initiating, responding or interacting with other parties or their electronic agents once it has been activated by a party, without further attention of that party.

While this Act proceeds on the paradigm that an electronic agent is capable of performing only within the technical strictures of its preset programming, it is conceivable that, within the useful life of this Act, electronic agents may be created with the ability to act autonomously, and not just automatically. That is, through developments in artificial intelligence, a computer may be able to "learn through experience, modify the instructions in their own programs, and even devise new instructions." Allen and Widdison, "Can Computers Make Contracts?" *9 Harv. J.L.&Tech 25* (Winter, 1996). If such developments occur, courts may construe the definition of electronic agent accordingly, in order to recognize such new capabilities.

The examples involving Bookseller.com and Automaker in the Comment to the definition of Automated Transaction are equally applicable here. Bookseller acts through an electronic agent in processing an order for books. Automaker and the supplier each act through electronic agents in facilitating and effectuating the just-in-time inventory process through EDI.

6. **"Electronic record."** An electronic record is a subset of the broader defined term "record." It is any record created, used or stored in a medium other than paper (see definition of electronic). The defined term is also used in this Act as a limiting definition in those provisions in which it is used.

Information processing systems, computer equipment and programs, electronic data interchange, electronic mail, voice mail, facsimile, telex, telecopying, scanning, and similar technologies all qualify as electronic under this Act. Accordingly information stored on a computer hard drive or floppy disc, facsimiles, voice mail messages, messages on a telephone answering machine, audio and video tape recordings, among other records, all would be electronic records under this Act.

7. **"Electronic signature."**

The idea of a signature is broad and not specifically defined. Whether any particular record is "signed" is a question of fact. Proof of that fact must be made under other applicable law. This Act simply assures that the signature may be accomplished through electronic means. No specific technology need be used in order to create a valid signature. One's voice on an answering machine may suffice if the requisite intention is present. Similarly, including one's name as part of an electronic mail communication also may suffice, as may the firm name on a facsimile. It also may be shown that the requisite intent was not present and accordingly the symbol, sound or process did not amount to a signature. One may use a digital signature with the requisite intention, or one may use the private key solely as an access device with no intention to sign, or otherwise accomplish a legally binding act. In any case the critical element is the intention to execute or adopt the sound or symbol or process for the purpose of signing the related record.

The definition requires that the signer execute or adopt the sound, symbol, or process with the intent to sign the record. The act of applying a sound, symbol or process to an electronic record could have differing meanings and effects. The consequence of the act and the effect of the act as a signature are determined under other applicable law. However, the essential attribute of a signature involves applying a sound, symbol or process with an intent to do a legally significant act. It is that intention that is understood in the law as a part of the word "sign", without the need for a definition.

This Act establishes, to the greatest extent possible, the equivalency of electronic signatures and manual signatures. Therefore the term "signature" has been used to connote and convey that equivalency. The purpose is to overcome unwarranted biases against electronic methods of signing and authenticating records. The term "authentication," used in other laws, often has a narrower meaning and purpose than an electronic signature as used in this Act. However, an authentication under any of those other laws constitutes an electronic signature under this Act.

The precise effect of an electronic signature will be determined based on the surrounding circumstances under Section 9(b).

This definition includes as an electronic signature the standard webpage click-through process. For example, when a person orders goods or services through a vendor's website, the person will be required to provide information as part of a process which will result in receipt of the goods or services. When the customer ultimately gets to the last step and clicks "I agree," the person has adopted the process and has done so with the intent to associate the person with the record of that process. The actual effect of the electronic signature will be determined from all the surrounding circumstances, however, the person adopted a process which the circumstances indicate s/he intended to have the effect of getting the goods/services and being bound to pay for them. The adoption of the process carried the intent to do a legally significant act, the hallmark of a signature.

Another important aspect of this definition lies in the necessity that the electronic signature be linked or logically associated with the record. In the paper world, it is assumed that the symbol adopted by a party is attached to or located somewhere in the same paper that is intended to be authenticated, e.g., an allonge firmly attached to a promissory note, or the classic signature at the end of a long contract. These tangible manifestations do not exist in the electronic environment, and accordingly, this definition expressly provides that the symbol must in some way be linked to, or connected with, the electronic record being signed. This linkage is consistent with the regulations promulgated by the Food and Drug Administration. 21 CFR Part 11 (March 20, 1997).

A digital signature using public key encryption technology would qualify as an electronic signature, as would the mere inclusion of one's name as a part of an e-mail message B so long as in each case the signer executed or adopted the symbol with the intent to sign.

8. "**Governmental agency.**" This definition is important in the context of optional Sections 17-19.

9. "**Information processing system.**" This definition is consistent with the UNCITRAL Model Law on Electronic Commerce. The term includes computers and other information systems. It is principally used in Section 15 in connection with the sending and receiving of information. In that context, the key aspect is that the information enter a system from which a person can access it.

10. "**Record.**" This is a standard definition designed to embrace all means of communicating or storing information except human memory. It includes any method for storing or com-

municating information, including "writings." A record need not be indestructible or permanent, but the term does not include oral or other communications which are not stored or preserved by some means. Information that has not been retained other than through human memory does not qualify as a record. As in the case of the terms "writing" or "written," the term "record" does not establish the purposes, permitted uses or legal effect which a record may have under any particular provision of substantive law. ABA Report on Use of the Term "Record," October 1, 1996.

11. **"Security procedure."**

A security procedure may be applied to verify an electronic signature, verify the identity of the sender, or assure the informational integrity of an electronic record. The definition does not identify any particular technology. This permits the use of procedures which the parties select or which are established by law. It permits the greatest flexibility among the parties and allows for future technological development.

The definition in this Act is broad and is used to illustrate one way of establishing attribution or content integrity of an electronic record or signature. The use of a security procedure is not accorded operative legal effect, through the use of presumptions or otherwise, by this Act. In this Act, the use of security procedures is simply one method for proving the source or content of an electronic record or signature.

A security procedure may be technologically very sophisticated, such as an asymmetric cryptographic system. At the other extreme the security procedure may be as simple as a telephone call to confirm the identity of the sender through another channel of communication. It may include the use of a mother's maiden name or a personal identification number (PIN). Each of these examples is a method for confirming the identity of a person or accuracy of a message.

12. **"Transaction."** The definition has been limited to actions between people taken in the context of business, commercial or governmental activities. The term includes all interactions between people for business, commercial, including specifically consumer, or governmental purposes. However, the term does not include unilateral or non-transactional actions. As such it provides a structural limitation on the scope of the Act as stated in the next section.

It is essential that the term commerce and business be understood and construed broadly to include commercial and business transactions involving individuals who may qualify as "consumers" under other applicable law. If Alice and Bob agree to the sale of Alice's car to Bob for $2000 using an internet auction site, that transaction is fully covered by this Act. Even if Alice and Bob each qualify as typical "consumers" under other applicable law, their interaction is a transaction in commerce. Accordingly their actions would be related to commercial affairs, and fully qualify as a transaction governed by this Act.

Other transaction types include:

1. A single purchase by an individual from a retail merchant, which may be accomplished by an order from a printed catalog sent by facsimile, or by exchange of electronic mail.

2. Recurring orders on a weekly or monthly basis between large companies which have entered into a master trading partner agreement to govern the methods and manner of their transaction parameters.

3. A purchase by an individual from an online internet retail vendor. Such an arrangement may develop into an ongoing series of individual purchases, with security procedures and the like, as a part of doing ongoing business.

4. The closing of a business purchase transaction via facsimile transmission of documents or even electronic mail. In such a transaction, all parties may participate through electronic conferencing technologies. At the appointed time all electronic records are executed electronically and transmitted to the other party. In such a case, the electronic re-

cords and electronic signatures are validated under this Act, obviating the need for " in person" closings.

A transaction must include interaction between two or more persons. Consequently, to the extent that the execution of a will, trust, or a health care power of attorney or similar health care designation does not involve another person and is a unilateral act, it would not be covered by this Act because not occurring as a part of a transaction as defined in this Act. However, this Act *does* apply to all electronic records and signatures *related* to a transaction, and so does cover, for example, internal auditing and accounting records related to a transaction.

SECTION 3. SCOPE.

(a) Except as otherwise provided in subsection (b), this [Act] applies to electronic records and electronic signatures relating to a transaction.

(b) This [Act] does not apply to a transaction to the extent it is governed by:

(1) a law governing the creation and execution of wills, codicils, or testamentary trusts;

(2) [The Uniform Commercial Code other than Sections 1-107 and 1-206, Article 2, and Article 2A];

(3) [the Uniform Computer Information Transactions Act]; and

(4) [other laws, if any, identified by State].

(c) This [Act] applies to an electronic record or electronic signature otherwise excluded from the application of this [Act] under subsection (b) to the extent it is governed by a law other than those specified in subsection (b).

(d) A transaction subject to this [Act] is also subject to other applicable substantive law.

See Legislative Note below B Following Comments.

Comment

1. The scope of this Act is inherently limited by the fact that it only applies to transactions related to business, commercial (including consumer) and governmental matters. Consequently, transactions with no relation to business, commercial or governmental transactions would not be subject to this Act. Unilaterally generated electronic records and signatures which are not part of a transaction also are not covered by this Act. See Section 2, Comment 12.

2. This Act affects the medium in which information, records and signatures may be presented and retained under current legal requirements. While this Act covers all electronic records and signatures which are used in a business, commercial (including consumer) or governmental transaction, the operative provisions of the Act relate to requirements for writings and signatures under other laws. Accordingly, the exclusions in subsection (b) focus on those legal rules imposing certain writing and signature requirements which will *not* be affected by this Act.

3. The exclusions listed in subsection (b) provide clarity and certainty regarding the laws which are and are not affected by this Act. This section provides that transactions subject to specific laws are unaffected by this Act and leaves the balance subject to this Act.

4. Paragraph (1) excludes wills, codicils and testamentary trusts. This exclusion is largely salutary given the unilateral context in which such records are generally created and the un-

likely use of such records in a transaction as defined in this Act (i.e., actions taken by two or more persons in the context of business, commercial or governmental affairs). Paragraph (2) excludes all of the Uniform Commercial Code other than UCC Sections 1-107 and 1-206, and Articles 2 and 2A. This Act does not apply to the excluded UCC articles, whether in "current" or "revised" form. The Act does apply to UCC Articles 2 and 2A and to UCC Sections 1-107 and 1-206.

5. Articles 3, 4 and 4A of the UCC impact payment systems and have specifically been removed from the coverage of this Act. The check collection and electronic fund transfer systems governed by Articles 3, 4 and 4A involve systems and relationships involving numerous parties beyond the parties to the underlying contract. The impact of validating electronic media in such systems involves considerations beyond the scope of this Act. Articles 5, 8 and 9 have been excluded because the revision process relating to those Articles included significant consideration of electronic practices. Paragraph 4 provides for exclusion from this Act of the Uniform Computer Information Transactions Act (UCITA) because the drafting process of that Act also included significant consideration of electronic contracting provisions.

6. The very limited application of this Act to Transferable Records in Section 16 does not affect payment systems, and the section is designed to apply to a transaction only through express agreement of the parties. The exclusion of Articles 3 and 4 will not affect the Act's coverage of Transferable Records. Section 16 is designed to allow for the development of systems which will provide "control" as defined in Section 16. Such control is necessary as a substitute for the idea of possession which undergirds negotiable instrument law. The technology has yet to be developed which will allow for the possession of a unique electronic token embodying the rights associated with a negotiable promissory note. Section 16's concept of control is intended as a substitute for possession.

The provisions in Section 16 operate as free standing rules, establishing the rights of parties using Transferable Records *under this Act*. The references in Section 16 to UCC Sections 3-302, 7-501, and 9-308 (R9-330(d)) are designed to incorporate the substance of those provisions into this Act for the limited purposes noted in Section 16(c). Accordingly, an electronic record which is also a Transferable Record, would not be used for purposes of a transaction governed by Articles 3, 4, or 9, but would be an electronic record used for purposes of a transaction governed by Section 16. However, it is important to remember that those UCC Articles will still apply to the transferable record in their own right. Accordingly any other substantive requirements, e.g., method and manner of perfection under Article 9, must be complied with under those other laws. See Comments to Section 16.

7. This Act does apply, *in toto*, to transactions under unrevised Articles 2 and 2A. There is every reason to validate electronic contracting in these situations. Sale and lease transactions do not implicate broad systems beyond the parties to the underlying transaction, such as are present in check collection and electronic funds transfers. Further sales and leases generally do not have as far reaching effect on the rights of third parties beyond the contracting parties, such as exists in the secured transactions system. Finally, it is in the area of sales, licenses and leases that electronic commerce is occurring to its greatest extent today. To exclude these transactions would largely gut the purpose of this Act.

In the event that Articles 2 and 2A are revised and adopted in the future, UETA will only apply to the extent provided in those Acts.

8. An electronic record/signature may be used for purposes of more than one legal requirement, or may be covered by more than one law. Consequently, it is important to make clear, despite any apparent redundancy, in subsection (c) that an electronic record used for purposes of a law which is *not* affected by this Act under subsection (b) may nonetheless be used and validated for purposes of other laws not excluded by subsection (b). For example, this Act does not apply to an electronic record of a check when used for purposes of a transaction governed by Article 4 of the Uniform Commercial Code, i.e., the Act does not validate so-called electronic checks. However, for purposes of check retention statutes, the same electronic record of the check is covered by this Act, so that retention of an electronic

image/record of a check will satisfy such retention statutes, so long as the requirements of Section 12 are fulfilled.

In another context, subsection (c) would operate to allow this Act to apply to what would appear to be an excluded transaction under subsection (b). For example, Article 9 of the Uniform Commercial Code applies generally to any transaction that creates a security interest in personal property. However, Article 9 excludes landlord's liens. Accordingly, although this Act excludes from its application transactions subject to Article 9, this Act would apply to the creation of a landlord lien if the law otherwise applicable to landlord's liens did not provide otherwise, because the landlord's lien transaction is excluded from Article 9.

9. Additional exclusions under subparagraph (b)(4) should be limited to laws which govern electronic records and signatures which may be used in transactions as defined in Section 2(16). Records used unilaterally, or which do not relate to business, commercial (including consumer), or governmental affairs are not governed by this Act in any event, and exclusion of laws relating to such records may create unintended inferences about whether other records and signatures are covered by this Act.

It is also important that additional exclusions, if any, be incorporated under subsection (b)(4). As noted in Comment 8 above, an electronic record used in a transaction excluded under subsection (b), e.g., a check used to pay one's taxes, will nonetheless be validated for purposes of other, non-excluded laws under subsection (c), e.g., the check when used as proof of payment. It is critical that additional exclusions, if any, be incorporated into subsection (b) so that the salutary effect of subsection (c) apply to validate those records in other, non-excluded transactions. While a legislature may determine that a particular notice, such as a utility shutoff notice, be provided to a person in writing on paper, it is difficult to see why the utility should not be entitled to use electronic media for storage and evidentiary purposes. *Legislative Note Regarding Possible Additional Exclusions under Section 3(b)(4).*

The following discussion is derived from the Report dated September 21, 1998 of The Task Force on State Law Exclusions (the "Task Force") presented to the Drafting Committee. After consideration of the Report, the Drafting Committee determined that exclusions other than those specified in the Act were not warranted. In addition, other inherent limitations on the applicability of the Act (the definition of transaction, the requirement that the parties acquiesce in the use of an electronic format) also militate against additional exclusions. Nonetheless, the Drafting Committee recognized that some legislatures may wish to exclude additional transactions from the Act, and determined that guidance in some major areas would be helpful to those legislatures considering additional areas for exclusion.

Because of the overwhelming number of references in state law to writings and signatures, the following list of possible transactions is not exhaustive. However, they do represent those areas most commonly raised during the course of the drafting process as areas that might be inappropriate for an electronic medium. It is important to keep in mind however, that the Drafting Committee determined that exclusion of these additional areas was not warranted.

1. **Trusts** (other than testamentary trusts). Trusts can be used for both business and personal purposes. By virtue of the definition of transaction, trusts used outside the area of business and commerce would not be governed by this Act. With respect to business or commercial trusts, the laws governing their formation contain few or no requirements for paper or signatures. Indeed, in most jurisdictions trusts of any kind may be created orally. Consequently, the Drafting Committee believed that the Act should apply to any transaction where the law leaves to the parties the decision of whether to use a writing. Thus, in the absence of legal requirements for writings, there is no sound reason to exclude laws governing trusts from the application of this Act.

2. **Powers of Attorney.** A power of attorney is simply a formalized type of agency agreement. In general, no formal requirements for paper or execution were found to be applicable to the validity of powers of attorney.

Special health powers of attorney have been established by statute in some States. These powers may have special requirements under state law regarding execution, acknowledgment and possibly notarization. In the normal case such powers will not arise in a transactional context and so would not be covered by this Act. However, even if such a record were to arise in a transactional context, this Act operates simply to remove the barrier to the use of an electronic medium, and preserves other requirements of applicable substantive law, avoiding any necessity to exclude such laws from the operation of this Act. Especially in light of the provisions of Sections 8 and 11, the substantive requirements under such laws will be preserved and may be satisfied in an electronic format.

3. **Real Estate Transactions.** It is important to distinguish between the efficacy of paper documents involving real estate between the parties, as opposed to their effect on third parties. As between the parties it is unnecessary to maintain existing barriers to electronic contracting. There are no unique characteristics to contracts relating to real property as opposed to other business and commercial (including consumer) contracts. Consequently, the decision whether to use an electronic medium for their agreements should be a matter for the parties to determine. Of course, to be effective against third parties state law generally requires filing with a governmental office. Pending adoption of electronic filing systems by States, the need for a piece of paper to file to perfect rights against third parties, will be a consideration for the parties. In the event notarization and acknowledgment are required under other laws, Section 11 provides a means for such actions to be accomplished electronically.

With respect to the requirements of government filing, those are left to the individual States in the decision of whether to adopt and implement electronic filing systems. (See optional Sections 17-19.) However, government recording systems currently require paper deeds including notarized, manual signatures. Although California and Illinois are experimenting with electronic filing systems, until such systems become widespread, the parties likely will choose to use, at the least, a paper deed for filing purposes. Nothing in this Act precludes the parties from selecting the medium best suited to the needs of the particular transaction. Parties may wish to consummate the transaction using electronic media in order to avoid expensive travel. Yet the actual deed may be in paper form to assure compliance with existing recording systems and requirements. The critical point is that nothing in this Act prevents the parties from selecting paper or electronic media for all or part of their transaction.

4. **Consumer Protection Statutes.** Consumer protection provisions in state law often require that information be disclosed or provided to a consumer in writing. Because this Act does apply to such transactions, the question of whether such laws should be specifically excluded was considered. Exclusion of consumer transactions would eliminate a huge group of commercial transactions which benefit consumers by enabling the efficiency of the electronic medium. Commerce over the internet is driven by consumer demands and concerns and must be included.

At the same time, it is important to recognize the protective effects of many consumer statutes. Consumer statutes often require that information be provided in writing, or may require that the consumer separately sign or initial a particular provision to evidence that the consumer's attention was brought to the provision. Subsection (1) requires electronic records to be retainable by a person whenever the law requires information to be delivered in writing. The section imposes a significant burden on the sender of information. The sender must assure that the information system of the recipient is compatible with, and capable of retaining the information sent by, the sender's system. Furthermore, nothing in this Act permits the avoidance of legal requirements of separate signatures or initialing. The Act simply permits the signature or initialing to be done electronically.

Other consumer protection statutes require (expressly or implicitly) that certain information be presented in a certain manner or format. Laws requiring information to be presented in particular fonts, formats or in similar fashion, as well as laws requiring conspicuous displays of information are preserved. Section 8(b)(3) specifically preserves the applicability of such requirements in an electronic environment. In the case of legal requirements that information be presented or appear conspicuous, the determination of what is conspicuous will be left to other law. Section 8 was included to specifically preserve the protective functions of such disclosure statutes, while at the same time allowing the use of electronic media if the substantive requirements of the other laws could be satisfied in the electronic medium.

Formatting and separate signing requirements serve a critical purpose in much consumer protection legislation, to assure that information is not slipped past the unsuspecting consumer. Not only does this Act not disturb those requirements, it preserves those requirements. In addition, other bodies of substantive law continue to operate to allow the courts to police any such bad conduct or overreaching, e.g., unconscionability, fraud, duress, mistake and the like. These bodies of law remain applicable regardless of the medium in which a record appears.

The requirement that both parties agree to conduct a transaction electronically also prevents the imposition of an electronic medium on unwilling parties See Section 5(b). In addition, where the law requires inclusion of specific terms or language, those requirements are preserved broadly by Section 5(e).

Requirements that information be sent to, or received by, someone have been preserved in Section 15. As in the paper world, obligations to send do not impose any duties on the sender to assure receipt, other than reasonable methods of dispatch. In those cases where receipt is required legally, Sections 5, 8, and 15 impose the burden on the sender to assure delivery to the recipient if satisfaction of the legal requirement is to be fulfilled.

The preservation of existing safeguards, together with the ability to opt out of the electronic medium entirely, demonstrate the lack of any need generally to exclude consumer protection laws from the operation of this Act. Legislatures may wish to focus any review on those statutes which provide for post-contract formation and post-breach notices to be in paper. However, any such consideration must also balance the needed protections against the potential burdens which may be imposed. Consumers and others will not be well served by restrictions which preclude the employment of electronic technologies sought and desired by consumers.

SECTION 4. PROSPECTIVE APPLICATION. This [Act] applies to any electronic record or electronic signature created, generated, sent, communicated, received, or stored on or after the effective date of this [Act].

Comment

This section makes clear that the Act only applies to validate electronic records and signatures which arise subsequent to the effective date of the Act. Whether electronic records and electronic signatures arising before the effective date of this Act are valid is left to other law.

SECTION 5. USE OF ELECTRONIC RECORDS AND ELECTRONIC SIGNATURES; VARIATION BY AGREEMENT.

(a) This [Act] does not require a record or signature to be created, generated, sent, communicated, received, stored, or otherwise processed or used by electronic means or in electronic form.

(b) This [Act] applies only to transactions between parties each of which has agreed to conduct transactions by electronic means. Whether the parties agree to conduct a transaction by electronic means is determined from the context and surrounding circumstances, including the parties' conduct.

(c) A party that agrees to conduct a transaction by electronic means may refuse to conduct other transactions by electronic means. The right granted by this subsection may not be waived by agreement.

(d) Except as otherwise provided in this [Act], the effect of any of its provisions may be varied by agreement. The presence in certain provisions of this [Act] of the words "unless otherwise agreed", or words of similar import, does not imply that the effect of other provisions may not be varied by agreement.

(e) Whether an electronic record or electronic signature has legal consequences is determined by this [Act] and other applicable law.

Comment

This section limits the applicability of this Act to transactions which parties have agreed to conduct electronically. Broad interpretation of the term agreement is necessary to assure that this Act has the widest possible application consistent with its purpose of removing barriers to electronic commerce.

1. This section makes clear that this Act is intended to facilitate the use of electronic means, but does not require the use of electronic records and signatures. This fundamental principle is set forth in subsection (a) and elaborated by subsections (b) and (c), which require an intention to conduct transactions electronically and preserve the right of a party to refuse to use electronics in any subsequent transaction.

2. The paradigm of this Act is two willing parties doing transactions electronically. It is therefore appropriate that the Act is voluntary and preserves the greatest possible party autonomy to refuse electronic transactions. The requirement that party agreement be found from all the surrounding circumstances is a limitation on the scope of this Act.

3. If this Act is to serve to facilitate electronic transactions, it must be applicable under circumstances not rising to a full fledged contract to use electronics. While absolute certainty can be accomplished by obtaining an explicit contract before relying on electronic transactions, such an explicit contract should not be necessary before one may feel safe in conducting transactions electronically. Indeed, such a requirement would itself be an unreasonable barrier to electronic commerce, at odds with the fundamental purpose of this Act. Accordingly, the requisite agreement, express or implied, must be determined from all available circumstances and evidence.

4. Subsection (b) provides that the Act applies to transactions in which the parties have agreed to conduct the transaction electronically. In this context it is essential that the parties' actions and words be broadly construed in determining whether the requisite agreement exists. Accordingly, the Act expressly provides that the party's agreement is to be found from all circumstances, including the parties' conduct. The critical element is the intent of a party to conduct a transaction electronically. Once that intent is established, this Act applies. See Restatement 2d Contracts, Sections 2, 3, and 19.

Examples of circumstances from which it may be found that parties have reached an agreement to conduct transactions electronically include the following:

A. Automaker and supplier enter into a Trading Partner Agreement setting forth the terms, conditions and methods for the conduct of business between them electronically.

B. Joe gives out his business card with his business e-mail address. It may be reasonable, under the circumstances, for a recipient of the card to infer that Joe has agreed to communicate electronically for business purposes. However, in the absence of additional facts, it would not necessarily be reasonable to infer Joe's agreement to communicate electronically for purposes outside the scope of the business indicated by use of the business card.

C. Sally may have several e-mail addresses B home, main office, office of a non-profit organization on whose board Sally sits. In each case, it may be reasonable to infer that Sally is willing to communicate electronically with respect to business related to the business/purpose associated with the respective e-mail addresses. However, depending on the circumstances, it may not be reasonable to communicate with Sally for purposes other than those related to the purpose for which she maintained a particular e-mail account.

D. Among the circumstances to be considered in finding an agreement would be the time when the assent occurred relative to the timing of the use of electronic communications. If one orders books from an online vendor, such as Bookseller.com, the intention to conduct that transaction and to receive any correspondence related to the transaction electronically can be inferred from the conduct. Accordingly, as to information related to that transaction it is reasonable for Bookseller to deal with the individual electronically.

The examples noted above are intended to focus the inquiry on the party's agreement to conduct a transaction electronically. Similarly, if two people are at a meeting and one tells the other to send an e-mail to confirm a transaction B the requisite agreement under subsection (b) would exist. In each case, the use of a business card, statement at a meeting, or other evidence of willingness to conduct a transaction electronically must be viewed in light of all the surrounding circumstances with a view toward broad validation of electronic transactions.

5. Just as circumstances may indicate the existence of agreement, express or implied from surrounding circumstances, circumstances may also demonstrate the absence of true agreement. For example:

A. If Automaker, Inc. were to issue a recall of automobiles via its Internet website, it would not be able to rely on this Act to validate that notice in the case of a person who never logged on to the website, or indeed, had no ability to do so, notwithstanding a clause in a paper purchase contract by which the buyer agreed to receive such notices in such a manner.

B. Buyer executes a standard form contract in which an agreement to receive all notices electronically in set forth on page 3 in the midst of other fine print. Buyer has never communicated with Seller electronically, and has not provided any other information in the contract to suggest a willingness to deal electronically. Not only is it unlikely that any but the most formalistic of agreements may be found, but nothing in this Act prevents courts from policing such form contracts under common law doctrines relating to contract formation, unconscionability and the like.

6. Subsection (c) has been added to make clear the ability of a party to refuse to conduct a transaction electronically, even if the person has conducted transactions electronically in the past. The effectiveness of a party's refusal to conduct a transaction electronically will be determined under other applicable law in light of all surrounding circumstances. Such circumstances must include an assessment of the transaction involved.

A party's right to decline to act electronically under a specific contract, on the ground that each action under that contract amounts to a separate "transaction," must be considered in light of the purpose of the contract and the action to be taken electronically. For example, under a contract for the purchase of goods, the giving and receipt of notices electronically, as provided in the contract, should not be viewed as discreet transactions. Rather such notices amount to separate actions which are part of the "transaction" of purchase evidenced by the contract. Allowing one party to require a change of medium in the middle of the transaction evidenced by that contract is not the purpose of this subsection. Rather this subsection is intended to preserve the party's right to conduct the next purchase in a non-electronic medium.

7. Subsection (e) is an essential provision in the overall scheme of this Act. While this Act validates and effectuates electronic records and electronic signatures, the legal effect of such records and signatures is left to existing substantive law outside this Act except in very narrow circumstances. See, e.g., Section 16. Even when this Act operates to validate records and signatures in an electronic medium, it expressly preserves the substantive rules of other law applicable to such records. See, e.g., Section 11.

For example, beyond validation of records, signatures and contracts based on the medium used, Section 7 (a) and (b) should not be interpreted as establishing the legal effectiveness of any given record, signature or contract. Where a rule of law requires that the record contain minimum substantive content, the legal effect of such a record will depend on whether the record meets the substantive requirements of other applicable law.

Section 8 expressly preserves a number of legal requirements in currently existing law relating to the presentation of information in writing. Although this Act now would allow such information to be presented in an electronic record, Section 8 provides that the other substantive requirements of law must be satisfied in the electronic medium as well.

SECTION 6. CONSTRUCTION AND APPLICATION. This [Act] must be construed and applied:

(1) to facilitate electronic transactions consistent with other applicable law;

(2) to be consistent with reasonable practices concerning electronic transactions and with the continued expansion of those practices; and

(3) to effectuate its general purpose to make uniform the law with respect to the subject of this [Act] among States enacting it.

Comment

1. The purposes and policies of this Act are

(a) to facilitate and promote commerce and governmental transactions by validating and authorizing the use of electronic records and electronic signatures;

(b) to eliminate barriers to electronic commerce and governmental transactions resulting from uncertainties relating to writing and signature requirements;

(c) to simplify, clarify and modernize the law governing commerce and governmental transactions through the use of electronic means;

(d) to permit the continued expansion of commercial and governmental electronic practices through custom, usage and agreement of the parties;

(e) to promote uniformity of the law among the States (and worldwide) relating to the use of electronic and similar technological means of effecting and performing commercial and governmental transactions;

(f) to promote public confidence in the validity, integrity and reliability of electronic commerce and governmental transactions; and

(g) to promote the development of the legal and business infrastructure necessary to implement electronic commerce and governmental transactions.

2. This Act has been drafted to permit flexible application consistent with its purpose to validate electronic transactions. The provisions of this Act validating and effectuating the employ of electronic media allow the courts to apply them to new and unforeseen technologies and practices. As time progresses, it is anticipated that what is new and unforeseen today will be commonplace tomorrow. Accordingly, this legislation is intended to set a framework for the validation of media which may be developed in the future and which

demonstrate the same qualities as the electronic media contemplated and validated under this Act.

SECTION 7. LEGAL RECOGNITION OF ELECTRONIC RECORDS, ELECTRONIC SIGNATURES, AND ELECTRONIC CONTRACTS.

(a) A record or signature may not be denied legal effect or enforceability solely because it is in electronic form.

(b) A contract may not be denied legal effect or enforceability solely because an electronic record was used in its formation.

(c) If a law requires a record to be in writing, an electronic record satisfies the law.

(d) If a law requires a signature, an electronic signature satisfies the law.

Source: UNCITRAL Model Law on Electronic Commerce, Articles 5, 6, and 7.

Comment

1. This section sets forth the fundamental premise of this Act: namely, that the medium in which a record, signature, or contract is created, presented or retained does not affect it's legal significance. Subsections (a) and (b) are designed to eliminate the single element of medium as a reason to deny effect or enforceability to a record, signature, or contract. The fact that the information is set forth in an electronic, as opposed to paper, record is irrelevant.

2. Under Restatement 2d Contracts Section 8, a contract may have legal effect and yet be unenforceable. Indeed, one circumstance where a record or contract may have effect but be unenforceable is in the context of the Statute of Frauds. Though a contract may be unenforceable, the records may have collateral effects, as in the case of a buyer that insures goods purchased under a contract unenforceable under the Statute of Frauds. The insurance company may not deny a claim on the ground that the buyer is not the owner, though the buyer may have no direct remedy against seller for failure to deliver. See Restatement 2d Contracts, Section 8, Illustration 4.

While this section would validate an electronic record for purposes of a statute of frauds, if an agreement to conduct the transaction electronically cannot reasonably be found (See Section 5(b)) then a necessary predicate to the applicability of this Act would be absent and this Act would not validate the electronic record. Whether the electronic record might be valid under other law is not addressed by this Act.

3. Subsections (c) and (d) provide the positive assertion that electronic records and signatures satisfy legal requirements for writings and signatures. The provisions are limited to requirements in laws that a record be in writing or be signed. This section does not address requirements imposed by other law in addition to requirements for writings and signatures See, e.g., Section 8.

Subsections (c) and (d) are particularized applications of subsection (a). The purpose is to validate and effectuate electronic records and signatures as the equivalent of writings, subject to all of the rules applicable to the efficacy of a writing, except as such other rules are modified by the more specific provisions of this Act.

Illustration 1: A sends the following e-mail to B: "I hereby offer to buy widgets from you, delivery next Tuesday. /s/ A." B responds with the following e-mail: "I accept your offer to buy widgets for delivery next Tuesday. /s/ B." The e-mails may not be denied effect solely because they are electronic. In addition, the e-mails do qualify as records under the Statute of Frauds. However, because there is no quantity stated in either record, the parties' agreement would be unenforceable under existing UCC Section 2-201(1).

Illustration 2: A sends the following e-mail to B: "I hereby offer to buy 100 widgets for $1000, delivery next Tuesday. /s/ A." B responds with the following e-mail: "I accept your offer to purchase 100 widgets for $1000, delivery next Tuesday. /s/ B." In this case the analysis is the same as in Illustration 1 except that here the records otherwise satisfy the requirements of UCC Section 2-201(1). The transaction may not be denied legal effect solely because there is not a pen and ink "writing" or "signature".

4. Section 8 addresses additional requirements imposed by other law which may affect the legal effect or enforceability of an electronic record in a particular case. For example, in Section 8(a) the legal requirement addressed is *the provision of information* in writing. The section then sets forth the standards to be applied in determining whether the provision of information by an electronic record is the equivalent of the provision of information in writing. The requirements in Section 8 are in addition to the bare validation that occurs under this section.

5. Under the substantive law applicable to a particular transaction within this Act, the legal effect of an electronic record may be separate from the issue of whether the record contains a signature. For example, where notice must be given as part of a contractual obligation, the effectiveness of the notice will turn on whether the party provided the notice regardless of whether the notice was signed (See Section 15). An electronic record attributed to a party under Section 9 and complying with the requirements of Section 15 would suffice in that case, notwithstanding that it may not contain an electronic signature.

SECTION 8. PROVISION OF INFORMATION IN WRITING; PRESENTATION OF RECORDS.

(a) If parties have agreed to conduct a transaction by electronic means and a law requires a person to provide, send, or deliver information in writing to another person, the requirement is satisfied if the information is provided, sent, or delivered, as the case may be, in an electronic record capable of retention by the recipient at the time of receipt. An electronic record is not capable of retention by the recipient if the sender or its information processing system inhibits the ability of the recipient to print or store the electronic record.

(b) If a law other than this [Act] requires a record (i) to be posted or displayed in a certain manner, (ii) to be sent, communicated, or transmitted by a specified method, or (iii) to contain information that is formatted in a certain manner, the following rules apply:

(1) The record must be posted or displayed in the manner specified in the other law.

(2) Except as otherwise provided in subsection (d)(2), the record must be sent, communicated, or transmitted by the method specified in the other law.

(3) The record must contain the information formatted in the manner specified in the other law.

(c) If a sender inhibits the ability of a recipient to store or print an electronic record, the electronic record is not enforceable against the recipient.

(d) The requirements of this section may not be varied by agreement, but:

(1) to the extent a law other than this [Act] requires information to be provided, sent, or delivered in writing but permits that requirement to be varied

by agreement, the requirement under subsection (a) that the information be in the form of an electronic record capable of retention may also be varied by agreement; and

(2) a requirement under a law other than this [Act] to send, communicate, or transmit a record by [first-class mail, postage prepaid] [regular United States mail], may be varied by agreement to the extent permitted by the other law.

Source: Canadian B Uniform Electronic Commerce Act

Comment

1. This section is a savings provision, designed to assure, consistent with the fundamental purpose of this Act, that otherwise applicable substantive law will not be overridden by this Act. The section makes clear that while the pen and ink provisions of such other law may be satisfied electronically, nothing in this Act vitiates the other requirements of such laws. The section addresses a number of issues related to disclosures and notice provisions in other laws.

2. This section is independent of the prior section. Section 7 refers to legal requirements for a writing. This section refers to legal requirements for the provision of information in writing or relating to the method or manner of presentation or delivery of information. The section addresses more specific legal requirements of other laws, provides standards for satisfying the more particular legal requirements, and defers to other law for satisfaction of requirements under those laws.

3. Under subsection (a), to meet a requirement of other law that information be provided in writing, the recipient of an electronic record of the information must be able to get to the electronic record and read it, and must have the ability to get back to the information in some way at a later date. Accordingly, the section requires that the electronic record be capable of retention for later review.

The section specifically provides that any inhibition on retention imposed by the sender or the sender's system will preclude satisfaction of this section. Use of technological means now existing or later developed which prevents the recipient from retaining a copy the information would result in a determination that information has not been provided under subsection (a). The policies underlying laws requiring the provision of information in writing warrant the imposition of an additional burden on the sender to make the information available in a manner which will permit subsequent reference. A difficulty does exist for senders of information because of the disparate systems of their recipients and the capabilities of those systems. However, in order to satisfy the *legal requirement* of other law to make information available, the sender must assure that the recipient receives and can retain the information. However, it is left for the courts to determine whether the sender has complied with this subsection if evidence demonstrates that it is something peculiar the recipient's system which precludes subsequent reference to the information.

4. Subsection (b) is a savings provision for laws which provide for the means of delivering or displaying information and which are not affected by the Act. For example, if a law requires delivery of notice by first class US mail, that means of delivery would not be affected by this Act. The information to be delivered may be provided on a disc, i.e., in electronic form, but the particular means of delivery must still be via the US postal service. Display, delivery and formatting requirements will continue to be applicable to electronic records and signatures. If those legal requirements can be satisfied in an electronic medium, e.g., the information can be presented in the equivalent of 20 point bold type as required by other law, this Act will validate the use of the medium, leaving to the other applicable law the question of whether the particular electronic record meets the other legal requirements. If a law requires that particular records be delivered together, or attached to other records, this Act does not preclude the delivery of the records together in an electronic communica-

tion, so long as the records are connected or associated with each other in a way determined to satisfy the other law.

5. Subsection (c) provides incentives for senders of information to use systems which will not inhibit the other party from retaining the information. However, there are circumstances where a party providing certain information may wish to inhibit retention in order to protect intellectual property rights or prevent the other party from retaining confidential information about the sender. In such cases inhibition is understandable, but if the sender wishes to enforce the record in which the information is contained, the sender may not inhibit its retention by the recipient. Unlike subsection (a), subsection (c) applies in all transactions and simply provides for unenforceability against the recipient. Subsection (a) applies only where another law imposes the writing requirement, and subsection (a) imposes a broader responsibility on the sender to assure retention capability by the recipient.

6. The protective purposes of this section justify the non-waivability provided by subsection (d). However, since the requirements for sending and formatting and the like are imposed by other law, to the extent other law permits waiver of such protections, there is no justification for imposing a more severe burden in an electronic environment.

SECTION 9. ATTRIBUTION AND EFFECT OF ELECTRONIC RECORD AND ELECTRONIC SIGNATURE.

(a) An electronic record or electronic signature is attributable to a person if it was the act of the person. The act of the person may be shown in any manner, including a showing of the efficacy of any security procedure applied to determine the person to which the electronic record or electronic signature was attributable.

(b) The effect of an electronic record or electronic signature attributed to a person under subsection (a) is determined from the context and surrounding circumstances at the time of its creation, execution, or adoption, including the parties' agreement, if any, and otherwise as provided by law.

Comment

1. Under subsection (a), so long as the electronic record or electronic signature resulted from a person's action it will be attributed to that person B the legal effect of that attribution is addressed in subsection (b). This section does not alter existing rules of law regarding attribution. The section assures that such rules will be applied in the electronic environment. A person's actions include actions taken by human agents of the person, as well as actions taken by an electronic agent, i.e., the tool, of the person. Although the rule may appear to state the obvious, it assures that the record or signature is not ascribed to a machine, as opposed to the person operating or programing the machine.

In each of the following cases, both the electronic record and electronic signature would be attributable to a person under subsection (a):

A. The person types his/her name as part of an e-mail purchase order;

B. The person's employee, pursuant to authority, types the person's name as part of an e-mail purchase order;

C. The person's computer, programmed to order goods upon receipt of inventory information within particular parameters, issues a purchase order which includes the person's name, or other identifying information, as part of the order.

In each of the above cases, law other than this Act would ascribe both the signature and the action to the person if done in a paper medium. Subsection (a) expressly provides that the same result will occur when an electronic medium is used.

2. Nothing in this section affects the use of a signature as a device for attributing a record to a person. Indeed, a signature is often the primary method for attributing a record to a person. In the foregoing examples, once the electronic signature is attributed to the person, the electronic record would also be attributed to the person, unless the person established fraud, forgery, or other invalidating cause. However, a signature is not the only method for attribution.

3. The use of facsimile transmissions provides a number of examples of attribution using information other than a signature. A facsimile may be attributed to a person because of the information printed across the top of the page that indicates the machine from which it was sent. Similarly, the transmission may contain a letterhead which identifies the sender. Some cases have held that the letterhead actually constituted a signature because it was a symbol adopted by the sender with intent to authenticate the facsimile. However, the signature determination resulted from the necessary finding of intention in that case. Other cases have found facsimile letterheads NOT to be signatures because the requisite intention was not present. The critical point is that with or without a signature, information within the electronic record may well suffice to provide the facts resulting in attribution of an electronic record to a particular party.

In the context of attribution of records, normally the content of the record will provide the necessary information for a finding of attribution. It is also possible that an established course of dealing between parties may result in a finding of attribution Just as with a paper record, evidence of forgery or counterfeiting may be introduced to rebut the evidence of attribution.

4. Certain information may be present in an electronic environment that does not appear to attribute but which clearly links a person to a particular record. Numerical codes, personal identification numbers, public and private key combinations all serve to establish the party to whom an electronic record should be attributed. Of course security procedures will be another piece of evidence available to establish attribution.

The inclusion of a specific reference to security procedures as a means of proving attribution is salutary because of the unique importance of security procedures in the electronic environment. In certain processes, a technical and technological security procedure may be the best way to convince a trier of fact that a particular electronic record or signature was that of a particular person. In certain circumstances, the use of a security procedure to establish that the record and related signature came from the person's business might be necessary to overcome a claim that a hacker intervened. The reference to security procedures is not intended to suggest that other forms of proof of attribution should be accorded less persuasive effect. It is also important to recall that the particular strength of a given procedure does not affect the procedure's status as a security procedure, but only affects the weight to be accorded the evidence of the security procedure as tending to establish attribution.

5. This section does apply in determining the effect of a "click-through" transaction. A "click-through" transaction involves a process which, if executed with an intent to "sign," will be an electronic signature. See definition of Electronic Signature. In the context of an anonymous "click-through," issues of proof will be paramount. This section will be relevant to establish that the resulting electronic record is attributable to a particular person upon the requisite proof, including security procedures which may track the source of the click-through.

6. Once it is established that a record or signature is attributable to a particular party, the effect of a record or signature must be determined in light of the context and surrounding circumstances, including the parties' agreement, if any. Also informing the effect of any attribution will be other legal requirements considered in light of the context. Subsection (b) addresses the effect of the record or signature once attributed to a person.

SECTION 10. EFFECT OF CHANGE OR ERROR. If a change or error in an electronic record occurs in a transmission between parties to a transaction, the following rules apply:

(1) If the parties have agreed to use a security procedure to detect changes or errors and one party has conformed to the procedure, but the other party has not, and the nonconforming party would have detected the change or error had that party also conformed, the conforming party may avoid the effect of the changed or erroneous electronic record.

(2) In an automated transaction involving an individual, the individual may avoid the effect of an electronic record that resulted from an error made by the individual in dealing with the electronic agent of another person if the electronic agent did not provide an opportunity for the prevention or correction of the error and, at the time the individual learns of the error, the individual:

(A) promptly notifies the other person of the error and that the individual did not intend to be bound by the electronic record received by the other person;

(B) takes reasonable steps, including steps that conform to the other person's reasonable instructions, to return to the other person or, if instructed by the other person, to destroy the consideration received, if any, as a result of the erroneous electronic record; and

(C) has not used or received any benefit or value from the consideration, if any, received from the other person.

(3) If neither paragraph (1) nor paragraph (2) applies, the change or error has the effect provided by other law, including the law of mistake, and the parties' contract, if any.

(4) Paragraphs (2) and (3) may not be varied by agreement.

Source: Restatement 2d Contracts, Sections 152-155.

Comment

1. This section is limited to changes and errors occurring in transmissions between parties B whether person-person (paragraph 1) or in an automated transaction involving an individual and a machine (paragraphs 1 and 2). The section focuses on the effect of changes and errors occurring when records are exchanged between parties. In cases where changes and errors occur in contexts other than transmission, the law of mistake is expressly made applicable to resolve the conflict.

The section covers both changes and errors. For example, if Buyer sends a message to Seller ordering 100 widgets, but Buyer's information processing system changes the order to 1000 widgets, a "change" has occurred between what Buyer transmitted and what Seller received. If on the other hand, Buyer typed in 1000 intending to order only 100, but sent the message before noting the mistake, an error would have occurred which would also be covered by this section.

2. Paragraph (1) deals with any transmission where the parties have agreed to use a security procedure to detect changes and errors. It operates against the non-conforming party, i.e., the party in the best position to have avoided the change or error, regardless of whether

that person is the sender or recipient. The source of the error/change is not indicated, and so both human and machine errors/changes would be covered. With respect to errors or changes that would not be detected by the security procedure even if applied, the parties are left to the general law of mistake to resolve the dispute.

3. Paragraph (1) applies only in the situation where a security procedure would detect the error/change but one party fails to use the procedure and does not detect the error/change. In such a case, consistent with the law of mistake generally, the record is made avoidable at the instance of the party who took all available steps to avoid the mistake. See Restatement 2d Contracts Sections 152-154.

Making the erroneous record avoidable by the conforming party is consistent with Sections 153 and 154 of the Restatement 2d Contracts because the non-conforming party was in the best position to avoid the problem, and would bear the risk of mistake. Such a case would constitute mistake by one party. The mistaken party (the conforming party) would be entitled to avoid any resulting contract under Section 153 because s/he does not have the risk of mistake and the non-conforming party had reason to know of the mistake.

4. As with paragraph (1), paragraph (2), when applicable, allows the mistaken party to avoid the effect of the erroneous electronic record. However, the subsection is limited to human error on the part of an individual when dealing with the electronic agent of the other party. In a transaction between individuals there is a greater ability to correct the error before parties have acted on it. However, when an individual makes an error while dealing with the electronic agent of the other party, it may not be possible to correct the error before the other party has shipped or taken other action in reliance on the erroneous record.

Paragraph (2) applies only to errors made by individuals. If the error results from the electronic agent, it would constitute a system error. In such a case the effect of that error would be resolved under paragraph (1) if applicable, otherwise under paragraph (3) and the general law of mistake.

5. The party acting through the electronic agent/machine is given incentives by this section to build in safeguards which enable the individual to prevent the sending of an erroneous record, or correct the error once sent. For example, the electronic agent may be programed to provide a "confirmation screen" to the individual setting forth all the information the individual initially approved. This would provide the individual with the ability to prevent the erroneous record from ever being sent. Similarly, the electronic agent might receive the record sent by the individual and then send back a confirmation which the individual must again accept before the transaction is completed. This would allow for correction of an erroneous record. In either case, the electronic agent would "provide an opportunity for prevention or correction of the error," *and the subsection would not apply*. Rather, the affect of any error is governed by other law.

6. Paragraph (2) also places additional requirements on the mistaken individual before the paragraph may be invoked to avoid an erroneous electronic record. The individual must take prompt action to advise the other party of the error and the fact that the individual did not intend the electronic record. Whether the action is prompt must be determined from all the circumstances including the individual's ability to contact the other party. The individual should advise the other party both of the error and of the lack of intention to be bound (i.e., avoidance) by the electronic record received. Since this provision allows avoidance by the mistaken party, that party should also be required to expressly note that it is seeking to avoid the electronic record, i.e., lacked the intention to be bound.

Second, restitution is normally required in order to undo a mistaken transaction. Accordingly, the individual must also return or destroy any consideration received, adhering to instructions from the other party in any case. This is to assure that the other party retains control over the consideration sent in error.

Finally, and most importantly in regard to transactions involving intermediaries which may be harmed because transactions cannot be unwound, the individual cannot have received any benefit from the transaction. This section prevents a party from unwinding a transaction after the delivery of value and consideration which cannot be returned or destroyed. For example, if the consideration received is information, it may not be possible to avoid the benefit conferred. While the information itself could be returned, mere access to the information, or the ability to redistribute the information would constitute a benefit precluding the mistaken party from unwinding the transaction. It may also occur that the mistaken party receives consideration which changes in value between the time of receipt and the first opportunity to return. In such a case restitution cannot be made adequately, and the transaction would not be avoidable. In each of the foregoing cases, under subparagraph (2)(c), the individual would have received the benefit of the consideration and would NOT be able to avoid the erroneous electronic record under this section.

7. In all cases not covered by paragraphs (1) or (2), where error or change to a record occur, the parties contract, or other law, specifically including the law of mistake, applies to resolve any dispute. In the event that the parties' contract and other law would achieve different results, the construction of the parties' contract is left to the other law. If the error occurs in the context of record retention, Section 12 will apply. In that case the standard is one of accuracy and retrievability of the information.

8. Paragraph (4) makes the error correction provision in paragraph (2) and the application of the law of mistake in paragraph (3) non-variable. Paragraph (2) provides incentives for parties using electronic agents to establish safeguards for individuals dealing with them. It also avoids unjustified windfalls to the individual by erecting stringent requirements before the individual may exercise the right of avoidance under the paragraph. Therefore, there is no reason to permit parties to avoid the paragraph by agreement. Rather, parties should satisfy the paragraph's requirements.

SECTION 11. NOTARIZATION AND ACKNOWLEDGMENT. If a law requires a signature or record to be notarized, acknowledged, verified, or made under oath, the requirement is satisfied if the electronic signature of the person authorized to perform those acts, together with all other information required to be included by other applicable law, is attached to or logically associated with the signature or record.

Comment

This section permits a notary public and other authorized officers to act electronically, effectively removing the stamp/seal requirements. However, the section does not eliminate any of the other requirements of notarial laws, and consistent with the entire thrust of this Act, simply allows the signing and information to be accomplished in an electronic medium.

For example, Buyer wishes to send a notarized Real Estate Purchase Agreement to Seller via e-mail. The notary must appear in the room with the Buyer, satisfy him/herself as to the identity of the Buyer, and swear to that identification. All that activity must be reflected as part of the electronic Purchase Agreement and the notary's electronic signature must appear as a part of the electronic real estate purchase contract.

As another example, Buyer seeks to send Seller an affidavit averring defects in the products received. A court clerk, authorized under state law to administer oaths, is present with Buyer in a room. The Clerk administers the oath and includes the statement of the oath, together with any other requisite information, in the electronic record to be sent to the Seller. Upon administering the oath and witnessing the application of Buyer's electronic signature to the electronic record, the Clerk also applies his electronic signature to the electronic record. So long as all substantive requirements of other applicable law have been fulfilled and are reflected in the electronic record, the sworn electronic record of Buyer is as effective as if it had been transcribed on paper.

SECTION 12. RETENTION OF ELECTRONIC RECORDS; ORIGINALS.

(a) If a law requires that a record be retained, the requirement is satisfied by retaining an electronic record of the information in the record which:

(1) accurately reflects the information set forth in the record after it was first generated in its final form as an electronic record or otherwise; and

(2) remains accessible for later reference.

(b) A requirement to retain a record in accordance with subsection (a) does not apply to any information the sole purpose of which is to enable the record to be sent, communicated, or received.

(c) A person may satisfy subsection (a) by using the services of another person if the requirements of that subsection are satisfied.

(d) If a law requires a record to be presented or retained in its original form, or provides consequences if the record is not presented or retained in its original form, that law is satisfied by an electronic record retained in accordance with subsection (a).

(e) If a law requires retention of a check, that requirement is satisfied by retention of an electronic record of the information on the front and back of the check in accordance with subsection (a).

(f) A record retained as an electronic record in accordance with subsection (a) satisfies a law requiring a person to retain a record for evidentiary, audit, or like purposes, unless a law enacted after the effective date of this [Act] specifically prohibits the use of an electronic record for the specified purpose.

(g) This section does not preclude a governmental agency of this State from specifying additional requirements for the retention of a record subject to the agency's jurisdiction.

Source: UNCITRAL Model Law On Electronic Commerce Articles 8 and 10.

Comment

1. This section deals with the serviceability of electronic records as retained records and originals. So long as there exists reliable assurance that the electronic record accurately reproduces the information, this section continues the theme of establishing the functional equivalence of electronic and paper-based records. This is consistent with Fed.R.Evid. 1001(3) and Unif.R.Evid. 1001(3) (1974). This section assures that information stored electronically will remain effective for all audit, evidentiary, archival and similar purposes.

2. In an electronic medium, the concept of an original document is problematic. For example, as one drafts a document on a computer the "original" is either on a disc or the hard drive to which the document has been initially saved. If one periodically saves the draft, the fact is that at times a document may be first saved to disc then to hard drive, and at others vice versa. In such a case the "original" may change from the information on the disc to the information on the hard drive. Indeed, it may be argued that the "original" exists solely in RAM and, in a sense, the original is destroyed when a "copy" is saved to a disc or to the hard drive. In any event, in the context of record retention, the concern focuses on the integrity of the information, and not with its "originality."

3. Subsection (a) requires accuracy and the ability to access at a later time. The requirement of accuracy is derived from the Uniform and Federal Rules of Evidence. The requirement of continuing accessibility addresses the issue of technology obsolescence and the need to update and migrate information to developing systems. It is not unlikely that within the span of 5-10 years (a period during which retention of much information is required) a corporation may evolve through one or more generations of technology. More to the point, this technology may be incompatible with each other necessitating the reconversion of information from one system to the other.

For example, certain operating systems from the early 1980's, e.g., memory typewriters, became obsolete with the development of personal computers. The information originally stored on the memory typewriter would need to be converted to the personal computer system in a way meeting the standards for accuracy contemplated by this section. It is also possible that the medium on which the information is stored is less stable. For example, information stored on floppy discs is generally less stable, and subject to a greater threat of disintegration, that information stored on a computer hard drive. In either case, the continuing accessibility issue must be satisfied to validate information stored by electronic means under this section.

This section permits parties to convert original written records to electronic records for retention so long as the requirements of subsection (a) are satisfied. Accordingly, in the absence of specific requirements to retain written records, written records may be destroyed once saved as electronic records satisfying the requirements of this section.

The subsection refers to the information contained in an electronic record, rather than relying on the term electronic record, as a matter of clarity that the critical aspect in retention is the information itself. What information must be retained is determined by the purpose for which the information is needed. If the addressing and pathway information regarding an e-mail is relevant, then that information should also be retained. However if it is the substance of the e-mail that is relevant, only that information need be retained. Of course, wise record retention would include all such information since what information will be relevant at a later time will not be known.

4. Subsections (b) and (c) simply make clear that certain ancillary information or the use of third parties, does not affect the serviceability of records and information retained electronically. Again, the relevance of particular information will not be known until that information is required at a subsequent time.

5. Subsection (d) continues the theme of the Act as validating electronic records as originals where the law requires retention of an original. The validation of electronic records and electronic information as originals is consistent with the Uniform Rules of Evidence. See Uniform Rules of Evidence 1001(3), 1002, 1003 and 1004.

6. Subsection (e) specifically addresses particular concerns regarding check retention statutes in many jurisdictions. A Report compiled by the Federal Reserve Bank of Boston identifies hundreds of state laws which require the retention or production of original canceled checks. Such requirements preclude banks and their customers from realizing the benefits and efficiencies related to truncation processes otherwise validated under current law. The benefits to banks and their customers from electronic check retention are effectuated by this provision.

7. Subsections (f) and (g) generally address other record retention statutes. As with check retention, all businesses and individuals may realize significant savings from electronic record retention. So long as the standards in Section 12 are satisfied, this section permits all parties to obtain those benefits. As always the government may require records in any medium, however, these subsections require a governmental agency to specifically identify the types of records and requirements that will be imposed.

SECTION 13. ADMISSIBILITY IN EVIDENCE. In a proceeding, evidence of a record or signature may not be excluded solely because it is in electronic form.

Source: UNCITRAL Model Law on Electronic Commerce Article 9.

Comment

Like Section 7, this section prevents the nonrecognition of electronic records and signatures solely on the ground of the media in which information is presented.

Nothing in this section relieves a party from establishing the necessary foundation for the admission of an electronic record. See Uniform Rules of Evidence 1001(3), 1002,1003 and 1004.

SECTION 14. AUTOMATED TRANSACTION. In an automated transaction, the following rules apply:

(1) A contract may be formed by the interaction of electronic agents of the parties, even if no individual was aware of or reviewed the electronic agents' actions or the resulting terms and agreements.

(2) A contract may be formed by the interaction of an electronic agent and an individual, acting on the individual's own behalf or for another person, including by an interaction in which the individual performs actions that the individual is free to refuse to perform and which the individual knows or has reason to know will cause the electronic agent to complete the transaction or performance.

(3) The terms of the contract are determined by the substantive law applicable to it.

Source: UNICTRAL Model Law on Electronic Commerce Article 11.

Comment

1. This section confirms that contracts can be formed by machines functioning as electronic agents for parties to a transaction. It negates any claim that lack of human intent, at the time of contract formation, prevents contract formation. When machines are involved, the requisite intention flows from the programing and use of the machine. As in other cases, these are salutary provisions consistent with the fundamental purpose of the Act to remove barriers to electronic transactions while leaving the substantive law, e.g., law of mistake, law of contract formation, unaffected to the greatest extent possible.

2. The process in paragraph (2) validates an anonymous click-through transaction. It is possible that an anonymous click-through process may simply result in no recognizable legal relationship, e.g., A goes to a person's website and acquires access without in any way identifying herself, or otherwise indicating agreement or assent to any limitation or obligation, and the owner's site grants A access. In such a case no legal relationship has been created.

On the other hand it may be possible that A's actions indicate agreement to a particular term. For example, A goes to a website and is confronted by an initial screen which advises her that the information at this site is proprietary, that A may use the information for her own personal purposes, but that, by clicking below, A agrees that any other use without the site owner=s permission is prohibited. If A clicks "agree" and downloads the information and then uses the information for other, prohibited purposes, should not A be bound by the click? It seems the answer properly should be, and would be, yes.

If the owner can show that the only way A could have obtained the information was from his website, and that the process to access the subject information required that A must have clicked the "I agree" button after having the ability to see the conditions on use, A has performed actions which A was free to refuse, which A knew would cause the site to grant her access, i.e., "complete the transaction." The terms of the resulting contract will be determined under general contract principles, but will include the limitation on A's use of the information, as a condition precedent to granting her access to the information.

3. In the transaction set forth in Comment 2, the record of the transaction also will include an electronic signature. By clicking "I agree" A adopted a process with the intent to "sign," i.e., bind herself to a legal obligation, the resulting record of the transaction. If a "signed writing" were required under otherwise applicable law, this transaction would be enforceable. If a "signed writing" were not required, it may be sufficient to establish that the electronic record is attributable to A under Section 9. Attribution may be shown in any manner reasonable including showing that, of necessity, A could only have gotten the information through the process at the website.

SECTION 15. TIME AND PLACE OF SENDING AND RECEIPT.

(a) Unless otherwise agreed between the sender and the recipient, an electronic record is sent when it:

(1) is addressed properly or otherwise directed properly to an information processing system that the recipient has designated or uses for the purpose of receiving electronic records or information of the type sent and from which the recipient is able to retrieve the electronic record;

(2) is in a form capable of being processed by that system; and

(3) enters an information processing system outside the control of the sender or of a person that sent the electronic record on behalf of the sender or enters a region of the information processing system designated or used by the recipient which is under the control of the recipient.

(b) Unless otherwise agreed between a sender and the recipient, an electronic record is received when:

(1) it enters an information processing system that the recipient has designated or uses for the purpose of receiving electronic records or information of the type sent and from which the recipient is able to retrieve the electronic record; and

(2) it is in a form capable of being processed by that system.

(c) Subsection (b) applies even if the place the information processing system is located is different from the place the electronic record is deemed to be received under subsection (d).

(d) Unless otherwise expressly provided in the electronic record or agreed between the sender and the recipient, an electronic record is deemed to be sent from the sender's place of business and to be received at the recipient's place of business. For purposes of this subsection, the following rules apply:

(1) If the sender or recipient has more than one place of business, the place of business of that person is the place having the closest relationship to the underlying transaction.

(2) If the sender or the recipient does not have a place of business, the place of business is the sender's or recipient's residence, as the case may be.

(e) An electronic record is received under subsection (b) even if no individual is aware of its receipt.

(f) Receipt of an electronic acknowledgment from an information processing system described in subsection (b) establishes that a record was received but, by itself, does not establish that the content sent corresponds to the content received.

(g) If a person is aware that an electronic record purportedly sent under subsection (a), or purportedly received under subsection (b), was not actually sent or received, the legal effect of the sending or receipt is determined by other applicable law. Except to the extent permitted by the other law, the requirements of this subsection may not be varied by agreement.

Source: UNCITRAL Model Law on Electronic Commerce Article 15.

Comment

1. This section provides default rules regarding when and from where an electronic record is sent and when and where an electronic record is received. This section does not address the efficacy of the record that is sent or received. That is, whether a record is unintelligible or unusable by a recipient is a separate issue from whether that record was sent or received. The effectiveness of an illegible record, whether it binds any party, are questions left to other law.

2. Subsection (a) furnishes rules for determining when an electronic record is sent. The effect of the sending and its import are determined by other law once it is determined that a sending has occurred.

In order to have a proper sending, the subsection requires that information be properly addressed or otherwise directed to the recipient. In order to send within the meaning of this section, there must be specific information which will direct the record to the intended recipient. Although mass electronic sending is not precluded, a general broadcast message, sent to systems rather than individuals, would not suffice as a sending.

The record will be considered sent once it leaves the control of the sender, or comes under the control of the recipient. Records sent through e-mail or the internet will pass through many different server systems. Accordingly, the critical element when more than one system is involved is the loss of control by the sender.

However, the structure of many message delivery systems is such that electronic records may actually never leave the control of the sender. For example, within a university or corporate setting, e-mail sent within the system to another faculty member is technically not out of the sender's control since it never leaves the organization's server. Accordingly, to qualify as a sending, the e-mail must arrive at a point where the recipient has control. This section does not address the effect of an electronic record that is thereafter "pulled back," e.g., removed from a mailbox. The analog in the paper world would be removing a letter from a person's mailbox. As in the case of providing information electronically under Section 8, the recipient's ability to receive a message should be judged from the perspective of whether the sender has done any action which would preclude retrieval. This is especially the case in regard to sending, since the sender must direct the record to a system designated or used by the recipient.

3. Subsection (b) provides simply that when a record enters the system which the recipient has designated or uses and to which it has access, in a form capable of being processed by that system, it is received. Keying receipt to a system accessible by the recipient removes the potential for a recipient leaving messages with a server or other service in order to avoid receipt. However, the section does not resolve the issue of how the sender proves the time of receipt.

To assure that the recipient retains control of the place of receipt, subsection (b) requires that the system be specified or used by the recipient, and that the system be used or designated for the type of record being sent. Many people have multiple e-mail addresses for different purposes. Subsection (b) assures that recipients can designate the e-mail address or system to be used in a particular transaction. For example, the recipient retains the ability to designate a home e-mail for personal matters, work e-mail for official business, or a separate organizational e-mail solely for the business purposes of that organization. If A sends B a notice at his home which relates to business, it may not be deemed received if B designated his business address as the sole address for business purposes. Whether actual knowledge upon seeing it at home would qualify as receipt is determined under the otherwise applicable substantive law.

4. Subsections (c) and (d) provide default rules for determining where a record will be considered to have been sent or received. The focus is on the place of business of the recipient and not the physical location of the information processing system, which may bear absolutely no relation to the transaction between the parties. It is not uncommon for users of electronic commerce to communicate from one State to another without knowing the location of information systems through which communication is operated. In addition, the location of certain communication systems may change without either of the parties being aware of the change. Accordingly, where the place of sending or receipt is an issue under other applicable law, e.g., conflict of laws issues, tax issues, the relevant location should be the location of the sender or recipient and not the location of the information processing system.

Subsection (d) assures individual flexibility in designating the place from which a record will be considered sent or at which a record will be considered received. Under subsection (d) a person may designate the place of sending or receipt unilaterally in an electronic record. This ability, as with the ability to designate by agreement, may be limited by otherwise applicable law to places having a reasonable relationship to the transaction.

5. Subsection (e) makes clear that receipt is not dependent on a person having notice that the record is in the person's system. Receipt occurs when the record reaches the designated system whether or not the recipient ever retrieves the record. The paper analog is the recipient who never reads a mail notice.

6. Subsection (f) provides legal certainty regarding the effect of an electronic acknowledgment. It only addresses the fact of receipt, not the quality of the content, nor whether the electronic record was read or "opened."

7. Subsection (g) limits the parties' ability to vary the method for sending and receipt provided in subsections (a) and (b), when there is a legal requirement for the sending or receipt. As in other circumstances where legal requirements derive from other substantive law, to the extent that the other law permits variation by agreement, this Act does not impose any additional requirements, and provisions of this Act may be varied to the extent provided in the other law.

SECTION 16. TRANSFERABLE RECORDS.

(a) In this section, "transferable record" means an electronic record that:

(1) would be a note under [Article 3 of the Uniform Commercial Code] or a document under [Article 7 of the Uniform Commercial Code] if the electronic record were in writing; and

(2) the issuer of the electronic record expressly has agreed is a transferable record.

(b) A person has control of a transferable record if a system employed for evidencing the transfer of interests in the transferable record reliably establishes that person as the person to which the transferable record was issued or transferred.

(c) A system satisfies subsection (b), and a person is deemed to have control of a transferable record, if the transferable record is created, stored, and assigned in such a manner that:

(1) a single authoritative copy of the transferable record exists which is unique, identifiable, and, except as otherwise provided in paragraphs (4), (5), and (6), unalterable;

(2) the authoritative copy identifies the person asserting control as:

(A) the person to which the transferable record was issued; or

(B) if the authoritative copy indicates that the transferable record has been transferred, the person to which the transferable record was most recently transferred;

(3) the authoritative copy is communicated to and maintained by the person asserting control or its designated custodian;

(4) copies or revisions that add or change an identified assignee of the authoritative copy can be made only with the consent of the person asserting control;

(5) each copy of the authoritative copy and any copy of a copy is readily identifiable as a copy that is not the authoritative copy; and

(6) any revision of the authoritative copy is readily identifiable as authorized or unauthorized.

(d) Except as otherwise agreed, a person having control of a transferable record is the holder, as defined in [Section 1-201(20) of the Uniform Commercial Code], of the transferable record and has the same rights and defenses as a holder of an equivalent record or writing under [the Uniform Commercial Code], including, if the applicable statutory requirements under [Section 3-302(a), 7-501, or 9-308 of the Uniform Commercial Code] are satisfied, the rights and defenses of a holder in due course, a holder to which a negotiable document of title has been duly negotiated, or a purchaser, respectively. Delivery, possession, and indorsement are not required to obtain or exercise any of the rights under this subsection.

(e) Except as otherwise agreed, an obligor under a transferable record has the same rights and defenses as an equivalent obligor under equivalent records or writings under [the Uniform Commercial Code].

(f) If requested by a person against which enforcement is sought, the person seeking to enforce the transferable record shall provide reasonable proof that the person is in control of the transferable record. Proof may include access to the authoritative copy of the transferable record and related business records sufficient to review the terms of the transferable record and to establish the identity of the person having control of the transferable record.

Source: Revised Article 9, Section 9-105.

Comment

1. Paper negotiable instruments and documents are unique in the fact that a tangible token B a piece of paper B actually embodies intangible rights and obligations. The extreme difficulty of creating a unique electronic token which embodies the singular attributes of a paper negotiable document or instrument dictates that the rules relating to negotiable documents and instruments not be simply amended to allow the use of an electronic record for the requisite paper writing. However, the desirability of establishing rules by which business parties might be able to acquire some of the benefits of negotiability in an electronic environment is recognized by the inclusion of this section on Transferable Records.

This section provides legal support for the creation, transferability and enforceability of electronic note and document equivalents, as against the issuer/obligor. The certainty created by the section provides the requisite incentive for industry to develop the systems and processes, which involve significant expenditures of time and resources, to enable the use of such electronic documents.

The importance of facilitating the development of systems which will permit electronic equivalents is a function of cost, efficiency and safety for the records. The storage cost and space needed for the billions of paper notes and documents is phenomenal. Further, natural disasters can wreak havoc on the ability to meet legal requirements for retaining, retrieving and delivering paper instruments. The development of electronic systems meeting the rigorous standards of this section will permit retention of copies which reflect the same integrity as the original. As a result storage, transmission and other costs will be reduced, while security and the ability to satisfy legal requirements governing such paper records will be enhanced.

Section 16 provides for the creation of an electronic record which may be controlled by the holder, who in turn may obtain the benefits of holder in due course and good faith purchaser status. If the benefits and efficiencies of electronic media are to be realized in this industry it is essential to establish a means by which transactions involving paper promissory notes may be accomplished completely electronically. Particularly as other aspects of such transactions are accomplished electronically, the drag on the transaction of requiring a paper note becomes evident. In addition to alleviating the logistical problems of generating, storing and retrieving paper, the mailing and transmission costs associated with such transactions will also be reduced.

2. The definition of transferable record is limited in two significant ways. First, only the equivalent of paper promissory notes and paper documents of title can be created as transferable records. Notes and Documents of Title do not impact the broad systems that relate to the broader payments mechanisms related, for example, to checks. Impacting the check collection system by allowing for "electronic checks" has ramifications well beyond the ability of this Act to address. Accordingly, this Act excludes from its scope transactions governed by UCC Articles 3 and 4. The limitation to promissory note equivalents in Section 16 is quite important in that regard because of the ability to deal with many enforcement issues by contract without affecting such systemic concerns.

Second, not only is Section 16 limited to electronic records which would qualify as negotiable promissory notes or documents if they were in writing, but the issuer of the electronic record must expressly agree that the electronic record is to be considered a transferable record. The definition of transferable record as "an electronic record that . . . the issuer of the electronic record expressly has agreed is a transferable record" indicates that the electronic record itself will likely set forth the issuer's agreement, though it may be argued that a contemporaneous electronic or written record might set forth the issuer's agreement. However, conversion of a paper note issued as such would not be possible because the issuer would not be the issuer, in such a case, of an electronic record. The purpose of such a restriction is to assure that transferable records can only be created at the time of issuance by the obligor. The possibility that a paper note might be converted to an electronic record and then intentionally destroyed, and the effect of such action, was not intended to be covered by Section 16.

The requirement that the obligor expressly agree in the electronic record to its treatment as a transferable record does not otherwise affect the characterization of a transferable record (i.e., does not affect what would be a paper note) because it is a statutory condition. Further, it does not obligate the issuer to undertake to do any other act than the payment of the obligation evidenced by the transferable record. Therefore, it does not make the transferable record "conditional" within the meaning of Section 3-104(a)(3) of the Uniform Commercial Code.

3. Under Section 16 acquisition of "control" over an electronic record serves as a substitute for "possession" in the paper analog. More precisely, "control" under Section 16 serves as the substitute for delivery, indorsement and possession of a negotiable promissory note or negotiable document of title. Section 16(b) allows control to be found so long as "a system employed for evidencing the transfer of interests in the transferable record reliably establishes [the person claiming control] as the person to which the transferable record was issued or transferred." The key point is that a system, whether involving third party registry or technological safeguards, must be shown to reliably establish the identity of *the* person entitled to payment. Section 16(c) then sets forth a safe harbor list of very strict requirements for such a system. The specific provisions listed in Section 16(c) are derived from Section 105 of Revised Article 9 of the Uniform Commercial Code. Generally, the transferable record must be unique, identifiable, and except as specifically permitted, unalterable. That "authoritative copy" must (i) identify the person claiming control as the person to whom the record was issued or most recently transferred, (ii) be maintained by the person claiming control or its designee, and (iii) be unalterable except with the permission of the person claiming control. In addition any copy of the authoritative copy must be readily identifiable as a copy and all revisions must be readily identifiable as authorized or unauthorized.

The control requirements may be satisfied through the use of a trusted third party registry system. Such systems are currently in place with regard to the transfer of securities entitlements under Article 8 of the Uniform Commercial Code, and in the transfer of cotton warehouse receipts under the program sponsored by the United States Department of Agriculture. This Act would recognize the use of such a system so long as the standards of subsection (c) were satisfied. In addition, a technological system which met such exacting standards would also be permitted under Section 16.

For example, a borrower signs an electronic record which would be a promissory note or document if it were paper. The borrower specifically agrees in the electronic record that it will qualify as a transferable record under this section. The lender implements a newly developed technological system which dates, encrypts, and stores all the electronic information in the transferable record in a manner which lender can demonstrate reliably establishes lender as the person to which the transferable record was issued. In the alternative, the lender may contract with a third party to act as a registry for all such transferable records, retaining records establishing the party to whom the record was issued and all subsequent transfers of the record. An example of this latter method for assuring control is the system established for the issuance and transfer of electronic cotton warehouse receipts under 7 C.F.R. section 735 et seq.

Of greatest importance in the system used is the ability to securely and demonstrably be able to transfer the record to others in a manner which assures that only one "holder" exists. The need for such certainty and security resulted in the very stringent standards for a system outlined in subsection (c). A system relying on a third party registry is likely the most effective way to satisfy the requirements of subsection (c) that the transferable record remain unique, identifiable and unalterable, while also providing the means to assure that the transferee is clearly noted and identified.

It must be remembered that Section 16 was drafted in order to provide sufficient legal certainty regarding the rights of those in control of such electronic records, that legal incentives would exist to warrant the development of systems which would establish the requisite control. During the drafting of Section 16, representatives from the Federal Reserve carefully scrutinized the impact of any electronicization of any aspect of the national payment system. Section 16 represents a compromise position which, as noted, serves as a bridge pending more detailed study and consideration of what legal changes, if any, are necessary or appropriate in the context of the payment systems impacted. Accordingly, Section 16 provides limited scope for the attainment of important rights derived from the concept of negotiability, in order to permit the development of systems which will satisfy its strict requirements for control.

4. It is important to note what the section does not provide. Issues related to enforceability against intermediate transferees and transferors (i.e., endorser liability under a paper note), warranty liability that would attach in a paper note, and issues of the effect of taking a transferable record on the underlying obligation, are NOT addressed by this section. Such matters must be addressed, if at all, by contract between and among the parties in the chain of transmission and transfer of the transferable record. In the event that such matters are not addressed by the contract, the issues would need to be resolved under otherwise applicable law. Other law may include general contract principles of assignment and assumption, or may include rules from Article 3 of the Uniform Commercial Code applied by analogy.

For example, Issuer agrees to pay a debt by means of a transferable record issued to A. Unless there is agreement between issuer and A that the transferable record "suspends" the underlying obligation (see Section 3-310 of the Uniform Commercial Code), A would not be prevented from enforcing the underlying obligation without the transferable record. Similarly, if A transfers the transferable record to B by means granting B control, B may obtain holder in due course rights against the obligor/issuer, but B's recourse against A would not be clear unless A agreed to remain liable under the transferable record. Although the rules of Article 3 may be applied by analogy in an appropriate context, in the absence of an express agreement in the transferable record or included by applicable system rules, the liability of the transferor would not be clear.

5. Current business models exist which rely for their efficacy on the benefits of negotiability. A principal example, and one which informed much of the development of Section 16, involves the mortgage backed securities industry. Aggregators of commercial paper acquire mortgage secured promissory notes following a chain of transfers beginning with the origination of the mortgage loan by a mortgage broker. In the course of the transfers of this paper, buyers of the notes and lenders/secured parties for these buyers will intervene. For the ultimate purchaser of the paper, the ability to rely on holder in due course and good faith purchaser status creates the legal security necessary to issue its own investment securities which are backed by the obligations evidenced by the notes purchased. Only through their HIDC status can these purchasers be assured that third party claims will be barred. Only through their HIDC status can the end purchaser avoid the incredible burden of requiring and assuring that each person in the chain of transfer has waived any and all defenses to performance which may be created during the chain of transfer.

6. This section is a stand-alone provision. Although references are made to specific provisions in Article 3, Article 7, and Article 9 of the Uniform Commercial Code, these provisions are incorporated into this Act and made the applicable rules for purposes of this Act. The rights of parties to transferable records are established under subsections (d) and (e). Subsection (d) provides rules for determining the rights of a party in control of a transferable record. The subsection makes clear that the rights are determined under this section, and not under other law, by incorporating the rules on the manner of acquisition into this statute. The last sentence of subsection (d) is intended to assure that requirements related to notions of possession, which are inherently inconsistent with the idea of an electronic record, are not incorporated into this statute.

If a person establishes control, Section 16(d) provides that that person is the "holder" of the transferable record which is equivalent to a holder of an analogous paper negotiable instrument. More importantly, if the person acquired control in a manner which would make it a holder in due course of an equivalent paper record, the person acquires the rights of a HIDC. The person in control would therefore be able to enforce the transferable record against the obligor regardless of intervening claims and defenses. However, by pulling these rights into Section 16, this Act does NOT validate the wholesale electrification of promissory notes under Article 3 of the Uniform Commercial Code.

Further, it is important to understand that a transferable record under Section 16, while having no counterpart under Article 3 of the Uniform Commercial Code, would be an "account," "general intangible," or "payment intangible" under Article 9 of the Uniform Commercial Code. Accordingly, two separate bodies of law would apply to that asset of the obligee. A taker of the transferable record under Section 16 may acquire purchaser rights under Article 9 of the Uniform Commercial Code, however, those rights may be defeated by a trustee in bankruptcy of a prior person in control unless perfection under Article 9 of the Uniform Commercial Code by filing is achieved. If the person in control also takes control in a manner granting it holder in due course status, of course that person would take free of any claim by a bankruptcy trustee or lien creditor.

7. Subsection (e) accords to the obligor of the transferable record rights equal to those of an obligor under an equivalent paper record. Accordingly, unless a waiver of defense clause is obtained in the electronic record, or the transferee obtains HDC rights under subsection (d), the obligor has all the rights and defenses available to it under a contract assignment. Additionally, the obligor has the right to have the payment noted or otherwise included as part of the electronic record.

8. Subsection (f) grants the obligor the right to have the transferable record and other information made available for purposes of assuring the correct person to pay. This will allow the obligor to protect its interest and obtain the defense of discharge by payment or performance. This is particularly important because a person receiving subsequent control under the appropriate circumstances may well qualify as a holder in course who can enforce payment of the transferable record.

9. Section 16 is a singular exception to the thrust of this Act to simply validate electronic media used in commercial transactions. Section 16 actually provides a means for expanding electronic commerce. It provides certainty to lenders and investors regarding the enforceability of a new class of financial services. It is hoped that the legal protections afforded by Section 16 will engender the development of technological and business models which will permit realization of the significant cost savings and efficiencies available through electronic transacting in the financial services industry. Although only a bridge to more detailed consideration of the broad issues related to negotiability in an electronic context, Section 16 provides the impetus for that broader consideration while allowing continuation of developing technological and business models.

[SECTION 17. CREATION AND RETENTION OF ELECTRONIC RECORDS AND CONVERSION OF WRITTEN RECORDS BY GOVERNMENTAL AGENCIES. [Each governmental agency] [The [designated state officer]] of this State shall determine whether, and the extent to which, [it] [a governmental agency] will create and retain electronic records and convert written records to electronic records.]

Comment

See Comments following Section 19.

[SECTION 18. ACCEPTANCE AND DISTRIBUTION OF ELECTRONIC RECORDS BY GOVERNMENTAL AGENCIES.

(a) Except as otherwise provided in Section 12(f), [each governmental agency] [the [designated state officer]] of this State shall determine whether, and the extent to which, [it] [a governmental agency] will send and accept electronic records and electronic signatures to and from other persons and otherwise create, generate, communicate, store, process, use, and rely upon electronic records and electronic signatures.

(b) To the extent that a governmental agency uses electronic records and electronic signatures under subsection (a), the [governmental agency] [designated state officer], giving due consideration to security, may specify:

(1) the manner and format in which the electronic records must be created, generated, sent, communicated, received, and stored and the systems established for those purposes;

(2) if electronic records must be signed by electronic means, the type of electronic signature required, the manner and format in which the electronic signature must be affixed to the electronic record, and the identity of, or criteria that must be met by, any third party used by a person filing a document to facilitate the process;

(3) control processes and procedures as appropriate to ensure adequate preservation, disposition, integrity, security, confidentiality, and auditability of electronic records; and

(4) any other required attributes for electronic records which are specified for corresponding nonelectronic records or reasonably necessary under the circumstances.

(c) Except as otherwise provided in Section 12(f), this [Act] does not require a governmental agency of this State to use or permit the use of electronic records or electronic signatures.]

Source: Illinois Act Section 25-101; Florida Electronic Signature Act, Chapter 96-324, Section 7 (1996).

Comment

See Comments following Section 19.

[SECTION 19. INTEROPERABILITY. The [governmental agency] [designated officer] of this State which adopts standards pursuant to Section 18 may encourage and promote consistency and interoperability with similar requirements adopted by other governmental agencies of this and other States and the federal government and nongovernmental persons interacting with governmental agencies of this State. If appropriate, those standards may specify differing levels of standards from which governmental agencies of this State may choose in implementing the most appropriate standard for a particular application.]

Source: Illinois Act Section 25-115.

See Legislative Note below B Following Comments.

Comment

1. Sections 17-19 have been bracketed as optional provisions to be considered for adoption by each State. Among the barriers to electronic commerce are barriers which exist in the use

of electronic media by state governmental agencies B whether among themselves or in external dealing with the private sector. In those circumstances where the government acts as a commercial party, e.g., in areas of procurement, the general validation provisions of this Act will apply. That is to say, the government must agree to conduct transactions electronically with vendors and customers of government services.

However, there are other circumstances when government ought to establish the ability to proceed in transactions electronically. Whether in regard to records and communications within and between governmental agencies, or with respect to information and filings which must be made with governmental agencies, these sections allow a State to establish the ground work for such electronicization.

2. The provisions in Sections 17-19 are broad and very general. In many States they will be unnecessary because enacted legislation designed to facilitate governmental use of electronic records and communications is in place. However, in many States broad validating rules are needed and desired. Accordingly, this Act provides these sections as a baseline.

Of paramount importance in all States however, is the need for States to assure that whatever systems and rules are adopted, the systems established are compatible with the systems of other governmental agencies and with common systems in the private sector. A very real risk exists that implementation of systems by myriad governmental agencies and offices may create barriers because of a failure to consider compatibility, than would be the case otherwise.

3. The provisions in Section 17-19 are broad and general to provide the greatest flexibility and adaptation to the specific needs of the individual States. The differences and variations in the organization and structure of governmental agencies mandates this approach. However, it is imperative that each State always keep in mind the need to prevent the erection of barriers through appropriate coordination of systems and rules within the parameters set by the State.

4. Section 17 authorizes state agencies to use electronic records and electronic signatures generally for intra-governmental purposes, and to convert written records and manual signatures to electronic records and electronic signatures. By its terms the section gives enacting legislatures the option to leave the decision to use electronic records or convert written records and signatures to the governmental agency or assign that duty to a designated state officer. It also authorizes the destruction of written records after conversion to electronic form.

5. Section 18 broadly authorizes state agencies to send and receive electronic records and signatures in dealing with non-governmental persons. Again, the provision is permissive and not obligatory (see subsection (c)). However, it does provide specifically that with respect to electronic records used for evidentiary purposes, Section 12 will apply unless a particular agency expressly opts out.

6. Section 19 is the most important section of the three. It requires governmental agencies or state officers to take account of consistency in applications and interoperability to the extent practicable when promulgating standards. This section is critical in addressing the concern that inconsistent applications may promote barriers greater than currently exist. Without such direction the myriad systems that could develop independently would be new barriers to electronic commerce, not a removal of barriers. The key to interoperability is flexibility and adaptability. The requirement of a single system may be as big a barrier as the proliferation of many disparate systems.

Legislative Note Regarding Adoption of Sections 17-19

1. Sections 17-19 are optional sections for consideration by individual legislatures for adoption, and have been bracketed to make this clear. The inclusion or exclusion of Sections 17-19 will not have a detrimental impact on the uniformity of adoption of this Act, so long as Sections 1-16 are adopted uniformly as presented. In some States Sections 17-19 will be unnecessary because legislation is already in place to authorize and implement govern-

ment use of electronic media. However, the general authorization provided by Sections 17-19 may be critical in some States which desire to move forward in this area.

2. In the event that a state legislature chooses to adopt Sections 17-19, a number of issues must be addressed:

A. Is the general authorization to adopt electronic media, provided by Sections 17-19 sufficient for the needs of the particular jurisdiction, or is more detailed and specific authorization necessary? This determination may be affected by the decision regarding the appropriate entity or person to oversee implementation of the use of electronic media (See next paragraph). Sections 17-19 are broad and general in the authorization granted. Certainly greater specificity can be added subsequent to adoption of these sections. The question for the legislature is whether greater direction and specificity is needed at this time. If so, the legislature should not enact Sections 17-19 at this time.

B. Assuming a legislature decides to enact Sections 17-19, what entity or person should oversee implementation of the government's use of electronic media? As noted in each of Sections 17-19, again by brackets, a choice must be made regarding the entity to make critical decisions regarding the systems and rules which will govern the use of electronic media by the State. Each State will need to consider its particular structure and administration in making this determination. However, legislatures are strongly encouraged to make compatibility and interoperability considerations paramount in making this determination.

C. Finally, a decision will have to be made regarding the process by which coordination of electronic systems will occur between the various branches of state government and among the various levels of government within the State. Again this will require consideration of the unique situation in each State.

3. If a State chooses not to enact Sections 17-19, UETA Sections 1-16 will still apply to governmental entities when acting as a "person" engaging in "transactions" within its scope. The definition of transaction includes "governmental affairs." Of course, like any other party, the circumstances surrounding a transaction must indicate that the governmental actor has agreed to act electronically (See Section 5(b)), but otherwise all the provisions of Sections 1-16 will apply to validate the use of electronic records and signatures in transactions involving governmental entities.

If a State does choose to enact Sections 17-19, Sections 1-16 will continue to apply as above. In addition, Sections 17-19 will provide authorization for intra-governmental uses of electronic media. Finally, Sections 17-19 provide a broader authorization for the State to develop systems and procedures for the use of electronic media in its relations with non-governmental entities and persons.

SECTION 20. SEVERABILITY CLAUSE. If any provision of this [Act] or its application to any person or circumstance is held invalid, the invalidity does not affect other provisions or applications of this [Act] which can be given effect without the invalid provision or application, and to this end the provisions of this [Act] are severable.

SECTION 21. EFFECTIVE DATE. This [Act] takes effect ....

UNIFORM ELECTRONIC COMMERCE ACT

Uniform Law Conference of Canada
Uniform Electronic Commerce Act[1]

Definitions

1. The definitions in this section apply in this Act.

(a) "electronic" includes created, recorded, transmitted or stored in digital form or in other intangible form by electronic, magnetic or optical means or by any other means that has capabilities for creation, recording, transmission or storage similar to those means and "electronically" has a corresponding meaning.

(b) "electronic signature" means information in electronic form that a person has created or adopted in order to sign a document and that is in, attached to or associated with the document .

(c) "Government" means

(i) the Government of [enacting jurisdiction];

(ii) any department, agency or body of the Government of [enacting jurisdiction], [other than Crown Corporations incorporated by or under a law of [enacting jurisdiction]]; and

[(iii) any city, metropolitan authority, town, village, township, district or [rural municipality or other municipal body, however designated, incorporated or established by or under a law of [enacting jurisdiction].]

Application

2. (1) Subject to this section, this Act applies in respect of [enacting jurisdiction] law.

(2)The [appropriate authority] may, by [statutory instrument], specify provisions of or requirements under [enacting jurisdiction] law in respect of which this Act does not apply.

(3) This Act does not apply in respect of

(a) wills and their codicils;

---

1 Reproduced with permission from the Uniform Law Conference of Canada.

(b) trusts created by wills or by codicils to wills;

(c) powers of attorney, to the extent that they are in respect of the financial affairs or personal care of an individual;

(d) documents that create or transfer interests in land and that require registration to be effective against third parties.

(4) Except for Part 3, this Act does not apply in respect of negotiable instruments, including negotiable documents of title.

(5) Nothing in this Act limits the operation of any provision of [enacting jurisdiction] law that expressly authorizes, prohibits or regulates the use of electronic documents.

(6) The [appropriate authority] may, by [statutory instrument], amend subsection (3) to add any document or class of documents, or to remove any document or class of documents previously added under this subsection.

(7) For the purpose of subsection (5), the use of words and expressions like "in writing" and "signature" and other similar words and expressions does not by itself prohibit the use of electronic documents.

Crown

3. This Act binds the Crown.

Interpretation

4. The provisions of this Act relating to the satisfaction of a requirement of law apply whether the law creates an obligation or provides consequences for doing something or for not doing something.

PART 1
PROVISION AND RETENTION OF INFORMATION

Legal recognition

5. Information shall not be denied legal effect or enforceability solely by reason that it is in electronic form.

Use not mandatory

6.(1) Nothing in this Act requires a person to use or accept information in electronic form, but a person's consent to do so may be inferred from the person's conduct.

(2) Despite subsection (1), the consent of the Government to accept information in electronic form may not be inferred by its conduct but must be expressed by

communication accessible to the public or to those likely to communicate with it for particular purposes.

Requirement for information to be in writing

7. A requirement under [enacting jurisdiction] law that information be in writing is satisfied by information in electronic form if the information is accessible so as to be usable for subsequent reference.

Providing information in writing

8.(1) A requirement under [enacting jurisdiction] law for a person to provide information in writing to another person is satisfied by the provision of the information in an electronic document,

(a) if the electronic document that is provided to the other person is accessible by the other person and capable of being retained by the other person so as to be usable for subsequent reference, and

(b) where the information is to be provided to the Government, if

(i) the Government or the part of Government to which the information is to be provided has consented to accept electronic documents in satisfaction of the requirement; and

(ii) the electronic document meets the information technology standards and acknowledgement rules, if any, established by the Government or part of Government, as the case may be.

Providing information in specific form

9. A requirement under [enacting jurisdiction] law for a person to provide information to another person in a specified non-electronic form is satisfied by the provision of the information in an electronic document,

(a) if the information is provided in the same or substantially the same form and the electronic document is accessible by the other person and capable of being retained by the other person so as to be usable for subsequent reference, and

(b) where the information is to be provided to the Government, if

(i) the Government or the part of Government to which the information is to be provided has consented to accept electronic documents in satisfaction of the requirement; and

(ii) the electronic document meets the information technology standards and acknowledgement rules, if any, established by the Government or part of Government, as the case may be.

Signatures

10. (1) A requirement under [enacting jurisdiction] law for the signature of a person is satisfied by an electronic signature.

(2) For the purposes of subsection (1), the [authority responsible for the requirement] may make a regulation that,

(a) the electronic signature shall be reliable for the purpose of identifying the person, in the light of all the circumstances, including any relevant agreement and the time the electronic signature was made; and

(b) the association of the electronic signature with the relevant electronic document shall be reliable for the purpose for which the electronic document was made, in the light of all the circumstances, including any relevant agreement and the time the electronic signature was made.

(3) For the purposes of subsection (1), where the signature or signed document is to be provided to the Government, the requirement is satisfied only if

(a) the Government or the part of Government to which the information is to be provided has consented to accept electronic signatures; and

(b) the electronic document meets the information technology standards and requirements as to method and as to reliability of the signature, if any, established by the Government or part of Government, as the case may be.

Provision of originals

11. (1) A requirement under [enacting jurisdiction] law that requires a person to present or retain a document in original form is satisfied by the provision or retention of an electronic document if

(a) there exists a reliable assurance as to the integrity of the information contained in the electronic document from the time the document to be presented or retained was first made in its final form, whether as a paper document or as an electronic document;

(b) where the document in original form is to be provided to a person, the electronic document that is provided to the person is accessible by the person and capable of being retained by the person so as to be usable for subsequent reference; and

(c) where the document in original form is to be provided to the Government,

(i) the Government or the part of Government to which the information is to be provided has consented to accept electronic documents in satisfaction of the requirement; and

(ii) the electronic document meets the information technology standards and acknowledgement rules, if any, established by the Government or part of Government, as the case may be.

(2) For the purpose of paragraph (1)(a),

(a) the criterion for assessing integrity is whether the information has remained complete and unaltered, apart from the introduction of any changes that arise in the normal course of communication, storage and display;

(b) the standard of reliability required shall be assessed in the light of the purpose for which the document was made and in the light of all the circumstances.

Whether document is capable of being retained

12. An electronic document is deemed not to be capable of being retained if the person providing the electronic document inhibits the printing or storage of the electronic document by the recipient.

Retention of documents

13. A requirement under [enacting jurisdiction] law to retain a document is satisfied by the retention of an electronic document if

(a) the electronic document is retained in the format in which it was made, sent or received, or in a format that does not materially change the information contained in the document that was originally made, sent or received;

(b) the information in the electronic document will be accessible so as to be usable for subsequent reference by any person who is entitled to have access to the document or who is authorized to require its production; and

(c) where the electronic document was sent or received, information, if any, that identifies the origin and destination of the electronic document and the date and time when it was sent or received is also retained.

Copies

14. Where a document may be submitted in electronic form, a requirement under a provision of [enacting jurisdiction] law for one or more copies of a document to be submitted to a single addressee at the same time is satisfied by the submission of a single version of an electronic document.

Other requirements continue to apply

15. Nothing in this Part limits the operation of any requirement under [enacting jurisdiction] law for information to be posted or displayed in a specified manner or for any information or document to be transmitted by a specified method.

Authority to prescribe forms and manner of filing forms

16. (1) If a provision of [enacting jurisdiction] law requires a person to communicate information, the minister of the Crown responsible for the provision may

prescribe electronic means to be used for the communication of the information and the use of those means satisfies that requirement.

(2) If a statute of [enacting jurisdiction] sets out a form, the [authority responsible for the form] may make an electronic form that is substantially the same as the form set out in the statute and the electronic form is to be considered as the form set out in the statute.

(3) A provision of [enacting jurisdiction] law that authorizes the prescription of a form or the manner of filing a form includes the authority to prescribe an electronic form or electronic means of filing the form, as the case may be.

(4) The definitions in this subsection apply in this section.

(a) "filing" includes all manner of submitting, regardless of how it is designated.

(b) "prescribe" includes all manner of issuing, making and establishing, regardless of how it is designated.

Collection, storage, etc.

17. (1) In the absence of an express provision in any [enacting jurisdiction] law that electronic means may not be used or that they must be used in specified ways, a minister of the Crown in right of [enacting jurisdiction] or an entity referred to in subparagraphs 1(c)(ii) [or (iii)] may use electronic means to create, collect, receive, store, transfer, distribute, publish or otherwise deal with documents or information.

(2) For the purpose of subsection (1), the use of words and expressions like "in writing" and "signature" and other similar words and expressions does not by itself constitute an express provision that electronic means may not be used.

Electronic payments

18. (1) A payment that is authorized or required to be made to the Government under [enacting jurisdiction] law may be made in electronic form in any manner specified by [the Receiver General] for the [enacting jurisdiction].

(2) A payment that is authorized or required to be made by the Government may be made in electronic form in any manner specified by the [Receiver General] for the [enacting jurisdiction].

PART 2
COMMUNICATION OF ELECTRONIC DOCUMENTS

Definition of "electronic agent"

19. In this Part, "electronic agent" means a computer program or any electronic means used to initiate an action or to respond to electronic documents or actions

in whole or in part without review by a natural person at the time of the response or action.

Formation and operation of contracts

20. (1) Unless the parties agree otherwise, an offer or the acceptance of an offer, or any other matter that is material to the formation or operation of a contract, may be expressed

(a) by means of an electronic document; or

(b) by an action in electronic form, including touching or clicking on an appropriately designated icon or place on a computer screen or otherwise communicating electronically in a manner that is intended to express the offer, acceptance or other matter.

(2) A contract shall not be denied legal effect or enforceability solely by reason that an electronic document was used in its formation.

Involvement of electronic agents

21. A contract may be formed by the interaction of an electronic agent and a natural person or by the interaction of electronic agents.

Errors when dealing with electronic agents

22. An electronic document made by a natural person with the electronic agent of another person has no legal effect and is not enforceable if the natural person made a material error in the document and

(a) the electronic agent did not provide the natural person with an opportunity to prevent or correct the error;

(b) the natural person notifies the other person of the error as soon as practicable after the natural person learns of the error and indicates that he or she made an error in the electronic document;

(c) the natural person takes reasonable steps, including steps that conform to the other person's instructions to return the consideration received, if any, as a result of the error or, if instructed to do so, to destroy the consideration; and

(d) the natural person has not used or received any material benefit or value from the consideration, if any, received from the other person.

Time and place of sending and receipt of electronic documents

23. (1) Unless the originator and the addressee agree otherwise, an electronic document is sent when it enters an information system outside the control of the originator or, if the originator and the addressee are in the same information system, when it becomes capable of being retrieved and processed by the addressee.

(2) An electronic document is presumed to be received by the addressee,

(a) when it enters an information system designated or used by the addressee for the purpose of receiving documents of the type sent and it is capable of being retrieved and processed by the addressee; or

(b) if the addressee has not designated or does not use an information system for the purpose of receiving documents of the type sent, when the addressee becomes aware of the electronic document in the addressee' s information system and the electronic document is capable of being of being retrieved and processed by the addressee.

(3) Unless the originator and the addressee agree otherwise, an electronic document is deemed to be sent from the originator's place of business and is deemed to be received at the addressee's place of business.

(4) For the purposes of subsection (3)

(a) if the originator or the addressee has more than one place of business, the place of business is that which has the closest relationship to the underlying transaction to which the electronic document relates or, if there is no underlying transaction, the principal place of business of the originator or the addressee; and

(b) if the originator or the addressee does not have a place of business, the references to "place of business" in subsection (3) are to be read as references to "habitual residence".

PART 3
CARRIAGE OF GOODS

Actions related to contracts of carriage of goods

24. This Part applies to any action in connection with a contract of carriage of goods, including, but not limited to,

(a) furnishing the marks, number, quantity or weight of goods;

(b) stating or declaring the nature or value of goods;

(c) issuing a receipt for goods;

(d) confirming that goods have been loaded;

(e) giving instructions to a carrier of goods;

(f) claiming delivery of goods;

(g) authorizing release of goods;

(h) giving notice of loss of, or damage to, goods;

(i) undertaking to deliver goods to a named person or a person authorized to claim delivery;

(j) granting, acquiring, renouncing, surrendering, transferring or negotiating rights in goods;

(k) notifying a person of terms and conditions of a contract of carriage of goods;

(l) giving a notice or statement in connection with the performance of a contract of carriage of goods; and

(m) acquiring or transferring rights and obligations under a contract of carriage of goods.

Documents

25. (1) Subject to subsection (2), a requirement under [enacting jurisdiction] law that an action referred to in any of paragraphs 24(a) to (m) be carried out in writing or by using a paper document is satisfied if the action is carried out by using one or more electronic documents.

(2) If a right is to be granted to or an obligation is to be acquired by one person and no other person and a provision of [enacting jurisdiction] law requires that, in order to do so, the right or obligation must be conveyed to that person by the transfer or use of a document in writing, that requirement is satisfied if the right or obligation is conveyed through the use of one or more electronic documents created by a method that gives reliable assurance that the right or obligation has become the right or obligation of that person and no other person.

(3) For the purposes of subsection (2), the standard of reliability required shall be assessed in the light of the purpose for which the right or obligation was conveyed and in the light of all the circumstances, including any relevant agreement.

(4) If one or more electronic documents are used to accomplish an action referred to in paragraph 24(j) or (m), no document in writing used to effect the action is valid unless the use of electronic documents has been terminated and replaced by the use of documents in writing. A document in writing issued in these circumstances must contain a statement of the termination, and the replacement of the electronic documents by documents in writing does not affect the rights or obligations of the parties involved.

(5) If a rule of [enacting jurisdiction] law is compulsorily applicable to a contract of carriage of goods that is set out in, or is evidenced by, a document in writing, that rule shall not be inapplicable to a contract of carriage of goods that is evidenced by one or more electronic documents by reason of the fact that the contract is evidenced by electronic documents instead of by a document in writing.

UNCITRAL MODEL LAW ON ELECTRONIC SIGNATURES (2001)*

Article 1. Sphere of application

This Law applies where electronic signatures are used in the context[1] of commercial[2] activities. It does not override any rule of law intended for the protection of consumers.

Article 2. Definitions

For the purposes of this Law:

(a) "Electronic signature" means data in electronic form in, affixed to or logically associated with, a data message, which may be used to identify the signatory in relation to the data message and to indicate the signatory's approval of the information contained in the data message;

(b) "Certificate" means a data message or other record confirming the link between a signatory and signature creation data;

(c) "Data message" means information generated, sent, received or stored by electronic, optical or similar means including, but not limited to, electronic data interchange (EDI), electronic mail, telegram, telex or telecopy; and acts either on its own behalf or on behalf of the person it represents;

(d) "Signatory" means a person that holds signature creation data and acts either on its own behalf or on behalf of the person it represents;

---

1 The Commission suggests the following text for States that might wish to extend the applicability of this Law:

"This Law applies where electronic signatures are used, except in the following situations: [. . .]."

2 The term "commercial" should be given a wide interpretation so as to cover matters arising from all relationships of a commercial nature, whether contractual or not. Relationships of a commercial nature include, but are not limited to, the following transactions: any trade transaction for the supply or exchange of goods or services; distribution agreement; commercial representation or agency; factoring; leasing; construction of works; consulting; engineering; licensing; investment; financing; banking; insurance; exploitation agreement or concession; joint venture and other forms of industrial or business cooperation; carriage of goods or passengers by air, sea, rail or road.

(e) "Certification service provider" means a person that issues certificates and may provide other services related to electronic signatures;

(f) "Relying party" means a person that may act on the basis of a certificate or an electronic signature.

Article 3. Equal treatment of signature technologies

Nothing in this Law, except article 5, shall be applied so as to exclude, restrict or deprive of legal effect any method of creating an electronic signature that satisfies the requirements referred to in article 6, paragraph 1, or otherwise meets the requirements of applicable law.

Article 4. Interpretation

1. In the interpretation of this Law, regard is to be had to its international origin and to the need to promote uniformity in its application and the observance of good faith.

2. Questions concerning matters governed by this Law which are not expressly settled in it are to be settled in conformity with the general principles on which this Law is based.

Article 5. Variation by agreement

The provisions of this Law may be derogated from or their effect may be varied by agreement, unless that agreement would not be valid or effective under applicable law.

Article 6. Compliance with a requirement for a signature

1. Where the law requires a signature of a person, that requirement is met in relation to a data message if an electronic signature is used that is as reliable as was appropriate for the purpose for which the data message was generated or communicated, in the light of all the circumstances, including any relevant agreement.

2. Paragraph 1 applies whether the requirement referred to therein is in the form of an obligation or whether the law simply provides consequences for the absence of a signature.

3. An electronic signature is considered to be reliable for the purpose of satisfying the requirement referred to in paragraph 1 if:

(a) The signature creation data are, within the context in which they are used, linked to the signatory and to no other person;

(b) The signature creation data were, at the time of signing, under the control of the signatory and of no other person;

(c) Any alteration to the electronic signature, made after the time of signing, is detectable; and

(d) Where a purpose of the legal requirement for a signature is to provide assurance as to the integrity of the information to which it relates, any alteration made to that information after the time of signing is detectable.

4. Paragraph 3 does not limit the ability of any person:

(a) To establish in any other way, for the purpose of satisfying the requirement referred to in paragraph 1, the reliability of an electronic signature; or

(b) To adduce evidence of the non-reliability of an electronic signature.

5. The provisions of this article do not apply to the following: [. . .].

Article 7. Satisfaction of article 6

1. *[Any person, organ or authority, whether public or private, specified by the enacting State as competent]* may determine which electronic signatures satisfy the provisions of article 6 of this Law.

2. Any determination made under paragraph 1 shall be consistent with recognized international standards.

3. Nothing in this article affects the operation of the rules of private international law.

Article 8. Conduct of the signatory

1. Where signature creation data can be used to create a signature that has legal effect, each signatory shall:

(a) Exercise reasonable care to avoid unauthorized use of its signature creation data;

(b) Without undue delay, utilize means made available by the certification service provider pursuant to article 9 of this Law, or otherwise use reasonable efforts, to notify any person that may reasonably be expected by the signatory to rely on or to provide services in support of the electronic signature if:

(i) The signatory knows that the signature creation data have been compromised; or

(ii) The circumstances known to the signatory give rise to a substantial risk that the signature creation data may have been compromised;

(c) Where a certificate is used to support the electronic signature, exercise reasonable care to ensure the accuracy and completeness of all material representations made by the signatory that are relevant to the certificate throughout its life cycle or that are to be included in the certificate.

2. A signatory shall bear the legal consequences of its failure to satisfy the requirements of paragraph 1.

Article 9. Conduct of the certification service provider

1. Where a certification service provider provides services to support an electronic signature that may be used for legal effect as a signature, that certification service provider shall:

(a) Act in accordance with representations made by it with respect to its policies and practices;

(b) Exercise reasonable care to ensure the accuracy and completeness of all material representations made by it that are relevant to the certificate throughout its life cycle or that are included in the certificate;

(c) Provide reasonably accessible means that enable a relying party to ascertain from the certificate:

(i) The identity of the certification service provider;

(ii) That the signatory that is identified in the certificate had control of the signature creation data at the time when the certificate was issued;

(iii) That signature creation data were valid at or before the time when the certificate was issued;

(d) Provide reasonably accessible means that enable a relying party to ascertain, where relevant, from the certificate or otherwise:

(i) The method used to identify the signatory;

(ii) Any limitation on the purpose or value for which the signature creation data or the certificate may be used;

(iii) That the signature creation data are valid and have not been compromised;

(iv) Any limitation on the scope or extent of liability stipulated by the certification service provider;

(v) Whether means exist for the signatory to give notice pursuant to article 8, paragraph 1 *(b)*, of this Law;

(vi) Whether a timely revocation service is offered;

(e) Where services under subparagraph *(d)* (v) are offered, provide a means for a signatory to give notice pursuant to article 8, paragraph 1 *(b),* of this Law and, where services under subparagraph *(d)* (vi) are offered, ensure the availability of a timely revocation service;

(f) Utilize trustworthy systems, procedures and human resources in performing its services.

2. A certification service provider shall bear the legal consequences of its failure to satisfy the requirements of paragraph 1.

Article 10. Trustworthiness

For the purposes of article 9, paragraph 1 *(f)*, of this Law in determining whether, or to what extent, any systems, procedures and human resources utilized by a certification service provider are trustworthy, regard may be had to the following factors:

(a) Financial and human resources, including existence of assets;

(b) Quality of hardware and software systems;

(c) Procedures for processing of certificates and applications for certificates and retention of records;

(d) Availability of information to signatories identified in certificates and to potential relying parties;

(e) Regularity and extent of audit by an independent body;

(f) The existence of a declaration by the State, an accreditation body or the certification service provider regarding compliance with or existence of the foregoing; or

(g) Any other relevant factor.

Article 11. Conduct of the relying party

A relying party shall bear the legal consequences of its failure:

(a) To take reasonable steps to verify the reliability of an electronic signature; or

(b) Where an electronic signature is supported by a certificate, to take reasonable steps:

(i) To verify the validity, suspension or revocation of the certificate; and

(ii) To observe any limitation with respect to the certificate.

Article 12. Recognition of foreign certificates and electronic signatures

1. In determining whether, or to what extent, a certificate or an electronic signature is legally effective, no regard shall be had:

(a) To the geographic location where the certificate is issued or the electronic signature created or used; or

(b) To the geographic location of the place of business of the issuer or signatory.

2. A certificate issued outside *[the enacting State]* shall have the same legal effect in *[the enacting State]* as a certificate issued in *[the enacting State]* if it offers a substantially equivalent level of reliability.

3. An electronic signature created or used outside *[the enacting State]* shall have the same legal effect in *[the enacting State]* as an electronic signature created or used in *[the enacting State]* if it offers a substantially equivalent level of reliability.

4. In determining whether a certificate or an electronic signature offers a substantially equivalent level of reliability for the purposes of paragraph 2 or 3, regard shall be had to recognized international standards and to any other relevant factors.

5. Where, notwithstanding paragraphs 2, 3 and 4, parties agree, as between themselves, to the use of certain types of electronic signatures or certificates, that agreement shall be recognized as sufficient for the purposes of cross-border recognition, unless that agreement would not be valid or effective under applicable law.

UNCITRAL DRAFT CONVENTION ON ELECTRONIC CONTRACTING[1]

United Nations General Assembly
A/CN.9/WG.IV/WP.108
18 December 2003

United Nations Commission on International Trade Law
Working Group IV (Electronic Commerce)
Forty-third session
New York, 15-19 March 2004

Legal aspects of electronic commerce

Electronic contracting: provisions for a draft convention

Note by the Secretariat

1. The Working Group began its deliberations on electronic contracting at its thirty-ninth session (New York, 11-15 March 2002), when it considered a note by the Secretariat on selected issues relating to electronic contracting (A/CN.9/WG.IV/WP.95). That note also contained an initial draft tentatively entitled "Preliminary draft convention on [international] contracts concluded or evidenced by data messages" (A/CN.9/WG.IV/WP.95, annex I).

2. At that time, the Working Group held a general exchange of views on the form and scope of the instrument, but agreed to postpone discussion on exclusions from the draft convention until it had had an opportunity to consider the provisions related to the location of the parties and contract formation (see A/CN.9/509, paras. 18-40). The Working Group then took up articles 7 and 14, both of which dealt with issues related to the location of the parties (see A/CN.9/509, paras. 41-65). After it had completed its initial review of those provisions, the Working Group proceeded to consider the provisions dealing with contract formation in articles 8-13 (see A/CN.9/509, paras. 66-121). The Working Group concluded its deliberations on the draft convention at that session

1 Reproduced with permission from the United Nations Commission on International Trade Law (UNCITRAL).

with a discussion of draft article 15 on availability of contract terms (see A/CN.9/509, paras. 122-125). The Working Group agreed, at that time, that it should consider articles 2-4, dealing with the sphere of application of the draft convention and articles 5 (Definitions) and 6 (Interpretation), at its fortieth session (see A/CN.9/509, para. 15).

3. The Working Group resumed its deliberations on the preliminary draft convention at its fortieth session (Vienna, 14-18 October 2002). The Working Group began its deliberations by a general discussion on the scope of the preliminary draft convention (see A/CN.9/527, paras. 72-81). The Working Group proceeded to consider articles 2-4, dealing with the sphere of application of the draft convention and articles 5 (Definitions) and 6 (Interpretation) (see A/CN.9/527, paras. 82-126).

4. The Secretariat thereafter prepared a revised version of the preliminary draft convention (A/CN.9/WG.IV/WP.100, annex I). The Working Group, at its forty-first session (New York, 5-9 May 2003), reviewed articles 1-11 of the revised preliminary draft convention (see A/CN.9/528, paras. 26-151). The Secretariat was requested to prepare a further revised version of the preliminary draft convention, for consideration by the Working Group at its forty-second session.

5. At its forty-second session (Vienna, 17-21 November 2003), the Working Group held a general discussion on the scope of the preliminary draft convention (see A/CN.9/546, paras. 33-38). The Working Group noted that a task force had been established by the International Chamber of Commerce to develop contractual rules and guidance on legal issues related to electronic commerce, tentatively called "E-terms 2004". The Working Group considered the work being undertaken by that task force as a useful complement to the work being undertaken by the Working Group to develop an international convention. The Working Group proceeded to consider the revised text of the preliminary draft convention (A/CN.9/WG.IV/WP.103, annex I). The Working Group reviewed articles 8-15 and requested a number of changes in connection therewith (see A/CN.9/546, paras. 39-135).

6. The annex to the present note contains the newly revised version of the preliminary draft convention, which reflects the deliberations and decisions of the Working Group at its previous sessions.

Annex[2]
Preliminary draft convention[3] on the use of data messages in [international trade] [the context of international contracts]

CHAPTER I. SPHERE OF APPLICATION

Article 1. Scope of application

1. This Convention applies to the use of data messages in connection with an existing or contemplated contract between parties whose places of business are in different States:

Variant A[4]

(a) When the States are Contracting States;

(b) When the rules of private international law lead to the application of the law of a Contracting State; or[5]

(c) When the parties have agreed that it applies.[6]

Variant B[7]

. . . when these States are parties to this Convention and the data messages are used in connection with an existing or contemplated contract to which,

---

2 The numbers in square brackets after the article numbers indicate the corresponding numbers in the previous version of the draft convention (A/CN.9/WG.IV/WP.103, annex).

3 The form of a convention represents a working assumption only (see A/CN.9/484, para. 124) and is without prejudice to a final decision by the Working Group as to the nature of the instrument.

4 This variant reflects the scope of application of the draft convention essentially as contained in earlier versions. By combining this variant with variant A of draft article Y, a contracting State would make it clear that the provisions of the draft convention apply to messages exchanged under any of the international conventions referred to therein, while preserving the possibility of excluding particular instruments, or adding other instruments as it sees fit.

5 This paragraph reproduces a rule that is contained in the provisions on the sphere of application of other UNCITRAL instruments. There have been objections to this rule on the grounds that such an expansion of the convention's field of application would significantly reduce certainty at the time of contracting owing to its inherent ex post facto nature (see A/CN.9/509, para. 38). At its forty-first session, the Working Group agreed to retain the subparagraph (see A/CN.9/528, para. 42). If the draft paragraph is retained, the Working Group would still need to consider whether reservations to this rule should be permitted, as was suggested at its forty-second session (see A/CN.9/528, para. 42). See also draft article X, paragraph 1.

6 This possibility is provided, for instance, in article 1, paragraph 2, of the United Nations Convention on Independent Guarantees and Stand-by Letters of Credit. The Working Group postponed a decision on this subparagraph until it had considered the operative provisions of the draft convention (see A/CN.9/528, paras. 43 and 44). The Working Group may wish to consider whether it should be possible for contracting States to exclude this provision through a declaration made pursuant to draft article X, paragraph 1.

7 This variant reflects variant 1 of a proposal that was submitted by Germany to the Working Group at its forty-second session (A/CN.9/WG.IV/XLII/CRP.2). Its practical effect would be to limit the applicability of the draft convention only to messages exchanged under the abovementioned conventions, with the possibility of individual exclusions by contracting States under variant C of draft article Y.

pursuant to the law of these States Parties, one of the following international conventions is to be applied:

Convention on the Limitation Period in the International Sale of Goods (New York, 14 June 1974) and Protocol thereto (Vienna, 11 April 1980)

United Nations Convention on Contracts for the International Sale of Goods (Vienna, 11 April 1980)

United Nations Convention on the Liability of Operators of Transport Terminals in International Trade (Vienna, 17 April 1991)

United Nations Convention on Independent Guarantees and Stand-by Letters of Credit (New York, 11 December 1995)

United Nations Convention on the Assignment of Receivables in International Trade (New York, 12 December 2001).

2. The fact that the parties have their places of business in different States is to be disregarded whenever this fact does not appear either from the contract or from any dealings between the parties or from information disclosed by the parties at any time before or at the conclusion of the contract.

3. Neither the nationality of the parties nor the civil or commercial character of the parties or of the contract is to be taken into consideration in determining the application of this Convention.

Article 2. Exclusions[8]

This Convention does not apply to the use of data messages [in connection with the following contracts, whether existing or contemplated] [in the context of the formation or performance of the following contracts]:

(a) Contracts concluded for personal, family or household purposes [unless the party offering the goods or services, at any time before or at the conclusion of the contract, neither knew nor ought to have known that they were intended for any such use];[9]

8 The last version of this draft article contained two variants reflecting alternative approaches for the treatment of consumer contracts. Variant A excluded consumer contracts by using the same technique that is used in article 2, subparagraph (a), of the United Nations Convention on Contracts for the International Sale of Goods (the "United Nations Sales Convention"). Variant B deferred to domestic law on consumer protection issues, without excluding consumer transactions from the draft convention (see A/CN.9/527, para. 89; see also A/CN.9/528, paras. 51-54). The present version of the draft article retains only the former variant A. The former variant B has been incorporated into draft article 3, as its content is more akin to that article, in its current formulation. The Working Group may wish to bear in mind that the entire draft article may become redundant if the Working Group chooses to define the scope of application of the draft convention along the lines of variant C of draft article 1, since the draft convention would then apply only to the exchange of data messages falling within the scope of those international conventions in accordance with their own rules on their scope of application.

9 The last phrase is in square brackets, since there was some support at the forty-first session of the Working Group to the suggestion that all the words after "household purposes" should be deleted (see A/CN.9/528, para. 52).

[(b) Contracts for the grant of limited use of intellectual property rights;][10]

(c) [*Other exclusions that the Working Group may decide to add.*][11] [Other matters identified by a Contracting State under a declaration made in accordance with article X].[12]

Article 3. Matters not governed by this Convention[13]

This Convention does not affect or override[14] any rule of law relating to:

[(a) The protection of consumers;][15]

---

10 This exclusion is in square brackets as the Working Group has not yet reached an agreement on the matter (see A/CN.9/527, paras. 90-93, and A/CN.9/528, paras. 55-60). The Working Group may wish to note that the International Bureau of the World Intellectual Property Organization sees no need for an exclusion clause with regard to contracts involving intellectual property rights (see A/CN.9/WG.IV/WP.106, para. 2).

11 This draft article might contain additional exclusions, as may be decided by the Working Group. Annex II of the initial draft (A/CN.9/WG.IV/WP.95) reproduced, for illustrative purposes and without the intention of being exhaustive, exclusions typically found in domestic laws on electronic commerce. Additional exclusions that had been proposed at the fortieth session of the Working Group and reiterated at the forty-first session, related to certain existing financial services markets with well-established rules resulting from specific regulations, standard agreements and practices, system rules or otherwise. Those exclusions included payment systems, negotiable instruments, derivatives, swaps, repurchase agreements (repos), foreign exchange, securities and bond markets, while possibly including general procurement activities of banks and loan activities (see A/CN.9/527, para. 95, and A/CN.9/528, para. 61). Additional exclusions proposed at the forty-first session included "real estate transactions, as well as contracts involving courts or public authorities, family law and the law of succession" (see A/CN.9/528, para. 63). The Working Group may wish to note, in that connection, that the United Nations Commission on International Trade Law (UNCITRAL), at its thirty-sixth session, decided to undertake work in the area of public procurement, including procurement by electronic means (see A/58/17, paras. 225-230). This may render an open-ended exclusion of "contracts involving courts or public authorities" inappropriate.

12 This phrase is an alternative formulation that would obviate the need for a common list of exclusions (see A/CN.9/527, para. 96).

13 The Working Group may wish to bear in mind that the entire draft article may become redundant, if the Working Group chooses to define the scope of application of the draft convention along the lines of variant C of draft article 1, since the draft convention would then apply only to the exchange of data messages falling within the scope of those international conventions in accordance with their own rules on their field of application.

14 This formulation has been used following a suggestion at the forty-first session of the Working Group that the words previously used ("This Convention is not concerned with") were inaccurate (see A/CN.9/528, para. 67).

15 Draft subparagraph (a) appears within square brackets, as it represents in some respects an alternative to draft article 2, subparagraph (a) (see A/CN.9/528, para. 52). Under this rule, consumer transactions would not be automatically excluded from the scope of the draft convention, but the provisions of the draft convention would not supersede or affect rules on consumer protection.

(b) The validity of the contract or of any of its provisions or of any usage [except as otherwise provided in articles [...]];[16]

(c) The rights and obligations of the parties arising out of the contract or of any of its provisions or of any usage;[17] or

(d) The effect, which the contract may have on, the ownership of rights created or transferred by the contract.[18]

Article 4. Party autonomy

The parties may exclude the application of this Convention or derogate from or vary the effect of any of its provisions [except for the following: . . .].[19]

CHAPTER II. GENERAL PROVISIONS

Article 5. Definitions[20]

For the purposes of this Convention:

(a) "Data message" means information generated, sent, received or stored by electronic, optical or similar means including, but not limited to, electronic data interchange (EDI), electronic mail, telegram, telex or telecopy;

---

16 Draft subparagraph (b) is derived from article 4, subparagraph (a), of the United Nations Sales Convention. The Working Group may wish to consider the relationship between the general exclusions under the draft article and other provisions that, for instance, affirm the validity of data messages, such as draft articles 8, 9 and 12 (see A/CN.9/527, para. 103).

17 The preliminary draft convention is not concerned with substantive issues arising out of the contract, which, for all other purposes, remains subject to its governing law (see A/CN.9/527, paras. 10-12). The Working Group may wish to consider whether this provision is still required, since the rule contained in the subparagraph might nevertheless be evident from the limited scope of the draft convention.

18 Draft subparagraph (d) is based, mutatis mutandis, on article 4, subparagraph (b), of the United Nations Sales Convention. Regardless of its final decision on draft articles 1 and Y, the Working Group may wish to consider whether this provision is still required, since the rule contained in the subparagraph might nevertheless be evident from the limited scope of the draft convention.

19 The Working Group has yet to consider whether some limitation to the principle of party autonomy is appropriate or desirable in the context of the preliminary draft convention, in particular in the light of provisions such as draft articles 9, paragraph 3, 11 and 15 (see A/CN.9/527, para. 109; see also A/CN.9/528, paras. 71-75). The earlier version of this article contained a second paragraph dealing with the agreement of the parties to the use of data messages in a contractual context. That provision has now been combined with draft article 8.

20 The definitions contained in draft paragraphs (a) to (e) are derived from article 2 of the UNCITRAL Model Law on Electronic Commerce. The definition of "electronic signature" corresponds to the definition of the same expression in article 2 of the UNCITRAL Model Law on Electronic Signatures. The definitions of "offeror" and "offeree" have been deleted, although the Working Group had tentatively retained them (see A/CN.9/527, para. 115). The Secretariat submits that those words have become superfluous in view of the reformulation of draft articles 8 and 13 (see A/CN.9/528, para. 106).

(b) "Electronic data interchange (EDI)" means the electronic transfer from computer to computer of information using an agreed standard to structure the information;

(c) "Originator" of a data message means a person by whom, or on whose behalf, the data message purports to[21] have been sent or generated prior to storage, if any, but it does not include a person acting as an intermediary with respect to that data message;

(d) "Addressee" of a data message means a person who is intended by the originator to receive the data message, but does not include a person acting as an intermediary with respect to that data message;

(e) "Information system" means a system for generating, sending, receiving, storing or otherwise processing data messages;[22]

(f) "Automated information system" means a computer program or an electronic or other automated means used to initiate an action or respond to data messages or performances in whole or in part, without review or intervention by a natural person each time an action is initiated or a response is generated by the system;[23]

[(g) "Electronic signature" means data in electronic form in, affixed to, or logically associated with, a data message, which may be used to identify the person holding the signature creation data in relation to the data message and indicate that person's approval of the information contained in the data message;[24]

---

21 The wording of this definition is taken from article 2, subparagraph (c), of the UNCITRAL Model Law on Electronic Commerce. It has been suggested to the Secretariat that it might be preferable to delete the words "purports to have been sent" and use instead the words "has been sent".

22 The Working Group may wish to consider whether this definition needs further clarification, in view of the questions that have been raised in connection with paragraph 2 of the former article 11 (currently article 10) (see A/CN.9/528, paras. 148 and 149, and A/CN.9/546, paras. 59-80).

23 This definition is based on the definition of "electronic agent" contained in section 2, paragraph 6, of the Uniform Electronic Transactions Act of the United States of America; a similar definition is also used in section 19 of the Uniform Electronic Commerce Act of Canada. This definition was included in view of the contents of draft article 14.

24 The initial draft contained in document A/CN.9/WG.IV/WP.95 included, as a variant to this provision, a general definition of "signature". Although the Working Group tentatively agreed on retaining both variants, the Secretariat suggests that it might be more appropriate, given the limited scope of the draft convention, to define only "electronic signatures", leaving a definition of "signature" for the otherwise applicable law, as had been suggested at the fortieth session of the Working Group (see A/CN.9/527, paras. 116-119).

[(h) "Place of business"[25] means [any place of operations where a person carries out a non-transitory activity with human means and goods or services;][26] [the place where a party maintains a stable establishment to pursue an economic activity other than the temporary provision of goods or services out of a specific location;][27]]

[(i) "Person" and "party" include natural persons and legal entities;][28]

[(j) Other definitions that the Working Group may wish to add.][29]

Article 6. Interpretation

1. In the interpretation of this Convention, regard is to be had to its international character and to the need to promote uniformity in its application and the observance of good faith in international trade.

2. Questions concerning matters governed by this Convention which are not expressly settled in it are to be settled in conformity with the general principles on

---

25 The proposed definition appears within square brackets since the Commission has not thus far defined "place of business" (see A/CN.9/527, paras. 120-122). At the thirty-ninth session of the Working Group, it was suggested that the rules on the location of the parties should be expanded to include elements such as the place of an entity's organization or incorporation (see A/CN.9/509, para. 53). The Working Group decided that it could consider the desirability of using supplementary elements to the criteria used to define the location of the parties by expanding the definition of place of business (see A/CN.9/509, para. 54). The Working Group may wish to consider whether the proposed additional notions and any other new elements should be provided as an alternative to the elements currently used or only as a default rule for those entities without an "establishment". Additional cases that might deserve consideration by the Working Group might include situations where the most significant component of human means or goods or services used for a particular business are located in a place bearing little relationship to the actual centre of a company's affairs, such as when the only equipment and personnel used by a so-called "virtual business" located in one country consists of leased space in a third-party server located elsewhere.

26 This alternative reflects the essential elements of the notions of "place of business", as understood in international commercial practice, and "establishment", as used in article 2, subparagraph (f), of the UNCITRAL Model Law on Cross-Border Insolvency.

27 This alternative follows the understanding of the concept of "place of business" in the European Union (see para. 19 of the preamble to Directive 2000/31/EC of the European Union).

28 During the preparation of the UNCITRAL Model Law on Electronic Commerce, it was felt that such a definition did not belong in the text of the instrument, but in its guide to enactment. As a convention would not normally be accompanied by extensive comments, the proposed definition has been included in the form of a provision, should the Working Group find such a definition necessary, particularly in view of provisions such as draft article 9, variant B, subparagraph 4 (b).

29 The Working Group may wish to consider whether definitions of other terms should be included, such as "signatory" (if variant B of draft article 10 (formerly 14) is adopted), "interactive applications", "electronic mail" or "domain name".

which it is based or, in the absence of such principles, in conformity with the law applicable [by virtue of the rules of private international law].[30]

Article 7. Location of the parties[31]

1. For the purposes of this Convention, a person's place of business is presumed to be the location indicated by that person [, unless the person does not have a place of business at such location [[and] such indication is made solely to trigger or avoid the application of this Convention]].

2. If a person [has not indicated a place of business or, subject to paragraph 1 of this article, a person][32] has more than one place of business, the place of business for the purposes of this Convention is that which has the closest relationship to the relevant contract and its performance, having regard to the circumstances known to or contemplated by the parties at any time before or at the conclusion of the contract.

3. If a person does not have a place of business, reference is to be made to the person's habitual residence.

4. The place of location of the equipment and technology supporting an information system used by a person in connection with the formation of a contract or the place from which such information system may be accessed by other persons, in and of themselves, do not constitute a place of business [, unless such legal entity does not have a place of business [within the meaning of article 5 (h)]].[33]

---

30 The closing phrase has been placed in square brackets at the request of the Working Group. Similar formulations in other instruments had been incorrectly understood as allowing immediate referral to the applicable law pursuant to the rules on conflict of laws of the forum State for the interpretation of a convention without regard to the conflict of laws rules contained in the convention itself (see A/CN.9/527, paras. 125 and 126).

31 The draft paragraph is not intended to create a new concept of "place of business" for the online world. The phrase in square brackets aims to prevent a party from benefiting from recklessly inaccurate or untruthful representations (see A/CN.9/509, para. 49), but not to limit the parties' ability to choose the Convention or otherwise agree on the applicable law. The two variants previously contained in the draft paragraph have been combined as the Working Group preferred the former variant A (see A/CN.9/528, para. 88). The words "manifest and clear" which the Working Group found to be conducive to legal uncertainty (see A/CN.9/528, para. 86), have been deleted.

32 It has been suggested to the Secretariat that the presumption contemplated in the draft article could also apply in the event that a party does not indicate its place of business. This suggestion has been inserted in square brackets, since the presumption contemplated in the draft article has been used in other UNCITRAL instruments only in connection with multiple places of business.

33 The draft paragraph reflects the principle that rules on location should not result in any given party being considered as having its place of business in one country when contracting electronically and in another country when contracting by more traditional means (see A/CN.9/484, para. 103). The draft paragraph follows the solution proposed in paragraph 19 of the preamble to Directive 2000/31/EC of the European Union (see also the overview of issues related to the location of information systems in A/CN.9/WG.IV/WP.104, paras. 9-17). The phrase within square brackets is only intended to deal with so-called "virtual companies" and

5. The sole fact that a person makes use of a domain name or electronic mail address connected to a specific country does not create a presumption that its place of business is located in such country.[34]

Article 7 bis [11]. *Information requirements*

Nothing in this Convention affects the application of any rule of law that may require the parties to disclose their identities, places of business or other information, or relieves a party from the legal consequences of making inaccurate or false statements in that regard.

CHAPTER III. USE OF DATA MESSAGES IN INTERNATIONAL CONTRACTS

Article 8. Legal recognition of data messages

1. Where a communication, declaration, demand, notice or request that the parties are required to make or choose to make in connection with an existing or contemplated contract, including an offer and the acceptance of an offer, is conveyed by means of data messages, such communication, declaration, demand, notice or request shall not be denied validity or enforceability on the sole ground that data messages were used for that purpose.

[2. Nothing in this Convention requires a person to use or accept information in the form of data messages, but a person's agreement to use or accept information in the form of data messages may be inferred from the person's conduct.][35]

---

not with natural persons, who are covered by the rule contained in draft paragraph 3. The Working Group may wish to consider whether draft paragraphs 4 and 5, which the Working Group agreed to retain for further consideration, should be combined in one provision (see A/CN.9/509, para. 59).

34 The current system for assignment of domain names was not originally conceived in geographical terms. Therefore, the apparent connection between a domain name and a country is often insufficient to conclude that there is a genuine and permanent link between the domain name user and the country (see A/CN.9/509, paras. 44-46; see also A/CN.9/WG.IV/WP.104, paras. 18-20). However, in some countries the assignment of domain names is only made after verification of the accuracy of the information provided by the applicant, including its location in the country to which the relevant domain name relates. For those countries, it might be appropriate to rely, at least in part, on domain names for the purpose of article 7, contrary to what is suggested in the draft paragraph (see A/CN.9/509, para. 58). The Working Group may wish to consider whether the proposed rules should be expanded to deal with those situations.

35 The provision reflects the idea that parties should not be forced to accept contractual offers or acts of acceptance by electronic means if they do not want to do so (see A/CN.9/527, para. 108). However, since the provision is not intended to require that the parties should always agree beforehand on the use of data messages, the second phrase provides that a party's agreement to transact electronically may be inferred from its conduct. The reference to "consent" has been replaced with the phrase "a person's agreement to use or accept information in the form of data messages" so as to avoid the erroneous impression that the draft paragraph refers to consent to the underlying transaction (see A/CN.9/546, para. 43).

Article 9. Form requirements

[1. Nothing in this Convention requires a contract or any other communication, declaration, demand, notice or request that the parties are required to make or choose to make in connection with an existing or contemplated contract to be made or evidenced in any particular form.][36]

2. Where the law requires that a contract or any other communication, declaration, demand, notice or request that the parties are required to make or choose to make in connection with a contract should be in writing, that requirement is met by a data message if the information contained therein is accessible so as to be usable for subsequent reference.[37]

3. Where the law requires that a contract or any other communication, declaration, demand, notice or request that the parties are required to make or choose to make in connection with a contract should be signed, or provides consequences for the absence of a signature, that requirement is met in relation to a data message if:

(a) A method is used to identify that person and to indicate that person's approval of the information contained in the data message; and

(b) That method is as reliable as appropriate to the purpose for which the data message was generated or communicated, in the light of all the circumstances, including any relevant agreement.[38]

Article 10. Time and place of dispatch and receipt of data messages[39]

1. The time of dispatch of a data message is the time when the data message [enters an information system outside the control of the originator or of the person

---

36 This provision incorporates the general principle of freedom of form contained in article 11 of the United Nations Sales Convention, in the manner suggested at the forty-second session of the Working Group (see A/CN.9/546, para. 49).

37 This provision sets forth the criteria for the functional equivalence between data messages and paper documents, in the same manner as article 6 of the UNCITRAL Model Law on Electronic Commerce. The Working Group may wish to consider the meaning of the words "the law" and "writing" and whether there would be a need for including definitions of those terms (see A/CN.9/509, paras. 116 and 117).

38 The draft paragraph recites the general criteria for the functional equivalence between handwritten signatures and electronic identification methods referred to in article 7 of the UNCITRAL Model Law on Electronic Commerce.

39 Earlier versions of the draft article followed more closely the formulation of article 15 of the UNCITRAL Model Law on Electronic Commerce, with some adjustments to harmonize the style of the individual provisions with the style used elsewhere in the draft convention. The current formulation reflects the deliberations of the Working Group at its forty-second session (see A/CN.9/546, paras. 59-86). The Working Group may wish to review the new formulation, in particular draft paragraph 2, with a view to ensuring that it is consistent in result with article 15 of the Model Law.

who sent the data message on behalf of the originator] [leaves an information system under the control of the originator or of the person who sent the data message on behalf of the originator], or, if the message had not [entered an information system outside the control of the originator or of the person who sent the data message on behalf of the originator] [left an information system under the control of the originator or of the person who sent the data message on behalf of the originator], at the time when the message is received.

2. The time of receipt of a data message is the time when the data message becomes capable of being retrieved by the addressee or by any other person named by the addressee. A data message is presumed to be capable of being retrieved by the addressee when the data message enters an information system of the addressee unless it was unreasonable for the originator to have chosen that particular information system for sending the data message, having regard to the circumstances of the case and the content of the data message.

3. A data message is deemed to be dispatched at the place where the originator has its place of business and is deemed to be received at the place where the addressee has its place of business, as determined in accordance with article 7.

4. Paragraph 2 of this article applies notwithstanding that the place where the information system is located may be different from the place where the data message is deemed to be received under paragraph 3 of this article.

Article 11 [12]. *Invitations to make offers*[40]

A proposal to conclude a contract made through one or more data messages which is not addressed to one or more specific persons, but is generally accessible to parties making use of information systems, including proposals that make use of interactive applications[41] for the placement of orders through such information system, is to be considered as an invitation to make offers, unless it

40 This provision deals with an issue that has given rise to extensive debate. At the forty-first session of the Working Group, it was noted that "there was currently no standard business practice in that area" (see A/CN.9/528, para. 117). The current text is inspired by article 14, paragraph 1, of the United Nations Sales Convention and affirms the principle that proposals to conclude a contract that are addressed to an unlimited number of persons are not binding offers, even if they involve the use of interactive applications. The Working Group may wish to consider, however, whether specific rules should be formulated to deal with offers of goods through Internet auction platforms and similar transactions, which in many legal systems have been regarded as binding offers to sell the goods to the highest bidder.

41 At its forty-second session, the Working Group noted that the expression "automated information system", which had been used in earlier versions of the draft article, did not offer meaningful guidance since the party that placed an order might have no means of knowing how the order would be processed and to what extent the information system was automated. The notion of "interactive applications", in turn, was considered to be an objective term that better described a situation apparent to any person accessing the system, namely that it was prompted to exchange information through that system by means of immediate actions and responses having an appearance of automaticity. It was noted that the term was not a legal term

clearly indicates the intention of the person making the proposal to be bound in case of acceptance.

Article 12 [14]. Use of automated information systems for contract formation[42]

A contract formed by the interaction of an automated information system and a person, or by the interaction of automated information systems, shall not be denied validity or enforceability on the sole ground that no person reviewed each of the individual actions carried out by such systems or the resulting agreement.

[Article 13 [15]. Availability of contract terms

[Variant A[43]

Nothing in this convention affects the application of any rule of law that may require a party that negotiates a contract through the exchange of data messages to make available to the other contracting party the data messages that contain the contractual terms in a particular manner, or relieves a party from the legal consequences of its failure to do so.]

[Variant B[44]

A party offering goods or services through an information system that is generally accessible to persons making use of information systems[45] shall make the

---

but rather a term of art highlighting that the provision focused on what was apparent to the party activating the system rather than on how the system functioned internally. On that basis, the Working Group agreed that the term "interactive applications" could be retained (see A/CN.9/546, para. 114).

42 This article has been redrafted as a non-discrimination rule, as requested by the Working Group at its forty-second session (see A/CN.9/546, paras. 128 and 129). The Working Group may wish to consider whether the provision should be supplemented by a general provision on attribution of data messages, including attribution of data messages exchanged by automated information systems (see A/CN.9/546, paras. 85, 86 and 125-127).

43 This variant has been added pursuant to a request by the Working Group in view of the controversy around the draft article (see A/CN.9/546, paras. 130-135). If this variant alone is retained, the Working Group may wish to consider placing the draft article in chapter I or II of the draft convention or even combining it with the current draft article 3.

44 This variant, which is based on article 10, paragraph 3, of Directive 2000/31/EC of the European Union, appears in square brackets, as there was no consensus on the need for the provision within the Working Group (see A/CN.9/509, paras. 123-125, and A/CN.9/546, paras. 130-135). If the provision is retained, the Working Group may wish to consider whether the draft article should provide consequences for the failure by a party to make available the contract terms and what consequences would be appropriate. In some legal systems the consequences might be that a contractual term that has not been made available to the other party cannot be enforced against it.

45 The Working Group may wish to consider whether these words adequately describe the types of situations that the Working Group intends to address in the draft article.

data message or messages which contain the contract terms[46] available to the other party [for a reasonable period of time] in a way that allows for its or their storage and reproduction.]

Article 14 [16]. *Error in electronic communications*

Variant A[47]

[Unless otherwise [expressly] agreed by the parties,][48] a contract concluded by a person that accesses an automated information system of another party has no legal effect and is not enforceable if the person made an error in a data message and:[49]

(a) The automated information system did not provide the person with an opportunity to prevent or correct the error;

(b) The person notifies the other party of the error as soon as practicable when the person making the error learns of it and indicates that he or she made an error in the data message;

[(c) The person takes reasonable steps, including steps that conform to the other party's instructions, to return the goods or services received, if any, as a result of the error or, if instructed to do so, to destroy such goods or services; and

---

46 The words "and general conditions" have been deleted as they appeared to be redundant. The Working Group may, however, wish to consider whether the provision should be made more explicit as to the version of the contract terms that needs to be retained.

47 This draft paragraph deals with the issue of errors in automated transactions (see A/CN.9/WG.IV/WP.95, paras. 74-79). Earlier versions of the draft article contained, in paragraph 1 of variant A, a rule based on article 11, paragraph 2, of Directive 2000/31/EC of the European Union, which creates an obligation for persons offering goods or services through automated information systems to offer means for correcting input errors, and required such means to be "appropriate, effective and accessible". The draft article was the subject of essentially two types of objections: one objection was that the draft convention should not deal with a complex substantive issue such as error and mistake, a matter on which the Working Group has not yet reached a final decision; another objection was that the obligations contemplated in article 14, paragraph 2, of the first version of the draft convention (as contained in A/CN.9/WG.IV/WP.95) were regarded as being of a regulatory or public law nature (see A/CN.9/509, para. 108). The Working Group may wish to consider whether the latter objection could be addressed by deleting the reference to an obligation to provide means for correcting errors and by contemplating only private law consequences for the absence of such means.

48 The Working Group may wish to consider whether the possibility of derogation by agreement needs to be expressly made or can result from tacit agreement, for instance when a party proceeds to place an order through the seller's automated information system even though it is apparent to such party that the system does not provide an opportunity to correct input errors.

49 This provision deals with the legal effects of errors made by a natural person communicating with an automated information system. The draft provision is inspired by section 22 of the Uniform Electronic Commerce Act of Canada. At the thirty-ninth session of the Working Group it was suggested that such provisions might not be appropriate in the context of commercial (that is, nonconsumer) transactions, since the right to repudiate a contract in case of material error may not always be provided under general contract law. The Working Group nevertheless decided to retain it for further consideration (see A/CN.9/509, paras. 110 and 111).

[(d) The person has not used or received any material benefit or value from the goods or services, if any, received from the other party.][50]

Variant B

1. [Unless otherwise [expressly] agreed by the parties,][51] a contract concluded by a person that accesses an automated information system of another party has no legal effect and is not enforceable if the person made an error in a data message and the automated information system did not provide the person with an opportunity to prevent or correct the error. The person invoking the error must notify the other party of the error as soon as practicable and indicate that he or she made an error in the data message.[52]

[2. A person is not entitled to invoke an error under paragraph 1:

(a) If the person fails to take reasonable steps, including steps that conform to the other party's instructions, to return the goods or services received, if any, as a result of the error or, if instructed to do so, to destroy such goods or services; or

(b) If the person has used or received any material benefit or value from the goods or services, if any, received from the other party.][53]

[*Other substantive provisions that the Working Group may wish to include.*][54]

---

50 Subparagraphs (c) and (d) appear within square brackets since it was suggested, at the thirty-ninth session of the Working Group, that the matters dealt with therein went beyond matters of contract formation and departed from the consequences of avoidance of contracts under some legal systems (see A/CN.9/509, para. 110).

51 See note 47.

52 This variant combines in two paragraphs the various elements contained in paragraphs 2 and 3 and subparagraphs (a)-(d) of the first version of the draft article (see A/CN.9/WG.IV/WP.95), as requested by the Working Group (see A/CN.9/509, para. 111).

53 See footnote 49.

54 Such additional provisions might include, beyond consequences for a person's failure to comply with draft articles 11, 15 and 16, an issue that the Working Group has not yet considered (see A/CN.9/527, para. 103), other issues dealt with in electronic commerce legislation, such as liability of information services providers for loss or delay in the delivery of data messages.

CHAPTER IV. FINAL PROVISIONS

[Article X. Declarations on exclusions[55]

1. Any State may declare at the time of the deposit of its instrument of ratification, acceptance, approval or accession that it will not be bound by subparagraph 1 (b) of article 1 of this Convention.][56]

2. Any State may declare at the time of the deposit of its instrument of ratification, acceptance, approval or accession that it will not apply this Convention to the matters specified in its declaration.

3. Any declaration made pursuant to paragraphs 1 and 2 of this article shall take effect on the first day of the month following the expiration of [six] months after the date of its receipt by the depositary.]

Article Y. Communications exchanged under other international conventions[57]

Variant A[58]

1. Except as otherwise stated in a declaration made in accordance with paragraph 2 of this article, a State Party to this Convention [may declare at any time

---

55 The Working Group has not yet concluded its deliberations on possible exclusions to the preliminary draft convention under draft article 2 (see A/CN.9/527, paras. 83-98). The draft article has been added as a possible alternative, in the event that consensus is not achieved on possible exclusions to the preliminary draft convention.

56 At its forty-first session, the Working Group agreed to consider, at a later stage, a provision allowing contracting States to exclude the application of subparagraph (b) of article 1, paragraph 1, along the lines of article 95 of the United Nations Sales Convention (see A/CN.9/528, para. 42).

57 The draft article is intended to offer a possible common solution for some of the legal obstacles to electronic commerce under existing international instruments, which had been the object of a survey contained in an earlier note by the Secretariat (see A/CN.9/WG.IV/WP.94). At the fortieth session of the Working Group, there was general agreement to proceed in that manner, to the extent that the issues were common, which was the case at least with regard to most issues raised under the instruments listed in variant A (see A/CN.9/527, paras. 33-48). If either variant B or variant C is adopted, the title of the draft article would need to be changed to "reservations".

58 This variant is intended to remove doubts as to the relationship between the rules contained in the draft convention and rules contained in other international conventions. It is not the purpose of this variant effectively to amend or otherwise affect the application of any other international convention. In practice, the draft article would have the effect of an undertaking by a contracting State to use the provisions of the draft convention to remove possible legal obstacles to electronic commerce that might arise under those conventions and to facilitate their application in cases where the parties conduct their transactions through electronic means.

that it][59] undertakes to apply the provisions of [article 7 and] chapter III[60] of this Convention to the exchange [by means of data messages] of any communications, declarations, demands, notices or requests [, including an offer and acceptance of an offer,] that the parties are required to make or choose to make in connection with or under any of the following international agreements or conventions to which the State is or may become a Contracting State:

Convention on the Limitation Period in the International Sale of Goods (New York, 14 June 1974) and Protocol thereto (Vienna, 11 April 1980)

United Nations Convention on Contracts for the International Sale of Goods (Vienna, 11 April 1980)

United Nations Convention on the Liability of Operators of Transport Terminals in International Trade (Vienna, 17 April 1991)

United Nations Convention on Independent Guarantees and Stand-by Letters of Credit (New York, 11 December 1995)

United Nations Convention on the Assignment of Receivables in International Trade (New York, 12 December 2001).

[2. Any State may declare at the time of the deposit of its instrument of ratification, acceptance, approval or accession that it will also apply this Convention to the exchange by means of data messages of any communications, declarations, demands, notices or requests under any other international agreement or convention on private commercial law matters to which the State is a Contracting State and which are identified in that State's declaration.][61]

3. Any State may declare at any time that it will not apply this Convention [or any specific provision thereof] to international contracts falling within the scope of [any of the above conventions.] [one or more international agreements, trea-

59 The language in square brackets is intended to give more flexibility in the application of the draft article, since, without such clarification, the provision might be read to the effect that an undertaking pursuant to the draft article needed to be assumed upon signature, ratification or accession and could not be expanded at a later stage. If these words are retained, a provision along the lines of paragraph 3 of draft article X may be needed also in draft article Y.

60 The specific reference to the substantive provisions of the draft convention contained in chapter III is intended to avoid the impression that the provisions on the scope of application of the draft convention would affect the definition of the scope of application of other international conventions. The Working Group may wish to consider whether the provisions of draft article 7, to which reference is made in square brackets, are also suitable for subsidiary (interpretative) application in the context of other international conventions, or whether they might interfere with the existing interpretation of those conventions.

61 Paragraph 1 of variant A is intended to make it clear that the provisions of the draft convention apply also to messages exchanged under any of the international conventions referred to therein. Paragraph 2 contemplates the possibility for a contracting State to extend the application of the new instrument to the use of data messages in the context of other international conventions.

ties or conventions to which the State is a Contracting Party and which are identified in that State's declaration.]

4. Any declaration made pursuant to paragraphs 1 and 2 of this article shall take effect on the first day of the month following the expiration of [six] months after the date of its receipt by the depositary.

Variant B[62]

1. Any State may at any time make a reservation to the effect that it shall apply this Convention [or any specific provision thereof] only to data messages in connection with an existing or contemplated contract to which, pursuant to the law of that State, a specific international convention clearly identified in the reservation made by that State is to be applied.

2. Any declaration made pursuant to paragraph 1 of this article shall take effect on the first day of the month following the expiration of [six] months after the date of its receipt by the depositary.

Variant C[63]

1. Any State may declare at any time that it will not apply this Convention [or any specific provision thereof] to data messages in connection with an existing or contemplated contract to which one or more of the international conventions referred to in article 1, paragraph 1, are to be applied, provided that the relevant conventions shall be clearly identified in the declaration made by that State.

2. Any declaration made pursuant to paragraph 1 of this article shall take effect on the first day of the month following the expiration of [six] months after the date of its receipt by the depositary.

[*Customary and other final clauses that the Working Group may wish to include.*]

---

62 This variant reflects variant 2 of a proposal that was submitted by Germany at the forty-second session of the Working Group (see A/CN.9/WG.IV/XLII/CRP.2). It is logically related to variant A of draft article 1. Its practical effect would be to limit the applicability of the draft convention only to messages exchanged under conventions specifically identified by contracting States.

63 This variant reflects variant 1 of a proposal that was submitted by Germany at the forty-second session of the Working Group (see A/CN.9/WG.IV/XLII/CRP.2). It is included in the event that the Working Group chooses variant B of draft article 1, so as to give the contracting States the possibility to exclude the application of the draft convention in respect of certain specific conventions.

INDEX

TOPICAL INDEX